Charles Sumner
and the Coming of the Civil War

Charles Sumner in the Early 1850's

Charles Sumner
and the Coming of the Civil War

David Herbert Donald

FAWCETT COLUMBINE • NEW YORK

TO

THE MEMORY OF MY GRANDFATHER

John Belford

LIEUTENANT

IN THAT BRAVE CIVIL WAR REGIMENT

The First Vermont Cavalry

PREFACE TO THE
1989 EDITION

❖

T HE republication of this book is evidence of the continuing fascination that our Civil War holds for Americans. A few years ago it seemed that interest in the Civil War and Reconstruction periods was waning. The excessive publicity and over-commercialization of the Civil War centennial celebrations dampened popular enthusiasm, while the publication of such massive, authoritative histories as Allan Nevins's *Ordeal of the Union*, Bruce Catton's *Centennial History of the Civil War*, and Shelby Foote's *The Civil War: A Narrative*,[1] discouraged younger historians from writing their own books on the period. During the late 1960's and 1970's, when the nation's energies were absorbed in the civil rights movement, the women's movement, and the Vietnam war, the flood of books on the Civil War diminished to a trickle, and, except in the South, interest in the nineteenth-century sectional conflict seemed little more than antiquarianism.

But the last few years have witnessed a remarkable revival of interest, both popular and scholarly, in the Civil War and Reconstruction era. The number of visitors to the national battlefield parks has reached a new high, and the sharp outcry over threatened commercial encroachments on the sites of Manassas and Antietam suggests the significance that American memory attaches to these hallowed military fields. Reenactments of Civil

---

[1] Allan Nevins, *Ordeal of the Union* (8 vols.; New York: Charles Scribner's Sons, 1947–1971); Bruce Catton *The Centennial History of the Civil War* (3 vols.; Garden City, N. Y.: Doubleday & Co., 1961–1965); Shelby Foote, *The Civil War: A Narrative* (3 vols.; New York: Random House, 1958–1974).

War battles, which dropped out of fashion after the centennial years, have resumed, and each year some forty thousand buffs, young and old, put on uniforms of blue or gray, pick up their muzzleloaders, and march off to present "living history" impressions of Civil War combat. In 1988 the largest reenactment in history was staged at Gettysburg.

Readers have turned back to books on the Civil War, attracted by important new studies that not merely retell the facts but recapture, with great immediacy, the experience of the war years. One thinks—to mention only a few, taken almost at random—of James Robertson's revealing life of A. P. Hill, of Emory Thomas's spirited recreation of "Jeb" Stuart, of Stephen W. Sears's fine, critical life of George B. McClellan, of Jean Harvey Baker's shrewdly sympathetic biography of Mary Todd Lincoln, of Gerald Linderman's and Reid Mitchell's disturbing analyses of soldiers' experiences, of James M. McPherson's absorbing narrative history of the war, of Leon Litwack's graphic reconstruction of the lives of ex-slaves during their first years of freedom, and of Eric Foner's eloquent account of Reconstruction.[2]

Fictional works on the war have made the conflict come alive for even more readers. William Safire's *Freedom* and Gore Vidal's *Lincoln* have reached hundreds of thousands. Even larger audiences have watched Peter Batty's brilliant documentary, "The Divided Union" and the television adaptation of Vidal's *Lincoln*. It is hardly surprising that *U.S. News and World Report* recently featured a cover story, "Reliving The Civil War," which asked "Why America's Bloodiest Conflict Still Grips Us 125 Years Later."[3]

Several years ago Robert Penn Warren offered the best an-

[2]James I. Robertson, Jr., *General A. P. Hill: The Story of a Confederate Warrior* (New York: Random House, 1987); Emory M. Thomas, *Bold Dragoon: The Life of J. E. B. Stuart* (New York: Harper & Row, 1986); Stephen W. Sears, *George B. McClellan: The Young Napoleon* (New York: Ticknor & Fields, 1988); Jean Harvey Baker, *Mary Todd Lincoln: A Biography* (New York: W. W. Norton and Co., 1987); Gerald F. Linderman, *Embattled Courage: The Experience of Combat in the American Civil War* (New York: The Free Press, 1987); Reid Mitchell, *Civil War Soldiers: Their Expectations and Their Experiences* (New York: Viking, 1988); James M. McPherson, *Battle Cry of Freedom: The Civil War Era* (New York: Oxford University Press, 1988); Leon Litwack, *Been in the Storm So Long: The Aftermath of Slavery* (New York: Alfred A. Knopf, 1979); Eric Foner, *Reconstruction: America's Unfinished Revolution* (New York: Harper & Row, 1988).

[3]Lew Lord and others, "In the Grip of the Civil War," *U.S. News & World Report*, August 15, 1988, pp. 48–59.

swer to that question: "The Civil War is, for the American imagination, the great single event of our history. Without too much
wrenching, it may, in fact, be said to *be* American history."[4]
Because the Civil War is so central in the American story, it is
essential that it be remembered not alone for its battles and its
military leaders but for the great social and intellectual movements that helped to bring the war about: the embattled proslavery defense in the South, which led the section to the disastrous
step of secession, and the antislavery movement in the North,
which insisted on curbing the South's "peculiar institution" as a
means of putting it on the road to ultimate extinction. Many
leaders of that Northern movement deserve a place in history—
William H. Seward, Salmon P. Chase, Benjamin F. Wade, Owen
Lovejoy, Wendell Phillips, to name just a few—but none more
completely embodied his section's values and more fully voiced
its goals than Charles Sumner. As Senator from Massachusetts
during the 1850's, Sumner became, as Carl Sandburg has said,
"the most perfect impersonation of what the South wanted to
secede from." Sumner's biography helps us to understand how
the Civil War came about and to appreciate the legacy it has left
us. Republication of *Charles Sumner and the Coming of the Civil
War,* is, then, a contribution to our ongoing search for national
self-understanding, and I hope that it will do something to explain
how the United States drifted into the bloodiest and most divisive
war in its history.

Not long ago a historian whose work I greatly respect remarked that at least once every two years he regularly rereads
each of the many books he has published. While I admire his
patience, I do not follow his practice. Indeed, once a book of mine
has been published, I rarely look at it except perhaps to verify a
quotation or a fact. Consequently it has been more than a quarter
of a century since I systematically read *Charles Sumner and the
Coming of the Civil War,* as I was obliged to do for the preparation of this new edition.

My first reaction was one of surprise that I once knew so much

---

[4]Robert Penn Warren, *The Legacy of the Civil War* (Cambridge: Harvard University
Press, 1961), p. 3.

that I have forgotten. I fear that I could not now pass an examination that required me to trace the transformation of the Massachusetts Conscience Whigs into Republicans. Nor could I readily remember the details of Charles Sumner's complex medical history during the years when he was recovering from Preston S. Brooks's assault.

In a way this distance from the book gives me a chance to see it in perspective and to reassess it. Of course I am troubled by the few factual inaccuracies that have turned up, and I am happy that these, together with an occasional typographical slip, have been silently corrected in this edition.[5] If it were possible to do so, I might introduce some other changes that, without essentially altering the character of the book, would reflect the findings of recent scholarship. For instance, if I were redoing all the footnotes, I no longer have to cite the 114 manuscript collections in the United States, Great Britain, and Canada which I searched for Sumner letters but could refer to the comprehensive microfilm edition of *The Papers of Charles Sumner*, edited by Beverly Wilson Palmer.[6] Drawing on Dale Baum's *The Civil War Party System: The Case of Massachusetts, 1848–1876*, I could now provide a fuller account of the Bird Club and other political groups that formed the basis of Sumner's political organization in Massachusetts.[7] And, following recent studies by William E. Gienapp, I could present a much more complete analysis of the social and economic composition of the Republican party, which Sumner helped create.[8]

Some other changes would reflect a difference in emphasis rather than new research. It is probably true, as one critic has

[5]Several kind readers—notably Professor Samuel Shapiro, of the University of Notre Dame—have pointed out these slips. In a highly critical essay, "The Pulitzer Prize Treatment of Charles Sumner" (*Massachusetts Review*, II [1961]:749–769), Louis Ruchames did not identify any factual errors in my book but charged that by selective quotations I misrepresented Sumner's life. This charge was parroted, without independent examination of the evidence, in Paul Goodman's "David Donald's *Charles Sumner* Reconsidered" (*New England Quarterly*, XXXVII [1964]: 373–387). Both these writers complained that I distorted Sumner's views by quoting only phrases and sentences from his writings, rather than paragraphs and pages. Few other readers, I believe, share their eagerness for more of Sumner's prose.

[6]*The Papers of Charles Sumner*, ed. by Beverly Wilson Palmer (85 reels; Alexandria, Virginia: Chadwyck-Healey, Inc.)

[7]Dale Baum, *The Civil War Party System: The Case of Massachusetts, 1848–1876* (Chapel Hill: The University of North Carolina Press, 1984).

[8]William E. Gienapp, *The Origins of the Republican Party, 1852–1856* (New York: Oxford University Press, 1987).

charged, that I have quoted more derogatory comments about Sumner than I have admiring tributes from his contemporaries.[9] In part this is because the most glowing praise was offered only after Sumner was safely dead, and its sincerity is suspect; it is also true that Sumner's critics were generally more interesting than his admirers. If a biographer, with limited space, has to choose between Carl Schurz's praise of Sumner's "moral courage" and the "sincerity of his convictions," and Henry Adams's remark that Sumner's mind "had reached the calm of water which receives and reflects images without absorbing them; it contains nothing but itself," can there be any doubt as to which he will include? Nevertheless, I wish I had been better able to portray Sumner as his best friends and admirers saw him: amiable, pure, earnest, and affectionate.

I wish, too, that I had written more fully about Sumner's relationships with some of the leading New England thinkers of his day. I have treated at some length the influence that William Ellery Channing exerted on Sumner, but I had much too little to say about his friendships with Ralph Waldo Emerson, Brownson Alcott, Orestes Brownson, Margaret Fuller, and others in the Transcendentalist group, and I did not adequately treat the role that Theodore Parker played as intermediary between Sumner and these reformers.[10]

But there are not many other changes that I would make if I were rewriting *Charles Sumner and the Coming of the Civil War.*[11] Most of the interpretations I advanced have stood the test of time. Since the publication of this book, and its companion volume, *Charles Sumner and the Rights of Man* (1970), no one else has felt impelled to write another biography of Sumner.

I believe, however, that what I intended to be one of the major contribution of this book to general American history has

---

[9]Gilbert Osofsky, "Cardboard Yankee: How Not to Study the Mind of Charles Sumner," *Reviews in American History,* I (1973): 597–599.

[10]For a preliminary exploration of this topic, see Bill Ledbetter, "Charles Sumner: Political Activist for the New England Transcendentalists," *Historian,* XLIV (1982):347–363.

[11]For instance, my account of Sumner's medical history after the Brooks assault is confirmed, in nearly every particular, by Laura A. White's "Was Charles Sumner Shamming, 1856–1859?" *New England Quarterly,* XXXIII (1960): 291–324, which appeared after this book went to press. William E. Gienapp's researches have supported my analysis of the importance that the Brooks assault on Sumner had in the 1856 election. Gienapp, "The Crime Against Sumner: The Caning of Charles Sumner and the Rise of the Republican Party," *Civil War History,* XXV (1979):218–245.

been somewhat overlooked. I conceived this biography as a case study of the American as reformer in politics, which would analyze the four essential elements needed for success in that role. The first, and most essential, of these is the existence of a real, palpable, and threatening evil that demands correction; for Sumner, after some experimentation with other causes, that was slavery. Another prerequisite is a body of public thought that can be mobilized against the evil. Sumner was able powerfully to appeal to widespread, if latent, beliefs of New Englanders in the equality of men and in the idea of Progress. Third, for a reform to take hold, there have to be cracks or fissures in the established social structure, where seeds of change can take root. In nineteenth-century New England, industrialization and urbanization presented challenges that divided the established leadership of the region and afforded younger people an opportunity to question the traditional politics of deference.

But, finally, for a reformer to be successful he must be deeply committed to his cause, not simply on intellectual or philosophical grounds but because of profound personal involvement. One of the main purposes of this book is to show that Sumner's decision to become a reformer, and his willingness to stick to his cause despite social isolation, hostile criticism, and even physical assault, were deeply rooted in his early family experiences. Because of this emphasis, one colleague half-jokingly remarked that *Charles Sumner and the Coming of the Civil War* was the most completely Freudian biography he ever read. In a sense he may have been right, for the book is informed by psychoanalytical insights—though not, I hope, marred by psychoanalytical jargon. But my purpose was anything but the kind of reductionism that is so often the mark of so-called "psychobiography." Instead it was, and is, my hope that *Charles Sumner and the Coming of the Civil War* can serve as a model to be tested by the life experiences of other American reformers.

David Herbert Donald

Lincoln, Massachusetts
19 August 1988

PREFACE TO THE
ORIGINAL EDITION

✤

THIS is the first biography of Charles Sumner to be written in fifty years. The neglect of Sumner has not been due to any unawareness of his importance in American history. The more familiar and dramatic episodes of his career spring readily to mind. For example, as Mr. Bruce Catton has recently reminded us in *This Hallowed Ground,* [1] Preston Brooks's assault upon Sumner in the Senate chamber in 1856 may be regarded as the first blow of the Civil War. Students recognize that Sumner's life touched upon virtually every significant movement in mid-nineteenth-century American history. He was an advocate of international peace; leader of educational and prison reform movements; organizer of the antislavery Whigs; a founder of the Republican party; the outstanding antislavery spokesman in the Senate during the 1850's; chief of the Radical Republicans during the Civil War; chairman of the Senate Committee on Foreign Relations during both the war and the Reconstruction years; a principal architect of the congressional program for reconstructing the conquered South; and pioneer in the Liberal Republican movement of 1872. In a period when senators often exercised more influence than presidents of the United States, Charles Sumner was one of the most potent and enduring forces in the American government.

Sumner's role in American history is unique. I can think of few, if any, other instances in which a "statesman *doctrinaire,*" as Charles Francis Adams, Jr., called Sumner—a man inflexibly com-

[1] New York: Doubleday & Company, Inc.; 1956, pp. 1–7.

mitted to a set of basic ideas as moral principles—has exercised political power in the United States. Sumner's career illustrates the problems the man of theories must confront when he becomes the man of action. He was further distinctive in that he alone of his contemporaries moved with equal assurance in the antithetical worlds of New England letters and of Washington politics. He was friend to both Ralph Waldo Emerson and Pierre Soulé. In addition, Sumner was almost the only nineteenth-century American politician who was nearly as widely known in Europe as in his own country. At a time when President Abraham Lincoln had to confess that he had no personal acquaintances abroad, Sumner knew practically every important political leader and literary figure in England, France, Germany, and Italy.

These were some of the reasons why I began research toward a biography nearly ten years ago. At the time I was, fortunately, not aware of the opinion Mr. Edward H. O'Neill, the historian of American biography, had rendered upon Sumner: "He had one of the most complex characters of any man in American public life, a character that requires not only industry but knowledge and genius for its proper interpretation."[2] Of the "genius" allegedly requisite I do not speak, but I can certainly agree that a Sumner biographer must exhibit industry. The published and manuscript records of his career are almost overwhelmingly voluminous. Sumner himself began the editing and publishing of his *Works*, which run to fifteen volumes,[3] but these include, I estimate, less than one half of his public utterances. His papers, which he bequeathed to Harvard University, total somewhere between 40,000 and 60,000 items. Most of these, of course, are letters to Sumner, for the senator's own letters are scattered through dozens of manuscript repositories in the United States, Canada, and Great Britain.

Finding Sumner materials has, indeed, been less a problem than assimilating them. I found, once I had begun this project, that I should have to know not merely something of Massachusetts and national politics, but a good deal of fields where I have

[2] *A History of American Biography* (Philadelphia: University of Pennsylvania Press; 1935), p. 68.
[3] *The Works of Charles Sumner* (Boston: Lee and Shepard; 1870–83). Another edition, misleadingly called *Charles Sumner: His Complete Works* (Boston: Lee & Shepard; 1900; 20 vols.) is in fact only a reprinting, with new introductory material, of the *Works*.

no technical training—constitutional law; rhetoric; medicine; and psychology. The following pages, I fear, reveal that I am still all too in expert in these matters, but I have tried to learn and, as my acknowledgments will show, I have been fortunate enough to have some of the best teachers in the world to help me.

I wish I could say that I have unraveled the riddle of Sumner and that I am now presenting the "definitive" biography. Of course I make no such claims. Virtually every sentence in the following chapters should have an interjected phrase like "it seems to me," or "to the best of my knowledge," or "in my opinion." Out of charity to the reader I have omitted such qualifiers; out of charity for the author he will supply them for himself.

While I was preparing this book, interested friends—perhaps recalling that a leading American jurist once called Sumner the most objectionable figure in American history—kept asking: "Is your biography going to be a sympathetic one?" I have never, I think, been able to answer the question satisfactorily. Certainly I started my research without conscious preconceptions or partialities. The longer I worked, the less relevant the question of sympathy became. After living with Sumner for a decade, after learning more about him than I know about any other human being, alive or dead—a great deal more, in some respects, than he ever knew about himself—I think of him almost as I would a member of my family. Rarely does it occur to one to ask whether he really "likes" his father or his mother or any other member of his family; these are the people with whom one lives, who are important in his life, and whom he tries to understand.

My purpose has been to understand Sumner and his motives, to recreate a very complex personality, not to hale him for trial before the bar of history. Where he was misinformed, or partially informed, or actually in error, I have not hesitated to set the record straight, but I have not felt it my proper function to sit in moral judgment upon his career, handing down verdicts of either praise or condemnation for his actions.

In trying to explain the motives underlying Sumner's actions, I am not making even an implicit judgment on the causes for which he fought. If—to make an assumption I carefully do *not* make in the following pages—Sumner took up the cause of prison reform solely in order to advance his own political career, his motive in no sense derogates from the desirability of reforming prisons; nor would the unworthiness of his motive keep him from doing valiant service in that worthy cause. In particular, I hope that no one will accuse me of sympathizing with Negro slavery because I have not interjected a little moral discourse after each of Sumner's orations to the effect that he was on the side of the angels. Surely in the middle of the twentieth century there are some things that do not need to be said.

While some readers may feel that I have gone much too far in exploring the depths of Sumner's mind, others may object that I have not explicitly discussed such ultimate questions as the causes of the Civil War. These matters, in my opinion, are beyond a biographer's proper competence. Certainly the debate about whether the Civil War was an "irrepressible conflict" or a "needless war" is not likely to be settled through a study of one participant in the sectional crisis, even of a key figure like Sumner. The more I have learned about the complexities of Sumner's personality and career, the less willing I have grown to generalize about other nineteenth-century American politicians.

If biography is to have a useful function in the historical craft, perhaps it is to steer us away from cosmic and unanswerable questions toward the intricacies of actuality. As André Gide once remarked, it is the part of wisdom to ask not why, but how events happen. I hope that it may be helpful in this biography to examine the way in which a single actor in a historical crisis arrived at his position of power. In 1845 any observer would have predicted that Sumner's chances for political success were much less than those of Robert C. Winthrop or Edward Everett, considerably inferior to those of John Gorham Palfrey or Charles Francis Adams. Yet, as the following chapters show, a series of developments—the Conscience Whig movement; the Free Soil party; the coalition of Democrats and antislavery men; the rise of nativism; the Preston Brooks assault; the factional disputes within the Republican party—sifted out Sumner's rivals and left him the unchallenged spokesman of his own state. The historical philosopher who could explain Sumner's triumph in terms of the interaction of forces, whether of economics, society, or personality, would have to be both daring and wise—and even then, perhaps, he might overlook the part that accident plays in selecting leaders.

I have concluded my book with 1861, when Sumner and his party finally attained power. These chapters form a self-contained unit. The uses to which Sumner and his associates put their power during the stormy Civil War and Reconstruction periods I expect to make the subject of a companion volume at a not too distant date.

A few words need to be added about the documentation of this book. Since, as Edward H. O'Neill correctly observed, Sumner's previous biographers[4] generally omitted "all facts and inferences that might adversely affect the character of their hero," I have placed little reliance upon earlier works, but have tried, wherever possible, to work with the original manuscript sources. I have, however, found a great deal of useful material in the standard four-volume *Memoir and Letters of Charles Sumner,* by Edward Lillie Pierce, his authorized biographer.[5]

Because Sumner's *Works* represent what the senator in the 1870's wished he had said, rather than what he actually said in earlier years, I have usually referred to the manuscripts or to the earliest pamphlet editions of his speeches.

A few liberties have been taken with some of the quotations in this book. Where Sumner, in haste, used "Comm[ttee]," "Gov[t]," "&," etc., I have spelled the words out. For easier reading I have also transposed the persons of a few quotations. Where Sumner may have written "my condition," I have said "his condition." I have also dispensed with most initial and terminal ellipses for quoted materials. Instead of writing: ". . . he was right. . . ." I have simply said: "He was right." In no case, of course, have I tampered with the meaning of any quoted passage.

[4]Previous biographies of Sumner include: D. A. Harsha: *The Life of Charles Sumner* . . . (New York: Dayton and Burdick; 1856); Jeremiah and J. D. Chaplin: *Life of Charles Sumner* (Boston: D. Lothrop & Co.; 1874); C. Edwards Lester: *Life and Public Services of Charles Sumner* (New York: United States Publishing Company; 1874); Elias Nason: *The Life and Times of Charles Sumner* (Boston: B. B. Russell; 1874); Anna Laurens Dawes: *Charles Sumner* (New York: Dodd, Mead & Co.; 1892); Archibald H. Grimke: *The Life of Charles Sumner* . . . (New York: Funk & Wagnalls Co.; 1892); Moorfield Storey: *Charles Sumner* (Boston: Houghton Mifflin Co.; 1900); George H. Haynes: *Charles Sumner* (Philadelphia: George W. Jacobs & Co.; 1909); and Walter G. Shotwell: *Life of Charles Sumner* (New York: Thomas Y. Crowell Company; 1910). A biographical essay written by Carl Schurz in the 1890's has recently been published: Arthur Reed Hogue (ed.): *Charles Sumner: An Essay by Carl Schurz* (Urbana: University of Illinois Press; 1951). For a critical appraisal of these and other writings, see Louis Ruchames: "Charles Sumner and American Historiography," *Journal of Negro History,* XXXVIII (1953), 139–60.

[5]Boston: Roberts Brothers; 1878–93. Hereafter cited as Pierce.

My footnotes are designed to give sources for specific statements and quotations, not to offer a general bibliography of pre-Civil War history, a task that would require a volume at least as long as the present one. Consequently these notes—though surely more than ample for most readers—do not adequately reflect my indebtedness to scholars who have written on nineteenth-century American history. For nearly every topic discussed in this book I could have referred to the works of Avery O. Craven, Oscar Handlin, Allan Nevins, Roy F. Nichols, James G. Randall, and others as excellent secondary sources. Fortunately the recent publication of the admirable *Harvard Guide to American History*[6] makes such citations here supererogatory.

[6]Edited by Oscar Handlin, et al., Cambridge: Harvard University Press; 1954.

ACKNOWLEDGMENTS

During the course of my ten years of research on Charles Sumner I have incurred many personal and professional obligations, which it is a pleasure to acknowledge. Perhaps my largest debt is to the staff of the Houghton Library, of Harvard University, where the voluminous Sumner manuscripts are housed. Without the permission of Mr. William A. Jackson to use and quote from these papers, the present book could not have been written, and without the courteous and efficient assistance of Miss Carolyn Jakeman my researches could not have been completed.

The staff of the Massachusetts Historical Society has been equally generous and equally helpful. Mr. Stephen T. Riley, the Director, has been an invaluable guide to that library's rich collections, and Miss Winifred Collins has efficiently handled my most time-consuming requests. I am grateful to the Trustees of the Adams Trust, and to Mr. Lyman Butterfield, the editor-in-chief of the Adams Papers, for permission to quote from the Adams Manuscripts, which I have read in microfilm.

During several summers of research in Washington I have invariably been treated with great kindness by the officials of the Library of Congress. I am particularly indebted to Mr. David C. Mearns, Mr. Robert Land, Dr. Elizabeth McPherson, and Dr. C. P. Powell of the Manuscripts Division; to Mr. Hirst Milhollen and Mr. Milton Kaplan, of the Prints and Photographs Division; and to Colonel Willard Webb, Chief of the Stack and Reader Service.

The full extent of my obligation to the scholars at The National Archives does not appear in this volume, but I must acknowledge my gratitude to Mr. W. Neil Franklin, Chief of the

Reader Service, to Mr. C. L. Lokke, of the Foreign Affairs Branch, and to Miss Josephine Cobb, of the Still Picture Branch.

Other librarians, too, have given freely of their time by help-ing me search out Sumner manuscripts or by solving difficult reference problems. Among those to whom I am particularly indebted for materials incorporated in this volume are: Miss Ellen F. Adams, of the Baker Library, Dartmouth College; Mr. T. D. Seymour Bassett, of the Wilbur Library, University of Vermont; Miss Elizabeth Biggert, of the Ohio State Archaeological and His-torical Library; Mr. Carey S. Bliss, of the Henry E. Huntington Library; Miss Alice H. Bonnell, of the Columbia University Li-brary; Miss Dorothy Bridgewater, of Sterling Library, Yale Uni-versity; Mr. Clarence Brigham, Director of the American Antiquarian Society; Professor Paul H. Buck, Librarian of Har-vard University; Miss Margaret E. Butterfield, of the Rush Rhees Library, University of Rochester; Mr. Alexander Clark, of the Firestone Library, Princeton University; Miss Georgia Coffin, of the Cornell University Library; Miss Charlotte D. Conover, of the New Hampshire Historical Society; Mr. Thomas DeValcourt, of the Craigie House Library; Mr. Kimball C. Elkins, of the Harvard University Archives; Mr. William Ewing, of the William L. Cle-ments Library, University of Michigan; Miss Margaret Flint, of the Illinois State Historical Library; Miss Clara E. Follette, of the Vermont Historical Society; Miss Hannah D. French, of the Wellesley College Library; Miss Mary Isabel Fry, of the Henry E. Huntington Library; Mr. Ebenezer Gay, of the Athenaeum, Bos-ton; Mr. Zoltán Haraszti, of the Boston Public Library; Mr. Robert H. Haynes, of the Harvard University Library; Mrs. Alice P. Hook, of the Historical and Philosophical Society of Ohio; Mr. Elmer M. Hunt, of the New Hampshire Historical Society; Miss Edna L. Jacobsen, of the New York State Library; Miss Hazel E. Joselyn, of the Baker Library, Dartmouth College; Miss Lucile Kane, of the Minnesota Historical Society; Mr. William Kaye Lamb, Do-minion Archivist, The Public Archives of Canada; Mr. Edward C. Lathem, of the Baker Library, Dartmouth College; Mr. Wilmer R. Leech, of the New York Historical Society; Miss Helen M. McFarland, of the Kansas State Historical Society; Miss Dorothy McKinley, of the Newberry Library; Mr. Watt P. Marchman, Di-rector of the Rutherford B. Hayes Library; Mr. Walter M. Merrill,

Director of the Essex Institute; Mr. Bradley Mitchell, of the Cornell University Library; Mr. Richard W. Morin, Director of the Baker Library, Dartmouth College; Mr. Robert Rosenthal, of the University of Chicago Library; Mr. W. O. Rourke, Director of the Buffalo Public Library; Miss Marian B. Rowe, of the Maine Historical Society; Miss Mattie Russell, of the Duke University Library; Miss Judith E. Sachs, of the Institute for Advanced Study; Miss Margaret Scriven, of the Chicago Historical Society; Mr. Clifford K. Shipton, Custodian of the Harvard University Archives; Mr. Lester G. Wells, of the University of Syracuse Library; Mr. R. N. Williams, II, Director of the Pennsylvania Historical Society; Mrs. Alene Lowe White, of the Western Reserve Historical Society; Mr. Walter Muir Whitehill, Director of the Athenaeum, Boston; Miss Constance Winchell, of the Columbia University Library.

I owe a very special debt of gratitude to my dear friend, Norma Cuthbert, of the Henry E. Huntington Library.

A number of collectors have generously permitted me to examine Sumner manuscripts in their possession: Mr. Charles Sumner Bird (who has since presented the Bird MSS. to Houghton Library); Mrs. E. C. Reeves; Mr. Boyd B. Stutler; and Mr. George H. Wettach. My indebtedness to Mr. Charles M. Segal, who has allowed me to make extensive use of his large collection of Sumner materials, is very heavy. Mr. Herbert W. Sumner, Jr., of Fair Lawn, N.J., and Mrs. Charles Sumner, of Baltimore, have greatly assisted me on genealogical matters.

My professional colleagues have been unvaryingly kind in responding to my numerous appeals for advice and assistance. Especially am I obligated to Professor Bernard Barber, of Barnard College; Professor I. H. Bartlett, of the Massachusetts Institute of Technology; Dean Jacques Barzun, of Columbia University; Dr. Saul Benison, of Columbia University; Mrs. Harry E. Pratt, of the Illinois State Archives; Mr. Bruce Catton, of *American Heritage;* Professor Sigmund Diamond, of Columbia University; Dr. Martin Duberman, of Yale University; Professor Fletcher M. Green, of the University of North Carolina; Professor Walter Harding, of Genesee State Teachers College; Professor Leonard W. Levy, of Brandeis University; Professor Dumas Malone, of the University of Virginia; Mr. Taylor Milne, Director of the Institute of Histori-

ACKNOWLEDGMENTS xxii

cal Research, London; Professor Allan Nevins, of the Henry E.
Huntington Library; Dean John G. Palfrey, of Columbia University; Professor Harold Schwartz, of Kent State University; Professor Hans L. Trefousse, of Brooklyn College; Professor Robert K.
Webb, of Columbia University; and Professor C. Vann Wood-
ward, of the Johns Hopkins University. Professor Frank Freidel,
of Harvard University, has aided me in innumerable ways and
most generously made his voluminous notes on the Francis
Lieber MSS. available to me.

To many younger scholars I am also profoundly indebted.
Three of my own doctoral students at Columbia University did
valiant service as research assistants during various stages of this
project: Mr. Albert Fein, of Long Island University; Mr. Grady
McWhiney, of the University of California (Berkeley); and Dr.
Irwin F. Unger, of Long Beach State College. Other Columbia
students have kept an eye out for Sumner materials during the
course of their own researches: Mr. Richard Abrams, of Columbia
University; Mrs. Helene Baer; Mrs. Sylvia Crane; Dr. Stanley P.
Hirshson, of Paterson State Teachers College; Dr. Ari A. Hoogen-
boom, of Pennsylvania State University; Mr. Edward Leonard, of
Iona College; Dr. Samuel Shapiro; and Mr. Theodore V. Theo-
bald. Mr. Frank Otto Gatell, a graduate student at Harvard University, has generously shared his findings in the Palfrey MSS. with
me.

There are not words adequate to acknowledge my obligation
to busy colleagues who took time from their own researches to
read this manuscript. My deepest debt is to Professors Richard
Hofstadter, of Columbia University, and Allan Nevins, of the
Henry E. Huntington Library, who read all of it; I have profited
throughout by their detailed and stimulating criticisms. In my
early chapters Professor Henry Steele Commager, of Amherst
College, caught numerous blunders, and I have drawn heavily
upon his profound knowledge of Joseph Story's career. My chapter on Sumner's European travels has benefited from the criticisms of Professor Herman Ausubel, of Columbia University, who
has also generously shared with me his researches in English
manuscript collections. Dean Roy F. Nichols, of the University of
Pennsylvania, gave me the benefit of his unparalleled expertness
in the politics of the 1850's by reading the last half of the book, and

the final three chapters have been greatly improved by the close critical reading given them by Professor David M. Potter of Yale University.

Through the kindness of Professor T. A. Larson, I have been privileged to examine the notes collected by the late Professor Laura A. White, of the University of Wyoming, for a projected biography of Sumner. Since I received access to these notes late in the course of my own researches, I found they generally referred to materials I had already examined, yet in a number of cases Miss White's jottings led me to fresh and useful sources.

For advice on medical aspects of Sumner's history I am greatly in debt to Dr. Bronson S. Ray, of the Cornell Medical Center, and to Dr. Julia L. Schneider, of the Neurological Institute of New York.

My publisher, Mr. Alfred A. Knopf, has given me constant encouragement in an undertaking that has at times seemed endless and overwhelmingly difficult.

For subventions without which the travel and research required for this book would have been almost impossible, I am indebted to the following organizations: the American Philosophical Society; the Columbia University Council for Research in the Social Sciences; the George A. and Eliza Gardner Howard Foundation; and the Henry E. Huntington Library. To the Institute for Advanced Study, and to its Director, Dr. Robert Oppenheimer, I am grateful for a stimulating year that provided me the ideal surroundings in which this manuscript was actually drafted.

My wife, Aïda DiPace Donald, has shared with me her research findings in New York newspapers and manuscript collections, and all my chapters have profited by the careful critical reading she gave them.

A great many others have assisted me on the later phases of Sumner's career. I hope to have the opportunity in a future volume to express my indebtedness to them.

CONTENTS

ILLUSTRATIONS

Charles Sumner
and the Coming of the Civil War

CHAPTER I

A Natural Coldness

❧

"T HESE jottings are made for friendly eyes," the newly elected
senator from Massachusetts wrote as a postscript to his autobiography, "to be used more or less, or not at all, as shall be thought
best." [1] The senatorial contest of 1851 had been the most embittered and prolonged in Massachusetts history, and Charles Sumner wished to repel charges that he was a political nonentity, a
mere rhetorician elected through an unholy and corrupt coalition. As his autobiographical notes had this practical purpose,
they naturally were not modest, and Sumner's old friend and
former Harvard professor, John Gorham Palfrey, to whom he entrusted them, was able to work them into a laudatory newspaper
sketch of the new antislavery senator as a statesman whose name
would illuminate "the historical page of the triumphs of Freedom
in the nineteenth century." [2] Touched by Palfrey's words, which,
in fact, merely echoed his own, Sumner was delighted by "that
beautiful sketch" of his career. "I felt a throb of gratitude to you,"
he wrote Palfrey, "but a deep feeling also of my own unworthiness. . . . As a composition your article is all that could be
desired. As a token of friendship more than I deserve." [3]

[1] Sumner's MS. autobiography [May 1851], John Gorham Palfrey MSS.
[2] Boston *Commonwealth*, May 16, 1851. Unless otherwise expressly indicated, all newspaper references are to daily editions.
[3] Sumner to Palfrey [May 1851], Palfrey MSS.

· 1 ·

Sumner's autobiographical jottings, like Palfrey's published tribute to him, were revealingly reticent. The new Massachusetts
senator stated that he had been born in Boston on January 6,
1811, but he had nothing else to say about his boyhood. Neither
here nor at any other time did he look back to the good old days
when Boston was a compact town of only 40,000 inhabitants,
most of whom knew each other by sight. He never told anecdotes
of playing in the mud flats of Back Bay, where now some of the
proudest houses in Boston rise. He had no tales of wandering on
the wharves, thronged with sailing ships manned by rough-
voiced sailors shouting in unknown tongues. He never remembered roaming through the markets, sniffing the exotic aroma of
tea from the Orient, tasting figs from Smyrna, and sampling bar-
rels of West Indies molasses through straws adeptly inserted
through the bungholes. He had no recollections of snowball fights
on the Common or of sledding down Beacon Hill across the main
thoroughfare of Washington Street in defiance of all traffic.
Sumner never had the feeling of his contemporary, Edward
Everett Hale, that Boston "was a good place in which to be born,
and a good place in which to grow to manhood." [4]

Sumner's autobiography was equally silent on his genealogy.
Though he knew that New Englanders had an almost Oriental
reverence for their ancestors and delighted in tracing family
lineages through assorted Patiences, Ashabels, and Eliphalets
back to the founders of Massachusetts Bay Colony, the newly
elected senator made no effort to exploit the fact that on both
sides of his family he could claim industrious and God-fearing
forebears who had settled in New England in the early 1630's.
He did not mention that his mother's grandfather had been an
extensive landholder, the surveyor of Hanover, in Plymouth
County, a town selectman, a member of the Revolutionary Committee on Public Safety, and later a state representative, or that
his maternal grandmother was a descendant of Governor William Bradford, of Plymouth. [5] Nor did he refer to the career of his

[4] Hale: A New England Boyhood (New York: Cassell Publishing Company;
1893), p. v.
[5] John S. Barry: A Historical Sketch of the Town of Hanover, Mass., with
Family Genealogies (Boston: Samuel G. Drake; 1853), pp. 319–35. Barry as-

paternal grandfather, Major Job Sumner, who quit his Harvard classes to fight under General Washington and after the Revolution served as United States commissioner to settle the accounts between the Confederation and Georgia.[6]

Any temptation Sumner may have had to proclaim himself the heir of the Puritans in politics was curbed by his knowledge that his father had been born out of wedlock.[7] Inbred, provincial Boston, where such scandals were never forgotten, would be all too likely to rake up the gossip about the dashing Major Sumner's failure to marry Esther Holmes, by whom he begat his one son. Remembering the grandson's fondness for oppressed races, Boston maiden aunts speculated—without any evidence whatever—that the mysterious Esther had been "partly of negro or Indian blood." [8] Prudently the new senator preferred to draw the veil over the whole subject of his genealogy: "It seems to me better to leave it all unsaid." [9]

More surprising was Sumner's silence about his parents. Of his father, Charles Pinckney Sumner, the son merely remarked that he "was a lawyer by profession . . . a person of literary taste and knowledge, of remarkable independence and sterling integrity." [1] The son's coolness reflected the fact that the father was a singularly unlovable man.[2] Presumably he had not always been so formal, so obdurately fixed in his ways. As a student at Harvard he had become a warm friend of young Joseph Story, of Salem, who inspired him to attempt verses in the stately tradi-

---

serted that Sumner's mother, Relief Jacob, was "probably of Jewish descent"; this allegation led Frank Preston Stearns (*Cambridge Sketches* [Philadelphia: J. B. Lippincott Co.; 1905], p. 180) to identify "the Hebrew element in Sumner's nature; the inflexibility of purpose, the absolute self-devotion, and even the prophetic forecast." Such a theory of inherited racial traits is, of course, highly unscientific. But, in any case, the Jewish strain in Sumner's ancestry is dubious. At no point in his career, when virtually every other possible weapon was used against him, were anti-Semitic charges raised.

[6] On Job Sumner see Pierce, I, 3–10; Records of the Harvard College Faculty, III, 258, 265; IV, 6, 60; sundry commissions and clippings in C. P. Sumner MSS. On the Sumner genealogy as a whole see William Sumner Appleton: *Record of the Descendants of William Sumner of Dorchester, Mass., 1636* (Boston; 1879).

[7] Ibid., p. 176.

[8] Robert Carter to E. L. Pierce, Dec. 1, 1877, E. L. Pierce MSS.

[9] Sumner's autobiography, Palfrey MSS. Cf. Sumner to George Sumner, July 15, 1842, Sumner MSS.

[1] Sumner's autobiography, Palfrey MSS.

[2] Pierce, I, 11–30; James Spear Loring: *The Hundred Boston Orators* (2nd ed.; Boston: John P. Jewett and Company; 1853), pp. 325–33.

tion of Alexander Pope's rhymed couplets. The friendship did not expire with college days, and in florid fashion Sumner claimed that he treasured Story's frequent letters as "truly the *balsam of friendship*, . . . infinitely more sacred than that which bedewed the hand of laughterloving *Venus*, when wounded by the sacrilegious shaft of *Diomed.*" Under Story's influence he became an ardent Jeffersonian, at a time when only Federalism was respectable in Massachusetts, and he even talked of editing a party newspaper in Boston.[3] But, by the time Charles Sumner was born, his father's feeble fires of rebellion had burned low. "I have now passed more than half the age of man," he wrote in 1811, at the age of thirty-five, "and the ambition of youth is in me now checked by the . . . cautious, and sober thoughts of age." The insecurity of his clouded birth and impoverished childhood, his comparative failure in his law practice, and his financial worries over his growing family he concealed behind an outward front of stiff and stilted formality. Long after the style had changed, he, like Major Thomas Melville, continued to wear a tricornered hat, and he retained to his death the punctilious eighteenth-century etiquette of saluting acquaintances upon the streets by "bowing low, touching his mouth with his hand, and waving it back to his side." His family rarely, if ever, saw him smile.[4]

His wife brought little more warmth to the Sumner household. Tall and stately, with a smooth olive complexion and lustrous brown eyes, Relief Jacob had been a twenty-five-year-old seamstress when she married, and she carried some of her spinster ways into her married life. She did not know how to express affection; not until after her death did Charles learn that she had always cherished a lock of his baby hair. Even her friends remarked that she was "distant" or that she had "the old-school dignity of manner," and she impressed on them her "evident superiority of mind."[5]

Doubtless it was the memory of his own cheerless home

[3] C. P. Sumner: *The Compass. A Poetical Performance at the Literary Exhibition in September, M,DCC,XCV, at Harvard University* (Boston: William Spotswood; 1795); C. P. Sumner to Story [c. 1797], C. P. Sumner MSS.

[4] C. P. Sumner to Thomas Kittera, Aug. 12, 1811, MS., Hist. Soc. of Penn.; Pierce, I, 30.

[5] A. W. N. Howard to Sumner, June 19, 1866, Sumner MSS.; Nason: *Sumner*, pp. 311–12; Boston *Traveller*, Apr. 21, 1874.

that made young Sumner, when a student at Harvard, describe
"The present character of the Inhabitants of New England" as
one of sobriety, industry, moral purity—and "a natural cold-
ness." [6] The very house in which he was born, on Bartolph (now
Irving) Street, was "respectable, and yet only above being humble." Like the two later homes the Sumners occupied on Hancock
Street, it lay north of that imaginary line that, as true Bostonians
used to say, divided the "bob" from the "nabob" side of Beacon
Hill. When Charles was a boy, his father's income was only
about $1,000 a year, and only Mrs. Sumner's frugality kept the
family from actual want. She could afford only iron knives and
forks for tableware, and she sent Charles to school wearing
coarse, chunky shoes and cheap sky-blue satinet clothes, "never a
nice fitting or handsomely appearing suit." [7]

Sumner's autobiography ignored not merely his undemon-
strative parents, but also his brothers and sisters. He himself was
a twin; he and his sister Matilda had been premature babies,
weighing only three and one-half pounds each, who were
scarcely expected to survive. Giving the daughter to a nurse's
care, Mrs. Sumner took the boy to feed at breast. Her decision to
separate the two children had lasting consequences; there never
grew up between Charles and Matilda that closeness of feeling
that so often characterizes twins. Though Matilda lived to the
age of twenty-one, Charles almost never mentioned her in any of
his voluminous letters. When she died, he coolly recalled the
anecdote of the Persian matron, who, told by her monarch that
she could "save from death *one* of her family and relatives,"
chose to sacrifice husband and children in order to save her old
and decrepit father, "saying that another husband and other children she might have, *but another father never.*" [8]

If Sumner hoped that Matilda's death would strengthen his
father's affection for him, he was mistaken; there were too many

[6] MS. essay dated June 19, 1830, Harvard Univ. Archives.
[7] E. Buckingham to Pierce, Nov. 27, 1874, Pierce MSS.; Allan Chamberlain:
Beacon Hill: Its Ancient Pastures and Early Mansions (Boston: Houghton
Mifflin Co.; 1925), p. 42; Stearns: *Cambridge Sketches*, p. 182. Sumner indig-
nantly denied reports that he had been "born in affluence and bred in elegance."
See his marginal annotations on *Speech of Gerrit Smith (to His Neighbors) in
Peterboro, N.Y., June 22d 1872*, in Smith MSS.
[8] Pierce, I, 113.

other rivals in the house. By 1827 Mrs. Sumner had produced nine children [9]—five boys and four girls—and through her skill as a mother and her patience as a nurse she brought them all past the age of adolescence. Toward his younger sisters, born many years after himself, Charles developed a real, if sometimes possessive, affection, but he felt his brothers, so much nearer his own age, as competitors. They seemed to have an easier time with his parents, and not so much was demanded of them. The oldest son, on the other hand, bearing the father's own name, was expected to do the impossible. "Charles," the father formally admonished him, "upon your discretion and good deportment, the happiness of my life will in no trifling measure depend." [1]

Earnestly Charles tried to gain his parents' love by living up to their expectations. But it seemed unfair that he should have to earn affection while it appeared to be heaped undeservingly to Albert and George, Henry and Horace. It was no wonder that Charles early came to find *King Lear* the most satisfying of Shakespeare's plays, for he could identify himself with Cordelia. Throughout his life his most frequently used quotation was the reproach of the mad king, which should have been directed against the faithless and undeserving Goneril and Regan, but instead fell upon the head of the inarticulate Cordelia: "Nothing will come of nothing."

· 2 ·

There was only one way in which Charles seemed able to win his father's esteem. He was not a handsome boy, or even a prepossessing one. Growing too rapidly, he had faulty muscular coordination and was poor at all sports except swimming. Boys laughed at him as "Gawky Sumner" and left him out of their play.[2] Shy and lonesome, Charles made up for these defects by becoming bookish. Both at the private school conducted by one of his aunts in the upper floor of the Sumner house and then at the neighborhood public school, teachers found Charles a quiet,

[9] For a list of the children, together with dates of birth and death, see Appleton: *Record of the Descendants of William Sumner*, p. 176.
[1] Aug. 10, 1828, copy, C. P. Sumner MSS.
[2] Stearns: *Cambridge Sketches*, p. 181.

intelligent lad.[3] Their teaching did not interest him, for he wanted to have a classical education like his father's and to understand the Latin phrases with which his parent elegantly larded his conversation. He listened eagerly to the older boys in the neighborhood who attended the Boston Latin School, and, saving up his coppers, he bought the Latin grammar and Liber Primus used in the first class. Without his parents' knowledge, he studied them at home, after school hours, and "came down to his father one morning as he was shaving, and astonished him by reciting and reading Latin."[4] His father, who had intended for Charles to receive only a brief English education, so that he could get to work earlier and help support the family, was touched, and, in August 1821, sent him to the Latin School.

Some of the boys who attended the Boston Public Latin School chafed at the meager educational fare provided by Benjamin Apthorp Gould and his assistants, and were unhappy at having "to commit to memory the uninteresting and unintelligible rules, exceptions, notes, and remarks, of which the school grammar was full,"[5] but Sumner rejoiced in this wonderful opportunity to become a learned man like his father, and for the five years of the course he seems to have been perfectly happy. The formidable list of required Latin classics, including Caesar, Cicero, Tacitus, Sallust, Vergil, and Horace, and the less extensive readings in Greek he managed without difficulty; indeed, he memorized great stretches of them, which he could quote, with or without provocation, to the end of his life. Repeatedly he won prizes for his translations, his Latin hexameters, and other exercises.[6]

At the same time he further emulated his father by becom-

[3] A modern psychologist, on the basis of rather dubious evidence, concludes that Sumner had an I.Q. of between 140 and 145. Catherine Morris Cox: *The Early Mental Traits of Three Hundred Geniuses* (Vol. II of *Genetic Studies of Genius*, ed. by Lewis M. Terman), pp. 731–2.
[4] Richard Henry Dana, Jr., Journal, Sept. 1854, Dana MSS.
[5] Edward Everett Hale (ed.): *James Freeman Clarke: Autobiography, Diary and Correspondence* (Boston: Houghton Mifflin Co.; 1891), p. 26.
[6] Pauline Holmes: *A Tercentenary History of the Boston Public Latin School, 1635–1935* ("Harvard Studies in Education," Vol. XXV; Cambridge: Harvard University Press; 1935), pp. 192, 194, 269–71. For a student debate in which Sumner participated see John O. Sargent, Diary, Mar. 11, 1826, MS., Harvard Univ. Archives.

ing an "ardent student of *history*," rising often before daybreak to
read Hume and Gibbon. Imitating his father's antiquarian passion for meticulously tabulating events that had happened on the
same day in the past, Charles, at the age of fourteen, drew up an
eighty-six-page chronological compendium of English history, including all the kings and their dates:

799 EGBERT succeds [*sic*] to the Kingdom of Wessex the most pow-
          erful of the Heptarchy and unites all the kingdoms together
          and
827 becomes the first king of England.
835 The Danes land in England but are defeated at Hangesdown
838 Egbert dies and is succeeded by ETHELWOLF who dies, and di-
          vided his
857 kingdom between his two sons. . . .[7]

The boy's real chance to impress his father, however, came
during his final year at the Latin School. With schoolboy curiosity
he went to hear Daniel Webster deliver an oration upon the recent deaths of Thomas Jefferson and John Adams. The hall was
packed, and Charles could not see the speaker. Taking advantage
of his size, the spindly youth dived to the floor and began working
his way on his hands and knees to the front of the auditorium.
He emerged just as Webster, in tribute to Jefferson, pronounced:
"*Felix, non vitae tantum claritate, sed etiam opportunitate mor-
tis.*" "Then I felt proud," Charles later recalled, "for I understood
the sentence; and I felt that I too belonged to the brotherhood of
scholars." Hurrying home, he told his father of Webster's quotation, and the elder Sumner went to his shelves and checked in
the *Agricola* of Tacitus to see if the boy had remembered it accurately. "We were both pleased to find that I had," Charles remembered, even after many years. "He showed the words to me
then, in their original application." [8]

Despite the son's obvious eagerness for learning, Charles
Pinckney Sumner did not originally plan to send him to college.
Even after he had given up his law practice in 1819 to accept
slightly more remunerative employment as deputy sheriff of Suffolk County, he felt too poor to send the boy to Harvard. Besides,

---

[7] Sumner's autobiography, Palfrey MSS.; Julia Hastings to Pierce, Oct. 19,
1874, Pierce MSS.; "A chronological Compendium of English History by Charles
Sumner. Copy-right secured Boston MDCCXXV. 1825," Sumner MSS.
[8] Boston *Beacon*, Jan. 26, 1878.

he thought, "The life of a scholar would be too sedentary and inactive for him." Perhaps remembering Major Job Sumner's career, he encouraged Charles to think of a military education, and
planned to enroll him as a student proctor in Captain Alden
Partridge's "American Literary, Scientific, and Military Academy"
at Middletown, Connecticut.[9]

But, on September 6, 1826, a sudden change occurred in
the Sumner fortunes. Governor Levi Lincoln appointed Charles
Pinckney Sumner sheriff of Suffolk County, which included Boston. It was a lucrative job—at least, more so than any Sumner
had ever held—and, on the income of about $2,000 a year, the
new sheriff felt able to sell his crowded house on Bartolph Street
and rent a larger establishment on Hancock Street. In 1829 he
purchased a thirteen-room, three-story house at No. 20 Hancock
Street, which became the family's permanent residence. The
new sheriff impressively donned his official uniform, which consisted of a tricornered hat, a blue coat with military facings,
yellow breeches, white tipped boots, and a neat side sword, and,
rejoicing in his unexpected elegance and wealth, even gave dinners twice a year to the governor and judges of the Commonwealth.[1]

His new position made it possible for C. P. Sumner to send
his oldest son to college. Confused by the abrupt change, and remembering his father's earlier, repeated injunctions that he must
not become a burden on the family finances, Charles continued
for a few days to declare that he really would prefer a free appointment to the United States Military Academy at West Point
to an expensive education at Cambridge, but his father, in September 1826, enrolled him at Harvard. To Governor Lincoln, his
"greatest earthly benefactor," the sheriff gave profuse thanks for
making it possible for Charles to follow the steps of his father
and grandfather: "Without your favor I should probably not have
sent a son to college or emerged from that humility of station
from which at the age of forty nine you saw fit to draw me."[2]

[9] Pierce, I, 43.
[1] Between 1831 and 1838 the sheriff's fees totaled $16,745.78. Notarized
statements, C. P. Sumner MSS. Edwin Coolidge to Sumner, Mar. 26, 1867, Sumner MSS.
[2] Pierce, I, 43-4; C. P. Sumner to Levi Lincoln, Jan. 21, 1834, copy, C. P.
Sumner MSS.

· 3 ·

Entering Harvard College marked no decided break in Charles Sumner's life. His father sent him to Cambridge with a Polonius-like letter: "Preserve therefore a good character: associate with those who have it: for those who have it are commonly the greatest proficients in literature and science, and will be not only patient but even gratified with your company. Shun those who have no good character of their own; they will not respect it in you. . . . " etc., etc., for pages and pages.[3] Every Sunday he required Charles to return to Hancock Street and give a report on the week's happenings at college. Sheriff Sumner kept a close watch upon his son's expenses, which ran to $177.86 for room, board, and fees during his first year at Harvard—almost precisely what the college catalogue stipulated as minimal—and he always seemed to know when Charles cut classes. Though by modern standards the boy's record of only three absences out of 580 classes, recitations, and chapel exercises during his first year seems remarkably perfect, his father grimly noted on his report card: "It is of little avail to have expensive and learned professorships established at college if a scholar does not devote his whole time to the duties prescribed."[4]

Even without his father's admonitions Charles could not have become lost at Harvard. The great majority of the 199 undergraduates in 1826 were New England youths like himself, many of them acquaintances from his Boston Latin School days. Certainly there was nothing in the curriculum to confuse him or any of the other thirty-five members of the freshman class. Their schedule was simple and unvarying. Rising for prayers before seven, they had a recitation in Greek and Latin before breakfast, which was at 8:30; their morning recitations in algebra and geometry were followed by dinner at one o'clock; Greek and Latin again occupied them until evening prayers and tea. On Saturdays declamations were substituted for mathematics, and the boys got the afternoon off. If the program was scarcely designed

[3] C. P. Sumner to Charles Sumner [1826], copy, C. P. Sumner MSS.
[4] Receipted bills, Sumner College Memorial Scrapbook, Harvard Univ. Archives; Nason: *Sumner*, pp. 34–5; printed statements of class attendance, 1826–7, Sumner College Memorial Scrapbook. Sumner's expenses reached their maximum, $226.73, during his junior year.

to inspire, neither did it perplex. There was, in fact, a kind of businesslike monotony about the whole proceeding. "No attempt was made to interest us in our studies," remembered James Freeman Clarke, who was in the class ahead of Sumner's. "We were expected to wade through Homer as though the Iliad were a bog, and it was our duty to get along at such a rate *per diem*." [5]

Sumner, to his own considerable disappointment, proved only a moderately competent student. The Livy and Horace and the smattering of Greek which the learned Professor J. S. Popkin required him to read he could manage easily; any boy trained at Gould's Latin School found these assignments "simply a dull school exercise." But, for mathematics, which made up such a large part of the curriculum, he, like his father, had no aptitude whatever. Nobody tried to explain to him that these studies had any interest or importance; no tutor in conic sections ever suggested "that these were the curves in which the planets and comets moved, and that by learning their laws we were able to determine, a thousand years beforehand, an eclipse of the sun or an occultation of Jupiter." Failing to grasp the first principles of mathematics, Sumner fell far behind as the course progressed. Bored, he left the pages of his algebra text uncut and committed by rote to memory the solutions to enough problems to pass the examinations. In succeeding years, as his class progressed under its rigidly prescribed curriculum to more advanced mathematical studies, Sumner learned even less from his teachers. Once to a professor who pursued him with questions, he replied candidly: "I don't know; you know I don't pretend to know any thing about mathematics." "Sumner!" exclaimed the teacher. "Mathematics! mathematics! Don't you know the difference? This is not mathematics. This is *Physics*." [6]

It is no wonder that Sumner's standing in his classes was only respectable [7] and that he graduated with no feeling of having undergone an exciting intellectual experience. In his four

[5] *A Catalogue of the Officers and Students of the School in Cambridge, Massachusetts. September, 1826* (Cambridge: University Press; 1826); Hal Bridges: *Iron Millionaire: Life of Charlemagne Tower* (Philadelphia: University of Pennsylvania Press; 1952), p. 13; Hale (ed.): *James Freeman Clarke*, p. 36.

[6] Hale: *A New England Boyhood*, p. 222; Pierce, I, 47–8.

[7] In his class rank lists (MS., Harvard Univ. Archives), which totaled the grades students received in all subjects, Sumner was never higher than fifteenth or lower than twenty-seventh in a class of about forty students.

years at Cambridge only the occasional lectures of George Ticknor on French and Spanish literature and the sound advice of Edward Tyrell Channing on rhetoric seem to have made any impression on him. If Harvard was in what its historian has called its Augustan Age in these last years of the Presidency of John Thornton Kirkland, Sumner was unaware of it, nor did the coming of a new President, Josiah Quincy, during his senior year immediately raise educational standards. "I am not aware that *any one single thing* is well taught to the Undergraduates of Harvard College," Sumner reflected with some bitterness a few years after he graduated. "Certainly I left it without knowing anything." [8]

Standing well below the first third of his class, Sumner was not elected to Phi Beta Kappa, and he was given such an insignificant part in the 1830 commencement exercises that he wished to decline it. Only firm pressure from his father compelled him to participate, along with three other undistinguished members of the graduating class, in what was called a "conference" on "The Roman Ceremonies, the System of the Druids, the Religion of the Hindoos, and the Superstitions of the American Indians." When his turn came, Sumner, defying all that Professor Channing had taught him about simplicity of rhetoric, announced that the Indians acknowledge "one Supreme Intelligence, who stretcheth forth the Heavens alone and spreadeth abroad the earth by himself—who binds the sweet influences of the Pleiades and looses the bands of Orion"—and so forth for quite a while. His long-suffering auditors, who endured more than six hours of undergraduate oratory that day, did not think Sumner's performance distinguished. [9]

Despite the uninspiring instruction and his inglorious record, Sumner, on the whole, found his Harvard years among the most enjoyable of his life. Though bound by the rigid curriculum and watched by the paternal eye of Sheriff Sumner, he began for

[8] George Ticknor to C. P. Sumner, July 7 [1828], Sumner MSS.; Samuel Eliot Morison, *Three Centuries of Harvard, 1636–1936* (Cambridge: Harvard University Press; 1936), Chaps. IX–XI; Sumner to Joseph Story, Sept. 24, 1839, Sumner MSS.

[9] Sumner's speech, Aug. 25, 1830, MS., Harvard Univ. Archives; "Order of Exercises for Commencement," Aug. 25, 1830, Sumner College Memorial Scrapbook; *Proceedings of the Massachusetts Historical Society*, V (2 ser., 1889–90), 202. Hereafter these *Proceedings* are cited as *MHSP*.

the first time to lead a life of his own. Merely to put on the undergraduate uniform of black-mixed coat and pantaloons ("By black-mixed," the regulations carefully specified, "is understood, black with a mixture of not more than one twentieth, nor less than one twenty-fifth part of white."), with "neck-cloth," hat, shoes, and even buttons of prescribed shape and color,[1] was to commence a new existence in which his family had no share.

He found independence giddily exhilarating and, in his junior year, even staged a private rebellion against the college authorities of a sort he had never had the audacity to attempt at home. Defying the college statutes that undergraduates must wear waistcoats of either "black-mixed" or white, he, perhaps in emulation of Daniel Webster's fancy senatorial costume, sported a vest of buff color. Summoned before the Parietal Board of college professors and tutors who dealt with such heinous infractions of the rules, Sumner coolly denied that the waistcoat was illegal; it "might need the manipulations of a laundress, but it was worn for the lawful color." Giving Sumner warning, the Parietal Board dismissed him, only to learn a few days later that he was still wearing the offending garment. After several additional hearings, during which the board entered upon Sumner's record an "admonition for illegal dress," the professors, wearied by Sumner's stubborn unwillingness to admit that he could be wrong, or perhaps impressed by his ability to argue, in the name of morality and justice, that buff was white, relented and voted "that hereafter Mr. Sumner's vest be considered by this Board white."[2]

Such moments of rebellion in Sumner's college career were few, for most of his days were happy. If he learned little from his teachers, he had the privilege of browsing independently in

[1] *Statutes and Laws of the University in Cambridge, Massachusetts* (Cambridge: University Press; 1826), p. 25.

[2] Boston *Commonwealth*, Feb. 18, 1871; printed statement of class attendance, 1828–9, Sumner College Memorial Scrapbook. This bit of bravado on Sumner's part may have been more of a joke than anything else, for the rest of his college record is remarkably free from infractions of discipline. Aside from being admonished for too frequent absence from public worship and for causing excessive noise on his velocipede (Harvard Faculty Records, XI, 20), he was not otherwise disciplined during four years of college. Miss Eleanor Tilton (*Amiable Autocrat: A Biography of Dr. Oliver Wendell Holmes* [New York: Henry Schuman; 1947], p. 34) errs in stating that Charles Sumner was punished for attending the theater; the offending party was T. H. Sumner, and the punishment was inflicted six months before Charles entered college.

the Harvard Library. During his freshman year he borrowed
more books than any other student in his class, books that had
little relation to the dull curriculum, but included *Don Quixote*,
many of Scott's novels, much of Washington Irving, and some
miscellaneous history. During the next three years he continued
to read assiduously, becoming especially fond of early English
poetry, great stretches of which he committed to memory.[3]

His classmates he found almost as instructive as his books.
He appears to have had no friends among the gay, charming
Southerners who attended Harvard.[4] Nor did he associate much
with the athletes, who performed gymnastic feats in the Delta.
Sumner's own physical exertions were confined to his weekly
walks into Boston, an occasional attempt at fencing, and an improbable affection for his velocipede, "a heavy, bone-breaking
machine, moved not by pedals but by thrusting the feet against
the ground," on which, at the expense of a pair of shoe soles, he
could race the stagecoach along Massachusetts Avenue.[5] Instead, he found more to his liking the studious New Englanders
who were destined to lead their region for the next decade. Sumner probably saw little of Ralph Waldo Emerson, who was listed
as a "resident graduate" during his freshman year, but Cornelius C. Felton and Edmund Quincy among the "Senior Sophisters," George S. Hillard and Robert C. Winthrop among the "Junior Sophisters," and Oliver Wendell Holmes, Benjamin R.
Curtis, and James Freeman Clarke among the sophomores were
to play major roles in his later career, as were John Lothrop
Motley and Wendell Phillips, who entered as freshmen in 1827.

Sumner picked his particular "chums," however, from the
members of his own Harvard class. Jonathan F. Stearns, of Bed-
ford, whose grandfather had taught Sumner's father, Charlemagne Tower, of Paris, N.Y., John W. Browne, of Salem, and
Thomas Hopkinson, of New Sharon, Maine, became the first

[3] Harvard College Library Charge Books, 1826-7, pp. 17, 27; *id.*, 1827-8, p.
34; *id.*, 1828-9, pp. 56-8, 82; *id.*, 1829-30, p. 64. Cf. Sumner's "Common-place
Book," Dec. 17, 1829, Harvard Univ. Archives.

[4] There is no reference to Sumner in Arthur H. Cole (ed.): *Charleston Goes
to Harvard: The Diary of a Harvard Student of 1831* (Cambridge: Harvard
University Press; 1940).

[5] Petition to Dr. Charles Follen, signed by Sumner and many other members
of the junior and sophomore classes [Dec. 17, 1827], Harvard College Papers,
II, 2 ser., 163; James Kendall Hosmer: *The Last Leaf* . . . (New York: The
Knickerbocker Press; 1912), pp. 19-22.

real friends he had ever had, and he learned from them that all social intercourse was not necessarily conducted with the gloomy formality that prevailed in the house on Hancock Street. Secure in the relaxed, affectionate company of these classmates, where there was no moody father or rival brother to pounce upon every careless word or to capitalize upon every failing, Sumner found that he had a hitherto undiscovered talent, conversation.

In fact, he commenced a career, destined to continue for more than half a century, as one of the greatest talkers in American history. Enthusiastically and with relentless persistence, he talked so much that his friends labeled him the "Chatterbox." In "the Nine," a harmless secret society that he and his closest friends formed, he discoursed on English universities, on the "Old English Writers," and like topics. In the Hasty Pudding Club, to which he was elected in his junior year, he was also loquacious, using, on one occasion, "not only the formidable engine of legal argument, but the two edged sword of satire, the poisoned darts of irony, and the barbed shafts of ridicule" in a mock trial of that "notorious felon alias Mr. Blackboard." [6] On an extended walking trip that he and three classmates undertook in the summer of his junior year, tramping across Massachusetts and on to Lake Champlain, he talked, laughed, sang, and talked some more, for nearly three uninterrupted weeks.[7] In the fortnightly junior and senior classes in declamation, held under Professor Channing's frosty eye, he learned to talk in public. Overcoming adolescent squeakiness by letting "his voice down in his throat" and cultivating a bass sonority, he became one of the best declaimers in the class, and his efforts were marked by his "great degree of earnestness" and his "entire freedom from any effort to make a *dash*." Sumner announced that he was devoted to "the *Divine Art*" of public speaking, and it was scarcely surprising that in one of the college exhibitions of his junior year he was given the part of the "pedantic Orator" in a Greek dialogue, with the significant lines: "For myself I confess the study of oratory—I boast to be 'a speaker of words.'. . . De-

[6] Bridges: *Iron Millionaire*, p. 16; Sumner to J. F. Stearns, Dec. 27, 1829, Sumner MSS.; Pierce, I, 55-6; Secretary's Records, Hasty Pudding Club, IX (June 26, 1829), 22-3. Cf. *id.*, IX, 1-5, 10, 38, 44.

[7] Sumner's pedestrian account of this walking trip, July 13-31, 1829, in the form of a journal is in the C. P. Sumner MSS.

mosthenes and Pericles . . . will be like stars to point out the pathway to glory and their glory will always be the object of my desire." [8]

· 4 ·

"I find it hard to untie the spell that knits me so strongly to college life," Sumner wrote more than a month after President Quincy had certified him as a Bachelor of Arts of Harvard College. His four years at Cambridge had given him a mastery of Greek and Latin and a fastidiousness in grammar and style which made him consider form more important than content, and they had left him with a total ignorance of science and mathematics, a desire to live like a gentleman, and an inability to support himself. Sadly he moped about his room in Holworthy Hall until the junior class took over, "parading around, the almost 'undisputed Lords and masters' of what we Seniors a day before alone enjoyed." [9]

Sumner's predicament was not an unusual one; like other Harvard graduates who did not have private fortunes he had to choose a profession. The alternatives were neither numerous nor inviting. The Christian ministry was never a possibility. Like his father, he held vaguely Unitarian views and sometimes attended King's Chapel. Despite all the compulsory chapel sermons at Harvard, he remained "unconvinced that Christ was divinely commissioned to preach a revelation to men and that he was entrusted with the power of working miracles." When pressed, he admitted to believing "that Christ lived when and as the Gospel says—that he was more than man (viz. above all men who had as yet lived) and yet less than God." But these were not subjects on which he thought, or cared to think, much. "I am," he explained to Stearns, "without religious feeling." [1] Medicine, to one as squeamish and as totally ignorant of science as Sumner, was also out of the question as a profession. Remembering his father's uninteresting and unsuccessful legal career, Sumner

---

[8] Sumner to Charlemagne Tower, Nov. 4, 1830, Tower MSS.; Pierce, I, 58; Translation of Greek Dialogue [Apr. 28, 1829], Sumner College Memorial Scrapbook.

[9] Pierce, I, 80–1.

[1] Sumner to Stearns, Jan. 12, 1833, Sumner MSS.

judged that "a *mere* lawyer" must be "one of the veriest wretches
in the world." "Dry items and facts, argumentative reports, and
details of pleadings must incrust the mind with somewhat of
their own rust." [2] For teaching school, that last resort of the lib-
eral-arts graduate, he quickly learned, after a three weeks' trial,
that he had "a natural hydrophobia." To be successful in that
"harrassing [sic], throat-cutting, mind-dissolving" occupation,
he thought, would require him to "gather up all the scraps and
rags of patience at his command—ram down into the very bot-
tom of his legs all temper and receive with the meekness of an
Ultra-orthodox-Quaker all vexations, crosses, ills to which school-
master flesh is heir to." [3]

Sheriff Sumner posed the real difficulty in his son's choice of
a career. Though a Harvard graduate, the boy was only nineteen
years old, and he desperately wanted to please his dour parent.
But, aside from vetoing Charles's romantic notion of leading "a
life of letters" and from sourly observing that he ought not to
"stand all day idle, dependent upon his Father for support," the
Sheriff did nothing either to direct or to encourage his son. "He
seems determined to let me shape my own course," Charles reported, with some exasperation, to Stearns; "so that if I am wise,
I shall be wise for myself and if I am foolish I alone shall
bear it." [4]

Lacking any direction from his father and any preference
of his own, Charles decided to spend the year after his graduation at home in individual study. Enthusiastically he planned a
program that would remedy the deficiencies of his Harvard
training and extend his interests. "I have doomed myself for
this year at least to hard labor," he wrote to a classmate. "I intend to diet on study—go to bed late and get up early and leave
none of my time unemployed. I have imposed upon myself the
task of reading as following—a course of Mathematics, not indeed so thorough as the Cambridge, but one which will give me
all I want to know . . . Juvenal and Tacitus (without ponies)
—a course of Modern History, Hallam's Middle Ages and Con-

[2] Pierce, I, 86.
[3] Sumner to Stearns, Feb. 13, 1831, Sumner MSS.; Sumner to Tower, Mar. 1,
1831, Tower MSS.
[4] C. P. James to Pierce, Jan. 7, 1877, Pierce MSS.; Sumner to Stearns, Feb.
13, and Aug. 7, 1831, Sumner MSS.

stitutional History, Roscoe's Leo and Lorenzo, Robertson's Charles V etc." "I shall," he pledged, "make labor my pleasure." [5]

This elaborate regimen, so enthusiastically begun, lasted only a month or so. For one thing, the boy had no place to study. At crowded No. 20 Hancock Street there was no privacy, and he was obliged to read in the family parlor, sitting, "like Chance amidst the little chaos around" of "children and chairs, bores and books, andirons and paper." Mathematics, when studied alone, proved no easier than in the classroom. The *roots* of Algebra," he learned, "when obtained, are but bitter," and after only a month he reported: "I have *ef*fected but little with those *af*-fected Equations—indeed I have but little *affection* for them." [6]

Eagerly he welcomed diversions. He spent hours writing long, tedious letters to his friends, so heavily encrusted with quotations from the classics that Browne begged him: "Be less lavish of your classic allusions, for so thickly was your epistle . . . bedizened with these gems that my mineralogy was all at fault —I could neither measure nor sort them." [7] In December 1830 he interrupted his study to dash off an essay on commerce for a contest sponsored by the Boston Society for the Diffusion of Useful Knowledge, and he had the honor of being summoned to the platform, on the evening the awards were announced, to receive the first prize, a set of the *Encyclopedia Americana*, from Daniel Webster himself, who called the author his "young friend."

Bored with study, Sumner for the first time began to take an interest in politics. When Sheriff Sumner entered the Antimasonic movement and publicly attacked the order, in which he had once risen to be a master Mason, as a danger to the republic, "a pillar of ice supporting a superstructure of marble," [8] Charles became an enthusiastic convert to the new party. "My *reason* has enlisted me in Anti-Masonry," he explained to Tower; "my *feelings* have nearly run away with my reason." Though he knew that a genteel Harvard graduate should keep "his mind wholly aloof from politics," it was impossible for him to do so: "My feelings, despite my reason, love them." [9]

[5] Sumner to Stearns, Sept. 28, 1830, ibid.
[6] Pierce, I, 84; Sumner to Stearns, Nov. 24, 1830, Sumner MSS.
[7] Browne to Sumner, Mar. 6, 1831, ibid.
[8] For Sheriff Sumner's many animadversions upon the masons see his manuscript notebook, titled "Miscellany," C. P. Sumner MSS.
[9] Sumner to Tower, June 10, 1831, Tower MSS.

The great disadvantage of all this disorganized activity was that it led nowhere. Sumner was, by his own admission, an ambitious young man; one of his college friends declared that he had "a pervading ambition,—not an intermittent, fitful gust of an affair, blowing a hurricane at one time, then subsiding to a calm, but a strong, steady breeze, which will bear him well on in the track of honor." [1] When he permitted himself to think that he had wasted nearly twelve months, he became the victim of "green-eyed melancholy and sickening musings." He engaged in adolescent brooding about death. "There is a most charming stillness in the grave, contrasted with the busy rolling hum above," he wrote with gloomy inappropriateness to Stearns, who was in the hospital; "no apprenticeship or long pupillage is there demanded." By May 1831 he was ready to admit defeat: "I've passed by a sorry time, progressed but little in those studies which my mind has been the whole while looking to; and enjoyed as little happiness as . . . a sensitive mind could glean from thoughts of negligences and misspent time." [2]

At last, in August, Sumner realized that he must make a choice, if only to appease his father, who stood always in the background silently disapproving his idleness. With considerable reluctance he decided to enroll in the Harvard Law School. His devotion to his new profession, however, was anything but single-minded. "I intend to give myself to the law, so as to read satisfactorily the regular and parallel courses," he explained to Tower, but he added that he intended also "to take hold of some of the classics—Greek, if I can possibly gird up my mind to the work,—to pursue historical studies,—to read Say and Stewart; all mingled with those condiments to be found in Shakespeare and the British poets." [3]

[1] Pierce, I, 83.
[2] Sumner to Tower, June 10, and May 27, 1831, Tower MSS.; Sumner to Stearns, Mar. [22], 1831, Sumner MSS.
[3] Pierce, I, 88.

CHAPTER II

You Were Meant
for Boston

❦

Sumner's three years in the Harvard Law School, he declared later, were "the happiest of my life." Originally reluctant to study the law, he soon discovered that it was his "true profession; the one in which the mind is the most sharpened and quickened, and the duties of which, properly discharged, are most vital to the interests of the country." He promptly gave up his vague hopes for a literary career and diverted his energies, with single-minded intensity, to his new occupation. The law, he found, offered him not merely personal satisfaction and professional advancement; it also opened for him a new circle of friends and gave him an entree into the best Boston society. After only one year in law school he was certain that he had found himself. "I become more wedded to the law, as a profession, every day that I study it." [1]

· 1 ·

The principal agent in this remarkable transformation was Joseph Story, the associate justice of the United States Supreme Court, who had infused new life into the Harvard Law School when he accepted the Dane professorship in 1829. Under Story's prodding, the college added John H. Ashmun to the faculty as Royall professor of law, purchased a sizable legal library, and

[1] Pierce, I, 108, 111, 117.

commenced work on a new building to house the classes and
library of the reinvigorated professional school. Enrollment
quickly increased. Benjamin R. Curtis, future justice of the Supreme Court, Timothy Walker, later one of the most influential
lawyers in Ohio, Thomas Hopkinson, who had held the highest
rank in Sumner's undergraduate class, and George S. Hillard,
shortly to become Sumner's close friend and partner, were
among those who flocked to Cambridge during these first years
of the Story-Ashmun regime. By the time Sumner entered, in
September 1831, enrollment in the law school totaled forty-
two.[2]

Sumner joined the law school with doubts about his profession and reservations about Story, who, he thought, was often
guilty of "mawkish sentimentality" and "bad taste."[3] But, once
he heard the Dane professor lecture, all his doubts vanished.
Never had Sumner encountered anybody so captivating as the
little pink-faced, cherubic professor who combed his pixie-like
wisp of curling blond hair on his forehead as he talked to his
students. Story seemed actually interested in teaching. The
sullen taciturnity of Sumner's father, the mechanical grading of
his recitations by Harvard teachers had never been anything like
this. Story did not ask students to repeat answers to routine questions upon the assigned text; he illuminated every line of it with
a running commentary, linking together his prodigious knowledge of the law, his broad acquaintance with literature, his personal experience in the Supreme Court, and his political prejudices in an altogether hypnotic and totally convincing fashion.

Immediately Story became Sumner's hero. Sumner admired
his erudition, his enthusiasm, his gaiety, his incessant and brilliant conversation, his concern for his students, which "warmed
the classes with ardor in their studies." Story he thought the
ideal teacher, "always ready and profuse in his instructions, anx-

[2] The best accounts of Story's life are William Wetmore Story: *Life and Letters of Joseph Story* . . . (Boston: Charles C. Little and James Brown; 1851), and Henry Steele Commager: "Joseph Story," *The Gaspar G. Bacon Lectures on the Constitution of the United States* (Boston: Boston University Press; 1953), pp. 33–94. On the Harvard Law School the standard works are Charles Warren: *History of the Harvard Law School and of Early Legal Conditions in America* (New York: Lewis Publishing Company; 1908), and *The Centennial History of the Harvard Law School, 1817–1917* (Harvard Law School Association; 1918).

[3] Sumner to Stearns, Sept. 25, 1831, Sumner MSS.

iously seeking out all the difficulties which perplexed the student and anticipating his wants, leaving no stone unturned by which the rugged paths of the law might be made smoother." Consequently the students, Sumner reported to Charlemagne Tower, "love him more than any instructor they ever had before. He treats them all as gentlemen, and is full of willingness to instruct. . . . The good scholars like him for the knowledge he distributes; the poor (if any there be), for the amenity with which he treats them and their faults." [4]

Identifying himself completely and enthusiastically with the judge, Sumner ran into the danger, common to all students of great teachers, of becoming a caricature of his professor. When Story was charmed by Fanny Kemble, the young English actress who moved Boston to flurries of tears, Sumner, in whom anything artistic was an acquired taste, promptly dropped his law studies to attend the theater. If Story was impressed by the earnest, learned German expatriate, Francis Lieber, to whom he introduced Sumner, his student promptly annexed Lieber as an admired friend, whose works he humbly praised and whose career he sought to forward by soliciting for him honorary degrees from Harvard, contracts with publishers, and puffs in the Boston newspapers. Lieber asked Sumner to serve as "part friend, part agent" for him in Boston, but the young lawyer promptly replied: "I will be *all* friend, and do for you as well as I can." Pleased by such adulation, Lieber told his wife: "Sumner, is one of the finest men I know of; he . . . studies hard and *deep*, and is withal enthusiastically devoted to me. He verily loves me." [5]

For Sumner, who had for so many years sought but never secured his father's approbation, winning Story's approval became a chief goal in life. The professor had merely to suggest some reading, to hint of some research, and Sumner dashed out

---

[4] *American Jurist*, XIII (Jan. 1835), 114; Pierce, I, 112.

[5] Sumner to Lieber, June 28, Aug. 25, and June 8, 1835, Sumner MSS.; Lieber to Matilda Lieber, Aug. 12, 1837, Lieber MSS. Sumner wrote the article praising Lieber in the Boston *Advertiser*, Aug. 24, 1835. Sumner met Lieber in Washington in 1834. For carefully documented accounts of his friendship with Lieber see Frank Freidel: "Francis Lieber, Charles Sumner, and Slavery," *Journal of Southern History*, IX (Feb. 1943), 75–93; and Freidel: *Francis Lieber: Nineteenth Century Liberal* (Baton Rouge: Louisiana State University Press; 1947), pp. 109–10, 141–2, 201–2, and *passim*.

to do it. As Story thought that a student should not parrot textbooks, but should investigate legal precedents for himself, Sumner dug assiduously in the law library. "In my studies," he reported proudly, "[I] never relied upon the textbooks, but went to
the original sources, read all the authorities and references,
whether treatises or decided cases—made myself acquainted
more or less, with every work of the common law, from the Year
Books in uncouth Norman down to the latest reports—could go
into the Law Library of many thousand volumes, and, if every
volume was in its place, could find any volume desired in the
dark." As Story thought lawyers should be acquainted not merely
with cases, but with the broad literature of the law, Sumner tried
to learn "the names of all the authors who have treated on the
different branches of the law, their various degrees of merit, and
how to consult them"; he read and digested the most important
books, paid less attention to slighter works, and gave "a transient
glance along the pages of others, like a dog drinking at the Nile
as he runs." [6]

When Story announced that a good lawyer must also be
broadly versed in literature, Sumner promptly agreed: "A lawyer must know every thing. He must know law, history, philosophy, human nature; and . . . he must drink of all the springs
of literature." His lawyer's commonplace book he filled not
merely with usable quotations from the fathers of the common
law, but with extracts from St. Augustine, Thomas Gray, Leibnitz, Thomas Burton, Edmund Burke, and Alexander Pope.
Sometimes there seemed to be so much work ahead that his eyes
would be blinded with reading. "Volumes upon volumes are to be
mastered, of the niceties of the law," he explained to Tower;
"and the whole circle of literature and science and history must
be compassed. For what is a lawyer, brim-full, though his head
may be, with statutes and precedents and points, if he lacks that
elegance and taste which will set off his own mind and infuse itself into every thing which passed through it." So diligently did
Sumner set himself to studying that his friends became seriously
concerned about his health, and his father was obliged to enter
one of his stately reproaches: "Charles, while you study the law,

---

[6] Sumner's autobiography, Palfrey MSS.; *American Jurist*, XIII (Apr. 1835),
388–9.

be not too discursive; study your prescribed course well. That is enough to make you a sound lawyer. You may bewilder your mind by taking too wide a range." But, Sumner, now under an influence more potent and more agreeable than his father's, continued avidly to read.[7]

In a day when the requirements of the Harvard Law School were not notably stringent, Sumner's exertions were naturally considered remarkable. Although his classes recited but three times a week when Story was away in Washington and but once a day even when Story was in Cambridge, and although there were no fixed standards of attendance and no written examinations, Sumner worked as though "every moment, like a filing of gold, ought to be saved." In his room in Divinity Hall, the most secluded of the college buildings, he saw few friends except Browne and Hopkinson, of his undergraduate class, who were also reading law; he seldom went into society; he rarely even returned to his home in Boston. Instead, he studied. He completed not merely all the prescribed books for the regular two-year course, but also the works recommended for supplementary reading "as far as the leisure and progress of the students may permit" and even most of the titles listed on the "parallel course," which were suggested "chiefly for private reading." [8]

Sumner's enthusiastic diligence won him the recognition he craved. Everybody agreed that this lanky, pale-faced youth, whose bloodshot eyes, muddy complexion, and harsh, constant cough indicated too serious application to his studies, would make a name for himself. His classmate Browne reported that after only a year of study Sumner had become "to the law what he used to be for history,—a repertory of facts to which we might all resort." Professor Ashmun, that precise opposite of Story, whose teaching relied less upon inspirational excitement than on "exactness of learning, . . . acuteness of mind and untiring perseverance" in drill, accepted the assiduous young student as a friend and almost an equal. Simon Greenleaf, Ash-

---

[7] Sumner to Stearns, Sept. 25 [1831], Sumner MSS.; Sumner's Commonplace Book, ibid.; Sumner: "The Lawyer's Commonplace Book," MS., Harvard Univ. Archives; Sumner to Tower, Sept. 29, 1831, Tower MSS.; Pierce, I, 98–9; C. P. Sumner to Sumner, Apr. 4, 1832, copy, C. P. Sumner MSS.

[8] Pierce, I, 111. Compare the list of books Sumner read during law school, 1831–4, in his "Lawyer's Commonplace Book," pp. 435–8, with the prescribed lists in Warren: Harvard Law School, I, 436–7.

mun's successor, grew equally fond of this eager, serious youth, whose 120 pounds seemed scarcely to cover his six-foot, two-inch frame, but whose burning zeal for the law was untiring.[9]

Most important of all, Sumner's goodhearted simplicity and eagerness to please promptly gained him the "affectionate intimacy and confidence of Story himself." Sumner became a regular visitor at the Story house, where the professor welcomed him "with a beaming face, and treated him almost as if he were a son." During Story's long absences in Washington, Sumner continued to drop in frequently to cheer up the lonely Mrs. Story and to give Latin lessons to young William Wetmore Story, for whom he developed an almost paternal affection.[1]

Story came to respect as well as to like the young man. Very early he was impressed by Sumner's organized industry. "He has a wonderful memory," he told President Quincy's family; "he keeps all his knowledge in order, and can put his hand on it in a moment." Rather than see so promising a student leave Cambridge after only two years of professional training, Story encouraged him to remain a third by naming him librarian of the law school, in which capacity Sumner was given "the pleasantest room in Cambridge," in the newly constructed Dane Hall, and by persuading the corporation to pay him $160 for cataloguing the law library.[2]

Soon Story entrusted Sumner with various small professional duties. When the judge had to go to Washington for the Supreme Court sessions, he turned over the proofreading of his *The Conflict of Laws* to his student, secure in the knowledge that Sumner would check all the quotations and citations and prod the printer into more rapid action.[3] So eager was Sumner to serve that the judge found it necessary to warn him: "You will

[9] Pierce, I, 99; *American Jurist*, XIII (Jan. 1835), 114; Sumner's autobiography, Palfrey MSS.; Sumner's passport, signed by Edward Everett, Nov. 18, 1835, C. P. Sumner MSS.

[1] Sumner's autobiography, Palfrey MSS.; Pierce, I, 108, 105–6; Sumner to Story, Jan. 20 [1834], Story MSS.; Andrew F. Rolle: "A Friendship across the Atlantic: Charles Sumner and William Story," *American Quarterly*, XI (Spring 1959), 40–57.

[2] Pierce, I, 103; Story to Sumner, July 12, 1833, Sumner MSS.; Sumner to Story, Dec. 18, 1833, Harvard Coll. Papers, VI, 2 ser., 69; Harvard Coll. Records, VII (1827–36), 342.

[3] Sumner to Story, Jan. 20 [1834], Story MSS. See also numerous letters from Sumner to Charles Folsom, concerning proofreading and indexing Story's books, Folsom MSS.

have to learn, that those, who are willing to labour for others, will never want ample employment, especially if their services are gratuitous; and you must begin to be chary of your intellectual, as well as physical strength." Still, knowing Sumner's fondness for obliging his friends, he continued to call on him for assistance. "There are not many, of whom I would venture to ask the favor of troubling themselves with my affairs," he told Sumner, "but I feel proud to think, that you are among the number, and I have . . . a heritable right to your friendship." [4]

Sumner, for his part, rejoiced at every opportunity to be of service. Every favor he performed gave him another excuse to write one of his long, affectionate letters to "My dearest Judge Story." "My happiness is materially dependent upon your regard and favorable estimate of my trifling labors," he ingenuously confessed. He was actually sorry to complete the proofreading and indexing of *The Conflict of Laws* because "it dissolves for the time the connection of confidence which, in my vanity, I imagined to be expressed, towards me, thereby." "Indeed," he added, "my whole relation to you has been, from the first, one of unlimited obligation on my part. Not a day—not an hour passes without some perception of your kindness coming into my mind. I can never express towards you the fullness of my feelings." [5]

· 2 ·

"For *once* . . . I have felt desolated and alone," Professor Greenleaf wrote Story in January 1834. "Sumner . . . has left me. I stoutly refused *ever* to bid him farewell." Though Sumner had reluctantly departed from Cambridge, he was not, in fact, cutting his ties with the law school, but carrying out a program advised by his professors. As Story and Greenleaf thought that a young attorney should, after his theoretical training, get practical experience in the office of some established lawyer, Sumner went, with Story's strong letter of recommendation, to study with Benjamin Rand, of Boston, whom he found "a thorough lawyer and at the same time a liberal lawyer—a jurisconsult." [6]

[4] Story to Sumner, Feb. 4, 1834, Sumner MSS.; Story: *Story*, II, 119–20.
[5] Sumner to Story, Jan. 20, and 30, Feb. 12, and undated [1834], Story MSS.
[6] Greenleaf to Story, Jan. 23, 1834; Sumner to Story, Jan. 20 [1834], ibid.

Following another of Story's suggestions, that a lawyer should not merely practice, but should contribute to the literature of his profession, Sumner, as early as July 1833, had commenced writing for *The American Jurist,* the best legal periodical in the United States at the time. As he settled into Rand's office, his contributions became more frequent. Some of his articles, such as a technical essay on "Can the assignee of a Scotch bond maintain an action in his own name in the courts of this country?" attracted favorable critical notice. In May 1834 he became joint editor of the journal, and his duties were heavy. To fill up the July issue, for instance, he himself had to write "upwards of 100 pages of pretty heavy print"—"no small labor," he thought.[7]

Then, too, Story and Greenleaf thought that a beginning lawyer should gain as broad an acquaintance as possible with his nation's judges and political leaders, and at their suggestion Sumner obediently made his first visit to Washington in 1834. Setting out in February, he stopped off in New York to call on Chancellor James Kent, whose *Commentaries* gave him a place alongside Story's in American jurisprudence, and the fastidious young attorney found the old judge "lively and instructive, but grossly ungrammatical." On his way through Maryland Sumner had his first sight of Negro slaves. "My worst preconception of their appearance and ignorance did not fall as low as their actual stupidity," he reported to his family. "They appear to be nothing more than moving masses of flesh, unendowed with any thing of intelligence above the brutes. I have now an idea of the blight upon that part of our country in which they live."

In Washington Sumner made the Supreme Court the center of his interest. Though few causes of importance were being argued, Sumner listened attentively as Francis Scott Key pleaded a case in which he relied "upon a quickness and facility of language rather upon research" and as Webster replied in a fashion that indicated he had not studied the case, even though half a million dollars was involved. The justices were more impressive, and Sumner, whose friendship with Story gave him "almost . . . a place in the court,—*persona standi in judico,* as Lord Stowell

<hr/>

[7] *American Jurist,* XI (Jan. 1834), 101–15; Sumner's autobiography, Palfrey MSS.; Henry Moore to Sumner, May 14, 1834, Sumner MSS.; Sumner to Tower, July 17 [1834], Tower MSS.

would say," not merely observed them on the bench, but also had
the privilege of dining with them regularly at their boarding
house, where they discussed judicial business over postprandial
Madeira. Sumner admired most of all the venerable chief justice, John Marshall, now within a year of his death, whom he
found "a model of simplicity . . . naturally taciturn, and yet
ready to laugh; to joke and be joked with." [8]

Compared with the court, everything else in Washington
seemed vulgar. President Andrew Jackson did not impress Sumner; "the old tyrant," he reported, "seemed to have hardly nerve
enough to keep his bones together." In Congress he found Henry
Clay's eloquence "splendid and thrilling" and admired John C.
Calhoun, who seemed "more than an orator . . . an honest and
able man, having earnestly at heart all that he was uttering, and
indifferent to the guise of his thought, so he could make them
understood." Even so, little about the congressional proceedings
attracted Sumner's interest, and after the court adjourned, he
found "nothing but dust and dullness" in Washington, "the cne
sweeping in volumes up and down the Avenue and the other pervading the Capitol." Under the tutelage of Story, who had conveniently forgotten his own earlier career as a Jeffersonian partisan and had now become John Marshall's chief support in the
Supreme Court,[9] Sumner developed, during his Washington
trip, a decided aversion to politicians and to "the unweeded garden in which they are laboring." "The more I see of *politics*," he
reported, in words that echoed Story's, "the more I learn to love
law." As he left the capital, he shook the dust off his feet. "I probably shall never come here again," he announced. "I have little
or no desire ever to come again in any capacity." [1]

By the fall of 1834 Sumner's advisers felt that he was ready
to begin his professional career. In September, having had his
title to the degree of Bachelor of Laws from Harvard College certified by President Quincy, his diligence in legal studies endorsed
by Greenleaf, and his "most unblemished character" vouched for

---

[8] Pierce, I, 132, 134–7, 141; Boston *Commonwealth*, Mar. 7, 1874.

[9] The change in Story's opinions, however, had been neither so abrupt nor
so marked as historians have sometimes pictured it. Commager: "Joseph Story,"
pp. 35–7, 58–9.

[1] Pierce, I, 136, 137, 139, 141–2; Sumner to Story, Mar. 20, and 21 [1834],
Story MSS.

by Rand, Sumner was admitted to the bar.[2] Immediately he
formed a partnership with George S. Hillard, another of Story's
favorite pupils, rented an office at No. 4 Court Street, and hung
out his shingle. On October 13 he had his first case, a minor suit
in the Boston municipal court. The Boston *Atlas* kindly noted
Sumner's first appearance at the bar and remarked that he was
"said to be more deeply read in the law than any other individual
of similar age." [3]

It is difficult to judge how successful Sumner's practice was
during the next three years. No business records exist of the
Hillard and Sumner partnership; court dockets are fragmentary
and unrevealing; later reminiscences are not entirely reliable. In
his autobiography Sumner himself claimed that his early practice was "considerable," that he promptly began earning an "income larger than that of any other person at the time so young
in his profession," and that as a result of his successes, he "was
soon invited into lucrative partnership with *three* eminent members of the profession." Theophilus P. Chandler, who had an office in the same building as Hillard and Sumner, agreed that
Sumner's practice was both successful and increasing. The fact
that only a year after Sumner was admitted to the bar, the
United States District Attorney for Massachusetts, Andrew Dunlap, invited him to become his partner, to handle all his cases
before the court of common pleas, the municipal court, and perhaps the district court, suggests that the young attorney's abilities were widely recognized.[4]

On the other hand, there are indications that Sumner was
less than overwhelmed with business. The remaining, scattered legal papers for these years suggest that most of his cases
were small matters—the drawing of a will, the settling of an
estate, etc.—and even these appear not to have been numerous.[5]
Clients could tell that Sumner was not at his best in the court-

[2] Harvard College Papers, VI, 2 ser., 224; certificate signed by Greenleaf,
Jan. 6, 1834, and certificate signed by Rand & Ashe, Sept. 2, 1834, MSS., Ameri-
can Antiquarian Society; certificate signed by J. G. Kendall, Sept. 3, 1834,
Sumner MSS.

[3] Oct. 14, 1834.

[4] T. P. Chandler to Pierce, Jan. 24, 1879, Pierce MSS.; Sumner to Story
[Jan. 1835], Story MSS.

[5] E.g., Sumner to Gustavus S. Drane, Oct. 24, 1835, MS., Segal Coll.; Boston
Commonwealth, Nov. 1, 1862,

room, for he thought too slowly to succeed at cross-examination and relied too heavily upon cited precedents to impress a jury. The envious claimed that he owed whatever business he did attract chiefly "to Judge Story's friendship and favor." He did not argue a case before the Massachusetts Supreme Judicial Court until 1837, and even after that, his appearances were rare.[6] Three years after he commenced practice, Sumner, in what may have been a bit of unintentional autobiography, advised a friend just admitted to the bar not to be discouraged by a seeming want of success. "The *first* year is no criterion," he argued. "Many of the *first years* of our first lawyers have been passed in the direst desolation, without the chance ray from a single client to enlighten their darkness."[7]

Sumner occupied his considerable spare time with professional writing, which he found more congenial than practice. He, Hillard, and Luther S. Cushing, whose office was just above Sumner's, now edited *The American Jurist,* and for almost every quarterly issue Sumner turned out long articles and shorter reviews on such topics as "Are Challenges to Jurors in Massachusetts Determinable by Triors?" "The Advocates Library in Edinburgh," and "The Juridical Writings of Sir James Mackintosh."[8] He also found time to write on legal subjects for the *North American Review* and the *American Monthly Review.*[9] Sumner's plan to edit, in fifteen or twenty volumes of 800 pages each, "the whole series of modern and ancient British chancery reports, in a condensed form," was interrupted when Dunlap, who was dying of tuberculosis, asked him to complete his *Practice in Admiralty.* Without interrupting his own practice, Sumner found time to check all of Dunlap's citations, to read the proofs twice, to prepare over one hundred pages of appendices, including sum-

6 Theophilus Parsons to Sumner [Apr. 1836], Sumner MSS.; 19 Pickering 202.

7 Sumner to "My dear George," Aug. 6, 1837, MS., Yale Univ. Sumner's attempt to add to his income by buying stock in a speculative land company failed, and he was left in debt. Sumner to W. C. Russell, Aug. 25, Sept. 4, and 20, 1835. Sumner MSS. He was obliged to borrow $1,100 from his father during his first few years at the bar. Will of C. P. Sumner, Apr. 5, 1839, Docket No. 32,151. Probate Court Office, Suffolk Co., Boston.

8 J. C. Perkins to Sumner, Nov. 3, 1837, Sumner MSS.; printed circular, enclosed in Sumner to James Kent, Apr. 30, 1836, Kent MSS.; *American Jurist,* XII (Oct. 1834), 330–40; XIII (Apr. 1835), 382–9; XIV (July 1835), 100–34.

9 *North American Review,* XLV (Oct. 1837), 482–4, 502–4; XLVI (Jan. 1838), 300–1; *American Monthly Review* (Boston), III (Apr. 1833), 315–27; (May 1833), 430–3.

maries of the rules of United States admiralty courts and a collection of practical forms to be used in admiralty proceedings,
which Sumner himself worked up from British and American
usage, to make the index, and to write a biographical preface
about Dunlap, who died before the book appeared.[1] Early in
1835 Sumner, appointed reporter for the United States Circuit
Court by Judge Story, who sensed that the young man was not
making a living at his practice, undertook an even more time-
consuming task. During the next two years he gathered, edited,
and oversaw the publication of two volumes that were known as
Sumner's Reports; a third volume appeared in 1841.[2]

If Sumner's friends were not worried because these literary
activities diverted him from actual practice at the Massachusetts
bar, where such giants as Rufus Choate were gaining both impressive incomes and national reputations and where younger
attorneys like Benjamin R. Curtis were rapidly establishing
themselves, it was because they planned a different future for
him. Even while he was in law school, Sumner's classmates had
predicted that through "the confidence, esteem, and friendship
of that truly great man," Story, Sumner would find his "employment probably in the science of the law" and would thus escape
its "drudgery." The hope was one that Sumner himself earnestly
shared. He had hated to leave the law school. "I could spend my
life, I believe, in this, as some call it, monkish seclusion," he confessed. Sumner's professors encouraged his aspiration. Greenleaf
was "full of lamentations" when Sumner left the school in 1834,
and Story, who missed his young friend even more, promised
him: "If the Law School succeeds I am sure you will be with us
again at no distant period."[3]

In fact, only a year after his graduation, Sumner was invited to return to the Harvard Law School. In 1835, when Story

---

[1] *American Jurist,* XIII (Apr. 1835), 490–1; Dunlap to Sumner, Feb. 14,
1835, Sumner MSS.; Sumner to Dunlap, June 8, 1835, Dunlap MSS.; Sumner to
Benjamin W. Stone, Aug. 15, 1836, ibid.; Sumner to C. S. Daveis, Aug. 8, 1836,
Daveis MSS.; Dunlap's *A Treatise on the Practice of Courts of Admiralty . . .*
(2nd ed.; New York: Jacob R. Halsted; 1850), pp. viii–xii. Sumner received
$500 for his labors on Dunlap's book.

[2] Richard Peters to Sumner, June 6, 1835, Sumner MSS.; Sumner's contract
with Hilliard, Gray & Co., Mar. 11, 1836, ibid. The title page read: *Report of
Cases Argued and Determined in the Circuit Court of the United States for the
First Circuit, By Charles Sumner, Reporter of the Court.*

[3] Pierce, I, 100, 119; Story to Sumner, Feb. 4, 1834, Sumner MSS.

was obliged to remain for longer than usual in Washington, President Quincy asked Sumner to teach his courses. The invitation came at just the time Dunlap offered him a partnership, but Sumner had no difficulty in making his choice. "The situation [in the law school], in a pecuniary point of view and on divers other accounts is far less acceptable than that offered by you," he explained to Dunlap; "yet my sense of duty, of respect to those who have treated me kindly, and some of my tastes and predilections do not allow me to decline it." Not only in 1835, but in the following year as well Sumner served as instructor in the law school, and in 1837, when both Story and Greenleaf were absent, he was for a time in sole charge of the Harvard Law School.[4]

Sumner lectured principally upon the Law of Evidence, using Starkie as a text, "expounding and commenting on the subject, step by step, and saying everything which occurred to him by way of illustration from the cases, from practice, history and legal anecdote," and upon the Law of Nations, "discussing the principles of International Law, the rights of war, of neutrals and the duties flowing therefrom, now running along the narrow lines which separate the cases with regard to domicil and the various kinds of property liable to capture, and now rejoicing in historical illustration or in some of the more expansive principles which are to be found in the elementary writers." One does not know how much his students learned, but the lecturer received invaluable training for a future career in the Senate Committee on Foreign Relations. Sumner also gave "some most righteous judgments in the moot-court," then, as always, an essential feature of a Harvard legal education. With every year of teaching he thought he gained "new confidence, as well as facility, and, perhaps, capacity."[5]

Though Sumner reported that the students were "in admirable order, most ardently engaging in work, and zealous after knowledge," he seems to have made no striking impression upon them. Doubtless many were disappointed that a novice was attempting to fill the place of Story and Greenleaf. Probably they

---

[4] Sumner to Dunlap [Jan. 1835], Dunlap MSS.; Sumner's autobiography, Palfrey MSS. Harvard paid Sumner $275 for his teaching services in 1835, $225 in 1835–6, and $150 in 1837. Harvard College Papers, VII, 2 ser., 99, 550; VIII, 204, 238.

[5] Sumner to Story, Jan. 18, and 25, and Feb. 5, 1837, Story MSS.

also recognized that Sumner, like every beginning teacher, was
only one assignment ahead of his students. Necessarily "he confined his talk to the given pages in the text book, but . . . did
not question the students or so develop the lecture as to present
anything new outside of the text book, or compel the students, by
his method, to hard and close study of the lesson." Still, they
found him "a ready and agreeable talker," and, on the whole, he
was "very popular with the students." [6]

Whatever the students thought, Sumner's professors valued
his services. Hearing through Greenleaf of Sumner's "complete,
and every way gratifying" success, Story as early as 1835 wrote
him frankly: "I hope this is but the beginning, and that one day
you may fill the chair which he or I occupy, if he or I, like auto-
crats, can hope to appoint our successor." Greenleaf shared his
colleague's hope and wrote Sumner, a little later: "Our earnest
desire is to have you occupy an additional professor's chair, with
Judge Story and myself, bringing into our institution all that
power and all the affluence of your mind, to bear upon the great
and increasing number of young men who come to us for instruction."

Their wish was also Sumner's desire. "You have thrown out
some hints with regard to my occupying a place with you and
the Judge at Cambridge," he replied to Greenleaf. "You know well
that my heart yearns fondly to that place, and that in the calm
study of my profession I have ever taken more delight than in
the pert debate at the bar." [7]

· 3 ·

Story's influence shaped not merely Sumner's professional career, but also his pattern of thought, his outlook on life, and even

[6] Most of these comments come from students who heard Sumner lecture
in 1843, when he again replaced Story, but they are doubtless applicable to his
earlier teaching experience as well. Warren: *Harvard Law School*, II, 26, 56.

[7] Story: *Story*, II, 189; Pierce, I, 380; II, 9. Sumner later claimed that he
"in 1835 was invited by President [Quincy] to the professorship of Moral Philosophy and political Economy in Harvard University—declined—afterwards was
again pressed, and asked if I would not entertain it, if coupled with a permanent
professorship in [the] Law School—declined." Sumner's autobiography, Palfrey
MSS. I have been unable to find anything to support this recollection, and as
there is considerable evidence to indicate that he desired just such a professorship, I am inclined to think his memory was at fault.

his gestures and his mannerisms. He did his best to mold his favorite pupil into the safe, conservative, respectable pattern of Boston Whiggery. The merchants of State Street began to speak of Sumner as a promising young man, who combined a proper respect for law and a belief in the indispensability of the legal profession [8] with a suitable disdain for popular politics and an outright contempt for the Jacksonian Democrats. Even in literature he exhibited a wholesome reverence for the classics and an ability to quote almost too extensively from the Latin sages. He held the reassuring conviction that the essays of the dangerous transcendentalist, Ralph Waldo Emerson, contained "exquisite sentences, images and phrases, but [were] a maze without a plan." The young lawyer seemed to hold no dangerous ideas on the subject of property, so basic to the Whig creed. Instead, he belittled the sermons of William E. Channing, who was beginning to advocate needed social reforms, as wanting "in the forms of logical discussion, and the close, continuous chain of reasoning," and even contributed an article to the *North American Review*, arguing that "the enterprise and generosity of the merchants" of the United States were the best contemporary manifestation of the "spirit of chivalry." [9] Clearly Sumner was doing all he could to fulfill the prophesy of a classmate, who dissuaded him from even thinking of locating his law office in another state. "I have always supposed that the place of your ultimate destination was certain," he had told Sumner. "You were made for Boston." [1]

As yet, however, Sumner's general acquaintance in Boston society was still limited. Though both Story and Hillard sponsored him, Sumner seemed an odd figure to those Bostonians who sedulously imitated English manners and considered conversation a fine art. "He was tall, thin, and ungainly in his movements, and sprawled rather than sat on a chair or sofa," William Wetmore Story recalled. "Nothing saved his face from ugliness but his white gleaming teeth and his expression of bright intelligence

[8] *North American Review*, XLV (Oct. 1837), 503.
[9] Sumner to Mrs. George Bancroft, Jan. 24, 1849, Bancroft MSS.; Pierce, I, 157; *North American Review*, XLVI (Jan. 1838), 115–16. Cf., however, T. Wemyss Reid: *The Life, Letters, and Friendships of Richard Monckton Milnes, First Lord Houghton* (New York: Cassell Publishing Company; 1891), I, 237–9.
[1] Pierce, I, 100.

and entire amiability." Everybody recognized Sumner's "simplicity, his perfect *naturalness*," as well as his intelligence, but it was not at all clear that these compensated for his social deficiencies.

Though Sumner talked incessantly to his close friends, he had no general conversation. He admitted that he had "no knowledge of music, and but little, scarcely any, ear for it," that he was ignorant "of the principles of art and of its history." Even poetry was "with him more an acquired taste than a natural one." He cared nothing for sports and could not talk of fishing, shooting, and rowing, or of horses and dogs. His intensity and seriousness dampened light conversation. He had no sense of humor; a censorious father and rival brothers had taught him that it was dangerous ever to let down his guard and that to laugh at himself was an admission of error. "He was," young Story declared, "totally put off his balance by the least *persiflage;* and, if it was tried on him, his expression was one of complete astonishment. He was never ready at a retort, tacked slowly, like a frigate when assaulted by stinging feluccas, and was . . . almost impervious to a joke." Oliver Wendell Holmes exaggerated only a little when he declared that if one told Sumner that the moon was made of green cheese, he would say: "No! it cannot be so," and proceed to give weighty reasons to the contrary.[2]

Sumner's most serious social handicap was his inability to converse with women. As a college senior he had been too timid to be introduced to President Quincy's youngest daughter, Anna, who had attained the venerable age of eighteen; he dared only to look on her "from afar with awe."[3] Now that he was a promising young lawyer, he still did not know how to act or what to say. He was not hostile to women. In fact, he held highly romantic notions about love, marriage, and the family. He firmly believed "that the only true love is love at first sight." Marriage, he was certain, would be a life of perpetual rapture. "One beautiful look of love from a wife or child must start a more exquisite thrill of happiness than comes from any distinction, literary or politi-

[2] Ibid., I, 106–7, 127, 237, 241; John T. Morse, Jr.: *Life and Letters of Oliver Wendell Holmes* (Boston: Houghton Mifflin Co.; 1896), II, 202–3.
[3] Pierce, I, 103. Sumner did, however, later overcome his shyness and converse with the Quincy sisters. M. A. DeWolfe Howe (ed.): *The Articulate Sisters* . . . (Cambridge: Harvard University Press; 1946), pp. 238–9.

cal." But, in such a partnership, he thought that a woman should know her role. "A female's place is at home," he somewhat heavily instructed his young sister Jane when she was but fourteen years old, "not abroad in the excited scenes of the world," and her principal charm should be the ability "to listen intelligently." [4]

But, Boston ladies showed a disconcerting unwillingness to listen. They wanted to talk themselves, to make witty remarks, and to engage in flirtatious conversation. Such creatures fascinated Sumner, but they were beyond his comprehension. How, to so awesome a being as a Boston lady, could one bare his soul? Could he ever dare to squeeze the universe into a ball and roll it to some overwhelming question? How his classmates mustered the courage to enter "Cupid's Tribunal" baffled him. Such delight was not for him, he grew convinced; it would be his fate to "tarry at the gate, beholding his associates enter one by one, waiting for Time when tired of detaining him to let him in." So terrifying were these formidable females that Sumner tried to avoid them. "It was in vain for the loveliest and liveliest girl to seek to absorb his attention," William Story declared. "He would at once desert the most blooming beauty to talk to the plainest of men." [5]

If Sumner was not at home in mixed society, he was exceptionally popular among men of his own age, who found him sincerely sympathetic, eager for friendship. Besides, as an unmarried man, he was always available. After graduating from the law school, he had moved from his father's crowded, gloomy house, and he and Luther Cushing rented a furnished room and took their meals at a restaurant. Later Sumner found living quarters in the Albion Hotel, on the corner of Beacon and Tremont streets, where his friends could always find him ready for a talk, a walk out to Cambridge—though he strode along at such a rate that few tried this more than once—or a midnight supper in one of the oyster houses.

"Among my chief delights have been my friends," Sumner declared in his autobiography. He had many of them, especially among his colleagues at the bar, nearly all of whom had a genuine affection for this serious, studious young man. Gradually he

[4] Sumner to Story, Feb. 12, 1837, Story MSS.; Sumner to Lieber, Oct. 13, 1837, Lieber MSS.; Sumner to Jane Sumner, Mar. 4, 1834, Sumner MSS.
[5] Sumner to Tower, Dec. 17, 1832, Tower MSS.; Pierce, I, 106–7.

built a smaller circle of specially cherished intimates. One, naturally, was his law partner, Hillard, whose dreamy, poetic look
and delicate, sickly constitution suggested that literature rather
than law should have been his vocation.[6] Another was Henry
Wadsworth Longfellow, Ticknor's successor at Harvard, whom
Sumner met while lecturing at the law school. Between the poet
and the lawyer there grew up an instant affection, which ripened
into the most enduring friendship of Sumner's life.[7] Frail, ailing
Henry R. Cleveland, who served for a time as proctor at Harvard
before feeble health compelled him to lead a life of idleness,
served as a sounding board for his more loquacious and excit-
able friends. Sumner thought him wholly admirable, combining "the choicest qualities of the heart and head—a truth and
purity of character, as unsullied as the lawn of the altar, with a
temper which is never ruffled and a constancy which never
fails." [8] In marked contrast was Sumner's fifth special friend,
Cornelius C. Felton, tall and stout, certainly the most jovial professor of Latin ever to teach at Harvard or anywhere else. His
"*fat,* and . . . his *fun,*" Sumner thought, made Felton an ideal
companion, and his "exilerating [sic] laugh, and his constant
flow of wit and kindliness" kept his friends from too much morbid
introspection.[9]

Sumner, Hillard, Longfellow, Cleveland, and Felton grew
so attached to each other that they formed a kind of informal
society, which they styled "The Five of Clubs." At their Saturday
dinner meetings they discussed the many interests they had in
common. In 1837 they were all less than thirty years old, and all
except Hillard were still unmarried. All aspired to be accepted
in Boston society, and, even though they lacked the wealth and
the family connections to move easily among the Winthrops, the
Curtises, and the Searses, they were recognized as promising

[6] Francis W. Palfrey: "Memoir of the Hon. George Stillman Hillard," *MHSP,*
XIX (June 1882), 339–45.
[7] The best account of Longfellow during these early years of his friendship
with Sumner is Lawrance Thompson: *Young Longfellow (1807–1843)* (New
York: The Macmillan Co.; 1938).
[8] Sumner to Sarah Perkins, June 9, 1837, copy, Henry Wadsworth Longfellow MSS.; *A Selection from the Writings of Henry R. Cleveland. With a
Memoir by George S. Hillard* (1844), pp. v–li.
[9] Sumner to George Washington Greene, Mar. 31, 1843, Greene MSS.;
Hillard: "Remarks on Felton's Death," *MHSP,* V (1862), 446–57; William
Watson Goodwin, in *The Cambridge Historical Society Publications, II: Proceedings, October 23, 1906–October 22, 1907,* pp. 117–30.

young men who might someday be admitted to the socially elect. But, it was chiefly their love of literature which drew the five together. Though only Longfellow was able to make a career for himself as a man of letters, the other four friends had also originally aspired to become writers, and, despite other occupations, all did make minor contributions to American literature. Eagerly they read and criticized each other's manuscripts, and loyally they published laudatory reviews of each other's books. These articulate friends thought so well of themselves that newspapers began to refer to them derisively as "The Mutual Admiration Society." [1]

Younger than any of his close friends, Sumner in the 1830's was the most endearing and ingratiating of the five. Nothing about him at the time suggested the inflexible zeal and moral terrorism of his later reform career. On the contrary, he was totally dependent upon his friends for affection and praise. A phrenologist who analyzed Sumner's character in 1835 by measuring the bumps on his head—and doubtless by collecting current opinion and gossip about him—declared that his "self esteem" was much too small; he was "not self poised and independent" enough. "You must rouse up your self respect," the phrenologist urged, prescribing that he overcome his shyness by attempting to speak in public. "You would be mild, bland, respectful, and pleasing," he promised Sumner, "if you could feel self-confidence enough to get well under weigh [sic]." Sumner's intimates would have agreed with this analysis. If Sumner could only overcome his diffidence and his willingness to be exploited by others, they believed he might make a name for himself. Longfellow was certain that Sumner's "very lovely character" was "full of talent; with a most keen enjoyment of life; simple, energetic, hearty, good." [2]

· 4 ·

Completely under Story's influence, Sumner in the 1830's seemed well on the way to becoming a Boston Brahmin, yet, paradoxically, it was Story's ideas that kept him from quite fitting

[1] Samuel Longfellow: *Life of Henry Wadsworth Longfellow With Extracts from his Journals and Correspondence* (Boston: Houghton Mifflin Co.; 1891), I, 253–4.

[2] Ibid., I, 304; Memorandum by T. Jones, Nov. 12, 1835, Sumner MSS.

into the dominant pattern of Boston society. Now growing old
and conservative, the judge tended to think of himself as the defender of nationalism and of property, the friend of Webster and
of Marshall, and to forget that in his younger days he had been
suspected of harboring dangerous, almost Jacobinical ideas. But,
Sumner, as a worshipful student, treasured every word the judge
had ever written and adopted every opinion he had ever expressed—including some that Story had himself discarded.

In his legal writings, for example, Sumner began to advocate certain mild reforms that Story had once endorsed in his
lectures, and, in his thorough-going fashion, carried them to an
extreme the judge had never contemplated. Remembering
Story's defense of the "intricate, but . . . exquisitely finished
system" of equity jurisprudence, Sumner, in his very first essay
for *The American Jurist,* challenged the State Street merchants'
reverence for the common law by suggesting that equity proceedings were more reliably just. In subsequent articles he pushed
the idea further, urging American lawyers to import "new principles from the broad field of ethics" and quoting with approval
an English judge's dictum: "Principles of private justice, moral
fitness and public convenience, when applied to a new subject,
make common law without a precedent." [3]

It was even more heretical for Sumner to prefer the com-
mentators on French and Roman law to Blackstone and Chitty,
those twin gods of Court Street. He recalled reading Story's pious
wish, expressed in an article published in 1817, "that the time is
not far distant, when [the writings of such jurisconsults as]
Pothier and Emerigon and Valin will be accessible in our native
tongue to every lawyer, and will be as familiarly known to them
as they now are to the jurists of continental Europe," and decided that a knowledge of the civil law should be considered a
mark of "enlarged liberality and intelligence." Even in petty municipal cases he attempted, to the considerable confusion of his
clients and the judges, to introduce concepts from continental
jurisprudence. In his Harvard lectures, too, Sumner exhibited
what he proudly called a "tincture of *Radicalism*" in preferring
the simple, all-inclusive rules of the civil code to the obscure

[3] William Wetmore Story (ed.): *The Miscellaneous Writings of Joseph Story*
(Boston: Charles C. Little and James Brown; 1852), p. 540; *American Jurist,* X
(July 1833), 227–37; XI (Apr. 1834), 321.

common law, "so shingled over with exceptions, that the rule can hardly be observed." [4]

Enthusiastically Sumner adopted Story's view that the law should be succinct and simple, but what was a moderate opinion in the judge became, in Sumner, a dogma. Story, for instance, had always been in favor of codifying Massachusetts law, so as to bring some measure of order into the conflicting, confused, and repetitious legislation of the Commonwealth. By the 1830's, though he still spoke of codification "with great ardor . . . and with confidence in its practicability," he derided the possibility of drawing up "a positive code, which shall be adequate to the business and rights and modifications of property in any one single age, unless the legislature can foresee every possible as well as every probable combination of circumstances applicable to every subject-matter in that age," and thought it best to advocate "only the reduction to a positive code of those general principles, . . . which . . . are now capable of a distinct enunciation." Sumner, on the other hand, treasured the judge's younger, more radical opinion that codification was not only possible, but might be "within the reach of a single mind successfully to accomplish," and he favored reducing the common law to the regularity and simplicity of the Code Napoleon. When the Massachusetts legislature in 1836 set up a commission, with Story at its head, to investigate the possibilities of codification, Sumner was delighted. He urged the judge, in naming his fellow commissioners, to "use the *young*," as "the old are prejudiced" against thorough-going legal reform. One of the young men he had in mind was Charles Sumner.[5]

To detect these faint notes of dissent in Sumner's think-

[4] Story (ed.): *Story's Miscellaneous Writings*, pp. 78, 281; *American Jurist*, XI (Jan. 1834), 265; XIV (Oct. 1835), 313; Sumner to Story, Jan. 18, 1837, Story MSS. It was doubtless this same "radicalism" that caused Sumner to disagree with Story's conservative opinion in the Charles River Bridge case. *MHSP*, XXXV (1901–2), 210–11.

[5] Sumner to Theophilus Parsons, undated [1836], MS., Boston Public Lib.; Story (ed.): *Story's Miscellaneous Writings*, pp. 239, 707, 709; Sumner to K. A. J. Mittermaier, Mar. 27, 1837, Sumner MSS.; Sumner to John A. Kasson, July 12, 1849, Charles Aldrich Coll.; Story to Edward Everett, Mar. 17, 1836, Everett MSS.; Parsons to Everett, Mar. 17, 1836, ibid.; Parsons to Sumner [Apr. 1836], Sumner MSS. On codification see Oscar and Mary Flug Handlin: *Commonwealth: A Study of the Role of Government in the American Economy: Massachusetts, 1776–1861* (New York: New York University Press; 1947), pp. 213–14; Leonard W. Levy, *The Law of the Commonwealth and Chief Justice Shaw* (Cambridge: Harvard University Press; 1957), pp. 196–202.

ing would have required a closer attention to his trivial court cases and his technical legal essays than any busy merchant of Boston was prepared to give, but Sumner's decision in 1837 to interrupt both his law practice and his teaching in order to travel in Europe was unmistakable evidence that this promising young lawyer did not accept the values of Boston as absolute. Nearly everybody was shocked by his plan. His father sourly disapproved. Puzzled by his willingness to throw up his promising prospects, his colleagues at the bar urged: "Do not think of going to Europe, until you shall become the head of your profession, as you will become, and rich, as you will be." Professor Greenleaf shook his head at Sumner's want of wisdom. President Quincy, remembering all too well that George Bancroft had returned from his European trip an effeminate dandy, told Sumner brusquely: "You will come home with a cane, moustaches and an additional stock of vanity—that's all." [6]

What was worse, Story disapproved. Sumner found the judge's position incomprehensible. It had been Story who originally caused him to fall "in love with *Europa*" [7]—just as it had been Story who had been the source of Sumner's quiet legal heresies. The judge had indeed taught that the well-rounded lawyer should travel abroad, but he himself never left the United States.

Story's views on the value of travel might change, but not Sumner's. Easily influenced initially to adopt an idea, he was, as the Harvard Parietal Board had discovered, inflexibly stubborn. By using almost the same words Story had employed in his lectures, he sought to bring the judge around. "Do . . . think of my strong desire, which dates back to my earliest days of memory—amounting almost to an instinct—to visit those scenes memorable in literature and history and to see, so far as it may be given to one so humble as myself, the great men that are already on the stage," he begged Story; "think, then, of the desire, which has arisen in maturer years, of obtaining a knowledge of languages, of observing the manners, customs and institutions of

[6] Richard Peters to Sumner, Dec. 29, 1836, Sumner MSS.; Sumner to Story, Feb. 10, 1840, ibid.

[7] Sumner to Lieber, Jan. 17, 1837, ibid. As a student in the law school, Sumner had pledged: "I will bond my services to any one for five years, who will furnish me with means sufficient to go to Europe and travel from one to two years in the old countries." N. F. Bryant to Pierce, Apr. 2, 1878, Pierce MSS.

other people than my own, particularly of noting in France and Germany the administration of justice and the course of legal institutions and in England frequenting Westminster Hall and drinking at the very bubbling fountain of the common law."

Rather against his own judgment, Story allowed himself to be convinced that Sumner planned to travel "not for *display* but for *purposes* of *education*," and he agreed to lend his young friend $1,000 for his journey. Samuel Lawrence, the textile magnate, and Congressman Richard Fletcher, a wealthy Boston lawyer, put up similar amounts.[8]

With his money in hand, Sumner turned to soliciting letters of introduction. From all his friends who had European acquaintances, even from friends of friends who had been abroad, he sought letters. By the time he was ready to leave, Sumner had "letters, under which a mail would groan." Story, Fletcher, C. S. Daveis, of Maine, David Hoffman, of Baltimore, and Horace Binney wrote to English lawyers and judges in his behalf; Caleb Cushing and Edward Everett to English politicians; Channing, Longfellow, Emerson, and Washington Allston to men of letters; Lieber to his many acquaintances in France, Germany, and Italy. "My supply of introductions is bountiful," Sumner at last reported; "the door of English life, law and literature [is] wide open to me." [9]

Sumner had hoped to sail in October 1837, but business detained him until December. As the time for departure grew near, he became increasingly excited about his prospects and increasingly troubled by the audacity of his course. Toward midnight of his last day on land, he wrote a troubled letter to Story, whose words had originally inspired the trip, but whose opinion of it was still far from favorable: "Your confidence and friendship are a life-blood to me. I hope these may not desert me. And may God grant that I may return from Europe with increased knowledge and added capacity for usefulness. If I do not, then, indeed, shall I have travelled in vain." [1]

[8] Sumner to Story, July 13, 1837, Story MSS.; Samuel Lawrence to Pierce, Jan. 3, 1876, Pierce MSS.

[9] Sumner to Lieber, Nov. 19, 1837, Sumner MSS.; Sumner to Daveis, Aug. 4, 1837, Daveis MSS.; Sumner to Longfellow, Aug. 18, 1837, Longfellow MSS.; Sumner to Jared Sparks, Oct. 28, 1837, Sparks MSS.; Sumner to Kent, Nov. 7, 1837, Kent MSS.; Sumner to Story, Nov. 7 [1837], Story MSS.

[1] Sumner to Story, Dec. 7, 1837, Story MSS.

CHAPTER III

The Life of Life

I TREMBLE with hope, anticipation and anxiety," Sumner wrote as he was about to begin his European tour.[1] His worry was entirely justified. One hundred years ago the physical perils that attended a trip abroad were numerous. On the transatlantic crossing, wooden sailing ships often suffered disastrously from fires or storms. Fortunately, the *Albany*, upon which he sailed from New York in December 1837, was a safe, swift ship, requiring but twenty days to reach Europe. Though the voyage was tranquil, Sumner suffered considerably from seasickness, which prostrated him before he lost sight of land. "Literally 'cabbined, cribbed and confined' in my berth I ate nothing, did nothing, and read nothing for three days," he reported to his Boston friends, with an invalid's interest in his own health. For more than a week after that he was too feeble to appear at the public table.

Isolated and lonely, he began to question the wisdom of this bold, almost rash, step he had taken "contrary to the advice of dear friends." Perhaps he had lost forever his chance to build a successful law practice. After all, he could not "throw off his clients and then whistle them back, 'as a huntsman does his pack.'"

[1] Sumner to Daveis, Dec. 7, 1837, Daveis MSS. Sumner's European trip is the most elaborately documented part of his life. His voluminous letters and detailed travel journals contain fascinating descriptions of most of the important leaders in British and Continental society, politics, and literature of the period. Fortunately many of these letters and most of Sumner's journal, except for a few passages considered slanderous or risqué, were printed in E. L. Pierce's *Memoir and Letters of Charles Sumner*, I, 213–380; II, 1–147. My purpose in this chapter is not to repeat this travelogue, but to discuss the effect of European travel upon Sumner's personality.

But, with better health and an appetite that returned "like a Bay of Fundy tide," he became more cheerful. Soon he was able to read, to study French, to walk the wet decks, and to play whist and chess with the other passengers. By the time the captain spied land, on Christmas night, Sumner's spirits were high. Each wave in the English channel seemed "to have a tale of interest or of glory." At any moment, he fancied, he might "catch a glimpse of Admiral Drake, slowly proceeding on his circuit of the globe, or of Robinson Crusoe, when as a runaway apprentice he left Hull, or Nelson sweeping on to the victories of the Nile and Trafalgar." He could hardly wait to go ashore. Joyfully he exclaimed: "The life of life seems to have burst upon me." [2]

· 1 ·

From the moment Sumner set foot in France he was prepared to admire everything. The docks at La Havre, bearing the inscription *An IX. Bonaparte 1ᵉʳ Consul,* were like a romantic introduction to the glories of French history. The room he rented for his first night in Europe, with its "floor of hexagon tiles partially covered with a neat rug-like carpet; with a bed plump and neat as imagination could picture, with a crimson coverlet and curtains," was wonderfully "un-American." The diligence, which carried him along the winding Seine to Rouen, was distinctively and excitingly French. The old cathedral at Rouen, with its thousands of historical associations, "its heaven-kissing spire, . . . its stained windows and the dim religious light, . . . its innumerable arches, . . . its altars, and above all its tombs and inscriptions," was alone enough, he declared, to repay the cost of his trip. The pictures in Rouen's rather mediocre museum had "a finish, a grace, an expression and subtlety of colouring" which made him "recall the collections of America as mere daubs." Everything about France, he concluded, breathed of antiquity. France was "all *old cheese,* mouldy, rotten and worm-eaten, but full of pregnancy and strength, as compared with the curdled milk of America." [3]

[2] Sumner to Hillard, Dec. 25, 1837, and Dec. 14, 1838, Sumner MSS.; Pierce, I, 214–15, MHSP, XV (2 ser.), 211–12; Sumner to Lieber, Mar. 9, 1838, Sumner MSS.

[3] Pierce, I, 217; MHSP, XV (2 ser.), 215; Sumner's Travel Journal, Dec. 29–30, 1837, Sumner MSS.

Only one thing interfered with his incipient love affair with France—his inability to master the French language. Though he had studied French at Harvard and had carefully reviewed his grammar before coming abroad, he discovered when he reached Paris that his "French was no more fit for use than a rusty gun-barrel." Calling upon Jean-Jacques Gaspard Foelix, the editor of the *Revue Etrangère de Législation et d'Economie Politique*, to whom he had a glowing letter of introduction, Sumner presented himself: "*Je m'appelle* Charles Sumner." Baffled by the accent, Foelix asked the stranger whether he had seen Mr. Sumner lately. The contretemps convinced Sumner that he should give up all idea of entering French society until he learned to make himself understood. With characteristic thoroughness, he employed not one, but two tutors, and spent hours each day in "laborious *artificial* conversation" with them. Every morning, in the hope of accustoming his ear to the spoken language, he sampled lectures at the Sorbonne or at the Collège de France. Evenings he went to the theater or opera, attempting to follow the rapid and elusive French in a libretto. His progress at times was discouraging. "That letter *u*," he exclaimed; "my lips refuse to utter it. I stumble over it constantly; and despair of being able to compass it." [4]

Debarred "from the society and scenes of this great metropolis" by his awkward linguistic handicap, Sumner, like many a more recent tourist, found consolation in sight-seeing in the company of fellow Americans. A true Bostonian, he gravitated naturally toward the New Englanders in Paris. He was delighted to find that the George Ticknors, who had just completed a triumphant tour of the Continent, were temporarily settled in the French capital, and the fact that Sumner brought them news and letters from Boston gave him an excuse to spend every evening of his first week in Paris at their lodgings. Soon he discovered even more congenial company in Dr. George Shattuck, another young Bostonian, who was completing his medical education in France. Sumner was so lonely that Shattuck was able to drag him to the Ecole de Médecine, where he saw "skeletons etc,

    [4] Pierce, I, 227; Sumner to Henry R. Cleveland, Jan. 30, 1837 [the date should be 1838], Cleveland MSS.; Sumner to Hillard, Jan. 6, 1837 [i.e., 1838], Sumner MSS.

all of which most thoroughly disgusted him," and to the great
hospital, the Hôtel Dieu, where, in spite of his shrinking "from
the sight of the knife, and the gush of blood," he witnessed "several operations for the stone" and where he nearly fainted among
those "shambles of death," the dissecting rooms.[5]

Gratefully concluding that Providence made him a lawyer
and not a doctor, Sumner soon found it pleasanter to stride about
the streets of Paris alone. Used to compact little Boston, he was
astonished to find the distances so gigantic. The galleries of the
Louvre, for instance, were so vast that he spent "four hours in
walking through them, not stopping to study anything." He longed
for time to investigate every street, every building of Paris. He
walked along the boulevards with his "mind swimming with the
excitement." "Great as my anticipations were," he reported to
Hillard, "they were greatly surpassed." [6]

Of course this very conventional young American from Puritan New England found much in France to shock him. On Sumner's first day in Paris, and a Sunday at that, he dashed out to
visit Frascati's, the largest gambling hell in the metropolis, which
the law was about to close permanently. He found it very exciting to see the roulette table, surrounded by intent gamblers, and
to watch the card games, where gold and silver were "spread
on the table to a vast amount," but he cautiously refrained from
betting so much as a franc. Nor were the young women moving
from table to table—"undoubtedly Cyprians," Sumner thought
—more enticing, though they possessed "considerable personal
attractions." Life in Paris gave Sumner a series of such titilla-
tions, unaccompanied by temptations. A singularly pure young
man with romantic notions of womanhood, he found "the im-
morality and total depravity" of the city at once fascinating and
revolting. "It is a perfect Sodom," he assured Hillard, "without
religion and without any morality between the sexes." [7]

Living abroad gave Sumner a new perspective on American
society. Like most Bostonians, he had been provincially conceited

[5] Sumner to Hillard, Jan. 6, 1837 [i.e., 1838], and Jan 13, 1838, Sumner
MSS.; George Ticknor, Journal, Jan. 1, 1838, Ticknor MSS.; Sumner's Travel
Journal, Jan. 10, and 31, Feb. 15, Mar. 21, 1838, Sumner MSS.
[6] Sumner's Travel Journal, Jan. 10, 1838, Sumner MSS.; Sumner to Hillard,
Jan. 13, and 30, 1838, ibid.
[7] Pierce, I, 225; Sumner to Hillard, Mar. 8, and Jan. 30, 1838, Sumner MSS.

when he sailed for Europe. If he did not precisely believe that
Boston was the hub of the universe, he did think that David
Sears's house on Beacon Street was the ideal type "of a palace,
the Athenaeum Gallery, of a collection of paintings, and the plas-
ter casts in the Athenaeum reading-room, . . . of a collection of
antiques." Paris taught him a lesson. "Never," he warned Hillard,
only two weeks after arriving in France, "exalt any building in
Boston . . . to the dignity of a *lion*, especially in the presence of
a foreigner. . . . Otherwise, rest assured he will laugh in secret
at the national vanity which could exalt such petty things into
objects of curiosity." Sumner began to suspect that other American beliefs were parochial. Though the sight of two or three Negroes, "dressed quite *à la mode,* and having the easy jaunty air
of young men of fashion" as they sat among the other students at
the Sorbonne struck him as very strange, he promptly decided
that French tolerance was superior to American racial proscription. "It must be," he concluded, "that the distance between free
blacks and the whites among us is derived from education, and
does not exist in the nature of things." [8]

Preoccupied with learning the French language and with
sight-seeing, Sumner almost forgot that he had come abroad with
the serious purpose of studying the civil law, perhaps in anticipation of a Harvard professorship when he returned. To be sure,
he had almost, from the day of his arrival, dropped in occasionally upon law lectures at the Sorbonne and at the Collège de
France, but his purpose was not so much to pursue a course of
study as to gain some personal impressions of the chief French
jurists and to improve his command of the language. During his
first two months he never got around to visiting the French
Chamber of Deputies or to attending the Paris courts.

Not until March did Sumner apply himself vigorously to
studying the French legal system. Though he still spoke falter-
ingly and "in defiance of all the rules of Grammar and pronunciation," he was now able to follow conversation easily, and he
began to present his letters of introduction to such lawyers as
Michel Chevalier, who had made an investigation of the American railroad system and later published a report of his travels,
the Baron de Gérando, the peer who was engaged in preparing

[8] Sumner to Hillard, Jan. 13, 1838, Sumner MSS.; Pierce, I, 241-2.

a massive treatise on philanthropy, and Jean Marie Pardessus, an internationally recognized authority on maritime law. Through their intercession he was assigned "a comfortable and honorable seat" at the Cour d'Assises and the Cour de Cassation, where for several weeks he followed cases carefully, drew diagrams of the courtrooms for his journal, and recorded strange or interesting details of French legal usage.[9]

Favorably predisposed toward continental jurisprudence, Sumner was impressed by what he saw. To his older friends at home, to be sure, he reported his opinions on the French law with circumspection. Story, who urged him to be skeptical of "all the visionary notions of Reformers" and to "value old principles more and innovation less," was doubtless pleased to hear that Sumner thought a French court "a laughable place," "a theatre, and all the judges, advocates, and parties 'merely players.' " In Paris, Sumner wrote the judge, "the learning of the profession is of the most shallow kind," and added: "Without vanity . . . I have several times felt that my acquaintance with the literature of French jurisprudence, and with the character and merits of its authors, was equal if not superior to that of many of the Frenchmen with whom I conversed." But, to Hillard, Sumner wrote his true opinion that the French Code, so grossly calumniated in America, offered "much greatly to admire." Doubtless a combination of French and English procedures would make the most desirable legal system, but, he concluded: "I am . . . *convinced,*—that if I were compelled to adopt the *whole* of either, without admixture, I should take the *French.*" It was clear that Professor Greenleaf's hope that Sumner would come back from Europe "cured of some *over*-tendencies to excess in legal reform" would not be realized. Instead, Sumner boasted: "I shall return, not simply a codifier, but a *revolutionist;* always ready however, I trust, to be illuminated by the superior wisdom of my friends." [1]

Though Sumner in his long letters to Story still spoke of his studies in Paris as leading ultimately to "a work presenting a *comparative view of the judicial institutions* of France, England, and America, particularly with a view to the theory of proofs and the

[9] Sumner to Hillard, Jan. 30, Mar. 21, and Apr. 10, 1838, Sumner MSS.
[1] Story to Sumner, May 22, 1838, ibid.; Pierce, I, 277, 288, 292; Sumner to Hillard, Apr. 10, 1838, Sumner MSS.; Greenleaf to Lieber, May 5, 1838, MS. bound in Vol. IX of "Pamphlets on Crime," Univ. of California Lib.

initiation of causes," in his heart he realized that preparing such
a book "would take months, perhaps years." During his brief stay
in Paris he did not, of course, secure anything like the formal
training in the civil law necessary for such a scholarly study,
though he had toured the courts with the same sight-seeing enthusiasm he had given the galleries of the Louvre, the studio of
David, the abattoir and the morgue. By May, when it came time
for him to leave France, he had quietly changed the purpose of
his European trip. Leaving Paris behind "with the liveliest regret,
and . . . with a thousand things undone, unlearned and un-
studied," he headed for England to "find a *vacation,*—the first I
have had for years." [2]

· 2 ·

"Land of my studies, my thoughts, and my dreams!" Sumner rapturously saluted England. "There, indeed, shall I 'pluck the life
of life.'" Arriving in London on May 31, he was almost at once
swept into the exciting round of English social life. By accepted
convention, each of his numerous letters of introduction entitled
its bearer to one dinner invitation, but Sumner proved so personable that many of his hosts insisted upon entertaining him again
and again. Justice John Vaughan, for example, to whom Sumner
presented a letter from Story, gave a dinner so that Sumner
could meet some other British judges. Charmed by his American
guest's behavior, he invited Sumner to accompany him to the Old
Bailey, where he sat beside the judge during the hearings, and
asked him to dine with the other magistrates of that court. "I received you first on Story's account," Vaughan exclaimed to the
young American, "but I keep you on your own; I like you very
much; indeed, if a judge may say so, I have an affection for you,
by G—d." [3]

As one invitation led to another, Sumner found "every moment of his time . . . absorbed and his mind almost in a *fever*"
of social excitement. "Aroused prematurely in the morning to
dress for breakfast," then one of the most fashionable forms of
British entertaining, he kept active in his giddy social whirl until

[2] Pierce, I, 290, 294, 295.
[3] Ibid., I, 294; Sumner to Story, July 12, 1838, Sumner MSS.

long after midnight. For want of time he abandoned the travel
journal with which he had so methodically begun his journey,
but his immensely detailed letters to his Boston friends were now
crammed with references to lords and ladies, barons and earls,
lord chancellors, and even an occasional duke or two. He became
an honorary member of the Garrick, the Travellers', the Athenaeum, and the Alfred clubs; the last, he boasted, was "the most
exclusive in London," and he was "the only untitled honorary
member" of it. At Westminster Hall, after declining repeated
invitations to sit on the bench, he was assigned a seat in the Ser-
geants' row at the Court of Common Pleas and in the Queen's
Counsel row at the Queen's Bench. He was admitted to the floor
of the House of Commons, and in the House of Lords he had a
regular place assigned him, on the steps of the throne, where he
could remain even during divisions. For the coronation of the
young Queen Victoria, for which admission to Westminster Ab-
bey was so eagerly sought that seats sold at the scalper's rate of
twenty-five guineas each, Sumner had no fewer than three tickets—one from a privy councillor and another from the Marquis
of Lansdowne—and he was able to give two away with "terrible
éclat." [4]

Soon Sumner knew everybody in the small world of London
society. He was impressed by Sir Robert Peel, "polished, graceful,
self-possessed, candid, or apparently candid, in the extreme," and
thought poorly of Lord John Russell, who reminded him of a pet-
tifogging attorney, since he wriggled as he spoke, "played with
his hat, [and] seemed unable to dispose of his hands or his
feet." At one breakfast he heard that "perfect model of a judge,"
Lord Denman, condemn the judicial wig as "the silliest thing in
England," and at the next he heard Justice James Allan Park ex-
claim that this sentiment "was all a piece of Denman's coxcombry
—that he wished to shew his person." Through Emerson's introduction he met Thomas Carlyle, who seemed to him "like an inspired boy," whose "thoughts . . . came from his apparently
unconscious mind, couched in the most grotesque style, and yet
condensed to a degree of intensity." With Walter Savage Landor,
"about 55, with an open countenance, firm and decided, with a

<hr>

[4] Sumner to Story, June 27, 1838, Sumner MSS.; Sumner to Hillard, June 14,
1838, ibid.; Lieber to Matilda Lieber, Aug. 1, 1838, Lieber MSS.

head grey and inclining to baldness" and "dressed in a heavy frock-coat of snuff colour, trowsers of the same and boots," he argued the comparative merits of Napoleon and Washington. At dinner at Lord Lansdowne's he encountered a sharp-voiced, articulate man of "about 40, rather short, and with a belly of unclassical proportions," who proved to be Thomas Babington Macaulay, just back from India and about to commence his history of England. "My acquaintance is most extensive—extensive beyond my most sanguine anticipations," Sumner reported complacently to Lieber. "All that is eminent in the law I know well, as well as some of the most prominent men in politics and in the church." [5]

The end of the London social and legal season in July was only the beginning of Sumner's conquest of Britain. During the summer, at the invitation of the presiding judges, he "travelled a part of the Home Circuit with Lord Denman, the Western with Baron Parke, the North Wales with Mr. Justice Vaughan, and the Northern with Baron Alderson." When he reached Chester, where Vaughan was holding assizes, the judge addressed him from the bench and called him to his side, where he sat for two hours. At Liverpool he dined one day "with the city corporation at a truly aldermanic feast in honor of the judges; the second, with the judges, to meet the bar; the third, with the Mayor at his country seat; the fourth, with the bar; the fifth, with Mr. Cresswell (the leader and old reporter) . . . , the sheriffs, etc."; the sixth, with John Arthur Roebuck, the young Radical who was later to become the Confederacy's best, if not wisest, friend in England. The English judges and lawyers, he found, were "indeed, a band of brothers," and they treated him not "as a young man, or a *junior brother,* but every way as an *equal.*" By September, when the courts adjourned, he could boast that he had seen "more of the English bar and of its practice, than ever before fell to a stranger." [6]

Sumner did not confine his interests to lawyers and courts.

[5] Pierce, I, 316; Sumner to Story, July 12 [continued July 17], and Aug. 18, 1838, Sumner MSS.; Sumner to Hillard, June 14, and July 3, 1838, ibid.; Sumner to Lieber, Sept. 3, 1838, ibid.

[6] Sumner to Benjamin Rand, Sept. 4, 1838, MS., Mass. Hist. Soc.; Sumner to Story, Aug. 12, 1838, Sumner MSS.; Pierce, I, 343; Sumner to Hillard, Dec. 4, 1838, Sumner MSS.; Sumner to Richard Fletcher, Sept. 10, 1838, Segal Coll.

In August he stopped off at Combe Florey for a visit with Sydney Smith, whom he considered "one of the most remarkable men of England," despite his baffling sense of humor. The witty clergyman was so pleased with this "remarkably agreeable modest well behaved American lawyer" that he sent Sumner with a glowing letter of introduction to his fellow founder of the *Edinburgh Review*, the Lord Advocate Sir John A. Murray. At Rydal Mount, Wordsworth entertained Sumner with tea and "sensible, instructive and refined" conversation. At Brougham Hall the eccentric Henry Brougham startled his American visitor by speaking "in the most disparaging terms of the aristocracy" and by lacing his conversation with " 'God!' 'good God!' 'by God'—'damned' etc.," and then impressed him by dashing off a letter in correct Latin and scrawling a Greek ode without referring to a dictionary.[7]

Almost as interesting as lawyers and literary lions to Sumner were English noblemen who had nothing but birth and wealth to recommend them. In Yorkshire he visited Baron Wharncliffe at Wortley Hall, set in a park of 1,800 acres, where deer grazed, and Sumner found the family, for all its wealth and titles, abounding in "good sense, pure Toryism, simplicity and affectionate intercourse." At Wentworth House he was the guest of Earl Fitzwilliam, who showed him an establishment so vast that there were stables for one hundred horses, and conservatories and aviaries which made the Boston Botanical Garden seem small. On a brief trip to Dublin, he was entertained by the Lord Lieutenant of Ireland, Lord Morpeth, oldest son of the Earl of Carlisle. At Holkham House the Earl of Leicester showed Sumner his priceless Vandykes, Titians, and Rubenses, but his guest was more interested in the "crabbed hand-writing" on "the darksome notes and memoranda" which the Earl's ancestor, Edward Coke, had left in the library.[8]

By the time Sumner returned to London in November, he was a social lion. He knew everybody—or everybody wanted to know him. George Shattuck, who came over from Paris and visited him, was astonished to find that Sumner, in the course of

[7] Sumner to Sarah P. Cleveland, Aug. 6, 1838, copy, Longfellow MSS.; Smith to Murray, Aug. 16, 1838, MS., J. Pierpont Morgan Lib.; Sumner to Hillard, Sept. 6, and 8, 1838, Sumner MSS.

[8] Sumner to Story, Oct. 24, 1838, Sumner MSS.; Sumner to Hillard, Oct. 27, 1838, ibid.; Sumner to Greenleaf, Nov. 2, 1838, ibid.

only six months in England, had become "acquainted with all
[the] distinguished . . . whigs, tories, radicals, judges, literary men of all grades and classes, scientific, professional men."
The acquaintance that I have is truly *prodigious*," Sumner himself exclaimed; "it is almost *unmanageable*." [9]

His days were "a constant succession of kindnesses and attentions of the most flattering and gratifying character," he
proudly wrote Story, "such as belong to a *Crown Prince*, rather
than to a person so humble as myself." He was the guest of the
Lord Mayor of London at the Guildhall dinner. At Windsor palace
he was given a private view of Victoria's rooms, "never shown except during the Queen's absence," and was privileged to hear
"the gals" in waiting upon Her Majesty complain "that there is
nothing but stale eggs in the Castle." He had breakfast with Samuel Rogers, the aged poet, who explained that it took him ten
times as long to write a sentence of prose as it did Wordsworth to
write one in verse. Henry Hallam, the historian, had him to dinner, and Harriet Martineau to an evening party. Richard Monckton Milnes, the poet, became a close friend. He accepted an invitation to visit the meretricious Countess of Blessington and see her
famous and scandalous ménage at Gore House, but snubbed two
of her attendant friends, Disraeli, whom he thought "one of the
most vulgar fops I ever saw," and Bulwer, with "his flash *falsetto*
dress, with high-heel boots, a white great coat . . . and a flaming blue cravat." Sir Charles Vaughan welcomed him to All Soul's
College at Oxford, and William Whewell entertained him at Cambridge.[1]

By February 1839, when he began to think of leaving England, Sumner was almost exhausted, and complained that he was
beginning "to tire of company and society." "I have sounded it in
all its depths and shallows," he explained to Hillard. "I have seen
it in some of its most splendid and fashionable, as well as literary
and intellectual phases." But, though he claimed to be bored, he
could not drag himself away until the end of March. After all, he
found, "the blood does dance to sit at meat with men gifted and
good, and more still, with ladies cultivated, refined and beautiful

[9] Sumner to Story, Aug. 18, 1838, ibid.; Shattuck to Miss E. E. Shattuck,
Feb. 21, 1839, Shattuck MSS.
[1] Sumner to Story, Aug. 18, 1838, Sumner MSS.; Sumner to Hillard, Nov. 16,
Dec. 4, and 28, 1838, ibid.

—to see the shifting shadows that crowd the countenance and catch the various conversation, perhaps to mingle in it and find your voice not unheeded." [2]

· 3 ·

Sumner left England in a shower of compliments. Lord Denman, urging him to return, declared: "No one ever conciliated more universal respect and good will." Lord and Lady Holland, Lord Lansdowne, and the Earl of Leicester declared that their homes were always open to him. Sydney Smith thanked him for coming, and added that it was an honor to be "thought well of on the other Side of the World by a Gentleman as honourable—and as enlightened" as Sumner. When Lord Brougham heard that Sumner was leaving, he exclaimed: "O God! must you go!" "Do you wonder that I quit England full of love and friendly feeling?" Sumner asked his American friends.[3]

They did not, but a good many did wonder at the extraordinary reception he had received. Sumner's social campaign in Britain, the historian Prescott concluded, was "more brilliant . . . than was ever achieved by any of his countrymen before." Felton wrote proudly: "Probably no other private American gentleman has enjoyed opportunities equal to yours." Sumner himself was almost as astonished as pleased by his social success. Could all this really be happening to "Charles Sumner, a poor scribe and lawyer of Boston?" he sometimes asked himself. Why should he, a "poor lawyer, hardly recognized at home, or if recognized, only received as a young man," be accepted upon intimate terms by "the very leaders and Queen's Counsel, the *elite* of the English bar" and by fashionable English society as well? [4]

It is not too difficult to learn the secret of Sumner's success. He had come to England at a most opportune time. In another decade the ubiquitous American tourist with his letters of introduction would become a bore and a nuisance, but as yet only a few, eminent Americans, such as Washington Irving and George

[2] Sumner to Hillard, Dec. 14, 1838, ibid.
[3] Denman to Sumner, Feb. 27, 1839, Sumner Autograph Coll.; Smith to Sumner, Aug. 16, 1838, ibid.; Pierce, II, 80–1.
[4] George Ticknor: *Life of William Hickling Prescott* (Boston: Ticknor and Fields; 1864), p. 364; Felton to Sumner, Nov. 5, 1838, Sumner MSS.; Sumner to Hillard, June 14, and Aug. 12, 1838, ibid.

Ticknor, had knocked at the doors of English society.[5] Further-more, English attitudes toward America were generally friendly, as in the 1830's the only source of friction between the two coun-tries was the Maine boundary line, about which, Sumner quickly found, nobody in England seemed to know or care.

Though the English were in a receptive mood and though Sumner's letters of introduction initially opened doors for him, he had to rely upon his own social resources to stay inside of them. These were, in fact, impressive. He was obviously of English de-scent. His appearance as well as his name lent truth to his re-peated protestation that when an American like himself went to England, "he was coming home,—coming, as it were, to his fa-ther's hearthstone." [6] This visitor looked not merely English, but handsome and personable as well. The lankness, clumsiness, and muddy complexion which had marred Sumner's adolescence had now disappeared, and with his regular features, smooth olive skin, dark brown flashing eyes, perfectly regular white teeth, and shock of dark brown hair, he looked like a strikingly healthy, vigorous young giant. The excellent tailors to whom he had im-mediately resorted had persuaded him to discard some of his more exuberant American clothing, and in his expensive, unob-trusive wardrobe he seemed almost English.

Yet, of course, the fact that Sumner was not English was one of his chief social assets. His hosts found that everything was delightfully new to him. The most demanding Englishman could not ask for a more assiduous sight-seer, or one in a more "constant state of astonishment and delight." Sumner's willing-ness to be pleased irritated choleric Thomas Carlyle, who defined Sumner as "the most completely nothin' of a mon that ever crossed my threshold,—naught whatsoever in him or of him but wind and vanity," but most Englishmen found it only proper that a visiting American should be impressed by all things British, and concluded that Sumner was "an amiable, sensible, high-minded, well-informed gentleman." [7]

[5] Robert E. Spiller, *The American in England during the First Half Century of Independence* (New York: Henry Holt & Co., Inc.; 1926).

[6] Pierce, I, 347.

[7] Ibid., I, 306, 309; Sara Norton and M. A. DeWolfe Howe: *Letters of Charles Eliot Norton with Biographical Comment* (Boston: Houghton Mifflin Co.; 1913), I, 422.

They found his naïveté delightful, and took pleasure in shocking this serious-minded young American. A true New Englander, Sumner was astonished to learn that Englishmen played cards for money. "Sober persons," he reported, with puzzlement, "make the sum six-pence on each *point*, a term which I do not understand, though I have gained several points as I have been told." He was upset, too, by the prevalence of swearing among the members of the English upper classes. Even more disconcerting was the lack of reticence upon subjects absolutely prohibited in Boston society. Sumner was greatly embarrassed when the Lady Georgiana Wortley told him that Lady John Russell "had gone to Brighton *to lie in*," and was covered with confusion when Lady Anson asked if he had "seen in Edinburgh the small room in which Mary Queen of Scots was *confined* with James." Most shocking of all was to hear Lady Morgan, in the presence of a young niece, assert "that it was time men should begin to think of children in the selection of their wives, and that they should be influenced by the same consideration that governed them when they *bought* a *mare to breed from*." [8]

But, if Sumner was easily shocked, he was even more easily taught. He promptly learned that "one would sooner commit the unpardonable sin than appear in boots" and that "every day should be *clean-shirt* day." Noting that the English aristocrats avoided using titles or even "Mr." except when addressing strangers, Sumner made their usage his lifelong habit. Willingly he accepted reproof from Englishmen. At a dinner party when Sumner mentioned that George Washington's "ashes still reposed at Mt. Vernon," he took with good grace Landor's chiding: "Why will you, Mr. Sumner, who speak with such force and correctness, employ a word which in the present connection is not English. Washington's body was never *burnt*—there are no ashes —say, rather, *remains*." Sumner's hosts found him uniformly enthusiastic in doing whatever they had planned for his entertainment, however strange it seemed to him. In Northumberland, though it was pouring rain, he uncomplainingly accompanied Archdeacon T. H. Scott in splashing out over the moors to hunt grouse; though their dogs started several coveys, neither man

[8] Sumner to Hillard, Oct. 27, and Nov. 16, 1838, and Jan. 23, 1839, Sumner MSS.

got a single bird all day, but Sumner shot a hare, which he formally entered in his host's game book. On a Christmas visit to Lord Fitzwilliam at Milton Hall, Sumner went fox hunting, again in a dreary rain, remained on horseback, at the imminent risk of life and limb, for seven or eight hours each day, received a bad fall, but cheerfully enjoyed the whole affair.[9]

The English found Sumner as reserved as he was agreeable. He was careful never to push himself forward. Though he presented many of his American letters of introduction, he was punctilious in not asking his English acquaintances for favors. "I have followed a rigid rule . . ." he explained. *"I have not asked an introduction to a single person—I have not asked a single ticket, privilege, or any thing of the kind from any body—I have not called upon anybody* (with one exception) *until I had been first called upon or invited."* Yet, he noted proudly: "I doubt if there is a man in England that I could not have been introduced to simply by expressing a bare wish."[1]

Sumner was also discreet. Some previous American travelers, notably James Fenimore Cooper and N. P. Willis, had published books on their Europen adventures which amounted to an invasion of the privacy of those who had entertained them. Carefully Sumner made it known that he "came abroad in no book-making spirit." As anything he wrote would present either an untrue picture of the men he had met or an offensive portrait that would tell all the truth, he would publish nothing at all. "For instance," he asked Hillard, who was urging him to do a book of travel essays, "could I say of O'Connell that he is a vulgar looking man with a foul breath; of Brougham, that he has a glorious head, but little heart, and that withal he has a vein of insanity, which, indeed, existed in his father and in a still-living sister, a fact unknown to the public at present entirely?"[2]

Gradually Sumner's English friends recognized that he had, apart from enjoying British society, only one purpose, to promote "the diffusion of the writings of any American calculated to in-

[9] Sumner to Hillard, July 3, Aug. 24, Sept. 6, and Dec. 25, 1838, ibid.; Sumner to George Sumner, Sept. 6, 1839, ibid.; T. H. Scott to Sumner, Feb. 5, 1839, Sumner Autograph Coll.
[1] Sumner to Story, July 15, 1838, Sumner MSS.; Sumner to Hillard, Aug. 12, 1838, ibid.
[2] Sumner to Hillard, Aug. 12, 1838, ibid.

spire respect . . . [for] liberal institutions." He advocated his friends' books with a zeal he did not show for himself. He tried to interest English publishers in Motley's poor novel, *Morton's Hope*, in Palfrey's lectures on Jewish antiquities, and in Richard Hildreth's *The Slave*, which anticipated *Uncle Tom's Cabin* by many years. Through his friendship with Monckton Milnes he secured the publication of the first serious article devoted to Emerson in a British periodical. He persuaded an English firm to bring out an edition of Lieber's *Political Ethics*. But most of all he tried everywhere to promote the reputation of Judge Story. In France he started a movement to elect Story to the Institute, even preparing himself a memoir of the judge in French; in England he saw that his important friends at the bar read and reviewed Story's works. "I perpetually keep in view," he wrote the judge, "the making of our jurisprudence known in England." [3]

Englishmen might have found these exertions for American law and letters objectionable in another person, but Sumner so clearly admitted the overwhelming superiority of the English in these, as in all other fields, that no one could take offense. Increasingly Sumner was becoming an Anglophile. He spent a good deal of his time abroad being embarrassed for his country and for his countrymen. From his English vantage point American politics seemed "inconceivably petty," smaller than "Tom Thumb's 'pint-pot.' " Like his English friends, he was horrified by the reports of frontier violence and vigilante gangs that appeared in the news from the United States. This American disregard of law, he sharply told Story, had "a gigantic importance" abroad, and he could not understand how reputable men at home could "stand by and smile, while the law is prostrated." [4]

When compared with Great Britain, Sumner concluded, the United States was lamentably lacking in culture. American social life was narrow and censorious. "One who mingles in the broad society of London and Paris," he informed Longfellow, rather loftily, "must be reminded, by sad contrast, of the narrow imper-

[3] Sumner to Story, Sept. 28, and Nov. 16, 1838, ibid.; Sumner to Richard Bentley, Dec. 3, 1838, Longfellow MSS.; Bentley to Sumner, Dec. 6, 1838, Sumner Autograph Coll.; James Pope-Hennessy, *Monckton Milnes: The Years of Promise, 1809–1851* (London: Constable; 1949), p. 115; Sumner to David B. Warden, May 28, 1838, Jan. 15, 1839, and Mar. 12, 1840, Warden MSS.

[4] Sumner to Hillard, Dec. 11, 1838, and July 26, 1839, Sumner MSS.; Sumner to Story, Oct. 4, 1838, ibid.

tinence that characterizes our town, where the colour of a gentleman's coat, and the habit of his shirt-collar or cravat are cardinal
topics of criticism." His fellow citizens were as lacking in independence as in taste. "Americans are sheep," Sumner scornfully
decided, "and follow the bellweather." American colleges were
shockingly deficient when compared to European universities.
"When shall we have an institution in America, where a person
may get an education?" he querulously asked. By European
standards, the professions in the United States were ill-trained.
The American bar, compared with the French and the English,
was "the poorest, most illiterate, and ungentlemanlike, of all the
three." Even the use of language in the United States was slov-
enly, Sumner complained, when a great writer like Longfellow
could in the middle of a beautiful poem "commit that *Americanism—'side-walk.'* " All in all, Sumner summarized, as he was
about to leave England: "Here, civilization has gone further than
with us," an opinion which was in no small measure responsible
for the warmth of his welcome in Britain.[5]

· 4 ·

Though Sumner's friends in Boston jokingly referred to him as
"the Earl," they were seriously troubled by the insistent note of
anti-Americanism which kept creeping into his letters. Greenleaf feared that he would "be so 'improved' by travel" that he
would not return "the simple, whole-souled, transparent, generous fellow we all love," and Longfellow wondered whether Sumner, when he came home, would not "find it somewhat hard, to
put his Pegasus into a yoke." [6]

Indignantly Sumner rejected suggestions that travel had
weakened his loyalty to the United States. "Grateful I am that
I am an American," he insisted, "for I would not give up the priceless institutions of my country (abused and perverted as they
are), the purity of morals in society, and the universal competence which prevails, in exchange for all that I have seen

[5] Sumner to Longfellow, Jan. 24, 1839, Longfellow MSS.; Sumner to Hillard,
July 26, 1839, and Mar. 18, 1840, Sumner MSS.; Sumner to Story, Sept. 24,
1839, ibid.; Sumner to William F. Frick, Aug. 4, 1839, ibid.; Sumner to Benjamin
Rand, Feb. 20, 1839, MS., Mass. Hist. Soc.

[6] Lieber to Hillard, Sept. 8, 1839, Lieber MSS.; Greenleaf to Lieber, Apr. 11,
1838, ibid.; Longfellow to Hillard, Aug. 16, 1838, photostat, Longfellow MSS.

abroad." "I am not yet entirely perverted by Europe," he protested, a bit too emphatically. "I have not ceased to be an American." [7]

To prove his point, and to counteract some of his earlier, more extreme pro-English statements, he wrote his Boston friends, rather repetitiously, that America was in many ways superior. "In England what is called society is better educated, more refined, and more civilized than what is called society in our country," he admitted, but "The true pride of America is in her middle and poorer classes, in their general health and happiness, and freedom from poverty, in their facilities for being educated, and in the opportunities to them of rising in the scale there." [8]

Doubtless Sumner sincerely believed these patriotic sentiments, but it is hard to see that he had any evidence to support them. Though he had an intimate and remarkable acquaintance among the English aristocracy, bar, and intelligentsia, though he had friends among all political parties and counted no fewer than four Cabinet members as personal friends, Sumner had, as some of his English acquaintances reminded him, seen "little of the middle ranks and masses" while abroad.[9] Interested in historic sights and aristocratic estates, he was insensitive to the less happy aspects of life in the early Victorian age. He visited no factories. He lived for months in London unaware of the slums around him. He showed no concern over the British government's failure to provide general elementary education, medical care, or sanitation. In fact, Sumner's animadversions against English society reflected not so much his experience abroad as his desire to appease his worried friends in Boston. His remark that the superiority of the American masses more than counterbalanced the excellence of the British upper classes was not really a profound reflection derived from his wide experience; it was a direct quotation of a remark he had heard Charles Buller make in a London drawing room and, what is more, it was the familiar theme of Francis J. Grund's *The Americans,* which Sumner had praised in the *North American Review* before he ever left Boston.[1]

[7] Pierce, I, 326; Sumner to Hillard, Mar. 9, 1839, Sumner MSS.

[8] Sumner to Hillard, Mar. 1, 1839, Sumner MSS.

[9] Joseph Parkes to Sumner, June 2, 1840, ibid.; W. S. Gilly to Sumner, Nov. 26, 1838, ibid.

[1] Similarly, Sumner's occasional remarks that the British ought to equalize suffrage and that primogeniture, "the worst thing in England," should be

Whatever he might tell his American friends, Sumner was, in fact, completely in love with England. Not even the raw London winter, with "murky, foggy days,—freighted with colds, catarrhs, and death," could disenchant him. He felt that he was living "in a land of imagination and not of reality," and he continued to enjoy his stay right up to the day for his departure to the Continent. When his English friends expressed envy because he was going to the sunny, warm south, he replied, with genuine feeling: "England is the *Italy* of an American." Leaving Britain, he explained, was for him "like quitting a *second country*." [2]

Almost immediately upon his arrival in France, Sumner found his affection toward England tested against loyalty to his own country. He learned that the United States minister, Lewis Cass, and many other Americans residing in Paris were seriously excited over the danger of a war between Great Britain and the United States. When in England, Sumner had been so absorbed by society that he was only casually aware that the perennial dispute over the Northeastern Boundary had erupted again, and he could not believe that anyone could take seriously "the undignified, illiterate and blustering" proclamation of the governor of Maine, claiming title to the whole area in dispute. Embarrassed that his countrymen were behaving so badly, Sumner had announced: "I would rather give up the whole state of Maine, and of Massachusetts to boot than to go to war." [3] But in Paris he discovered that the dispute, which he had so easily brushed aside, was indeed a dangerous one, and his loyalties were divided.

Believing that "*peace* is the duty of nations before all things," Sumner, at Cass's suggestion, immediately commenced research upon the points at dispute between England and America and within a very few days produced a long and learned essay that attempted to settle impartially the rival boundary claims. The article showed that whatever Sumner had learned in Europe, he had not forgotten his law; it was a careful, scholarly, perspicuous

abolished so as "to break the aristocracy," are not real social criticism on his part, but are merely echoes of the ideas of his friends among the moderate Radicals, Joseph Parkes and George Grote. Sumner to Hillard, Jan. 12, 1839, ibid.; Sumner to Story, Mar. 18, 1839, ibid.

[2] Pierce, II, 52, 81; Sumner to Story, June 27, 1838, and Mar. 9, 1839, Sumner MSS.

[3] Sumner to J. O. Sargent, Mar. 15, 1839, J. O. Sargent MSS.; Sumner to Richard Fletcher, Mar. 20, 1839, copy, Sumner MSS.

statement of the main points in the intricate and prolonged dispute. More significant was the fact that Sumner, after all the flattering attentions he had received in England, found himself enthusiastically "stating the *American side*" of the argument. "I endeavored to look at it candidly," he naïvely explained to Lord Morpeth, "and I cannot resist coming to the conclusion that we are right." Delighted at this *"most complete and satisfactory statement of our side that had ever appeared,"* Cass had it published in *Galignani's Messenger,* which was widely circulated throughout Europe.[4]

Having convinced himself of the justice of the American claim, Sumner was sure he could persuade his recent hosts in England to agree with him. The British he had found to be an eminently reasonable people. If Americans would only cease their vulgar agitation and base their case upon a "clear, correct and dignified ground," he was certain they would overcome the general ignorance and indifference of the English. Characteristically, Sumner did not believe that the accredited American diplomats abroad could influence British opinion; the United States minister in London, Andrew Stevenson, was, after all, a man of no particular social standing, who certainly had never been admitted to the circles in which Sumner had moved. Against the advice of both Cass and Stevenson, Sumner tried to settle the Maine boundary dispute by personal diplomacy. Buttonholing every influential English politician who came to Paris during these weeks, widely distributing his *Galignani* article to his British friends, and writing "to some *thirty* persons of influence in British politics, soliciting their attention to this subject," Sumner was sure his exertions would help keep the peace. "I thought," he explained to Stevenson, "considering what I had seen and enjoyed there, that nobody was more called upon to contribute his mite to the great cause of peace than myself." [5]

Leaving Paris at the end of April 1839, Sumner did not tarry to observe the consequences of his shirt-sleeve diplomacy. Had he done so, he might have realized that his friendships, valuable as they were as a social and intellectual bridge between America

[4] Sumner to Hillard, Apr. 15, 1839, Sumner MSS.; Pierce, II, 87.

[5] Sumner to Everett, Mar. 18, 1839, Everett MSS.; Sumner to Stevenson, Apr. 10, and 19, 1839, Stevenson MSS.; Cass to Stevenson, Apr. 10, 1839, ibid.; Sumner to Sir Charles Vaughan, Apr. 19, 1839, Vaughan MSS.

and England, were not an effective means of settling grave political issues between the two nations. He could have observed, too, that his arguments, however lucid or accurate, were ineffectual in persuading the English government to act against its national interest. But these were lessons Sumner would only learn, with a shock, some twenty years later, during the Civil War.

· 5 ·

"I have supped full of society, and am tired of bright lights," Sumner had announced as he left London for Italy. "I have scores of letters to all sorts of people on my *route,* but am sated with society, and shall look at *things.*" The month he delayed in Paris in order to write on the boundary dispute kept him from breaking his resolve, for he arrived in Italy during the hot summer months when "everybody" was leaving it. "Man's season was over," he remarked sentientiously, "but I may truly say, God's was come." [6]

Sumner rejoiced that he had come at the slack social season, for he could devote his unlimited energy to serious sight-seeing. With the same thoroughness he had once demonstrated in cataloguing the Harvard law library, he set himself to mastering the language, literature, and history of Italy. Every day he followed a strict schedule: "rose at 6½ o'clock; threw myself on my sofa, with a little round table near well-covered with books—read undisturbed till about 10, when the servant brought on a tray my breakfast—two eggs done *sur le plat,* a roll and cup of chocolate . . . rang the bell, and my table was put to rights, and my reading went on—often till 5 and 6 o'clock in the evening, without my once rising from the sofa. . . . At 5 or 6 got up, stretched myself—dressed to go out—dined in a garden under a mulberry tree, chiefly on fruits, salads, and wine . . . walked. . . . After an ice-cream . . . to my books again. . . ."

During his four months in Italy he tried to read everything. He studied, in the original, all of Dante, Tasso, Boccaccio, Manzoni, and Alfieri, and most of Machiavelli, Guicciardini, Goldoni, and Foscolo as well, generally working with several "different editions, and going over a monstrous mass of notes and annotations."

[6] Sumner to Hillard, Apr. 15, and Mar. 1, 1839, Sumner MSS.; Sumner to George Ticknor, Sept. 15, 1839, Ticknor MSS.

By October he thought himself master of the language. "There is no Italian which I cannot understand without a dictionary; there is hardly a classic in the language of which I have not read the whole, or considerable portions." [7]

With his time so employed, Sumner found his stay in Italy all too short. He tried to hoard his hours by ignoring as much as possible of modern Italy, which depressed him. Like most American tourists, he was annoyed that he could not leave his rooms "without being surrounded with half a dozen squalid wretches, with most literally scarcely a rag to cover their nakedness." As bad as the poverty was the superstition. At a single village church he was proudly shown "the skeletons of *twenty five* saints dressed in silk, . . . a part of a cushion that belonged to the Mother of the Virgin Mary and also a part of a sandal of *Joseph*." This "perversion of Christianity," he decided in disgust, was an "uncouth imposture," and he willingly turned to "the thrilling . . . antient classical sites and things." [8]

For company in his sight-seeing Sumner looked to the little colony of Americans resident in Italy. With Bostonian fastidiousness he spotted other American tourists—a record crowd of 375 poured into Rome in 1839—by "their dirty shirts—their nasal conversation—their want of the manner either of the scholar or the man of the world," and in their presence pretended to speak only French and Italian. But a semipermanent resident like George W. Greene, the American consul at Rome, who was both a grandson of General Nathanael Greene and a friend of Longfellow, was different. Promptly concluding that "our country has not *five* men his peers" in scholarship, Sumner annexed Greene as his constant companion and cicerone during his three months in Rome. Together they walked each evening to the Forum, or to St. Peter's, or out to one of the gates of Rome; they used to sit together for hours on a broken column along the Via Sacra or a rich capital in the Colosseum and reconstruct in fancy the history that had passed before these mute marbles. [9]

Greene introduced Sumner to the numerous American artists then living in Italy. At Florence he met Horatio Greenough,

[7] Sumner to Hillard, Sept. 29, 1839, Sumner MSS.; Pierce, II, 118.
[8] Sumner to Hillard, May 19, 1839, Sumner MSS.; Sumner to Story, Sept. 4, 1839, ibid.
[9] Sumner to Hillard, Sept. 29, 1839, ibid.

and, recognizing the famous sculptor as a "high priest of the Temple of Art," approached him as "a mere neophyte, one of the humblest worshippers, who kneel between the posts of the door." Greenough proved not to be a formidable personage after all, but "a wonderful fellow—an accomplished man," and Sumner, who was unable to distinguish between personal and aesthetic feelings, concluded that he was "master of his art, . . . the most accomplished artist alive." Soon he ventured, almost as an equal, to offer suggestions about the details of Greenough's "masterly" but startlingly nude statue of George Washington.[1] Sumner found Hiram Powers less impressive than Greenough, for the Cincinnati artist had "not gone beyond bust-making" and his works seemed "quite pretty, but rather tame and insignificant." Far more interesting was the relatively obscure Thomas Crawford, to whose studio in Rome Greene brought Sumner. Greatly taken by Crawford personally, excited at the idea of discovering a hitherto unknown, and convinced by Greene that the "Orpheus" on which Crawford was working would be "one of the most remarkable productions that have come from an artists of his years in modern times," Sumner promptly started a campaign to have his friends in Boston purchase or publicize the sculptor's works. "If you cannot order a statue," he told Longfellow, "you can at least write an article."[2]

Absorbed in his studies of literature, history, and art, Sumner broke away from Italy with great reluctance. "I regret that I left so many things unseen, and saw so little of many others worthy to be studied and pondered,—food for thought and imagination," he wrote Greene in farewell. Like many another American visitor to that enchanting land, he had fancies of going back to the United States, "collecting together some of the savings of a few years," and returning to Italy to "live in the sight of all that is fine in art, and under this beautiful sky, and die in peace."

[1] Ibid.; Sumner to Greenough, Nov. 8, 1839, and Jan. 8, 1839 [the date should be 1840], photostats of MSS. in the possession of Mrs. Sylvia Crane, New York City. See also Otto Wittman, Jr.: "The Italian Experience (American Artists in Italy, 1830–1875)," *American Quarterly*, IV (Spring 1952), 3–15, and Van Wyck Brooks: *The Dream of Arcadia: American Writers and Artists in Italy, 1760–1915* (New York: E. P. Dutton & Co., Inc.; 1958), esp. Chaps. iii–viii.

[2] Pierce, II, 111–12; Sumner to Hillard, July 26, 1839, Sumner MSS.; Sumner to Longfellow, July 26, 1839, Longfellow MSS.; Sumner to W. H. Prescott, June 28, 1839, Prescott MSS.

As unconscious evidences of his wish to remain, Sumner carelessly left belongings behind him at every place he stopped during his last few weeks in Italy: "a silk handkerchief at one, a cambric one at another, a shirt at another, and an umbrella at a fourth; to say nothing of a pair of gloves." [3]

Uncertainty about his future, as well as love for Italy, was behind his reluctance to depart. "I begin to tremble about myself," he confessed to Story. "I look with great anxiety to my professional prospects." Cheerfully he tried to predict that when he got back to Boston, he could easily "renew the labors which I have for the while forsaken" and "grasp resolutely the plough which I have left in the furrough [sic]," but, in more realistic moods, he recognized that his European trip had permanently affected his prospects at the bar. "I think of that tide, whose ebb I declined to take, which might have floated me on to fortune—that is, to worldly success," he wrote Greenleaf ruefully, "and I fear that I have lost it forever." Ahead of him now could lie only a life of "unchanging drudgery" at "the great grindstone of the law." [4]

These distressing reflections hung darkly over the remaining few months of Sumner's European travels. Not even the fact that Prince Metternich showered him with civilities in Vienna, that the Crown Prince of Prussia received him in Berlin, or that in Heidelberg the jurists Mittermaier and Thibaut welcomed him as an equal and addressed him as *Herr Professor* could make him forget that he had so shortly to return to America. In his heart he wanted to stay in Germany "all the winter, pursuing his studies, and mingling in this learned and gay world," but Story, Greenleaf, and Hillard all urged him to come home. Even more pressing was the advice of his pocketbook. "I have spent more than five thousand dollars," he calculated, "and I cannot afford to travel longer." Reluctantly he admitted that it was time to "close this charmed book." [5]

Returning to England in March 1840, Sumner had a final fling in English society. London he found "more mighty, magnifi-

---

[3] Sumner to Greene, Dec. 30, 1839, Greene MSS.; Sumner to Hillard, Sept. 29, 1839, Sumner MSS.; Pierce, II, 118.

[4] Sumner to Story, Sept. 24, 1839, Sumner MSS.; Sumner to Greenleaf, Nov. 2, 1838, and Jan. 21, 1839, ibid.; Pierce, II, 126.

[5] Sumner to Story, Feb. 10, 1840, Sumner MSS.; Sumner to Hillard, Dec. 25, 1839, and Mar. 18, 1840, ibid.; Pierce, II, 133.

cent, and fascinating than ever." He had not been forgotten during his travels on the Continent, and his friends overwhelmed
him with invitations. He had time to visit only a few—"the Lans-
downes, Duke and Duchess of Sutherland (the most beautiful
woman in the world), Mrs Norton, Lady Seymour (both beautiful in the extreme); [Abraham] Hayward, Sydney Smith, [Nas-
sau] Senior, Fonblanque, Milnes, . . . the [George] Grotes,
Charles Austin (more brilliant than ever), the Wortleys, etc."
But "I must leave all this," he sternly told himself. "If I do not
force myself away, I shall not be able to go." [6]

Sailing from Portsmouth on April 3, Sumner spent the slow
four-week voyage reflecting upon his past triumphs and future
prospects. His very wardrobe proclaimed that he was now a cosmopolitan man. His "trowsers, waist-coats, frock-coat, and blue
evening coat" came "from London—black evening coat from Berlin . . . boots from Paris—where else can boots be made?
. . . huge *pelt-stiefel* from Vienna and distant Hungary—hat
from Rome—*thick* travelling-cap from New York—*thin* one from
Marseilles—surtout from Paris—cloak from Boston—the good
old cloak, that has 'braved the battle and the breeze' so long." His
thoughts were of a similarly composite character. Though he
protested that he was "still a *believer* in our institutions," he
could not help thinking that, when compared to Europe, America
looked "sad enough—vulgar, petty, grovelling." He professed eager anxiety to return to his professional life, "to plunge at once
. . . in *medias res*," but he also admitted that he anticipated
"mortification, disappointment, perhaps defeat." Difficult as it
would be "to step from the pinnacle of this world's society to . . .
the stern realities of American life," he was certain that he had
benefited by his travels. "My tour has stimulated my ambition,"
he told Lieber, "taught me my ignorance—and enabled me to direct my future studies." [7]

[6] Sumner to Hillard, Mar. 18, and 28, and Feb. 11, 1840, Sumner MSS.
[7] Sumner to Story, Mar. 24, and Feb. 10, 1840, ibid.; Sumner to Hillard, Feb.
8, 1840, ibid.; Sumner to Lieber, Sept. 12, 1839, Lieber MSS.

CHAPTER IV

The Iron Curtain

❦

MY EUROPEAN drama is wound up," Sumner lamented as he returned to Boston. "The iron curtain has fallen upon it." Even before he left Europe, he had begun to dread going back to his "lot . . . of stern uninteresting employ, vulgar contacts dealing with magnified trifles, inhaling bad air, moiling in formal documents, trudging, drudging." His misgivings, he now discovered, had been more than justified. Boston was not London, and the Athenaeum not the Uffizi. Sadly Sumner complained of "the littleness of American life." His only solace was in his "recollections —thoughts—thick-coming fancies." Each morning as he dressed, he returned in imagination to the scenes of his European triumphs, and as he walked down Beacon Hill to his office, he let his mind wander back to "the memory of his Roman life—the happiest days he ever passed." [1]

· 1 ·

There was, one might think, no good reason for Sumner's discontent. He returned from Europe in fine health and excellent appearance. A strikingly handsome young man, whose London tailor dressed him to perfection, Sumner was the rage among adolescent girls in Boston, who swooned over him as "fascinating" and nicknamed him "Hyperion." [2] Some of their older sisters thought him equally glamorous.

[1] Sumner to Lieber, July 6, 1840, Sumner MSS.; Sumner to Cleveland, Aug. 27, 1839, Cleveland MSS., Richard Monckton Milnes to Sumner, Aug. 24 [1840], Sumner MSS.; Sumner to Samuel Gridley Howe, May 31, 1844, ibid.

[2] Anna R. Palfrey to Mrs. John G. Palfrey, Nov. 19, 1840, Palfrey MSS.; Anna R. Palfrey to Sarah H. Palfrey, Nov. 20, 1840, ibid.

Boston was ready to welcome Sumner enthusiastically. Among the stanchly pro-English residents of Beacon Hill, Sumner's almost royal reception abroad more than counterbalanced his humble origins and gave him a "halo never acquired by domestic sanctity." Everybody wanted to hear of his European adventures. George Ticknor, who had moved in the same elevated social circles abroad—and who consequently knew how difficult they were of access—invited Sumner to his mansion on Park Street and had the traveler "sitting up with him night after night, till 12 o'clock," retelling his successes. Wanting to hear Sumner's story while it was still fresh, Samuel Lawrence begged him to spare a day for a visit to Lowell. Even Ralph Waldo Emerson emerged from his transcendental brooding to invite Sumner to Concord. It was not a happy encounter. Sumner, who professed complete incomprehension of what, if anything, transcendentalism meant, regretted that "the great mystagogue" failed to lead out "his winged griffins to take us into the Empyrean," and Emerson, equally disappointed, thought that his "talkative countryman" had "brought nothing home but names, dates, and prefaces." [3]

But for most Bostonians these were quite enough, and they rejoiced in hearing Sumner relive his social successes abroad. Nathan Appleton, the great textile manufacturer, welcomed him as an equal. At Charles P. Curtis's mansion on Mt. Vernon Street Sumner was a dinner guest-of-honor along with Daniel Webster, Jeremiah Mason, and Rufus Choate. The historian Prescott, whose *Ferdinand and Isabella* Sumner had helped to publicize abroad, commenced a lifelong friendship for the young traveler. To symbolize his social acceptance, Sumner became a regular attendant at Mrs. Ticknor's weekly soirees, where, he reported smugly: "There is always a circle of the best people in our town." [4]

Sumner's domestic life was also more satisfactory than before his trip. The worst of his family difficulties had been re-

[3] Henry Adams: *The Education of Henry Adams* (New York: Modern Library, Inc.; 1931), p. 30; C. S. Daveis to Sumner, May 21, 1840, Sumner MSS.; Samuel Lawrence to Sumner, May 9, 1840, ibid.; Sumner to Longfellow [Aug. 9, 1840], Longfellow MSS.; Felton to Longfellow, Aug. 7, 1840, ibid.; *The Correspondence of Thomas Carlyle and Ralph Waldo Emerson, 1834–1872* (Boston: James R. Osgood and Company; 1883), I, 300.

[4] *MHSP*, XLIV, 338; Sumner to Cleveland, Apr. 3, 1841, copy, Longfellow MSS.

solved when his father died while Sumner was in Italy. The relations between Charles and his father had steadily worsened during the 1830's. As Sheriff Sumner grew older, he became more
morose and domineering, and the very word "home" came to have
sad connotations for his son. During the more than two years
Sumner spent abroad, he exchanged few letters with his family.
"Where Charles is now and what his designs [are] I am ignorant," the sheriff had to confess in January 1839. When the news
of his father's death reached Charles a few months later, he professed "unfeigned sorrow," but added rather coolly: "I cannot affect to feel entirely the grief that others have on such a bereave-
ment." His closest friends did not write him letters of condolence.
"What your father has been to you, you have not disguised from
me," Cleveland said frankly. "That you are not as deeply afflicted
by his death as you would have been if he had been like a father
to you I cannot suppose." [5] When Sumner returned to Boston, he
went, not to the hotel where he had previously lived, but back to
No. 20 Hancock Street.

Altogether Charles found his new domestic arrangements
the most satisfactory he had ever known. Mrs. Sumner, to whom
the sheriff had left his entire estate, was, to be sure, a bit parsi-
monious and tended to make the house a "large rookery that is
perpetually cawing" by entertaining too many of the "old crones"
who were her relatives, but she was a good manager and was
willing to foot Charles's bills. The two surviving Sumner daughters helped make the house cheerful, for during Charles's absence Mary had become a delicate and handsome young woman
and Julia a bright girl of thirteen. Sumner took a strong interest
in both, and he offered to surrender any future share in his father's legacy in order to give them the best education the country could afford. He was proud to escort Mary to concerts and social affairs and even unbent to play with "Jule," as he called his
youngest sister. "There was," said Julia many years later, "a world
of love and tenderness within him,—often hidden under a cold

[5] Sumner to Hillard, Dec. 8, 1837, Sumner MSS.; C. P. Sumner to George
Sumner, Jan. 19, 1838 [the date should be 1839], copy, C. P. Sumner MSS.;
Pierce, II, 109; Cleveland to Sumner, May 2, 1839, copy, Longfellow MSS.
Sumner's letters have been carefully mutilated to excise nearly all references to
his difficulties with his father.

exterior, or apparently crusted over with a chilling coat of reserve." [6]

The absence of Sumner's two older brothers from the house on Hancock Street unquestionably made life easier for him. Albert, who had married a rich widow, had his own luxurious mansion in New York and a summer place at Newport. George had sailed to Europe as supercargo on a trading vessel that docked in Russia. By a combination of charm, effrontery, and good fortune he met Tsar Nicholas, whose kindly attentions launched the young American upon his travels in Europe, Asia, and Africa.[7] Charles watched his brother's social progress with a mixture of approval and irritation. Though he conceded that George was remarkably intelligent, he felt that he lacked "respect for education and educated men" and feared he might publish a book of travels, "which may give a young man some notoriety, but which a man of established character would hardly like to own." As George reached Italy and announced plans for visiting France and England as well, Charles became worried and asked Greene to give a confidential report on his brother's appearance and manners. "Brother as he is," Charles announced, "I shall not presume to present him to my friends in . . . these countries unless I feel assured that he is *entirely presentable*." [8] Presentable or not, George was to remain in Europe for the next fifteen years, and Charles had no rival in his own house.

There seemed no good reason why professionally as well as personally Sumner should not be content in Boston. His office at No. 4 Court Street was waiting for him, as was his law partner and closest friend, Hillard. During the first four months after his return from Europe, he engaged in no legal business, except to substitute for Hillard for a few days, but, with the opening of the fall term of court, he settled back into his office routine. He made it a point to be at his desk punctually at nine o'clock in the morning and to remain at work until two; then, after an hour and a

[6] Sumner to George Sumner, Jan. 1, 1844, and July 13, 1839, Sumner MSS.; Julia Sumner Hastings to Pierce, Nov. 10, 1874, Pierce MSS.; Pierce, II, 158.
[7] Robert C. Waterston: "Memoir of George Sumner," *MHSP*, XVIII (1880–1), 189–223.
[8] Sumner to Greene, Jan. 4, 1840, Greene MSS.; Sumner to Hillard, Sept. 29, 1839, Sumner MSS.; Sumner to George Sumner, July 8, 1838, ibid.

half for lunch, he returned to his office, where he stayed until
night. "Never at any time, since I have been at the bar," he
proudly reported to Lieber, "have I been more punctual and faithful. Po[c]ket that, ye croakers! who said that Europe would spoil
me for office-work." Hillard agreed: "Sumner is behaving like a
very good boy, nailed to his desk like a bad cent to a grocer's
counter—not that the parallel holds throughout." [9]

After an absence of twenty-nine months, Sumner had, of
course, to start his law practice almost anew, but clients were
soon flocking to his office. Some were referred to him by Greenleaf, whose practice was heavy. Others came because of Sumner's erudition in the more esoteric branches of legal lore.[1] A few
probably thought his intimacy with Story might be helpful in
cases tried before the Federal Circuit Court. Through the influence of his English friends, the British consul in Boston, T. C.
Grattan, retained Sumner to defend a number of cases where
English vessels were sued for searching alleged American slave
traders off the coast of Africa.[2] But the most important part of
Sumner's practice came from such leading merchants as Thomas
and Edward Wigglesworth, Henry Lee, T. C. Thwing, Stephen H.
Perkins, Nathan and Samuel Appleton, G. R. Minot, and Zachariah Silsbee, who thus gave practical evidence that Sumner had
arrived in Boston society.[3]

Only a month after returning to practice, Sumner was able
to report that he was doing very well. He had, he announced complacently, "already disposed of one weighty matter, say ($50,-
000)," by giving his opinion on a legal point that had escaped
all other Boston attorneys to whom the case had been submitted.
At the December 1841 term of the United States District Court
he appeared in twenty-four cases to defend Boston merchants
and won them all.[4] At the same time he was arguing eleven cases

[9] Sumner to Lieber, Sept. 23, 1840, Sumner MSS.; Hillard's postscript on
Sumner to Sarah P. Cleveland, Oct. 2, 1840, copy, Longfellow MSS.
[1] Law Reporter, III (Feb. 1841), 383–6; IV (Dec. 1841), 301–3; IV (Jan.
1842), 342–9.
[2] Ibid., IV (May 1841), 33–4; J. C. Perkins to Pierce, Nov. 16, 1875, Pierce
MSS.
[3] U.S. District Court, Record Books, XXV, 251, 256–61, 263–5, 270–4, 278–9,
etc. (MS., Federal Records Center, Dorchester).
[4] Sumner to Cleveland, Sept. 23, 1840, copy, Longfellow MSS.; U.S. District
Court, Docket Book, December 1841, Nos. 32–6, 38–40, 42 (MS., Federal Records
Center, Dorchester); U.S. District Court, Record Books, XXV, 251–79, passim.

before the United States Circuit Court, where he often served as
junior counsel to such leaders of the bar as Greenleaf, Franklin
Dexter, and Charles G. Loring.[5] Sumner was not modest about
his legal merits, and he assessed his fees accordingly. "I charged
one client yesterday as *part* of my fee in one case $600," he told
Lieber in December 1841. "He had the grace to say that it was no
more than he expected and not so much as I deserved." [6]

Sumner was promptly recognized as an expert in certain
special branches of his profession. Everybody admitted that "in
what may be called the literature of the law, the curiosities of
legal learning," he had no rival in Boston. In cases involving
British and Continental precedents other attorneys often drew
upon his prodigious memory. He was at his best in suits that
hinged upon historical research, as, for instance, in the much
litigated dispute over the Massachusetts–Rhode Island boundary.
Serving as junior counsel to Rufus Choate, he diligently ransacked musty volumes of town records to learn just what had
been the original bounds of the Bay Colony. In cases where Sumner thought some basic principle of justice was at stake he
showed himself relentlessly persistent. Retained in litigation over
a patent for friction matches, Sumner concluded that his opponents were "ignorant, impudent and unprincipled," and, in suits
that stretched over a period of five years, fought them as though
he were defending the nation's fundamental liberties.[7]

When Sumner had time to relax after his work, he found his
intimate friends in "The Five of Clubs" as congenial as ever. Longfellow, Cleveland, Felton, and Hillard had held only occasional
meetings while Sumner was abroad, but when he reappeared in
Boston, all the old warmth of friendship was instantly rekindled.
Night after night they gathered in "delightful Gaudiolum" to hear
Sumner retell his adventures. On one occasion Sumner "discoursed in one continuous flow" from four o'clock in the after-

5 U.S. Circuit Court, Docket Book, Term beginning October, 1841, Nos. 25–6,
31–2, 43, 93, 99–103 (MS., Federal Records Center, Dorchester).

6 Sumner to Lieber, Dec. 10, 1841, Sumner MSS.

7 *Law Reporter*, VII (May 1844), 58; Fanny Appleton Longfellow, Journal,
Jan. 6, 1844, Longfellow MSS.; Jared Benson, Jr., to Sumner, Dec. 27, 1852,
Sumner MSS.; Samuel Gilman Brown: *The Works of Rufus Choate with a
Memoir of His Life* (Boston: Little, Brown & Co.; 1862), I, 74; Sumner to
Hillard [Sept. 25, 1841], Sumner MSS.; Pierce, II, 149–50. See the elaborate legal
documents in William Brooks versus Ezekiel Byam et al., before the United
States Circuit Court, 1841–5 (MS., Federal Records Center, Dorchester).

noon until eleven at night, when Hillard protested that listening
to him was "like being under Niagara," but the friends vicari-
ously enjoyed even the minutiae of Sumner's travels.[8]

Quickly "The Five of Clubs" fell back into the pattern of regular Saturday meetings. In addition, of course, Sumner saw Hillard every day. Nearly every Sunday he drove out to Cambridge
to visit Longfellow. More rarely he went to Pine Bank, Cleveland's home, to which illness more and more confined him. From
the Feltons he had a standing invitation: "Whenever you have
no other engagement, . . . jump into the omnibus, and come
out." With their growing intimacy, the friends adopted nicknames
for each other. Cleveland was "Hal"; Felton, "Corny"; Longfellow,
partly because he was so short, "Longo." Sumner to his friends
was "Charley," sometimes "Carl" or "Karliken," but most often, in
tribute to his triumphs among the European nobility, "Don
Carlos."

Without the slightest restraint, the friends talked over
everything together. They listened to Longfellow read his poetry
before he had it published, so as "to tread with iron heel" upon
it and "winnow out the chaff." With Cleveland they sympathized
in his illness, and with Hillard, that "young Hamlet in our own
times with a dark destiny hanging over him," in his unhappy
marriage and frustrated aspirations for a literary career. They
shared the joy of Felton, who always seemed "perfectly happy
just like a child with both hands full of flowers," and they echoed
when he gave one of his "resounding laughs, containing at least
one hundred cubic feet of laughter." [9] And to Sumner his friends
gave what he needed most of all—unreserved affection and unqualified praise.

· 2 ·

During the first few months after his return from Europe, Sumner seemed to settle securely into his niche in Boston society. Bos-

---

[8] Longfellow, Journal, Apr. 6, May 9, and 12, 1840, Longfellow MSS.

[9] Felton to Sumner, Oct. 26, 1840, Sumner MSS.; Longfellow to Sumner
[Oct. 1841], Longfellow MSS.; Longfellow to Cleveland, Jan. 4, 1843, photostat,
ibid.; Longfellow to Greene, Aug. 6, 1838, ibid.; Hillard to Longfellow, July 2,
1842, ibid.; Hillard: "Memoir of Cornelius Conway Felton," MHSP, X (1867-9),
367.

tonians began to think of him as a man with a promising future. He would be, they felt, a leader in Massachusetts, less, perhaps, in the tradition of Daniel Webster and Rufus Choate, both vigorous lawyer-politicians, than in that of Edward Everett or George Ticknor, scholarly gentlemen with European connections.[1]

Some Bostonians, to be sure, felt that Sumner had been spoiled by his European success. After listening to Sumner hold forth for hours upon his adventures, Fanny Appleton, the daughter of the textile magnate, judged that he was *"tant soit peu gâté* by the great civilities he has met with in England, at least for his own happiness and contentedness in this limited society and sphere," and wondered: "Has he any thing in his head beside a marvellous memory and a quantity of musty law-learning hanging to it to give him such renown and astonishing success?" Even Longfellow was at first inclined to think that Sumner's head had been a little turned by European applause, and deplored Sumner's "un-American" sneers at Boston, his "Flings at the College," and his " 'Jeringen! bring me my gaiters' style of conversation." [2]

Tongues began to wag more rapidly when Sumner, only a few months after his return, paid a public call on Fanny Ellsler, the dancer who exhibited to Boston with equal nonchalance her tight-clad legs and her "manager," who was notoriously reputed to be her lover. Sumner further drew all the hornets of scandal about his ears by taking Fanny on a drive through the countryside.[3]

In fact, Boston was needlessly alarmed. Sumner had called on Fanny not in order to shock society, but to honor letters of introduction which Harriet Grote and other English friends had written about the dancer. After Boston was scandalized, he continued to see her through sheer stubborn bravado, but he was doubtless relieved when she moved on to engagements elsewhere, for he was careful never again to put himself in such a compromising role.

[1] Adams: *Education of Henry Adams*, p. 30.
[2] Fanny Appleton to Lieber, June 12, 1840, Longfellow MSS.; Longfellow, Journal, May 7, and June 2, 1840, ibid. Cf. William Kent: *Memoirs and Letters of James Kent* (Boston: Little, Brown & Co.; 1898), p. 261.
[3] Sumner to Lieber, Sept. 22, 1840, Sumner MSS.; Sumner to Cleveland, Sept. 23, 1840, copy, Longfellow MSS. Cf. Sumner to Henry Wikoff, Oct. 11, 1844 [misdated 1834], in J. C. Derby: *Fifty Years Among Authors, Books and Publishers* (New York: G. W. Carleton & Co.; 1884), p. 373.

Though Sumner did not desire to disrupt Boston society, he did wish to impress it, and his letters from his friends in Europe gave him frequent opportunities. Henry Reeve, Tocqueville's translator and friend, made Sumner his only transatlantic correspondent and assured him: "You are continually talked of in Europe." The George Grotes, Joseph Parkes, and other moderate Radicals wrote him in almost every mail. Sydney Smith continued a cordial exchange of letters, reminding Sumner: "You occupy a large corner of Mrs. Sydney's heart." In one transatlantic mail, received just after the English elections of 1841, Sumner was both amused and pleased to count "four letters, all from MP's, who have lost their seats." His friends were proud of his European fame, and they rejoiced with him when the *London Quarterly Review*, in December 1840, announced that Sumner's recent triumphs in Britain offered "decisive proof that an American gentleman, without official rank or wide-spread reputation, by mere dint of courtesy, candour, an entire absence of pretension, an appreciating spirit, and a cultivated mind, may be received on a perfect footing of equality in the best English circles, social, political, and intellectual." [4]

In playing his part as a bridge between European and American society, Sumner spent a great deal of his time serving as cicerone to visiting foreigners, who came introduced by letters from his English acquaintances. Sometimes his guests were private gentlemen of no great consequence, who wanted merely to see the sights of Boston and be entertained for dinner. More often they were celebrities, for whom Sumner exerted himself. When Lord Ashburton's suite visited Boston, during the course of negotiating the Webster-Ashburton Treaty, Sumner was chosen to give them a special tour of the city. He also took Sir Charles Lyell out for an evening drive, and when the English geologist saw fireflies for the first time, Sumner obligingly caught a hatful for him. [5]

In 1841, when Lord Morpeth decided to visit America, Sum-

[4] Reeve to Sumner, Nov. 1, 1840, Sumner MSS.; Harriet Grote to Sumner, Jan. 31 [1841], ibid., Sumner to Nathan Appleton, Aug. 4 [1841], Appleton MSS.; *London Quarterly Review*, XLVII (Dec. 1840), 19. The article was by Abraham Hayward.

[5] Sumner to Story [1841], Story MSS.; Thomas Brown to Sumner, Mar. 27, 1844, Sumner MSS.; Abbott Lawrence to Sumner, Aug. 29 [1842], ibid.; Sumner to Hillard, July 15, 1842, ibid.

ner virtually suspended all business for several weeks in order to
entertain his friend. On the day Morpeth landed, Sumner gave
him a conducted tour of Boston. They climbed to the top of the
State house, where Sumner pointed out "the various spots illus-
trated in the early progress of the War of independence with the
proper feelings of a true and liberal American." Then they visited
the legislature, toured the courts, where Sumner presented his
guest to Story, inspected the city hall, and met the mayor. "In the
course of the walk," Morpeth recorded in his diary, "Sumner introduced me far and near." After dinner, Sumner took the Englishman for a drive through the suburbs, calling on the Cleve-
lands, taking coffee with the Storys, and inspecting historical
sights along the route. In the evening Sumner presented his
friend to the Great Panjandrum of Boston Society, George Ticknor.[6]

This was but the first of many strenuous days of sight-seeing
and visiting. Boston took at once to Morpeth. He was, as Longfellow said, "a very pleasant, jolly, sociable, ruddy-faced man,
with gray hair, blue coat, and red waistcoat,—a laughing bachelor of forty." Besides, he was an English lord. Everybody wanted
him for parties, receptions, and dinners, and everywhere he
went, Sumner stood in useful attendance, identifying names and
faces for him and reminding him of whether he had previously
met the guests to whom he was introduced. When Morpeth left
Boston at the end of December, he could not part from such a
"fast and firm friend" without emotion. The following fall, after
Morpeth had concluded his tour of America, Sumner again
dropped all business to spend a final week in New York with the
Englishman. They had, as Prescott laughingly said, "a perpetual
wake,—wake, indeed, for you don't seem to have closed your eyes
night or day. Dinners, breakfasts, suppers, 'each hue,' as Byron
says, 'still lovelier than the last.' "[7]

When Charles Dickens came to America in 1842, he, too,
made Sumner his guide and friend. A strikingly contrasted pair

      [6] Morpeth, Diary, Oct. 21, 1841, copy, Houghton Lib. Cf. Morpeth's *Travels
in America* . . . (New York: G. P. Putnam's Sons; 1851), pp. 8–14.
      [7] Longfellow: *Longfellow*, I, 410; Charles Francis Adams: *Richard Henry
Dana: A Biography* (Boston: Houghton Mifflin Co.; 1890), I, 29–30; Morpeth,
Diary, Dec. 27, 1841, and Sept. 25–9, 1842, MS., Houghton Lib.; Ticknor: *Prescott*,
p. 373.

they made as they strode over the cobblestones of Boston: Sumner, tall, serious, and intent, dark-haired and olive-skinned; Dickens, gay and free-and-easy, with his "fine bright face, blue eyes, and long dark hair." Together they climbed Copp's Hill and inspected the monument on Bunker Hill; they went with Longfellow to hear Father Taylor, prototype of Melville's Father Mapple, preach; they repeatedly dined, wined, and ate midnight oyster suppers together. Sumner served as a kind of social shield for Dickens and protected him from some of the cruder importunities of his admirers. As Dickens left for the West, he begged his new friend to accompany him, for, as he reported to their English friends: "Sumner is of great service to me." [8]

Sumner's friendly exertions were not confined to Englishmen. He continued to promote the fortunes of the still poor and unrecognized American sculptor, Thomas Crawford, whom he had met in Rome. Recognizing that a reputation in England would give an American artist great prestige, he pressed Sir Charles Vaughan and other British acquaintances to commission Crawford to make portrait busts. After much exertion, he persuaded Ticknor, the Lawrences, and other wealthy Bostonians to purchase Crawford's "Orpheus" for the Athenaeum, at a cost of $2,500. He himself superintended the repair of minor damages the statue suffered in being shipped across the Atlantic, vetoed the idea of exhibiting it in the Athenaeum's usual gallery, where the cross lights would kill its effect, and persuaded the directors to erect a little house on the grounds, where the statue could be shown against mahogany brown walls and in diffused lighting. As Boston gaped appreciatively over Crawford's curiously unbalanced figure of Orpheus, accompanied by its melancholy Cerebus, which looked embarrassed over its superfluity of heads, Sumner sought further to assist his friend by publishing a glow-

---

[8] Henry James: *William Wetmore Story and His Friends from Letters, Diaries, and Recollections* (Boston: Houghton Mifflin Co.; 1903), I, 58; Longfellow: *Longfellow*, I, 414; Edward F. Payne, *Dickens Days in Boston* (Boston: Houghton Mifflin Co.; 1927), pp. 7, 29, 42–3, 45–9, 59, 61; Edgar Johnson: *Charles Dickens: His Tragedy and Triumph* (New York: Simon and Schuster, Inc.; 1952), I, 360, 367–8, 371, 373; Walter Dexter (ed.): *The Letters of Charles Dickens* (Bloomsbury: The Nonesuch Press; 1938), I, 379, 406. For Sumner's similar attentions to the actor Macready, see William Toynbee (ed.): *The Diaries of William Charles Macready, 1833–1851* (London: Chapman and Hall, Ltd.; 1912), II, 235, 238–40.

ing account of his sculpture in the Boston *Advertiser* and in the
New York *Democratic Review*.[9]

Not all of Sumner's efforts for his friends were equally successful, but they were sincere and enthusiastic. He continued to
batter his French acquaintances with proposals to elect Justice
Story to the French Academy.[1] For his crusty friend Francis Lieber, who was teaching at South Carolina College, which Sumner
considered an exile "undisturbed by the foot of civilization," he
ran errands, bought books, and interviewed publishers. Lieber,
who was, as Rufus Choate said, "the most fertile, indomitable, un-
sleeping, combative and propagandising person of his race," relentlessly exploited Sumner's good nature and drew interminably
upon his time, yet he was greatly aggrieved when his every letter
was not promptly answered, his too frequent proposals for publishing books proved impracticable, and his nudging hints that he
ought to receive a chair at Harvard were not acted upon. Finally
even Sumner was goaded by Lieber's reproaches into protesting
"that in judging my conduct, my desire to serve you, at all times
and in all ways, *you do me injustice*," but his good nature quickly
reasserted itself, and, making allowance for Lieber's loneliness,
he reassured him: "Remember I shall always be over-happy in
doing anything I can for you."[2] It was no wonder that in Boston
men said: "Charles Sumner's friends are like other men's brothers."[3]

· 3 ·

Despite all these indications that Sumner could settle comfortably into Boston society, surrounded by a warm circle of admiring friends, he was an unhappy man. After the immediate exalta-
tion of returning to America and telling of his European adventures wore off, he fell more and more into moods of self-pity and
loneliness. His friends described him as "rather depressed, and

[9] Sumner to Ticknor, Sept. 15, 1839, Ticknor MSS.; Sumner to Hillard, July
26, 1839, Sumner MSS.; Pierce, II, 304; Boston *Daily Advertiser*, May 8, 1844;
The United States Magazine, and Democratic Review, XII (May 1843), 451–6.
[1] Sumner to Warden, June 20, 1841, Warden MSS.
[2] Sumner to Lieber, Dec. 10, 1840, May 12, 1841, and Jan. 20, 1842, Sumner
MSS.; Choate to Sumner, Jan. 7, 1842, ibid.
[3] John Kenyon to Sumner, Dec. 29 [1844], ibid.

weary with the great Ixion wheel of life," and he felt that he was a black cistern of melancholy. "You cannot fathom the yawning depths of my soul," he exclaimed to Longfellow. "I am *alive;* that is, continue to draw breath, and stride through the streets. But what is this? I am becoming every day duller and duller; I have nothing to say to any body. I am like an extinct volcano." [4]

Some part of Sumner's depression was probably caused by financial worries. Before he went to Europe, he had incurred a debt of $1,200 in an unfortunate land speculation, and he had borrowed $3,000 more from Story, Fletcher, and Samuel Lawrence in order to go abroad. As soon as Sumner returned to law practice, he began applying his earnings to these debts, but he seemed never to make quite enough. Finally in 1844 he gave up the struggle and persuaded his mother to pay his creditors. [5]

It soon became obvious that Sumner was not making a brilliant success of his legal career. In exceptional cases he excelled, but he had little interest in routine common-law practice. "I paid the bill of costs, without understanding it," he confessed to a colleague at the end of a case, "and I sometimes believe that it is not in my power to understand anything, which concerns such matters." Prospective clients found him uninterested as well as uncomprehending. His desk was almost constantly surrounded by admiring, talking literary acquaintances. Longfellow and Felton made his office their regular headquarters when they came into Boston, and Lieber, on his frequent summer visits from South Carolina, was at No. 4 Court Street from morning until night. Sumner would suspend business for a morning to debate with the elder Richard Henry Dana whether Washington Allston had written the finest poetry of modern times. Even if a client found Sumner alone, he was unlikely to win his full attention, for at the slightest provocation Sumner would launch into a long-winded reminiscence of his European adventures, recalling "in a dreamy way the irrelevant as well as the relevant incidents . . . connected with it." [6]

---

[4] Sumner to Cleveland, Apr. 3, 1841, copy, Longfellow MSS.; Longfellow, Journal, Apr. 10, 1844, ibid.; Sumner to Longfellow [May 12, 1843], ibid.; Sumner to Howe, undated, Sumner MSS.

[5] Sumner to Cleveland, Sept. 23, 1840, Cleveland MSS.; Samuel Lawrence to Sumner, Apr. 2, 1844, Sumner MSS.; Pierce, I, 199.

[6] Sumner to J. C. Perkins, June 14, 1844, Sumner MSS.; Mellen Chamberlain, Jr., Diary, Apr. 12, and Nov. 15, 1847, MS., Boston Public Lib.; Sumner to

Though Sumner's friends tried to convince themselves that he only needed time to rise to the head of the bar, prospective clients knew better, and they took their business to hard-working, untraveled lawyers like Benjamin R. Curtis, C. G. Loring, and Benjamin F. Butler, or to the deans of the profession, Choate and Jeremiah Mason. Despite his brilliant beginning in 1841, Sumner's business fell off sharply. He seems to have had no cases before the Federal District Court in Boston during the next five years. Nor was he listed as attorney in any cases before the Supreme Judicial Court of Massachusetts during these years. Even before the United States Circuit Court, where his friendship with Judge Story might be presumed to have some weight, he had little practice. From the eleven cases he argued in the fall term of Story's court in 1841 his business declined to three in 1842 and then to two in 1843; after that, except for the friction match case which was continued until 1845, his name does not appear on the docket books. Two years after he came home from Europe, Sumner's practice was so small that he happily accepted an appointment, procured through Story's influence, as a United States commissioner in bankruptcy proceedings, and he and Hillard made their "living on the blood and tears of those victims." [7]

More quickly than his friends, Sumner recognized that his future as a practicing lawyer would be, at best, one of unrewarding mediocrity. "Though I earn my daily bread," he confessed to Lieber in 1840, "I lay up none of the bread of life. My mind, soul, heart are not improved or invigorated by the practice of my profession; by overhauling papers, old letters, and sifting accounts, in order to see if there be any thing on which to plant an action. The sigh will come, for a canto of Dante, a Rhapsody of Homer, a play of Schiller." [8]

Lacking clients, Sumner occupied his time in seeing the third volume of his *Reports* through the press. When Judge Story fell sick, Sumner took his place in the Harvard Law School for a

---

Hillard, Aug. 5 [1840], Sumner MSS.; Edwin Percy Whipple: *Recollections of Eminent Men . . .* (Boston: Houghton Mifflin Co.; 1893), pp. 209–13.

[7] Docket Books of U.S. Circuit Court and U.S. District Court (MS., Federal Records Center, Dorchester); Francis Bassett to Sumner, Feb. 2, 1842, Sumner MSS.; Hillard to Lieber, Mar. 24, 1842, Lieber MSS. It is possible, of course, that Sumner served as junior counsel in some cases during these years when his name was not listed on the docket books.

[8] Sumner to Lieber, Sept. 23, 1840, Lieber MSS.

fortnight in 1840 and again in 1843. He employed his abundant leisure and extensive energy in writing articles and reviews for the *Law Reporter* which unconsciously revealed how little he was interested in the details of daily practice. He expressed pain that an editor of Sir James Mackintosh's *A Discourse on the Study of the Law of Nature and Nations* had given notes translating the numerous, difficult Latin quotations in the work as, he observed snobbishly: "Few persons will attempt the text, who can desire any such assistance as is here volunteered." Reviewing the latest volume of New Hampshire supreme-court reports, he ignored all points of law and fretted about the judges' "use of a barbarism, like 'loaned.'" "The verb *to loan* in all its inflections," he ruled, "is not only vicious in respect of taste, but it is superfluous. We trust it will be discountenanced from the bench." [9]

However satisfying, such legal diversions were decidedly not remunerative, and Sumner began to think that a public office might prove more profitable than private practice. Alexander H. Everett, who had some influence with the administration of President James K. Polk, tried to get Sumner appointed Chief Clerk in the Department of State, but James Buchanan, the new Secretary, declared that he was "rather unwilling to appoint a gentleman, with whom he had no personal acquaintance." Story, too, tried to assist his impecunious friend by having him chosen reporter of the United States Supreme Court, and Sumner was enthusiastic about the job, which would give him "$3,000 for two months' work, . . . besides an opportunity of taking business in the highest court of the country." Announcing that he disliked "most cordially the *principle* and *practice* of office-seeking" and that he had "no disposition to join that 'army offensive,' which is perpetually crying 'Give, give,'" he nevertheless solicited the support of Justice John McLean. "I could not decline to present myself, in a proper way, and on a proper occasion, as one of the candidates for the office." But illness kept Story from attending the Supreme Court in 1842–3, and there was little other support for Sumner's candidacy. Through what he characteristically concluded was "a cabal among the loco [foco] judges of the Su-

[9] Report of Treasurer, Mar. 31, 1841, Harvard Coll. Papers, X, 2 ser., 213; Harvard Coll. Records, VII (1837–46), 197; Sumner to Lieber, July 11, 1843, Sumner MSS.; *Law Reporter*, VI (Dec. 1843), 380; VII (May 1844), 48–51. Cf. also Sumner's essay on "The Number 'Seven,'" ibid. VI (Apr. 1844), 529–41.

preme Court," a new reporter of Democratic antecedents was appointed.[1]

• 4 •

But Sumner's financial insecurity was not the real cause of his unhappiness. After all, he was a bachelor with moderate living expenses; his legal work did bring in some income, he had free room and board, and he could always call on his mother's help in real emergencies. Sumner's comparative failure at the bar was less a cause than a symptom of his deeper, more mysterious discontents.

When Sumner returned from Europe, he found that for the first time in his life he was obliged to stand alone, without the guidance and support from some older man who could give direction to his career. His father was dead. Justice Story remained a good friend, but no longer exhibited the same paternal interest in Sumner's career. There was no estrangement between the two, but they were gradually drifting apart. During Sumner's two years abroad, Story had grown older and feebler, and his interests had become centered on the new crop of students who were attending the Harvard Law School. He had been troubled by Sumner's legal "radicalism," which echoed his own early but now rejected views, and concerned over his decision to go abroad; now he was puzzled by Sumner's failure to succeed at his practice. When Sumner went to see the judge in Cambridge, he always found the warmest welcome; but there were no more prophecies about a Harvard law professorship for him.[1a]

For a time it seemed that Samuel Gridley Howe would take Story's place in Sumner's life. Sumner had known Howe casually since 1837, when the two men, at considerable personal risk, helped quell an anti-Irish riot on Broad Street, but not until his return from Europe were they thrown frequently together. Howe,

[1] A. H. Everett to Sumner, Mar. 26, 1846, Sumner MSS.; Sumner to McLean, Feb. 2, 1843, McLean MSS.; Sumner to Cleveland, Feb. 17, 1843, Cleveland MSS.; McLean to Story, Jan. 25, 1843, Story MSS.

[1a] When Story died a few years later, Sumner cooly observed that his passing "has been keenly felt by friends, the profession and the public; but, in this busy life, new interests arise to take the place of those that have disappeared, and the world soon learns to forget its benefactors." Sumner to Lord Morpeth, Mar. 29, 1846, Carlisle MSS.

who was more than a decade older in years and seemingly a generation older in experience, seemed positively heroic to Sumner.
The younger man thrilled to hear Howe's tales of fighting for the
Greeks in their war for independence and of assisting the Poles in
their revolution against Prussia. Now the distinguished head of
the Perkins Institute for the Blind, Howe was still a knight-errant
of reform, and Sumner worshipfully concluded that his new
friend possessed "intelligence and experience of no common order, all elevated and refined by a chivalrous sense of honor, and a
mind without fear." [2]

At Sumner's urging, Howe was made a member of "The
Five of Clubs," replacing Cleveland, who went to Cuba for his
health, but Sumner spent more time with him than with all the
other members, who were either married or lived outside of Boston. "Bachelors both," Sumner explained, "we drive and ride together—and pass our evenings far into the watches of the night
in free and warm communion." At loose ends when summer came
and other friends were out of town, he and Howe used every evening to "mount their horses or jump into a gig and career through
the country for two hours," returning to eat ices and strawberries
and to "chat, wherein, are remembered things, experiences and
hopes of all sorts, [which] absorb the remainder of the evening."
Often they spent the night together at Howe's quarters in South
Boston, and "Chev" (as intimates nicknamed Howe) had fond
memories of Sumner, "his straps unbuttoned, his waistband also,
his feet in my red slippers, a glass of orvieto in his hands, his
sweet smile on his lips . . . as he used to sit in my easy chair."
When they went to bed, they left the door between their rooms
open, so that they could continue their conversation into the
drowsy hours. [3]

The two friends addressed each other in terms of intimacy
verging upon endearment. When "Chev" was out of town, Sumner felt desolate and wrote him: "I lack the consciousness of

[2] Laura E. Richards (ed.): *Letters and Journals of Samuel Gridley Howe*
(Boston: Dana Estes & Company; 1909), II, 97–8; Sumner to Lieber, May 12,
and June 3, 1841, Sumner MSS.

[3] Sumner to Lieber, June 27, and July 13, 1842, Sumner MSS.; Howe to
Sumner, Feb. 2, 1844, Howe MSS. For a perceptive study of Howe, which casts
much light on Sumner, see Harold Schwartz: *Samuel Gridley Howe, Social Reformer, 1801–1876* (Cambridge: Harvard University Press; 1956).

your presence, and the sense of security, which it gave me." Howe
fondly reassured him: "I love thee better than thou ever lovedst
me—better even I believe than any of the numerous friends who
spring up around thee wherever thou plantest thy foot." With as
much truth as humor Hillard reported on the progress of Sumner's new friendship. "He is quite in love with Howe and spends
so much time with him that I begin to feel the shooting pains of
jealousy." [4]

Seeing Howe as "the soul of disinterestedness," who had
"purged his character from all considerations of *self*," Sumner
tried to imitate his friend in his career of bettering society. Admiringly he observed the Doctor's work with the blind, and faithfully he visited the Perkins Institute to observe the progress he
was making with the education of the deaf-blind girl, Laura
Bridgman, even though Laura privately complained: "Sumner
is not gentle like Dr. . . . Why does Dr want Sumner to come
here if he is not gentle. . . . I do not love or like Sumner. . . ."
Howe called Sumner's attention to the important work Horace
Mann was doing to rejuvenate the public schools of the Commonwealth, and Sumner enthusiastically endorsed Mann's ideas of
nonsectarian education: "Let us put an iron heel upon the serpent
of religious bigotry trying to hug our schools in its insidious coil."
With his civic interests aroused, he became secretary of the Emigration Society, designed to ease the problems of the Irish immigrants who were beginning to pour into Boston, joined the Prison
Discipline Society, and attended the meetings of the Peace Society.[5]

Though powerfully influential, Howe could not quite fill the
place that Sumner's father and later Judge Story had played in
his life. For one thing, Howe resolutely refused to be an older
man directing a young friend's career. On the contrary, he insisted that it was he who derived inspiration from Sumner. "It has
never been my lot to know a man more perfectly loyal to truth,
right and humanity," he assured his friend. "You are my junior by

[4] Sumner to Howe, June 25, 1850, MS., Huntington Lib.; Howe to Sumner,
May 4, 1843, Sumner MSS.; Hillard to Longfellow, May 16, 1842, Longfellow
MSS.
[5] Schwartz: *Howe*, p. 108; Sumner to Howe, May 31, 1844, Sumner MSS.;
Sumner to R. H. Dana, Sr., Feb. 22 [1842], Longfellow MSS.

many years, but to you I owe many of the feeble aspirations which I feel for progress upwards and onwards in my spiritual nature." [6]

Howe also had other aspirations, which needed, and received, no encouragement from Sumner. He fell in love. In the summer of 1841 Julia Ward, oldest daughter of a prosperous New York merchant, visited Boston, and Howe was immediately captivated. With a perfect oval face, creamy complexion, blue eyes, and startlingly red hair, Julia was as beautiful as she was talented; she wrote poetry, read French, German, and Italian, and sang operatic arias so well that friends called her Diva. Though he was eighteen years her senior, Howe promptly commenced a serious courtship and during the next two years made frequent visits to New York. [7]

With friendly generosity Howe wanted Sumner to share his experience of falling in love. After all, there were three daughters in the Ward household, the "Three Graces of Bond Street," and if Howe had singled out Julia for himself, Sumner could choose the dark, exotic-looking Louisa or the gentle, self-effacing Annie. The fact that Sumner was thirty-one and that Annie and Louisa were seventeen and eighteen, respectively, seemed no insuperable barrier to the Doctor; there was a greater disparity between his and Julia's ages.

Willingly Sumner allowed himself to be carried along—up to a point. He accompanied Howe in his pilgrimages to "the Trinity of Bond Street," and helped attend the Ward sisters wherever they went. He unbent amazingly. When Felton gave a party for Julia and her friend Mary Dwight, Sumner was actually flirtatious. After dinner, Julia reported, "Sumner got Mary and me under a curtain, held it down, called us his dear wives, and said it was the commencement of his domestic bliss." In December 1842 Sumner, Howe, and Felton all went to New York to greet Longfellow, who was returning from Europe, and the Ward sisters welcomed them with much rejoicing. The three maidens, the two Harvard professors, the veteran of the Greek wars, and Sumner played blindman's buff, and, Sumner reported coyly: "Who

[6] Richards: *S. G. Howe*, II, 252.
[7] Schwartz: *Howe*, Chap. viii; Louise Hall Tharp: *Three Saints and a Sinner* (Boston: Little, Brown & Co.; 1956), Chap. viii.

should I catch . . . but the lovely Louisa? and who should catch me, in the same game, but the same paragon of loveliness?" Felton shrewdly noted the "unerring skill [with which] Howe caught Julia, and Sumner, Louisa; and . . . the length of time they spent in determining who their captives were; a question they did not presume to decide until they had made the most minute phrenological examination of their beautiful heads." Encouraged, Howe had "strong hopes that Charley may be warmed by the star second in magnitude in the Constellation of Bond Street." [8]

Sumner shyly assured his friends that there was ground for these hopes. He spoke rapturously of "warm hearted, simple and affectionate" Louisa and of "gentle, simple, sweet, confiding" Annie. When Lieber visited Boston in 1843, he found that Sumner had no other topic of conversation. "We spoke so much of love, and my soul turned to that so spontaneously," Sumner apologized, "that whenever I sought to wake another cord, it was in vain." A devoted wife, he decided, would be better than "an Indian argosy." "I would walk on foot round the earth, to find a woman who would love me with . . . truth," he exclaimed. "Oh! with what ardour I would pour my gushing affections into her soul," he wrote, with grimly inappropriate imagery, "as the Parthians filled the head of Crassus with the gold he loved too well." [9]

For all his protestations, Sumner took no steps toward finding a wife. Once he realized that Louisa Ward was no sisterly adolescent, but a marriageable young woman, he declared frankly: "I have no desire in that quarter," and he was relieved when she went to Europe, where she shortly met her future husband, Sumner's friend Crawford. Available women did not interest Sumner. He declined to begin a correspondence with one female admirer, and he showed total indifference to the highly eligible Mary Dwight, whom his friends constantly threw at his head. But, on a trip to Philadelphia, he reported that he "met the most fascinating woman I have ever seen in America—

[8] Sumner to Lieber, Sept. 5, 1841, and Dec. 8, 1842, Sumner MSS.; Julia Ward to Annie and Louisa Ward [1842], Howe MSS.; Felton to Cleveland, Nov. 28, 1842, copy, Longfellow MSS.; Howe to Lieber, Aug. 17, 1842, Lieber MSS.
[9] Sumner to Lieber, July 18, and Dec. 8, 1842 [Sept. 1843], and Aug. 31, 1841, Sumner MSS.; Sumner to Longfellow, July 10, 1842, Longfellow MSS.

beautiful as morning, with the *esprit* of France . . . and the glowing soul of the South." But he discovered: "Alas! she is married—to a senator in Congress." He was similarly bewitched by the former Euphemia Van Rensselaer, of New York, a "peerless creature." "I fell in love with that beautiful creature," he gushed to Howe. "The first moment I saw her I felt that she had a warm heart, a pure and etherial [sic] nature, a clear intellect, and a soul as graceful as her person." She, too, was quite happily married. So regularly did the pattern recur that Lieber concluded sagely: "The truth is you dont wish for love, but delight in amatory cro[a]king. . . . How else is it that you are always, not once, smitten with women out of reach?" [1]

Friends were genuinely concerned about the "cage of celibacy" in which Sumner was trapped. Felton's and Hillard's select "committee upon his domestic relations" was a little more than a joke. Felton urged Sumner to get married before he turned into "a solitary monument, in the deserts of life, like one of the strong Sphinxes, in the wastes of Aegypt, buried all but the *head*, in the unfruitful, parched and parching sands . . . staring out upon the appalling loneliness with deadened eyes." Howe thought Sumner was simply too timid. "You do love," he argued, "you are all love—you have more of love in you than any man I ever knew." Action was all that was required. "Go straight up to Beacon Street; walk around the Common; seek out the sweetest girl you meet; join her at the second round, and offer yourself to her; insist upon her accepting you, and carry off her troth before you are thrice around." [2]

But Julia Ward, with shrewd feminine intuition, knew the case was hopeless and said that Sumner had *"no heart."* Though Sumner indignantly protested: "I have a *heart*—it is not my fault if all its throbbings have been in vain," her judgment came near the mark. Easily falling in love with ineligible women, he set up impossible standards for those whom he might win. Sam Ward, Julia's worldly wise brother, diagnosed Sumner's difficulty. "He is

[1] Sumner to Fanny Longfellow, Oct. 20, 1843, Longfellow MSS.; Louisa Bullard to Charles Eliot Norton, May 19, 1843, Norton MSS.; Sumner to Hillard, Jan. 29, 1841, Sumner MSS.; Sumner to Howe, Oct. 1, 1843, ibid.; Lieber to Sumner, Oct. 15, 1843, Lieber MSS.

[2] Sumner to Palfrey [Oct. 1845], Palfrey MSS.; Felton to S. G. and Julia Howe, May 23, 1843, copy, Howe MSS.; Felton to Sumner, Apr. 2, 1844, Sumner MSS.; Howe to Sumner, Feb. 2, 1844, Howe MSS.; Richards: *S. G. Howe*, II, 193-4.

like the Sultan in the Arabian tale who sent a mirror out to reflect the face of an unsullied virgin—He requires nevertheless that he should be master—superior in intellect." Sumner was in fact protecting himself against possible rejection and humiliation. In his father's embittered household he had learned that he must never let down his guard; yet how could he fall in love or propose marriage without opening himself to scorn or even ridicule? Perhaps it might have been easier could he have courted a girl in humble station, like his mother, but the society in which he now moved demanded that his wife be educated, intelligent, and probably wealthy. These were the very women Sumner found most frightening, for they inspired in him, he confessed, "a certain awe, and a sense of [their] superiority, which makes me . . . anxious to subside into my own inferiority, and leave the conversation to be sustained by other minds." [3]

Reluctantly, broodingly, he watched others take the step he dared not take. It was a bitter blow when Howe became engaged to Julia in February 1843. "God bless you both! You will strengthen each other for the duties of life; and the most beautiful happiness shall be yours," he exclaimed in his letter of congratulations, but privately he was deeply troubled: "I am about to lose a dear friend; for the intimate confidence of friendship may die away, when love usurps the breast, absorbing the whole nature of a man." He could only hope that Howe would not entirely forget him and that in time Julia might come to accept him, too. Though Julia promptly assured Sumner that he had not lost but gained a friend by the engagement, she had deeper reservations. At her wedding reception "her natural roguery broke out, and seeing Sumner bent over, and intently engaged in talking to a lady, she could not help slipping two or three silver spoons into his coat pocket." Then, jestingly, she accused him of attempting to steal something belonging to herself. [4]

[3] Sumner to Lieber, Sept. 22, 1842, Sumner MSS.; Ward to Longfellow, Jan. 14, 1842, Longfellow MSS.; Sumner to Hillard, Sept. 12, 1844, Sumner MSS.
[4] Laura E. Richards and Maud Howe Elliott: *Julia Ward Howe, 1819–1910* (Boston: Houghton Mifflin Co., 1916), I, 76; Sumner to Samuel Ward, Feb. 21, 1843, Howe MSS.; Julia Ward to Sumner [Feb. 21, 1843], Sumner MSS.; Longfellow to Sarah P. Cleveland [Apr. 19, 1843], photostat, Longfellow MSS. Vexed by the amount of time Howe spent writing letters to Sumner during their honeymoon, Julia exclaimed: "Sumner ought to have been a woman and you to have married her." Howe to Sumner, Sept. 11, 1844, Howe MSS.

• 5 •

"I am all *alone—alone*," Sumner lamented, as Howe's marriage and honeymoon trip to Europe left him without that paternal counsel he needed to direct his life. Howe wrote him "strangely confidential" letters from Europe, announcing: "The torrent of affection which is continually flowing from my heart toward the new object of my love diminishes not by one drop the tide of feeling which swells within my bosom at the thought of thee dear Sumner: I love thee not less because I love her more," but Sumner was inconsolable. "My friends fall away from me," he grieved. "I lead a joyless life, with very little sympathy." [5]

During the tense months of Howe's courtship and marriage Sumner had grown to be an increasingly difficult person to live with. At home he was almost as domineering as his father had been. Constantly he reproached and scolded his younger brothers and sisters who remained at home. Only Mary, now a tall, gentle girl of nearly twenty, escaped his censorious advice, perhaps because it was already clear that she was gradually dying of tuberculosis. But Horace, the youngest brother, "a very good youth, of moderate capacity and no ambition and little energy," but with "an affectionate temper, [an] unworldly disposition and [a] feminine purity and delicacy of feeling," was a constant vexation to his drivingly ambitious brother.[6] Henry, who felt that Charles's meddling had thwarted one of his love affairs, lived in open enmity with his older brother, to whom he refused to speak.[7] Little Julia was subjected to nothing more than tedious admonitions about education and cleanliness until she grew up and began to have ideas of her own. Then Charles objected so strenuously to

[5] Sumner to Lieber, July 13, and Oct. 6, 1843, Sumner MSS.; Fanny Longfellow, Journal, Mar. 26, 1844, Longfellow MSS.; Howe to Sumner, May 13, 1843, Howe MSS.

[6] Hillard to Lieber, July 23, 1850, Lieber MSS.; undated clipping from Boston *Journal*, Pierce Scrapbooks; Sumner to George Sumner, May 15, 1844, Sumner MSS.; Sumner to George Sumner, June 19, 1849, Segal Coll. Horace was for a time a member of Brook Farm; then he worked a year or two on a New Hampshire farm; finally he was shipped off to Italy, where it was hoped he would strengthen his health and broaden his limited intelligence. In Italy he became a friend of the Marchioness Ossoli (Margaret Fuller). (Horace Sumner to "Dear Madame Ossoli," undated, Fuller MSS.) Returning to America on the same ship, they were both lost off Fire Island, July 19, 1850. Sumner to Henry David Thoreau, July 31, 1850, MS., Abernethy Lib., Middlebury Coll.

[7] Sumner to George Sumner, June 1, July 16, and Oct. 7, 1846, and Nov. 16, 1847, Sumner MSS. Henry died in South Orange, N.J., May 5, 1852.

her engagement to the "plain but sensible" Dr. John Hastings that he forbade the physician to visit the house, and Julia had to make a scene in order to win her right to receive her lover when and how she liked.[8]

Lonely and discouraged, Sumner grew increasingly sensitive. He began to suspect that people were saying unkind things about him, and, except when he was with his few intimate friends, he stalked through Boston's streets as though he were in panoply of prickly, defensive armor. He conducted social intercourse with extreme punctiliousness. "He would never submit to any discourtesy from others," Peleg W. Chandler remembered, "and required that they should observe the rules which he rigidly adhered to himself." When David Sears, one of the richest and most influential men in Boston, heard a distorted account of something Sumner supposedly had said reflecting upon the Sears family, Sumner icily refused to explain or to make amends. "Mr. Sears owes me an ample apology, for allowing me to be talked of in such a way," he stonily informed Hillard, and he stood on his dignity until Sears, learning the truth from other sources, wrote him a formal letter expressing regret at the misunderstanding.[9]

Soon Sumner convinced himself that he was surrounded by dangerous enemies in Boston society. Though he had been an intimate of the Ticknors since his return from Europe, he came to think, for reasons that are not at all clear, that Ticknor had "a peculiar prejudice and ill will" toward him. Once Sumner suspected a slight, he magnified every occurrence, real or fancied, into an insult. The turn of a phrase in conversation, the casual laughter that might drift out as he entered one of Ticknor's soirees would be enough to persuade him that there was a conspiracy against him. Sumner's close friends reproached him for being too sensitive. "Here you are, a man with full grown powers, circled by loving friends, with every thing to stimulate you, and above all with the priceless blessing of fine health," Cleveland chided. "Will you be driven to despondency by the apparent

[8] Julia Ward Howe to "Aunt Lou," Oct. 28, 1853, Howe MSS.; Pierce, II, 157. Julia, who married Hastings in 1854, was the one member of the family who outlived Charles. She died in California, May 29, 1876.

[9] Pierce, II, 254; Sumner to Hillard, Jan. 24, and 27, 1841; Prescott to Sumner, Jan. 25, and 27, 1841; Sears to Sumner, Jan. 14, 1841, Sumner MSS.

treachery of a few friends, or the tittering nonsense of a few girls." But Sumner was implacable. The gulf between him and the Ticknors, he felt, was "growing broader every day." Soon he convinced himself that Ticknor, whom he had earlier considered the chief ornament of Boston arts and letters, was "the impersonation of *refined* selfishness." While men like Howe were doing good works, Sumner sneered, Ticknor "sits in his rich library, and laps himself in care and indulgence, *doing* nothing himself, treating unkindly the works of those who *do,* looking down upon all, himself having no claim to be regarded, except as a man of *promises*—never, in a life no longer short, redeemed." In a society so small and closely knit as Boston's, such remarks quickly got back to Ticknor's ears, and the essential justice of Sumner's characterization made them rankle. By 1843 friends warned Sumner not to call at Park Street, lest he be shown the door.[1]

Unhappy at home and in society at large, Sumner sought comfort in the company of his closest friends, but even here, it seemed, fate was constricting his circle. Felton was too wholesome and hearty to give Sumner much sympathy in his black moods. Hillard was preoccupied by his own unhappiness, Cleveland was dying in Cuba, and Howe was honeymooning in Europe.

Only Longfellow was left, and at Craigie House in Cambridge, where Sumner's visits were so regular that he was known as "the Sunday *male,*" the two friends read together and talked long and affectionately. Sumner could take solace in the fact that Longfellow, too, had suffered reverses. He had fallen in love with Fanny Appleton, daughter of Nathan Appleton, when they met in Germany in 1836. Her black eyes and dark auburn hair had driven the young Harvard professor into importunate wooing, which met with prompt rejection. Longfellow's loss was Sumner's gain, for the two could now pool their loneliness.[2]

But Sumner was soon to be deprived even of this comfort. In 1842 Longfellow sailed for Europe to recover his health and his spirits. Soon he reported to Sumner a significant dream: the two men were in bed together, and when Sumner mentioned "a

---

[1] Sumner to Longfellow, May 14, 1842, Longfellow MSS.; Cleveland to Sumner, Apr. 7, 1843, Cleveland MSS.; Sumner to Lieber, Jan. 29, 1844, Sumner MSS.; Howe to Sumner [Apr. 10, 1843], Howe MSS.

[2] Julia Ward Howe to Longfellow, undated, Longfellow MSS.; Thompson: *Young Longfellow*, pp. 235–8, 250–62; Edward Wagenknecht: *Longfellow: A Full-Length Portrait* (New York: Longmans, Green & Co., Inc.; 1955), pp. 223–7.

certain person's name," Longfellow fell on Sumner's neck and wept, exclaiming: "I am very unhappy." In the dream Sumner was "buried up to his neck in sand," but Longfellow was not—as he promptly demonstrated when he returned to America and won Fanny Appleton's hand, leaving his friend buried in his celibacy.[3]

When Longfellow announced his approaching marriage, Sumner, already prostrated by Howe's recent wedding, could only conceal his dismay by pretending to be dull and indifferent to his friend's great happiness. He compelled himself to write Fanny his "most sincere, most cordial, most affectionate congratulations," but he was, in fact, heartbroken and desolate. "Howe has gone," he reproached Longfellow, "and now you have gone, and nobody is left with whom I can have sweet sympathy. . . . What shall I do these long summer evenings? And what will become of those Sabbaths, sacred to friendship and repose?" The Longfellows, who had no intention of giving up their friends just because they were married, took pity on Sumner and invited him to accompany them on their wedding trip to the Catskills. He accepted, and, on the train, read to the newlyweds Bossuet's funeral orations.[4]

Sumner tried to forget his unhappiness in work. He treated his body, as Lieber remarked, "like an iron pot which may be night and day over fire," without remembering even that would wear out. By the fall of 1843, the disastrous year in which both Howe and Longfellow were married, Sumner's friends were worried about his health; the fact that his sister Mary was dying of tuberculosis and that his brother Henry was coughing blood indicated the danger. Howe begged him to abandon "that morbid and unnatural state of mind which made you careless of whether you should live or die," and, as a physician, sternly directed him to stop "working hard all day, eating and drinking without regard to time or quality, or quantity; sitting up two thirds of the night, using up the whole store of nervous power accumulated by one night's sleep, and anticipating that of the next day by forced loans."[5]

[3] Longfellow to Sumner, June 24, 1842, copy, Longfellow MSS.
[4] Sumner to Longfellow [May 12, 1843]; Sumner to Fanny Appleton, May 11, 1843; Fanny Longfellow to Sumner [July 1843]; Fanny Longfellow, Journal, Aug. 8, 1843, ibid.
[5] Lieber to Hillard, Nov. 11, 1844, Lieber MSS.; Howe to Sumner, Dec. 1843, Howe MSS.

But Sumner, instead of cutting down his load, increased it. In April 1844, against his better judgment and as though to punish himself, he signed a contract with Little & Brown to edit twenty volumes of Francis Vesey's chancery reports. For the sum of $2,000 he agreed to furnish copy for a volume every fortnight; as there were twenty-seven printers in the Little & Brown plant waiting to set the books in type, there could be no delay. Felton exclaimed that Sumner would have to "take the veil" and retire from the world while he performed this Herculean task. "I imagine you wearing a shirt set sharp with steel pens by day; and at night, catching brief snatches of rest in proof-sheets, with black-letter folios for your pillows," he punned, "while, like Saint Antony [sic], you are haunted by Devils, and tempted by the lucious forms of imaginary oysters, in every variety." [6]

The labor was indeed arduous, for Sumner attempted to annotate Vesey with citations to later English and American chancery cases and to add biographical sketches of the English judges and lawyers mentioned in the reports. For two months he was able to keep up the work and saw four volumes through the press. The physical strain did not relieve his mental depression, for Longfellow found him "in a desperate mood of Werterismus, wishing that some one would shoot [him] through the heart." In June his body rebelled, and he went to bed with a cold and fever. Attempting to resume work too soon, he had a serious relapse, and his physicians diagnosed tuberculosis, which was killing pallid, delicate Mary, confined in the room adjacent to his. [7]

Though there were, in fact, no apparent symptoms of consumption, Sumner's doctors were ready to declare his case hopeless. His friends came to Hancock Street to pay him final visits and to offer what kindly services they could. "There are so few like him upon earth," mourned Sam Ward, "that I cannot believe God really means to deprive humanity of so noble an example of all that is good and high-minded and pure." [8]

[6] J. C. Perkins to Pierce, Nov. 16, 1875, Pierce MSS.; Little & Brown to Sumner, Apr. 1, and 2, 1844, Sumner MSS.; Felton to Sumner, Apr. 10, 1844, ibid.; Longfellow, Journal, Apr. 4, 1844, Longfellow MSS.
[7] Law Reporter, VII (May 1844), 57–8; Longfellow, Journal, July 3, 1844, Longfellow MSS.; Hillard to Sarah P. Cleveland, July 31, 1844, copy, ibid.; Pierce, II, 308.
[8] Ward to Longfellow, July 28, 1844, Sumner MSS. Cf. Ticknor: Prescott, p. 241.

At the end of July, to everyone's surprise, Sumner began to mend. Relieved by the news that his Harvard classmate, J. C. Perkins, had agreed to take over the labor of editing Vesey, he began to feel that his physicians' verdict had been premature, and decided that his disease was only "a slow, nervous fever, brought on by sitting and studying at his desk, till after the clock struck two at night." His mood of depressed loneliness lifted when he learned of how his numerous friends had gathered around his bedside. As Hillard said: "It was worth while to approach the gates of the grave, to have such assurances of affection and regard as was [sic] showered upon him." [9]

Accustomed to the most vigorous health, Sumner felt that recovery should come overnight. Obliged to "assume the character of an invalid, watch the wind and skies, wrap up his throat, . . . take medicines, and listen to the vacillating opinions of his physicians," he suspected that he might, after all, be suffering from some dread ailment. "I begin to feel . . . that I have a shattered constitution," he confessed to Howe, "and that health has flown from me, perhaps forever." Death he did not fear, but throughout his life he had a terror that some lingering illness would leave him "but half a man." [1]

A fall vacation in the Berkshires helped take his mind off his symptoms, and while he rode horseback, flirted mildly with the neighboring belles, and played at archery with Fanny Kemble, his body gradually recuperated. By late November he was back at his office, editing the remaining volumes of Vesey and appearing in courts. He celebrated his recovery by appearing in the friction match case, in which he had taken so strong an interest, and his ten-hour summation speech to the jury was evidence that he was physically as strong as ever.[2] But he continued to suffer from his deep spiritual malaise.

[9] Pierce, II, 309; Sumner to Sarah P. Cleveland, July 31, 1844, copy, Longfellow MSS. There is not sufficient evidence to warrant a medical diagnosis of Sumner's illness. For similar "identity crises" in the lives of other young men about Sumner's age, see Erik H. Erikson: *Young Man Luther* (London: Faber and Faber Ltd., c. 1958), pp. 38–45.

[1] Sumner to Howe, Aug. 27, 1844, Sumner MSS.

[2] Sumner had edited Vols. I–IV of Vesey before his collapse. Perkins edited Vols. V, VII–X, and XII, and Charles B. Goodrich, Vol. XI. Sumner, after his recovery, edited Vols. VI and XIII–XX. Sumner to Tower, Dec. 4, 1844, Tower MSS.

CHAPTER V

An
Outrageous Philanthropist

❦

Sumner's "spirits are not good I am sorry to say," Hillard reported several months after he seemed fully recovered from his breakdown, "and life seems to have less and less attractions for him as he grows older." Failing to win professional success, failing to keep the social approbation on which he thrived, and, worst of all, failing to find security from these blows in domestic happiness, Sumner became bored, frustrated, and lonely. The reverses he had suffered during the four years since his return from Europe would have disconcerted any man; to Sumner they were catastrophic. "To me friendship, sympathy and kindness are a peculiar necessity of my nature," he recognized, "and I can have few losses greater than the weakening of any of these bonds." The death of his sister Mary, the only member of his family for whom he had a deep attachment, pointed up the meaningless of his own life. "I dwell often on the image of her beauty, of her sweet nature, and of her most serene soul," he wrote a few months after her funeral, "and feel that it would have been far better, had the health, which was unexpectedly renewed in my veins, been bestowed upon her in my stead." [1]

Genuinely troubled by Sumner's unhappiness, his friends tried to cheer him up. Henry and Fanny Longfellow welcomed

[1] Hillard to Sarah P. Cleveland, Dec. 1, 1844, copy, Longfellow mss.; Sumner to Longfellow, May 14, 1842, ibid.; Sumner to Sarah P. Cleveland, Jan. 31, 1845, Cleveland mss.

him as a regular weekend guest at Craigie House; Hillard endlessly sympathized with him; Felton regaled him with oysters
and outrageous puns. Howe, when he got back from Europe,
favored more active measures. He thought it best to divert Sumner's interest from his personal problems into the constructive
channels of civic reform.

• 1 •

Philanthropy was not something new to Sumner in 1844. Ever
since his return from Europe he had been under the influence
of William Ellery Channing, the father of organized benevolence
in Boston. It is difficult to explain the enormous influence this
frail, aging spokesman for liberal religion exercised over New
Englanders of Sumner's generation. Certainly it was not his appearance that won him a following. As Longfellow unkindly remarked, Channing "is one of the funniest looking individuals you
meet in the streets; as he wears a blue camlet wrapper, silver-
bowed spectacles; a shawl round his neck, and an enormous hat,
coming down over his eyes and ears, like an extinguisher." Nor
was he in the conventional sense an orator, for "his voice was soft
and musical, not loud or full in its tones," and he carefully refrained from rhetorical display. Quiet, sickly, and cautious, Channing was a philosopher whose ideas had neither great originality
nor brilliance. Yet he managed to be, as Emerson said, the
"Bishop" for the "New" in Massachusetts thought and society.[2]

Learning of Channing's enormous European reputation
while abroad, Sumner was prepared to overcome his initial distrust of the minister, and when Hillard, who was secretary of the
Federal Street congregation, brought his friend to the informal
weekly discussions Channing held at his Mount Vernon Street
mansion, Sumner was totally captivated. In Channing he found
an older man, of the same generation as his father and Justice
Story, whom he could revere as "one of the purest, brightest,
greatest minds of this age." Unlike Sheriff Sumner, Channing was

[2] Longfellow to his father, Jan. 3, 1841, Longfellow MSS.; Sumner: *The
Scholar, The Jurist, The Artist, The Philanthropist . . .* (Boston: William D.
Ticknor and Company; 1846), pp. 65–6. For Channing's enormous influence in
New England, see Gladys Brooks: *Three Wise Virgins* (New York: E. P. Dut-
ton & Co., Inc.; 1957), and Arthur W. Brown: *Always Young for Liberty*
(Syracuse: Syracuse University Press; 1956), Chap. xv.

"a saint-like character," always kindly and benevolent. Unlike Story, the minister did not become conservative as he grew older, but instead "as he advanced in life, his enthusiasm seemed to brighten, his soul put forth fresh blossoms of hope, his mind opened to new truths," namely, social reforms.[3]

Where Channing led, Sumner followed. He adopted all of the minister's arguments; he shared his concern over prison reform, education, international peace, and Negro slavery. It seemed to him positively heroic that the great Unitarian should continue to battle for social justice despite his age and obviously failing health. When Channing died in 1842, Sumner felt his loss more deeply than he had the death of his own father. Channing's "soul was of rectitude and courage 'all compact,'" he wrote. "What seemed to me a sight almost sublime, was this weak old man, almost fading out of life, with a voice affected by the debility of his frame, uttering words that pass mountains and seas, overcoming the impediments of distance and boundaries, and . . . pleading trumpet-tongued for humanity, for right, for truth."[4]

During Channing's lifetime, Sumner's own activities in social reform had been unobtrusive. Perhaps the very fact that he was a loved, respected member of the minister's circle kept him from being angry with society. Certainly Channing exercised a restraining hand upon his disciples, warning "that there is danger of pushing principles to extreme" and "that there must be a compromise between the Ideal and the Actual." Under such moderate guidance, Sumner had been a reformer only in the limited sense that he shared Howe's interest in the deaf and dumb and Mann's concern with education. He had also published letters in the "respectable daily," the Boston *Advertiser*, defending the British navy's right to search suspected American slave traders, and he had assisted Channing in preparing *The Duty of the Free States*, a pamphlet that attacked Secretary of State Webster's conten-

[3] Pierce, II, 223, 227; Sumner: *The Scholar, The Jurist, The Artist, The Philanthropist*, p. 67.

[4] Henry Marion Hall (ed.): "Longfellow's Letters to Samuel Ward," *Putnam's Monthly*, III (Nov. 1907), p. 166. On Channing as a social reformer, see William H. Channing: *Memoir of William Ellery Channing* . . . (Boston: Wm. Crosby and H. P. Nichols; 1848), III, Chaps. iii–v, and David P. Edgell: *William Ellery Channing: An Intellectual Portrait* (Boston: Beacon Press; 1955), pp. 150–201.

tion that the American flag protected even a slave ship on the high seas. But further Sumner was not prepared to go, and, despite numerous invitations, he took no public position as leader of any reform cause.[5]

By 1844, however, his reluctance had vanished. Irritated at the "toryism and donnishness" of Boston society, he was becoming increasingly restive. Both his European successes and his American failures taught him that a social order dominated by George Ticknor was not necessarily utopian. The darker his own personal prospects became, the greater grew his willingness to recognize a duty to improve society.[6]

The first reform cause in which Howe involved him was the common-schools controversy. Horace Mann was in serious trouble. His *Seventh Annual Report* charged that the famous Boston public schools were dulling students' minds through rote memorization and injuring their bodies through daily atrocious floggings. Outraged, the Principals' Association of Boston published an attack upon Mann's report. Angry and unwell, Mann issued a "Reply" to "this association—alias *Club* for eating and drinking and telling bawdy stories." As all Boston eagerly watched the fight, the embattled teachers published a "Rejoinder," and Mann retaliated with an "Answer to the 'Rejoinder.' "[7]

Always fond of losing causes, Howe plunged into the controversy on Mann's side, and, doubtless thinking that it would distract Sumner's mind from his woes, he brought his best friend along with him. He worked out a plan to have Mann's backers chosen to the Boston School Committee in the fall elections;

[5] Boston *Advertiser*, Jan. 4, and Feb. 10, 1842. See the reply of J. C. Perkins, ibid., Jan. 21, 1842. On this controversy see Hugh G. Soulsby: *The Right of Search and the Slave Trade in Anglo-American Relations, 1814–1862* ("Johns Hopkins University Studies in Historical and Political Science," Vol. XI, No. 2; Baltimore: The Johns Hopkins Press; 1933), esp. pp. 58–77. On Sumner's interest in the *Creole* affair see George Ticknor: *Life, Letters, and Journals* (Boston: James R. Osgood and Company; 1876), II, 199; Pierce, II, 194, 202, 205, 208, 210; Channing to Sumner, May 24, 1842, Sumner MSS.; Boston *Advertiser*, Apr. 18, 1842; Sumner to Lord Morpeth, Jan. 18, and Mar. 29, 1842, Carlisle MSS.

[6] Pierce, II, 214; III, 3–4. Cf. Eric Hoffer: *The True Believer: Thoughts on the Nature of Mass Movements* (New York: New American Library of World Literature, Inc.; 1958), pp. 22–3.

[7] Louise Hall Tharp: *Until Victory: Horace Mann and Mary Peabody* (Boston: Little, Brown & Co.; 1953), p. 203; Francis Bowen to Sumner, Dec. 14, 1844, Sumner MSS. The best treatment of the common schools controversy is in Schwartz: *Howe*, Chap. ix.

then, with a whip over the obdurate schoolmasters, they could insist upon progressive teaching methods. For Ward 4 Howe put up Sumner, despite vigorous objections from East Bostonians, who also belonged to that ward, against a candidate of "so little popularity, with the people." Though Howe's machine pushed Sumner's nomination through the Whig convention, the dissidents afterward ran a candidate of their own, a Baptist clergyman from East Boston. With the normal Whig majority split, Sumner was defeated in this his first trial for elective office.[8]

As Sumner was not elected to the school committee, he could have no part in Howe's 1845 campaign of harrying the Boston schoolmasters, but now that his interest was aroused, he did all he could elsewhere to assist Mann. In January he persuaded twenty-four leading Boston merchants and literary figures to sign a public letter he drafted praising Mann's "noble ardour, . . . marvellous application, undissipated and unwearied, [and] various labors, shrinking from no details or drudgery of duty." Mann's gratitude for this "most beautiful and touching letter" spurred Sumner to further exertions. Along with four other admirers of Mann's he petitioned the state legislature to appropriate $5,000 to construct normal schools, one of Mann's favorite projects, which the Boston principals were ridiculing; the five petitioners promised to match the state grant with an equal sum raised by private subscription.[9]

When the governor signed the bill in March, Sumner was sure there could be no difficulties ahead. Westfield, Bridgewater, and Northampton all were ready to pledge $1,000 if selected as a normal school site; Theodore Lyman had secured promises of another thousand; and Charles Brooks, one of Sumner's fellow petitioners, said he could raise the remainder on the Boston exchange "in five minutes." Fearing to delay the enterprise and hoping to assist Mann, then in the bitterest stage of his quarrel with the Boston teachers, Sumner borrowed the needed $5,000 on his own personal note, and presented the sum to the Board of Educa-

---

[8] Schwartz: *Howe*, pp. 127–9; Henry Greenleaf Pearson: *The Life of John A. Andrew: Governor of Massachusetts, 1861–1865* (Boston: Houghton Mifflin Co.; 1904), I, 45–6; Pierce, II, 324–5.

[9] Draft of a letter to Mann in Sumner's writing [Jan. 13, 1845], Sumner MSS.; Mann to the Members of the Committee, Jan. 13, 1845, ibid.; Mary Mann to Sumner [c. Jan. 20, 1845], ibid.; Boston *Post*, Jan. 28, 1845.

tion, relying upon the subscribers and the other friends of the common schools to repay him.

It was a noble gesture, but once Sumner had paid the money, the others lost interest and the subscriptions stopped coming in. The buildings went up, the normal schools opened, and Mann paid tribute to the "active and leading agency" that Sumner had "had in executive measures which have led to this beneficial result." But Sumner was once again heavily in debt. When his note was due, more than a year after the buildings had been finished, he could not pay it. In anger, he turned upon the others who had helped sponsor the project. "It seems to me rather hard that I should be thus left in the lurch by our committee, and particularly by individuals on it who have never contributed their full quota, and who are themselves rich, too. I . . . am less able than any member of the committee to pay this deficiency out of my own pocket. . . . It seems to me, therefore, that I may properly devolve upon the members of the committee . . . the duty of meeting this deficit." [1]

· 2 ·

Such an initial experience in reform might have dampened the zeal of anyone except Sumner, but, in his unhappy mood, he found defeat almost as satisfying as victory. From Channing he had learned to expect reverses when the spirit of benevolence came into conflict with "the infinite, intense thirst for gain and accumulation" prevalent in Massachusetts. The "stone-blindness of the multitudes" was no cause for defeatism. "Amidst the disappointments which may attend individual exertions," Sumner argued, in words that paraphrased Channing's, "let us recognize . . . that whatever is just, whatever is humane, whatever is good, whatever is true . . . in the golden light of the Future, must prevail." [2]

Unquestioningly Sumner shared Channing's faith in prog-

[1] Sumner to Mann, June 5, and 13, 1845, Mann MSS.; Pierce, II, 327–38.
[2] Channing: *Channing*, III, 55, 264; Sumner: *The Law of Progress* . . . (Boston: William D. Ticknor & Company; 1849), p. 44. I am deliberately disregarding chronology in the following discussion of Sumner's philosophy of reform. His opinions did not change between 1844 and 1850, and his more carefully considered utterances, which were made later in this period, give the best insight into his pattern of thought.

ress. From his own personal dark defeatism he found solace in the bright future of humanity. Like Channing, he rejected the "want of faith in improvement . . . found . . . chiefly among what are called 'the better classes.' " He chafed impatiently at the Beacon Hill residents who lamented that commercial supremacy was shifting to uncultured New York, that political power had fallen to the unwashed Jacksonian masses, and that Boston itself was being invaded by hordes of Catholic Irish. He dissented from Joseph Story's mournful opinion: "The Republic is daily sinking. . . . I have lost my confidence in the practical administration of our government. . . . I am in utter despair . . . I can see little or no ground of hope for our country." Such a melancholy want of faith in man, he agreed with Channing, sprang from a want of faith in God, and he thrilled to the great preacher's challenge: "In such a world, who shall set limits to change and revolution?" [3]

Convinced by Channing, Sumner believed that "man, as an individual, is capable of indefinite improvement, so long as he lives." Eagerly he welcomed all advances in knowledge which might promote human betterment. For a time he shared with Mann and Howe an enthusiasm for phrenology, as the pseudo science justified a challenge to the "granite, felspar, hornblende, and mica State Orthodoxy" of Massachusetts.[4] If phrenology was right, "surrounding circumstances" had "an important, if not controlling influence" in shaping men. It must be, Sumner concluded, with his usual passion for carrying an argument to its logical extreme, the external circumstances of climate which made the Ethiopian black and the New Englander white, and it was no less true "that the minds of persons . . . take their complexion from predominating influences; and the forms even of . . . the character are modified by external circumstances." If environment made man, evil could be eliminated. By creating a society where "knowledge, virtue, and religion prevail," even "the

[3] Channing: *Channing*, III, 132–3; Story to Sumner, Jan. 16, 1839, and Feb. 6, 1842, Sumner MSS.; Story: *Story*, II, 518–20.
[4] Sumner to Longfellow, May 15, 1842, Longfellow MSS.; Mary Mann: *Life of Horace Mann* (Boston: Walker, Fuller, and Company; 1865), pp. 111, 124, 132; Harold Schwartz: "Samuel Gridley Howe as a Phrenologist," *American Historical Review*, XVII (Apr. 1952), 644–51. Cf. John D. Davies: *Phrenology, Fad and Science: A 19th-Century American Crusade* (New Haven: Yale University Press; 1955), esp. p. 3.

most forlorn shall grow into forms of unimagined strength and beauty." [5]

But the reformer, Sumner believed, must not be concerned with individuals; "the good of the whole human family, its happiness, its development, its progress" should be his objective. From Channing he borrowed unquestioningly the postulates that "states and nations . . . were amenable to the same moral law as individuals" and, therefore, that *what is wrong for an individual is wrong for a state.*" [6]

In an elaborate address delivered at Union College in 1848, Sumner summarized his thinking on reform. Citing Leibnitz, Descartes, Pascal, Turgot, and Condorcet as prophets, he announced "The Law of Progress" as "a *discovery* of our age." "The tocsin of monarchy and injustice of all kinds," progress ordained that indefinite improvement be "the Destiny of man, of societies, of nations, and of the Human Race." The lesson of history was "Onward forever." [7]

As the "Age of Humanity" was waiting in the wings, it was the duty of the reformer to usher it on stage. From Channing, who had supplied so much of his philosophy of progress, Sumner derived his view of the proper role of the reformer. As a first step a would-be philanthropist must make certain that he himself was uncontaminated by any legal or moral connection with the evils he wished to destroy. "Let us wash our hands of the great guilt" became the constant refrain of Sumner's speeches. [8] Pure himself, the reformer must then stir up public opinion, "which insensibly operates every where, like the gentle droppings of water and produces mighty results." Others would join him in proclaiming a *"moral blockade"* against the wrong, and, as "the soul of all effective laws is an animating public sentiment," the laws that

[5] Sumner to George Putnam, Apr. 1848, author's copy, Sumner MSS.; Sumner: *Law of Progress*, p. 32.

[6] Sumner: *The Scholar, The Jurist, The Artist, The Philanthropist*, pp. 55, 59.

[7] Sumner to Greene, May 10, 1848, Greene MSS.; Sumner: *Law of Progress*, pp. 12, 28. A recent scholar calls the "Law of Progress" address "the most adequate and significant treatment of the subject" to appear in America during Sumner's generation. Arthur Alphonse Ekirch, Jr.: *The Idea of Progress in America, 1815–1860* (New York: Columbia University Press; 1944), p. 258.

[8] E.g., Sumner: *Works*, I, 157. Cf Channing's justification of his petition for the abolition of slavery in the District of Columbia: "I wished by some public act to disclaim all participation in the national guilt. . . ." Channing: *Channing*, III, 187.

tolerated evil would themselves be changed. To charges of uto-
pianism, Sumner replied firmly: "The Utopias of one age have
been the realities of the next." [9]

• 3 •

Though Sumner himself thought that his ideas had revolutionary
implications, few of his contemporaries were alarmed by his
views.[1] If rarely heard on Beacon Hill, the word "progress" came
naturally to the lips of Americans of Sumner's generation. For
years Bostonians had heard orators expatiate on "The Progresive
Character of Mankind" or "Progressive Improvement in the Condition of Man." [2] Sumner's views seemed a bit extravagant, but
quite pardonable in a young man, especially as he was careful to
exclude Comte, Saint-Simon, and Fourier from the legitimate
prophets of progress, which, in his opinion, must not "shake *property*." Besides, Sumner announced, his law of progress "shews
that all change must come gradually—I am tempted to add
peacefully." [3]

Far from being disturbed, respectable Bostonians approved
of Sumner's growing interest in civic affairs, and to indicate their
commendation, Mayor Thomas A. Davis and his council invited
the young lawyer to deliver the city's 1845 Fourth of July oration.
It was a considerable honor, for Boston's city fathers had made it
a practice since 1783 to assign the principal speech on these occasions to "young men of promising genius." Harrison Gray Otis,
John Quincy Adams, and Josiah Quincy had delivered the oration
in earlier years; more recently Charles Francis Adams, Hillard,
and Mann had made their formal bows before the Boston public
in this fashion.[4]

[9] Sumner to Lieber, Oct. 26, 1837, Lieber MSS.; Sumner: *The Scholar, The
Jurist, The Artist, The Philanthropist*, p. 59; Sumner: *The War System of the
Commonwealth of Nations* . . . (Boston: Ticknor, Reed, and Fields; 1849), pp. 8,
29.

[1] Lieber, to be sure, grumbled that Sumner's "Law of Progress" oration
was "peculiarly superficial" because the speaker had not "paid sufficient attention to retrograde nations and times." Lieber to Hillard, May 19, 1850, Lieber
MSS.; Lieber's undated note on the cover of *The Law of Progress* in The Johns
Hopkins Univ. Lib.

[2] Alexis de Tocqueville: *Democracy in America*, ed. by Phillips Bradley
(New York: Vintage Books, Inc.; 1956), II, 78; Ekirch: *Idea of Progress*, pp.
67, 73.

[3] Dawes: *Sumner*, pp. 104–6; Sumner to George Sumner, May 16, 1848,
Sumner MSS.; Sumner to Greene, May 10, 1848, Greene MSS.

[4] Davis to Sumner, Apr. 24, 1845, Sumner MSS.; Pierce, II, 338–9. Prior to
1783 the annual oration had been delivered on March 5, to commemorate the

Inexplicably, Sumner was reluctant to accept. As he later recalled, he *"peremptorily declined"* at first and agreed only when the mayor himself suggested that he had "kept aloof from public affairs in an unbecoming manner." Even after he had promised to give the oration, he had inner misgivings about the assignment. He delayed so long before commencing his preparation that Felton had repeatedly to remind him that his "numerous and distinguished audience" might determine his entire future career. Not until the middle of June did he settle down to real work, when he began "reading books like Briareus, fifty abreast," but even so, his manuscript was completed only on the eve of the holiday.[5]

In accepting the invitation to speak, Sumner had informed the mayor that his topic would be International Peace. His choice was not an unexpected one, as for years he had had an active, though quiet, interest in the peace movement. One of his earliest memories was of an address Josiah Quincy delivered before the Peace Society in the Old South Church; though only nine years old at the time, Sumner received from it "a deep and lasting impression" of the horrors of war. Shortly after he left college, hearing an address by William Ladd strengthened Sumner's antiwar convictions. His trip abroad intensified his dislike of militarism. He found European military installations and fortifications shocking and thought it would be better if the millions of soldiers were out "building . . . railways and other internal improvements, instead of passing the day in carrying superfluous muskets." When he returned to the United States, he joined the Peace Society, which Channing had helped found, and became a member of its executive committee. With most Bostonians he shared a concern over American saber-rattling in the 1840's, and he deplored with equal vigor the "insidious" plan of the South to annex Texas and carve from it "great slaveholding States" and the abominable intrigue to seize the disputed Oregon Territory, "not worth a groat to us." "For myself," he declared in private letters, "I hold all wars unjust and un-Christian."[6]

Boston Massacre. For a complete list of the speakers to 1852 see Loring: *The Hundred Boston Orators.*

[5] Sumner to George Putnam, Apr. 1848, author's copy, Sumner MSS.; Felton to Sumner [June? 1845], ibid.; Hillard to Sarah P. Cleveland, June 15, 1845, copy, Longfellow MSS.

[6] Sumner to Putnam, Apr. 1848, author's copy, Sumner MSS.; Ralph Volney Harlow: *Gerrit Smith, Philanthropist and Reformer* (New York: Henry Holt &

If the Boston city officials knew of these opinions, they were not at all perturbed by them, but went ahead with their plans for a customary rousing holiday celebration. Even nature seemed to co-operate. July 4 was a beautiful, cool day, and a partial news-paperman reported: "We doubt whether any part of our blessed country showed a fairer sight than the Boston common on the morning" of the holiday. "Magnificent flags" hung along the streets, and the ships in the harbor displayed colorful pennants. The United States warship *Ohio*, visiting in the port, "was beauti-fully dressed with flags, from the tops of her tall masts to the water's surface."

At about 10:30 the city authorities, led by the mayor and the orator of the day, began the procession from City Hall. They were followed by representatives of the Sons of Temperance, the Catholic Sunday Schools, the Veteran Cod Association, the Irish Charitable Relief Society, and by throngs of gaily dressed school children. More than 2,000 persons filed into Tremont Temple to hear the oration. On the platform, behind the speakers' chairs, was a choir of one hundred schoolgirls, dressed in white, ready to sing the national anthem. The Washington Light Guards, the uniformed officers of the Massachusetts militia, and officers of the United States army and navy occupied the seats just in front of the platform. After introductory prayers, the Declaration of Independence was "most effectively and impressively read." The celebration seemed to be going off "beautifully and harmoni-ously." [7]

Then Sumner rose to deliver his oration, which he titled "The True Grandeur of Nations." Carefully dressed for the occa-sion in a long-tailed blue coat with gilt buttons, white waistcoat, and white trousers, he had never looked so well in his life. Tall, erect, his clean-cut features saved from sternness by the smile that occasionally lit up his intelligent face, the thirty-four-year-old lawyer seemed to many of his audience the perfection of manly beauty.[8] With great ease and spirit he began: "It is in

Co., Inc.; 1939), p. 107; Pierce, II, 82, 278, 301, 314; Sumner to Howe, Dec. 31, 1843, Sumner MSS.

[7] Boston *Post*, July 7, 1845.

[8] *Dinner Commemorative of Charles Sumner and Complimentary to Ed-ward L. Pierce. Boston, December 29, 1894* (Cambridge: John Wilson and Son; 1895), p. 23; Fanny Longfellow to Nathan Appleton, July 5, 1845, Longfellow MSS.

obedience to an uninterrupted usage in our community that, on
this Sabbath of the Nation, we have put aside the common
cares of life and seized a respite from the neverending toils of
labor, to meet in gladness and congratulation, mindful of the
blessings transmitted from the Past, mindful also, I trust, of the
duties to the Present and the Future." [9] As the deep voice rolled
out the swelling periods, Sumner's hearers settled themselves
comfortably to listen.

Abruptly they were startled. After denouncing the annexation of Texas as an attempt "in this land of boasted freedom, to
fasten by new links the chains which promise soon to fall from
the limbs of the unhappy slave" and branding the American demand for Oregon as "a presumptuous assertion of a disputed
claim to a worthless territory," Sumner bluntly announced his
theme: "IN OUR AGE THERE CAN BE NO PEACE THAT IS NOT HON-
ORABLE: THERE CAN BE NO WAR THAT IS NOT DISHONORABLE."

For nearly two hours the orator, ignoring the uneasy whis-
perings of the military men just in front of him and the occasional
hisses from the crowd, proceeded to develop this proposition.
Speaking entirely from memory, except when he referred to his
notes for statistics, he enumerated the evils of war. This "monstrous and impious usage" was "utterly ineffectual to secure or advance" justice; it produced only "wasted lands, ruined and fam-
ished cities, and slaughtered armies." What was even worse, it
destroyed human nature, for war was "a temporary adoption, by
men, of the character of wild beasts, emulating their ferocity, rejoicing like them in blood."

Why, then, were wars still fought? Sumner asked. Partly because men had a mistaken belief in their necessity; partly because they relied upon the "feeble tapers that glimmer in the
sepulchres of the Past," rather than upon "those ever-burning
lights" of present progress. Still another reason was the support
the Christian Church gave to warfare. A mistaken view of honor
and "a selfish and exaggerated *love of country*" also perpetuated

[9] Unless otherwise noted, all quotations in the following paragraphs are
from the contemporary pamphlet edition of *The True Grandeur of Nations*
(Boston: William D. Ticknor and Company; 1845), which is considerably
different from the often revised and somewhat subdued version that appears
in Sumner: *Works*, I, 1–132. The manuscript of Sumner's address (Sumner
MSS., Houghton Lib.) differs in only slight verbal matters from the pamphlet
version.

the martial spirit. "Our country, be she *right or wrong*," announced Sumner, was "a sentiment dethroning God and enthroning the Devil."

But perhaps the weightiest cause of conflict was "the costly *preparations* for war, in time of peace." With their armies and navies, their cannon and their fighting ships, nations were like "the wild boar in the fable, who whetted his tusks on a tree in the forest, when no enemy was near, saying that in time of peace he must prepare for war." Even the United States government, Sumner noted, spent more than seven times as much for "*peaceful preparations for war*" as for "all other purposes whatsoever."

And for what purpose were these warlike preparations? the orator continued. The army of the United States, trained in "farcical and humiliating exercises," performed no useful function. Its officers were educated at that "seminary of idleness and vice," West Point. Similarly, the navy had no purpose, for it would be "an unavailing defence against any serious attack." As for the militia, he announced, addressing himself directly to the officers in front of him, though they might dress "in padded and well-buttoned coats of blue, 'besmeared with gold,' surmounted by a huge mountain-cap of shaggy bear skin, and with a barbarous device, typical of brute force, a tiger, painted on oil-skin tied with leather to their backs," they were not even competent to put down a street riot, much less to defend a nation.

Americans, Sumner concluded, must recognize that the true grandeur of nations lies, not in warfare, but "in moral elevation, enlightened and decorated by the intellect of man." Then would come the "true golden age." "Then," declared the orator in a final burst of rhetoric, "shall the naked be clothed and the hungry fed. Institutions of science and learning shall crown every hill-top; hospitals for the sick . . . shall nestle in every valley; while spires of new churches shall leap exulting to the skies. . . . The eagle of our country, without the terror of his beak, and dropping the forceful thunderbolt from his pounces, shall soar with the olive of Peace, into untried realms of ether, nearer to the sun."

Immediately following the oration, Sumner, the city officials, and the invited guests repaired to Faneuil Hall for the customary July 4 dinner, and here the animosity that had been accumulating while the orator spoke exploded. Thirteen toasts were given, and nearly all the responses showed hostility toward Sumner and his ideas. Even his friend Palfrey announced that "he was not, on the fourth of July, willing to forget that Massachusetts sent one soldier for every three to the armies which fought the battles of independence." J. C. Park, of the state senate, bitterly attacked Sumner for the inappropriateness of his oration and for the rudeness with which he had assailed the military men present, the invited guests of the city, as "so many lions, tigers, or other wild beasts." Adjutant General Oliver praised the American Revolution as a defensible and desirable war, which "gave to the world a new nation, . . . permitting to each man the right to think, act and speak whatever he lawfully may, he himself being the best and only judge of the fitness of time, place and presence." The allusion was not missed.

The most weighty of all the rebukes came from Congressman Robert C. Winthrop, who spoke authoritatively for the Whig oligarchy of Massachusetts. Feeling that Sumner "seemed to contemplate non-resistance and dissolution of the Union," he replied to a toast by bluntly stating his own doctrine: "Our Country, whether bounded by Sabine or Del Norte—still our Country— to be cherished in all our hearts—to be defended by all our hands."

To keep the audience from becoming vicious, the toastmaster, Sumner's friend P. W. Chandler, decided "to throw the whole thing into broad farce" and "began by criticizing the oration, and asked what more or better you could expect from an old bachelor. How could a man who never knew anything of domestic broils feel competent to speak of war? What were the discomforts of a camp to a washing day at home?" This kind of coarse nonsense tickled the crowd, and Chandler even got some applause for the toast: "The orator of the day. However much we may differ from his sentiments, let us admire the simplicity, manliness and ability with which he has expressed them."

Sumner rose and "said he would not follow the apple of discord which he appeared to have thrown out." Instead he replied with another toast: "The youthful choristers of the day—May their future lives be filled with happiness, as they have filled our hearts to-day with the delights of their music." [1]

[1] Boston *Post*, July 7, 1845; Winthrop to J. H. Clifford, Jan. 7, 1846, copy, Winthrop MSS.; Chandler to Pierce, Aug. 27, 1877, Pierce MSS.

· 4 ·

His Fourth of July oration, Sumner objectively reported a few weeks later, "was delivered to a large and applauding audience, and has been received . . . by some persons with very great favor, and by others with condemnation. It is admitted on all sides to be bold and fearless, and many who condemn its sentiments praise its style."[2]

Many influential persons were outraged by "The True Grandeur of Nations." Samuel A. Eliot, former mayor of the city and treasurer of Harvard College, stiffly remonstrated with Sumner for sacrificing "a reputation for good judgment and civility" to "the applause of thousands of excited and enthusiastic persons." He summarized the opinion of Beacon Hill: "The young man has cut his own throat." A "Citizen of Boston" published an irate pamphlet attacking Sumner as a theorist, questioning his taste in presenting a Peace Society oration on such an occasion, ridiculing his "harsh and unpolished . . . involved and obscure" style, and riddling his faulty logic and history. L. M. Goldsborough, of the United States navy, angrily challenged Sumner's statistics on American expenditures for armaments and branded the oration as a "collation of irrelevant shreds and patches . . . exceedingly deficient in manliness, originality, and accuracy." The Boston Post rebuked Sumner for his "mixture of monomania, sophistry and presumption" in delivering on the Fourth of July "a discourse appropriate perhaps for an insane Quaker in his dotage."[3]

Many of Sumner's friends were distressed by his oration. Nathan Appleton, a practical man whose income depended upon the importation of Southern cotton into the port of Boston, was unwilling "to leave our harbors unprotected and to rely for safety on the character of non-combatism." Like President Quincy,

---

[2] Sumner to Sarah P. Cleveland, Aug. 15, 1845, copy, Longfellow MSS.

[3] Eliot to Sumner, Aug. 19, 1845, Sumner MSS.; Allan Nevins: Ordeal of the Union (New York: Charles Scribner's Sons; 1947), I 393; Remarks Upon an Oration Delivered by Charles Sumner Before the Authorities of the City of Boston, July 4th, 1845. By a Citizen of Boston (Boston: Wm. Crosby & H. P. Nichols; 1845), esp. pp. 8, 15; Goldsborough: A Reply . . . to an Attack Made Upon the Navy of the United States, . . . In which a Brief Notice is Taken of the Recent Fourth of July Oration, Delivered at Boston, by Charles Sumner (Portsmouth: C. W. Brewster; 1845), esp. pp. 18, 22; Boston Post, Aug. 21, 1845.

he was troubled by the extremism of Sumner's views, but conceded: "It is sometimes necessary to 'cut beyond the wound' . . . to go for the whole in order to get half." Remembering "the Poles, and the negroes at the South," Horace Mann thought there were some cases where "people would be justified, before the holiest tribunal, for declaring and waging even the most extirminating [sic] war." "By all those who fought and bled at Marathon; by those who fought at Morgarten and Bannockburn; by those who fought and bled at Bunker's Hill," Prescott denied Sumner's proposition that all wars were dishonorable. Lieber sneered at Sumner as "a new Archangel Michael with a flybrush instead of a sword," and Chancellor Kent gave opinion that Sumner's oration, though "beautifully classic and eminently benevolent," revealed his mind to be "diseased manifestly . . . on certain subjects." [4]

Two dissents cost Sumner more pain than all the other criticism combined. Justice Story, now within a few weeks of his death, read the oration and disagreed with Sumner. Too kindly to be harsh upon a favorite pupil, whom he had treated as a member of his family and had once destined to be his successor in the Harvard Law School, Story admitted the justice of Sumner's strictures upon war and praised his "exalted mind . . . and enlarged benevolence." But he added firmly: "In my judgment war is under some . . . circumstances not only justifiable, but an indispensable part of public Duty. . . . In the extent, to which you press your doctrines, they are not in my judgment defensible." Congressman Winthrop, quasi-official representative of the Massachusetts Whig party, also vigorously dissented. He wrote Sumner that his toast at the July 4 dinner had been no offhand remark; defensive wars were justifiable, and the American Revolution had been worth its cost in blood. [5] The doors of both Boston and the Harvard Law School were closing in Sumner's face.

Sumner gained some comfort from the fact that many peo-

[4] Appleton to Sumner, Aug. 11, 1845, Sumner MSS.; Mann to Sumner, Sept. 8, 1845, ibid.; Ticknor: *Prescott*, p. 377; Lieber to Sumner, June 25, 1845, Lieber MSS.; C. H. Van Tyne (ed.): *The Letters of Daniel Webster* . . . (New York: McClure, Phillips & Co.; 1902), p. 334. Many of the letters Sumner received on this occasion are printed in W. C. Ford (ed.): "Sumner's Oration on the 'True Grandeur of Nations,' July 4, 1845," *MHSP*, L (1916–17), 249–307.

[5] Story to Sumner, Aug. 11, 1845, Sumner MSS.; Winthrop to Sumner, July 9, 1845, ibid.; Sumner to Winthrop, July 6, 1845, Winthrop MSS.

ple did approve his peace doctrines. Requests for copies of the oration poured in from all parts of New England, from New York, and from as far west as Kentucky and Ohio. Many of his enthusiastic correspondents were embattled, doctrinaire reformers, a group with whom he had hitherto had little contact. Such antislavery crusaders as William Lloyd Garrison, Gerrit Smith, and J. M. McKim praised the oration. Theodore Parker, the hard-hitting Unitarian heretic, barred from most of Boston's pulpits because of his daring social and theological ideas, initiated a correspondence with Sumner, lauding him "for so nobly exposing the evils of war, its worthlessness and its waste." The principal figure in the American Peace Society, Elihu Burritt, the learned blacksmith, who was now organizing a world crusade to outlaw war, wrote Sumner simply: "The cause of Peace dates principally from your oration." [6]

The Peace Society immediately asked to republish the oration, and it rapidly went through six editions. A copy was sent to each member of Congress, in the hope that it might help avert a threatened war with England over the Oregon boundary. Abroad, too, the speech had a large audience. In Liverpool the Peace Society published an edition of 7,500 copies, sending them to the Queen, the Duke of Wellington, Sir Robert Peel, and other notables. Five or six editions were printed in London, and near the Royal Exchange, news venders hawked it as ha'penny a copy as "Sumner's Speech agin war with England." [7]

From two continents grateful words of praise rolled in. "That oration will live," a Boston admirer predicted. "It will be a textbook for hundreds. . . . Should you never do anything else, than you have now done—you will not have lived in vain." [8]

Sumner pretended to be indifferent to both the censure and the praise his oration elicited. In fact, however, he shrank sensitively under the unaccustomed criticism. During the weeks fol-

[6] Parker to Sumner, Aug. 17, 1845, Sumner MSS.; Burritt to Sumner, Nov. 19, 1845, ibid.

[7] John W. Tatum to Sumner, Mar. 9, 1854, ibid.; Christina Phelps: *The Anglo-American Peace Movement in the Mid-Nineteenth Century* ("Columbia University Studies in History, Economics, and Public Law," No. 330, New York: Columbia University Press; 1930), p. 71; Merle E. Curti: *The American Peace Crusade, 1815–1860* (Durham: Duke University Press; 1929), pp. 121–2; William Hayden to Sumner, June 19 [1846], Sumner MSS.

[8] R. C. Waterston to Sumner, July 7, 1845, Sumner MSS. Merle Curti (*American Peace Crusade*, p. 120) agrees that the oration had an "epoch-making significance in the history of the peace movement."

lowing July 4 he spent much of his time writing long, troubled letters explaining and defending his positions. To add to his discomfort he developed boils—one, as Felton pointed out, "on the shoulder, just where the epaulette is worn, and another on the side, where the sword hangs." [9]

He was genuinely surprised by the storm he had stirred up. He had intended nothing more than an oratorical display of fairly common opinions that he earnestly shared. Neither now, or at any time during his later career, did he make any great claim to be an original thinker. A hostile critic complained with some justice that the oration contained "nothing new in its sentiments, its arguments, or its illustrations," though he went too far in calling it "a birds-nest built out of materials gathered from all quarters, and without any great scrupulousness or delicacy as to their quality or value." Even an admirer pointed out that Sumner's oration contained the same ideas as Channing's sermons.[1] Channing had observed that war "turns man into a beast of prey"; Sumner called war "a temporary adoption, by men, of the character of wild beasts." "Justice and force have little congeniality," Channing preached; Sumner, weighing war's "sufficiency as a mode of determining justice between nations," found "that it is a rude appeal to force or a gigantic game of chance, in which God's children are profanely dealt with as a pack of cards." Channing and Sumner used identical words in condemning any American conflict with England as a civil war between brothers. On other points Sumner echoed the ideas, and sometimes the very words, of William Ladd, William Jay, and other advocates of international peace.[2]

Nor was Sumner's oration distinguished for its logical force. The historical incidents, classical quotations, and statistics on military expenditures which he cited were, properly speaking, not arguments at all, but illustrations of generalizations so obvious as to require no proof.[3] Everybody agreed that wars are un-

[9] Felton to Longfellow, Aug. 9, 1845, Longfellow MSS.
[1] *Remarks upon an Oration Delivered by Charles Sumner . . . By a Citizen of Boston*, pp. 8–9; John Tappan to Sumner, July 5, 1845, Sumner MSS.
[2] *The Works of William E. Channing* (Boston: James Munroe and Company; 1841), IV, 55; V, 118; Sumner: *True Grandeur of Nations*, pp. 9, 81. Sumner acknowledged his borrowing in his elaborate annotations.
[3] R. Elaine Pagel and Carl Dallinger: "Charles Sumner," in William Norwood Brigance (ed.): *A History and Criticism of American Public Address* (New York: McGraw-Hill Book Co.; 1943), pp. 751–76.

fortunate, bloody, and undesirable; everybody knew that preparations for war are expensive. The oration was the earliest public demonstration of Sumner's propensity for what might be called illogical logicality, his tendency to extend a principle to its utmost limits. Given the assumption that war is bad, Sumner thought it followed that all wars are equally bad. As a nation, like an individual, should do only what is good, the United States should always and under all circumstances eschew war.

No one could have taken Sumner's "The True Grandeur of Nations" as a practical guide to world peace. Except for passing references to a possible congress of nations and to international arbitration, Sumner said nothing about how wars were to be prevented. The oration was a perfect example of Channing's technique of reform through verbal exorcism, through public disapproval of an institution considered wrong. On the practical question of how even this verbal outlawing of war could be secured, Sumner's sole advice was: "*Believe* that you can do it, and you *can* do it." [4]

If it is not hard to understand why the oration exasperated so many of Sumner's hearers, the acclaim it received from reformers is also easy to explain. To the leaders in the peace crusade, whose writings had been distinguished more for good intentions than for good grammar, "The True Grandeur of Nations" seemed a marvel of learning and rhetoric. Sumner lent reputability to the peace movement, for he spoke as one who had "enjoyed the rare advantages of having graduated at Harvard; studied law with Justice Story; and, withal, basked in the allurements of foreign climes." [5]

The eloquence of the address, too, made a tremendous impression upon his audience. Sumner's emphasis upon Christian truths, his simple faith that a nation must obey the same moral law as an individual, his invocation of faith, justice, and duty reminded his older listeners of the half-forgotten principles on which New England had originally been founded; his appeal to progress inspired the young. If the ideas in the oration were not new, the rhetoric in which they were clad was fresh and original. One cannot, of course, separate the oration from the orator. Sum-

---

[4] Sumner: *Works*, I, 129.
[5] Goldsborough: *A Reply . . . to an Attack Made Upon the Navy*, p. 22.

ner's handsome presence, his obvious sincerity, his deep, convincing voice, his flashing eye kindled with righteousness—all gave magic to words that read coldly upon the printed page.

The circumstances under which Sumner delivered his oration lent it additional interest and importance. "Had it been delivered before a Peace Society," Sumner's sharpest critic declared, "we should never have raised our . . . voice against it." But Sumner spoke, it seemed, in the very mouth of the cannon. Since he was, as Wendell Phillips once remarked, like "a cat without smellers," it was not, in fact, so much audacity as insensitivity to the weight and edge of his own words that led Sumner to look the city's military guests in the eye and denounce "the pride, pomp and circumstance of glorious war" or to point to the frowning guns of the warship in the harbor and ask: "What is the use of the Navy of the United States?" But his listeners thought it an act of high moral courage. "You mistake your vocation, my dear Sumner," one of his friends wrote him. "You should be a soldier and a general—The bravery which led you to declare such a doctrine on such a day would secure you laurels and arches." As the Boston essayist E. P. Whipple summarized: "The great success of Sumner was due to the fact that this oration was studiously framed so as to be utterly *in*appropriate to the occasion." [6]

· 5 ·

Though Felton warned that Elihu Burritt and his peace reformers were "sentimental idiots . . . with their cant and fee-faw-fum," Sumner relished their praise, which was all the more grateful because respectable Boston disapproved of him. He pledged eternal devotion to a cause he had hitherto only cautiously endorsed, and, holing up in Felton's Cambridge house for several weeks, carefully revised his oration, adding citations, appendices, arguments, and footnotes in Greek, Latin, French, and Italian. "You have no idea what an arsenal of peace arms my home has become," Felton joked. "Lives of William Penn, Sermons on War, tracts of the American Peace Society, journals anti-every-thing, Scriptural arguments, estimates of the costs of navies and

[6] *Remarks upon an Oration Delivered by Charles Sumner . . . By a Citizen of Boston*, p. 30; B. D. Silliman to Sumner, Sept. 8, 1845, Sumner MSS.; Whipple: *Recollections of Eminent Men*, p. 213.

armies, besides a great many smaller arms—the pistols, hand grenades, cutlasses and so forth of the Peace Establishment— are arranged in every part of the house—upstairs, downstairs, in the attic, and in the cellar." [7]

During the next four years Sumner rarely neglected an occasion to depict the grandeur of peace and the horror of war. In 1846 he devoted a large part of his Phi Beta Kappa oration at Harvard to lauding Channing for understanding "that the fairest flowers cannot bloom in soil moistened by human blood." The following summer he urged the students at Amherst to recognize that as all God's "children are brethren, . . . ALL WAR BE- COMES FRATRICIDAL." In newspaper letters he protested against the governor's appearing in church accompanied by an "escort of his fellow-citizens, dressed in strange harlequin garments, and with burnished weapons of war," and he implored the Massachusetts clergy not to "lend themselves to the fanfaronade of a militia celebration" on the traditional Artillery Election Day. [8]

Sumner's most ambitious contribution to the peace crusade was a long oration titled "The War System of the Commonwealth of Nations," which he delivered to the American Peace Society in 1849. Very proud of this address, Sumner was convinced that he had not merely cogently restated all the old arguments against war, but had put the peace movement on a "thoroughly *practicable* foundation." Actually, he mostly summarized, with rhetorical flourishes, the conventional peace advocates' picture of war as a "damnable profession—a trade of barbarians," and urged, in almost precisely the same words William Ladd had used years before: "The most complete and permanent substitute for War would be a Congress of Nations, and a High Court of Judicature organized in pursuance thereof." [9]

If Sumner made any contribution to the ideas of the peace movement, it was his theory that war should be outlawed through international law. For years he had been struck by the

[7] Felton to Sumner [July? 1845], Sumner MSS.; Felton to Longfellow, Aug. 9, 1845, Longfellow MSS.

[8] Sumner: *The Scholar, The Jurist, The Artist, The Philanthropist*, pp. 63–4; Sumner: *Fame and Glory* . . . (Boston: William D. Ticknor and Company; 1847), p. 38; Boston *Chronotype*, Nov. 7, 1847; Boston *Semi-Weekly Courier*, Dec. 20, 1847.

[9] Sumner to George Sumner, June 19, 1849, Segal Coll.; Sumner to Amasa Walker, June 29, 1849, Walker MSS.; Sumner: *The War System*, pp. 20, 60. Cf. William Ladd: "Essay on a Congress of Nations . . . ," in *Prize Essays on a Congress of Nations* (Boston: Whipple & Damrell; 1840), p. 521.

fact that the law of nations recognized war as a means, even if a last, unhappy means, by which countries could secure their rights. This, in Sumner's opinion, was comparable to the barbarous usage of permitting individuals to resort to force, as in dueling, to redress wrongs. Just as municipal law outlawed violence between citizens, and the American Constitution outlawed violence between states, so should international law ban war as "impious, monstrous and unchristian." Once the law of nations was changed, war would disappear, and with it "forts, navies, armies, military display, military chaplains and military sermons." [1] The difficulties involved in changing international law or in yielding national sovereignty to some international organization never occurred to Sumner. He was concerned with principles, not with mechanics.

Thoroughly pleased with his own efforts in behalf of peace, Sumner was distressed that so few of his close friends took him seriously as a thinker on international affairs. Only Hillard and Longfellow really approved his course; Richard Henry Dana, Jr., spoke for the rest when he declared that Sumner's views on peace were "in inextricable confusion." When they questioned Sumner, he was repeatedly obliged to modify his positions. Though he insisted that he was voicing Christian principles in denouncing war, he maintained that the strength of his argument was "entirely independent of the texts of the Gospels." Though he repeatedly praised the Quakers for understanding that force availed nothing against *unarmed virtue* and *truth*," he declared that he was not a nonresistant. He thought a purely defensive war unlikely, "at least in our age, and with reference to our country," but, when closely cross-examined, he was obliged to admit that nations, like individuals, did have the right to self-defense. "If sorrowfully, necessarily, the sword may be taken as the instrument of Justice," Sumner finally restated his position, "it can never be *the Arbiter of Justice*." In effect, this meant that Sumner thought all war was horrible and that he opposed aggressive wars. [2]

[1] *MHSP*, L, 264; Sumner to George Putnam, Apr. 1848, author's copy, Sumner MSS.; Sumner: *War System*, pp. 13, 23.

[2] Dana to Julia Ward Howe, Feb. 9, 1876, Howe MSS.; Sumner: *The War System*, p. 6; Sumner to Winthrop, July 6, 1845, Winthrop MSS.; *MHSP*, L, 262; Sumner to Everett, Sept. 7, 1846, Everett MSS.; Sumner to R. H. Dana, Jr., [August 1845], Dana MSS.; Sumner's undated memorandum, enclosed in Amasa Walker, to Sumner, June 4 1849, Sumner MSS.

However much Sumner's friends approved these more cautiously stated views, his Peace Society associates were greatly disappointed in his watered-down opinions. While publicly praising Sumner's "War System" oration as "the mightiest word for peace that has yet been spoken," the pacifist editor of the *Christian Citizen* privately rebuked Sumner for lowering the standard of the Peace Society by admitting the possibility of a defensive war. In the eyes of extreme nonresistants Sumner was becoming merely another man who favored peace, not a Peace Society man.[3]

Though Sumner continued to announce that the outlawing of war was "the question of *our age*," especially important because the economies of disarmament offered European nations the only practical way of curing their ills and "of meeting *socialism*," he drifted away from the peace movement after 1849. The European Revolutions of 1848 caused him to see that inflexible advocacy of peace often meant support of the reactionary status quo. In these contests between tyranny and liberty, he announced, "all our sympathies must be with Freedom, while, in our sorrow at the unwelcome combat, we confess that victory is only less mournful than defeat." Retaining a nominal affiliation with the peace movement down into the 1850's, and occasionally sponsoring international mediation or arbitration, Sumner gradually came to feel that this cause was less important than other reforms. "One evil at a time," he said, and turned to other crusades.[4] When war came in 1861, America's foremost peace advocate solidly supported the military measures of the Union government.

· 6 ·

Even before Sumner became famous as a peace advocate, he had become fiercely involved in a dispute over penal reform. Like all

[3] Curti: *American Peace Crusade*, p. 122; Thomas Drew to Sumner, June 11, and 20, 1849, Sumner MSS.; Sumner to Amasa Walker, June 11, 1849, Walker MSS. On factionalism in the peace movement see Curti: *American Peace Crusade*, Chap. iv, and Alice Felt Tyler: *Freedom's Ferment: Chapters in American Social History to 1860* (Minneapolis: University of Minnesota Press; 1944), pp. 409–13.

[4] Sumner to George Sumner, May 16, 1848, Sumner MSS.; Sumner to Joshua R. Giddings, Aug. 20, 1849, Giddings-Julian MSS.; Sumner: *The War System*, p. 66; Sumner: *Works*, II, 393–7; Sumner to Henry Richards, Apr. 4, 1854, Sumner MSS.; G. C. Beckwith to Sumner, Feb. 21, 1861, ibid.

the other crusades in which Sumner engaged, improvement of prisons was considered a perfectly respectable interest even by eminently conservative Bostonians. Since 1825 the Boston Prison Discipline Society, which was run by its influential secretary, Louis Dwight, issued reports "that served as penal textbooks for governors, legislators, and prison officers throughout the country." Such Boston leaders as A. A. Lawrence and John T. Bigelow belonged to the society, subscribed generously to its funds, and attended its public meetings each spring during Anniversary Week, when Dwight reported on the cheering progress of the good cause.[5]

Though Sumner was too young to take any active role in these proceedings until the 1840's, his interest in penal reform, like his concern for education and international peace, had been aroused many years earlier. As editor of *The American Jurist* he had entered into correspondence with such penologists as Lieber, Alexis de Tocqueville, N. H. Julius, of Prussia, and Joseph Adshead, of England. After his return from Europe, his "friend, and . . . idol," Channing, urged him to take a more vigorous interest in prisons, and Sumner accompanied Dorothea Dix, another of the great minister's disciples, on her visits to expose the shocking state of Massachusetts jails and asylums.[6]

If Sumner's ideas about penal reform derived largely from Channing, his impetus for action, once again, came from Howe. Shocked to find that, after decades of agitation by the Boston Prison Discipline Society, the idiots, the feeble-minded, and the insane of Massachusetts were still being herded into noisome jails along with hardened criminals, Howe concluded that the reform society itself needed reformation. As early as 1842 he and Sumner eyed the well-paid secretaryship of the society as an ideal haven for their friend Lieber, who was discontented in his South

[5] Blake McKelvey: *American Prisons: A Study in American Social History Prior to 1915* (Chicago: University of Chicago Press; 1936), Chap. i, esp. pp. 9–10; Stewart Holbrook: *Dreamers of the American Dream* (Garden City, N.Y.: Doubleday & Company, Inc.; 1957), pp. 240–3.

[6] Pierce, II, 227; Channing: *Channing*, III, 25–9; Francis Tiffany: *Life of Dorothea Lynde Dix* (Boston: Houghton Mifflin Co.; 1890), p. 75; Helen E. Marshall: *Dorothea Dix: Forgotten Samaritan* (Chapel Hill: University of North Carolina Press; 1937), p. 95. On European interest in American prisons see Frank Thistlethwaite: *The Anglo-American Connection in the Early Nineteenth Century* (Philadelphia: University of Pennsylvania Press; 1959), pp. 88–9.

Carolina exile, and contemplated making "a severe onslaught on the incumbent." [7]

Not until the collapse of his personal happiness and his severe physical breakdown in 1844 could Sumner be persuaded actively to enter upon a crusade to oust Dwight. When he turned his full attention to the Boston Prison Discipline Society, he found, in his new mood of pessimism and disillusionment, that Dwight embodied everything that was wrong about Boston: he was a part of the inbred ruling aristocracy; he was "*lazy to the last degree*"; he was provincial and bigoted; he knew "nothing of the European mind." [8] Dwight's narrow-mindedness, Sumner thought, was clearly exhibited in his attitude toward the rival systems of prison discipline which prevailed in the United States in the 1840's. In the separate system, best exemplified in the Eastern Penitentiary at Cherry Hill, Philadelphia, each prisoner was confined in an absolutely isolated, separate cell. The rival congregate system, developed at Auburn and Sing Sing, New York, also isolated prisoners in separate cubicles at night, but during the day they marched, in lock step, and worked together, but with all communication prohibited by the ever present threat of the lash.[9] The bitter rivalry between the partisans of the two systems had deep emotional undertones. As the Pennsylvania plan was so much more expensive than the Auburn system, the argument involved the perennial battle between the idealistic reformer and the practical administrator concerned with money. As European governments tended to admire the separate system while American states more often followed the congregate plan,

---

[7] Howe to Lieber, Aug. 17, and Sept. 5, 1842, Lieber MSS. On Howe and prison discipline see Schwartz: *Howe*, pp. 147–9. Sumner at this point joined the Prison Discipline Society and donated $2.00. *Eighteenth Annual Report of the Board of Managers of the Boston Prison Discipline Society* (Boston: Damrell and Moore; 1843), p. 109.

[8] Sumner to Howe [July 27, 1846], Sumner MSS.; Sumner to Francis Wayland, May 30, 1845, Wayland MSS.

[9] Tyler: *Freedom's Ferment*, pp. 265–85; O. F. Lewis: *The Development of American Prisons and Prison Customs, 1776–1845* (Albany; 1922); Harry Elmer Barnes: *The Evolution of Penology in Pennsylvania* (Indianapolis: The Bobbs-Merrill Company, Inc.; 1927); Negley K. Teeters and John D. Shearer: *The Prison at Philadelphia Cherry Hill: The Separate System of Prison Discipline, 1829–1913* (New York: Columbia University Press; 1957), esp. pp. 201–23. By modern standards both systems were strikingly inhumane. If the Auburn plan seemed ideally devised for turning out hardened criminals, the Pennsylvania system, as Barnes remarks (p. 291), could make serious pretensions only to converting its inmates into Robinson Crusoes, "broken and unoffending hermits."

the controversy became partly one between cosmopolitanism and nationalism.

An idealist who prided himself upon never counting the cost, an internationalist who was much influenced by such European penologists as Tocqueville, Sumner was horrified to find that Dwight had committed the Boston Prison Discipline Society to unrelenting warfare against the Pennsylvania system and that his reports had become an arsenal for advocates of the Auburn plan. After unsuccessfully attempting to remonstrate with the secretary in private, he decided that Dwight must go.

The first stage of Sumner's assault upon the unsuspecting Dwight came during the annual meeting of the Prison Discipline Society at Park Street Church in May 1845, which promised to be the usual cut-and-dried affair. Dwight, "a stout person, with a hard, red face and a dogmatic manner," read extracts from his report, and John T. Bigelow made some animadversions upon the Pennsylvania system. At this point, when the customary formal motion to accept the secretary's report was expected, Sumner rose and claimed the floor. Unceremoniously he "mounted upon the rail of his pew, and passed rapidly from pew to pew till he stood upon the platform." Most of the audience did not recognize the tall and rather slender young man, "with a shock of black hair not very carefully arranged, dressed in a blue frock-coat, buttoned, with a velvet collar," and even Francis Wayland, the president of the society, had to inquire his name.

Not waiting for an introduction, Sumner seized the lectern and launched into an arraignment of Dwight and his report. He showed "how the Pennsylvania system was regarded by all the governments of Europe . . . and argued that it was not right for the Boston Prison Discipline Society to continue to malign and misrepresent a system which most of the members had had no means of examining." For half an hour he continued, carrying his audience with him. Though Dwight retorted angrily, Sumner's motion to refer the secretary's report to a select committee was adopted; furthermore, the committee, to which both Sumner and Howe were appointed, was authorized to visit Philadelphia and inspect the system Dwight had so energetically condemned.[1]

During the months following his unexpected appearance

[1] Pierce, III, 81–2; Boston *Post*, May 28, 1845; Howe to Lieber, May 28, 1845, Lieber MSS.; G. B. Emerson to Dorothea L. Dix, May 27, 1845, Dix MSS.

before the Prison Discipline Society, Sumner continued his agitation against Dwight and won some converts for his views. Thus
far he had surprised, but not alienated, Boston society. A large
body of expert opinion agreed with him that the Pennsylvania
system was greatly preferable, and even a stalwart conservative
like Nathan Hale, editor of the Boston *Advertiser*, thought
Dwight wrong in serving as an advocate of the Auburn plan.[2]
In October 1845 the special committee spent three days at the
Eastern Penitentiary, and Sumner returned more than ever convinced of the virtues of the separate system. Although the Society refused to print Howe's minority report praising the Pennsylvania plan, many Bostonians still had an open mind. Even George
Ticknor was willing to concede that Howe's report was a "most
important one," and A. A. Lawrence talked of subsidizing its publication.[3]

Sumner's extremism soon alienated most of this good will.
He insisted upon pushing his arguments to the uttermost. As all
penologists thought that criminals should not be permitted to
contaminate each other through conversation, he argued that
the Pennsylvania system, being more separate than the Auburn
system, was superior "on grounds of reason, independent of experience." "If separation be desirable," he asked with his usual
logic, "should it not be complete?"[4]

Even more disturbing to most Bostonians was Sumner's
newly discovered propensity to engage in personalities with
those who disagreed with him. At the May 1846 meeting of the
Prison Discipline Society he launched into an hour-long attack
upon Dwight. Ostensibly paying tribute to the secretary's labors
for the convict, he in fact minimized them in his repeated ironi-
cal references to Dwight's "indefatigable" exertions. Angrily Sumner drew up his indictment: Dwight had suppressed communications hostile to the congregate system; he had misquoted
authorities; he had ignored the painstaking reports of foreign
observers; he had misrepresented European penology. "If the

[2] Dorothea L. Dix: *Remarks on Prisons and Prison Discipline in the United
States* (Philadelphia: Joseph Hite & Co.; 1845), pp. 76–7; Francis Lieber: *A
Popular Essay on Subjects of Penal Law* . . . (Philadelphia; 1838), p. 90;
Schwartz: *Howe*, pp. 147–9; Hillard to Dorothea L. Dix, Feb. 9, 1846, Dix MSS.

[3] Sumner to Lieber, Dec. 15, 1845, Sumner MSS.; Sumner to A. A. Lawrence,
June 29, 1846, Lawrence MSS.; Ticknor: *Life, Letters and Journal*, II, 228.

[4] Sumner: *Works*, I, 165–71, 173.

facts and authorities to which I have referred, were withheld intentionally," Sumner charged, "it was most uncandid; if through ignorance, the ignorance was gross." Dwight's reports were "lies," *"wilful and unwarrantable perversions of truth."*

All Boston was shocked by the intemperance of Sumner's vituperation. Something, it seemed, had transformed this hitherto exceptionally agreeable, accommodating young man into a master of invective, whose words, uttered with fierce moral indignation, had the power to wound. Many observers thought they detected Sumner's real animus when he interrupted his tirade against Dwight to take an entirely gratuitous fling at Winthrop, whose July 4 toast still rankled: " 'Our country, right or wrong' is a cry that rises from the hoarse conclaves of politics. Let its spirit never intrude into any association like ours. Let none of us say, 'Our Society, right or wrong.' " [5]

Appointed to a committee to investigate Dwight's alleged misdeeds, Sumner and his friends spent much of the summer of 1846 agitating against the secretary. When Dwight's supporters refused to participate in the inquiry, Sumner and Hillard, who had persuaded President Wayland to go along with them, drew up a report showing up Dwight as "one of those singular individuals whose self esteem leads them to believe they are religious, honest and industrious, while in reality they are selfish, jesuitical and lazy." Not content with undermining Dwight at home, Sumner roused up his European friends against him. When Dwight attended the Frankfurt International Penitentiary Congress during the summer, Sumner's allies "out-generaled" him and prevented him from stating his case abroad; when he stopped in England on his way home, English penologists, all acquaintances of Sumner, snubbed the secretary. [6]

All these maneuvers were merely preliminary to the next annual meeting of the society, which opened in Tremont Temple on May 25, 1847. Dwight's report was more than ever hostile

[5] Hillard to Dorothea L. Dix, June 30, 1846, Dix MSS.; Boston *Advertiser*, May 28, 1846; Boston *Courier*, May 30, 1846; Sumner to Wayland, May 30, 1846, Wayland MSS.

[6] Howe to Lieber, July 30, 1846, Lieber MSS.; Richard Rathbone to Sumner, July 3, 1846, Sumner MSS.; N. H. Julius to Sumner, July 8, 1846, ibid. George Sumner, who was in Paris, published a letter at this time defending the separate system on the basis of recent French experiments in penology. *Mr. Sumner's Letter* (City of Boston, *City Document*, No. 11; 1846).

to the Pennsylvania system, and for the third consecutive year Sumner rose to reply. Loftily he moved that the secretary's report be tabled and that, instead, the society adopt resolutions announcing that it was not "the pledged advocate of the Auburn system" and praising the directors of the Eastern Penitentiary as "sincere, conscientious and philanthropic fellow-laborers." [7]

This time Dwight and his friends were prepared to put down Sumner as a brash interloper. Dwight himself opened the counteroffensive; Francis C. Gray was ready with facts and reasons to uphold the congregate system; and J. T. Stevenson, a representative of the textile manufacturers of Lowell, with whom Sumner was already at odds politically, ridiculed Sumner's logic. Most weighty of all was Eliot, "pompous and Boston personified," who was, as he reminded his hearers, a man of considerable importance—a former mayor of the city; treasurer of Harvard College; senator of the Commonwealth; treasurer of the Society. He did not need to remind them that he spoke not merely for himself, but for his large family connections—the Dwights, the Guilds, the Willises, the Curtises, the Ticknors—and for Boston respectability itself.[8]

The debates stretched over eight evenings (May 25–June 23) and as they became increasingly embittered, they attracted an enormous amount of public attention. On some nights more than 2,000 persons filled Tremont Temple, ostensibly to hear the merits of rival prison systems discussed, in reality to watch the antagonists "bait each other like dogs and bulls." "Night after night . . . the discussions have proceeded," one regular attendant reported, "until they are become the only evening amusement of the city." [9]

The drama of the debate lay in the fact that Sumner, nearly unaided, was taking on in a single fight all the organized powers that ruled Boston. He had alienated most of the moderates in the society and now had virtually no supporters besides Howe and Hillard. As the debates progressed, Howe spoke up

---

[7] E. D. Cheney to Pierce, Jan. 16, 1877, Pierce MSS.; Boston *Semi-Weekly Courier*, May 27, 1847.

[8] Elaborate accounts of the debates were carried in the Boston *Advertiser*, June 1, 1847, and in the Boston *Whig*, June 10, 12, 19, and 23, 1847.

[9] Mary Lesley Ames (ed.): *Life and Letters of Peter and Susan Lesley* (New York: G. P. Putnam's Sons; 1909), I, 151.

manfully, but he was no orator, and newspapers correctly belittled his efforts as "petulant, rambling, discursive, touching
everything and discussing nothing." Hillard was even less effective, for after a newspaper ridiculed the irritable, scolding tone
of his one speech as the prerogative of a person who appeared
"to be mid-way between the sexes" and who had, therefore, "the
right of exercising the privilege of the softer portion of humanity" whenever he felt testy, he lapsed into silence.[1]

Even without allies Sumner put up a magnificent fight, but
as the debates wore on, his temper grew increasingly acerb. With
renewed bitterness he repeated all his old charges against the society; even the loyal Hillard had to admit that his friend was
"not altogether conciliatory." Toward Eliot, Sumner manifested
positive venom. Striking through the treasurer at the Boston oligarchy, Sumner riddled Eliot's "vanity or self-esteem" which had
led him to intermeddle in subjects of which he was ignorant, and,
borrowing "something of his frankness, without his temper,"
sharply deflated his pretensions to be a philanthropist. Turning
on the platform so as to face Dwight directly, Sumner now explicitly charged that the secretary was lazy, inefficient, and extravagant. It would be hard, Sumner argued, to show that the
society was doing "any thing of much importance beyond the
publication of its annual report, a pamphlet of about one hundred pages." "Between its flimsy covers," Sumner shouted derisively, "is all that we have done." Flapping the pages of Dwight's
offending report high in the air above his head, he sneered: "Our
three thousand dollars have been wrapt here as in a napkin."[2]

As the protracted debate went on, arguments wore thread-
bare and the audience drifted away. At last somebody proposed
as a compromise that the society would pledge itself not to advocate any special system of prison discipline. Sumner accepted the
resolution; his opponents refused to concede anything. Finally,
on July 22, in a surprise move, made after most of the members
had left the hall for the evening, one of Eliot's relatives proposed
to lay the whole question on the table. There, despite entreaties

[1] Boston *Semi-Weekly Courier*, June 7, 1847; Boston *Post*, June 4, and 9,
1847.
[2] Longfellow, Diary, June 18, 1847, Longfellow MSS.; George Bemis, Diary,
June 29, 1847, Bemis MSS.; Hillard to Lieber, June 10, 1847, Lieber MSS.; Sumner: *Works*, I, 496–7; Boston *Semi-Weekly Courier*, June 3, 1847; Pierce, III, 89.

from Sumner, it remained. The next year, in a move designed to illustrate the solidity of Boston society, George Ticknor and George T. Curtis were elected to the board of managers of the society, Eliot was made president, and Dwight, who was suffering from a nervous breakdown, was re-elected secretary, a post he continued to hold until his death in 1854. In 1848, at Ticknor's suggestion, it was voted to hold no further public meetings of the Boston Prison Discipline Society.[3]

Sumner felt that he had accomplished something by his foray. Prison authorities in Philadelphia praised him; the New York Prison Discipline Society invited him to make an address; Tocqueville, Julius, and Adshead all supported his views in Europe. "The weight and influence of the Society abroad have already been broken—partly through our exertions," he reported, adding, with grim jubilation: "Mr. Dwight, the secretary, has become insane, whether incurably so or no, I do not know." [4]

But for these victories, if such they were, Sumner had a price to pay. Sumner's "inconceivable effrontery," his "brazen audacity," and his "vituperative declamation" made him a marked man. For his "close twisted cord of charge, imputation and innuendo, so scandalously interwoven" against Dwight, respectable Boston had an explanation: "The only supposition which will relieve him from the charge of being a malignant defamer of other men's reputation, is that of having a disordered intellect." "The scorpion sting of that speech," the newspapers predicted, "will be turned on its author." [5]

Far more than his activities for education or peace, Sumner's efforts in the prison-discipline dispute caused him to be banned from Boston society. For Beacon Hill George Ticknor said the last word. The principles of the Boston oligarchy, he announced, were "right, and its severity towards disorganizers, and social democracy in all its forms, is just and wise. . . . Unsound opinions must be rebuked, and you can no more do that, while you treat their apostles with favor, than you can discourage bad

[3] Boston *Advertiser*, Aug. 5, 1847; Sumner to George Sumner, May 30, 1848, Sumner MSS.

[4] Sumner to George Sumner, May 30, 1848, Sumner MSS.; Sumner to Alexis de Tocqueville, Sept. 15, 1847, ibid.

[5] Boston *Post*, June 2, 1847.

books at the moment you are buying and circulating them." [6] Though Ticknor lived until 1871, he never again spoke to Sumner.

Boston had an even sharper way of making Sumner feel its disapproval. On September 10, 1845, Joseph Story died, and a new Dane Professor had to be chosen for the Harvard Law School. It was a post about which Sumner had dreamed for years. Both Story and Greenleaf had virtually promised it to him; his trip to Europe had really been undertaken to fit him for teaching civil and international law. After Story's funeral, Sumner published in the Boston *Advertiser* an eloquent tribute to his departed friend—which incidentally happened to point up his own qualifications as friend of "the chief jurists of our time, in the classical countries of jurisprudence, France and Germany." His mail was full of letters that assumed that he would be named to the chair.[7] But Daniel Webster was said to oppose the appointment, and President Edward Everett acquiesced in the Corporation's unanimous choice of William Kent, son of the New York Chancellor.

Nor when Kent resigned after only two years was the post offered to Sumner. Chief Justice Lemuel Shaw declared that Sumner, in his temporary teaching assignments in the law school, "had not . . . rendered himself and his services acceptable to the students." [8] But in a private letter to Lieber, Kent explained the Corporation's action: "Sumner has become an outrageous Philanthropist—neglecting his Law, to patch up the world—to reform prisoners and convicts—put down soldiers and wars— and keep the solar system in harmonious action. . . . The conservative Corporation of Harvard College . . . consider Sumner in the Law-school, as unsuitable as a Bull in a china-shop." [9]

[6] Ticknor: *Life, Letters, and Journals*, II, 235.

[7] Sumner: *Works*, I, 144; John Jay to Sumner, Nov. 8, 1845, Sumner MSS.; Charles Sedgwick to Sumner, Nov. 28, 1845, ibid.; Sumner's autobiography, Palfrey MSS.

[8] Theodore Sedgwick to Sumner, Oct. 29, 1845, Sumner MSS.; Everett to Sumner, Aug. 22, 1846, ibid.; Lemuel Shaw to Everett, Sept. 14, 1849, Harvard College Papers, XV, ser. 2, 133.

[9] Kent to Lieber, June 15, 1847, Lieber MSS.

CHAPTER VI

Let the Lines Be Drawn

❧

M_{Y NAME}," Sumner modestly declared in 1845, "is connected somewhat with two questions, which may be described succinctly as those of peace and slavery. To these may be added prison-discipline." In all three reform movements the pattern of his participation was precisely the same. He started by holding ideas most New Englanders shared. Through the influence of Channing, his views on international peace, on prison discipline, and on slavery came to be more carefully thought out and more articulately expressed, but not until personal unhappiness increased Sumner's sensitivity to social injustice did he take an active part in agitating these issues. Once he appeared before the public, he was attacked, and the more he was criticized, the more inflexible his opinions became. Carrying his ideas to extremes, he alienated moderate opinion and placed himself, as George Ticknor announced, "outside the pale of society." [1]

· 1 ·

For as long as Sumner could remember, he had detested slavery. His father taught him that Negroes deserved not merely freedom, but equality and happiness as well. "It will do us no good to make the blacks as free as the whites," Sheriff Sumner de-

---

[1] Sumner to George Putnam, Apr. 1848, author's copy, Sumner MSS.; Pierce, III, 119.

clared, "unless we learn to have good feelings toward them, and treat them as well." Reading Lydia Maria Child's *An Appeal in Favor of that Class of Americans Called Africans*, a tract published in 1833, further helped convince Sumner of the injustice of both slavery and racial discrimination. He found his first actual sight of slaves, on his trip to Washington in 1834, shocking, and he was outraged by the bullying proslavery tone Calhoun's disciples adopted during the 1830's. In 1836 he wrote to Lieber: "We are becoming abolitionists at the North fast." [2]

Sumner's European travels had further strengthened his belief that the United States must abolish slavery. [3] Everywhere abroad he was told that slavery was his country's disgrace. At the Collège de France he heard a savant declare "that all the races of men have a common origin, [and] that of course they must be substantially alike at present," and at the Sorbonne he saw a practical illustration of this theory in the easy intermingling of Negroes and whites in the same law classes. In Italy at the Convent of Palazzuola, where he and Greene spent a few quiet days, he noted the "freedom, gentleness, and equality" with which the friars treated "an Abyssinian, very recently arrived from the heart of Africa, whose most torrid sun had burned upon him." When Sumner returned to America, he made all his friends cognizant of his "hatred of slavery." [4]

His views were anything but unique, for virtually everyone in Massachusetts shared them. Though the Democratic leaders of the state, dependent upon pro-Southern national administrations for patronage, were quiet on the question of slavery, every influential Massachusetts Whig spoke out openly against the

[2] C. P. Sumner's notebook titled "Miscellany," p. 78, C. P. Sumner MSS.; Lydia Maria Child to Sumner, July 7, 1856, Sumner MSS.; Sumner to Lieber, Jan. 9, 1836, ibid.

[3] Sumner to J. O. Sargent, Nov. 20, 1838, J. O. Sargent MSS. Years later John Forster circulated a rumor that Sumner, on his European trip, had been an apologist for slavery. Norton and Howe (eds.): *Letters of Charles Eliot Norton*, I, 422. Sumner's contemporary letters, such as that to Sargent, refute the charge. Sumner himself explicitly denied the story and suggested that Forster had probably remembered some words of George Sumner. John Bigelow: *Retrospections of an Active Life* (New York: Doubleday, Page & Company; 1913), IV, 76.

[4] Pierce, I, 247–8; II, 261; Theodore Sedgwick to Sumner, Oct. 11, 1842, Sumner MSS. Bitterly Sumner rejected the pretensions of Calhoun and his followers: "The Southerners, and slave-owners are Chinese in character; theirs is the celestial empire; and all who do not buy and sell human sinews are outer barbarians." Sumner to Lord Brougham, May 15, 1844, Brougham MSS.

South's peculiar institution. "I regard slavery as one of the greatest evils, both moral and political," Daniel Webster asserted in his famous reply to Hayne. Abbott Lawrence, Webster's rival for the control of Massachusetts Whiggery, announced that he had been "born an abolitionist," that "we were all abolitionists." In 1837 the Whig-dominated Massachusetts Senate, with near unanimity, adopted resolutions opposing the admission of additional slave states and demanding, in the name of "the principles of the Revolution and humanity," the abolition of slavery in the District of Columbia.

Massachusetts men differed, of course, on the best way to oppose slavery. Conservatives feared that direct agitation against slavery would undermine the Constitution and hoped that the slow processes of time would bring freedom to the Negro. A large segment of moderate opinion followed Webster, who admitted that "domestic slavery of the Southern States is a subject within the exclusive control of the States themselves," but frankly announced his "unwillingness to do anything that shall extend the slavery of the African race on the continent, or add other slaveholding States to the Union." Only a handful of extremists agreed with William Lloyd Garrison, who called for an immediate end to slavery throughout the land.[5]

Sumner was not one of these Garrisonians. Though he had subscribed for the *Liberator* since 1835, he did not approve its "vindictive, bitter, and unchristian" tone. Secure in the respectable, Whiggish society of Boston, Sumner appears never to have met Garrison before 1845. "Of the many abolition meetings held in Boston" during these martyr years of the antislavery movement, Garrison himself stated: "Mr. Sumner's presence was never recognized at any one of them. Why he never came—at least among the curious to hear—I know not."[6]

[5] Claude Moore Fuess: *Daniel Webster* (Boston: Little, Brown & Co.; 1930), II, 32, Boston *Whig*, June 19, 1846; Henry Wilson: *History of the Rise and Fall of the Slave Power in America* (Boston: Houghton Mifflin Co.; 1872), I, 370, 591.

[6] Garrison to Pierce, Oct. 25, 1876, Pierce MSS.; Garrison to Edmund Quincy, Aug. 16, 1872, Garrison MSS., Smith Coll. In the 1870's, angry with Sumner, Garrison doubted that he had ever subscribed for the *Liberator*, but more reliance can be placed on Sumner's positive contemporary statement: "The earliest newspaper that I remember to have subscribed for was the *Liberator*." Sumner to George Putnam, Apr. 1848, author's draft, Sumner MSS. Cf. Wendell Phillips, in *Twenty-First Annual Report Presented to the Massachusetts Anti-Slavery Society* . . . (Boston; 1853), p. 122; Sumner to Lord Morpeth, Jan. 29, 1847, Carlisle MSS.

Sumner's indifference to Garrisonianism did not mean a coolness to the cause of antislavery. In this, as in all other reform impulses, he followed Channing, who defied conservative Boston opinion in praising Garrison's followers as "advocates of the principles of freedom, justice, and humanity," but was himself unwilling to become an abolitionist. Unable to endorse the Garrisonians' blanket indictment of all slaveholders, to adopt their motto of "Immediate Emancipation," or to approve their "showy, noisy mode of action," Channing agreed that slavery was "radically essentially evil" and argued that Northerners should first dissociate themselves from this great sin and then plead the cause of the slave before that "grand moral tribunal, before which all communities stand, and must be judged." Under this "moral blockade" slaveholders would come to realize that they were condemned by "those great principles of justice and charity, with which the human heart is everywhere beginning to beat." [7]

Sumner's ideas on slavery were essentially an elaboration of Channing's. Unlike the Garrisonians, who denounced the Constitution as a proslavery document and desired no union with slaveholders, Sumner prided himself upon his "strong attachment to the Constitution and the Union." "Thank God!" he exclaimed, "the Constitution of the United States does not recognize man as *property.*" "The laws that sanction slavery are *local* and *municipal* in their character," he argued. Antislavery men, therefore, could not properly "seek, either through their own Legislatures or through Congress, to touch slavery in the States where it exists."

Opponents of slavery should not, on the other hand, "feel called upon to suppress their sympathy for the suffering slave." Sumner himself urged Longfellow to publish his "Poems of Slavery," and he tried in 1842 to get Boston lawyers to pledge that they would boycott claimants who attempted to recover fugitive slaves on Massachusetts soil. "The moralist, the statesman, the orator, the poet, all in their several ways and moods," he argued, should express their disapproval of slavery and thus "surround the Southern States with a *moral blockade.*"

There were also more direct ways in which antislavery men

[7] Channing: *Remarks on the Slavery Question, in a Letter to Jonathan Phillips, Esq.* (Boston: James Munroe and Company; 1839), pp. 5, 11–12; Brown: *Always Young for Liberty,* pp. 222–41.

could strike at the South's peculiar institution. Barred by the Constitution from attacking the domestic institutions of the slave states, they could properly and legally act wherever slavery was "a *national* evil, for which . . . the *nation* and all its parts are responsible." Specifically, as United States law established slavery in the District of Columbia and in the territories, regulated the interstate and coastal slave trade, and controlled the rendition of fugitive slaves, these were legitimate objects for Northern action. Another possibility, he noted ominously, lay in the fact that "the Constitution may be amended so that it shall cease to render any sanction to Slavery."

In 1846 Sumner summarized his antislavery position:

I think Slavery a sin, individual and national; and think it the duty of each individual to cease committing it, and, of course of each State, to do likewise. Massachusetts is a party to slave-holding, and is responsible for it, so long as it continues under the sanction of the Constitution of the United States. I would leave it to the *local* laws of each State. If the South persists in holding slaves let it not expect Massachusetts to aid or abet in the wrong. I cannot be a slave-holder; nor can I help upholding [i.e., to uphold] slaveholding.[8]

· 2 ·

Up until his illness of 1844 Sumner, though he did not conceal these antislavery opinions, took no part in agitating the issue. He did not "express in public his opposition to Slavery," he explained, because "there never had . . . been any occasion in which he was disposed to participate," because he could not "coincide in views with those who conducted the Anti-Slavery movement," and because he "had no relish for the strife of politics." [9]

He had been, in fact, quite content with the course Massachusetts Whig leaders were following on questions concerning slavery. He was enthusiastic about John Quincy Adams's "grand" fight against the Gag Rule, which choked off antislavery petitions

[8] Sumner to George Putnam, Apr. 1848, author's copy, Sumner MSS.; Pierce, II, 204; Sumner to Joshua R. Giddings, Dec. 21, 1846, Giddings MSS.; Boston *Advertiser*, Jan. 10, 1843; Sumner to Cleveland, Nov. 28, 1842, copy, Longfellow MSS.; Sumner to Maria Weston Chapman, Nov. 30 [1842], Weston MSS.; MHSP, LVII, 196. In Chap. IX, *infra*, I have given a more elaborate analysis of Sumner's antislavery theories.
[9] Sumner to George Putnam, Apr. 1848, author's copy, Sumner MSS.

to the House of Representatives. The ex-President, he cheered, "has rallied the North against the South, has taught them their right, and opened their eyes to the *bullying* (I dislike the word, as much as the thing) of the South." Though he deplored Webster's proslavery *Creole* letter and feared that he lacked "sympathy with the mass,—with humanity, with truth," his record seemed "clear, massive and statesmanlike" when compared with the "weakness and bad faith" of President John Tyler or the proslavery platform of the Democratic presidential candidate, James K. Polk, that "pot house politician, vulgar, ignorant, wayward." [1]

But, in 1844 a national emergency, which coincided with Sumner's personal crisis, shocked him out of his complacency and brought him actively into politics. Like Channing, he had for several years watched with growing concern the movement to annex the Republic of Texas to the United States. Neither he nor his Whig contemporaries in Massachusetts could see the annexation scheme in the calm second glance of history; he failed to comprehend that the migration of American settlers into Mexican territory had been but a part of the national westward movement, that the Texas revolution had been inspired by genuine grievances against Mexico, and that annexation was not the result of a proslavery conspiracy. Instead, he believed that Southern slaveholders, by playing upon the "prejudice, selfishness, and vanity" of President Tyler, had persuaded him to sign the treaty of annexation, and he rejoiced when the Senate rejected that "ditch-delivered drab." Tyler's subsequent maneuver to annex Texas through joint resolutions of the two houses of Congress Sumner thought clearly unconstitutional, but he feared that if elected, Polk, that "4th rate lawyer," would acquiesce in the proslavery scheme. [2]

In all these opinions Sumner was in complete agreement with the leaders of the Massachusetts Whig party. The movement to annex Texas deeply stirred the latent antislavery sentiment of New England. Not merely the Liberty party, which cam-

[1] Sumner to Lieber, Feb. 21, 1841, and July 18, 1842, ibid.; Pierce, II, 223; Sumner to Horatio Greenough, Sept. 16, 1841, copy, Sumner MSS.; Sumner to George Sumner, Feb. 28, 1846, ibid.
[2] Sumner to Howe, May 31, 1844, ibid.; Sumner to George Sumner, June 1, 1844, ibid.

paigned in 1844 upon a platform explicitly repudiating annexation, fought the Texas scheme; all segments of Massachusetts Whiggery did likewise. Abbott Lawrence, Nathan Appleton, and other cotton manufacturers attempted in March 1844 to start a free-state protest against annexation, and dropped their project only because of the difficulty of securing co-operation from Whigs in other states. When the Massachusetts General Court assembled in January 1845, it voted that the Commonwealth would "never by any act or deed give her consent to the further extension of slavery to any portion of the world." Even more significant was an allegedly nonpartisan public meeting held in Faneuil Hall on January 29, where an enthusiastic crowd adopted resolutions denouncing "the iniquitous project in its inception and in every stage of its progress, its means and its end, and all the purposes and pretenses of its authors." [3]

Sumner attended this anti-Texas rally, and he enthusiastically applauded its resolutions. There for the first time he heard Garrison, whose words "fell in fiery rain" upon the audience, and he noted that even in this Whig-controlled assembly there was "a very respectable number . . . in favor of a dissolution of the Union, in the event of the Annexation of Texas." As the joint resolution for annexation was pushed through Congress in February 1845, Sumner felt that anti-Texas sentiment had lifted public opinion "to a new platform of Anti-Slavery." By fall he reported to Lieber: "The Anti-Slavery element is becoming the controlling power in our state, and, I doubt, if any person could be sent [to Congress] who was not in favor of earnest efforts for the abolition of slavery under the Federal Constitution." [4]

Even while Sumner was predicting "Massachusetts will never give her vote for another slaveholder," the Whig opposition to Texas began to dwindle. All along, astute observers had noted that the most conspicuous figures in the anti-Texas movement were not the regular party chieftains, but a group of younger, more idealistic, and generally somewhat disaffected "Young Whigs." Such men as Charles Francis Adams, the son and grand-

---

[3] Martin Bauml Duberman: "Charles Francis Adams, 1807–1851" (unpublished Ph. D. dissertation, Harvard Univ.; 1957), pp. 250–1; Wilson: *Slave Power*, I, 622–3. Webster helped draft the resolutions, but was not present at the meeting.

[4] Sumner to Story, Feb. 5, 1845, Sumner MSS.; Sumner to Lieber, Nov. 19, 1845, ibid.

son of Presidents of the United States, Stephen C. Phillips, a Salem merchant with political aspirations, John G. Palfrey, formerly professor of theology at Harvard and currently Secretary of State to the Commonwealth, Henry Wilson, the Natick cobbler turned politician, and Hillard, who aspired to membership in the state legislature, appeared most frequently as spokesmen of the group, with which Sumner early identified himself. But Webster, Choate, Everett, Winthrop, Abbott Lawrence, and Nathan Appleton, the real leaders of Massachusetts Whiggery, rarely took public part in these protests. These practical politicians quickly recognized that they were facing an accomplished fact; after Congress passed the annexation resolution, what was the point of further resistance? Factious opposition would only serve to split the Whig party and to alienate Southern congressmen at just the time when President Polk was urging a downward revision of the tariff seriously injurious to New England manufacturing. More important in the minds of some Massachusetts Whigs than even the manufacture of cotton was the manufacture of a Whig presidential candidate for 1848, as both Webster and Abbott Lawrence aspired to the White House.[5]

Still a political amateur, Sumner was insensitive to these shifting currents of expediency. For him it was enough that the annexation of Texas was wrong; the authoritative spokesmen for the Massachusetts Whig party had said so. Characteristically he had committed himself to a principle, and he continued with it to extreme conclusions long after it was abandoned by its originators. In "The True Grandeur of Nations" oration on July 4, 1845, Sumner thought that he was merely announcing good Whig doctrine in condemning as "mean and cowardly" both the annexation and the war that threatened to result from it. So like a Whig stump speech were parts of Sumner's address that some in the audience thought he was making a bid for public office. When old John Quincy Adams read the "highly wrought, learned, ingenious diatribe," he concluded: "Mr. Sumner takes a lofty flight and promises to be a politician." [6]

But at the dinner following the speech, Winthrop bluntly

[5] Pierce, III, 105. On the "Young Whig" movement I have greatly profited by reading Mr. Frank Otto Gatell's admirable " 'Conscience and Judgment': The Bolt of the Massachusetts Conscience Whigs," a seminar paper prepared under the direction of Professor Frederick Merk at Harvard University.
[6] J. Q. Adams, Diary, Aug. 13, 1845, Adams MSS.

announced that Sumner was out of step. "Our country—whether bounded by Sabine or Del Norte . . . ," he toasted, rebuking not merely the orator of the day, but all of the "Young Whig" group.

The switch in the official Massachusetts Whig position placed Sumner's friends in a serious dilemma. Genuinely concerned over the expansion of slavery, and deeply troubled over the approaching war with Mexico, they hoped even after annexation to continue "an agitation against the admission of Texas as a *Slave State*," [7] but to do so in the face of Winthrop's explicit warning might mean cutting themselves off from the Whig party, to which they were bound by ancient ties of loyalty and from which they, in the overwhelmingly Whiggish state of Massachusetts, must expect any future public honors or offices.

Moreover, continued agitation of the Texas issue would inevitably throw the "Young Whigs" into closer contact with the despised and distrusted abolitionists, who had plans for exploiting the anti-Texas sentiment for their own ends. The "Young Whigs" had invited Garrison and his followers to participate in the original Faneuil Hall rally in order to demonstrate that all elements in Massachusetts were opposed to annexation. When the Garrisonians in return asked them to speak at a nonpartisan rally designed to continue the anti-Texas agitation, the "Young Whigs" had difficulty in declining. Once publicly connected with the abolitionist-sponsored movement, Adams, Palfrey, Wilson, and Sumner found it necessary to become increasingly active in it, lest it be taken over by the Garrisonians, who hoped to divert the aroused public interest into their own program for the immediate abolition of slavery and the dissolution of the Union.

Too prominently associated with the anti-Texas drive to retreat, too distrustful of their new abolitionist allies to be silent, the "Young Whigs" behaved as a kind of junto. They thought of themselves as "conspirators," bound by a firm discipline. Palfrey, the senior statesman of the little group, handed down rulings on the duties "our brotherhood" demanded, and Charles Francis Adams, whose cool, balanced mind planned their strategy, required that the members chasten their "personal views . . . into entire obedience to the sacrificing nature of our mission." [8]

[7] Sumner to Lieber, Nov. 19, 1845, Sumner MSS.
[8] C. F. Adams, Diary, Dec. 3, 1846, and Apr. 12, 1847, Adams MSS.

Sumner was a willing and prominent member of the group. Winthrop's rebuke, far from abashing him, increased his stubborn opposition to Texas and to any war with Mexico. As he had no conscious political aspirations, he hesitated less than did Wilson, Adams, Palfrey, or Phillips in challenging the Whig oligarchy of Massachusetts. With antislavery views more advanced than those of most of his new friends, he was not embarrassed to associate with the abolitionists, and his warm friendship with Wendell Phillips, Garrison's right-hand man, made him an ideal go-between. In the conspiratorial tone of the "Young Whig" enterprise, its secrecy, and its danger, Sumner found a sense of security, of belonging to a group with a mission.[9] Enthusiastically he began pushing the "Young Whig" ideas to an extreme, and his political allies were disturbed by his radical tone. Adams thought that, "too much led by his visions," Sumner needed "constantly the guiding and superintendence of a man more worldly wise."[1]

But even Adams was forced to admit that if Sumner had "not sufficient every day steadiness of mind to do well the work of infantry," he performed "with success as a pioneer." He helped organize and edit the little newspaper the anti-Texas leaders published, *The Free State Rally and Texas Chain-Breaker*, and he served efficiently on a state committee appointed in the fall of 1845 to arouse Massachusetts opinion against the admission of Texas as a slave state. In planning the large rally of anti-Texas Whigs, abolitionists, and Liberty party men, to be held in Faneuil Hall on November 4, Sumner was particularly active. When the spokesmen of the mutually distrustful co-operating groups were unable to agree upon resolutions to be adopted at the meeting, Sumner produced a compromise draft, eloquently denouncing "this wicked scheme" of annexation, undertaken "for the atrocious purpose . . . of increasing the market for human flesh," the consummation of which would "cover the country with disgrace, and make us all responsible for crimes of gigantic magnitude."[2]

The long-heralded meeting took place on a dark and stormy

---

[9] Cf. Eric Hoffer: *The True Believer*, pp. 60–1.

[1] C. F. Adams, Diary, Mar. 1, 1847, Adams MSS.

[2] Ibid., Mar. 8, 1847; *Free State Rally . . .*, Nov. 20, 1845, p. 2; draft of resolutions in Sumner's handwriting [c. Nov. 4, 1845], Palfrey MSS.; Sumner: *Works*, I, 149 ff.

night—weather suitable for so foul a plot, Democrats claimed. There was, nevertheless, a respectable attendance, and, with Charles Francis Adams in the chair, the proceedings, carefully divided among the sponsoring groups, went off smoothly. After Palfrey read the resolutions Sumner had drafted, Garrison, Wendell Phillips, and the Reverend W. H. Channing spoke for the abolitionists, H. B. Stanton for the Liberty party, and Hillard and Sumner for the Conscience Whigs. "All in very tolerable temper," Adams noted in his diary, with his customary restraint, "and some in a high style of oratory." [3]

For Sumner the occasion was far more important than Adams's arid diary record indicated. Testing his aptitude for oratory, which he had discovered only on July 4, he made his first political speech. It was brief and effective. He begged his hearers to put "aside all distinctions of party" and to subordinate all political and economic questions to "the supreme requirements of religion, morals, and humanity," and he proposed again Channing's idea of a moral blockade against evil. He did not suggest interference "with any institution of the Southern States," or modification of "any law on the subject of Slavery anywhere under the Constitution." But, to admit slaveholding Texas to the Union would implicate his dearly loved Massachusetts in wrong. "By welcoming Texas as a Slave State we make slavery our own original sin." "Let us wash our hands of this great guilt," he urged. "God forbid that the votes and voices of Northern freemen should help to bind anew the fetters of the slave! God forbid that the lash of the slave-dealer should descend by any sanction from New England! God forbid that the blood which spurts from the lacerated, quivering flesh of the slave should soil the hem of the white garments of Massachusetts." [4] Antislavery in Massachusetts had found a new voice.

· 3 ·

It was not a voice welcomed by conservative Boston Whiggery. The regular party leaders now openly discountenanced further agitation of the Texas question. Abbott Lawrence announced:

[3] C. F. Adams, Diary, Nov. 4, 1845, Adams MSS.
[4] Sumner: Works, I, 152, 155-7.

"A majority of the people have decided in favor of annexation, and . . . Texas now virtually composes a part of our Union." Pointing to the presence at the Faneuil Hall rally of "a great number . . . of those who have distinguished themselves as members of the abolition party," Nathan Appleton refused to give further support to the anti-Texas movement. "I consider the question settled," he declared. Whig leaders blocked Henry Wilson's attempt to push anti-annexation resolutions through the state senate, and were unmoved by E. Rockwood Hoar's spirited pronouncement: "It is as much the duty of Massachusetts to pass resolutions in favor of the rights of man as in the interests of cotton." If obliged to be either "Cotton Whigs" or "Conscience Whigs"—as the "Young Whigs" henceforth designated themselves—Boston leaders had no hesitation in making a choice. Shortly after the Faneuil Hall meeting, Edmund Dwight took Sumner aside, told him of the party's decision to discourage further discussion of the Texas issue, and "gave him very good advice not to go into this abolition movement in disguise." [5]

Warning Sumner to cease agitating the Texas issue was the most certain way of making him do just the opposite. In his opinion the regular Whig leaders were blind to the proslavery plot that was being hatched. In December Texas was admitted to the Union, a slaveholding state. In April 1846 General Zachary Taylor's men, marching into territory claimed by both the United States and Mexico, were fired upon. War, announced President Polk, had begun through the shedding of American blood upon American soil, and American armies started to slice off great segments of Mexico's northern empire.

In New England it was an unpopular war, and Conscience Whigs, who had hitherto been a tiny minority, suddenly found they had many supporters, especially in the strongly antislavery rural districts of Massachusetts. Taking advantage of the aroused public opinion, Palfrey, Adams, S. C. Phillips, Wilson, and Sumner prepared to renew and expand their agitation against slavery. In May they purchased a nearly derelict Boston daily newspaper, *The Whig,* as organ for their faction, which had been inhospitably

[5] Abbott Lawrence to C. F. Adams, Nov. 17, 1845, copy in Adams's Diary of the same date, Adams MSS.; Appleton to C. F. Adams, Palfrey, and Sumner, Nov. 10, 1845, author's copy, Appleton MSS.; Wilson: *Slave Power,* II, 117–18; C. F. Adams, Diary, Nov. 22, 1845, Adams MSS.

treated in the *Advertiser* and the *Atlas,* the two principal Boston Whig papers, and had received only grudging recognition in the more tolerant *Courier.* Palfrey and Phillips contributed three fifths of the capital; Adams, in addition to putting up the rest of the money, agreed to serve as editor; and Sumner and Wilson, who were both poor, promised to write for the newspaper.[6]

"The Whig principles of Massachusetts, such as they have been declared at every authorized assembly of the party since 1840, will be . . . the guides of this paper," Adams announced in his inaugural editorial on June 1, 1846. He and his friends were trying to lose the taint of disunionism acquired during the previous year by association with the Garrisonians and to establish themselves as true Whigs. "We do not believe," Adams announced firmly to a correspondent who proposed that the free states separate from the slaveholding South, "that a division would be productive of permanent benefit to either party, whilst on the other hand, it would originate innumerable evils to both." Even more positive was the *Whig's* rebuke to the Liberty party men, with whom Sumner and his associates had formerly worked so amiably. Third parties, Adams asserted editorially, "are productive of a much greater share of evil to the community, than they can be of good. . . . We . . . never did and cannot now put any confidence in Mr. [James G.] Birney," the Liberty party's presidential candidate.[7]

The real purpose of the newspaper, of course, was not so much to demonstrate that the Conscience Whigs were still Whigs, but to prove that they were the only true Whigs in Massachusetts. Relentlessly Adams ridiculed the professed antislavery sentiments of such regular party leaders as Abbott Lawrence and Nathan Appleton. "Thinking more of sheep and cotton than of Man," "truckling to expediency in every thing, for the sake of . . . slaveholding gold," these two cotton textile manufacturers, Adams asserted, had used their influence "to keep down in Massachusetts the growing restlessness under the domination of the slave power." They had sabotaged the movement "for a general union of the members of all parties . . . in opposition to the annexation of Texas." To Lawrence and his money-making

---

[6] C. F. Adams, Diary, May 23, 1846, Adams MSS.
[7] Boston *Whig,* Aug. 20, and July 9, 1846.

schemes, "wholly unworthy of the noble aim of the Pilgrim race," the *Whig* attributed "the manifest degeneracy which prevails among . . . our politicians, a tone which blusters about the rights of sheep and falls into the softest whisper when dealing with the rights of man." [8]

However scathing or eloquent, the *Whig's* attacks upon Appleton and Lawrence lacked any real urgency, for neither of the manufacturers held public office in 1846; their control over the Whig party in Massachusetts, though real, was tacit and informal and beyond the reach of public opinion. To make their attack felt, Adams and his allies needed a more immediate target, and they found one in Congressman Winthrop. With his ancient family, great wealth, excellent education, and undeviating loyalty to the Whig party, Winthrop was obviously being groomed as successor to Daniel Webster and Edward Everett; the weight of his responsibilities had already made him, as Tom Appleton thought, "the dullest and most unelastic of companions, the perfection of prudence and respectability." Neither great nor strong, Winthrop was, in Hillard's words, "a man of decencies, decorums and proprieties." [9] In his cold, formal way he held antislavery principles, and he lived by them as well as an ambitious politician, who would ultimately need Southern votes for national office, could. Originally opposed to the annexation of Texas, Winthrop was placed in a serious dilemma by the declaration of war against Mexico. Through Democratic parliamentary ingenuity, the bill providing necessary supplies for Taylor's army had a preamble asserting that the war they were fighting had been caused by Mexican aggression. As a Northern antislavery man, Winthrop could not conscientiously vote for the preamble, but as a Whig politician who remembered the fate of the Federalists who had opposed the War of 1812, he could not refuse to vote supplies. Fourteen of his Massachusetts colleagues in the House voted against the bill, but Winthrop, together with one other congressman from Essex County, finally decided to support it. [1]

[8] Ibid., July 3, and 31, Aug. 7, and 21, and Sept. 18, 1846.
[9] T. G. Appleton to Nathan Appleton, Aug. 4 [1850], Appleton MSS.; Hillard to Lieber, Sept. 9, 1850, Lieber MSS.
[1] The best accounts of Winthrop are Robert C. Winthrop, Jr.: *Memoir of Robert C. Winthrop* (Boston: Little, Brown & Co.; 1897), and Daniel D. Levenson: "Robert C. Winthrop: A Study of a Whig Conscience" (unpublished honor's thesis, Harvard Univ.; 1954).

At last Adams had his issue. Winthrop, the *Whig* announced on July 16, had "set his name in perpetual attestation of a false-hood"; he had given "a positive sanction of the worst acts of the Administration." The attack ruffled Boston; Adams began to hope that people might even subscribe to the *Whig* for such spicy read-ing. But when the *Advertiser* issued a massive rebuttal of the *Whig's* changes against Winthrop, Adams called for help.[2]

At this point Sumner entered the controversy. To defend Adams and the *Whig,* he renewed the assault upon Winthrop. Unctuously protesting high regard for the congressman and faith in his integrity, Sumner, under the pseudonym "Boston," announced boldly that Winthrop, in voting for the war bill, had "told a lie" and had committed "gross disloyalty to Truth and Freedom." A week later he continued the attack, again under his pseudonym, this time in the columns of the *Courier.* Taking the questionable charges made in his first letter as proved, Sumner now went on to make even more serious accusations. Winthrop, he proclaimed, had voted for *"an unjust war, and national false-hood, in the cause of slavery";* he had supported what was un-questionably "the darkest act in our history." [3]

The violence of these assaults took Winthrop by surprise. He was ready for the hostility of Charles Francis Adams, who, he thought, aspired to replace him in Congress. But the mysterious "Boston" articles, written by "an accomplished person [who] does his work with elegance," made him writhe. Speculation sug-gested Wendell Phillips or Theodore Parker as author, but Win-throp thought both lacked the polish and finesse of his assailant. For a time he suspected Hillard. It was with reluctance that he came to believe that the author was Sumner, who in April 1846, only six months earlier, had been Winthrop's guest in Washing-ton and had "parted with many expressions of obligation on his part, which would seem at odds with . . . so much personal unkindness." [4]

After gossip had identified Sumner as author of the "Bos-ton" articles and "A True Whig" replied to him in the *Courier,* he thought it expedient to explain his motives directly to Winthrop.

---

[2] Pierce, III, 114; C. F. Adams, Diary, July 15–16, 1846, Adams MSS.

[3] Boston *Whig,* July 22, 1846; Boston *Courier,* July 31, 1846.

[4] Winthrop to J. H. Clifford, July 24, Aug. 2, and 3, 1846, copies, Winthrop MSS.

The congressman must believe, Sumner declared in a personal letter, that the articles were written "under the impression of duty." Their anonymity, he rather feebly protested, was "less from any disposition to withhold my name, than because that is the customary [use] made with communications" in the newspapers. "I hope," Sumner concluded, "in doing what I have done, I have not in any way been disloyal to those pleasant relations, which I have always had the happiness of cherishing with you, and which I trust may always continue." [5]

Hurt, Winthrop replied that Sumner's articles were "ungenerous and unjust"; he had been "grossly and wantonly wronged by them." He objected to their "intentional offensiveness . . . , and their obvious design, not to sustain a principle or vindicate the truth, but to rob him, personally, of that 'spotless reputation, which is the purest treasure mortal times afford.'" Coolly he ended his reply by sharing Sumner's regret at the interruption of their "pleasant relations" and with a vague "hope that circumstances may occur, which may enable us to restore them without sacrifice of self-respect on either side." [6]

Never willing to yield a point, Sumner prepared a reply to Winthrop's "very crusty and illtempered" letter. He denied any personal animus toward the congressman. Winthrop's toast at the July 4, 1845, dinner had originally aroused Sumner's suspicions. "I would have cut off my right hand rather than utter such a sentiment," Sumner passionately exclaimed. Winthrop's toast was promptly followed by his vote "for an *unjust war.*" Adams had felt obliged to discuss the issue in the *Whig*, the *Advertiser* had made support of Winthrop's vote a party test, and Sumner had entered the controversy at the urging of the editor of the *Courier*. He hoped that it was not too late for Winthrop to put behind him the pinchbeck "notability, acquired in the displays of party politics" and to exercise his powers "in the highest causes of Humanity and Right." [7]

Three days after Sumner sent this private letter to Win-

[5] Boston *Courier*, Aug. 1, 1846; Sumner to Winthrop, Aug. 5, 1846, Winthrop MSS.

[6] Winthrop to Sumner, Aug. 7, 1846, Sumner MSS.

[7] C. F. Adams, Diary, Aug. 10, 1846, Adams MSS.; Sumner to Winthrop, Aug. 10, 1846, Winthrop MSS. The editor of the *Courier* denied that he either incited or approved Sumner's articles. J. T. Buckingham to Winthrop, Oct. 13 [1846], Winthrop MSS.

throp, his third "Boston" article appeared in the *Courier*. Winthrop, Sumner now announced, was a modern Pontius Pilate. "Mr. Winthrop's vote was wrong," "Boston" protested. "It was wrong by the law of nations, and by the higher law of God. . . . It cannot be forgotten on earth; it must be remembered in heaven. Blood! blood! is on the hands of the representative from Boston. Not all great Neptune's ocean can wash them clean." [8]

Furious, Winthrop retorted with a letter that terminated all relations with Sumner for the next sixteen years. Sumner's articles, he declared, were full of "the coarsest personalities" and "the grossest perversions"; they assailed not merely Winthrop's acts, but his motives and his integrity. "I am willing to believe that you have not weighed the force of your own phrases," Winthrop added, with unusual perspicacity. "Your 'periculosa facilitas' has betrayed you. Your habitual indulgence in strains of extravagant thought and exaggerated expression, alike when you praise and when you censure, has, perhaps, impaired your discrimination in the employment of language." But, after such abuse, Winthrop could not maintain social relations with Sumner. "My hand," he said bluntly, "is not at the service of any one, who has denounced it, with such ferocity, as being stained with blood." [9]

The Conscience Whigs' assault upon Winthrop was only a part of their larger effort to seize control of the state-party machinery. They planned their strategy with care and secrecy. Looking ahead to the Massachusetts Whig convention announced for September 1846, they took great pains to see that their faction was well represented at the primary meetings that chose the members of the state assembly. The regular party leaders were surprised, for the newspapers noted with puzzlement how many "gentlemen who were never before seen in a political caucus, took part in the proceedings." At the Boston primary meeting, when Abbott Lawrence made the conventional Whig talk about the need for a higher tariff and internal improvements, the Conscience group sent Sumner to the stand to reply. It was, he announced, "the first meeting of the kind he had ever attended," but he was not abashed by the novelty of his situation. Lawrence

[8] Boston *Courier*, Aug. 13, 1846.
[9] Winthrop to Sumner, Aug. 17, 1846, Sumner MSS.

"had spoken for the material interests of the community—and no man, he was sure, could better do it." But Sumner, for the Conscience Whigs, had another, higher theme, "the moral interests which were at stake." The Whig party was one of freedom, he declared; at the approaching convention the Massachusetts party must reassert "the essence of Whig principles . . . the idea that all men were created free and equal." The regular party leaders managed to control a majority of the delegates named to the state convention, but Sumner, Adams, Hillard, and a handful of other young insurgents also secured places.[1]

With seats in the Boston delegation, a newspaper behind them, and much support in the strongly antislavery rural districts, the Conscience Whigs carefully planned their tactics in the state convention, which met in Faneuil Hall on September 23. The Cotton Whig leaders had arranged for Winthrop to be called to the stand while the committee on resolutions was preparing the platform. Secretly the Conscience Whig junto organized a counter demonstration, a demand from the floor to have Sumner speak. As the delegates cheered their respective spokesmen, the two factions engaged in a tug of war, and the admirably organized Conscience Whigs won.

Bounding to the platform, Sumner enunciated the "Antislavery Duties of the Whig Party." Strikingly dressed in his blue waistcoat and white trousers, his voice passionate with sincerity, Sumner implored his fellow delegates to put the Declaration of Independence, the Constitution, and the Union ahead of "obsolete ideas" like the protective tariff and internal improvement. "The Whigs," he announced, "are, or ought to be, the party of Freedom." Their watchword must be "REPEAL OF SLAVERY UNDER THE CONSTITUTION AND LAWS OF THE NATIONAL GOVERNMENT." They should seek to abolish slavery in the District of Columbia, to end slavery in the national territories, to terminate the slave trade, to refuse admission to new slave states, and to amend the Constitution so as to reach slavery elsewhere. Their leaders "must not be Northern men with Southern principles, nor Northern men under Southern influence." Their motto should not be 'Our party, *howsoever bounded,*'" he added, in a gratuitous gibe at Winthrop, "but 'Our party, bounded always by the Right.'"

[1] Boston *Whig*, Sept. 10, 1846; Boston *Courier*, Sept. 11, 1846.

Sumner concluded by urging Webster to join the Conscience group, adding to his titles as "defender of the Constitution" and "Defender of Peace" another, higher title, "never to be forgotten on earth or in heaven,—*Defender of Humanity*." [2]

When Winthrop got the floor after this elaborate and effective speech, he refrained from discussing "some incidental questions connected with this war," on which "there have been differences of opinions among friends at home," and entered upon a pallid and ineffectual review of Democratic financial measures, objectionable to New England manufacturers. The longer he spoke, the more certain it appeared that the Conscience Whigs would stampede the convention.

Promptly and shrewdly the Cotton Whigs replanned their strategy. While Winthrop was speaking, they inserted strong antislavery plans into their proposed platform. Though the determined Conscience Whigs attempted to move a substitute set of resolutions, most members of the convention could not distinguish between the rival platforms. Further to distract attention, the Cotton Whigs, at the crucial moment of the debates, staged a demonstration to bring Daniel Webster to the stand, "under an elaborate attempt to down every thing with acclamation." Puzzled and confused, the majority of the delegates followed the regular party leaders, rejected the Conscience Whig resolutions, and enthusiastically applauded Webster's plea for party solidarity: "For my part, in the dark and troubled night that is upon us, I see no star above the horizon promising light to give us, but the intelligent, patriotic, united Whig Party of the United States." [3]

Depressed by the failure of the Conscience Whigs, Sumner was by no means ready to give up his crusade against Winthrop. When Boston Whigs unanimously renominated the congressman, he toyed with accepting the Liberty Party nomination to run against him, but Adams's advice that "it would not do for him to go out and in the Whig party at pleasure" made him abandon the idea. Instead, he convinced himself that it was his duty to publish a summary and review of his controversy with Winthrop. In a long public letter to the congressman, this time issued over Sumner's own signature, he branded Winthrop's vote for the war

[2] Boston *Courier*, Sept. 24, 1846; Sumner: *Works*, I, 304–16.
[3] Boston *Whig*, Sept. 24–5, 1846; C. F. Adams, Diary, Sept. 23, 1846, Adams MSS.

bill as not merely "the most wicked in our history," but "one of the most wicked in all history." "Rather than lend your hand to this wickedness," Sumner objurgated the congressman, "you should have suffered the army of the United States to pass submissively through the Caudine Forks of Mexican power,—to perish, it might be, like the legions of Varus." [4]

After such a letter, Sumner could hardly have been surprised when a group of the younger Conscience Whigs in Boston, led by John A. Andrew, decided to bolt the party and offer him an independent nomination to Congress. Discreetly out of town when the nomination was made, Sumner found that his friends in the junto doubted its wisdom, as his enemies could now claim that personal ambition had all along been behind his letters attacking Winthrop. Hastily he withdrew, announcing: "I have never on any occasion sought or desired public office of any kind. . . . My tastes are alien to official life; and I have long been accustomed to look to other fields of usefulness." Howe, who realized that the contest was hopeless, took Sumner's place as the independent nominee. The abortive demonstration cost Winthrop hardly a vote; instead, it stimulated his friends and the Whig party generally to extraordinary efforts, and he was triumphantly re-elected. [5]

· 4 ·

"That a man who but yesterday professed to be my friend, and who was filling my ears with all sorts of phrases of devotion and admiration, should turn upon me with such ferocity, denounce me so publicly and grossly, and pursue me with such relentless malignity," Winthrop thought, "is almost inconceivable." The other leaders of the regular Whig party in Massachusetts had no such difficulty in conceiving Sumner's motives. Bostonians of the George Ticknor sort said openly that Sumner had "taken his position on reform questions in order to get a notoriety and prominence, greater than he could get otherwise so soon" and that he

[4] C. F. Adams, *Diary*, Sept. 29, and Oct. 2, 1846, Adams MSS.; Sumner: *Works*, I, 317–29.
[5] Andrew to Sumner, Oct. 30, 1846, Sumner MSS.; "To the Voters of Massachusetts," photostat of a broadside in Levenson: "Winthrop," facing p. 64; Boston *Whig*, Oct. 30–1, and Nov. 2, 1846; Boston *Courier*, Nov. 2, 1846; Schwartz: *Howe*, pp. 160–1; Edward Everett to A. H. Everett, Oct. 30, 1846, letterbook copy, Everett MSS.

was trying "to make himself thus early the chief of a growing party, and get earlier into power than he could by other tracks which are occupied by older men." Congressman George Ashmun attributed the entire Conscience Whig movement to the personal ambitions of its leaders. "If [S. C.] Phillips could be made Governor, [Judge Charles] Allen Senator, and Adams Representative from Suffolk, with such small chance for anything less which might fall to Sumner," he cynically suggested, "the trouble [over antislavery in the Whig party] would be at an end." [6]

Indignantly the Conscience Whigs denied such unworthy motives, and none more passionately than Sumner. "I have no personal motive to gratify in this controversy," he assured Winthrop. "I seek no office of any kind for myself, or for any friend." Though Sumner's own repeated assertions that he was not, and never would be, an office-seeker may be discounted, it is harder to dismiss the unanimous testimony of his close friends that Sumner was, as the critical Hillard said, "perfectly disinterested" in his antislavery agitation. Not even opponents could suggest any specific office for which Sumner was ambitious. Some credence must be given to Sumner's own considered opinion that his reform activities had hampered, rather than forwarded, his opportunities for political advancement. With dignity he answered a critic who suggested that self-promotion was his goal:

At the time my "position was taken in the Reform questions" few persons of my age in this community could behold wider openings for himself than I could, and few had declined more various opportunities. I was connected by relations of amity and confidence with those whose influence would have been most important to one seeking personal advancement. . . . I had often been solicited to take part in public affairs, and by members of different political parties. I had been thought of as a proper person for offices, academic, professional, judicial and diplomatic. . . . Surely, if mine were the ambition that has been suggested, I should not have neglected these advantages; most certainly I should not have renounced them, in pursuit of a vulgar notoriety. [7]

[6] Winthrop to J. H. Clifford, Feb. 14, 1847, copy, Winthrop MSS.; George Putnam to Sumner, Jan. 26, 1848, Sumner MSS.; Ashmun to Winthrop, Sept. 27, 1846, Winthrop MSS.

[7] Sumner to Winthrop, Aug. 10, 1846, Winthrop MSS.; MHSP, XVII, 195; Hillard to Dorothea L. Dix, Nov. 26, 1846, Dix MSS.; Sumner to George Putnam, Apr. 1848, copy, Sumner MSS.

Far from consciously plotting an easy route to power, Sumner was surprised to find himself a controversial figure and a leader of a political faction. In his own eyes he was a moderate and a man of good will. Reluctantly, but necessarily, he had stepped forward to defend Right at a time when the leaders of his party appeared about to endorse Wrong. In the controversies that followed, he had tried to keep his temper. He had, he thought, made it his inflexible rule *"never to question the motives of others."* "Well aware that where freedom of thought exists, differences must ensue," Sumner informed a critic, "I have always desired that these should be tempered by mutual kindness and forbearance, so that we might all at least 'agree to disagree.' " [8]

It is easy to understand why Sumner's enemies were infuriated by what they took to be his cant, which they found more objectionable than his criticisms, but Sumner was not being consciously disingenuous. A child of provincial New England, where small beer poets were compared to Shakespeare, and where poor George Hillard, who published a travel journal and an edition of Spenser's poems, was termed one of the sweetest and most enduring writers of the English language, Sumner shared his section's propensity for superlatives. Brought up under the spell of Daniel Webster and Edward Everett, he fell easily into the orator's natural tendency to use the exaggerated contrasts that made for rounded periods. When he praised, he seemed, as Lieber caustically observed, unable to "reign [sic] in the prancing steed of laudation." He compared his friend Channing to Pascal, the lexicographer John Pickering, to Erasmus. Similarly, when Sumner condemned, he condemned utterly. Totally insensitive to the power of his own words, he could not see why Winthrop should be so angry at having his vote called not merely bad, but *"the worst act that was ever done by a Boston representative."* [9]

But something more than mere rhetorical extravagance is required to account for the tone that pervades Sumner's early speeches. Edward Everett, noting the timing of Sumner's belated

[8] Sumner to George Putnam, Apr. 1848, author's copy, Sumner MSS.
[9] Lieber to Sumner, June 14, 1846, Lieber MSS.; Lieber's notes in his copy of Sumner's *The Scholar, The Jurist, The Artist, The Philanthropist,* in the Univ. of California Lib.; Freidel: *Lieber,* p. 238; Sumner to Nathan Appleton, Aug. 11, 1846, Appleton MSS.

entry upon the reform stage, tartly judged that his crusading zeal resulted from his failure to get Story's chair in the Harvard Law School.[1] Such an explanation is, of course, far too simple, yet it is true that a whole series of personal disasters and professional failures during the early 1840's had turned Sumner against the Boston society he once so admired. His inner state of mind was reflected in the rhetoric of his orations, in the frequent images of destruction and mutilation which recurred in his speeches. His references to "nations, now prostrate on the earth with bloody streams running from their sides," to "Blood! blood! . . . on the hands of the representative from Boston," to the "blood which spurts from the lacerated, quivering flesh of the slave," are ample, if unintentional, evidence of the deep anger that drove him on. It was not chance that singled out Robert C. Winthrop as the first object of Sumner's attack; perhaps his real offense lay less in his vote on the Mexican War than in the mere fact that he was a Winthrop.

Whatever the motives that initially brought Sumner into the political field, pride and stubbornness kept him there. When Winthrop and his allies unexpectedly took offense at the "Boston" letters, Sumner would not admit that he was to any degree at fault. All he had done, in his own estimation, was "gently and kindly to put [Winthrop] right; not defend him; not let him deceive himself into the belief that he has done anything but *wrong*." Sumner had not greatly changed since the Harvard Parietal Board attempted to prove to him that his buff waistcoat was not white. As William Kent shrewdly observed: "Sumner is a man of the loveliest temper and kindest and most generous heart; but he is Utopian as Horace Greele[y], and obstinate as a mule." [2]

That a man as dependent as Sumner upon approbation should defy Boston society was, however, something that stubbornness could not alone account for. If his former acquaintances snubbed him, his activities in the Conscience Whig group gave him a fresh sense of power and a new feeling of belonging. He seemed actually to enjoy his role as political pariah and social outcast. "The great questions to which he is giving himself," Hillard

[1] Everett, Diary, May 10, 1856, Everett MSS.
[2] Sumner to Nathan Appleton, Aug. 11, 1846, Appleton MSS.; Sumner to Longfellow, [Aug. 1846], Longfellow MSS.; William Kent to James Kent, Nov. 14, 1846, Kent MSS.

noted shrewdly, "have, at least, one salutary effect: that of breaking the spell of self-brooding melancholy which hung over him." [3]

Sumner's antislavery activities cost him some friends, but they also won him a new, fatherly adviser. Ex-President John Quincy Adams, now ending his long, controversial career, had apparently hardly known Sumner before he delivered "The True Grandeur of Nations." Though Adams could not approve of Sumner's pacifism, he did, out of sheer love of combat, rejoice that the young speaker had "set all the vipers of Alecto ahissing, by proclaiming the Christian Law of universal Peace and Love." Sumner's slashing attacks upon the Boston Brahmins further endeared him to the old President, for all the Adamses shared a suspicious hostility toward State Street. Finding in Sumner's eloquence and audacity something akin to his own notoriously bad temper and stubborn disposition, the elder Adams began to praise him as a young man who would "contribute largely to redeem the spirit of the free people of the Union from the dastardly servility to the slave-monger oligarchy into which they have . . . almost unconsciously fallen." [4]

Always responsive to praise, Sumner became Adams's adoring admirer. He had always extolled the ex-President's "unquestioned purity of character, and remarkable attainments, the result of constant industry," but in earlier years, when under the influence of Beacon Hill, he had objected "most strenuously to his manner, and to some of his expressions and topics, as unparliamentary and subversive of the rules and order of debate." Now he rejoiced in the very violence and vituperation with which Adams conducted his congressional campaign against slavery. Whenever the old President was in Quincy, Sumner came out to sit at his feet, and he undiscriminatingly adopted all of Adams's opinions, from his enthusiastic nationalism to his injunction that a statesman should *"Never accept a present."* Throughout the remainder of his career Sumner was to echo Adams's doctrines that the Declaration of Independence, with its pledge of universal human equality, was as much a part of the public law of the land as the Constitution; that an antislavery congressman was not obliged

---

[3] Hillard to Lieber, July 3, 1849, Lieber MSS.
[4] J. Q. Adams, Diary, Aug. 13, 1845, Aug. 27, and 31, 1846, Adams MSS.; J. Q. Adams to Sumner, Aug. 29, 1846, Sumner MSS. Cf. C. F. Adams to Pierce, June 6, 1877, Pierce MSS.

to uphold the fugitive slave acts, as "in swearing to support the Constitution, he swore to support it as he understood it, and not as other men understood it"; and that in the event of civil war the federal government could use martial law to abolish slavery.[5]

The aging ex-President was delighted by so diligent a student, whose enthusiastic admiration was in contrast with the cool detachment of his own son, and he earnestly urged the younger man to enter public life. When Sumner objected that he "was unwilling to renounce literature," Adams predicted: "You will enter public life; in spite of yourself." In some senses he regarded Sumner as his successor. "I see you have a mission to perform," he saluted his disciple at the beginning of his political career. "I look from Pisgah to the promised Land. You must enter upon it." [6]

• 5 •

There was little in the election returns of 1846 to justify President Adams's prediction. The Conscience Whigs were so soundly defeated that Sumner, during the next six months, was able to carry on his antislavery agitation only through incidental remarks in the course of his peace crusade, his prison discipline fight, and his several addresses before lyceums. He was particularly proud of his success in insinuating his political opinions from the lecture platform to groups that customarily banned discussion of current issues. In an ostensibly historical discourse on "White Slavery in the Barbary States," delivered before the Mercantile Library Association, he compared *the old mercantile interest* that had once prevented the English from exterminating slavery in Tripoli with New England's traffickers in cotton, and likened the Algerine pirates to the Southern slaveholders.[7]

[5] Sumner to Howe, Dec. 31, 1843, Sumner MSS.; Sumner to Lieber, Feb. 21, 1841, ibid.; David L. Child: *Homes of American Statesmen* (New York: Alfred W. Upham; 1860), p. 333; Sumner to Joshua R. Giddings, Dec. 21, and 30, 1846, Giddings MSS.; Sumner: *Duties of Massachusetts at this Crisis. A Speech . . . delivered at the Republican Convention at Worcester, Sept. 7, 1854* (Boston; 1854), p. 6. On Adams's political ideas see George A. Lipsky: *John Quincy Adams: His Theory and Ideas* (New York: Thomas Y. Crowell Company; 1950), esp. Chap. xii, and David Donald: "Abraham Lincoln: Whig in the White House," in Norman A Graebner (ed.): *The Enduring Lincoln* (Urbana: University of Illinois Press; 1959), pp. 63–6. The definitive study of Adams's career as congressman and antislavery leader is Samuel Flagg Bemis's masterly *John Quincy Adams and the Union* (New York: Alfred A. Knopf, Inc.; 1956).

[6] Sumner's autobiography, Palfrey MSS.; Child: *Homes of American Statesmen*, p. 333; J. Q. Adams to Sumner, Aug. 29, 1846, Sumner MSS.

[7] Sumner: *Works*, I, 389, 460–1.

"In Sumner's alphabet just now there are only two words Slavery and Mexican War," Hillard complained in February 1847. "He does nothing but write paragraphs for the newspapers and letters without number. Business he utterly neglects and the only persons he sees with any interest are those with whom he is in communication on these points." Sumner's practice virtually disappeared, and with it his interest in the law. Looking back a bit sentimentally upon his "early days of precocious judical enthusiasm," he was obliged to admit that his mind had flowed completely into other channels.[8]

Increasingly Sumner's Court Street office became "a sort of *reunion* for the ultra liberals" of Massachusetts. Almost every day Adams, Wilson, Phillips, Allen, and other Conscience Whig leaders dropped in for long conferences, and Hillard, who had law business to attend to, gave up the outer office to his partner and retreated to the back room. State legislators of pronounced antiwar or antislavery opinions began showing up at these sessions, and Sumner in turn started to attend their caucuses in the State House. As most of these were rural legislators without great legal lore or literary gifts, they often asked him to draft their motions and bills. For example, it was Sumner who drew up the resolutions that served as a platform for the Conscience Whigs in the legislature; they denounced the Mexican War as "a war of conquest, so hateful in its objects, so wanton, unjust, and unconstitutional in its origin and character," called for "the country to retire from the position of aggression which it now occupies towards a weak, distracted neighbor," and demanded that the national government undertake "all constitutional efforts for the destruction of the unjust influence of the slave power, and for the abolition of slavery within the limits of the United States."[9]

Sumner also became a kind of middleman between the Massachusetts Conscience Whigs and the national leaders of the political antislavery movement. He was in confidential correspondence with Salmon P. Chase, of Ohio, and John P. Hale, of New Hampshire, both of whom were trying to fuse the antislavery elements of all parties into a new national organization. On his frequent trips to New York, he came to know John A. Dix, John Bigelow, William Cullen Bryant, and other leaders of the "Barn-

[8] Hillard to Lieber, Feb. 16, 1847, Lieber MSS.; Pierce, III, 55, 75–6.
[9] Howe to Lieber, Mar. 15, 1847, Lieber MSS.; Boston *Whig*, Sept. 17, 1847.

burners," the dissatisfied antislavery Democrats who followed ex-
President Martin Van Buren. Closest of all Sumner's new political
friends was Joshua R. Giddings, of Ohio, who was John Quincy
Adams's chief lieutenant in the antislavery struggles in the national House of Representatives. Through Gidding's frequent letters Sumner was able to keep his Massachusetts associates
informed of the latest Washington political gossip, the rumors
about the next presidential candidates, and the strategy of the
tiny but vocal antislavery minority in Congress.[1]

Naturally Sumner's chief political interest during 1847 was
in Massachusetts, where an embittered rivalry between two
groups of Conservative Whig leaders gave the Conscience Whigs
an unexpected opportunity. Hoping to be the Whig presidential
candidate in 1848, Webster made a stately tour through the
South, wooing slaveholders' votes and in the process, Sumner
thought, humbling himself and stultifying his state.[2] But, even
while Webster was angling for the nomination, a group of moneyed Whigs in his own state, headed by Abbott Lawrence and
Nathan Appleton, were resolved that he would never get it. They
were tired of paying Webster gratuities to keep him in public
office; they felt that he had sacrificed the interests of their textile
industry to his own selfish ambition; and, at least in the case of
Lawrence, they considered themselves worthy of the offices that
Webster had so long pre-empted. If unencumbered by Webster,
they thought they could speedily come to terms with Southern
and Western Whigs on the really important issues of tariffs, internal improvements, and banking. Tired of defeat and remembering that the one successful Whig candidate had been a military man, they looked to the Mexican War to produce their
nominee. After the victory at Buena Vista on February 22,
General Zachary Taylor was their man, with Abbott Lawrence
for Vice-President.[3]

[1] Both George W. Julian: *The Life of Joshua R. Giddings* (Chicago: A. C.
McClurg and Company; 1892), and Richard W. Solberg: "Joshua Giddings:
Politician and Idealist" (unpublished Ph. D. dissertation, Univ. of Chicago;
1952) contain detailed accounts of the Sumner-Giddings friendship. The former
includes many of the letters the two men exchanged.

[2] Sumner to Lieber, May 3, 1847, Sumner MSS.

[3] Surprisingly little has been written about the Webster-Lawrence an-
tagonism, which began when Webster refused to resign from John Tyler's
cabinet and was exacerbated by Webster's jealousy of Henry Clay in 1844. As
the leading figures in both factions were careful to maintain a public semblance

The Conscience Whigs, holding a balance between these rival regular factions, found themselves courted by both, and in their political inexperience they had difficulty in keeping their independent position. Early in 1847 Webster's spokesmen approached them with an invitation to join in preventing the renomination of Senator "Honest John" Davis, whose untimely loquacity during the previous session of Congress had killed the Wilmot Proviso, which was designed to exclude slavery from all lands acquired by the Mexican War. Sumner and his friends rejoiced to think that Webster shared their condemnation of Davis's "vacillation and treachery," but they soon learned that his real purpose was to strike at Lawrence through his henchman, Davis.[4]

At the same time, the Lawrence faction showed unusual kindness to the Conscience Whigs. A full year after most Beacon Hill doors were closed to Sumner, Abbott Lawrence still entertained him and his antislavery associates. After Webster's friends determined to force an endorsement of his presidential candidacy through the state Whig convention in 1847, Lawrence's attentions to the conscience junto became increasingly assiduous. When Sumner, Adams, Phillips, Palfrey, and Allen were chosen by primary meetings to attend the state convention, the Conscience Whigs naïvely attributed their success to the carelessness or stupidity of the regular Whig managers, but in fact the Lawrence group was happy to have them serve as hatchet men against Webster.[5]

When the convention met in Springfield on September 29, the Webster men were apparently in full control. Desirous of a

---

of agreement, little appeared in the newspapers about their differences. But see A. B. Darling: *Political Changes in Massachusetts, 1818–1848* ("Yale Historical Publications," Vol. XV, New Haven: Yale University Press; 1925), pp. 325–6; James Schouler: "The Whig Party in Massachusetts," *MHSP*, L (1916–17), 39–53; Hamilton Andrews Hill: *Memoir of Abbott Lawrence* (Boston; 1883), pp. 73–9.

[4] Sumner to Giddings, Feb. 1, and 5, 1847, Sumner MSS.; C. F. Adams, Diary, Feb. 6, and 8, 1847, Adams MSS.

[5] This judgment is admittedly based only upon inferential evidence. C. F. Adams in his diary (Sept. 15, 1847, Adams MSS.) attributed the "unexpected victory" of the Conscience leaders to "some error in tactics" on the part of their opponents and to the disturbing presence of liquor dealers at the caucus. He could not explain, however, how the regular party leaders, who were presumably defeated when Sumner, Adams, et al., were elected delegates, were able promptly to regain control of the caucus and squash resolutions proposed by Sumner which would have embarrassed Taylor's supporters. For a report of the caucus proceedings see the Boston *Advertiser*, Sept. 16, 1847.

unanimous endorsement of Webster as Massachusetts' favorite
son, they were willing to forget "their horror at the youthful Anti-
Slavery *escapades* of the juvenile portion of the party" and to permit Sumner and his friends to speak at great length, provided
they did not disturb Webster's chances. But by prearrangement
the Conscience Whigs, with the tacit approval of Lawrence's
backers, upset the program by moving that it was "inexpedient to
recommend a nomination of candidates for the Presidency and
Vice Presidency." To appease the strong antislavery element that
backed the motion, Webster's friends on the platform committee
worked desperately to produce a set of resolutions acceptable to
the Conscience minority. While they labored, Webster himself
took the stand, and, keeping a careful eye on the door through
which the committee must return to the convention with their
compromise scheme, he delivered one of the most remarkable
and agile speeches of his career. The longer the committee delayed, the more articulate Webster's antislavery opinions became. By the end of two hours, the *Liberator* gibed, a miracle had
occurred. "He who had gone up, as men thought, the Oldest of
the Old Whigs, came down again younger than the Youngest! His
youth was renewed like the eagle's. . . . He had never been an
Old Whig at all. He had always indulged in a Conscience. The
Wilmot Proviso was not Mr. Wilmot's, after all, but Mr. Webster's
thunder." [6]

Thus far Sumner and his friends had unwittingly served
Lawrence well. Even though the convention finally accepted a
resolution endorsing Webster, they had compelled him to make
antislavery statements that would certainly injure him in the
South, and they had demonstrated that Massachusetts was anything but unanimously behind her favorite son.

But, having used the Conscience Whigs to destroy Webster,
the Lawrence faction was now ready to discard them. When Palfrey moved "That the Whigs of Massachusetts will support no
men as candidates for the offices of President and Vice President,
but those who are known by their acts or declared opinions to be
opposed to the existence of Slavery," Lawrence's friends, who had
sat complacently silent while Webster was under attack, furiously

[6] C. F. Adams, Diary, Sept. 29, 1847, Adams MSS.; Boston *Advertiser*, Sept.
30, 1847; *The Liberator*, Oct. 8, 1847.

fought back, lest the resolution jeopardize the chances of the slaveholding Zachary Taylor. In the acrimonious debate, Sumner again clashed directly with Winthrop. While Sumner was speaking, the congressman made a "sullen and impudent interruption," and Sumner flashed back with scornful denunciation of one who could "say, with detestable morality, 'Our party, *right or wrong.*'" "Loyalty to principle is higher than loyalty to party," Sumner warned. "Whatever the final determination of this Convention, there are many here to-day who will never yield support to any candidate, for Presidency or Vice-Presidency, who is not known to be against the extension of Slavery, even though he have freshly received the sacramental unction of a 'regular nomination.'"[7]

Defeated by the Lawrence machine, the Conscience Whigs did not fully understand what had happened to them. Puzzled by the fact they were able to destroy the genuinely antislavery Webster, but were impotent against the proslavery Taylor, they feebly explained their final failure by the early departure from the convention of country delegates, who supposedly went home to milk the cows. Regardless of the causes of the fiasco, they were sure of the consequences. The Conscience Whigs left Springfield, aware that they could never attend another Whig convention.

Sumner, for one, did not leave the party with great reluctance. He had never been "an ultra Whig," but he had hoped that the old party would become an antislavery organization. His quarrel with Winthrop had disillusioned him, and as early as January 1847 he had thought it "more than probable that we shall be obliged to enter the next Presidential contest with our own candidate." A new political movement might extricate the Conscience group "from our present uncomfortable position, of political association with those who really hate us more [than] they hate the Locofocos."[8] "Let the lines be drawn," he urged after the Springfield convention. "The sooner the better."[9]

[7] Boston *Whig*, Oct. 1, 1847; Linus B. Comins to Sumner, Mar. 22, 1861, Sumner MSS.; Sumner: *Works*, II, 61–2.

[8] "Locofoco" was originally a term applied to the antimonopoly wing of the New York City Democrats, but by the 1840's Whigs used it as a smear word for all members of the Democratic party.

[9] Sumner: *Works*, II, 76; Sumner to Giddings, Jan. 6, 1846 [the date should be 1847], and Dec. 1, 1847, Giddings MSS.

CHAPTER VII

Glacial Solitude

I AM TIRED of the anomalous position which is forced upon dissenting Whigs here in Massachusetts," Sumner exclaimed a few months after his defeat in the Springfield convention. "Let us have an open field, and direct battle, instead of private assassination and assault which is our lot here—suspected, slandered, traduced by those who profess to call themselves Whigs." If the Conscience Whigs would face the fact that they had no future in a party dominated by Abbott Lawrence and Nathan Appleton, they would look elsewhere for political allies. "Unexpected combinations" with other antislavery groups, of Democratic, Liberty, and even abolitionist antecedents, might be worked out. Even if a new political party could not be formed immediately, Sumner thought, "all of us, who are in earnest in our opposition to slavery, should cultivate kindly relations with each other—in view of some future association." [1]

· 1 ·

Though the Conscience leaders as early as 1847 were prepared to bolt the Whig party rather than support a slaveholding candidate, and though the Cotton Whigs announced that their departure would be a welcome "sluice way through which, the Whig party could run off a good deal of cumbersome material, and thereby purify itself," [2] the farewells were protracted and acrimonious.

Undeterred by the triumph of the Lawrence faction in the

---

[1] Sumner to Chase, Oct. 1, 1847, and Feb. 7, 1848, Chase MSS., Lib. of Cong.
[2] T. N. Brewer to William Schouler, May 1848, William Schouler MSS.

state convention of 1847, the Conscience Whigs continued to attack Winthrop, now especially vulnerable as he was the Whig
candidate for speaker of the national House of Representatives.
After consulting with other members of the junto, Palfrey, who
had recently been elected to Congress, joined with one or two
other antislavery Whigs to vote against Winthrop, and his action
almost cost Massachusetts the speakership.

Though respectable Boston felt "ineffable contempt and disgust" at Palfrey's course, Sumner rejoiced in his "courage, firmness and *conscience*." [3] When the *Atlas* and the *Advertiser* attacked Palfrey for his vote, the Conscience clique came to his
defense. Adams and S. C. Phillips praised Palfrey in the *Whig*,
and Sumner in anonymous letters in the *Courier* extolled his independence and integrity as among the state's "brightest posses-
sions, more precious far than all the distinctions of office, or the
rewards of political success." [4]

The venom with which the Cotton Whigs replied indicated
that they had already singled out Sumner as the most dangerous,
and perhaps the most exposed, of the Conscience leaders. The
editor of the influential Boston *Atlas*, William Schouler, publicly
ridiculed Sumner's "cant," his "inordinate vanity and self-con-
ceit," his "puerile self-consequence," his "vagrant theories, and
transcendental abstractions," and, most of all, his "personal
malignity" in attacking Winthrop. [5]

"I feel the bitter personality of this attack upon myself more
than I thought I should ever again feel anything a newspaper
could say," Sumner admitted to Palfrey. [6] His friends appeared indifferent to the "envenomed" attacks Schouler was making. Phillips finished his series of articles against Winthrop and fell silent.
Adams supported Sumner vigorously until February, when John
Quincy Adams died. Touched by Winthrop's obviously sincere
admiration of his father and by his many kindnesses to the Adams
family, he then dropped the quarrel.

[3] Sumner to Palfrey, Dec. 8, and 10, 1847, Palfrey MSS.; Ezra Lincoln to
William Schouler, Dec. 12, 1847, William Schouler MSS. For a thorough study of
the Palfrey-Winthrop controversy see Frank Otto Gatell: "Palfrey's Vote, the
Conscience Whigs, and the Election of Speaker Winthrop," *New England Quarterly*, XXXI (1958), 218–31.
[4] Boston *Semi-Weekly Courier*, Dec. 23, 1847.
[5] Boston *Atlas*, Jan. 3, 27, and 29, 1848.
[6] Sumner to Palfrey, Jan. 27, and 31, 1848, Palfrey MSS.

Desperately casting about for assistance, Sumner turned to Giddings, that "master of us all in antislavery matters." The Ohio congressman told him a new reason why Palfrey had been correct in opposing Winthrop: "At a meeting of the Whig members of the House of Representatives, held on the morning on which our present war with Mexico was declared, Mr. Winthrop made a speech urging the whole party to vote for the war. While the bill was pending in the House, he went among his colleagues and personally urged them to sustain the bill, containing one of the most flagrant falsehoods ever uttered by a deliberative body." Without trying to check the facts, Sumner rushed into print with Gidding's charges.[7]

He paid for his precipitancy. Informed by Winthrop himself that Giddings's accusation was false, Schouler, in the *Atlas*, bluntly branded Sumner's story as a lie and connected it with the "vindictiveness" and "malignity" of his previous attacks. Frantic, Sumner begged Giddings for proof of his charges. But Giddings delayed; then he expressed qualms about appearing publicly in the controversy; and finally he sent along a weak collection of statements from congressmen who disagreed as to whether a caucus had been held, whether Winthrop had been present, and whether he had spoken in favor of the war bill. Even Sumner had to admit that Giddings's proofs were "less strong than he had anticipated." Schouler triumphantly noted that they were "frivolous." "As for Sumner," wrote one wealthy Boston merchant at the end of the controversy, "the more I hear about him, . . . the more difficult it is for me to believe him to be an honest man."[8]

· 2 ·

In attacking Winthrop, Sumner and his allies were really striking at the Cotton Whigs who were promoting the nomination of Zachary Taylor for President in 1848. None of the Conscience group could support the slaveholding Taylor, and Sumner, with his peace principles, was especially hostile to any military man. In his curiously naïve way he called on Abbott Lawrence, promi-

7 Boston *Whig*, Jan. 15, 1848.
8 Boston *Atlas*, Jan. 27, and Mar. 17, 1848; Sumner to Giddings, Feb. 3, 10, and 11, and Mar. 25, 1848, Giddings MSS.; J. H. Clifford to Winthrop, Mar. 27, 1848, Winthrop MSS.

nently mentioned as a likely running mate for Taylor, in the hope of convincing him that the general was not entitled to the Presidency.

"I am your friend," Sumner informed the manufacturer. "I have faith in the sincerity, the goodness and generosity of your nature. I do not believe you actuated . . . by a desire for the Vice Presidency . . . ; and I now plead with you to withdraw from this movement in which you are involved."

Genially Lawrence replied: "*What can I do about it;* I AM IN UP TO THE EYES."

Righteously Sumner retorted: "Get out of it. . . . It is never too late to begin to do right." [9]

But it was hard even for the Conscience Whigs to know what was right for 1848. They were opposed to Taylor, but the other possible candidates for the Whig nomination all had weaknesses. General Winfield Scott had antislavery sentiments, but Sumner objected to him as another "instrument of this atrocious war." Justice John McLean, of the United States Supreme Court, was popular among conservatives, but the Conscience group doubted his antislavery zeal. For a time Sumner was enthusiastic about Senator Thomas Corwin, who had eloquently denounced the Mexican War, but the Ohioan proved reluctant to commit himself to the rigid antislavery doctrines of the Conscience group. The newly elected senator from New Hampshire, John P. Hale, was entirely willing to endorse their principles, but he had no general popularity and was tainted by his previous acceptance of a Liberty nomination. Conscience Whig leaders began to think that the most attractive possibility to defeat Taylor was Daniel Webster, whose campaign they had so effectively sabotaged only the previous year. Henry Wilson openly announced that Webster was his first choice for the Presidency, and even Sumner had an occasional "fit" of "the mania of Mr. Webster," until Charles Francis Adams reconvinced him that Webster lacked moral principles.[1]

[9] Sumner to Nathan Appleton, Aug. 31, 1848, copy, Sumner MSS.
[1] Sumner to Giddings, May 6, 1848, Nov. 1, 1847, and July 28, 1847, Giddings MSS.; Sumner to Lieber, Mar. 22, 1847, Sumner MSS.; Sumner to S. P. Chase, Feb. 7, 1848, Chase MSS., Lib. of Cong.; Sumner to Thomas Corwin, Sept. 7, 1847, copy, Sumner MSS.; Sumner to Giddings, Feb. 19, 1847, ibid.; Sumner to Palfrey [Apr. 23, 1848], Palfrey MSS.; Wilson to Webster, May 31, 1848, Webster MSS., Dartmouth Coll.; Adams, Diary, Mar. 29, 1848, Adams MSS.

Even while hoping that the Whig convention would come up with a candidate of acceptable antislavery views, the Conscience leaders were exploring the possibilities of uniting the dissatisfied Whigs, the Liberty party men, and the antislavery Democrats into a third party. Sumner joyfully welcomed the prospect of such a union. "Let us all join in earnest labor," he urged, "not against *each other*—but against *Slavery*." To the dismay of his more cautious associates, he came actually to desire the disruption of the Whig party. "The truth is," Charles Francis Adams sourly remarked, "Sumner is impulsive and ardent and this carries him perpetually to an extreme." [2]

Sumner played an important role in the informal pre-convention discussions of a united antislavery front. As he held no political position and had no known political aspirations, he could talk with Democrats and Liberty men with less likelihood of committing the other members of his group; at the same time, the other Conscience Whigs knew that his tendency to converse "upon abstract points" concerning lofty principles "would keep him out of the range of imprudence as to passing events." [3] There was also the practical consideration that Sumner, alone of the Conscience group, had close friends among the "Barnburners," the New York antislavery Democrats, and could discuss the possibilities of fusion in intimacy and privacy with "Prince John" Van Buren, son of the ex-President, John Bigelow, and William Cullen Bryant.[3a] In addition, Sumner's agitation in behalf of edu-

[2] Boston *Whig*, Jan. 19, 1847; Sumner to Giddings, Jan. 22, 1847, Giddings MSS.; Adams, Diary, Jan. 21, 1848, Adams MSS. Frank Otto Gatell's " 'Conscience and Judgment'; The Bolt of the Massachusetts Conscience Whigs," *The Historian*, XXI (1958), 18–45, is the best study of the formation of the Free Soil party in Massachusetts.

[3] C. F. Adams, Diary, Jan. 20, 1848, Adams MSS.

[3a] New York Democrats who were enthusiastic about reform were called "Barnburners" in allusion to the fable of a man who burned his barn in order to get rid of the rats. Their conservative opponents were called "Hunkers" because they allegedly forgot their principles in hungering after office. The story of New York politics in the 1840's is very complex, but in a general way it can be said that the Barnburners, who rallied about Martin Van Buren and his son, were strongly opposed to slavery. Alienated by President Polk's course, they formed the backbone of the Free Soil party in New York in 1848. After 1849 most of them returned to the Democratic party. Some Barnburners were later to become prominent in the Republican party, though others, most notably the Van Burens, remained stanchly Democratic. Herbert D. A. Donovan: *The Barnburners* (New York: New York University Press; 1925); William Trimble: "Diverging Tendencies in New York Democracy in the Period of the Locofocos," *American Historical Review*, XXIV (1919), 396–421; Ernest P. Muller: "Preston King: A

cation, peace, and prison reform had won him many admirers
in the Liberty party, and John Greenleaf Whittier, who was not
only a poet, but a principal political leader among Massachusetts
abolitionists, had become one of his warmest friends.[3b]

The importance of such personal contacts became apparent
as the two national parties began to break up during the summer
of 1848. When the Democrats nominated Lewis Cass in May,
antislavery men repudiated him as a tool of the South, and the
New York "Barnburners" bolted the party. Throughout New England, antislavery Whigs, anticipating Taylor's success in the Philadelphia convention, were preparing to join the insurgent movement. There was going to be "an organized revolt at the North,"
Sumner predicted. "We in Massachusetts are maturing it in advance; the same is doing in Ohio. If so, there will be a new party,
having some *principles*, and looking to the good of Humanity." [4]

When the Whig convention brushed aside antislavery protests and nominated Taylor, the Conscience junto swiftly moved
to create a new party. Sumner and Adams promptly circulated a
call for a convention to meet at Worcester on June 28; all Massachusetts voters opposed to both Taylor and Cass were invited.
During the few weeks before the convention, planning for the
new party consumed all of Sumner's time. Through Giddings and
Dr. Gamaliel Bailey, the editor of the *National Era* in Washington, he tried to synchronize developments in Massachusetts with
antislavery movements in other states. Spurring along the "Barnburners," Sumner helped persuade ex-President Martin Van Buren
to write letters that, despite their customary ambiguity, could be
interpreted as endorsing antislavery. He persuaded Whittier that
Hale, the Liberty candidate, was hopeless as a coalition leader and
must be withdrawn.[5]

Political Biography" (unpublished Ph. D. dissertation, Columbia Univ.; 1957);
Walter L. Ferree: "The New York Democracy: Division and Reunion, 1847–
1852" (unpublished Ph. D. dissertation, Univ. of Pennsylvania; 1953); Martin
Lichterman: "John Adams Dix, 1798–1897" (unpublished Ph. D. dissertation,
Columbia Univ.; 1952).

[3b] J. Welfred Holmes: "Whittier & Sumner: A Political Friendship," *New
England Quarterly*, XXX (1957), 58–72.

[4] C. F. Adams, Diary, May 27, 1848, Adams MSS.; Sumner to George Sumner, May 30, 1848, Sumner MSS.

[5] Sumner to Palfrey, June 8, 1848, Palfrey MSS.; Boston *Whig*, June 19,
1848; John Albree (ed.): *Whittier Correspondence from the Oak Knoll Collections, 1830–1892* (Salem: Essex Book and Print Club; 1911), pp. 97–100.

Sumner, as Hillard cynically observed, expected the union of antislavery factions to produce "a new political Jerusalem," and he attended the Worcester convention in a spirit of dedication to a noble cause. The crowd was impressively large, and it responded enthusiastically to vigorous speeches by Giddings, Adams, and Charles Allen. When Sumner was called to the platform, he was powerfully stimulated by his audience and made one of the most effective addresses of his life. A revolution was occurring in American politics, he announced. All the old party issues—the tariff, the bank, internal improvements—were dead. Neither of the old parties dared face the one real remaining issue —the extension of slavery into territory recently acquired from Mexico. Nobody could expect anything from the Democrats under Cass. From the Whig party more might have been anticipated, but it had been perverted from its true principles by a "secret influence which went forth from among ourselves." Taylor's nomination had been procured by a "conspiracy" between Southwestern and Northeastern politicians, "between the cotton-planters and flesh-mongers of Louisiana and Mississippi and the cotton-spinners and traffickers of New England,—between the lords of the lash and the lords of the loom." Consequently, it was time to abandon both the old parties and form a new organization based upon the truth and the right. Then would a new era dawn. "Politics and morals, no longer divorced from each other, become one and inseparable in the holy wedlock of Christian sentiment." [6]

It was well for Sumner that he had the power of self-deception, for the great crusading army he thought he was organizing was, even in Massachusetts, a mongrel assortment of disgruntled Conscience Whigs, a few Webster followers, furious that their chief had been spurned at Philadelphia, some patronage-hungry Democrats, assorted Liberty men, and other disaffected persons. In other states the amalgam was even more curious. In New York the Free Soil forces, under their veneer of antislavery, were mostly the followers of Martin Van Buren, who, as President, had discountenanced the abolition of slavery in the District of Co-

[6] Hillard to "My dear Rogers," Dec. 29, 1847, MS., Mass. Hist. Soc.; Boston *Courier*, June 29, 1848; Boston *Atlas*, June 29, 1848; Boston *Whig*, June 29, 1848; Boston *Advertiser*, June 30, 1848; C. F. Adams, Diary, June 28, 1848, Adams MSS.; Sumner: *Works*, II, 81, 87.

lumbia and had upheld the right of Southern postmasters to burn abolitionist mail. None of these discords and inconsistencies troubled Sumner; he was marching to Zion.

At the national Free Soil convention, which met in Buffalo in early August, Sumner's role was an unimportant one. He was not a delegate, because the Massachusetts representation had to be carefully apportioned among former Whigs, former Democrats, and former Liberty men, and none of these groups considered Sumner as representing their distinctive interests. Nevertheless, he attended the convention as a spectator and watched the enthusiastic delegates nominate Van Buren for President. When there was some talk of inviting Sumner to address an open-air rally, he declined, as he was unaccustomed to speaking without first having memorized a carefully prepared script, and fled, with Charles Francis Adams's oldest son, to Niagara Falls. During their absence Adams was nominated Vice-President.[7]

Returning to Massachusetts with the delegation, Sumner prepared to stump the state in defense of the Free Soil ticket. Everywhere his arguments were the same. The Democratic nominee, Cass, did "not represent the principle of *Freedom.*" The Whig candidate was a successful general, but a man ignorant and inexperienced in civil affairs. In contrast was the Free Soilers' Martin Van Buren, that "veteran statesman, sagacious, determined, experienced, who, at an age when most men are rejoicing to put off their armor, girds himself anew, and enters the lists as champion of Freedom." Obliged to admit that antislavery men had hitherto consistently opposed the ex-President, Sumner rationalized manfully: "It is not for the Van Buren of 1838 that we are to vote, but for the Van Buren of *to-day.*" Men were less important than principles, anyway, and the Free Soil party was "The Party of Freedom," long desired by John Quincy Adams and William Ellery Channing. "Their spirits hover us, and urge us to

[7] R. H. Dana, Diary, July 18, 1848, Dana MSS.; Adams: *Dana*, I, 135–6. On his way to Buffalo, Sumner conferred with New York politicians and, with their approval, tried to interest Edward Everett and John McLean in the second place on a ticket with Van Buren. Everett firmly refused to leave the Whig party, and McLean entrusted his fortunes at the convention to Salmon P. Chase. Sumner to McLean, July 31, 1848, McLean MSS.; Francis P. Weisenburger: *The Life of John McLean: A Politician on the United States Supreme Court* (Columbus: Ohio State University Press; 1937), p. 136; Sumner to Everett, July 31, 1848, Everett MSS.; Everett to Sumner, Aug. 4, 1848, Sumner MSS.; J. A. Briggs to Pierce, Feb. 6, 1877, Pierce MSS.; Adams, Diary, Aug. 9, 1848, Adams MSS.

persevere," Sumner concluded his addresses. "Let us be true to the moral grandeur of our cause." [8]

The Free Soilers discovered that politics demanded organization as well as oratory. Patricians like Dana and Phillips made excellent speeches, but the necessary behind-the-scenes work called for a shrewd, opportunistic politician like Henry Wilson. Though most of the Conscience group scorned Wilson because of his reputation for deviousness and his low social standing, Sumner, who welcomed all allies from all quarters, had no repugnance to working with him. He helped Wilson organize the first Massachusetts state convention of the new party, which met on September 7, and became the chairman of its state central committee.[9]

Inevitably when district conventions met and named candidates for Congress, Sumner was invited to run in the Boston district. As in 1846, he hesitated. To run against Winthrop would re-open all the old quarrels of the past two years; it would renew suspicions that he had been acting for revenge or for personal advancement. Sumner "stands now, as he himself feels, at just the most critical point of his life," Longfellow noted on October 22. "Shall he plunge irrevocably into politics, or not? . . . From politics, as a career, he still shrinks back. When he has once burnt his ships there will be no retreat. He already holds in his hands the lighted torch." [1]

In fact, though Sumner still protested vigorously that he had no desire for office, that his life had other objectives, that he contemplated some great historical work that would occupy his future time (though he never commenced one),[2] his protestations were wearing thin. This time feelings of duty, ambition, and revenge obliged him to accept the nomination in a platitudinous letter declaring: "Morals is the soul of all true politics." [3]

Thoroughly absorbed in politics, Sumner was not discouraged when the Free Soil ticket carried no state in the fall elections and won no electoral votes. "The public mind has been

[8] Outline of a speech delivered at various places during the 1848 campaign, Sumner MSS.; Boston *Republican*, Oct. 19, 1848; Sumner: *Works*, II, 144–5.
[9] Boston *Advertiser*, Sept. 8, 1848; Boston *Republican*, Sept. 8, 1848.
[1] Longfellow, Diary, Oct. 22, 1848, Longfellow MSS.
[2] Sumner to Samuel Lawrence, Nov. 29, 1848, copy, Sumner MSS.
[3] Boston *Republican*, Oct. 28, 1848.

stirred on the subject of slavery to depths never before reached,"
he argued cheerfully; "and much information with regard to the
Slave-Power has been diffused in quarters heretofore ignorant of
this enormous tyranny." Not even Winthrop's victory in the congressional election, held on November 14, just after the presidential balloting, checked Sumner's enthusiasm. He had known
from the start that his candidacy was hopeless, and he found
some consolation in the fact that the Free Soiler tickets in Massachusetts drew a respectable vote. "If we have not reached the
anticipations of the more sanguine," he wrote Giddings, "we have
disappointed all the calculations of our enemies. We have . . .
taken our place, before the Cass party, as the *second* party. First
we are in principles; I trust we shall soon shew ourselves *first* in
numbers." [4]

· 3 ·

"I have spoken a great deal . . . and with a certain effect,"
Sumner reviewed the 1848 campaign in a letter to his brother.
"As a necessary consequence, I have been a mark for abuse. I
have been attacked bitterly; but I have consoled myself by what
J. Q. Adams said to me . . . 'No man is abused whose influence
is not felt.' " [5]

He could have no doubt that Beacon Hill felt his influence.
Nathan Appleton, a kinsman by marriage and father-in-law of
Sumner's best friend, Longfellow, had tried to maintain his
friendship with Sumner even when other Boston doors were
closed to the young agitator, but he found intolerable the accusation that a conspiracy of Southern slaveholders and New England cotton millers, "the lords of the lash and the lords of the
loom," had brought about Taylor's nomination. Curtly Appleton,
who was both one of the largest textile manufacturers in the
United States and a firm supporter of Taylor's candidacy, asked
whether Sumner had any evidence for such a charge or whether
it was "a mere rhetorical flourish." For several weeks Sumner refused to reply because of Appleton's lordly tone; then he composed a long review of the evidence which sustained his accusa-

---

[4] Sumner to Chase, Nov. 16, 1848, Chase mss., Lib. of Cong.; Sumner to
Giddings, Nov. 10, 1848, Giddings mss.
[5] Sumner to George Sumner, Nov. 15, 1848, Sumner mss.

tion.[6] Appleton found in the reply only reports, impressions, newspaper columns and gossip—"very *skimble skamble stuff*, in the way of evidence"—and declared that Sumner had not proved any "conspiracy," much less an "unholy" one. In the past, Appleton added, he had watched Sumner's course "more in sorrow than in anger." Now the time for charity had passed; he could only regard Sumner as a malignant liar. Henceforth when the textile manufacturer visited his daughter at Craigie House, Longfellow carefully warned Sumner to stay away.[7]

Another old friend, Samuel Lawrence, who had once helped finance Sumner's trip to Europe, also took umbrage at the "lords of the loom" conspiracy charge. "How an intelligent Massachusetts man could have given utterance to these words," Lawrence wrote angrily, "is beyond my comprehension . . . you appear in the eyes of your friends as a demagogue." Once again Sumner tried to defend himself; his objective in political life, he said, was not to advance himself, but "to introduce into politics the principles of Christianity." Savagely Lawrence retorted: "Your desire 'to intro[duce] into Politics the principles of Christianity' is so strong that . . . you have joined a Faction whose leaders . . . are [Henry] Wilson . . . and Mr. Martin Van Buren!!!!" "You and I never can meet on mutual ground," Lawrence concluded. "I can contemplate you only in the character of a Defamer of those you profess to love, and an enemy to the permanency of this Union."[8]

Even Sumner's more intimate friendships were disrupted by politics. Of the Five of Clubs only Howe fully sympathized with Sumner's Free Soil activities; Longfellow, though deeply antislavery, was uninterested in political warfare; and Hillard and Felton were on the Whig side. With little of the old comradely spirit left, the club sometimes failed to meet for months on end. "A pity these meetings should be so interrupted," Longfellow lamented. "Nothing but politics now! Oh where are those genial days, when literature was the theme of our conversation!"[9]

[6] For copies of both sides of this correspondence, which stretched from July 4 through August 31, 1848, see the Sumner-Appleton MSS.

[7] Appleton to Sumner, Sept. 4, 1848, copy, Appleton MSS.; Longfellow to Sumner [June 1849], Longfellow MSS.

[8] Lawrence to Sumner, Nov. 7, and Dec. 4, 1848, Sumner MSS.; Sumner to Lawrence, Nov. 29, 1848, copy, ibid.

[9] Longfellow, Diary, Dec. 27, 1845, and Sept. 17, 1848, Longfellow MSS.

Though Felton continued to protest undying affection for his "Dearly Beloved Charley," he found it increasingly difficult to get along with Sumner. When Sumner announced that William Lloyd Garrison was "an angel, that we are entertaining unawares," Felton, related by marriage to the most conservative families in Boston, snapped back that Garrison was "a demon." Unable to bear contradiction, Sumner accused the professor "of no longer sympathizing with him"; Felton, in turn, complained that Sumner was "running into all manner of extravagances and vitiating his naturally sweet disposition." Year by year their relations grew worse. When Felton tried to defend the Whig view of political affairs, Sumner treated him like a heckler in an audience, "rushing and sweeping over him in argument, as if he were nobody," and the outraged Harvard Latinist protested that he could not and would not "stand this over-bearing and down-bearing proceeding any longer." Sumner, he complained, was becoming so intolerant as "to think that difference from his opinions can only proceed from a bad head or a corrupt heart." "It almost seems," he added bitterly, "as if the *love of man* meant [to Sumner] the *hatred of men*." In 1850, when Sumner charged him with being "vindictive, bitter and unchristian" toward the friends of true liberty, Felton exclaimed that he would not endure "language . . . that gentlemen should not address to housebreakers and pickpockets," and broke off social intercourse.[1]

Hillard, too, was drifting away from Sumner. He had sympathized with Sumner's earlier views; he had admired the moral fervor of "The True Grandeur of Nations," supported Sumner in the prison discipline controversy, and helped rally anti-Texas sentiment in 1845. But, as Sumner became increasingly rabid on these subjects, Hillard, restrained by frail health, a gentle and conciliatory disposition, and his friendship for the Ticknors, held back.[2] With genuine anguish he watched Sumner become increasingly absorbed in politics, for he did not think his partner well fitted for a life of action. "Sumner," he astutely observed, "is

[1] Ibid., Dec. 26, 1845, May 16, 1847, and Dec. 19, 1849; Felton to Sumner, Jan. 27 [1846], Sumner MSS.; Sumner to Felton, Apr. 9, 1850, copy, Sumner MSS.; Felton to Palfrey, Sept. 13, 1850, Palfrey MSS.; Felton to Howe, Apr. 11, 1850, Howe MSS.

[2] Hillard analyzed his own weaknesses in letters to Lieber, Sept. 28, 1835, and Jan. 6, 1860, Lieber MSS.

so much occupied with thoughts of how the world is to be made
better, that he does not pause to consider and observe what the
world really is." [3]

As Sumner regarded anything short of unqualified approval
as little less than a personal affront, he came to regard Hillard
with increasing coolness. In the spring of 1847, when Hillard
was seriously ill and confined to his house for eight days, Sumner
did not take time to visit him. [4]

A few months later Hillard sailed to Europe for his health,
and, upon his return, he moved his law practice to new quarters.
"Sumner was so absorbed in politics," he explained, "and his
office was such a rendezvous for abolitionists, free soilists and
all other *ists*, that it was quite impossible to think of doing any
business there." He did not break off all contact with Sumner, but
kept up a thin, formal relationship. "We have made up our fagots
for life, and we will not wrangle or 'establish raws' upon subjects
on which we shall never agree," he told Sumner, "but will respect
each other's intellectual rights and accept each other's convictions as facts." [5]

· 4 ·

Though Sumner spoke of himself as being excluded from virtually every house on Beacon Hill and loudly bewailed his social
isolation, he was not, in fact, without friends. Even in the best
Boston society there were a few families, like the Josiah Quincys,
the John Lodges, and the W. H. Prescotts, who continued to welcome him.

If politics excluded Sumner from the Ticknor circle, they
made him the more welcome in the Adams family. [6] While the old
President was alive, he always greeted Sumner with tremulous
enthusiasm. Charles Francis Adams was naturally more reserved, but he encouraged Sumner to come out to Quincy for

[3] Hillard to Lieber, Nov. 25, 1846, ibid.
[4] Hillard to Lieber, Feb. 16, 1847, ibid.
[5] Hillard to Lieber, Dec. 5, 1848, ibid; Pierce, III, 250–1.
[6] Sumner also became increasingly intimate with Theodore Parker and
Ralph Waldo Emerson, who invited him to edit the new transcendalist journal,
The Massachusetts Quarterly Review. Theodore Parker to Sumner [1846], Sumner MSS.; Rusk (ed.): *Emerson Letters,* III, 391–4; Ralph L. Rusk: *The Life of
Ralph Waldo Emerson* (New York: Charles Scribner's Sons; 1949), p. 324.

dinner every Friday or Saturday. To the older Adams boys,
John, Henry, and Charles Francis, Jr., the embattled Sumner,
fighting for the cause of Truth and Virtue, was a heroic figure, a
"boy's ideal of greatness; the highest product of nature and art."
Of course, upon occasion, they grew restive under Sumner's mor-
alizing and took advantage of his want of humor. At dinner once
Sumner attempted "in his rather direct way" to instill into young
Henry Adams a love for historical study. "Why, Henry," he said
solemnly, "I am sure you would never let a slice of pudding stand
in your way to a slice of history!" When John pertly replied:
"You bet your life, Mr. Sumner, he wouldn't let it stand in the way
long," Sumner's face presented a picture of puzzled bafflement.
But, for all Sumner's seriousness, they admired him greatly;
years later Charles Francis Adams, Jr., declared that he "owed far
more to Charles Sumner than to all of the Harvard professors
put together." [7]

With the Howes, too, Sumner continued on terms of closest
intimacy. Julia, to be sure, sometimes found it a strain to have to
prepare the kind of "neat little dinner" he liked—"soup, salmon,
sweetbreads, roast lamb and pigeon, with green peas, potatoes *au
maitre d'hotel*, spinach, and salad, . . . pudding and blanc-
mange, then strawberries, pineapple, and ice-cream, then coffee,
etc." More than once she was vexed when Sumner persuaded her
husband to go out campaigning, leaving her alone in South Boston with a houseful of small children. She used to sing to her
babies:

> Rero, rero, riddety rad;
> This morning my baby caught sight of her Dad.
> Quoth she, "Oh Daddy, where have you been?"
> "With Mann and Sumner, a-putting down sin!"

Still, she admitted Sumner's purity of character and true friendship for her husband and concluded that he was "funny, but very
good and kind."

Her children adored Sumner—as children nearly always
did. They scrambled over his massive frame and called him "the
harmless giant." For years one of the Howe daughters used Sum-

[7] Henry Adams: *Education*, p. 31; *Pierce Dinner*, p. 40; Charles Francis
Adams: *Charles Francis Adams, 1835–1915: An Autobiography . . .* (Boston:
Houghton Mifflin Co.; 1916), p. 37.

ner's stately figure as a unit of measure, saying "that a thing was so much higher or lower than Mr. Sumner." [8]

Howe himself remained everything Sumner could desire in a friend—devoted, sympathetic, adulatory. He rejoiced when Sumner was victorious, and comforted him when he was in despair. "I know not where you may be, or what you may be about," he wrote once when Sumner was sulking during a depressed mood, "but I know what you are *not* about; you are not seeking your own pleasure, or striving to advance your own interests. You are, I warrant me, on some errand of kindness, some work for a friend or for the public." [9]

When Sumner wished to assume a less Olympian pose, he could always go out to the Longfellows' house in Cambridge. Giving Sumner unquestioning admiration and love, the Longfellows tried to divert his mind from politics. On his regular Sunday visits he inspected the improvements Longfellow was making at Craigie House, and he was especially charmed by the new shower bath the poet installed in his dressing room. Standing nude under it, ready to pull the string, he would announce to Longfellow: "This is a kind of Paradise."

"And you a kind of Adam!" replied the poet.

"With all my ribs," laughed Sumner, attempting a rare witticism, and then he let the deluge descend.[1]

The Longfellow children, too, loved Sumner, and no sooner did he settle into his favorite rocking chair at Craigie House than one of the three little daughters would snuggle in his lap. They liked his stately attempts at humor, and giggled hysterically when he would ceremoniously open a door for one of the tiny children with a grand wave of his hand and a sonorous "*In presequas.*" The Longfellow boys were a bit more restive under Sumner's solemnity, and objected strongly to his elephantine humor in taking a child's hand, grinding his thumb into the back of it until the pain was unbearable, and then releasing it with a laugh.

The entire Longfellow family at times found Sumner inex-

[8] Richards and Elliott: *Julia Ward Howe*, I, 121, 127–8, 152; Richards: *S. G. Howe*, II, 228.

[9] Richards: *S. G. Howe*, II, 189–91.

[1] Longfellow, Diary, June 14, 1846, Longfellow MSS. Ernest Longfellow, who did not like Sumner very much, erroneously remembered that he stepped into the shower fully clad and got drenched. *Random Memories* (Boston: Houghton Mifflin Co.; 1922), p. 22.

pressibly, if unintentionally, funny, and they long remembered
the occasion when Sumner, strolling in the garden after dinner,
decided to pet a calf tethered in the yard. In his "bucolic moment
of enthusiasm for the fascinations of rural life," Sumner—"he
who knows not grass from grain," Longfellow laughed—seized
the rope and pulled the calf nearer and nearer, saying "Come
here! Come here!" With a sudden leap the "idyl[l]ic animal"
sprang away; "there is a glimmer of gray gaiters high in air, and
prone lies the philanthropist on the sod." "So much for cockney
ruralizing," laughed Fanny, while Henry mercilessly compared
Sumner's position with that of the Free Soil party. Dignity gravely
wounded, Sumner turned majestically upon young Charlie, who
was guffawing wildly: "When a friend meets with an accident
you ought not to laugh at him; you ought to pity, and sympathize
with him!" [2]

Still, their laughter was in good fun, not in malice, for Sumner was truly welcome at Craigie House. "I am delighted to see
him so often," Longfellow wrote in his diary; "the face of a friend,
and such a friend! is what one cannot see too much of; never
enough." [3]

In spite of such a circle of genuine friends, Sumner never
ceased to grieve that Boston society had turned against him.
"There was a time," he once remarked when driving down Beacon Street, "when I was welcome at almost every house within
two miles of us, but now hardly any are open to me." Though he
was still "rarely without a pocket-full of letters from duchesses or
noblemen in England," he now had no one to read them to. He
felt absolutely alone. "His solitude was glacial," Henry Adams remembered, "and reacted on his character. He had nothing but
himself to think about." [4]

The role of martyr came easily to Sumner. Since childhood
he had felt that he was discriminated against, imposed upon, and
unjustly attacked. "I cannot but think how many *rubs* it is my for-

[2] Annie Longfellow Thorp: "A Little Person's Little Memories of Great
People" (MS. in the Longfellow MSS.); Ernest Longfellow: *Random Memories*,
p. 21; Longfellow, Diary, Nov. 4, 1849; Fanny Longfellow to Mary and Tom,
Nov. 5, 1849, Longfellow MSS.
   [3] Longfellow, Diary, June 12, 1846, ibid. Cf. Fanny Longfellow's affectionate
references to Sumner. Edward Wagenknecht (ed.): *Mrs. Longfellow: Selected
Letters and Journals of Fanny Appleton Longfellow*, pp. 124, 152, and 175.
   [4] Henry Adams: *Education*, pp. 30–1.

tune to receive," he lamented. Surely no one else suffered quite so much, and so undeservedly. When gossip spread the story that his brother George was a Russian spy, Sumner, instead of denouncing the canard, merely reflected that George's trials were nothing compared to "the fiery torrents" to which he himself had been exposed. The malignant powers of evil seemed to have concentrated their forces upon him. "Why," he sadly questioned, "if . . . I render no evil, and say no evil, am I the mark for so much? I cannot turn my bosom away from my most intimate friends without receiving a shaft. I begin to feel a distrust of everybody. Nobody is true; and all the words of kindness which drop, like fresh coin, from the lips of those I meet, are counterfeit." [5]

But, instead of collapsing under what he regarded as a combination of persecutors, this holy, blissful martyr thrived upon his torments. When left alone to the "tranquil pursuits and tranquil pleasures" he claimed he craved, Sumner was often ill. But, as soon as he became active in politics and became Boston's " 'caput lupinum' against whom every body was throwing a stone," his health amazingly was restored. Hillard's analysis of Sumner was, as usual, shrewd: "His mind and character require the stimulus of something outward and exoteric, some strong pressure, to take him out of himself and prevent him from a morbid habit of inactive brooding. He is a man of moral enthusiasm; made to identify himself with some great Cause and accept and surrender himself to it unconditionally." [6]

Despite his embattled isolation, which he interpreted as social martyrdom for the sake of high principle, Sumner was happier than he had been for years. He received much comfort from his friends—and perhaps even more from his enemies. "Amidst these troubles," he admitted, "I think I have found a higher satisfaction than I have experienced in any former period of my life, derived partly from the intensity of occupation but more from the intimate conviction that I was doing my duty." [7] "The world with ignorant or intolerant judgment may condemn," he added smugly; "the countenances of companions may be averted; the

[5] Sumner to Palfrey, Feb. 22, 1848, Palfrey MSS.; Sumner to Greene, July 28, 1849, Greene MSS.; Sumner to Howe [Apr. 24, 1845], Sumner MSS.
[6] Hillard to Lieber, Apr. 14, 1847, Dec. 5, 1848, and Mar. 28, 1849, Lieber MSS.
[7] Sumner to Mrs. George Bancroft, Jan. 24, 1849, Bancroft MSS.

hearts of friends grow cold; but the consciousness of duty done will be sweeter than the applause of the world, than the countenance of companion, or the heart of friend." [8]

• 5 •

The outcome of the 1848 election posed political as well as personal problems for Sumner. Massachusetts Free Soil leaders were sharply divided over the future course of their party. The more distinguished Conscience Whigs, such as Adams, Phillips, and Dana, wanted the party to maintain an absolutely independent course, without *"making terms"* with either Democrats or Whigs.[9] They were proud of the nearly 40,000 votes the new party had attracted in its first presidential contest. Its following was well distributed throughout the state. Van Buren had received an absolute majority of votes in forty-one of the Commonwealth's 312 towns, drawing his heaviest support from the Worcester area in central Massachusetts, which was unhappy at being forcibly drawn into the economic orbit of Boston. Free Soil voting, moreover, followed a pattern that offered considerable promise for the future. Instead of supporting Sumner's theory that antislavery votes came from the declining rural sections of Massachusetts, the election returns showed that the party had won pluralities in only six towns in the three western, most rural counties, but had carried such growing industrial centers as Worcester, Leicester, Fitchburg, and Grafton. Nor, even within the cities, was the Free Soil vote a limited, one-class following. In Boston, for example, Sumner's vote was widely scattered, coming about equally from rich and poor wards, from native American and heavily Irish precincts. There was, in other words, opportunity in Massachusetts for a broadly based, permanent Free Soil party to develop, if only it kept itself unentangled.[1] "The truth is," said Adams, one of the

[8] Sumner to Samuel Lawrence, Nov. 29, 1848, copy, Sumner MSS.

[9] Dana, Diary, Sept. 9, 1849, Dana MSS.

[1] MS. election returns for gubernatorial and presidential races, 1848, Mass. State Archives; Boston *Republican*, Nov. 15, and 22, 1848. I have found no significant statistical correlation between the percentage of Free Soil votes and the size of towns, their relative rank as manufacturers of woollens, cotton goods, or shoes, or the percentage of foreign-born inhabitants. A ward-by-ward statistical analysis of Sumner's vote in Congressional District No. 1 (Boston) similarly reveals no significant relationship between Free Soil vote and the wealth of the inhabitants (calculated upon the basis of the number of persons per housing

chief advocates of a permanent, independent third party, "the democratic and Whig parties are the Scylla and Charibdis of our principles and we must guard equally against both." [2]

When men like Adams, Phillips, Palfrey, and Dana permitted themselves to contemplate any political alliance, they looked naturally back toward the Whig party, from which they had originally come. They still had friends in the old party. Some of the original Conscience group, like Horace Mann, had never severed Whig connections; fearing to imperil both his much needed congressional salary and his work in Massachusetts education, he had remained neutral in the 1848 presidential campaign. Now that the election was over, Mann counseled the healing of the breach between Free Soilers and Whigs. "With what power such men as Phillips and Palfrey . . . and Sumner, could act upon the whigs," he argued persuasively, "if they did not stand in a hostile attitude toward them?" Even the Cotton Whigs, perturbed by the 1848 defection, were willing to forget the past and welcome the erring brothers home. Winthrop, who had suffered most from the Boston antislavery politicians, wanted to leave the door open to reconciliation; "silence is the best policy," he urged. [3]

But some of the less socially prominent Free Soil politicians, men like Henry Wilson, John B. Alley, Francis W. Bird, and E. L. Keyes, who had performed the ward-by-ward work of organizing the party in 1848, hoped for a very different sort of alliance. Recognizing that practically all the conspicuous orators in the Massachusetts Free Soil movement had come from the Whig party, they also knew that fully forty-five per cent of its voters were former

---

unit), the number of Irish residents, or the number of foreign-born voters. I do not suggest that the Free Soilers won many converts among the Irish, who later became bitter opponents of all antislavery groups, but in 1848 relatively few Irish were allowed to vote. Francis DeWitt (comp.): *Abstract of the Census of the Commonwealth of Massachusetts . . . 1855* (Boston: William White; 1857); Francis DeWitt (comp.): *Statistical Information Relating to Certain Branches of Industry in Massachusetts . . . 1855* (Boston: William White; 1856); *Report and Tabular Statement of the . . . State Census of Boston, May 1, 1850 . . .* (City Document, No. 42, Boston: John H. Eastburn; 1850). For a careful study of the Irish in Boston politics during this whole period see Oscar Handlin: *Boston's Immigrants, 1790–1865: A Study in Acculturation* (Cambridge: Harvard University Press; 1941), Chap. 7.

[2] Adams, Diary, Oct. 8, 1850, Adams MSS.

[3] Mann to Samuel Downer, Mar. 21, 1850, Mann MSS.; Winthrop to Everett, Jan. 31, 1849, Everett MSS.

Democrats, whose antislavery was merely one plank in their platform of opposition to all special privilege everywhere.[4] "Our beloved Commonwealth" is at present governed by as perfect a
monied aristocracy as ever existed," one of these embattled
equalitarians wrote Palfrey; "wealth and not men governs." These
voters were never going to join the Whig party. Instead, they felt,
the Free Soilers should combine with the Democrats to "check and
alleviate this evil" of moneyed monopoly.[5]

Sumner's position in this intraparty struggle over the future
of the Free Soil movement was crucial. As one of the original
Conscience leaders, who had repeatedly announced: "I am willing to be in a *minority* in support of our principles,"[6] he could
have given decisive strength to an independent third-party movement. As he had occupied such a prominent position during
three years of warfare against the Cotton Whigs, his colleagues
who wished to re-cement the Whig party would first have to gain
his consent. To those who favored a coalition with the Democrats, Sumner was even more important. His support would break
the united front of old Conscience Whig leaders—Adams, Palfrey, Phillips, Dana, and the rest—opposed to such a fusion. As
"the classical ornament of the anti-slavery party,"[7] Sumner with
his learning and his legal knowledge would give dignity to such
a coalition, and his strong personal following among the young
men, the women, and the clergymen of the Commonwealth
would add to its strength. During the months after the 1848 election, therefore, Sumner was "approached by all parties."[8]

He found all three possibilities attractive. He liked the idea
of an independent party; he secretly hankered for a restoration
of his ties with Boston Whiggery; but he also thought well of a
coalition with the Democrats. Never more than a "weak and pas-
sive Whig," he had always leaned slightly toward Democratic
economic policies, so far as he understood them. As early as 1837

---

[4] William Gleason Bean: "The Transformation of Parties in Massachusetts
. . . from 1848 to 1860" (unpublished Ph. D. dissertation, Harvard Univ.;
1922), pp. 32–3. (Hereafter cited as Bean: "Party Transformations.") For somewhat different figures see Darling: *Political Changes in Massachusetts*, pp.
354–7.
[5] James Russell to Palfrey, Dec. 15, 1848, Palfrey MSS.
[6] Sumner to Giddings, Feb. 1, 6, and 25, 1847, Sumner MSS.
[7] Henry Adams: *Education*, p. 31.
[8] Adams, Diary, May 14, 1850, Adams MSS.

he had disagreed with Judge Story's opinion in the Charles River Bridge case, which upheld the rights of corporate monopoly, and had agreed with the Jacksonian view of Chief Justice Taney that economic opportunity should be available to all.[9] More than most Massachusetts Whigs, he had always had friends in the Democratic party, in his own state, in New York, and, most recently, in Ohio, where Salmon P. Chase had just been elected to the Senate by a Democratic-Free Soil coalition.[1] With his growing ambition, Sumner must have realized that an independent antislavery party had no chance to win offices, that he could look to the Whig hierarchy for no future favors, and that fusion with the Democrats could be politically profitable, as it had paid off in the election of Free Soilers to Congress from Connecticut and Vermont, as well as from Ohio.

Shortly after the election of 1848 Sumner began making statements he once would have condemned as Jacksonian demagoguery. He shocked his friends by declaring that American democracy had more to fear "from the corruption of wealth than from mobs." He grew enthusiastic about the European revolutions of 1848, of which he regarded the Free Soil movement as an American counterpart, and hoped that they would destroy the outrageous social and economic injustices that had, to tell the truth, seemed anything but outrageous to him only a few years earlier when he visited England.[2]

Borrowing from the Jacksonian Democrats the idea of equal opportunity and from the French revolutionary spirit the phrase "Equality before the Law," Sumner in 1849 challenged the legality of segregated schools in Boston. In the famous Roberts case, Sumner pointed out the obvious physical inferiority of the school provided for Negroes, but he rested his argument chiefly upon the harmful psychological and sociological consequences of segregation. Anticipating Supreme Court decisions made more than a century later, he argued that both white and Negro children suffered from attending separate schools. Whatever facili-

[9] *MHSP*, XXXV (1901–2), 210–11.
[1] Albert Bushnell Hart (ed.): *Diary and Correspondence of Salmon P. Chase (Annual Report of the American Historical Association,* 1902, Vol. II), pp. 183–4; Sumner to Chase, Feb. 27, 1849, Chase MSS., Lib. of Cong.
[2] Pierce, III, 230; Sumner to Longfellow [Jan. 26, 1850], Longfellow MSS.; Sumner to George Sumner, Oct. 23, 1849, Sumner MSS.

ties were provided, "the separate school is not an equivalent.
. . . The matters taught in the two schools may be precisely the
same, but a school devoted to one class must differ essentially in
spirit and character from that Common School known to the
law, where all classes meet together in Equality." [3] Though Chief
Justice Lemuel Shaw and the Supreme Judicial Court did not
adopt these arguments, based as they were on philosophical
and psychological grounds rather than on common-law precedents, Sumner was content with his fight. As Palfrey said:
"When a question of vast social and constitutional bearings can
be thus brought to the responsible decision of the Courts of Justice, there is good hope that the right will prevail." Only six years
later the Massachusetts legislature, dominated by Sumner's
friends, outlawed racial segregation in all public schools in the
Commonwealth. [4]

In his new, equalitarian mood, Sumner did not mind that
Whigs branded his opinions as "nothing more or less than old
fashioned Jacobinism, or new-fashioned loco-focoism, dressed up
in more gentlemanlike habiliments than they were wont to
wear." He welcomed "any associates from any quarter." He was
sure that the Free Soilers could trust "the instincts of *personal
freedom*" among the Democrats to bring them ultimately to the
cause of antislavery. [5]

As chairman of the Free Soil state executive committee,
Sumner was in a position to help steer the party into the coalition
with Democrats, so much desired by Henry Wilson. In an address, "To the Friends of Freedom in Massachusetts," issued just

[3] Sumner: *Works*, II, 327–76. Two recent, careful scholars conclude that
"Sumner's argument before Shaw deserves to be included in a volume of great
documents on American democracy, for its nobility of sentiment, literary excellence, and grasp of principles which have been validated by modern soci-
ology." Leonard W. Levy and Harlan B. Phillips: "The *Roberts* Case: Source of
the 'Separate but Equal' Doctrine," *American Historical Review*, LVI (1956),
510–18.

[4] For Shaw's decision in the *Roberts* case see Helen Tunnicliff Catterall
(ed.): *Judicial Cases Concerning American Slavery and the Negro* (Washing-
ton: Carnegie Institution; 1936), IV, 512–14. Sumner served without fee in the
Roberts case. For further details on this significant case see: Sumner to George
Sumner, Dec. 10, 1849, Sumner MSS.; Chase to Sumner, Dec. 14, 1849, ibid.;
The Liberator, XX (Apr. 26, 1850), 67; XIX (Dec. 7, 1849), 1951; *Eighteenth
Annual Report, Presented by the Massachusetts Antislavery Society . . . 1850*
(Boston; 1859), p. 48; Palfrey to Sumner, Dec. 12, 1849, Palfrey MSS.

[5] Boston *Republican*, Nov. 12, 1849; Felton to Palfrey, Sept. 13, 1850, Palfrey MSS.; Dana, Diary, Sept. 8, 1849, Dana MSS.

after Taylor's victory in 1848, he stressed that the basic principle of Free Soil was "dear to real Democrats from its connection with the name of Thomas Jefferson," and regularly during the next twelve months he praised "the united regenerated Democracy of the North." [6]

By the 1849 Free Soil state convention Sumner and Wilson were prepared to take the party into a formal alliance with the Massachusetts Democrats. While Wilson managed the floor of the convention, Sumner, as chairman of the committee on resolutions, urged the delegates in opposing slavery not to forget another sort of tyranny, the "selfish, grasping, subtle" money power of the Commonwealth. His resolutions favored "a cheaper system of postage; the abolition of all unnecessary offices and salaries; the election of Post Masters and all other civil officers . . . by the people; the retrenchment of the expenses and patronage of the Federal Government; the improvement of Rivers and Harbors; and . . . the free grant to actual settlers, of reasonable portions of the public lands," and concluded with a fling at "the tendency of the legislation of the Commonwealth to consolidate wealth in corporations." The phrases could have been borrowed from any radical Democratic manifesto of the previous decade, and Massachusetts Whigs saw in Sumner's resolutions "an insidious appeal to class prejudices—an attempt to rouse the hatred of the poor against the rich, and to organize the vulgar passions of envy and jealousy into political action." But, under Wilson's skillful management, the convention, despite some reluctance on the part of Adams and some other former Whigs, swallowed the resolutions without gagging. [7]

When the Massachusetts Democrats, sore because the Southern wing of their party had deserted Cass in 1848 and supported Taylor, simultaneously adopted resolutions affirming opposition "to slavery in every form and color" and declaring that Congress had no power to institute slavery in the territories acquired from Mexico, the groundwork for coalition between the two parties in Massachusetts had been laid. [8]

[6] Boston *Semi-Weekly Republican*, Dec. 28, 1848, and July 25, 1849.
[7] Sumner: *Works*, II, 282–321; C. F. Adams, Diary, Sept. 11–12, 1849, Adams MSS.; Boston *Semi-Weekly Republican*, Sept. 15, 1849; Felton to Palfrey, Sept. 13, 1850, Palfrey MSS.
[8] Bean: "Party Transformations," p. 36.

CHAPTER VIII

A One-Idead
Abolitionist Agitator

❦

As A MORAL movement, our cause naturally appeals to good men of all party complexions," Sumner wrote, just before the 1849 Massachusetts elections. "With us fusion is complete." The election returns proved him a bad prophet. Arrangements for the Democratic-Free Soil coalition had been hastily and imperfectly made, and only in some of the eastern counties were formal fusion tickets placed before the voters. Free Soilers of Whig background were distrustful of what the Boston *Atlas* called a "corrupt bargain" with their life-long political adversaries. Democrats, too, were suspicious of their new allies. The Whigs carried the state by a heavy plurality, and Free Soil votes declined five per cent from 1848. The only comfort for the coalitionists was the fact that the Democratic and Free Soil votes if combined made up fifty-two per cent of the total. Fusion had not worked, but it was still possible.[1]

· 1 ·

National events played directly into the hands of the Massachusetts coalitionists. The Free Soilers had watched unsympathetically as the Taylor administration proved itself incompetent to handle the delicate issues arising from the Mexican War. Dis-

[1] Sumner to Chase, Sept. 18, and 25, 1849, Chase MSS., Lib. of Cong.; Boston *Atlas*, Oct. 22, and 25, and Nov. 1, 1849; MS. election returns, 1849, Mass. State Archives.

counting Southern threats of secession, they, like many Massachusetts Democrats and Whigs, thought that the compromise measures Henry Clay proposed in January 1850 were quite unnecessary concessions to the slaveholders. Sumner was especially aggrieved by the harsh new fugitive slave bill, which was a part of the compromise, and he urged Free Soilers not to "sacrifice one jot or tittle of our principles" even to conserve the Union.[2] Naturally, therefore, antislavery men were horrified when Daniel Webster, on March 7, endorsed Clay's proposals in a massive oration designed to foster national feeling and allay sectional strife.

For once Massachusetts was virtually unanimous in disapproving the course of her distinguished senator. Antislavery men compared his placating of the Southerners to "the ineffable meanness of the lion turned spaniel in his fawnings on the masters whose hands he was licking for the sake of the dirty puddings they might have to toss to him." Sumner agreed that Webster was an "archangel ruined" or "a traitor to a holy cause," comparable only to Judas Iscariot, Strafford, or Benedict Arnold.[3] It was more significant that Boston Whiggery, though, of course, in gentlemanly tones, disapproved of Webster's course as "madness." The powerful Boston *Atlas* openly criticized the Seventh of March speech; not a member of the Massachusetts congressional delegation defended the Senator's views; Winthrop said Webster's speech "would have killed any Northern man except himself." [4]

Angered by opposition to his opinions, Webster vigorously backed the compromise measures and publicly informed Massachusetts that it must conquer its "prejudices" against a strong fugitive slave act. He was furious over Winthrop's mild dissent from his position, and announced that he would "much prefer to see a respectable Democrat elected to Congress, than a professed Whig, tainted with any degree of Free Soil doctrines, or aboli-

2 Sumner to Palfrey, Feb. 15, 1850, Palfrey MSS.; Adams: *Dana*, I, 172; Boston *Semi-Weekly Republican*, Mar. 2, 1850.

3 Nevins: *Ordeal of the Union*, I, 291; Pierce, III, 213–14.

4 T. N. Brewer to William Schouler, Mar. 8, 1850, William Schouler MSS.; Godfrey Tryggve Anderson: "The Slavery Issue as a Factor in Massachusetts Politics from the Compromise of 1850 to the Outbreak of the Civil War" (unpublished Ph. D. dissertation, Univ. of Chicago; 1944), p. 12; Everett, Diary, May 2, 1850, Everett MSS.

tionism." After the sudden death of Taylor, when the new President Millard Fillmore named Webster Secretary of State, adherence to the compromise measures became the test of genuine Massachusetts Whiggery.[5]

The result was to close the door to any possible return of Free Soil dissidents to the Whig party. On the contrary, Webster did all he could to oust from the party men like Horace Mann, who were infected with the antislavery heresy. When the governor appointed Winthrop to succeed Webster in the Senate, and a new election for congressman had to be held in the Suffolk district, Webster personally intervened to keep the Boston Whigs from naming an uncommitted candidate, who might be acceptable to the Boston *Atlas* and other dissidents, and forced the selection of Samuel A. Eliot, Sumner's opponent in the prison discipline quarrels, who was known to endorse every one of the compromise measures, including the fugitive slave act.[6]

To oppose Eliot, the Boston Free Soilers once more nominated Sumner. He had not the slightest hope of winning, for he considered Webster's Seventh of March speech as part of the wave of reaction sweeping over both America and Europe after the liberal strivings of 1848. Still, he announced, his sense of duty did not permit him to refuse any service to the cause of liberty. Other Free Soilers showed a remarkable indifference to his candidacy. A scheduled rally at Faneuil Hall had to be canceled because the invited speakers, "pleading it was no use to waste their breath in such uphill work," did not attend, and his entire campaign consisted of newspaper publication of a rather tepid letter of endorsement by Richard Henry Dana, Jr., and a more vigorous one from David Wilmot. Sumner received fewer than 500 votes.[7]

Eliot's victory, which showed that Webster was firmly in control of Massachusetts Whiggery and that reconciliation with

[5] Webster to "My Dear Sir" [Aug. 11, 1850], Webster MSS., Dartmouth Coll.; Phil Shelton to S. Draper, May 9, 1850, Thurlow Weed MSS.; Webster to Fillmore, Oct. 14, 1850, Fillmore MSS.

[6] Boston *Atlas*, Aug. 14, 1850; Samuel Downer to Mann, Aug. 7, 1850, Mann MSS.

[7] Sumner to William Bates and James W. Stone, Aug. 12, 1850, MS., Boston Public Lib.; Samuel Downer to Mann, Aug. 16, 1850, Mann MSS.; Adams, Diary, Aug. 14, 1850, Adams MSS.; Boston *Traveller*, Aug. 17, 1850; Boston *Atlas*, Aug. 20, 1850.

the Conscience junto was ruled out, strengthened Wilson's desire for a fusion with the Democrats. During the summer of 1850 Sumner's office was the scene of frequent and often acrimonious meetings of the Free Soil leaders. As the fall elections would determine the naming not merely of the next governor, lieutenant governor, president of the state senate, and speaker of the house of representatives, but also of the United States senator to succeed Winthrop, Wilson wanted a formal coalition with the Democrats. Virtually all the original Conscience Whig leaders, who considered Massachusetts Democrats "the shameless apologists of . . . extreme profligacy," condemned such a scheme as "a renunciation of all moral character." So strong were Adams, Dana, and Palfrey against fusion that Wilson, rather than split the party, finally dropped his plan, and on September 10 the caucus compromised on a milk-and-water resolution "forbidding the central organization [of the Free Soil party] from any action [in support of coalition], . . . and leaving the individuals in the minor elections to act as they may deem most advisable." [8]

In all these negotiations Sumner's role was ambiguous. A far better politician than even his friends believed, he knew the advantages of rowing toward his objective with muffled oars. Though aware of Sumner's theoretical faith in the instincts of the Democracy, Adams, Dana, and Palfrey thought that he was opposed to coalition; he always said that any union with the Democrats must be upon the basis of Free Soil principles. He wrote a letter to Wilson, intended to be read at the Free Soil caucus, discouraging "any departure from our customary course, which did not enlist the sympathies of all who have thus far acted together in our movement." He thought it "a step of questionable propriety for our State Committee . . . to enter into an arrangement . . . with the Democrats as to the disposition of offices," and announced that he was "unwilling to be a party to any such bargain." [9]

But, even while making public disclaimers, Sumner was quietly co-operating with Wilson's plans. He left town so as not to be present at the September 10 caucus, where he would have

[8] Samuel Downer to Mann, Aug. 21, 1850, Mann MSS.; Adams, Diary, Aug. 10, and Sept. 10, 1850, Adams MSS.
[9] Sumner to Wilson, Sept. 9, 1850, in Boston *Journal*, Mar. 16, 1874.

had to show his hand, and his letter opposing coalitions, a convenient thing to have on record and one which Wilson carefully
preserved, was deliberately not read to the assembled Free Soil
leaders. Sumner's closest political friends, who were the most active promoters of the coalition, let the party work horses know,
unofficially but definitely, that he was behind the plan.[1]

Adams judged that Sumner, in these maneuvers, exhibited
"some want of character," but it is more realistic to assume that
he was, as he later admitted, "swept along by the current without
looking at these things as he should have done."[2] Uncertain in
his own mind about the propriety of a coalition, he found it easy
to agree both with Adams's theory and with Wilson's practice.

Unconsciously, personal considerations swung him over to
Wilson's side. In all plans for dividing the spoils with the Democrats, the Free Soil managers expected to secure the full-term
United States senatorship, and as early as August 1850 Sumner
was mentioned as the most likely nominee, the only prominent
Conscience Whig whom Democrats could stomach. Careful never
to mention his aspirations, Sumner began behaving suspiciously
like a candidate. Protesting that public office was not within the
field of his ambition, he nevertheless admitted that it "can be
welcome when it comes entirely unsought," and reflected that the
Senate chamber was "a mighty pulpit from which the truth can
be preached."[3] In case anyone had forgotten that Sumner had
never been a strong Whig and had often co-operated with the
Democrats, the two handsomely bound volumes of his speeches,
which he published at this strategic time, proved the point.[4] And,
on a long summer's evening at Swampscott beach, he allowed
John Greenleaf Whittier to convince him that if duty called, he
could not refuse to have his name considered for high office.[5]

At the state Free Soil convention, which met in Boston on

[1] Samuel Downer to Mann, Sept. 3, 1850, Mann MSS.; Adams, Diary, Sept.
2, and Nov. 16, 1850, Adams MSS.

[2] Adams, Diary, Oct. 12, 1850, and Jan. 12, 1851, Adams MSS.

[3] Sumner to Greene, Nov. 2, 1849, Greene MSS.; Sumner to George Sumner,
Apr. 18, 1849, Sumner MSS.; Sumner to Howe, Aug. 27, 1850, ibid.; Pierce, III,
212.

[4] *Orations and Speeches* (2 vols.; Boston: Ticknor, Reed, and Fields; 1851).

[5] Nason: *Sumner*, p. 142; Whittier to Pierce, Feb. 16, 1878, Pierce MSS.;
Samuel T. Pickard: *Life and Letters of John Greenleaf Whittier* (Boston:
Houghton Mifflin Co.; 1907), I, 351, 355–6; John A. Pollard: *John Greenleaf
Whittier: Friend of Man* (Boston: Houghton Mifflin Co.; 1949), pp. 217–19.

October 3, Sumner made what was virtually an announcement of his candidacy in a speech that attempted simultaneously and somewhat contradictorily to prove that he was willing to co-operate with the Democrats and that his antislavery principles were simon-pure.[6] His theme was the new Fugitive Slave Act, adopted with the approval of Daniel Webster. One of the worst measures in history, it ranked with the tyranny of Appius Claudius, Louis XIV, Charles I, and George III. President Millard Fillmore in signing it had sunk to the "depths of infamy." "Better far for him had he never been born; better far for his memory, and for the good name of his children, had he never been President!" Sumner proclaimed. The fugitive slave bill—Sumner would never call it an act of Congress because he thought it unconstitutional and hence void—would never be executed in Boston. Public opinion, "like the flaming sword of the cherubim at the gates of Paradise, turning on every side, . . . shall prevent any SLAVE-HUNTER from ever setting foot in this Commonwealth."

Turning from the wrongs of the past to a program for the future, Sumner called for the abolition of the fugitive slave laws, the end of slavery in the District of Columbia, the exclusion of slavery from all the national territories, the abolition of the domestic slave trade, and the overthrow of the slave power in politics, "so that the Federal Government may be put openly, actively and perpetually on the side of Freedom." To these labors he welcomed "men of all parties and pursuits, who wish well to their country, and would preserve its good name." Of their candidates the people should demand not party allegiance, but "tried character and inflexible will." "Three things at least they must require; the first is *back-bone;* the second is *back-bone;* and the third is *back-bone.*" [7]

---

[6] Sumner seems to have made virtually the same speech at the Free Soil convention in Boston on October 3, 1850 (*Orations and Speeches,* II, 396–420) and at the Faneuil Hall rally to ratify the Free Soil nominations on November 6 (*Works,* II, 398–424; Boston *Traveller,* Nov. 11, 1850). The speech combined phrases and ideas he had repeatedly tested on previous public occasions (Cf. *Works,* II, 423; Boston *Republican,* Nov. 12, 1849). The quotations in the following paragraphs are from *Orations and Speeches,* II, 403, 408, 412, 415, 418, and 420.

[7] Here again Sumner was using a catchy phrase he had often previously tested. Cf. Pierce, III, 214, 219, 278. He must have been disconcerted by the fact that Joshua Leavitt, who preceded him in addressing the Free Soil convention, also stressed the need for "backbone."

Sumner's speech was received with vast enthusiasm, partly
because he was known to be in favor of coalition, but the Adams-
Palfrey-Dana bloc was still strong enough to block Wilson's plans
for running a joint ticket with the Democrats.[8] In the campaign
that followed the nominations, state-wide fusion was quietly
abandoned; Democrats and Free Soilers in many towns co-operated in selecting candidates for local offices, but technically and
officially their alliance extended no further. When the votes
were counted, the Whigs had a heavy plurality, but the Democrats and Free Soilers together had a slight majority of all votes.
As no candidate for governor or lieutenant governor received a
majority, the election fell to the state legislature, where no party
had clear control.

· 2 ·

If the state government was to be organized, two of the three
parties had to work together. Delighted with the outcome of the
election, Wilson, Keyes, and Bird reverted to their idea of sharing offices with the Democrats. During the six weeks following
the election, there was much buzzing back and forth between
Free Soil and Democratic headquarters, and a plan was readied
for presentation to the legislative caucuses of the two parties,
held on the last day of 1850. With Free Soil backing, the Democrats would elect their candidate for governor, George S. Boutwell, the lieutenant governor, the speaker and other officers of
the House of Representatives, a majority of the governor's council; in addition they would receive the short-term United States
senatorship, the few remaining weeks of Webster's term which
Winthrop was filling. The Free Soilers would get the presidency
of the state senate, the remaining members of the governor's
council, and the six-year United States senatorship, commencing
March 4. On January 7 a Free Soil caucus, by a vote of eighty-
four to one, nominated Sumner senator, and the following day
the Democrats, with only six dissenting votes, accepted him.[9]

[8] Adams, Diary, Oct. 3, 1850, Adams MSS.
[9] For a detailed history of the coalition see Henry Wilson's article in the
Boston *Commonwealth*, Jan. 30, 1851. Two senatorial elections were before the
legislature, one short-term, to replace Winthrop, whose appointment expired
with the assembling of the legislature, the other for the same seat for the six-
year term beginning March 4, 1851. Robert S. Rantoul, a Democrat, was elected
for the short term.

As the details of these arrangements became public, Massachusetts erupted in a blaze of denunciation of this "contemptible coalition," which was "usurping power in opposition to the will of a majority of the people." It is hard to believe that this tone of outraged surprise was genuine. Insiders had known even the details of the proposed coalition as early as August 1850. Despite the official silence of the Free Soil convention, their campaign sheet, which Bird edited, had openly announced that the antislavery men would give state offices to the Democrats if they could have the triumph of electing a Free Soiler to the seat of Daniel Webster. The Democratic state convention had explicitly endorsed coalition. These plans certainly were not concealed from the Whigs. The Whig state central committee, on November 8, had issued a circular urging every Massachusetts businessman "to use all the influence he can over those in his employ, or in any way under his control" to crush the Democratic-Free Soil coalition at the polls. Throughout the campaign, Whig papers grimly anticipated that Free Soilers would support a series of Democratic reform measures—amending the state constitution, limiting the hours of workingmen, changing the charter of Harvard College—in order to exclude Winthrop from the Senate and choose "some one inferior in ability and influence" in his stead.[1]

Nor was the identity of that "some one" much in doubt. Sumner's name was mentioned during the canvass as the likely Free Soil candidate, and when he heard the election returns, he told Longfellow that he would probably be the next senator. On the day after the election, Seth Webb, Jr., one of Sumner's young Free Soil admirers, dashed off a note to him:

> I called to tell you *such* good news. We have
> carried everything in the state—senate sure,
> house nearly certain, Governor, *Senator* and all—
> You are bound for Washington this winter.[2]

[1] Springfield *Republican*, Jan. 10, 1851; Boston *Advertiser*, Jan. 10, 1851, and Oct. 9, 1850; Samuel Downer to Mann, Aug. 22, 1850, Mann MSS.; Boston *Commonwealth*, Jan. 14, 1851; Bean: "Party Transformations," p. 57; Thomas Henry O'Connor: "Cotton Whigs and Union: The Textile Manufacturers of Massachusetts and the Coming of the Civil War" (unpublished Ph. D. dissertation, Boston Univ.; 1958), p. 125; Boston *Atlas*, Oct. 12, 1850.

[2] Longfellow, Diary, Nov. 10, 1850, Longfellow MSS.; Seth Webb, Jr., to Sumner [Nov. 1850], Sumner MSS.

If the surprise over the division of spoils was somewhat spurious, the anger was entirely real. Henry Wilson's maneuver had the effect of splitting all three of the state parties. The Whigs had the least difficulty assuming a public attitude toward the coalition. Their newspapers denounced it as "a combination of opposing elements, like oil and water," having "no principle in common but the spoils of office." The most "dishonorable, disgraceful and immoral" means were being used to make Sumner senator; if he should be elected, his only claim to his seat would be "that he was ignobly shuffled through the forms of an election, by the machinery of a political gambling table." [3]

In private, however, the Whig position was a good deal more complex. Though about 165 Whigs in the House of Representatives could be counted on to support Winthrop in ballot after ballot, most were less than enthusiastic about their candidate. The Boston wing of the party was "heart and soul" behind Daniel Webster, who demanded total acquiescence in the Compromise of 1850 and blamed Winthrop's failure to endorse the Fugitive Slave Act for the Whig defeat at the polls. Indeed, Winthrop seemed so badly tinged with abolitionism that some of Webster's supporters actually preferred Sumner, "on the desperate grounds of *the worse, the better*." Keeping a close watch on Massachusetts affairs and purging from federal office any daring souls who supported Sumner, Webster himself wished to lead Massachusetts Whigs into a new political organization "of Union men of all parties." Hence Webster's supporters showered social attentions upon Governor Boutwell, whose inaugural message gratifyingly endorsed the compromise, and praised the "highly honorable" course of Democrats opposed to the coalition. [4]

More numerous, but less highly placed, were the Massachu-

[3] Boston *Advertiser*, Jan. 7, and 18, 1851; Boston *Courier*, Jan. 16, 1851.
[4] E. M. Wright to H. L. Dawes, Nov. 27, 1850, Dawes MSS.; Webster to Fillmore, Apr. 13, 1851, and Nov. 18, 1850, Fillmore MSS.; A. A. Lawrence to Charles Devens, Feb. 17, 1851, copy, Lawrence MSS.; Moses Stuart to Webster, Apr. 18, 1851, Webster MSS., Dartmouth Coll.; Winthrop to Julius Rockwell, July 31, 1851, Julius Rockwell MSS.; Webster to Peter Harvey, May 4, 1851, copy, Everett MSS.; Edward Casneau to J. A. Andrew, Mar. 30, 1861, Andrew MSS.; Van Tyne (ed.): *Webster Letters*, p. 445; Boston *Courier*, Jan. 17, 1851; A. A. Lawrence to Boutwell, Jan. 17, 1851, copy, Lawrence MSS.; Boutwell to Lawrence, Jan. 23, 1851, ibid.; Samuel Bridge to Caleb Cushing, Feb. 19, 1851, Cushing MSS.; *The Liberator*, XXI (Jan. 24, 1851), p. 13.

setts Whigs who felt that Webster's course was ruinous, that Winthrop could never be elected, and that an understanding should be reached with Free Soilers of Whig background. George Morey, chairman of the Whig state central committee, speaking for the majority of the Whigs outside of Boston, spread the word that many Whigs might be willing to support Charles Francis Adams for the Senate.[5]

Democratic difficulties were equally intense and far more difficult to conceal. Without question, most Massachusetts Democrats favored coalition as "the only means available to break down a dynasty of wealth and aristocracy, such as existed no where else in this country; and the only mode of securing a new constitution, and certain important reforms in [the] state legislation; and by changing the public officers throughout the state, to equalize political power, and teach a class of men for the first time that their right to office was not hereditary and perpetual." The United States senatorship was not of great importance to these Democrats, but, of the possible Free Soil nominees, Sumner was their "decided favorite," as party managers promised that he was sound on *all the great measures of Democracy*, from Jefferson's time downward." [6]

But a powerful, articulate Democratic minority, led by Caleb Cushing, objected to sending "a red-hot Abolitionist, . . . like a firebrand, for six years, into the senate chamber of the United States." Shrewdly keeping quiet during the preliminary negotiations, Cushing gave tacit consent to the coalition until the Free Soilers helped elect Boutwell governor; he then called his friends into a separate caucus and announced that the election of a "one-idead abolitionist agitator" like Sumner would be a "death-stab to the honor and welfare of the Commonwealth." Cushing's thirty-odd "Indomitables" held the balance of power between Sumner and Winthrop. For a time Cushing considered promoting his own election to the Senate; then he planned to run the conservative Whig, Edward Everett; but mostly he used his power, with

---

[5] Adams, Diary, Nov. 16, 1850, and Feb. 6, 1851, Adams MSS.; Springfield *Republican*, Jan. 31, 1851.

[6] Samuel Downer to Mann, Dec. 15, 1850, and Jan. 9, 1851, Mann MSS.; Whiting Griswold in Boston *Post*, Mar. 20, 1855; Springfield *Republican*, Feb. 8, 1851. Cf. Fred Harvey Harrington: *Fighting Politician: Major General N. P. Banks* (Philadelphia: University of Pennsylvania Press; 1948), pp. 10–13.

great effect, to intimidate the coalitionist Democrats. Under his pressure, backed by stern letters from Cass and other leading Democrats, Boutwell, who had been elected by Free Soil votes, announced: "I am not pledged to elect Mr. Sumner, I am not pledged to defeat him. The subject is in the control of the Legislature." [7]

The Free Soilers were better able to keep their legislative delegation in line behind the coalition, but behind the scenes they, too, were seriously split. For the former Democrats in the party, ex-Governor Marcus Morton objected that Wilson seemed determined "to exclude every Freesoil democrat from any important office." The senatorship was Morton's special grievance. Sumner, who "had genius but not the soundest judgment . . . learning but not practical knowledge," was a Whig. Privately Morton lobbied with the Free Soilers of Democratic extraction, and publicly he urged the legislature to reject all "*caucusses* [*sic*], *compromises* and *coalitions*." [8]

Considerably more influential was the continuing opposition of the former Conscience Whigs who had all along fought coalition and who resented Wilson's leadership of the Free Soil party, S. C. Phillips exhibited "considerable jealousy" over the pertinacity with which Sumner's name was pressed for the senatorship, to the exclusion of older and more prominent members of the party, like himself. [9] Palfrey, too, continued to fight the coalition. Scheduled to become editor of the new Free Soil newspaper, the *Commonwealth*, which was to start publication in Boston on January 1, 1851, Palfrey, in December, circulated a printed letter to all members of the incoming General Court. He opposed voting for Boutwell; he thought the importance of having an anti-

[7] Samuel Dexter Bradford: *Works* (Boston: Phillips, Sampson & Company; 1858), p. 294; T. J. Whittemore to Cushing, Nov. 29, 1850, Cushing MSS.; Boston *Post*, cited in Boston *Advertiser*, Jan. 8, 1851; Boston *Transcript*, Mar. 13, 1851; Everett, Diary, May 15, 1851, Everett MSS.; Boutwell: *Reminiscences of Sixty Years in Public Affairs* (New York: McClure, Phillips & Co.; 1902), I, 119. Cf. Claude M. Fuess: *The Life of Caleb Cushing* (New York: Harcourt, Brace & Co.; 1923), II, 100–4.

[8] Marcus Morton, Letterbooks, III, 60, 62, 89, 90–1; Morton: *Letter Addressed to the Free Soil and Democratic Members of the Legislature of Massachusetts* (Taunton; 1851), p. 7; Boston *Commonwealth*, Mar. 18, 1851. In a letter to Sumner (Mar. 12, 1851, Sumner MSS.) Morton denied lobbying against his election.

[9] Springfield *Republican*, Jan. 1, 1851. Cf. Phillips to Sumner, Jan. 9, and 12, 1851, Sumner MSS.; Adams, Diary, Jan. 9, 10, and 12, 1851, Adams MSS.

slavery senator "overrated," as his influence would be "very much crippled" by the manner of his election, and his protests against slavery would in any case "be crushed under an overwhelming proslavery majority" in Washington. He counseled the Free Soilers to keep their principles untarnished and to wait for another election.[1]

Palfrey's attack not merely disrupted plans for the *Commonwealth*, which had hastily to be entrusted to the less skillful editorial team of Bird, Richard Hildreth, and Elizur Wright, but it almost split the Free Soil party. His letter was known to have the support both of Richard Henry Dana and of Charles Francis Adams,[2] who was at a critical moment in his career. Disliking the state-wide coalition, and confessing a "lurking jealousy of Sumner's purity of purpose," Adams thought that he could probably be elected to the Senate himself with Whig support. After some soul-searching, he concluded that it would not be fitting for an Adams to be party to such a scheme: to Sumner, "who is rising in the world a little abrasion of this sort will do no harm, whilst to me who am constantly contrasted with my predecessors, it would be discreditable." Finally convincing himself that Sumner was not intriguing for the office, Adams issued a public letter in which he rejoiced that the present arrangement would elect "one of our ablest and most honest and most inflexible advocates" to the United States Senate, replacing "one, whose loose private and wavering public career has done more . . . to shake the principles and unsettle the highest policy of puritan New England than that of any man known to its history."[3]

· 3 ·

In all these crosscurrents of politics, Sumner maintained an attitude of reserve bordering upon indifference. "I was brought forward contrary to my express desires," he wrote his brother. "The nomination was forced upon me." Phillips or Adams, his "seniors

---

[1] Palfrey: *To the Members of the General Court of Massachusetts for the Year 1851*, a pamphlet marked "Confidential."

[2] Adams and Dana "entirely concurred" in Palfrey's reasoning, but did not favor the distribution of his letter. Adams, Diary, Dec. 26, 1850, Adams MSS.

[3] Adams, Diary, Nov. 14, and 16, 1850; *The Liberator*, XXI (Jan. 17, 1851), p. 9.

and betters" in the Free Soil movement, should have been the party's standard-bearer. "I never directly or indirectly suggested a desire for the place, or even a willingness to take it," he told John Bigelow. "I do not desire to be senator." [4]

Though he had "implicit faith in the propriety of the Coalition," he kept "aloof from all the arrangements at the State House, making no suggestion on any points or persons." Unwilling to solicit the endorsement even of the Free Soilers, he was immovably averse to wooing the Democrats. Four separate Democratic committees called on him. To all he replied: "I do not desire to be Senator. . . . I would not move across the room to take the post. . . . It must seek me—and . . . if it finds me, it will find me *an absolutely independent man,* without any pledge or promise." [5]

With outward equanimity Sumner chronicled the fluctuations in his own fortunes as the two houses of the legislature began their separate ballotings. On the first ballot in the House of Representatives, on January 14, Democratic defections kept him five votes from a majority, and his position did not improve during the next two days, when four additional ballots were taken. Though Wilson was furious, Sumner remained bright and cheerful. He thought the chance for his election now "lost beyond recovery," but declared he felt "no personal disappointments." [6]

When the state senate elected Sumner on January 22, he became cautiously optimistic.[7] But the five ballots held in the House of Representatives on January 23–24 showed that he was still far from election. The Whigs held firmly for Winthrop; the Free Soilers voted unanimously for Sumner, as did most of the Democrats; but between twenty-five and thirty "Indomitable" Democrats, following Cushing, threw away their votes upon other candidates.

While practically all public business in Massachusetts was

[4] Sumner to George Sumner, Feb. 23, 1851, Sumner MSS.; Frank Preston Stearns: *The Life and Public Services of George Luther Stearns* (Philadelphia: J. B. Lippincott Co.; 1907), p. 84; Pierce, III, 233; Bigelow: *Retrospections,* I, 105–6.

[5] Sumner to Dana, [1851], Dana MSS.; Sumner to Mann, Jan. 11, 1851, Mann MSS.; Bigelow: *Retrospections,* I, 106; Boston *Traveller,* Apr. 21, 1874.

[6] Springfield *Republican,* Jan. 15, 1851; Boston *Commonwealth,* Jan. 16, and 20, 1851; Adams, Diary, Jan. 14, 1851, Adams MSS.; Bigelow: *Retrospections,* I, 106.

[7] Richards, *S. G. Howe,* II, 335.

suspended, politicians of all factions attempted to rally their forces. Believing Boutwell "a timid, cunning, time-serving *trimmer*," Free Soilers tried to bully him into support of the coalition, by which his own election had been secured. At the same time they hoped to rally public opinion behind their candidate by publishing fulsome articles in the *Commonwealth* about Sumner's qualifications for office, his unquestioned Americanism, and his reverence for the Constitution and the Union. The Whigs, more practically, started a fund, for which Amos A. Lawrence, Ezra Lincoln, and William Appleton subscribed, to relieve Whig members of the legislature whose businesses at home were suffering during the protracted sessions of the General Court. The fund, Lawrence piously explained, was "not intended to be used for influencing any member in an improper manner," but he confided to Congressman Eliot: "Everything is being done to prevent Sumner's election . . . that can be." [8]

When voting resumed on February 7, Sumner still lacked two votes of election. A week later, on the fourteenth ballot, his strength had declined, and he needed nine votes. Despondent, Sumner wrote a letter to Wilson urging "the friends of Freedom in the Legislature . . . to transfer their support to some other candidate, faithful to our cause." "I have searched my heart, and have its response," he wrote to George at this time. "I do not desire to be Senator. My ambition is to live without office." [9]

Not one of Sumner's friends, and, indeed, few of his opponents, doubted that he was remaining creditably aloof from the election contest. Hillard, now a leading Whig politician, admitted that his former partner "behaved very well" by refusing "to retract any thing, to modify any thing or to promise any thing." Charles Francis Adams, who was not given to kindliness, agreed that it was "impossible for any body to have acquitted himself more honorably under circumstances of great trial." Palfrey, strongly opposed to the whole coalition scheme, wrote Sumner: "No one acquainted with your course in this matter, can ever say that it has not been most high and honorable." [1]

[8] Ibid., II, 338; Boston *Commonwealth*, Feb. 3–6, 1851; Ezra Lincoln and H. J. Gardner to A. A. Lawrence, Feb. 10, 1851, Lawrence MSS.; Lawrence to Ezra Lincoln, Samuel A. Eliot, and William Appleton, Feb. 10, 1851, copies, ibid.

[9] Sumner: *Works*, II, 430; Sumner to George Sumner, Feb. 23, 1851, Sumner MSS.

[1] Hillard to Lieber, Jan. 31, 1851, Lieber MSS.; Adams, Diary, Mar. 16, Apr. 1, and 24, 1851, Adams MSS.; Palfrey to Sumner, Feb. 25, 1851, Palfrey MSS.

Sumner as a Young Man

Miniature (2" x 2½") by an unknown artist

MASSACHUSETTS HISTORICAL SOCIETY

Boston about 1830: A View from Dorchester Heights

Joseph Story

Painting by Chester Harding

Sumner in 1839

Bust by Thomas Crawford

MASSACHUSETTS HISTORICAL SOCIETY

Henry Wadsworth Longfellow

Samuel Gridley Howe

Cornelius C. Felton

George S. Hillard

Painting by William Hillard, c. 1865

FRIENDS IN THE FIVE OF CLUBS

Sumner in 1846

Woodcut from a crayon drawing made by Eastman Johnson

Robert Charles Winthrop

Painting by George P. A. Healy

MASSACHUSETTS HISTORICAL SOCIETY

Daniel Webster
THE NATIONAL ARCHIVES

SPOKESMEN OF BEACON HILL

George Ticknor
MASSACHUSETTS HISTORICAL SOCIETY

John Quincy Adams

THE NATIONAL ARCHIVES

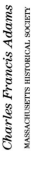

Charles Francis Adams

MASSACHUSETTS HISTORICAL SOCIETY

Henry Wilson

THE NATIONAL ARCHIVES

RIVAL MASSACHUSETTS FREE SOILERS

Sumner during His First Term in the Senate

Salmon P. Chase

Stephen A. Douglas

Edward Everett

William H. Seward

SENATE LEADERS OF THE 1850's

Preston S. Brooks

SOUTHERN CHIVALRY — ARGUMENT VERSUS CLUB'S.

The Brooks Assault

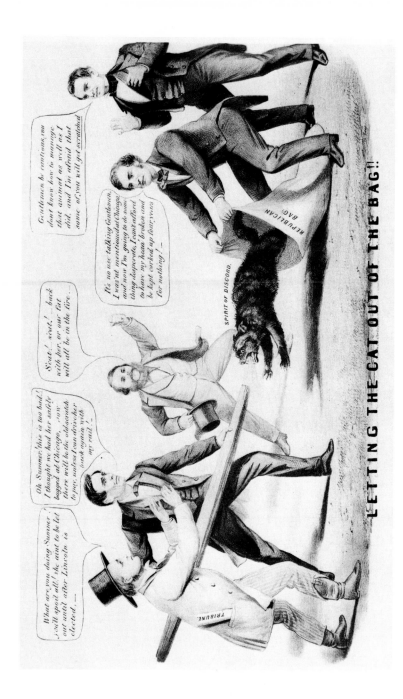

Republican Reaction to "The Barbarism of Slavery" Speech, 1860

Sumner at the Outbreak of the Civil War

At the same time that they credited the purity of Sumner's intention, practically nobody really believed his protestations of not wanting the senatorship. The eagerness with which he followed every detail of the coalition negotiations seemed to Adams to make "his pretensions of utter indifference rather ridiculous." "He is," Adams shrewdly remarked, "manifestly wound up" in desiring the office, "without being himself conscious of it." [2]

There is, in fact, considerable evidence to indicate that Sumner genuinely desired the senatorship and that he did all he honorably could to attain it. Even while he asserted that the senatorship properly belong to Adams or Phillips—both, incidentally, impossible candidates, as they opposed the coalition and were unacceptable to the Democrats—he admitted: "I feel that it would, to a certain extent, be a vindication of me against the attacks to which . . . I have been exposed." Sumner's refusal to dicker with Caleb Cushing reflected his high-spirited independence; but it also showed his political sagacity, as to keep Adams, Palfrey, Phillips, and Dana in the party, he had to convince them that he would maintain Free Soil principles uncontaminated. In January, to counter Marcus Morton's charge that he was a disunionist, Sumner wrote a letter for circulation among the legislators, announcing that he proposed "to wait and work patiently under and through the Constitution" in fighting slavery. The next month, when the Negro Shadrach was seized on the streets of Boston as a fugitive slave, Sumner cautiously declined to assist Dana in defending him because, he frankly admitted, of "the effect it might have on the pending senatorial election." But, when it became clear that Massachusetts opinion was outraged by the arbitrariness and cruelty of the arrest, Sumner apparently decided that high principle was good politics. In the next fugitive slave case, in early April, he instantly came to the defense of Thomas Sims and helped, unsuccessfully, to plead for his release.[3]

Doubtless Sumner was sincere in his February 22 letter, offering to withdraw from the senatorial contest, but he must have

---

[2] Adams, Diary, Feb. 7, and 29, 1851, Adams MSS. Cf. H. W. Beecher, in New York *Tribune*, May 31, 1856.

[3] Pierce, III, 233; Sumner: *Works*, II, 429; Adams: *Dana*, I, 183; Boston *Courier*, Apr. 12, 1851. On the Sims case see Leonard W. Levy: *Chief Justice Shaw and the Law of the Commonwealth* (Cambridge: Harvard University Press; 1957), pp. 92–104.

known that his declination would not be accepted. Though a number of Free Soilers began to murmur: "If we cant get Sumner, we must go for some one whom we can elect," everybody recognized that Phillips, the only other candidate seriously mentioned, would draw even fewer Democratic votes than Sumner. The Free Soilers, as Adams pointed out, had no choice but "to sustain their candidate until they get assurances from either side that they can elect another, who will suit them." Sumner's withdrawal was, accordingly, suppressed.[4]

Unresolved and apparently unresolvable, the senatorial deadlock continued through March and well into April. The House of Representatives took occasional votes, but Sumner came no nearer a majority. Violent charges and countercharges were hurled back and forth in the legislature. The Free Soilers blamed that "slimy snake" Marcus Morton for the stalemate, and Henry Wilson published a blast at the ex-governor's "croaking, paltering . . . duplicity." On both sides there were accusations of corruption. The Whigs were charged with employing their vast resources to buy up legislators, and the coalitionists, in return for votes for Sumner, were said to have pledged a $2,000,-000 state loan to the Troy and Greenfield Railroad, which was trying to tunnel under the Hoosac Mountain in order to give northwestern Massachusetts direct railroad connections with New York and the West.[5]

The truth of such charges, so freely made through the protracted balloting, is difficult to ascertain. Wealthy Whigs did subscribe funds to charter special trains for bringing in absent members of the legislature, to pay their expenses while in Boston, and to stir up anticoalition sentiment in town meetings, but the amounts involved were so small and the records of the transactions were so publicly kept that it is hard to think of this as actual bribery.[6] The story connecting the Free Soilers with the Hoo-

[4] Charles Allen to Sumner, Feb. 7, 1851, Sumner MSS.; Richards: *S. G. Howe*, II, 341; Howe to Palfrey, Feb. 13, 1851, Palfrey MSS.; Adams, Diary, Mar. 19, 1851, Adams MSS.

[5] Richards: *S. G. Howe*, II, 344; Boston *Commonwealth*, Feb. 22, Mar. 18, and 25, 1851; Boston *Transcript*, Mar. 14, 1851; Springfield *Republican*, Apr. 2, 1851; Boston *Advertiser*, Apr. 3, 1851.

[6] Ezra Lincoln to A. A. Lawrence, Mar. 7, 1851, Lawrence MSS.; memorandum, listing donors and amounts, Mar. 14, 1851, ibid. The sum subscribed was only $500.

sac tunnel scheme, which was to drain the Massachusetts treasury for the next quarter of a century, is almost certainly false. In private correspondence both Whigs and "Indomitable" Democrats declared that the report deserved "no Credit whatever." [7]

A larger issue was the Whig contention that the coalition itself was corrupt. If the charge was correct, the guilt of the Free Soilers was not palliated by the fact that similar coalitions were occurring in other states. Nor was it an extenuating circumstance that some of the Whigs had themselves contemplated just such a coalition with the Free Soilers or that Webster wished a union with conservative Democrats. Nor were Sumner's skirts cleared by the fact that he had not personally arranged or intrigued for his nomination. After all, as William Kent caustically reminded him, he could not have been run against his will, or, as gruff Francis Lieber put it, a man whose house is being used as a brothel is not innocent because he claims ignorance of that fact.[8]

But the Whig accusation was based upon two premises—that the senatorship was the chief goal of the coalition, and that the Free Soil and Democratic parties shared no principles—and neither was true. Most of the Democrats thought reform of the Massachusetts state government the essential object of the coalition; they were willing to surrender the senatorship to the Free Soilers because it was not important or useful in their plans of state reform. Many of the Massachusetts Free Soilers had originally been Democrats, and they shared that party's hostility to the "money power" in the Commonwealth, and, on the other hand, the Democrats—like practically all citizens of Massachusetts—shared the Free Soilers' opposition to the further extension of slavery. It seemed equitable, therefore, that the Democrats, interested in state reform, should get the state offices, and the Free Soilers, interested in the national question of slavery, should get the senatorship. The resulting union had about as much coherence of principle as any major American party ever does—and rather more than the Whig party in Massachusetts

---

[7] W. A. Hawley to H. L. Dawes, Apr. 5, 1851, Dawes MSS.; D. N. Carpenter to Caleb Cushing, Apr. 21, 1851, Cushing MSS.

[8] William Kent to Sumner [Oct. 1851], Sumner MSS.; Lieber to Hillard, Jan. 30, 1852, Lieber MSS.

had at this time. Inexpedient and unwise the coalition may have been, but not corrupt.[9]

If the Whig charge that the coalition was "unprincipled" was not tenable, the Free Soil counterclaim that some weighty principle of antislavery was involved in Sumner's election was equally dubious. Whatever idealism the Free Soilers may have had in the beginning had disappeared by the time two dozen ballots were taken, each followed by higgling for office and spoils. As their moral fervor effervesced, Free Soil leaders behaved, said Hillard, "like a woman, who has sold her person for money, going the next morning and . . . saying 'I was a virgin and I agreed to sleep with you for so many dollars and I have slept with you and now I want you to pay me.'"[1]

With diminishing hopes and waning enthusiasm, the struggle continued through April. The Webster Whigs were immovable, wanting nothing more than to prevent any election at all, expecting that the fall elections would bring in an anticoalition legislature.[2] Cushing, whose wing of the Democratic party depended upon national patronage, was equally inflexible; the fall elections meant nothing to him. But the majority of the Democrats and the Free Soilers were becoming desperate; in only a few weeks the legislature would have to adjourn, without having passed any significant legislation, without having secured any state reforms, and without even having elected a senator. On such a record, defeat would be certain in November.

When balloting was resumed on April 23, there were slight indications that a break might be in sight. During the three weeks since the last vote, Free Soilers had been agitating to have town meetings instruct their representatives to vote for Sumner, and at least one Whig, the member from Fall River, obeyed the instructions and was now ready to vote for the coalition candidate. There may have been some outside influence brought on Whig representatives; Thurlow Weed, the Whig boss of New York, was said to have persuaded a few Massachusetts Whigs to vote for Sumner because, as part of a bargain, Free Soilers had

9 The soundest treatment of the coalition and the senatorial election is Bean: "Party Transformations," Chap. 4.
1 Hillard to Lieber, Jan. 31, 1851, Lieber MSS.
2 B. R. Curtis to Webster, Feb. 23, 1851, Curtis MSS.; Abbott Lawrence to Nathan Appleton, Feb. 14, 1851, MS., Houghton Lib.

induced New York "Barnburners" to allow Hamilton Fish to be chosen senator from New York. Not a few Whigs were responsive to such pressure because Webster was now demanding that they abandon Winthrop and vote for a more thoroughgoing advocate of the Compromise of 1850. Rather than kill their party by backing a supporter of the Fugitive Slave Act, these Whigs preferred to see Sumner elected.[3]

With so many subtle forces at work, the political experts were prepared for a shift of votes on the twenty-first ballot, and when it was taken, shortly after noon on April 23, it was announced that Sumner had received 195 votes, a majority of the votes cast, and was elected. Free Soil representatives went "as crazy as a parcel of school boys just entered upon a vacation," and all over the city their supporters began to celebrate. While Sumner was having dinner with the Adamses at their Mt. Vernon Street home, visitors began pouring in to congratulate him. But, as the legislature did not adjourn, doubts about the election began to rise, and young Henry Adams was sent off to the Statehouse to learn the facts. He found that one printed ballot bearing Sumner's name had also been lightly penciled "John Mills, of Springfield." Under Whig pressure this doubtful ballot was given to Mills, the votes were recounted, and Speaker N. P. Banks announced that there was still no choice. As Henry Adams told the news, the Adams family lamented, but "Sumner did not to appearance change a muscle nor a tone." "In self-command," the elder Adams noted admiringly, "he certainly is fit for a politician much more than I am."[4]

The House of Representatives took two more ballots that day, all marked by great irregularities. On one of them there were two more votes than there were legislators. Coalitionists accused Whigs, and Whigs blamed coalitionists. Whoever was at fault, Sumner was no nearer election.

On April 24 the legislature reassembled in an atmosphere of great tension. On the twenty-fifth ballot there were again two

[3] George F. Hoar: *Autobiography of Seventy Years* (New York: Charles Scribner's Sons; 1903), I, 186; John Bigelow to Sumner, Apr. 2 [1851], Sumner MSS.; Springfield *Republican*, Apr. 25, 1851; Thomas M. Foote to Millard Fillmore, May 2, 1851, Fillmore MSS.; Adams, Diary, Apr. 23, 1851, Adams MSS.
[4] Boston *Advertiser*, Apr. 23, 1851; Springfield *Republican*, Apr. 24, 1851; Adams, Diary, Apr. 23, 1851, Adams MSS.

more votes than there were representatives present. After much wrangling, the house adopted a Whig proposal that on future ballots each member must cast his vote in a sealed envelope, so that it would be impossible for these extra ballots to be slipped in. Shortly after noon, the twenty-sixth ballot was taken. This time Sumner received 193 of the 385 votes cast, a majority of precisely one, and was declared elected.[5]

While great excitement prevailed at the State house, Henry Adams, who had been watching the voting attentively, slipped out and ran home to inform his parents of the triumph. Sumner was there, seated at the dining table with the Adams family. Breathless, Henry told his glorious news. "It was," he reflected more than half a century later, "probably the proudest moment in the life of either."[6]

While Whigs gloomily remained indoors, throngs of Free Soilers and Democrats began to congregate in the streets. By nightfall perhaps 10,000 people were milling about the *Commonwealth* office on the corner of Washington and State streets; the three upper stories of the building were illuminated, flags were stretched across the streets, and one hundred rockets were sent up to announce the victory. Henry Wilson spoke in praise of the election he, more than any other person, had brought about, and when hecklers interrupted him with shouts for Daniel Webster, the Union, and the Constitution, he turned on them with the taunt: "The victory this day consummated dates from the 7th of March, 1850, when that great man stood up in the Senate and repudiated the long-cherished sentiments of Massachusetts." In

[5] "Election of U. S. Senators in Massachusetts, 1788–1895," in *Massachusetts Year Book*, II (1896), 43–4. After close study of all the extant voting records, I am obliged to conclude with "Warrington" (Springfield *Republican*, Jan. 31, 1863): "It is impossible to tell how the election was finally effected, that is to say, by what change of vote." As all the ballots were secret, as a number of blank ballots were cast, and as there were several absentees, no one can say which person cast the deciding vote that gave Sumner his majority. The calculation of the *Advertiser* (Apr. 25, 1851) that one Whig and two "Indomitable" Democrats voted for Sumner on the last ballot seems plausible. In that case, there is room for the rival claims of Nathaniel Doane, of Harwich, a Whig; of Henry A. Hardy, of South Danvers, a Democrat (Boston *Commonwealth*, Jan. 31, 1863); and of Israel Haynes, of Sudbury, a Democrat (affidavit of Leander Haynes, Jan. 3, 1895, Pierce MSS.)—all of whom said they cast the deciding ballot.

[6] Henry Adams: *Education*, p. 51.

the privacy of his diary, Charles Francis Adams vindictively agreed that the election marked

the downfall of Mr. Webster. Nothing in the ordinary course of events will now avail to set him up again before nature shall remove him. His career on the whole has been rather that of a mountebank than of a statesman; a moral character degraded by the lowest sensualities and by the upmost rapacity. . . . Not a fit emblem of puritan Massachusetts. Sumner will come much nearer to it.

"The event of this day," Adams predicted, "constitutes probably an era in the present movement." [7]

Massachusetts Whiggery agreed. Webster himself was "grieved and mortified" by the results, and there were long faces and deep swearing in State Street. The day after the election some men, and more children, wore black crepe on their sleeves to commemorate the death of pure government in the Commonwealth. Whig newspapers, almost without exception, deplored the election, through the blackest of frauds, of an impractical theorist opposed to the principles of the American Constitution.[8] Nathan Appleton thought Sumner's election was "the most fatal blow to . . . popular suffrage that [had] been inflicted," and Winthrop felt that Sumner, despite his "professions of purity and disinterestedness," had "done more to demoralize and debauch the young men of our State by his example and by his success, than any man of modern days." In an effort to challenge the validity of Sumner's election, or at least to neutralize in advance any influence he might exert in the Senate, Benjamin R. Curtis drew up a public indictment, signed by all the Whig members of the legislature, denouncing the coalition as "a factious conspiracy," at once immoral and illegal.[9]

[7] "The Diary of William Read, a Boston Physician, April, 1851," *Proceedings of the Bostonian Society*, 1902, p. 38; Boston *Commonwealth*, Apr. 25, 1851; Adams, Diary, Apr. 24–5, 1851, Adams MSS.

[8] Webster to Stephen M. Allen, June 11, 1851, Webster MSS., Dartmouth Coll.; Hillard to Lieber. Apr. 24, 1851, Lieber MSS.; Nevins: *Ordeal of the Union*, I, 392; Henry Adams: *Education*, p. 51; extracts from the *Atlas, Advertiser*, and *Courier* in Boston *Globe*, Mar. 13, 1874.

[9] Nathan Appleton to Fanny Longfellow, May 23, 1851, Appleton MSS.; Winthrop to Hamilton Fish, Apr. 29, 1851, Fish MSS.; Winthrop to Everett, May 21, 1851, Everett MSS.; Everett to B. R. Curtis, May 1, 1851, ibid.; Samuel Hooper to Franklin Haven, May 4 [1851], Webster MSS., Houghton Lib.; Curtis: *To the People of Massachusetts* (Boston; 1851). Curtis (p. 8) argued that the

In the storm of triumph and abuse, Sumner gave not the slightest evidence of personal exultation over the result. Escaping as soon as he could from his congratulating visitors, he fled to the privacy of Longfellow's house in Cambridge, where he remained in retirement during the victory celebrations. Thoroughly exhausted by the prolonged contest, he seemed "more saddened than elated" by success. Sumner thrived under persecution, and flourished when battling overwhelming odds; victory had a flat taste. The responsibilities of his new position already seemed oppressive, and just after the election, he told a young friend: "I am by no means sure this result is best, either for the country or for me." "Most painfully do I feel my inability to meet the importance which has been given to this election and the expectation of enthusiastic friends," he lamented. "If I should fail through faithlessness," he declared, "I feel that I should go far to destroy all confidence in man." [1]

---

coalition was "a misdemeanor, punishable by indictment." Everett tried to persuade Henry Clay to present the Whig protest to the United States Senate. Everett to Clay, Dec. 3, 1851, Everett MSS. Cf. Benjamin R. Curtis, Jr. (ed.): *A Memoir of Benjamin Robbins Curtis* . . . (Boston: Little, Brown & Co.; 1879), I, 138–50.

[1] Longfellow, Diary, Apr. 24–5, 1851, Longfellow MSS.; Fanny Longfellow to Nathan Appleton, May 4, 1851, ibid.; Sumner to Epes Sargent, Apr. 29, 1851, Epes Sargent MSS.; Sumner to C. M. Ellis, Apr. 28, 1851, MS., Mass. Hist. Soc.; A. B. Muzzey: *Reminiscences and Memorials* . . . (Boston: Estes and Lauriat; 1883) p. 224; Pierce, III, 247; Sumner to Mann, Apr. 28, 1851, Mann MSS.

CHAPTER IX

The Slave of Principles

❧

"YOUR PARTING benediction and God-speed, mingling with mother's, made my heart overflow," Sumner wrote his sister Julia as he left for Washington in November 1851 to begin his first session of Congress. "For myself, I do not desire public life; I have neither taste nor ambition for it; but Providence has marked out my career, and I follow." [1] During the months since his election his repugnance for a political career had increased, for he realized that his position in Washington would be ambiguous and difficult. He had been chosen by a coalition widely condemned as unprincipled and immoral. A Free Soiler, he would be a member of a tiny and despised minority in the Senate. With no previous experience in any legislative body, he would be obliged to carry on his antislavery agitation against the opposition of veteran parliamentarians, and at a time when all outstanding national issues appeared to have been settled and when all the leaders of both major parties discountenanced further sectional controversy.

Even the purely formal ceremony of being sworn in as senator, when the first session of the Thirty-Second Congress assembled on December 1, suggested the embarrassments that lay ahead of Sumner. Each of the other five new senators had his credentials presented, as was customary, by his senior colleague from his own state. But "Honest John" Davis, the other Massachusetts senator, perhaps mindful of Webster's fury, overslept

[1] Pierce, III, 259.

that morning, and Sumner was obliged to turn to Michigan's Lewis Cass, his oldest personal acquaintance in the Senate. All the other new senators were introduced with "I beg leave to present . . ." or "I desire to present. . . ." Cass merely announced: "I have been requested to present the credentials of Charles Sumner, a Senator elect from the State of Massachusetts." [2]

· 1 ·

Bostonians, said Oliver Wendell Holmes, "all carry the Common in our heads as the unit of space, the State House as the standard of architecture, and measure off men in Edward Everetts as with a yardstick." Comparing Washington with this ideal, Sumner found it sadly wanting. "I am sick at heart with what I see here," he complained only a few weeks after assuming his new duties. "The tone of society . . . is inexpressibly low." There was, in fact, little to commend Washington in the 1850's. From the broken-down hackney coaches that served for public transportation to the huge unfinished Capitol building, everything seemed impermanent and incomplete. "The whole place looks run up in a night," a British observer wrote, "like the cardboard cities which Potemkin erected to gratify the eyes of his imperial mistress on her tour through Russia; and it is impossible to remove the impression that, when Congress is over, the whole place is taken down, and packed up again till wanted." [3]

Making the best of the capital's poor offerings, Sumner rented a bedroom and sitting room in a private house on New York Avenue, between Fourteenth and Fifteenth streets, for which he paid thirty-five dollars a month. As the rooms were "well appointed for Washington, retired, and yet conveniently situated," he felt himself "better lodged than any member of Congress, who has not a house of his own." [4]

Moving to Washington did not alter Sumner's routine of liv-

[2] Cong. Globe, 32 Cong., 1 Sess., 2–3.

[3] Morse: Holmes, II, 157; Sumner to Dorothea L. Dix, Dec. 26, 1851, Dix MSS.; Edward Dicey: Six Months in the Federal States (London: The Macmillan Co.; 1863), I, 93–9. Dicey's description, written during the 1860's, was equally applicable to the previous decade.

[4] Charles Eames to Sumner, Sept. 28, 1851, Sumner MSS.; Sumner to George Sumner, Apr. 19 [1852], ibid.

ing. Rising about seven o'clock each morning, he invariably took
a cold-water bath in his hat-shaped tub, shaved with cold water, and set to work as soon as he had dressed. Between eight
thirty and nine he had breakfast served him in his rooms, a
hearty meal of tea, toast, eggs, fruit, and pancakes and butter.
He did not eat again until the evening meal, which in Washington was between four and six. After first trying the food at Willard's Hotel, he arranged a regular mess with Count Sibbern, the
Swedish minister to the United States, and Judge John A. Rockwell, of Connecticut, at a nearby French restaurant. Sumner's
tastes were simple, but far from ascetic. A porterhouse steak,
dressed with oysters and accompanied by bread and butter and
a glass of claret, was his standard dinner, though he also liked
corned beef and cabbage. Not all the temperance preachments
of Horace Mann could make him abstain from wine, but he almost never touched hard liquor. Though he might occasionally
light an after-dinner cigar to keep a guest from feeling uncomfortable, he did not smoke or chew tobacco.[5]

Promptly Sumner fell into an unvarying schedule of work.
Walking the mile between his lodgings and the Capitol, he made
it a point to be in his place each morning when the Senate was
called to order, and to stand during the chaplain's prayer. Once
in his seat, he remained there, following the debates closely and
permitting nothing to distract his attention. Of course, as a
freshman member belonging to a third party, he did not have
the frequent business visitors who beseiged the more influential
senators and summoned them into the corridors for whispered
conferences. Nor were the insignificant committee assignments
given him—the lowest ranking positions in the revolutionary
claims and canals and roads committees—a drain on his time.
With little to do but listen and study, Sumner tried to learn the
rules of debate and the temper of his associates.

The Senate in 1851 was not a distinguished body. Calhoun

[5] A. B. Johnson: "Recollections of Charles Sumner," *Scribner's Monthly*,
VIII (1874), 474–5; Johnson: "Charles Sumner," *Cosmopolitan*, III (1887),
407; IV (1887), 48; G. M. Samson: "Senator Sumner in his Washington Home,"
Pierce MSS.; Sumner to Longfellow, Jan. 11, 1852, Longfellow MSS.; Sumner to
George Sumner, Apr. 19 [1852], Sumner MSS.; Mann to Samuel Downer, Feb.
10, 1852, Mann MSS.

was dead; Clay put in a single appearance, on the day Sumner was sworn in, but took no part in the debates; Webster was in the State Department. Thomas Hart Benton, who had just been defeated for re-election, told Sumner "that he had come to the Senate too late. All the great issues and all the great men were gone. There was nothing left but snarling over slavery, and no chance whatever for a career." [6] As Sumner settled into the Senate seat formerly occupied by Jefferson Davis, of Mississippi, the faces around him seemed to confirm Benton's prognosis. Such mediocrities as Solomon W. Downs, of Louisiana, Thomas J. Rusk, of Texas, and Charles T. James, of Rhode Island, made up most of the Senate.

Besides Sumner, there were only two other Free Soil senators. He doubted the integrity of John P. Hale, of New Hampshire, whose Senate career was more remarkable for his "long speeches, loud professions, Scriptural quotations, funny anecdotes, vehement denunciations" than for any legislative achievements, and could never work closely with him. Salmon P. Chase, of Ohio, with whom Sumner had been co-operating since 1848, was a more reliable ally. Sumner thought him "a tower of strength," whose mere presence would "confirm the irresolute, quicken the indolent, and confound the trimmers," and was pleased to have his Senate seat just in front of Chase's, on the Democratic side of the chamber. [7]

Sumner made only a few friends among the other Northern senators. Cass was too old and too selfish to be more than formally courteous, and Stephen A. Douglas, the leader of the Western Democrats, struck Sumner as a vulgar upstart. The New York senators he liked. In William H. Seward he found "those congenial sentiments, on things higher than party" which made "a peculiar bond of friendship." Though Sumner feared that Seward placed loyalty to the Whig party ahead of antislavery principles, he knew he had a firm ally in Mrs. Seward, who was an outright abolitionist. The aristocratic and wealthy Hamilton Fish,

[6] Haynes: *Sumner*, p. 139.

[7] John T. Morse, Jr. (ed.): *Diary of Gideon Welles, Secretary of the Navy under Lincoln and Johnson* (Boston: Houghton Mifflin Co.; 1909), I, 150; Adams, Diary, Nov. 27, 1852, Adams MSS.; Sumner to Chase, Feb. 7, and 27, 1849, Chase MSS., Lib. of Cong.

of New York, who was also serving his first term, was very cordial to Sumner. Though in private Fish had deplored the defeat of Winthrop, he graciously made Sumner feel almost a member of his Washington household.[8]

Oddly enough it was the Southerners whom Sumner found the best company in Washington. They seemed not to hold his antislavery opinions against him—after all, many Northerners made antislavery speeches when running for Congress—but welcomed him with gracious cordiality. Before long Sumner boasted that Pierre Soulé, the extreme state-rights senator from Louisiana, was his best friend in the Senate: "We deeply sympathize and stand firmly together." Soon he was also on excellent terms with Andrew Pickens Butler, whose seat adjoined Sumner's. The good-natured South Carolina senator took a fancy to his new colleague and frequently asked him to verify classical quotations he planned to use in his speeches. In his stiff Boston way Sumner grew fond of the old man, with his genial red face and his long silver-white hair standing on end, as though charged with electricity; he condescended to say that "if he had been a citizen of New England [Butler] would have been a scholar, or, at least, a well educated man." [9]

Even with Southern women, who dominated Washington society, Sumner was initially popular. They puzzled him, for their lighthearted repartee often went over his humorless head. To a friend who noted his inability to reply to a Southern belle's quips, Sumner confessed as they were walking home after the party: "I have *l'esprit d'escalier* and my retorts do not come until I am well-nigh down the flight of stairs." But, in formal calls, where he could arrange his thoughts in advance, he shone. Carefully not obtruding his antislavery views upon his Southern hostesses, he discoursed with "much Greek fire" and numerous "set pieces." Mrs. Jefferson Davis recalled that he talked learnedly to her of "the Indian mutiny, lace, Demosthenes, jewels, Seneca's morals,

---

[8] Sumner to Seward, Oct. 22, 1851, Seward MSS.; Fish to Winthrop, Apr. 26, 1851, Winthrop MSS.

[9] Lieber to Hillard, Mar. 2, 1852, Lieber MSS.; Carl Schurz: *The Reminiscences of Carl Schurz* (New York: Doubleday, Page & Company; 1917), II, 35; Ben: Perley Poore: *Perley's Reminiscences of Sixty Years in the National Metropolis* (Philadelphia: Hubbard Brothers; 1886), I, 408–9; James Redpath to Elias Nason, Apr. 10, 1874, MS. owned by Mr. Boyd B. Stutler.

intaglios, the Platonian theory," and once gave her "quite an interesting résumé of the history of dancing." [1]

Though Sumner was sometimes lonely in Washington and often missed the Longfellows and the Howes, he was soon caught up in a faster social whirl than had been his fortune in Boston since 1845. In a single week during his first month in the Senate, for instance, he dined, in succession, with the French minister, President Fillmore, Francis P. Blair, Robert Walsh, and Henry A. Wise.[2] He thrived upon the attentions and compliments that came his way, and his Boston friends found him growing "more egotistical than ever." It was not without cause that the Earl of Carlisle (Lord Morpeth) had warned Sumner after his election to the Senate: "Do not ever get dry, and big, and pompous, like some whom you . . . find your neighbors there." [3]

• 2 •

Sumner was resolved to prove himself no one-idead abolitionist agitator, but a practical, businesslike senator. He spent as much time as possible studying Luther Cushing's *Manual of Parliamentary Procedure*, the *United States Statutes at Large*, and the previous Senate debates recorded in the *Congressional Globe*. As his correspondence increased, he took pride in answering all important letters in his own hand, scrawling off a few widely spaced lines in immediate reply to most inquiries. Normally Sumner worked in his rooms from nine in the evening until midnight, but, when preparing a speech, he would often write all night. With his powerful physique he seemed never to tire, and after a bath and a complete change of clothing, he felt able to work on through the next day.[4]

Sumner was not "anxious to make a display in Congress"

[1] Marian Gouverneur: *As I Remember* . . . (New York: D. Appleton and Company; 1911), p. 243; Varina Howell Davis: *Jefferson Davis* . . . (New York: Belford Company; 1890), I, 557–8.

[2] Sumner to Longfellow [Dec. 28, 1851], Longfellow MSS. Blair was the Democratic strategist, former editor of the *Globe*; Walsh, a literary man who had once edited the *National Gazette*; Wise, a naval officer and Edward Everett's son-in-law.

[3] Adams, Diary, May 23, 1852, Adams MSS.; Carlisle to Sumner, Feb. 29, 1851, Sumner MSS.

[4] *Pierce Dinner*, pp. 58–9; Johnson: "Recollections," *Scribner's Monthly*, VIII (1874), 475–6.

during his first session,[5] but he felt called upon to make his maiden speech as early as December 10. The occasion was the arrival in America of Louis Kossuth, exiled leader of the Hungarian revolution. Whether because of the pathos of the Hungarian cause, Kossuth's unexpected eloquence in English, or the exile's handsome appearance (considerably aided by the black wig that concealed his grizzled hair), Americans went wild about him. Everybody wanted to give him an official welcome to the capital of the United States, but in the Senate the resolutions of greeting became involved with Southern fears that Kossuth was antislavery and with reverence for George Washington's noninterventionist teachings.

Sumner decided that his voice could help settle the controversy, and he made what Charles Francis Adams called an "admirably delivered and very impressive" speech. First he welcomed Kossuth as the servant of Freedom: "Whosoever serves this cause, wheresoever he may be, in whatever land, is entitled . . . to the gratitude of every true American bosom, of every true lover of mankind." But what he gave with one hand, he promptly took away with the other. An official reception for Kossuth, he argued, must not be understood as "encouraging any idea of belligerent intervention in European affairs"—precisely the objective on which Kossuth had come to America.[6]

Though Howe, veteran of Greek and Polish revolutions, protested that this was "the speech of Lawyer Sumner, Senator Sumner—not of generous, chivalrous, high-souled Charles Sumner," champion of liberty, Sumner's first Senate speech was generally received with favor. The friendly Massachusetts *Spy* declared that "his bland manners and deep toned melodious voice" had disarmed all criticism and left "an impression for scholarship, good sense, and soul."[7] Even the Boston *Atlas*, a stanchly Whig paper, joined in the chorus of praise.

"If I were disposed to regard my speech in other light than as a *duty done*," Sumner wrote home complacently, "I might be pleased with what is addressed to me." The elders of the Senate

---

[5] Ticknor: *Prescott*, p. 355.

[6] Adams, Diary, Dec. 10, 1851, Adams MSS.; Sumner: *Works*, III, 3–9.

[7] Richards: *S. G. Howe*, II, 360; Massachusetts *Spy* (weekly edition), Dec. 31, 1851. C. F. Adams approved the speech; Henry Wilson was disappointed in it.

crowded about him as he finished, beaming congratulations. Southerners like Henry S. Foote, of Mississippi, joined James Shields, of Illinois, in praising the new senator, and Cass condescended to say that he was not ashamed to have presented Sumner's credentials. "Many have told me," Sumner proudly wrote Howe, "that they never saw any senator listened to with superior attention than I was throughout." [8]

Having found his voice, Sumner did not wait long to use it again. In January 1852, when the Senate was discussing a proposed land grant to build a railroad in Iowa, Sumner, to everybody's surprise, joined in the debate as a defender of the project. Doubtless remembering Webster's exposition of New England's friendship for the West, in his Second Reply to Hayne, Sumner announced that it was becoming that he, as "a Senator from one of the old States," should speak in behalf of Iowa. Previously coached by his messmate, Judge Rockwell, he argued that the Western states suffered because the United States government kept the public lands exempt from taxation. As federal gifts of land for schools, asylums, and other purposes did not repay these states for their loss in taxes, they had a claim in equity for grants such as the one under discussion. [9]

This time Sumner's speech did not escape criticism. Senators from the landless states were unenthusiastic about legislation that would benefit only the West. Senator Joseph R. Underwood, of Kentucky, declared that all Sumner's statistics and computations were wrong; in addition, his comparison of the United States public lands to English crown lands, which were taxed, was un-American. "The Yankees are great inventors and great manufacturers," the Kentuckian sneered, "but such a mental invention, such a mental manufacture as this, I never met with before." [1]

Taking to heart Winthrop's warning that Sumner was "a Jesuit of the first water," who must not be given "the *prestige* of acknowledged success, in order to make him all the more dangerous to us," the Massachusetts Whig press energetically de-

---

[8] Sumner to Dana, Dec. 14, 1851, Dana MSS.; Sumner to Howe, Dec. 14, 1851, Sumner MSS.
[9] Sumner: *Works*, III, 12–32; Sumner to Palfrey, Feb. 11, 1852, Palfrey MSS.
[1] *Cong. Globe*, 32 Cong., 1 Sess., Appendix, 222, 225.

nounced Sumner. The *Atlas* pronounced his speech "uninteresting and heavy, . . . unsound and visionary"; the *Advertiser* called his ideas "entirely novel, and . . . extremely questionable." A correspondent of the latter paper, claiming that Sumner was favoring the Western states at the expense of New England, concluded: "We have sent into the national councils men of such universal philanthropy that our own immediate interests would seem to be the last in their concern." [2]

"I am not disturbed by Boston criticism," Sumner retorted angrily, though his letters reveal that he was writhing under the attacks. Peevishly he complained that nobody in Massachusetts had really studied his speech; only the *Commonwealth*, which had a tiny circulation, had bothered to print it. Earnestly he tried to convince such doubting friends as Adams, Palfrey, and Prescott that his argument was "original and unanswerable." His, he insisted, was "the most important speech for the West uttered in Congress for 10 years." [3]

· 3 ·

Sumner's "Justice to the Land States" speech was, in fact, neither so gross a betrayal of New England as his opponents charged, nor so daring a vindication of justice as Sumner himself thought. The subject of public lands was not one about which he had thought very deeply or cared very much. He spoke on the land question in order to impress his fellow senators with his "reserve, familiarity with the place, and the discussion of other subjects" than slavery. [4]

He attempted to make his speech a model of rhetoric, an example of the proper style and argument for congressional oratory. Considering an appearance upon the Senate floor a public performance, he carefully prepared every detail in advance. Like Daniel Webster, he thought he should "present his best thoughts,

---

2 Winthrop to John Davis, Dec. 13, 1851, Davis MSS.; extracts from Massachusetts newspapers in Boston *Commonwealth*, Jan. 31, Feb. 4, Mar. 11, and 22, 1851.

3 Sumner to Longfellow, Feb. 2, 1852, Longfellow MSS.; Sumner to Epes Sargent, Mar. 13, 1852, Epes Sargent MSS.; Sumner to Howe, Feb. 1, 1852, Sumner MSS.

4 Sumner to Howe, Feb. 14, 1852, Sumner MSS.

his best manner, [and] his best garb when he addressed his fellow-men." At a time when most senators wore black frock coats, Sumner affected light-colored English tweeds; his "favorite costume was a brown coat and light waistcoat, lavender-colored or checked trousers, and shoes with English gaiters."

Sumner's manner was as carefully chosen as his clothing. "Habit," he used to say, "is everything," and he declared he "never allowed himself, even in the privacy of his own chamber, to fall into a position which he would not take in his chair in the Senate." The irreverent might wonder how he looked in a nightshirt, but adherence to this rule made Sumner one of the most conspicuously dignified figures in the Senate chamber. Six feet two inches tall, weighing about 185 pounds, with a broad chest and well-knit figure, he looked the senator incarnate.

In most of his speeches in Congress, Sumner assumed the faintly condescending air of a pedagogue instructing backward children, and as he explained the rudimentary principles of justice to his colleagues, he customarily stood with his left hand on his hip, his right hand toying with an eyeglass. When he became more excited, his most frequent movement was to toss his high-piled, luxuriant brown hair back from his forehead by a swift motion of his head. His gestures were forceful rather than graceful, and Longfellow criticized him for standing "like a cannoneer . . . ramming down cartridges." [5]

Like most of his Senate colleagues, Sumner had little facility in extemporaneous debate, and both pride and belief in the importance of his ideas impelled him to write out and memorize his principal addresses. The later rumor that Sumner rehearsed his speeches at night before a full-length mirror, employing a Negro servant to hold a lamp so that he could better practice his gestures, had no foundation in fact and was probably not intended seriously. Very often, however, when committing a speech to memory, he would mutter phrases to himself, pacing back and forth in his bedroom or lying on his bed. With his incredibly fast and accurate memory, he was able to learn by heart pro-

[5] Noah Brooks: *Washington in Lincoln's Time* (New York: The Century Co.; 1895), pp. 24–5; "Lord Acton's American Diaries," *The Fortnightly Review*, CXVII (1922), 75; Mrs. W. S. Robinson: *"Warrington" Pen-Portraits* . . . (Boston: Lee and Shepard; 1877), p. 57; Dawes: *Sumner*, p. 224; Longfellow, Diary, Mar. 2, 1847, Longfellow MSS.

longed passages, even those including statistics and elaborate legal citations.[6]

Sumner's oratory was highly formal, in a style that was already considered a little old-fashioned. Professor Edward T. Channing, at Harvard, had taught him that orators should follow the classical Greek and Latin pattern of exordium, narration, partition, proof, refutation, and peroration, and nearly all his addresses used precisely this structure.[7] From Professor Channing, too, he had learned that an orator must always have "his points fixed and always visible, his statements almost laboriously distinct," and even in a short, minor effort like his speech on public lands he clearly listed his principal propositions before proceeding to develop them. As a result, virtually all Sumner's addresses had a blocky quality; the careful enumeration of points to be made, the repetition of those points in the course of the argument, and the recapitulation of the same points in the summary gave clarity at the expense of fluency and grace. Sumner was aware of this effect and cultivated it. He advised Horace Mann to follow the same pattern: "Let your points be clear; and the arrangement careful—divided, and sub-divided. These resting places help the understanding of a long document." [8]

To his sentence structure Sumner gave the same careful attention he devoted to his outline. In an age of oratorical solemnity, nobody expected him to be conversational. He deliberately strove to achieve a sonority of expression comparable to that of Edmund Burke, his model in oratory. Sumner's long, complex sentences, with their high proportion of Latin derivatives, gave his addresses a style "that would have been more at home in the days of Cicero and Quintilian than in contemporary life." [9] Early in his public-lands speech, for instance, he declared:

I have no inclination to go into these matters at length, even if I were able; but entertaining no doubt as to the requirements of policy and

[6] Brooks: *Washington in Lincoln's Time*, p. 25; A. B. Johnson to Pierce, Nov. 27, 1894, Pierce MSS.; E. L. Pierce in *Century Magazine*, XLIX (1895), 792.

[7] The best discussion of Sumner's oratory, to which I am much indebted, is Pagel and Dallinger: "Charles Sumner," in Brigance (ed).: *History and Criticism of American Public Address*, II, 751–76.

[8] Edward T. Channing: *Lectures Read to the Seniors in Harvard College* (Boston: Ticknor and Fields; 1856), p. 71; Sumner to Mann, June 23, 1850, Mann MSS.

[9] Pagel and Dallinger: "Charles Sumner," p. 764.

of justice in the present case, and in all like cases, seeing my way clearly before me by lights that cannot deceive, I hope in a few words to exhibit these requirements and to make this way manifest to others.

Though long, Sumner's sentences were considerably shorter than those of the orotund Rufus Choate and Daniel Webster.[1] The thundering clauses, the intricately balanced phrases, and the poetic effusions of these orators Sumner belittled as "scarlet, green-baize, holyoke flower stuff," and he tried to follow Channing's advice and keep his metaphors to a minimum.[2] In his speech on the public lands, for instance, he allowed himself only one real flight of rhetoric, predicting that if the projected railroad was built, the Missouri River, that "distant giant stream, mightiest of the earth, leaping from its sources in the Rocky Mountains, will be clasped with the Atlantic in the same iron bracelet."

In selecting his words, Sumner applied the same standards of restraint. He joined Professor Channing's war to defend the purity of the English language, and sternly scorned neologisms and technical terms. Such phrases as "poke fun" or "folks" he considered hopelessly vulgar.[3] Endlessly he revised his speeches, first in manuscript, again when they appeared in the *Congressional Globe*, and still further when he included them in his published collections of orations. In a single paragraph of an 1855 address, for example, he altered "glimpses" to "glances," "utterances" to "tones," "complete" to "carry through," and "different aspects" to "different heads."[4] Sumner felt that the care he took

[1] As a sample, I have found that Sumner in the introduction and peroration of his public-lands speech and of his Kansas-Nebraska speech averaged 33 words per sentence. Choate's average sentence contained 37 words. John W. Black: "Rufus Choate," in Brigance (ed.): *American Public Address*, I, 546. Wendell Phillips, the only orator of his generation who was colloquial and informal, averaged only 22.98 words per sentence. Raymond H. Barnard: "An Objective Study of the Speeches of Wendell Phillips," *The Quarterly Journal of Speech*, XVIII (1932), 578.

[2] Sumner to Longfellow [Nov. 1848], Longfellow MSS.

[3] Channing: *Lectures*, pp. 218–32; Richards: *S. G. Howe*, II, 389–90. In the Longfellow MSS. there is a set of proofs of *Evangeline*, bearing numerous marginal verbal corrections and suggestions by Sumner, which show his minute attention to purity of style.

[4] The manuscript of Sumner's "The Antislavery Enterprise" address is in the New York Historical Society; an early revision of the paragraph occurs in Sumner: *Recent Speeches and Addresses* (Boston: Higgins and Bradley; 1856), pp. 479–80; Sumner's final revision is in his *Works*, IV, 10–11.

in such matters was very important; he was proud to be a purist.

Instead of using vivid words or ornate sentences, Sumner relied for rhetorical effect upon four other devices. He used statistics to an extent that no modern audience would endure. In his brief address on public lands, for example, he rattled off the number of acres of public lands in the United States, their rate of sale, the amount of state taxes that might have been levied against them, and the total of federal grants to schools, universities, and asylums in the Western states. As a second device, he relied heavily upon quotations, especially from the classics, from English literature, and from medieval historians. Apparently he felt that no speech, however brief, was complete without one good Latin quotation. Though his political advisers in Massachusetts warned him that every Latin phrase he used cost him a vote, and though Hillard complained that his quotations often had no more relevance than the mysterious "Selah" of the Psalmist, Sumner was unwilling to conclude even a lesser effort such as the public-lands speech without a resounding

> *Quam bene Saturno vivebant rege; priusquam*
> *Tellus in longas est patefacta vias.*[5]

Sumner's speeches also gained force from rhetorical exaggeration, though it is hard to know when he was consciously extravagant and when he had convinced himself of his own statements. In his public-lands speech he announced that the projected railroad would make "the distant post of Council Bluffs . . . a suburb of Washington." Welcoming Kossuth, he compared the Hungarian to William Wallace, William Tell, and George Washington, and asserted that the exile's recent reception in England had been grander than any victory won by Julius Caesar or William the Conqueror. Finally, Sumner's oratory drew strength from the epithets he coined. A very high proportion of the anti-slavery men's armory of slogans came from Sumner's speeches: "Freedom National," "The Backbone Party," "The Crime Against Kansas," "The Barbarism of Slavery," and the like.

Though enemies like Winthrop complained that Sumner's

---

[5] J. W. Stone to Sumner, Dec. 16, 1851, Sumner MSS.; Hillard to Lieber, Dec. 30, 1851, Lieber MSS. Helpfully, Summer gave the Senate his source (Tibullus, *Eleg. Lib.*, I.iii.35,36) and translated for the nonscholars: "How well they lived while Saturn ruled—before the earth was opened by long ways!"

speeches were "stuffed full of sentimental commonplaces and exaggerated truisms and inflated affectations," and though less scholarly opponents of slavery like Ben Wade and Zach Chandler sneered at Sumner as one of "them literary fellers," whose oratory had "no bones in it," [6] the Massachusetts senator came to be recognized as the most eloquent congressional spokesman of the antislavery cause. No doubt a large part of Sumner's contemporary repute stemmed simply from the fact that he was a vigorous, handsome man who boldly dared speak out with impassioned sincerity against the majority. Doubtless, too, the high seriousness with which Sumner regarded himself and his mission contributed to his following; he agreed entirely with Professor Channing that an orator "must have a deep and sustained interest in what he is saying" and that he "must believe that he is uttering what others ought to hear and take to heart." [7] If a sense of humor is a handicap in American political life, Sumner was singularly unencumbered. Considering the earnestness of the warfare against the slavery, he could not understand how Wendell Phillips permitted humorous remarks to crop up in his speeches. "Did you ever see a joke in one of my speeches?" he sternly asked a young friend.

"No sir, I think I never did," was the unhesitating reply.

"Of course you never did," returned Sumner triumphantly. "You might as well look for a joke in the book of Revelations." [8]

With his high seriousness, Sumner seemed to true believers a reincarnation of some Old Testament prophet. Unlike Seward, who seemed constantly verging on frivolity, or Chase, whose personal ambition stained his eloquence, or Wade, who was crude and unclassical, Sumner carried absolute conviction to antislavery men. "What a glittering far-darting irresistable [sic] Ethuriel lance you have poised in the lists to tilt with the foes of Freedom!" wrote one of these admirers after Sumner's first antislavery speech in the Senate. "From the depths of my soul I say that your oration came like a new morning to one who was wandering

[6] Winthrop to John Davis, Dec. 13, 1851, Davis MSS.; Gouverneur: *As I Remember*, p. 241; Nevins: *Ordeal of the Union*, I, 395. Benjamin F. Wade was senator from Ohio (1851–69); Zachariah Chandler was senator from Michigan (1857–75, 1879).

[7] Channing: *Lectures*, p. 71.

[8] C. H. Brainerd: "Reminiscences of Charles Sumner," unidentified clipping, Sumner Scrapbooks.

in darkness; and so lighting up the Constitution that the Fathers gave, as to call forth all my reverence for them and for you." [9]

· 4 ·

To elicit such encomiums, however, Sumner had to speak on subjects more stirring than public lands. He presumably had been elected to the Senate in order to vindicate the cause of antislavery. Though he repeatedly refused to give any pledges to politicians, he had made a deep moral commitment by promising Theodore Parker and the antislavery radicals that as senator he would be "in morals, not in politics." In a rather unnecessary public letter accepting his office, he had announced, as from on Mt. Sinai: "Since true politics are simply morals applied to public affairs, I shall find constant assistance from those everlasting rules of right and wrong which are a law alike to individuals and communities." [1]

While Massachusetts conservatives eagerly watched Sumner's course for evidences to support their predictions that he would "betray the very men who have elevated him, give the lie to all his own professions and promises, and acknowledge that he has been an agitator merely for the purpose of obtaining office," antislavery men were equally worried lest he prove the accuracy of Hosea Biglow:

> So, wen one's chose to Congriss, ez soon ez he's in it,
> A collar grows right round his neck in a minnit,
> An' sartin it is thet a man cannot be strict
> In bein' himself, wen he gits to the Deestrict,
> For a coat thet sets wal here in old Massachusetts,
> Wen it gits onto Washington, somehow askew sets. [2]

Both groups of observers thought they had evidence that Sumner, now that he was entrenched in his office for six years, was cooling toward antislavery. Just after his election, he paid a courtesy call upon Millard Fillmore—that same Fillmore whom

[9] Benjamin F. Presbury to Sumner, Sept. 14, 1852, Sumner MSS.

[1] John Weiss: *Life and Correspondence of Theodore Parker* (New York: D. Appleton and Company; 1864), II, 111; Sumner: *Works*, II, 440.

[2] Winthrop to Everett, May 21, 1851, Everett MSS.; James Russell Lowell: *The Biglow Papers* . . . (Cambridge: George Nichols; 1848), p. 49.

he had once assigned to the "depths of infamy" for signing the
Fugitive Slave Act—when the President visited Boston. In the fall
elections of 1851 he refused to take an active part in supporting
the coalition that had just chosen him to the Senate.[3]

Once in Washington, Sumner seemed to be edging his way
into the Democratic party. He favored "fraternizing fully with
Democracy" in the 1852 campaign, and was reported to desire
the disbanding of the Free Soil party.[4] Even after the Whigs nominated a strong antislavery candidate, Winfield Scott, Sumner
thought Massachusetts Free Soilers should keep themselves "*absolutely uncommitted*," because he looked "for light from the Democratic side." When the Democrats nominated the proslavery
Franklin Pierce, Sumner still refused to support Scott, and
backed the third-party candidacy of John P. Hale, which was admittedly hopeless, but which might prevent the Whigs from regaining control of the Massachusetts legislature.[5]

While these undercover political maneuvers were known
only to a few of Sumner's intimates, every Massachusetts antislavery man was conscious of Sumner's slowness to make a demonstration in the Senate against slavery. Garrisonians thought
they had provided him with the perfect occasion when they sent
him a petition demanding the release of Drayton and Sayres, two
antislavery men imprisoned in the Washington jail for having
attempted to smuggle some fugitive slaves out of the District
of Columbia.

Sumner failed to present the petition to the Senate. Wendell

[3] Massachusetts *Spy* (Worcester), Oct. 1, 1851; *The Liberator*, XXI (Oct. 3,
1851), 160; Sumner to George Sumner, Sept. 30, 1851, Sumner MSS.

[4] Everett to Abbott Lawrence, Jan. 6, 1852, copy, Everett MSS.; F. P. Blair
to Martin Van Buren, Jan. 2, 1852, Van Buren MSS.; George Allen: *Reminiscences* (Worcester: Putnam and Davis; 1883), pp. 99–100. E. L. Pierce (III,
314) brands Allen's recollections as "not authentic," but they do at least prove
that contemporaries thought Sumner was ready to abandon the Free Soil party.

[5] Sumner to Amasa Walker, Jan. 9, 1852, Walker MSS.; Sumner to Henry
Wilson, Jan. 10, 1852, Wilson MSS.; Sumner to Mann, June 4, 1852, Mann MSS.;
Sumner to F. W. Bird, June 20, 1852, Bird MSS. At the same time, however,
Sumner wrote: "My hope is to have a third candidate, by whose support we
may openly declare our principles, but of democratic inclinings so as to draw
from Democrats rather than Whigs, and thus, so far as we can, consistently
with our principles, discriminate in favor of Scott." Sumner to Howe, July 4,
1852, Sumner MSS. Consequently he urged Chase to run. Chase to E. S. Hamlin,
July 19, 1852, Chase MSS., Lib. of Cong. There seems no reason to accuse Sumner of duplicity; he was simply so thrilled at being for the first time on the
"inside" of presidential politics that he veered from side to side, and his letters
reflected the views of the person he had most recently been talking to.

Phillips warned him that antislavery men were restive, and *The Liberator* expressed "surprise and regret," but he still did not act. At the April 1852 meeting of the Norfolk County Antislavery Society, Garrison himself introduced resolutions declaring that the senator's silence was "inexplicable," and, though Phillips and one or two others tried to defend Sumner, a vote of censure was adopted. Garrison followed it by a sharp assault in *The Liberator*, titled: "Inquiry after a 'Back-Bone.'" After four and one-half months in the Senate, he pointed out, Sumner had "yet to utter his first word of disapproval of slavery in general, or the Fugitive Slave Law in particular"; he had failed even to present the Drayton-Sayres petition, though it had been in his hands for nearly three months.[6]

In fact, Sumner was working hard to get Drayton and Sayres released by presidential pardon. Realizing that any public clamor would be the surest way of preventing Fillmore from acting, he withheld the Garrison petition. While the case was before the President, Sumner could make no public statement about it, and could not, indeed, even reply to petitioners so notoriously indiscreet as the Garrisonians. Fillmore moved with exasperating slowness, and not until August 11 did he sign the pardon. Fearing that Southerners would attempt to rearrest the two prisoners, Sumner, just as soon as the pardon was issued, hastened to the jail, put Drayton and Sayres in a carriage under the protection of an armed friend, and sped them on their way to the North and to freedom.[7]

The *Commonwealth* could now claim that Sumner had demonstrated that "efficient and practical private action" was preferable to "mere public agitation, which would, perhaps, have retarded instead of advancing . . . liberation" of Drayton and Sayres, but the Garrisonians were unappeased. They cared less for the liberty of Drayton and Sayres than for a denunciation of slav-

    [6] Wendell Phillips to Sumner, Mar. 15, and Apr. 27 [1852], Sumner MSS.; *The Liberator*, XXII (Mar. 19, 1852), 47, and XXII (Apr. 23, 1852), 66; W. I. Bowditch to Sumner, Apr. 22, 1852, Sumner MSS.
    [7] Boston *Commonwealth*, Aug. 24, 1852; Sumner to George Bemis, Apr. 17, 1852, Bemis MSS.; Sumner: *Works*, III, 49–63; Sumner to Howe, May 21, 1852, Sumner MSS.; J. H. Clay Mudd to Caleb Cushing, June 30, 1856, Cushing MSS.; Sumner to Pierce, May 7, 1852, Sumner MSS. Walter C. Clephane: "Lewis Clephane: A Pioneer Washington Republican," *Records of the Columbia Historical Society*, XXI, 267–9.

ery from the Senate. In November 1850, at Faneuil Hall, they reminded Sumner, he had pledged instant action against the Fugitive Slave Law; now "Almost seven months has he sat in the U.S.
Senate, yet not a syllable has he uttered against that Bill; though
men, women and children are hunted daily, and ruthlessly shot
down or dragged back to bondage." On all other subjects—public
lands in Iowa, abolition of the grog ration in the navy, inexpen-
sive international postage—he was eloquent; only on slavery did
he maintain his "strange, extraordinary and inexcusable silence."
"Surely," Garrison shrilled, "this is 'the play of Hamlet, with the
part of Hamlet omitted by particular request.'" Even Phillips,
who tried to sustain his friend, was obliged to condemn his course
as "impolitic and wrong," and Theodore Parker warned that "poor
Sumner" was in "imminent deadly peril": "If he does not speak,
then he is *dead—dead—dead!*" [8]

These attacks were the more annoying to Sumner because
conservative Whigs seized upon them as evidence that he cared
less for humanitarian reform than for his own political advancement. At Boston dinner tables Edward Everett sneeringly com-
mented upon the new senator's silence, and Hillard, hearing that
Southern senators liked Sumner, smartly remarked: *"Yes! now
they find he is a man that will never do them any harm."* Winthrop, vindictive toward the "perfect lickspittle" who was his successor in the Senate, in the early summer published a volume of
Addresses and Speeches containing a supplementary note that
ridiculed Sumner's "mysterious and prudent silence." "It is quite
too late for him," Winthrop jeered, "to explain away this signal
'disloyalty to Freedom,' as he has been accustomed to call it; . . .
the fact will remain on the record, in most ridiculous, or, as some
will think, in most lamentable contrast, both with his ferocious attacks upon others, and with his fervent professions for himself." [9]

At first Sumner's Free Soil friends were willing to let him
choose his own time for speaking out against slavery. Though
they warned the senator not to get lost in a "dismal Sahara of si-

[8] Boston *Commonwealth*, Aug. 12, 1852; Phillips to Sumner, Apr. 27 [1852],
Sumner MSS.; *The Liberator*, XXII (June 11, 1852), 94; XXII (June 18, 1852),
98; Weiss: *Parker*, II, 213.

[9] Everett, Diary, July 6, 1852, Everett MSS.; Parker to Sumner, Aug. 4, 1852,
Sumner MSS.; Winthrop to J. H. Clifford, Nov. 20, 1851, copy, Winthrop MSS.;
Winthrop: *Addresses and Speeches on Various Occasions* (Boston: Little, Brown
& Co.; 1852), pp. 770-1.

lence," they were not greatly troubled by Garrison's original assault. But as summer drew on and Sumner still did not speak,
Howe and Frank Bird began to grumble about his silence, and
Adams said that the party had made a mistake in expecting
Sumner to be "a leader when he was only an orator." At the end
of June, Wilson wrote Sumner bluntly: "You must not let the
session close without speaking. Should you do so you would be
openly denounced by nine tenths of our people." [1]

Behind Wilson's agitation lay deep-seated Free Soil dis-
gruntlement over the operation of the coalition. Antislavery men
in the legislature had faithfully co-operated with the Democrats
in passing laws dealing with corporations, banks, and mechanics'
liens. But the Democrats had failed to help then enact the personal liberty bill that Sumner and Dana had drafted to protect
fugitive slaves; they had failed to adopt resolutions attacking the
Fugitive Slave Act; they had failed to do anything about slavery.
To justify the coalition to their antislavery followers, Free Soil
leaders could point to only one achievement—the election of
Sumner to the Senate. And now silent Sumner seemed to be sell-
ing them out. "Do not for Heaven's sake fail to speak, cost what it
may of effort and trouble," Wilson implored him. "I tell you
frankly that our people are in a state of disappointment and almost of despair. . . . For God sake do not keep us in this state
longer than you can help it. . . ." [2]

Sumner had, as a matter of fact, intended all along to speak
on the question of slavery, and his failure to do so early in the
session reflected not dereliction of duty, but an inexperienced
political judgment. "In view of the singular misapprehension of
my character and position, and of the fact that I have several
years before me in which to labor," he explained to his friends,
"I desire by early caution and reserve, and by strengthening myself on other subjects, to place myself in a position to speak from
a vantage-ground when at last I do speak." He expected to attack the Fugitive Slave Act *"last* of all in this session." [3]

[1] J. W. Stone to Sumner, Jan. 25, 1852, Sumner MSS.; Wilson to Sumner,
Mar. 9, and June 29, 1852, ibid.; Bird to Sumner, July 3, 1852, ibid.; Richards:
S. G. Howe, II, 382–3; Adams, Diary, May 5, 1852, Adams MSS.
[2] R. H. Dana, Jr., to Sumner, fragment of a letter written about June 1852,
Sumner MSS.; Wilson to Sumner, Aug. 3, 1852, ibid.
[3] Sumner to Palfrey, Feb. 11, 1852, Palfrey MSS.; Sumner to Howe, Feb. 14,
1852, Sumner MSS.

His plan was thoroughly unrealistic. First of all, it failed to take into consideration the anxieties of his Massachusetts constituents. Had be been a senator of many years' service, his plea that antislavery men should trust his judgment might have carried weight. But, in a freshman senator, silence gave strength to doubts about the coalition and fortified Free Soilers who had felt all along that Adams, Palfrey, or S. C. Phillips should have been their party's choice.[4]

Furthermore, Sumner misjudged himself and his capacities. It proved hard to find an opportunity for an antislavery oration. "Subjects of debate here are like waves on the beach," he complained. "You expect to leap into one, which comes rolling on, but it has already given way or been lost in another." The longer he delayed, the more difficult it became to speak out. When both major parties, in the spring of 1852, adopted platforms condemning further agitation of the slavery question, he realized that an attack on the Fugitive Slave Act would precipitate a fierce brawl. Sumner, who had uttered many a violent word from the platform, had rarely engaged in face-to-face debate, and he was unsure of his powers. Moreover, he was, as Horace Mann said, "amazingly sensitive to praise," and hated to lose the esteem of the Senate and the friendship of the Southerners whom he had taken such pains to cultivate. Dejected and unhappy as June and his hoped-for time to attack slavery approached, Sumner became ill with diarrhea, undoubtedly of nervous origin, and for a fortnight was too feeble to precipitate a debate.[5] The two following weeks afforded him no opportunity to get the floor.

Finally, on July 27, under enormous pressure from his constituents, Sumner moved the immediate repeal of the Fugitive Slave Law of 1850. The next day, when he asked consent to speak on his motion—a permission required by the Senate rules, but customarily extended as a matter of courtesy—the very senators whom he had considered his warmest friends objected. Butler declared that Sumner's resolution was "merely a pretense to give him an opportunity to make an oratorical display before the

[4] For sharp Free Soil criticisms of his course see Wilson to Sumner, Aug. 3, 1852, ibid., and Theodore Parker to Sumner, Aug. 4, 1852, ibid.
[5] Sumner to George Sumner, Apr. 1, 1852, ibid.; Sumner to Howe, July 4, 1852, ibid.; Mann to Howe, July 27, 1852, Mann MSS.; Mann to Samuel Downer, July 27, 1852, ibid.; Mann to Mary Mann, Aug. 10, 1852, ibid.

Senate, and . . . wash deeper and deeper the channel through which flow the angry waters of agitation." Other Southerners warned that Sumner's motion was "equivalent to . . . a resolution to dissolve the Union." For the northern Democrats, Douglas announced that he would not "extend any act of courtesy to any gentleman to . . . fan the flames of discord that have so recently divided this great people." By a vote of thirty-two to ten the Senate refused Sumner permission to speak.[6]

Massachusetts antislavery papers were indignant against "this insult to the State of Massachusetts," which should make every citizen's "blood curdle with shame, or boil with indignation." Sumner's correspondents branded the Senate's action as "characteristically mean," "contemptible," and Seward fumed that it was "wicked and base." The Southerners, announced the *Commonwealth*, "dare not hear him, because they dread their own consciences."[7]

However consoling such balm, Sumner was "mortified and dejected" by his defeat. Nor were his spirits cheered when Cass, Soulé, Fish, and several other senators who had voted against hearing him sidled up and expressed their regrets. They had toward him the best will in the world, they declared, but their party platforms bound them not to permit further agitation of the slavery question during the presidential campaign. Senator James M. Mason, of Virginia, was more forthright. After silencing Sumner, he told the Massachusetts senator patronizingly: "You may speak next term."

"I must speak this term," Sumner replied firmly.

"By God, you shan't," Mason retorted.

"I will," promised Sumner, "and you can't prevent me."[8] His boast was mostly bravado, for the session was near its end and he was not likely to have another opportunity.

Sumner's unsuccessful attempt to speak failed to silence his critics in Massachusetts. Garrison's denunciations became so vituperative that Seward urged him to restrain his indignation. The

[6] *Cong. Globe*, 32 Cong., 1 Sess., 1934, 1950–3.
[7] Boston *Commonwealth*, July 31, and Aug. 2, 1852; E. A. Stansbury to Sumner, July 29, 1852, Sumner MSS.; John Jay to Sumner, July 30, 1852, ibid.; Frederick W. Seward: *Seward at Washington . . . 1846–1861* (New York: Derby and Miller; 1891), p. 190.
[8] Pierce, III, 292; Dana, Diary, Sept. 11, 1852, Dana MSS.

Democratic Boston *Post* called Sumner's motion a "contemptible dodge," intended to avoid a real discussion of slavery, and the Worcester *Palladium* agreed that Sumner "went into the matter cat-footed," without real intent of forcing a vote on the Fugitive Slave Law. Even the pious protest of the *Commonwealth* that "No well-informed man has any reason to distrust Mr. Sumner's devotion to the cause of freedom" lost its force when the same paper demanded that he "introduce at once a bill for the repeal of the Fugitive Slave Law, and let the slave drivers take, if they dare, the responsibility of silencing him." [9]

Sumner squirmed restlessly under the criticism. Distressed "by the evident impatience of distant friends . . . and the extravagant expectations" they had of him, he angrily reminded the Free Soilers that he had never sought the senatorship, that he had taken it "only as an independent man," unfettered by any claims or pledges. But, in the privacy of a letter to his brother George, he recognized that he had lost his "native independence of position, by becoming the holder of a public office," and that he must speak. [1]

Anxiously he sought an opportunity to deliver his prepared speech. Every subject in the world seemed to come before the Senate except slavery. "My ship is in a *terrible calm*," he wrote Whittier, "like that of the Ancient Mariner." His one opportunity was likely to come just at the end of the session, when he might be able to move an amendment to the civil appropriations bill and claim, as a matter of parliamentary right, an opportunity to speak in defense of his motion. Such a course, Sumner recognized, would have dangers: if the presiding officer failed to recognize him, or if he ruled his amendment not germane to the bill under discussion, there would be no other chance to speak this session. To allay Southern suspicions, Sumner cultivated an air of resignation; he cleared off all the books and papers from his desk and gave no hint that he had an antislavery speech in the top drawer. "*But I shall speak*," he promised his friends in confidence. "For a long time I have been prepared to handle the Fugi-

9 *The Liberator*, XXII (Aug. 13, 1852), 130; Theodore Parker to Seward, Aug. 11, 1852, Seward MSS.; Boston *Commonwealth*, Aug. 2, 6, and 9, 1852.
1 Sumner to Longfellow [Aug. 1852], Longfellow MSS.; Sumner to Dana, Aug. 13, 1852, Dana MSS.; Sumner to George Sumner, Aug. 18, 1852, Sumner MSS.

tive Slave Bill at length. By the blessing of God it shall be done." [2]

On August 26, as the Senate was debating the appropriations bill, Senator Hunter, for the appropriations committee, introduced an amendment for payment of "the extraordinary expenses" incurred by officials in enforcing the laws of the United States. The presentation of this amendment, designed to cover the expense of executing the Fugitive Slave Act, was precisely the opportunity for which Sumner had been waiting. Promptly he submitted an amendment of his own, to the effect that no part of any appropriation should be spent for carrying out the Fugitive Slave Act, "which said act is hereby repealed." [3]

Seizing the floor, he demanded to be heard "not as a favor, but as a right," and quickly launched into his prepared oration. No political platforms could keep him from discussing slavery, he boasted: "The slave of principles, I call no party master." [4] These principles impelled him to denounce the inconsistent, absurd, tyrannical effort to crush opposition to the Fugitive Slave Bill. He would, he promised, reveal that bill in its true enormity and prove that by the original intentions of the founders of the republic, slavery was a sectional institution and freedom national.

• 5 •

During the months while he prepared and memorized his "Freedom National" speech, Sumner had considered and reconsidered the best strategy for attacking slavery. Undoubtedly he was tempted to adopt an extreme abolitionist position. Sumner had a streak of what Lieber called "jacobinical abstraction"; he was the "statesman *doctrinaire*," who seized upon a single idea and carried it to its most extreme conclusion. He liked to fancy himself the descendant of the Separatists of the English revolution, who uncompromisingly contended "for religious, intellectual, and political emancipation." As their heir, he boldly announced that slavery was wrong. "There is no offense against religion, against morals, against humanity, which, in the license of this enormity, may not stalk 'unwhipt of justice.'" Therefore it must be de-

[2] Sumner to Whittier, Aug. 13, 1852, copy, Whittier MSS.; Dana, Diary, Sept. 11, 1852, Dana MSS.

[3] *Cong. Globe*, 32 Cong., 1 Sess., 2,371.

[4] The entire speech is in Sumner: *Works*, III, 95–196.

stroyed. Constitutional provisions and congressional enactments which tried to support this barbarous evil were offenses "against the Divine Law" and must not be obeyed. If it was argued that the rights of slaveholders had been settled by numerous laws and precedents, Sumner answered: "*Nothing . . . can be settled which is not right.*" If it was argued that insuperable practical difficulties forbade emancipation, he replied simply: "The Antislavery Enterprise is right; and the right is always practicable." [5]

Yet, however intense Sumner's Come-Outer spirit, he could never join Garrison and Phillips in denouncing the Constitution as a proslavery document and desiring the disruption of the Union. The basic influences upon his life had all been conservative. His father had taught him unquestioningly to respect the law. Judge Story had inculcated a lawyerlike reverence for precedents, and his *Commentaries on the Constitution* permanently impressed upon Sumner the values of American nationalism. W. E. Channing had urged him to follow a cautiously conservative course, even in reform. John Quincy Adams had been one of the great American nationalists.

With such teachers it was natural that Sumner should think of himself not as a radical extremist, but as a "Conservative Reformer," an American equivalent of Edmund Burke. Sumner even fancied he bore a physical resemblance to the great Irishman, and, later in life, insisted upon having his collected *Works* issued in bindings precisely like those of the standard American edition of Burke's. On questions where he had no great emotional stake, he often spoke with a genuinely conservative accent. He urged Massachusetts reformers seeking to alter the state's ancient constitution to remember that "Institutions are formed *from within, not from without.*" "They spring from custom and popular faith, silently operating with internal power," he added in the best Burkean manner, "not from the imposed will of a lawgiver." He could become eloquent in defending prescriptive usage. The Missouri Compromise, for instance, whatever its original merits, had "by long acquiescence become part of our fundamental law, irrepealable by common legislation." Similarly he refused to vote

[5] Lieber to Hillard, Jan. 16, 1851, Lieber MSS.; *Pierce Dinner*, p. 47; Sumner: *Works*, III, 191, 271-2, 291; II, 413; IV, 24.

against a subsidy to the notorious Collins steamship line on the ground that though he would not favor initiating such a grant, it was unwise and unfair constantly to agitate an already settled question. He was given to reminding his hearers that there were often "proper occasions for compromise." [6]

The difficulty with applying a conservative attitude to the slavery question was the fact that history, precedent, and law all seemed to favor the continuation, or even the extension, of the South's "peculiar institution." For over sixty years the Congress had protected slavery in the coastal slave trade, had admitted new slave states, had guaranteed slavery in the District of Columbia, and had authorized the seizure of fugitive slaves in the North; for over sixty years the courts had upheld all these acts. It was not clear how any disciple of Burke, believing in the organic growth and slow evolution of institutions, could act against slavery.

Sumner's task was to make conservative means lead to radical ends. He had to show that the supporters of the Compromise of 1850, who spoke of themselves as conservative unionists, were in fact extreme sectionalists, while the antislavery agitators, so often accused of radical sectionalism, were the true nationalists. His "Freedom National" speech carefully formulated these ideas and outlined his antislavery philosophy and program; in other speeches during the next decade he was to elaborate the points he made in this 1852 address, but he never varied his basic approach.[7]

To establish his argument, Sumner analyzed both the general question of federal protection of slavery and the specific problem of fugitive slave laws "in the light of history and of reason." In effect, he appealed from history drunk to history sober. Not merely precedents of the last sixty years, but the broader perspectives of American growth since the seventeenth century were relevant. The American nation, as Sumner saw it, had originated in the conflict between Puritan and Cavalier in England, a struggle between right and wrong, democracy and aristocracy. The

6 A. B. Johnson: "Charles Sumner," *Cosmopolitan*, IV (1887), 40; Sumner to J. T. Fields, July 7, 1866, Fields MSS.; Sumner to Longfellow, July 8, 1869, Longfellow MSS.; Sumner: *Works*, III, 252–3, 315; New York *Times*, Mar. 2, 1855.

7 For this reason I am presenting, in the following pages, a composite analysis of Sumner's antislavery thought, citing, without chronological differentiation, speeches made between 1848 and 1855.

contest was continued in the New World. The founders of New England, especially the builders of that "just and generous Commonwealth," Massachusetts, carried on the Puritan tradition; the fathers of Virginia had the vices of the Cavaliers, which multiplied after the introduction of Negro slaves. New England had inspired the American Revolution; her troops had won the nation's independence despite "the imbecility of Southern States," palsied by slavery. In the ardor of revolution the best of the Southerners came to see that slavery was pernicious; Jefferson, Washington, Madison, and Patrick Henry had favored abolition.[8]

The United States was thus born in an atmosphere of freedom for all men. The Declaration of Independence, that "Great Charter of our country," which embodied "in immortal words, those primal truths to which our country pledged itself with baptismal vows as a Nation," proclaimed liberty to all. The Northwest Ordinance, by which the Founding Fathers carefully excluded slavery from all the western territories then owned by the federal government, attested their devotion to liberty. So also did the Constitution, which carefully did not mention the words "slave" or "slavery," but which instead incorporated the Declaration of Independence in its preamble, pledging to "promote the general welfare, and secure the blessings of Liberty to ourselves and our posterity." When Washington was inaugurated, "Slavery had no national favor, existed nowhere on the national territory, beneath the national flag, but was openly condemned by Nation, Church, Colleges, and Literature of the time." [9]

From this high point of virtue there had, of course, been a decline. "The generous sentiments which filled the early patriots, giving to them historic grandeur, gradually lost their power." The slave masters "availed themselves of this indifference." In collaboration with the Northern "mercantile interests," they used "the skillful tactics of party" and "succeeded, through a long succession of years, in obtaining the control of the National Government, bending it to their will." The United States, as a result, was "not now what it was in the beginning"; "it has shrunk in character." [1]

[8] Sumner: *Works*, III, 133, 230, 386, 396.
[9] Ibid., III, 111, 127, 292.
[1] Sumner: *The Landmark of Freedom: Speech . . . in the Senate, February 21, 1854* (Washington; 1854), p. 11.

The remedy lay not in ending the Union, as the Garrisonians proposed, but in reverting to the policy of the Founding Fathers. Once the national government resumed its true position and gave no positive countenance to slavery, the South's "peculiar institution" must cease in the national territories, in the District of Columbia, and in the coastal slave trade; there would be no more slave states admitted; and "The Union Flag of the Republic will become once more the flag of freedom, and at all points within the national jurisdiction will refuse to cover a slave." [2]

When Americans cleared their minds of proslavery fallacies, Sumner thought they would see that the Constitution, as well as the Founding Fathers, spoke for liberty. He did not accept the tenuous reasoning that led Lysander Spooner and a few other antislavery men to argue that the Constitution, properly interpreted, actually abolished slavery throughout the United States.[3] Sumner was never willing to admit that in time of peace "the National Government has power under the Constitution to touch Slavery in the States." But he did insist, following Lord Mansfield's opinion in the Sommersett case (1772), which ended slavery in England, that the institution was "so *odious, that nothing can be suffered to support* it but POSITIVE LAW." Once men recognized the "essential barbarism" of slavery, no one could "be so absurd as to imagine, infer, suppose, conjecture, surmise, fancy, guess or presume that Slavery can have any sanction in words [of the Constitution] which do not plainly and unequivocally declare it." [4]

There were, Sumner boldly contended, no such words. Concealing the nationalistic views he had learned from Story and from John Quincy Adams, he, like most other antislavery politicians, resorted to an extremely strict interpretation of the Constitution to prove his point. As the Tenth Amendment stated that the powers of the United States government are "not general or universal, but special and particular," Congress could not establish slavery in the national territories or protect it in the District

[2] Sumner: *Works:* III, 129. Cf. *supra,* pp. 133–4.

[3] Lysander Spooner: *The Unconstitutionality of Slavery* (Boston: Bela Marsh; 1860), Chap. 8; William Goodell: *Views of American Constitutional Law, and Its Bearing upon American Slavery* (2nd ed.; Utica: Lawson & Chaplin; 1845), p. 77; Dwight L. Dumond (ed.): *Letters of James Gillespie Birney, 1831–1857* (New York: D. Appleton-Century, Inc.; 1938), II, 834.

[4] Sumner to A. P. Brown, Sept. 9, 1860, Garrison MSS., Boston Public Lib.; Sumner: *Works,* III, 105.

of Columbia without some explicit grant of power, and this did not exist in the Constitution. Any attempt of Congress to exercise jurisdiction over such matters was a threat to "all the rights of the States." Sumner called upon the Northern state governments to resist such "intrusive and offensive encroachment on State Rights"; he praised the Virginia Resolutions of 1798; and once or twice he even used Calhoun's word and asked for "nullification" of the Fugitive Slave Law. Slavery in America, he argued, was a creature of municipal or state law, with which the national government could have nothing to do.[5]

Not even the clause of Article IV providing for the rendition of fugitives, the constitutional basis of the fugitive slave laws of 1793 and 1850, gave the United States government power to protect slavery. Both these laws were, first of all, unconstitutional because they violated the Fifth Amendment, guaranteeing that no person could be deprived of life, liberty, or property without due process of law, and the Seventh Amendment, providing for jury trials. But, in fact, no conceivable fugitive slave law could be constitutional, because Article IV only recognized the right of rendition, but did not give Congress power to enforce that right. The fugitive slave clause was designed to promote interstate comity; it was "merely *a compact between the States, . . . conferring no power on the Nation.*" The existing fugitive slave acts must be stricken from the statute books, and "*Each State, in the exercise of its own judgment, will determine for itself the precise extent of obligation assumed.*"[6]

It is extremely difficult to judge the validity of these arguments, which Sumner made the basis of his antislavery agitation throughout the 1850's. There is much justification for his view that the framers of the Constitution did not intend to protect slavery, much less extend it to the national territories.[7] But Sumner did not adequately distinguish between the private opinions of the Founding Fathers and their public actions toward slavery, and he incorrectly identified their mild antislavery sentiments

[5] Sumner: *Works*, III, 125–6; Weiss: *Parker*, II, 140; Sumner to Byron Paine, Jan. 18, 1856, Paine MSS. Lieber thought that Sumner had become "*a genuine nullifier.*" Lieber to Hillard, Oct. 28, 1852, Lieber MSS.

[6] Ibid., III, 186–8.

[7] Allan Nevins: "The Constitution, Slavery and The Territories," in *The Caspar G. Bacon Lectures on the Constitution of the United States, 1940–1950* (Boston: Boston University Press; 1953), pp. 95–141.

with the abolitionism of later decades. His contention that slavery
had to be the creature of positive law and that in the United
States it depended upon local, not national, legislation found support in the opinions of leading Southern and Northern judges,[8]
but it did not necessarily follow that the federal government had
to adopt an antislavery attitude. Practically all the Southerners in
the Senate argued from the same premise that the federal government had no power to intervene against slavery anywhere.[9]
Sumner's arguments against the constitutionality of the fugitive
slave acts, though ingenious, were never sustained by the courts.
Massachusetts Chief Justice Lemuel Shaw, United States Supreme Court Justices Joseph Story, Levi Woodbury, and John Mc-
Lean, and Chief Justice Roger B. Taney were among those who
upheld the validity of the 1793 and 1850 fugitive slave laws.[1]

Critics noted that there was nothing new in Sumner's antislavery arguments. Sumner's stress on the antislavery views of
the Founding Fathers had been common Liberty party propaganda; Salmon P. Chase made the same case in 1845. His argument that the federal government had no constitutional right to
protect slavery had been a mainstay of Joshua R. Giddings's
speeches for years and was a plank in the 1848 Free Soil national
platform. Sumner's ideas about the unconstitutionality of the fugitive slave laws had been anticipated by Robert Rantoul, his
predecessor in the Senate, and his due-process and jury-trial
arguments could be traced back further, to Chase's briefs in the
Matilda case of 1837 and the Van Zandt case of 1846.[2] Sumner

[8] E.g., 18 Pickering, 211, 215; J. C. Hurd: *The Law of Freedom and
Bondage in the United States* (Boston: Little, Brown & Co.; 1858), I, 576.

[9] It was not until later, when Southerners sought a federal slave code for
all the territories, that they argued that slavery was "the common law of the
thirteen States of the Confederacy at the time they burst the bonds that united
them to the mother country." Hurd: *Law of Freedom and Bondage*, I, 573.

[1] Shaw, in 7 Cushing 285; Story, in 16 Peters 539; Woodbury, in 5 Howard
229; McLean, in 2 McLean 611; Taney, in 21 Howard 506. It should be noted,
however, that in none of these cases did the Court decide upon the precise issues
Sumner posed. A recent close student concludes, with Sumner, that "the provisions of the clause dealing with fugitives from service patently vest no power in
Congress to which that body . . . might give effect by legislation." Levy: *The
Law of the Commonwealth and Chief Justice Shaw*, p. 99.

[2] Cf. Salmon P. Chase and Charles Dexter Cleveland: *Anti-Slavery Addresses of 1844 and 1845* (London: Sampson Low, Son, and Marston; 1867),
pp. 76–7; Joshua R. Giddings: *Speeches in Congress* (Boston: John P. Jewett
and Company; 1853), pp. 336–7; Kirk H. Porter and Donald Bruce Johnson
(eds.): *National Party Platforms, 1840–1956* (Urbana: University of Illinois
Press; 1956), p. 13; Luther Hamilton (ed.): *Memoirs, Speeches and Writings*

himself recognized that most of his ideas were derivative; his mind, he frankly admitted, was "a cistern, not a fountain." It was, therefore, unkind of Wendell Phillips, addressing the American Antislavery Society, to claim that with the possible exception of one minor point, Sumner had introduced "no train of thought or argument, and no single fact in the whole ["Freedom National"] speech, which has not been familiar in our meetings and essays for the last ten years." Horace Mann gave a fairer appraisal of Sumner's role as an antislavery thinker: "The subject has been so extensively discussed already that he has an immense amount of material put into his hands. This position will require not originality . . . but skill in using, and this is his *forte*." [3]

It was not Sumner's constitutional arguments that gave strength to his antislavery addresses, but his vision of an emancipated America. He sought first to arouse "an enlightened, generous, humane, Christian public opinion" in the free states, so that the whole North would join in the "moral blockade" against slavery. Then the United States government, under Northern leadership, would withdraw its protection from the hated institution, and the "Slaveholding Oligarchy, banished from the National Government, and despoiled of ill-gotten political consequence, without ability to punish or reward," would sink into impotence. Slavery itself might "linger in the States as a local institution," but eventually "the citizens of the Slave States, where a large portion have no interest in Slavery," would realize that just as "A blade of grass would not grow where the horse of Attila had trod," so could no "true prosperity spring up in the foot-prints of the slave." The non-slaveholding whites, then, would force "open the gates of

---

of Robert Rantoul, Jr. (Boston: John P. Jewett and Company; 1854), pp. 740–1; Jacobus ten Broek: *The Antislavery Origins of the Fourteenth Amendment* (Berkeley: University of California Press; 1951), p. 38; Salmon P. Chase: *Reclamation of Fugitives from Service: An Argument . . . in the Case of Wharton Jones vs. John Van Zandt* (Cincinnati: K. P. Donough & Co.; 1847), pp. 89–92. Lysander Spooner: *A Defence for Fugitive Slaves . . .* (Boston: Bela Marsh; 1850) also anticipated many of Sumner's arguments. Practically all Sumner's points had been included in Horace Mann's Feb. 28, 1851, speech in the House of Representatives (Mann: *Slavery: Letters and Speeches* [Boston: B. B. Mussey & Co.; 1851], pp. 390–472), but numerous letters in the Mann MSS., 1849–50, show that Sumner was the source of his legal arguments and citations.

[3] Thomas Wentworth Higginson: "Charles Sumner," *The Independent*, XXVI (Apr. 2, 1874), 1; *Twenty-First Annual Report of the American Antislavery Society* (Boston; 1853), p. 111; Phillips to Sumner, Mar. 7, 1853, Sumner MSS.; Mann to Howe, July 27, 1852, Mann MSS.

Emancipation in the Slave States." To assist in this redemption, Sumner was willing to compensate the slave owners at national expense; nothing was due to them, but, so great was his hatred of slavery, he "could not hesitate to build a Bridge of Gold, if necessary for the retreating fiend." [4]

After emancipation, the South would once again come into fraternal relations with the rest of the nation, abandoning its sectional institutions and prejudices. Soon, too, the "profane assumptions of race" would disappear, though Sumner was careful to declare that he did not wish "to change human nature, or to force any individual into relations of life for which he is not morally, intellectually, and socially adapted," and that one must not assume "that a race, degraded for long generations under the iron heel of bondage, can be taught at once all the political duties of an American citizen." Though Sumner was willing to explore plans "for opening our neighboring tropical lands to the colonization of people of the African race," he thought that most of the Negroes, free and contented, would remain in the South as "a dependent and amiable peasantry." [5]

· 6 ·

During the three and three-quarters hours Sumner held the Senate floor in delivering his "Freedom National" speech, the galleries filled with spectators who had heard that an important oration was being given, and many members of the House of Representatives thronged the Senate floor. Webster, though old and ill and within two months of death, came in to listen. Sumner triumphantly noticed his presence and gloated that he, not the Secretary of State, was now the spokesman of Massachusetts. Rest-

[4] Sumner: *Works*, II, 312; III, 133, 459, 540; IV, 27, 32; Sumner to A. F. Rockwell, Mar. 23, 1854, Rockwell MSS., Lib. of Cong. Mann had used the "Bridge of Gold" phrase in 1850. Mann: *Slavery*, p. 278; it was derived from Byron's: "a golden bridge is for a flying enemy" (*The Deformed Transformed*, pt. II, sc. 2).

[5] Sumner: *Works*, III, 509; IV, 24; Sumner to J. R. Lowell, Dec. 14, 1857, Lowell MSS.; Boston *Times*, Apr. 12, 1874. Frederick Douglass complained that Sumner failed to recognize "the entire manhood and social equality of the colored people." Douglass to Sumner, Apr. 24, 1855, Sumner MSS. There is no necessary inconsistency between Sumner's position on Negro equality in his Senate speeches and his Roberts argument. He wished to remove all *legal* barriers that sustained racial discrimination, not to enforce social equality for the Negro.

lessly Webster moved from one side of the chamber to another, and after about an hour, he left, black and scowling.

Throughout the long speech the attention of the audience was unbroken, and as Sumner reached his peroration, many ladies in the gallery, and at least one senator as well, were in tears. Gracefully concluding with some "words of Oriental piety" —"Beware of the groans of the wounded souls. Oppress not to the utmost a single heart; for a solitary sigh has power to overset a whole world"—Sumner resumed his seat amid "unbounded" applause.[6]

Immediately Senator Jeremiah Clemens, of Alabama, rose to urge that no reply be made to Sumner's remarks: "The ravings of a maniac may sometimes be dangerous, but the barking of a puppy never did any harm." But Senator George E. Badger, of North Carolina, irritated apparently as much by the manner as the content of Sumner's address, attacked this "elaborate oration, carefully written, studied, committed to memory, and interspersed in various parts with curious quotations from modern learning and ancient lore, and every now and then dignified and adorned with Latin quotations, which, when the Senator did not condescend to translate them into English, I presume were very unintelligible to most of the members of this body." As the constitutionality of the fugitive slave laws had been unchallenged since 1793, Sumner's speech was designed for "mischievous purposes," not for the promotion of constructive legislation. "Never, sir, since I have been a member of this body," the veteran senator declared, "has the Senate witnessed such an exhibition."

Though leaders of both parties wanted to cut off the debate, it inevitably broadened. Stephen A. Douglas asserted that Sumner was not attacking the Fugitive Slave Act; he was assaulting the Constitution. Senator John B. Weller, of California, announced that this was the first abolitionist speech he had ever listened to and, as it was "so handsomely embellished with poetry, both Latin and English, so full of classical allusions and flourishes," he had found it more palatable than he had fancied possible; but he could see no purpose in Sumner's speech unless it was to incite riots in the Northern states.

[6] Horace Mann to Mary Mann, Aug. 27, 1852, Mann MSS.; Dana, Diary, Sept. 11, 1852, Dana MSS.

Sumner was not entirely without defenders. Hale told the Senate that in this one speech Sumner had placed "himself side by side with the first orators of antiquity, and as far ahead of any living American orator as freedom is ahead of slavery." And Chase loyally defended his friend's speech as opening "AN ERA in American history."

Gradually the debate widened into a general discussion of the approaching presidential election. Sumner, exhausted by his oration, said very little more. When at last a vote was taken on his motion to repeal the Fugitive Slave Act, there were only four "ayes"—Hale, Chase, Ben Wade, and himself.[7]

[7] *Cong. Globe*, 32 Cong., 1 Sess., Appendix, 1,113–25. A number of other genuine antislavery men in the Senate—Seward, Fish, Hannibal Hamlin, etc.— refrained from supporting Sumner's motion lest it imperil the chances of Whig presidential candidate Winfield Scott. For Badger's reactions to the speech see Lawrence F. London: "George Edmund Badger: His Last Years in the United States Senate, 1851–1855," *North Carolina Historical Review*, XV (1938), 231–50.

CHAPTER X

Outside of Any Healthy
Political Organization

S UMNER believed that his "Freedom National" oration was a
triumph. When the debate ended, Democratic Senator James
Shields, of Illinois, complimented him warmly, and John H.
Clarke, a Rhode Island Whig, declared that the speech would "be
a text-book when they were dead and gone." William H. Polk, of
Tennessee, who may have been pulling Sumner's leg, said that
the address "was the greatest triumph of genius, he had ever
known," and Soulé, who claimed to be "familiar with all the efforts of Wilberforce, and others against slavery in the British
Parliament," vowed that Sumner's oration was the greatest of
them all. Avid for praise, Sumner passed these remarks along to
his friends. "Be assured I receive these things with humility," he
assured Longfellow as he related the more extravagant of these
compliments. "I am satisfied to labor in the cause and not in
vain." [1]

In Massachusetts, as well as in the Senate chamber, the
speech seemed to have made a great impression. Such conservative papers as the Boston *Atlas*, *Advertiser*, *Courier*, and *Post* did

[1] Bigelow: *Retrospections*, I, 126; Sumner to Longfellow [Aug. 1852], Longfellow MSS.

not print it or even deign to comment upon it editorially, but Bay State voters read it in full in the *Commonwealth,* the *National Era,* or the New York *Post,* or purchased the pamphlet version, which quickly ran through five editions. The oration was "glorious," Henry Wilson wrote; it was "masterly," said Wendell Phillips. It seemed to restore him "to his full tide of popularity with the masses" of Massachusetts Free Soilers. When Sumner went home in September, they staged a rally at the door of his Hancock Street house and welcomed the returning hero "with the heartiest and most enthusiastic plaudits, long continued." "Now," rejoiced Theodore Parker, "you have done yourself Justice and put yourself out of the reach of attack from friend or foe." [2]

Tired from the long session, Sumner wanted to bask in his new popularity and to rest for three months until the next session of the Senate began. He looked forward to having dinner with his close friends, to meeting Arthur Hugh Clough, the visiting English poet, to sea-bathing with the Longfellows at Newport, to a cool, leisurely trip up Lake Champlain into Canada.

Instead, he found himself beset by importunate demands to aid the coalition in the fall elections. Free Soilers were at first plaintive, then strident, in their reproaches when, after making a brief appearance before the state Free Soil convention on September 15, he persisted in his vacation plans. "Every motive of interest, of gratitude, and of humanity" ought to impel him to support his own party, one angry correspondent wrote the *Commonwealth.* "Cannot Sumner . . . submit to some personal inconvenience in defence of the glorious truths embodied in our platform?" asked another. Howe warned that party leaders strongly felt: "That you ought 'to take the stump.' That the party has claim upon you in faith, honor. That you cannot disregard the claim with[out] risking your hold upon the confidence and regard of the party. That many influential men are already disaffected towards you in consequence of your reluctance to come forward. . . . That some who tried hard to secure your election to Congress swear they would work as hard to put you out."

[2] Boston *Commonwealth,* Sept. 6, and 10, 1852; John Bigelow to Sumner, Sept. 5, 1852, Sumner MSS.; J. W. Stone to Sumner, Dec. 27, 1852, ibid., Wilson to Sumner, Sept. 5, 1852, ibid.; Phillips to Sumner, Sept. 3 [1852], ibid.; Samuel Downer to Mann, Aug. 28, 1852, Mann MSS.; Parker to Sumner, Aug. 27, 1852, Sumner MSS.

More briefly, but bluntly, Henry Wilson said that Sumner was wrong to remain silent. When the Whigs regained control of the Massachusetts government in the fall elections, Free Soilers blamed Sumner.[3]

For the next eight years Sumner's life was to exhibit this same pattern: after doing everything he could to battle slavery in the Senate, he returned to Massachusetts only to find that distrust of his motives was as widespread as ever. Each demonstration he made against slavery was followed by renewed, ever more strident calls for further agitation. He could never satisfy his critics.

Though Sumner grew "very sore" under these incessant demands, and thought that each of his major addresses should have sufficiently demonstrated his antislavery zeal, his peculiar political position inevitably exposed him to such criticism. He was not sufficiently identified with any group to have its unqualified confidence. Whigs, of course, hated him and considered his antislavery protestations a pious front for self-promotion. So did the conservative, anticoalitionist Democrats. Abolitionists never fully trusted him because he did not meet their tests for doctrinal purity. Even the Free Soilers doubted his loyalty. As the chief recipient of benefits from the coalition, Sumner could never fully win the confidence of the small but influential group of anticoalitionists, such as Adams, Palfrey, Phillips, and Dana, who were trying to oust Wilson, that "third rate man, with the arts of a first rate demagogue," and restore the party to its original independent stand. At the same time, Wilson and his associates, recognizing that Sumner's friendships and social ties bound him to the Adams clique, demanded that he repeatedly demonstrate his loyalty to the coalition by "active participation in their hopes, their fears, their reverses and their successes."[4]

· 1 ·

The Senate session of 1852–3 afforded few opportunities for such demonstrations. In the quiet, lame-duck term, which opened on

[3] Boston *Commonwealth*, Oct. 27, and Nov. 2, 1852; Howe to Sumner [Oct. 1852], Howe MSS.; Pierce to Sumner, Dec. 6, 1852, Sumner MSS.

[4] The best account of the intraparty Free Soil feuds is in C. F. Adams's Diary. See entries for Sept. 6, and 11, and Nov. 10, and 25, 1852; also Samuel Downer to Mann, Feb. 16, 1853, Mann MSS.

December 7, the only interesting development was the plan of Southern expansionists to purchase Cuba from Spain. Though Sumner was thoroughly conversant with the scheme, he could not make a public protest, for all the debates were held in secret session, and he vainly attempted to have the rule of secrecy lifted. Aside from advocating the abolition of the grog ration in the navy, proposing lower international postage rates, and securing a small pension to a Massachusetts widow of a Revolutionary war veteran, Sumner had nothing to do. He could not even make a show of busy-work in committees, for he and Chase received no assignments because both Democratic and Whig caucuses agreed that they were "outside of any healthy political organization." [5]

Obliged to be silent, Sumner came under renewed attacks at home. The Garrisonians, discovering that his "Freedom National" speech had upheld the Constitution, decided that he was no better than Webster. Indeed, said Parker Pillsbury to the Massachusetts Antislavery Society: "Webster's fall was not so deplorable as that of Charles Sumner." Charles Francis Adams, concluding that Sumner was a prisoner of his own reputation, fearful of making another speech on slavery lest it fail to live up to the first, thought he "was never formed to be a political leader." Even more harshly Palfrey concluded that Sumner's mission in Washington had "failed by reason of his own reputation, and of his social tendencies, which relax his energies." When resolutions were introduced in the General Court deploring Sumner's exclusion from committee assignments as a slap at the sovereign state of Massachusetts, Wilson's faction let them die, declaring: "We are fools to defend those, who wont defend us or themselves." [6]

Sumner became petulant under these strictures. He was sure that his motives were pure; he knew that he was doing all that anybody could. His critics failed to recognize that he kept constant vigil in the Senate against proslavery plots. They did not understand that a senator had to have an occasion to make a ma-

[5] Everett, Diary, Dec. 22, 1852, Everett MSS.; Sumner: *Works,* III, 212–15; Pierce, III, 320.

[6] *Twenty-First Annual Report Presented to the Massachusetts Anti-Slavery Society* . . . (Boston; 1853), p. 86; A. G. Browne to Sumner, Feb. 14, 1853, Sumner MSS.; Samuel Downer to Mann, Feb. 16, 1853, Mann MSS.; Adams, Diary, Apr. 23, and 26, 1853, Adams MSS.

jor address and that each of his important antislavery orations required weeks to prepare and commit to memory. They did not realize that corruption, intemperance, and slavery were the dominant trinity in Washington, against which his efforts too often proved unavailing. His assailants had forgotten that he never wanted to come to the Senate, that he was not a politician; they ignored all that he had already done and said in Congress for the cause of freedom, even "though not ripening in any immediate fruit." "If among my discouragements," he wrote in soreness of spirit, "shall be alienation or distrust at home, I will try to bear this, and keep on in my duty." [7]

Sore and sensitive, Sumner did not re-examine his own course to see whether he might possibly have been at fault; he never outgrew the bitter lesson of his childhood that it was dangerous to admit the possibility of error. Nor did he reply directly to his critics. Characteristically, he vented his anger upon a bystander, much as a child in a temper tantrum will beat the wall or the floor. There was no little truth in the shrewd remark of a Boston spinster that Sumner was a "specimen of prolonged and morbid juvenility." [8]

Independent-minded, crusty Francis Lieber became the object of Sumner's wrath. For years the two men had gradually been drifting apart. Lieber thought Sumner's peace orations vapid, illogical, and impractical, and his antislavery agitation nothing less than Jacobinical. He regretted his friend's election to the Senate as "bad for Sumner, for Boston . . . for Congress, for the Union, for the country." [9]

Though Sumner was not a man to suffer dissent gladly, he tried for a long time to keep up his friendship with Lieber. As his Senate duties occupied more and more of his time, he wrote fewer and briefer letters; often he would only mark a few lines in a newspaper or pamphlet which he thought might specially interest the South Carolina professor.

All this, to Lieber, was perfectly insulting. Sumner's hasty notes he thought worse than no letters at all. All too often the

---

[7] Dana, Diary, Apr. 25, 1853, Dana MSS.; Sumner to Charles List, Dec. 5, 1852, Robie-Sewall MSS.

[8] Hillard to Lieber, Dec. 24, 1850, Lieber MSS.

[9] Lieber to Hillard, May 4, and Apr. 28, 1851, ibid.; Lieber to Sumner, May 20, 1851, ibid.

newspapers the senator forwarded contained marked passages lauding himself to the skies. To Lieber, who was fond of comparing himself to Grotius and Montesquieu, such egotism was disgusting. Equally revolting and more dangerous were the shocking articles "about ill-treated negroes marked with thick lines" which Sumner kept sending. They not merely endangered Lieber's standing in South Carolina; they seemed to brand Lieber himself as responsible for the slave system. "Is it nothing to me that Fate has put me hither and that I pass my life with a smarting pain the whole day and year," Lieber indignantly protested to Hillard; "have I made slavery? Have I praised it?" After nearly three years of being pelted with antislavery missives, Lieber, in 1853, asked Sumner to stop. Government reports and personal letters he would always welcome, but, he told Sumner: "If you have really no time to write to me, pray do not remind me of you in that peculiar manner." [1]

His protest reached Sumner as he was suffering most acutely from Massachusetts criticism and was looking for somebody to attack. Swiftly he retorted that Lieber had no right to complain, as he had become "the apologist of slavery."

Lieber was furious, but, remembering that "Sumner uses words as boys do stones," to "break windows and knock down flowerpots, while he all the time plays the offended," he wrote denying that he was a defender of slavery.

With the icy reserve Sumner always assumed when he was furious, he replied curtly that he was "right glad" if indeed Lieber was not a slavery apologist. Lieber refused to answer so offensive a communication and broke off the correspondence and the friendship.[2]

· 2 ·

Sumner's irritability was by no means assuaged by the fact that after a long, frustrating session of Congress, he was obliged to come home in the summer of 1853 and take an active part in

[1] Lieber to Dorothea L. Dix, Apr. 18, 1858, ibid.; Lieber to Hillard, Mar. 16, 1853, ibid.; Lieber to Sumner, May 2, 1853, ibid.

[2] Lieber to Hillard, May 29, and June 7, 1853, ibid. For a careful, perceptive analysis of the reasons for the break between the two see Freidel: *Lieber*, pp. 265–6.

Massachusetts politics. Defeated in the 1852 elections by the Whigs, the coalition had nevertheless managed to carry its proposal for calling a convention to amend the ancient constitution of Massachusetts. Howe convinced Sumner that serving in this convention would restore his popularity with the Free Soilers, and Wilson staged his election as a delegate from Marshfield, where Webster had lived.[3]

When the convention met at the State house in May, Sumner was conspicuously present, and Wilson had him named chairman of the committee on the Bill of Rights. Several times he presided over the assembly when it met in committee of the whole. Not until June 21 did he take an active part in the debates, making during the concluding weeks "two beautiful, classical, high-toned orations" on the Bill of Rights and the system of representation. But, unfamiliar with the issues and puzzled by the swiftness with which the debates ranged from one strange topic to the next, he exercised little influence in the convention. "Sumner has held his own as an orator," Richard Henry Dana, Jr., noted. "As a debater, a worker, an influential member, he has not succeeded. He takes but little active part, and seems to have a fear of taking the floor, except on leading subjects, and after great preparation."[4]

But it was not so much personal inadequacy as political embarrassment that limited Sumner's role. This convention of 1853, though numbering among its members such extraordinary talents as Choate, Dana, Anson Burlingame, N. P. Banks, Wilson, and Benjamin F. Butler, and including three state governors, two United States senators, ten congressmen, and seventy-nine members of the state senate, was anything but an impartial, judicious effort to improve the venerable constitution of 1780. Sponsored by the leaders of the recently defeated coalition, the convention was in fact a political move designed to break down the dominance of the Whig party in the state. As Boston, voting as a single election district, regularly sent a solid phalanx of forty-four

[3] Howe to Sumner, Feb. 1, 1853, Howe MSS.; Wilson to Sumner, Mar. 5, 1853, Sumner MSS. The fact that Wilson ran Sumner in Marshfield, where he was chosen in preference to Webster's own son, suggests that Wilson was aware of Sumner's mild flirtation with the antislavery Whigs (Adams, Diary, Nov. 10, and 25, 1852, Adams MSS.) and was deliberately arranging a victory that Whigs could only regard as an insult to Webster's memory. Hillard to Lieber, Mar. 1853, Lieber MSS.

[4] Boutwell: *Reminiscences*, I, 227; Adams: *Dana*, I, 247.

Whig members to the General Court, coalition leaders resolved
to divide all cities into several election districts. Because Whig
mill owners were intimidating their employees, the coalitionists
wanted to institute the secret ballot. As the coalitionists knew that
their strength was in the central and western parts of the Commonwealth, while the Whigs generally carried the larger cities of
the eastern section, they planned to reshuffle the system of representation so as to give two thirds of the representatives to the one
half of the state's population living in towns smaller than 4,500
inhabitants. All in all, it is difficult to resist the conclusions of opponents that the coalitionists intended to produce "a party Constitution, not a state Constitution." [5]

While the coalitionists wanted to use the Constitutional Convention of 1853 to strike at Whiggery, they also hoped to consolidate their power within their own parties. Boutwell made of
the convention an excuse for seizing control of the Massachusetts Democratic machine. Wilson, too, used it in an attempt to
force the old Conscience Whigs like Adams, Palfrey, and E. Rockwood Hoar—none of whom was elected to the convention—out
of the Free Soil party. Both Wilson and Boutwell gained support
from the Troy and Greenfield Railroad interests, which were willing to exchange votes of delegates from northwestern Massachusetts in exchange for state loans to construct the Hoosac tunnel. [6]

In this web of interests and ambitions, Sumner's position was
acutely uncomfortable. If he opposed coalition plans for revising

[5] The best analyses of the convention are: James Schouler: "The Massachu-
setts Convention of 1853," *MHSP*, XVIII (2 ser.; 1903), 30–48; Samuel Eliot
Morison: "History of the Constitution of Massachusetts," in *A Manual for the
Constitutional Convention, 1917* (Boston: Wright & Potter Printing Co.; 1917),
pp. 41–63; Bean: "Party Transformations," Chap. 6; Samuel Shapiro: "Richard
Henry Dana, Jr.: A Biography" (unpublished Ph. D. dissertation, Columbia
Univ.; 1958), Chap. 6; Jean Carol Kenney: "An Analysis of Political Align-
ments in Massachusetts as Revealed in the Constitutional Convention of 1853"
(unpublished M.A. thesis, Smith Coll.; 1951). See also: A. Poole (comp.):
Poole's Statistical View of the Convention . . . (Boston: White and Potter;
1853); Michel Brunet: "The Secret Ballot Issue in Massachusetts Politics from
1851 to 1853," *New England Quarterly*, XXV (1952), 354–62; *Discussions on the
Constitution Proposed to the People of Massachusetts by the Convention of 1853*
(Boston: Little, Brown & Co.; 1854). The detailed convention proceedings may
be consulted in *Official Report of the Debates and Proceedings in the State Convention, Assembled May 4th, 1853, to Revise and Amend the Constitution of the
Commonwealth of Massachusetts* (Boston: White & Potter; 1853).

[6] *Discussions on the Constitution*, p. 203. Cf. Edward C. Kirkland: "The
Hoosac Tunnel Route: The Great Bore," *New England Quarterly*, XX (1947),
88–113.

the constitution, he would be turning against the very men who elected him to the Senate—and Henry Wilson never permitted him to forget his debt to them. If he supported the revisions, he would take on "the responsibility of a set of schemes about which he was never even consulted." If he remained silent, everybody would think him incompetent.[7]

With his remarkable talent for rationalization, Sumner managed to convince himself that expediency and justice coincided, and he squarely endorsed most of the coalition's proposals. He came out enthusiastically for the Hoosac tunnel as "a glory to the Commonwealth, and a mighty channel of trade and travel." He contrived, with less enthusiasm, to support the coalitionists' plans to take representation away from Boston and give it to the central and western towns. The true basis for representation, Sumner declared in a speech to the convention on July 7, should ideally be founded "absolutely upon equality" so as to make "all men, in the enjoyment of the electoral franchise, whatever their diversities of intelligence, education, or wealth, and wheresoever they may be within the borders of the Commonwealth, whether in small town or in populous city, absolutely equal at the ballot-box." But, he swiftly backtracked, this system of equal representation could not be advantageously instituted "unless supported by the permanent feelings and conditions of the people." As the practice of giving Massachusetts small towns disproportionate influence had sprung "from custom and popular faith, silently operating with internal power, not from the imposed will of a lawgiver," he announced in Burkean rhetoric, no radical change in the admittedly inequitable system should be tried at present, but instead the rural towns should be given even more representation so as to protect the Commonwealth against the "commercial feudalism" of the big cities.[8]

Even after this public demonstration of loyalty, coalition leaders, perhaps still convinced that he was inwardly disaffected, drove him with a tight checkrein. When Sumner tried to make a flowery little speech on the origins of the Bill of Rights, most of the delegates were ready to listen, but coalitionists, headed by

[7] Longfellow, Diary, May 3, 1853, Longfellow MSS.; Sumner to W. W. Story, Aug. 2, 1853, MS., Huntington Lib.; Adams, Diary, June 4, 1853, Adams MSS.
[8] *Debates of the Massachusetts Convention*, III, 20–1; Sumner: *Works*, III, 229–58.

Boutwell and Bird, invoked the fifteen-minute limit imposed upon debaters. Then, to demonstrate their power to the senator, they relaxed the rule so that he could finish, but Sumner, peeved, peremptorily refused to continue with his prepared address.[9]

Wilson and the other Free Soil managers rather hoped that Sumner would take no part in the campaign to ratify the new constitution, so that they would have an excuse for reading him, along with Palfrey and Adams, out of the party. But Sumner surprised them by undertaking the most extensive speaking tour he had made since 1848. He made eighteen major addresses, speaking in every section of the state and reaching, as he believed, "more persons than have ever before been addressed in the same time by one man in Massachusetts." Though his address was long and technical, his hearers stayed through more than two hours of his oratory and even applauded as he announced ponderously: "I have now refuted, as I think, the twelfth argument brought against a new constitution. I pass to the thirteenth objection." [1]

Whatever effect Sumner may have had upon his audiences, he at least succeeded in convincing himself of the merits of the new constitution, and with all the zeal of a new convert he keenly resented criticisms of the reforms it proposed. The opposition of "the Boston cabal, whose home is State Street, and whose breath is Silver Grey Websterism," he had anticipated. He was not seriously disturbed when Attorney General Caleb Cushing issued a "ukase," condemning the coalition as "a fatal error" and warning Massachusetts Democrats that continued support of "persons engaged avowedly in the persistent agitation of the slavery question" would be considered "hostile in the highest degree to the determined policy of the [Pierce] Administration." Nor was he surprised that the Boston Irish, under Bishop John B. Fitzpatrick, mobilized to fight a new constitution that would have banned state support for sectarian schools.[2] But, when some of his old

---

[9] *Debates in the Massachusetts Convention*, III, 373–6; Schouler: "The Massachusetts Convention of 1853," p. 39.

[1] Pierce to Sumner, Jan. 23, 1854, Sumner MSS.; Sumner to Seward, Nov. 15, 1853, Seward MSS.; Thomas Wentworth Higginson: *Part of a Man's Life* (Boston: Houghton Mifflin Co.; 1905), p. 86.

[2] Sumner analyzed the opposition to the new constitution in letters to Seward, Nov. 15, 1853 (Seward MSS.), to Whittier, Nov. 21, 1853 (Albree: *Whittier Correspondence*, pp. 121–2), and to E. L. Pierce, Dec. 18, 1853 (Sumner MSS.). Cf. Handlin: *Boston's Immigrants*, pp. 204–5.

Free Soil allies expressed doubts about the proposed constitution, they came too close to the very questions Sumner had suppressed in his own mind, and he turned upon them with disproportionate bitterness.

Charles Francis Adams was the first to feel his anger. In November Adams explained to the citizens of Quincy his reasons for opposing the new constitution; it had little to commend it, and the inequitable system of representation was alone enough to condemn it. In a pointed reference, Adams claimed that his "honored friend, Charles Sumner," had started out with the impregnable principle of "*democratic equality of numbers*," but, allowing himself to be led astray by "the siren song of expediency," had "bowed his neck to the iron rod of party." Sumner was indignant, and not until Dana persuaded Adams to explain that he did not mean to "imply the smallest disrespect" to Sumner or any "dereliction of principle," did the two men resume social relations, and then for months they were on a rather distant footing.[3]

More angry and more lasting was Sumner's rupture with his old friend Palfrey, who was bitter that the coalitionists did not run him for governor, and hurt that he had not been chosen to the convention. Denying that he was imputing any dishonorable motives to the framers of the new constitution, Palfrey, signing himself "A Free Soiler from the Start," published a pamphlet vigorously attacking that document. Deeply hurt, Sumner complained to Dana of Palfrey's inexplicable course, but toward the offender himself he maintained an icy silence until after the election and the defeat of the new constitution. Ready to weep over the defeat of a plan that "would have broken the back-bone of the Boston oligarchy, the stumbling-block of all reform and especially of all Anti-slavery," Sumner blamed this "severe calamity" upon Palfrey, who, he said, could hardly "by any future services repair the wrong he has done to our cause." Palfrey's tentative efforts toward reconciliation were rebuffed, and for a long while after Sumner returned to Washington, he ignored the friendly notes Palfrey continued to send him. Finally, after Palfrey had gone to what he considered "the very verge of humiliation," Sumner con-

[3] Clipping from Boston *Advertiser*, in Adams, Diary, Nov. 4, 1853; Dana, Diary, Nov. 20, and 27, 1853, Dana MSS.; Adams to Sumner, Nov. 21, 1853, copy, Adams MSS.; Adams, Diary, Nov. 21–2, 24, 1853, ibid.

sented to resume relations, though he frankly informed his friend "that it seems to me that Freedom in Massachusetts has received from you a more deadly blow than from any other living citizen of our Commonwealth." The coolness between the two men continued, and their old cordiality was not revived for years.[4]

When the new session of Congress opened in December 1853, Sumner's political fortunes were at a new low. The coalition that had elected him to office had again been defeated, this time so decisively that the plan for Free Soil–Democratic fusion in Massachusetts was finally abandoned. The recent campaign caused many of the old Conscience Whig group to doubt, as did Adams and Palfrey, Sumner's political morality and to suspect that he lacked "the main requisite, sagacity and penetration." The Whigs continued in control of the state government, and Edward Everett, the new Whig senator from Massachusetts, was able to prevent Sumner from receiving any responsible committee assignments.[5] "Eheu! Eheu!" Sumner lamented. "For a while we must eat our political bread in great humility."

· 3 ·

"This Congress is the worst—or rather promises to be the worst—since the Constitution was adopted," Sumner wrote in December 1853; "it is the 'Devil's Own.'" He and Chase were now the only Free Soil members in the heavily Democratic Senate, and so hopeless was their position that rumors of Sumner's impending resignation were widely circulated.[6] As the session got under way, it was clear that his only role would be the frustratingly negative one of opposing every proposal of the Pierce administration and

[4] See the copies of the following letters in the Palfrey MSS.: Palfrey to Sumner, Nov. 29, 1853, Jan. 3, June 1, 13, and 23, 1854; Sumner to Palfrey, June 6, and 14, 1854; also Palfrey to Dana, Sept. 12, 1854, copy, ibid.

[5] Adams, Diary, Nov. 28, 1853, Adams MSS. As the Democrats gave Chase committee assignments at this session, Seward proposed that the Whig caucus include Sumner in its lists. Everett objected that he "could not consent to his being regarded as a Whig." Eventually the Whigs left vacant two posts at the foot of the committees on pensions and on enrolled bills, which the Democrats filled with Sumner's name. Seward: *Seward at Washington, 1846–1861*, p. 212; Everett, Diary, Dec. 10, 1853, Everett MSS.

[6] Pierce, III, 361; Buffalo *Commercial Advertiser*, Jan. 7, 1854; Boston *Commonwealth*, Dec. 12, 1853.

of everlastingly introducing petitions for cheaper international postage.[6a]

Sumner grew morose and sensitive. He quarreled bitterly with Everett, and only the tact of Mrs. Hamilton Fish patched up the dispute.[7] With suspicious eye he observed his fellow senators, certain that every move indicated a proslavery plot.

In January 1854 his worst suspicions seemed to receive corroboration. Stephen A. Douglas, the Democratic chairman of the Senate committee on territories, introduced a measure for organizing a territorial government for Nebraska. The new territory, which included both the present states of Kansas and Nebraska, was one from which slavery had been excluded by the Missouri Compromise of 1820, but Douglas's bill provided that "all questions pertaining to slavery in the Territories, and in the new States to be formed therefrom, are to be left to the decision of the people residing therein," and that the states to be formed from the territory, when applying for admission to the Union, should be received "with or without slavery" as their constitutions provided.

Instantly alarmed, Sumner proposed an amendment that would reaffirm the Missouri Compromise ban on slavery in the Nebraska territory. His maneuver was a hopeless one, intended to arouse public opinion against Douglas's bill; in fact, his amendment may have inadvertently been a disservice to freedom, as it also alerted Southern senators to the ambiguities of Douglas's proposal. Yielding to their pressure, Douglas, on January 23, introduced a substantially revised version of his bill, providing for two separate territorial governments in the region, and specifically asserting that the prohibition on slavery in the Missouri Compromise was "inoperative" because it had been "superseded by the principles of the legislation of 1850."[8]

6a In private conversation Sumner suggested adding an arbitration clause to a proposed commercial treaty between Great Britain and the United States, but both Secretary of State William L. Marcy and British minister J. F. Crampton agreed that, however desirable, the amendment would be defeated if Sumner sponsored it. Crampton to Earl of Clarendon, Jan. 1, 1854, Clarendon MSS.

7 Sumner to Mrs. Fish, Jan. 9, 1854, copy, Fish MSS.; Everett to Mrs. Fish, Jan. 9, 1854, copy, ibid.

8 The Missouri Compromise, which admitted Missouri to the Union as a slave state, prohibited slavery in all the rest of the territory acquired by the Louisiana Purchase which lay north of 36°30'. Thus it had been agreed since 1820 that Kansas and Nebraska would be organized as free territories. The

Even before the measure assumed its final form, Sumner was spreading the alarm that "the Nebraska bill opens anew the whole slavery question." He did not, actually, know very much about these territorial questions, nor had he hitherto exhibited any passionate concern over the fate of Nebraska. Assuming that the Missouri Compromise forever barred slavery from the region, he had failed to vote for its organization as a free territory in the previous Congress.[9] Nor did Sumner have any comprehension of the "whole broad complex of reasons, half-reasons, and quarter-reasons" behind Douglas's measure: "the disorganized, discontented state of the Democratic party, lacking both leader and policy; the obligation resting upon 'Young America' for bold, trenchant action; his own legitimate ambition to become President; the demand of the Northwest for a Pacific Railroad, with the consequent necessity for settling the Kansas-Nebraska country to furnish its future path; the fear of Missouri slaveholders lest they be surrounded on three sides by freesoil territory; [Missouri Senator David R.] Atchison's stubborn assertion that he would let Nebraska 'sink in hell' before he would see it organized on a basis excluding slaveholders with their property; and Atchison's ability to rally a solid block of Southern Senators behind him."[1] But to Sumner most of these factors were not merely unknown; they were irrelevant. All that mattered was that Douglas's bill permitted slaves in territory hitherto dedicated to liberty.

He needed no further evidence of the atrocity of Douglas's proposal, and even before the Southerners pushed the "Little Giant" into an explicit repeal of the Missouri Compromise, Sum-

---

Compromise of 1850 permitted the inhabitants of the New Mexico territory and the Utah territory, acquired through the War with Mexico, to decide the question of slavery for themselves by promising: "That, when admitted as a State, the said territory . . . shall be received into the Union, with or without slavery, as their constitution may prescribe at the time of their admission." Douglas claimed that by endorsing this principle of "popular sovereignty" in 1850, Congress had tacitly overruled the Missouri Compromise prohibition on slavery. For a defense of Douglas's argument see Harry V. Jaffa: *Crisis of the House Divided: An Interpretation of the Issues in the Lincoln-Douglas Debates* (New York: Doubleday & Company, Inc.; 1959), pp. 133–46.

[9] Pierce, III, 361. Sumner, Chase, and Seward all failed to vote when the Nebraska organization bill was defeated by a small margin on March 3, 1853. *Cong. Globe*, 32 Cong., 2 Sess., 1,117.

[1] Nevins: *Ordeal of the Union*, II, 102, 106. Cf. James C. Malin: *The Nebraska Question, 1852–1854* (Lawrence, Kans.; 1953); Roy F. Nichols: "The Kansas-Nebraska Act: A Century of Historiography," *Mississippi Valley Historical Review*, XLIII (1956), 187–212.

ner joined with Chase, Giddings, and three other antislavery congressmen to draw up an "Appeal of the Independent Democrats in Congress to the People of the United States." This skillful paper, written by Chase from a rough draft supplied by Giddings and then given a final literary revision by Sumner,[2] was a brilliantly effective piece of antislavery propaganda. Arraigning the bill "as a gross violation of a sacred pledge; as a criminal betrayal of previous rights; as part and parcel of an atrocious plot to exclude from a vast unoccupied region immigrants from the Old World and free laborers from our own States, and convert it into a dreary region of despotism, inhabited by masters and slaves," the "Appeal" begged free-state residents who thought of settling in the West, the German-born immigrants who had hopes of finding farms there, and Christians and Christian ministers everywhere to oppose the "monstrous plot." Douglas, so the "Appeal" charged, was actuated by "the mere hazards of a presidential game"; hoping to win Southern support, he was willing "permanently [to] subjugate the whole country to the yoke of a slaveholding despotism."

While the "Appeal" was secretly being distributed, Douglas moved for prompt consideration of his bill. Sumner and Chase, disturbed by the apparent apathy in the North and wishing their address to have a maximum effect, requested Douglas to delay the debate for a week, ostensibly so that they could give it further study, and the Illinois senator courteously agreed.[3] That same afternoon the "Appeal" appeared in Washington newspapers, and Douglas, learning that the very senators who had so blandly asked for delay were circulating what he considered gross libels upon himself and his favorite measure, grew choleric over their hypocrisy.

When the debate opened on January 30, he shrewdly turned his wrath to political purposes. By identifying all opposition to his measure with the intemperate and sometimes inaccurate "Ap-

[2] Julian: *Giddings*, p. 311.
[3] The best accounts of the Kansas-Nebraska debates are in Nevins: *Ordeal of the Union*, II, Chaps. 3–4; George Fort Milton: *The Eve of Conflict: Stephen A. Douglas and the Needless War* (Boston: Houghton Mifflin Co.; 1934), Chaps. 7–9; Albert J. Beveridge: *Abraham Lincoln, 1809–1858* (Boston: Houghton Mifflin Co.; 1928), II, Chap. 3.

peal," and by singling out the two Free Soil senators as the leaders of that opposition, he tried to consolidate behind him moderate opinion in both North and South. Ten times in his opening speech he denounced Chase and Sumner as the "abolition confederates." They were, he shouted, "the pure, unadulterated representatives of Abolitionism, Free Soilism, Niggerism in the Congress of the United States." He stigmatized the "Appeal of the Independent Democrats" as "an abolition manifesto," "a negro movement," "a wicked fabrication," "a gross falsification," "an atrocious falsehood."

Pushing ahead with driving, galloping speed, Douglas would not permit his enemies to explain their course. An interruption from Chase he brushed aside, as the senator, he claimed, had "violated all the rules of courtesy and propriety." He allowed Sumner barely a moment to declare that in signing the "Appeal" he had been judging "the act, and not its author" and that he still considered the measure "a soulless, eyeless monster—horrid, unshapely, and vast." [4]

In the ensuing bitter and vituperative debate, which occupied the Senate for most of the next month, Douglas ably marshaled on his side many moderate Northern senators and all but two of the slave-state senators. From the outset it was clear that, backed by the patronage of the Pierce administration, the bill would easily pass the Senate.

Because of Douglas's tactics, leadership of the opposition fell not to conservative Whigs, like Edward Everett, or even to Whigs of known antislavery views, like Seward, who gave one stiff, formal oration against the measure, but had little more to do with the debates, but to Chase and Sumner. Chase led the attack in an able speech that, in effect, was an amplification of the "Appeal." Knowing that it was impossible to defeat the bill in the Senate, he hoped to expose its inconsistencies and implications, to induce moderates to speak out against it, and, chiefly, to delay proceedings until Northern sentiment could be aroused. "It is *Slavery* that renews the strife," he asserted; he hit strongly at Douglas's argument that the Compromise of 1850 "superseded" the Missouri Compromise; and he denied that Douglas's "great

[4] *Cong. Globe*, 33 Cong., 1 Sess., 282.

principle" of squatter sovereignty could settle the territorial question. "What kind of popular sovereignty is that which allows one portion of the people to enslave another portion?" he asked.

Aside from raising minor questions about Indian tribes in the Nebraska territory, other opponents of the bill closely imitated Chase's argument. "You have seen them on their winding way," Douglas taunted, "meandering the narrow and crooked path in Indian file, each treading close upon the heels of the other, and neither venturing to take a step to the right, or left, or to occupy one inch of ground which did not bear the foot-print of the Abolition champion."

Sumner, both because he wanted moderate senators to voice their opposition to the Kansas-Nebraska bill first and because he was always slow in preparation, did not take the floor until February 21. By this time, he thought, Douglas's arguments had "been already amply refuted by able Senators." Nevertheless, he plunged ahead and, taking as his text a verse from Deuteronomy: "Cursed be he that removeth his neighbor's landmark," he titled his oration "The Landmark of Freedom." Declaring that the Kansas-Nebraska bill had been "precipitated . . . upon the Senate, at a moment of general calm, and in the absence of any controlling exigency, and then hurried to a vote in advance of the public voice," he condemned it, first of all, as "the infraction of solemn obligations originally proposed and assumed by the South . . . as a covenant of peace." The South had profited by the Missouri Compromise; the slave states of Missouri and Arkansas attested that. But now, "with the consideration in its pocket, it repudiates the bargain which it forced upon the country." In the second place, Douglas's bill, by permitting the extension of slavery, was "a flagrant and extravagant departure from the original policy of our fathers," and Sumner recapitulated his argument that the Founding Fathers had dedicated the nation to antislavery principles.

Douglas's bill, he concluded, was another of "the melancholy tokens of the power of slavery, under our political system." Slavery "loosens and destroys the character of Northern men, even at a distance—like the black magnetic mountain in the Arabian story, under whose irresistible attraction the iron bolts, which held together the strong timbers of a stately ship, were drawn out, till the whole fell apart, and became a disjointed wreck." Comparable was the Northern man from whom slavery had drawn the iron of principle; he became "that human anomaly— *a Northern man with Southern principles.*" After a burst of applause from the galleries, Sumner quickly ended. Douglas and his allies could pass the bill, he prophesied, but they could not settle the slavery question by their act. "Sir"—he repeated his favorite maxim—*"nothing can be settled which is not right."* [5]

Douglas promptly replied to Sumner's charges. Giving little attention to Sumner's unquestionably correct arguments that the Compromise of 1850 was not intended to supersede the Missouri Compromise and that Douglas's bill did reopen the floodgates of sectional controversy, the "Little Giant" adroitly seized upon weaknesses in his opponent's case. The Missouri Compromise, he pointed out, was not a "compact," as Sumner had claimed; it was an act of Congress which could be repealed by any succeeding Congress. If prescription sanctified the Missouri Compromise, Douglas sharply observed, the same might be said of the Fugitive Slave Law, which Sumner wanted repealed. It was "truly refreshing," he bitingly remarked, to hear a man like Sumner, who had protested so earnestly against the compromise measures of 1850, now bear testimony "to their beneficial effects in restoring peace, harmony, and fraternity to a distracted country." Sumner's attempt to attribute abolitionist views to the Founding Fathers Douglas dismissed casually as another of those "mere essays against slavery." [6]

Nor was the "Little Giant" one to endure a personal affront in silence. Sumner's hit at "a Northern man with Southern principles" had sounded very telling in the course of his speech, but, a short time later, when Douglas, bristling with anger, demanded to know whether the senator had intended a personal reference, Sumner sat silent. "He says nothing," Douglas gloated; "he has not the candor to admit it nor the courage to deny it." Then, triumphantly, he reminded the Senate that the phrase was not

[5] Sumner: *Landmark of Freedom*, pp. 2, 4, 8–9, 13, 14.
[6] *Cong. Globe*, 33 Cong., 1 Sess., Appendix, 326; James Ford Rhodes: *History of the United States from the Compromise of 1850* . . . (New York: The Macmillan Co.; 1893), I, 454.

new with Sumner; it had been conspicuously applied to Martin Van Buren—Sumner's candidate for the Presidency in 1848.[7]

The bitterness of Douglas's rebuttal indicated that "The Landmark of Freedom" had made a considerable impression. Even proslavery Senator Badger, of North Carolina, congratulated Sumner upon his "master-piece of oratory; perfect in its arrangements, in its historical elucidation and in its eloquent delivery"—though adding that it lacked "one thing; it was on the wrong side." Conservative Whigs like Edward Everett and William Seaton, editor of the *National Intelligencer*, thought the speech "extremely pertinent and conclusive." Chase called it "a splendid effort," and Seward enthusiastically praised it as "very brilliant, magnificent and effective." Complacently Sumner wrote Longfellow: "I have occasion to be satisfied with the reception of my speech." [8]

Particularly cheering was the news of its reception in Massachusetts. Though the Hunker newspapers of Boston failed to comment editorially on Sumner's speech, even they felt obliged to print the flattering telegraphic reports of its enthusiastic reception. The *Commonwealth* published a large extra edition containing the speech, and it was promptly exhausted by the universal and extraordinary demand. Massachusetts readers who could not get the *Commonwealth* read the speech in full in the New York *Herald*, the New York *Tribune*, and the New York *Times*. Sumner's oration was read to factory hands in Millbury, Massachusetts, as they worked, and extracts from it appeared in the *Transcript*, which fashionable Bostonians saw at tea time. "Since the introduction of this infamous bill into the Senate," Charles Francis Adams wrote the senator, "your position here has undergone a most sensible change, even those who have been most opposed to you, now acknowledge that you speak the voice of Massachusetts." [9]

Most gratifying of all was the change of opinion that seemed

[7] Everett, Diary, Apr. 6, 1854, Everett MSS. Sumner himself had been using the phrase since 1846. See *supra*, p. 147.

[8] Boston *Commonwealth*, Mar. 1, 1854; Sumner to Longfellow, Mar. 2, 1854, Longfellow MSS.; Everett, Diary, Feb. 21, 1854, Everett MSS.; Chase to Pierce, Mar. 12, 1854, Sumner MSS.; Seward: *Seward at Washington, 1846–1861*, p. 223.

[9] J. D. Baldwin to Sumner, Feb. 26, 1854, Sumner MSS.; A. H. Waters to Sumner, Mar. 4, 1854, ibid; Dana to Sumner, Feb. 26, 1854, ibid.; Adams to Sumner, Mar. 14 [1854], ibid.

to be occurring in Massachusetts Whiggery. Massachusetts conservatives had supported the Compromise of 1850 only because of Webster's assurance that it was necessary to save the Union.[1] Now it appeared that the South was plotting to extend slavery not merely to remote New Mexico, but to the fertile plains of Kansas, where Massachusetts farmers had expected to find free land, and Massachusetts manufacturers new markets.[2] Angrily Whigs cried that the price of Union was too great. At a Faneuil Hall meeting, held the day after Sumner spoke, Winthrop announced, to great applause, that he could not now support all the compromise measures of 1850—meaning the Fugitive Slave Law—and Samuel A. Eliot denounced the Kansas-Nebraska bill as "a deliberate breach of the plighted faith of the nation." [3]

In their new mood, Boston Whigs had little patience with their cautious, conservative representative, Edward Everett, whom they had sent to the Senate to checkmate Sumner. Indisposed to controversy, Everett hesitated long before declaring himself on the Kansas-Nebraska bill, and when he did come out in opposition, his muted attacks on the measure and his great courtesy toward Douglas made his efforts seem feeble when compared to the forceful directness of Chase, Seward, and Sumner. Everett's course, his own brother-in-law grumbled, proved him "stuff not good enough to wear in rainy weather, though bright enough in sunshine." Even a loyal Whig like Hillard thought Everett's speech "like a boned turkey—the knife goes clean through." When Everett, afflicted by kidney stones, was obliged to leave the Senate chamber during the long evening session of March 3, when the bill finally passed, Boston Whigs said that he had shirked the vote, and cruelly laughed that a man with so much gravel should be without grit.[4]

As Everett declined, Sumner rose. Daily he received dozens of enthusiastic letters, many from constituents who had hitherto

[1] But, for some economic considerations that made the Compromise palatable to them see David D. Van Tassel: "Gentlemen of Property and Standing: Compromise Sentiment in Boston in 1850," *New England Quarterly*, XXIII (1950), 307–19.

[2] Cf. Philip S. Foner: *Business and Slavery: The New York Merchants and The Irrepressible Conflict* (Chapel Hill: University of North Carolina Press; 1941), Chap. 5.

[3] New York *Tribune*, Feb. 24, 1854.

[4] Pierce, III, 370; Hillard to Lieber, Mar. 2, 1854, Lieber MSS.; George Sumner to Sumner [Mar. 1854], Sumner MSS.

opposed his course. With charming naïveté he took handfuls of
the complimentary messages over to the Sewards and read them
aloud, so that his friends could see that he was truly loved and
wanted by Massachusetts.[5]

Strengthened by such support, he began to thrive under the
attacks made upon him on the Senate floor, and more than once
ventured, without having prepared and memorized a formal
speech, to enter into the debates. Courteously but firmly he corrected Senator Butler, who misrepresented the status of slavery
in colonial Massachusetts, and with more acerbity he denied
Senator Moses Norris's allegation that he had counseled violence
in resisting the fugitive slave laws.

By the time the Kansas-Nebraska bill came up for final vote
in the Senate, Sumner felt ready to tangle with Douglas himself,
but he found the "Little Giant" a more formidable foe than his
subordinates. In a memorable Senate session that lasted for seventeen consecutive hours, Douglas reached a height of eloquence
and vindictiveness. Summarizing the arguments for his bill,
Douglas refuted the charges made by its opponents. Toward Sumner and Chase, whom he held responsible for the anti-Nebraska
sentiment sweeping through the North, he was overbearingly in-
solent. When Sumner tried to explain his views on the Missouri
Compromise, Douglas shouted him down and, with temper flar-
ing, denounced him and Chase: "You degrade your own States.
. . . You have stimulated [the people] to these acts [of opposition to the Nebraska bill], which are disgraceful to your State,
disgraceful to your party, and disgraceful to your cause." If Sumner dared impeach his motives, Douglas snarled: "I must be permitted to remind the Senator from Massachusetts that I did not
enter into any combinations or arrangements by which my character, my principles, and my honor, were set up at public auction
or private sale in order to procure a seat in the Senate of the
United States!"

Sumner, who always shrank "instinctively from any effort
to repel a personal assault," rose to deny that he had come
"into this body by any waiver of principles; by any abandonment
of my principles of any kind; by any effort or activity of my own,
in any degree."

5 Seward: *Seward at Washington, 1846–1861*, p. 226.

Douglas sneeringly rejected his explanation: "As well might the receiver of stolen goods deny any responsibility for the larceny, while luxuriating in the proceeds of the crime, as the Senator to avoid the consequences resulting from the mode of his election while he clings to the office." "I regret," Douglas added unctuously, "that the Senator should now, by a violation of all the rules of courtesy and propriety, compel me to refresh his mind upon these unwelcome reminiscences." [6]

Though Sumner had announced that he intended once more to enter the debate in opposition to the bill, he now took Seward's advice and did not speak again. At 4:55 in the morning of March 4, the Senate passed Douglas's bill, by a vote of thirty-seven to fourteen, with Sumner's vote in the negative. It was still dark when Sumner and Chase left the Capitol together, but Douglas's sympathizers in the city were firing cannon to celebrate his triumph. "They celebrate a present victory," said Chase, turning to his companion, "but the echoes they awake will never rest till slavery itself shall die." [7]

· 4 ·

"The North, through this Administration, is delivered bound, hand and foot to the South," Sumner grieved, but as long as he felt that Massachusetts was behind him, he was not despondent. "For a while Freedom is defeated," he admitted, "but I turn to the country and to God and do not despair." [8]

His opportunity to make another onslaught against slavery came when Mrs. Harriet Beecher Stowe, acting upon a hint in the "Appeal of the Independent Democrats," devoted some of her royalties from *Uncle Tom's Cabin* to the collection of a *"united clerical protest of New England"* against the Nebraska act.[9] Solemnly, "in the name of Almighty God, and in his presence," the clergymen denounced Douglas's bill as "a great moral wrong, . . . a breach of faith, . . . a measure full of danger to the Union, and

---

[6] *Cong. Globe,* 33 Cong., 1 Sess., Appendix, 234, 309, 332, 335-6.
[7] Sumner to S. Hale, Mar. 22, 1854, MS., N. H. Hist. Soc.; Pierce, III, 361; J. W. Schuckers: *The Life and Public Services of Salmon Portland Chase* (New York: D. Appleton and Company; 1874), p. 156.
[8] Sumner to R. C. Waterston, Mar. 21, 1854, Waterston MSS.; Sumner to J. Wingate Thornton, Mar. 9, 1854, Segal Coll.
[9] Mrs. Stowe to Sumner, Feb. 23, 1854, Sumner MSS.

exposing us to the righteous judgements of the Almighty." When completed, the petition formed a scroll 200 feet long. To avoid the imputation that this was an abolitionist manifesto, its sponsors asked Edward Everett to present it to the Senate. With a notable want of enthusiasm, he did so, and even when Douglas sprang up to denounce "political preachers" who were "desecrating the pulpit, and prostituting the sacred desk to the miserable and corrupting influence of party politics," Everett presented a cautious apology, rather than a manly defense of the petitioners.

Sumner looked on in anger, but while his colleague had the petition in charge, he felt that he should not intervene. But when Everett, ill and unhappy, went home to Boston and, a few weeks later, resigned his seat, Sumner saw his chance. Eagerly he welcomed some late signatures to the clergymen's petition, and on May 25, when the Senate prepared to give its final approval to the Kansas-Nebraska bill, as amended in the House, he gained the floor, ostensibly to present the petition, actually to vindicate the preachers who signed it. He would not, he announced, attempt "anything like a defence of the clergy. They need no such thing at my hands. There are men in the Senate justly eminent for eloquence, learning, and ability; but there is no man here competent, except in his own conceit, to sit in judgment on the clergy of New England." The Senators who had been "so swift with criticism and sarcasm" against these petitioners might profit by their example. Perhaps Senator Butler, who was "not insensible to scholarship, might learn from them something of its graces." Perhaps Senator James M. Mason, of Virginia, who found "no sanction under the Constitution for any remonstrance from clergymen, might learn from them something of the privileges of an American citizen." Perhaps Douglas himself, "who precipitated this odious measure upon the country, might learn from them something of wisdom."

Predicting the direst consequences from the Kansas-Nebraska act, Sumner announced that it was "at once the worst and the best which Congress ever acted": "It is the worst bill, inasmuch as it is a present victory of Slavery. . . . It is the best bill on which Congress ever acted; for it . . . annuls all past compromises with Slavery, and makes all future compromises impossible. Thus it puts Freedom and Slavery face to face, and bids them grapple. Who can doubt the result?" [1]

The very next day gave an answer to Sumner's question. On May 26 a throng of citizens assembled in Faneuil Hall to protest the arrest of a pitiable fugitive slave named Anthony Burns. Incited by Wendell Phillips and Theodore Parker, they mobbed the courthouse, where Burns was imprisoned, and tried to force an entrance. They were repelled, but only after they had killed one of the temporary guards appointed by the United States marshal. Promptly President Pierce ordered troops to Boston, and on June 2 they escorted the trembling fugitive through the crepe-hung streets lined with hostile spectators down to the ship that waited to carry him back to Virginia and to slavery. [2]

Sumner's enemies blamed him for the outbreak. Ignoring the fact that telegraphic reports of his speech did not reach Boston until the day after the Burns riot, they pointed to his prediction that the Nebraska bill would "broadcast through the land, dragons' teeth, which . . . will . . . fructify in civil strife and feud." Sumner, claimed the pro-administration Washington *Union,* had given the command for the Burns mob. The Washington *Star* warned: "If Southern gentlemen are threatened and assaulted, while legally seeking to obtain possession of property for the use of which they have a solemn constitutional guaranty, . . . *certain Northern men now in our midst* will have to evince a little more circumspection . . . in their walk, talk, and acts. . . . *Let Sumner and his infamous gang* feel that he cannot outrage the fame of his country, counsel treason to its law, incite the ignorant to bloodshed and murder, and still receive the support and countenance of the society of this city, which he has done so much to vilify." [3]

New England grew excited over the implicit threat. The seizure of Burns and the attempt to intimidate Sumner, wrote one formerly conservative Boston Whig, had unified "the good

---

[1] Henry M. Dexter to Pierce, Apr. 15, 1885, Pierce MSS.; Sumner: *Final Protest for Himself and the Clergy of New England against Slavery in Kansas and Nebraska* (Washington; 1854), pp. 4–6.

[2] The best account of the Burns case is Samuel Shapiro: "The Rendition of Anthony Burns," *Journal of Negro History,* XLIV (Jan. 1959), 34–51.

[3] Sumner: *Works,* III, 348.

men of all parties in a common sentiment of hostility to the encroachments of the slave power." Joseph Hawley, future governor of Connecticut, offered to come to Washington and defend Sumner. "I have revolvers and can use them," he announced. "Should you fall," one admiring correspondent told the senator, "you will . . . kindle a fire of freedom that will blaze and burn the length and breadth of the land the light of which will irradiate the fartherest corners of the earth." [4]

Confident in the support of his constituents, Sumner paid little attention to the threats—except to see that they received suitable publicity. Not even a Southern attempt to insult him in the restaurant where he regularly dined frightened him. "The Administration organs tried to stir a mob against me," he calmly told Mrs. Seward, "and some evil-disposed persons expressed a desire to put a bullet through my head; but I was never for a moment disturbed." He continued to walk unarmed from his lodgings to the Capitol, and to friends who urged him to take precautions, he replied: "I am here to do my duty and shall continue to do it without regard to personal consequences." [5]

Far from deterring Sumner, the threats made him the more eager to renew his war on slavery. Feeling "humbled in the dust" by the outcome of the Burns case, he planned again to demand the repeal of the odious Fugitive Slave Act. Then he would move "for the complete annulling by the North of all the other compromises." "Slavery will be discussed with us *as never before*," he promised Theodore Parker. [6]

Sumner did not have an opportunity to make the formal oratorical assault he had intended, however, for inadvertently his new colleague, Julius Rockwell, Everett's successor, started a fresh debate on slavery when he presented a petition of 2,900 Massachusetts citizens asking repeal of the Fugitive Slave Law. Southern senators objected to its reception because some of its signers had been members of the Burns rescue mob, who, "with

[4] George Livermore to Sumner, June 1, 1854, Sumner MSS.; Joseph R. Hawley to Sumner, May 31, 1854, ibid.; C. S. Macreading to Sumner, June 2, 1854, ibid.

[5] Sumner to Mrs. W. H. Seward, June 17, 1854, Seward MSS.; Sumner to Longfellow [June 2, 1854], Longfellow MSS.

[6] Sumner to James Freeman Clarke, June 10, 1854, Clarke MSS.; Sumner to Dana, June 4, 1854, Dana MSS.; Bigelow: *Retrospections*, I, 136; Weiss: *Parker*, II, 146.

treason in their hearts, and with knives in their hands," had resisted "the constituted authorities of the country."

Intervening to assist his colleague, Sumner boldly answered Southern threats that repeal of the fugitive slave laws would dissolve the Union. "If the Union be in any way dependent on an act . . . so revolting in every regard," he announced, "then it ought not to exist." He himself would continue "with joy and satisfaction" to work for repeal of the obnoxious law. As for the signers of the petition, something must be pardoned them because they were citizens of Massachusetts. Could Massachusetts, the home of Faneuil Hall, where John Adams and Joseph Warren had thunderously spoken for liberty, of Bunker Hill, of Lexington and Concord, be expected to tolerate the "disgusting rites" by which a "slave-hunter from Virginia" doomed a fellow man to bondage? Just as Massachusetts had annulled the Stamp Act, so would it refuse to enforce the Fugitive Slave Law.[7]

While Sumner was speaking, Butler came into the Senate chamber, and as he listened to Sumner's conclusion, he grew angrier and angrier. Seizing the floor, he denounced Sumner's speech as one "whose whole style, tone, and character does not become *a Senate.*" "If we repeal the fugitive slave law," Butler demanded, turning to Rockwell, "will the honorable Senator tell me that Massachusetts will execute the provision of the Constitution without any law of Congress? . . . Would they send fugitives back to us after trial by jury, or any other mode?" As Rockwell remained silent, Butler turned upon Sumner. "Will this honorable Senator tell me that he will do it?"

"Does the honorable Senator ask me if I would personally join in sending a fellow-man into bondage?" Sumner replied. " 'Is thy servant a dog, that he should do this thing?' "[8]

Furious, Butler began berating Sumner for saying that it was "a dog's office to execute the Constitution of the United States." Promptly Mason, of Virginia, joined him, shouting that Sumner had "rudely, wantonly, grossly assailed" the dignity of the Senate by his "vapid, vulgar declamation," the utterance "of a fanatic, one whose reason is dethroned." Pettit, of Indiana,

---

[7] Sumner: *Defense of Massachusetts* . . . (Washington; 1854), pp. 3–6.

[8] Wendell Phillips had earlier made effective use of this same biblical quotation. Oscar Sherwin: *Prophet of Liberty: The Life and Times of Wendell Phillips* (New York: Bookman Associates, Inc.; 1958), p. 219.

cried that Sumner ought to be expelled for declaring that he would spit on his solemn oath to support the Constitution, an oath Sumner had sworn "upon the holy Evangelists of God, kissing the book, giving seal and sanction" to the asseveration.

"Never!" Sumner interjected angrily. "Never!"

"You . . . said you would not maintain the Constitution of the United States—" Pettit retorted.

From his seat, Sumner interrupted: "I said I recognized no obligation in the Constitution of the United States to bind me to help to reduce a man to slavery." [9]

"Sir," Pettit addressed the chair, "I am inclined to believe that, in a moral point of view, that Senator cannot find one beneath himself. . . . He . . . has sunk . . . to a depth of humiliation and degradation which it would not be enviable for the veriest serf or the lowest of God's creation to occupy."

Two days later, on June 28, when the debate was resumed, Pettit renewed his assault upon Sumner, and Stephen Mallory, of Florida, joined him. Even more vindictive was Clement C. Clay, Jr., of Alabama, who called Sumner a "serpent," a "filthy reptile," a "leper," a Uriah Heep, and urged that he be ostracized and placed "in that nadir of social degradation which he merits."

Forcefully Sumner defended himself. He was not faithless to his oath to support the Constitution. "No such thing. Sir, I swore to support the Constitution as I understood it; nor more, nor less." For his interpretation of his oath he could cite not merely his own mentor, John Quincy Adams, but that Democratic sage, Andrew Jackson. Sumner thought the Constitution imposed no duty upon him, either as an individual or as a senator, to assist in returning fugitive slaves. Remembering the Southerners' aversion to the slave trade, he asked scathingly: "How many there are, even in this body, if, indeed, there be a single Senator, who would stoop to any such service? Until some one rises and openly confesses his willingness to become a Slave-

[9] The Senate spent much time two days later discussing precisely what words Sumner had used. This version is the one Sumner himself gave to the Senate reporter. Pettit charged that Sumner had falsified the Senate's records. Southern senators pretended to believe that Sumner had declared he had no obligation to obey the Constitution of the United States. What he clearly meant —and, according to most Northern senators, what he said—was that he did not recognize that the Constitution imposed upon him a duty to return fugitive slaves. *Cong. Globe*, 33 Cong., 1 Sess., 1,549–51, 1,557.

Hunter, I will not believe there can be one." Pausing dramati-
cally, he waited, but no Southerner volunteered.[1]

Throughout his reply Sumner maintained a tone of bitter
personal vindictiveness, coupled with a hauteur infuriating to
his opponents. Intending to be "as severe as an overseer's lash,"
he rebuked the "plantation manners" of Butler and of Mason;
doubtless "in the characteristic fantasy of the moment" they fancied themselves not in the United States Senate, but on "a plantation well stocked with slaves, over which the lash of the overseer
had full sway." Sneeringly he turned upon Mason, who, "with
imperious look, and in the style of Sir Forcible Feeble," had tried
to question Sumner's interpretation of the Fugitive Slave Law.
As father of that "soulless monster," Mason might be presumed to
know something about its constitutionality; in fact, he was ignorant of all knowledge of law. Knowing "something of his conversation, something of his manners, something of his attainments,
something of his abilities, something of his character," Sumner
boldly invited comparison of his own legal knowledge and personal character with those of the Virginian's. From Pettit, Mallory, and Clay, Sumner turned away scornfully. They were "best
answered by silence; best answered by withholding the words
which leap impulsively to the lips." [2]

When Sumner sat down, Clay sprang to his feet to declare
that he, for one, was willing to accept Sumner's challenge; he
had the moral courage to declare that he would assist in the rendition of a fugitive slave. Sumner turned upon him witheringly:
"Then let the Senator say the immoral courage." [3]

As the debate ended, there was serious talk of attempting
to expel Sumner for perjury and treason, but a quiet canvass
showed that sufficient votes could not be obtained. Unquestionably Sumner emerged from the controversy with new stature.
Hitherto he had been regarded merely as an elaborate and
learned orator; now he had proved that, when aroused, he could
fight back in debate. Henceforth Southern senators tended to
leave him alone in respectful silence, while cutting him socially.
The very next day he presented another petition for the repeal

[1] Sumner: *Defense of Massachusetts*, pp. 8–9.
[2] Ibid., pp. 7, 12–14, 15–16; Sumner to Earl of Carlisle, Oct. 30, 1854,
Carlisle MSS.
[3] *Cong. Globe*, 33 Cong., 1 Sess., 1,554.

of the Fugitive Slave Act, and this time his Southern opponents, to get rid of the subject, quietly referred it to the appropriate committee.[4]

Respect from the South was matched by an overwhelming demonstration of affection and trust from the North. Sumner's "matchless eloquence and power," the New York *Times* announced, had carried the day; "his triumph was complete." "You have given the heaviest blow you ever struck to the slave-holding Oligarchy," Wilson congratulated him. "Dont I feel proud to think that I had a humble part in placing you in the Senate?" "You have done gallantly," Dana echoed. "You don't know how rejoiced I am that a Northern gentleman and scholar has met them in the true spirit of a cavalier."[5]

Flushed with praise, Sumner had never been so radiantly happy, so completely triumphant. Though exhausted by the long session and by the heat of the Washington summer, he was, nevertheless, for the first time in his Senate career, anxious to spend his vacation campaigning in Massachusetts. Surely the North was now aroused. It was time to forget "all past differences on Tariff, Internal improvements and other things" and form "a *Grand Junction* party" in the North which would "take the control of the Government."[6]

· 5 ·

"I find myself 'a popular man,'" Sumner reported enthusiastically upon his return to Boston. "If my election to the Senate were now pending before the million of educated people whom I now represent, I should be returned without any opposition." All over the North, Free Soilers, Whigs, and antislavery Democrats were combining into anti-Nebraska coalitions, and a "fusion" convention of Massachusetts antislavery elements in July adopted the name "Republican." "At last there seems to be an awakening of the North," Sumner confidently exclaimed. "Good!"[7]

4 Ibid., pp. 1,567–68.
5 New York *Times*, June 30, 1854; Wilson to Sumner, July 2, 1854, Sumner MSS.; Dana to Sumner, July 2, 1854, ibid.
6 Sumner to Howe, July 22, 1854, ibid.; Bigelow: *Retrospections*, I, 135; Sumner to Amasa Walker, Apr. 26, 1854, Walker MSS.
7 Pierce, III, 406; Sumner to Mrs. W. H. Seward, June 17, 1854, Seward MSS.

At the regular nominating convention of the new party, held in Worcester in September, Sumner lashed out at the national administration in what even his critics admitted was an "eloquent, and forcible, and bitter" address. Avoiding Latin phrases and quotations from the classics, he branded the Kansas-Nebraska act as an atrocity paralleled only by the Burns case, where Federal authorities had converted the Boston courthouse "into a fortress and barracoon," guarded by "heartless hirelings" and "a prostituted militia." Against such proslavery aggressions, there must be union of all true Northern men. Neither Democrats nor Whigs could effectively battle the slave power. "Unseduced and unterrified," Northern voters must go forth "As *Republicans* . . . to encounter the *Oligarchs* of Slavery." [8]

Elated by applause and carried away by his own oratory, Sumner saw in the Republican convention at Worcester the vanguard of the armies of freedom; it was instead, as Adams acidly noted, merely "a drum and fife [corps] without followers." Democrats, deterred by Cushing's "ukase" from further collaboration with antislavery men, did not join the new organization. It did not embrace all of the Free Soilers, for Wilson, who was running for governor, tried to exclude Adams, Palfrey, Dana, and other former Conscience leaders from the new party. Nor did many Massachusetts Whigs join the Republicans. Opposed to the Kansas-Nebraska act, they distrusted Sumner's extreme views and suspected Wilson's "party *alliances* and *manoeuvres*." Like Seward in New York and Abraham Lincoln in Illinois, more than one Massachusetts antislavery man decided: "I can do my duty more efficiently and sincerely as the parties now stand . . . as a Whig than in any other way." [9]

So feeble was the enthusiasm for the new party that Republican leaders did not dare let Sumner campaign for its candidates, fearing that they could not attract audiences for him. The senator had come home from Washington "full of fight on the Slavery

[8] Boston *Advertiser*, Sept. 8, 1854; Sumner: *Duties of Massachusetts at This Crisis* . . . (n.d.).

[9] Adams to Bird, Oct. 16, 1854, copy, Adams MSS.; Bird to Sumner, Apr. 16, 1854, Sumner MSS. On Free Soil factionalism see A. G. Browne to Sumner, Feb. 22, 1854, Sumner MSS.; Dana to Sumner, Feb. 26, 1854, ibid.; Adams to G. Bailey, Sept. 2, 1855, copy, Adams MSS. For the Whig position see Boston *Advertiser*, Sept. 8, 1854; C. G. Loring to Sumner, Mar. 14, 1854, Sumner MSS.; T. D. Eliot to Sumner, Sept. 13, 1854, ibid.

question" and expecting to take the stump, but he found himself idle and unwanted as the election drew near.[1]

The November election returns revealed the reason behind the apathetic Republican campaigning. Henry Wilson had sold his party out. Becoming aware that a new secret organization, technically known as the Order of the Star Spangled Banner, but generally called Know-nothings, was combining the discontented factions of all parties into a powerful anti-immigrant, anti-Catholic movement, Wilson had joined a nativist lodge and had thrown his strength behind Henry J. Gardner, the Know-nothing candidate for governor. In return he secured a pledge that, if successful, the Know-nothings would elect him to the Senate as Sumner's colleague. Gardner received an unprecedented majority of nearly 33,000 votes, and the new legislature consisted of one Whig, one Democrat, one Republican—and 377 Know-nothings. Surely, wrote Rufus Choate, "Any thing more low, obscene, feculent, the manifold heavings of history have not cast up. We shall come to the worship of onions, cats and things vermiculate." [2]

Though Sumner was surprised by the extent of the Know-nothing victory, he had, of course, been aware for some time of the existence of the nativist movement. Some of his strongest political supporters had been active in it, for there had always been a strong nativist tinge to Massachusetts antislavery. From the beginning, Free Soilers had objected not merely to slaveholders in the South, but to Northern manufacturers and businessmen, economically tied to the South's "peculiar institution," who were altering the structure of New England society. Sumner's 1848

---

[1] Samuel Downer to Mann, Oct. 26, 1854, Mann MSS. Sumner occupied his spare time preparing an elaborate lecture on Granville Sharp, the English abolitionist. Sumner: *Works*, III, 479–519.

[2] Robinson: *Pen Portraits*, p. 63. Of the extensive literature on the Know-nothing movement in the North, I have found the following most helpful: Ray Allen Billington: *The Protestant Crusade, 1800–1860* (New York: The Macmillan Co.; 1938), Chaps. 15–16; Handlin: *Boston's Immigrants*, Chap. 7; Bean: "Party Transformations," Chaps. 8–10; Bean: "Puritan Versus Celt, 1850–1860," *New England Quarterly*, VII (1934), 70–80; George H. Haynes: "A Chapter from the Local History of Knownothingism," *New England Magazine*, XV (1896–7), 82–96; Haynes: "A Know Nothing Legislature," *Annual Report of the American Historical Association, 1896*, I, 177–87; Harry J. Carman and Reinhard H. Luthin: "Some Aspects of the Know-Nothing Movement Reconsidered," *South Atlantic Quarterly*, XXXIX (1940), 213–34.

theory of a conspiracy between the Lords of the Loom and the Lords of the Lash precisely expressed the dual suspicions of Massachusetts antislavery men. From hostility to manufacturing and corporations it was an easy step to opposition to cities and their working-class population. The transition was easier because by the 1850's factory workers in Massachusetts were predominantly immigrants. During the decade after 1846 over 100,000 Irish entered the Bay State; by 1855 they formed twenty-five per cent of Worcester's population and a majority of Boston's. Cruelly exploited by American employers, compelled to live in virtual ghettos, clinging to Catholicism, the Irish became a visible symbol of the forces that were transforming an unwilling New England.

Both temperamentally and intellectually Sumner disliked this nativist movement, which he feared might "break up the whole Northern combination and . . . give the South another lease of national ascendency." After the election of 1854, he talked confidentially with Adams and S. C. Phillips about rebuilding a fresh, independent antislavery party in Massachusetts, uncontaminated by Wilson and other Know-nothings. When the nativist legislature in 1855 elected Wilson to the Senate, Sumner was not a little regretful.[3]

But, whatever he said in private, Sumner took great care not to offend the powerful new order. Recognizing that most Massachusetts antislavery men, and practically all his special political backers, were now Know-nothings, he refrained, even in private letters, from condemning its course. Mildly and unaccusingly he explained the Know-nothing success in Massachusetts: "The people were tired of the old parties and they have made a new channel." Bolder politicians came out bluntly against the nativist party; Stephen A. Douglas, for instance, condemned it as early as July 4, 1854. But Sumner held his peace and, in January 1855, presented to Congress, without explanation or disclaimer, a petition of Massachusetts citizens seeking to impose a tax of $250 per head on immigrants. When a leading Unitarian

[3] Sumner to "My Dear Sir," Dec. 7, 1854, MS., Univ. of Chicago; Adams, Diary, Sept. 16, and Nov. 16, 1854, Adams MSS.; S. C. Phillips to Sumner, Nov. 15, 1854, Sumner MSS.; W. H. Whitcomb to Sumner, Jan. 16, 1855, ibid.; Everett, Diary, Feb. 9, 1855, Everett MSS.; Pierce to Mann, Jan. 18, 1855, Mann MSS.

minister urged Sumner to become Massachusetts' champion
not merely against slavery, but against nativist bigotry, he received no reply.[4]

Sumner's silence showed how worried he was becoming
about his own political future. Governor Gardner was no sooner
elected than he began scheming to use his office, and the Know-
nothing movement, to secure his own election as Sumner's successor. As Sumner could not conscientiously advocate nativist
principles, and as, in any case, he had delayed too long to assume
leadership in the Know-nothing movement, he was once again
in the exposed position of a senator without a political machine
behind him.

The new session of Congress, which assembled in December 1854, offered him no chance to recover his fortunes. There
were no angry sectional contests, which would give him opportunities for enunciating principles or for assaulting the South.
On only one day did the debates turn to the slavery question.
Sumner seized his chance to declare that "no temptation, no in-
ducement," could induce him "in any way to sanction the return
of any man to Slavery," but after the heated quarrels of the previous session, that was hardly news. Deciding that the best thing
he could do would be to follow a friend's advice and present
"matters of business" to the Senate so as to demonstrate that he
knew "a great many things outside . . . of peace and war, and
slavery," he started introducing resolutions for the payment of
bounties to fisheries, the erection of a new marine hospital in
Boston, and the guaranteeing of wages to seamen in case of
shipwreck.[5]

Feeling his popularity slipping, Sumner became increasingly
unhappy as the session drew to an end and he had no opportunity to recover lost ground. In such a mood, even his good friends
found him unbearable. When Seward, eager to promote New
York constituents' interests in an election year, asked him to support a subsidy for the Collins Steamship Line, Sumner declared

[4] Sumner to Mrs. Hamilton Fish, Nov. 15, 1854, Fish MSS.; Adams, Diary,
Oct. 25, 1854, and Mar. 24, 1855, Adams MSS.; Cong. Globe, 33 Cong., 2 Sess.,
178; John Weiss to Sumner, May 8, 1855, Sumner MSS.
[5] Sumner: The Demands of Freedom Speech . . . in the Senate . . . February 23, 1855 (n.d.), p. 8; P. W. Chandler to Sumner, Feb. 17, 1855, Sumner
MSS.

that there was not sufficient economic justification for the measure. Then Seward urged him to vote for the measure as a personal favor. Loftily Sumner replied that he had not been sent to the Senate to get Seward re-elected. Losing his self-command, Seward exclaimed: "Sumner, you're a damned fool." The two men did not speak for months.[6]

Returning North in March, as the term ended, Sumner tried to rally public opinion behind him by delivering a lecture on "The Antislavery Enterprise: Its Necessity, Practicability, and Dignity." After giving the address in several smaller Massachusetts cities, and in Auburn and Albany, New York, he delivered it in May at the huge Metropolitan Theater in New York City, which was crammed with enthusiastic listeners. Shout upon shout of applause greeted Sumner as he stepped to the lectern, and his audience was carried away by his "magnificent presence, . . . physically as well as mentally a giant, and symmetrical as his own orations, the grand organ-music of his voice, bearing to the heart the intense conviction that it comes deep out of the heart; the calm strength of his delivery, breathing the conscious assurance of eventual victory; the thunderbursts of eloquence." [7]

Sumner's brilliant and successful appearance in New York may have convinced him that "a general union of the antislavery elements on a broad foundation" was in the offing, but when he returned to Massachusetts, he was disillusioned. Bay State politics were "in a perfect muss." One objective reporter listed some of the turbulent ingredients: "Whig party nowhere. Democratic very small. Free Soil small. Republican small. Antipope and antislave large. Rum party pretty large, very active. Temperance pretty large, and doubtfull [sic]—pure Native Americanism small, and active. Catholic perfectly quiet." A new secret order called Know-Somethings, opposed to the Know-nothings, but also devoted to upholding Freedom, Protestantism, and Temperance, helped confuse the situation. "There is material to work upon,"

[6] Worthington Chauncey Ford (ed.): *Letters of Henry Adams (1858–1891)* (Boston: Houghton Mifflin Co.; 1930), p. 87; Sumner to Hamilton Fish, Apr. 28, 1855, copy, Fish MSS. Characteristically, Sumner did vote for the bill, after all, and even published a little speech explaining his stand. *Cong. Globe*, 33 Cong., 2 Sess., Appendix, 313; New York *Times*, Mar. 2, 1855.

[7] Sumner: *Works*, IV, 1–51; newspaper reaction clipped in *The Liberator*, XXV (May 18, 1855), 79; XXV (May 25, 1855), 81. Because of unusual public demand, Sumner repeated his lecture in Manhattan and gave it also in Brooklyn.

a veteran politician concluded sardonically. "No man knows what will come out of it." [8]

So uncertain was the political situation, Sumner decided that he had a clear duty—to remain aloof from all factions by making a prolonged trip to the West. After stopping to see his old friend Horace Mann at Antioch College, and visiting Chase in Cincinnati, Sumner crossed into Kentucky, where he made his first real acquaintance with the South's "peculiar institution," which he had so often denounced. Guided by Cassius M. Clay, the Kentucky antislavery leader, he saw the bluegrass country at the loveliest time of the year, and he found much he could admire and much he could never forget. The magnificent pastures and the cattle made a strong impression on him, and he was astonished to find the slave quarters so snug and comfortable. But, at Lexington he watched a slave auction on the courthouse steps, where a Negro was "compelled to open his mouth and show his teeth, like a horse"; his stagecoach was delayed so that the driver could "help lick a nigger"; at a hotel meal he had "to witness the revolting spectacle of a poor slave, yet a child, almost felled to the floor by a blow on the head from a clenched fist." Prudently keeping his reactions to himself, he traveled south to Mammoth Cave, then to Nashville, and on to St. Louis. [9]

Willingly leaving the slave states behind him, Sumner took a slow steamboat trip up the Mississippi River, stopping off at numerous places. At Davenport, Iowa, his horse ran away, and the buggy in which he was riding "was dashed against the projecting rails of a zig-zag fence, with such tremendous force that it whirled some ten or twelve feet into the air, and turning several complete somersets, came down upon the ground with . . . Sumner under its wreck." Suffering only from bad bruises, he continued to Minneapolis, where he made quite a favorable impression even upon his political opponents. At Milwaukee he visited Sherman M. Booth, who was contesting the constitutionality of the Fugitive Slave Act, and was cordially welcomed by his "hosts of admiring friends." After short trips to Chicago and to

[8] Samuel Downer to Mann, Aug. 25, 1855, Mann MSS.
[9] Sumner to William Schouler [June 1855], Segal Coll.; Pierce, III, 417-19; Sumner: *Works*, IV, 64. During the 1855 campaign the Boston *Post* charged that Sumner, while in Kentucky, had been so impressed by the "perfect happiness and contentment" of the Negroes that "he could but confess that his previous belief concerning slavery had been . . . wholly incorrect." Sumner promptly issued "a point-blank contradiction." Boston *Post*, Nov. 15-16, and Dec. 14, 1855.

Detroit, where he again flirted with Senator Cass's handsome, marriageable daughter, he made a steamboat tour of the Great Lakes before returning to New England for a brief vacation in the White Mountains. Not until September 6 did he return to Boston, having traversed eleven free states and three slave states.[1]

Prolonged as his vacation had been, it was not long enough to permit him to escape from the complexities of Massachusetts politics. Some changes, to be sure, had occurred during his absence. The defeat of the Know-nothings in the Virginia gubernatorial election gave promise that political nativism was but a transient phenomenon, and more and more politicians mustered courage to denounce it. In Massachusetts the new party, with its unwieldy majority of untrained legislators, had, despite a remarkable record of constructive, democratic achievements, lost favor, partly because of a notorious investigation of the state's convents and nunneries. So unpopular was the party by early summer of 1855, Charles Francis Adams observed, "that a disavowal of sympathy with them *now* would be liable to the suspicion of being prompted by a wish to escape odium."[2]

Wilson had reverted to his original strong antislavery position and, resenting Southern domination of the Know-nothing party, led an exodus of Northern nativists from the party's national convention. Upon his return to Massachusetts, he started elaborate negotiations to bring together all groups known to be opposed to slavery. Gardner, willing to accept support from any quarter, promised to join in the hope of securing re-election as governor. Wilson extended a special invitation to Winthrop, as the leader of conservative Whiggery, "to take the lead in forming a victorious Republican party." For a while it looked as if antislavery Whigs, anti-Nebraska Democrats, Know-nothings, and Free Soilers would all combine at the convention called for Worcester on September 20.[3]

[1] Ibid., July 21, 1855; James Shields to Hamilton Fish, Nov. 25, 1855, Fish MSS.; Milwaukee *Sentinel*, July 17–18, 1855; Theodore Calvin Pease and James G. Randall (eds.): *The Diary of Orville Hickman Browning* ("Collections of the Illinois State Historical Library," Vol. XX, Springfield: Illinois State Historical Lib.; 1925), I, 192; W. Preston to Hamilton Fish, Sept. 5, 1855, Fish MSS.; Sumner to Gerrit Smith, Aug. 28, 1855, Smith MSS.

[2] Adams to G. Bailey, Apr. 15, 1855, copy, Adams MSS.

[3] For details on the break-up of the Know-nothing party and the origins of Massachusetts Republicanism see Bean: "Party Transformations," Chap. 11; Wilson: *Slave Power*, II, Chap. 32.

Sumner had kept himself studiously ignorant of these developments during his long vacation, but, on his return, he faced a difficult decision. Fearing both the "corrupt tactics" of Governor Gardner, who was seeking re-election as a steppingstone to the Senate, and the hostility of Wilson, who was promising men like Winthrop "the honors of success" if they joined the fusion movement, he anticipated that either the success or the failure of the Worcester convention might imperil his Senate seat. Firmly he declined to attend.[4]

The Republican convention proved not to be so dangerous as Sumner had expected. Winthrop and the Boston Whigs refused to attend, chiefly because they distrusted Wilson and Sumner. Lacking another candidate, Wilson swore renewed fidelity to Sumner's interests, and pledged: "If I live and God gives me power Sumner goes back to the Senate."[5] Through Wilson's management and Dana's shrewd parliamentary maneuvering, the convention adopted a platform that contained no nativist appeals, and, after a hard fight, it passed over Gardner and nominated Julius Rockwell for governor.

When Gardner bolted the Republican party and ran as a Know-nothing candidate, Sumner clearly had no choice but to campaign for Rockwell. His decision was made easier by the fact that the nativist movement had drastically changed its composition since 1854; now it no longer drew chiefly from the antislavery small towns of the interior, but from the conservative Whigs of eastern Massachusetts. Late in the campaign he delivered an address at nine principal cities throughout the state. "Are you for Freedom, or are you for Slavery?" he asked his audiences. To combat the slave power, which he could now describe firsthand, Massachusetts could not rely upon the Democratic party, which was sustaining "the tyrannies and perfidies of the Slave Oligarchy," or upon the Whigs, "the Rip Van Winkles of our politics." Nor could the Know-nothings lead in the fight for freedom. Boldly, if belatedly, Sumner attacked the party for its policy of racial and religious proscription. "I am not disposed to place any check upon the welcome to foreigners," he declared. "Ourselves the children of the Pilgrims of a former generation, let us not

[4] Adams, Diary, Sept. 6, and 17, 1855, Adams MSS.; Wilson: Slave Power, II, 433.

[5] Boutwell: Reminiscences, I, 118; H. Kriesman to Sumner, Sept. 18, 1855, Sumner MSS.

turn from the Pilgrims of the present. . . . A party, which, beginning in secrecy, interferes with religious belief, and founds a discrimination on the accident of birth, is not the party for us." Only the Republican party, whose cornerstone was Freedom, whose "broad, all-sustaining arches" were Truth, Justice, and Humanity, was "the fit shrine for the genius of American Institutions." [6]

Although friendly newspapers spoke of the "rapturous applause" Sumner received, the hostile press was probably more accurate in describing the cool reception given the "modern Cicero." The Republican "fusion" party proved, as an opponent had predicted, "a mere resuscitation of the Radical Free-Soil party with an impotent *infusion* of a portion of the Whigs." [7] In 1855, as in the previous year, the new party made a poor showing at the polls, and Gardner, combining nativism and Whiggery, was re-elected.

"It is humiliating that this American faction should have thus triumphed," Sumner lamented. The Know-nothing victory threatened to become a personal humiliation, for Gardner's friends began loudly demanding that both Sumner and Wilson "voluntarily" resign from the Senate or be "instructed out of their seats . . . made to feel the embarrassment of their position, representing . . . a faction which never had a majority or even a plurality of the votes of the people of Massachusetts, and which the people have condemned anew with indubitable emphasis at the recent election." Gardner talked of asking the legislature to choose a new United States senator—preferably himself—even though Sumner's term did not expire until 1857. [8]

"Gardner is after your place," Theodore Parker warned Sumner as the Senate met in December 1855. "He has one eye . . . on the *Senatorship*. His chances are not contemptible. . . . The more decided your course is against slavery, and the further you depart from the Hunkers, the more secure is your position." [9]

But, for weeks the new session of Congress gave Sumner no

[6] Sumner: *The Slave Oligarchy and Its Usurpations* . . . (Washington: Buell & Blanchard [1855]).

[7] Pierce, III, 421; Sumner: *Works*, IV, 62; Boston *Post*, Oct. 30, and Nov. 3, 1855; J. H. Clifford to Winthrop, Aug. 31, 1855, copy, Winthrop MSS.

[8] Sumner to Seward, Nov. 11, 1855, Seward MSS.; Adams, Diary, Nov. 9, 1855, Adams MSS.; Boston *Advertiser*, Nov. 10, 1855; Boston *Post*, Nov. 17, 1855; Hillard to Lieber, Nov. 19, 1855, Lieber MSS.

[9] Weiss: *Parker*, II, 158.

opportunity to distinguish himself. During the long stalemate in the choice of a speaker of the House of Representatives, which held up all important business for two months, he had to content himself with behind-the-scenes negotiations. In December 1855 he went into conference with Chase, representing the Western "Independent Democracy," N. P. Banks, of the Northern Know-nothings, and Francis Preston Blair, Sr., of the "Barnburner" faction, on the "means for an organization of the AntiNebraska forces for the presidential election." Though carefully reticent on presidential possibilities, he talked with John Charles Frémont, that daring "pathmarker of the West," who was often mentioned as the most likely nominee of the new Republican party. Enthusiastically Sumner endorsed the "strong and yet moderate, conservative and yet progressive" declaration of principles adopted at the preliminary Republican convention, which assembled at Pittsburgh on February 22.[1]

Though politicians knew of these activities, the general public in Massachusetts was unaware of them and thought that Sumner was doing nothing in the Senate. Boldly the Boston *Courier* taunted "our mute representative," and even Sumner's friends began, rather despairingly, to hope "that his long silence is only ominous to the foes of freedom." [2]

Frustrated in Congress, Sumner closely watched Gardner's plot to stage a premature election of his successor. The Boston *Courier* enthusiastically supported the governor's plan, and the Democratic *Post*, welcoming dissension among its opponents, egged it along. Though the Boston *Atlas* and the Boston *Advertiser* manfully battled the scheme, and though Sumner's closest advisers in the State house advised him that Gardner was not likely to succeed, the senator was worried. "Do not believe me too sensitive," he assured Howe. "I am the representative of a great cause and a powerful party, both of whom suffer when I suffer." [3]

[1] Seward to Thurlow Weed, Dec. 31, 1855, Weed MSS.; William Ernest Smith: *The Francis Preston Blair Family in Politics* (New York: The Macmillan Co.; 1933), I, 323–4; Gamaliel Bailey to Chase, May 8, 1856, Chase MSS., Hist. Soc. of Penn.; Boston *Post*, Apr. 3, 1856; Sumner to Henry J. Raymond, Mar. 2, 1856, Raymond MSS.

[2] Boston *Courier*, Mar. 5, 1856; Thomas Baldwin to Seward, Apr. 11, 1856, Seward MSS.

[3] Boston *Courier*, Mar. 15, 1856; Boston *Post*, Mar. 11, 1856; Seth Webb, Jr., to Sumner, Mar. 19, 1856, Sumner MSS.; J. W. Stone to Sumner, Mar. 20, and

Unable to make an antislavery demonstration, Sumner again tried to win his constituents' confidence by paying even more assiduous attention than ever to their desires and petitions. Never before did he so carefully distribute public documents and the free flower seeds to which congressmen were entitled. Never before had he so persistently presented Massachusetts claims and memorials. Never had he so energetically prepared bills that would directly benefit his home state—bills for the construction of a new customs house at Plymouth, for the improvement of the Taunton River, for the protection of Cape Cod harbors, etc., etc.

But somehow mere attention to business did not restore Sumner's waning fortunes. Neither did his attempt to start a major foreign policy debate by challenging the President's right to abrogate a treaty with Denmark excite much enthusiasm. Equally unpromising was Sumner's attempt to remind his constituents of his past services by publishing a volume of his *Recent Speeches*. Despite prodding from Howe and Longfellow, who subsidized the publication, Ticknor & Fields were reluctant to issue the volume unless they could include, as Howe reported to Sumner, "something which they can *call* a last speech . . . [to] help sell the book." [4]

The advice of publishers and politicians for once coincided. If Sumner was to regain his political strength in Massachusetts, he had once again to agitate the slavery question. Providentially, a burning issue came to hand, for the mails brought in reports of proslavery aggressions and outrages in the newly organized territory of Kansas. In the middle of March, when Douglas, with his "vulgar swagger," ushered in the debate on Kansas, Sumner instantly resolved that he would reply, in an "elaborate speech," using "plain words." Confidentially he reassured Theodore Parker: "I shall pronounce the most thorough philippic ever uttered in a legislative body." [5]

28, 1856, ibid.; Adams to Sumner, Apr. 1, 1856, ibid.; Dana to Sumner, Mar. 14, 1856, ibid.; J. B. Alley to Sumner, Mar. 14, 1856, ibid.; Sumner to Howe, Dec. 28, 1855, ibid.

[4] Howe to Sumner, Apr. 2, 1856, ibid.

[5] Sumner to Gerrit Smith, Mar. 18, 1856, Smith MSS.; Sumner to Longfellow, Apr. 7, 1856; Weiss: *Parker*, II, 179.

CHAPTER XI

The Crime Against Kansas

T RULY—TRULY—this is a godless place," Sumner lamented
as the Thirty-Fourth Congress got under way. The friends of
Freedom seemed thoroughly demoralized by the "Know Nothing
madness." "In the House we are weak," Sumner reported; "in the
Senate powerless." Stephen A. Douglas, whom Sumner thought
"a brutal vulgar man without delicacy or scholarship [who] looks
as if he needed clean linen and should be put under a shower
bath," was undisputed master of the Democratic majority in the
Senate. Aspiring for the Presidency, Douglas appeared ready to
support any proslavery aggressions. "We have before us a long
season of excitement and ribald debate," Sumner predicted, as
Douglas opened the discussion of Kansas affairs in March 1856,
"in which the Truth will be mocked and reviled." [1]

For months Sumner's mails had been full of urgent letters
about the ominous developments in Kansas. As his correspondents gave him the story, the peaceable settlers in that remote
frontier area were industrious Northerners, especially those
brought out under the sponsorship of the New England Emigrant Aid Company. They had formed "an association of sincere
benevolence, faithful to the Constitution and laws, whose only
fortifications are hotels, school-houses, and churches; whose
only weapons are saw-mills, tools, and books; whose mission is

---

[1] Sumner to Gerrit Smith, Mar. 18, 1856, Smith MSS.; Sumner to John P.
Hale, Mar. 1, 1856, Segal Coll.; James Redpath to Elias Nason, Apr. 10, 1874, MS.
owned by Mr. Boyd B. Stutler.

peace and good will." But, the South, determined to create a new slave state in Kansas, had banded together "murderous robbers from Missouri," "hirelings, picked from the drunken spew and vomit of an uneasy civilization," commanded by that Catiline, former Senator David R. Atchison, of Missouri. They had invaded the territory "as an 'army with banners,' organized in companies, with officers, munitions, tents, and provisions, as though marching upon a foreign foe, and breathing loud-mouthed threats that they would carry their purpose, if need be, by the bowie-knife and revolver." Under their reign of terror a hideous proslavery government had been set up with the support of the proslavery President Pierce. Outraged by this brutality and usurpation, high-minded free-state immigrants had formed their own rival free-soil government at Topeka.[2]

With the coming of spring, Sumner's Kansas correspondents anticipated fresh outbreaks of violence. Our "citizens are in arms to defend the dearest rights of Americans," one embattled Northern immigrant warned. "Preparations of the most warlike kind are in progress," wrote another, "men enrolled, munitions of war collected in the western counties of Missouri, for the purpose of invading Kansas. My dear sir—HELP US." [3]

Completely trusting these private sources of information, Sumner was indignant when Douglas presented the Democratic version of these same events to the Senate. According to the "Little Giant," Kansas was a land where immigrants, chiefly and naturally from the adjacent slave state of Missouri, had been peacefully settling since the adoption of his Kansas Nebraska Act in 1854. But, the New England Emigrant Aid Company, an abolitionist conspiracy, had brought in hordes of antislavery men, armed with Sharps rifles and pledged to use them against the peaceful Southerners. Despite this interference, despite the attempt of the abolitionist interlopers to set up an unconstitutional government, the legitimate settlers of Kansas had organized a

---

[2] Sumner: *Kansas Affairs: Speech . . . in the Senate of the United States, May 19, 1856* (New York: Greeley & McElrath; 1856), pp. 8–9, 11, 18. All subsequent references to *The Crime Against Kansas* are to this contemporary pamphlet edition, published at the New York *Tribune* office and widely circulated.

[3] Henry P. Waters to Sumner, Topeka, Dec. 6, 1855; Mrs. Hanna Ropes to Sumner, Lawrence, Jan. 22, 1856; Samuel F. Tappan to Sumner, Jan. 18, 1856—all MSS. in Kansas Hist. Soc.

territorial government, drawn up a body of fundamental law, which naturally borrowed from the code of Missouri and included protection for slaveholders, and now they sought recognition from Congress. Only a partisan desire to continue sectional strife into the coming presidential campaign could keep Congress from approving at once this "Law and Order" government in Kansas and from crushing out its abolitionist rivals.

Certain that Douglas's picture of events in Kansas was totally incorrect, Sumner did not pause to consider that his own version of happenings on that remote frontier might be equally distorted. Like the rest of the senators, he was unaware that the Kansas struggle involved not merely freedom and slavery, but also land speculations, bitter rivalries over the location of the territorial capital, and personal ambitions of would-be congressmen from the territory. He did not understand that there was no ineradicable hostility between Southern pioneers in this region, virtually all of whom were non-slaveholders, and free-state settlers, who wanted forever to ban free Negroes from Kansas. Disorder there was, and some bloodshed, but up to 1856 there had been scarcely more of either than was normal on any frontier.[4]

At any time it would have been difficult for congressmen to arrive at such an objective view of the Kansas difficulties; certainly it was impossible for them to do so in 1856, a presidential year. As the Democrats were committed to the principles of popular sovereignty, and as Douglas was one of the principal presidential possibilities, they had little choice but to uphold the "Law and Order" party and to brand the rival free-state government of Kansas as revolutionary. On the other hand, the opponents of the administration, who were slowly coalescing into the new Republican party, had little in common except hostility to popular sovereignty; they necessarily argued that it was unsuccessful in Kansas, the territory where it had been most conspicuously applied.[5]

Outraged by the bullying tone in which Douglas began the

[4] James C. Malin: *John Brown and the Legend of Fifty-Six* ("Memoirs of the American Philosophical Society," Vol. XVII, Philadelphia: The American Philosophical Soc.; 1942); James G. Randall: *Lincoln the President: Springfield to Gettysburg* (New York: Dodd, Mead & Co.; 1945), I, 83, 92.

[5] Andrew Wallace Crandall: *The Early History of the Republican Party, 1854–1856* (Boston: Richard G. Badger; 1930), Chap. 3.

debate, Sumner was delighted when Seward promptly countered
by a demand for the immediate admission of Kansas as a free
state under the Topeka constitution. As the discussion grew angrier and extended over several weeks, he was heartened to
find more and more Northern senators joining in the attack on
Douglas.

From the opening of the debate Sumner had planned a plea
for Kansas, "that distant plundered territory," but it was not until nearly two months later that he claimed the Senate floor. In
the interval he had been preparing an elaborate oration that he
intended not merely as a defense of the free-state government
of Kansas, but as a vindication of himself and of Massachusetts.
Remembering the slurs Southerners had cast upon his state in
the Kansas-Nebraska debates two years earlier, he borrowed from
the Library of Congress histories of North Carolina, South Carolina, and Georgia, so as to be prepared to exhibit the past failings
of the South. Recalling the enormous popular acclaim he had
received from his sharp attacks on Butler, Mason, and Douglas
in those same debates, he carefully included a personal assault
upon each of these enemies, and, so that his quotations would be
correct, he borrowed the Library of Congress's *Don Quixote.*[6]

[6] Sumner to Longfellow, Apr. 7, 1856, Longfellow MSS.; Receipts for Books,
Library of Congress Records, 1855–7, pp. 49, 181. My imputation of motives here
is admittedly speculative, yet it is hard to find any other reason why Sumner assailed these three senators in "The Crime Against Kansas." Douglas, to be sure,
had been the leading administration spokesman during the debates, but Mason
had said little, and Butler, who had spoken more often, had maintained a
gravely solemn tone. The speech itself contains considerable internal evidence
to show that Sumner, as he wrote it, was thinking back to the acrimonious 1854
debates. Attacking Douglas, he said: "But I go back now to an earlier occasion,
when . . . he threw into this discussion . . . personalities most discreditable to
this body." In his final fling at Mason, Sumner mentioned: ". . . on a former
occasion I did something to exhibit the plantation manners which he displays."
I cannot accept Butler's conclusion that Sumner's "mortified vanity, arising from
former conflicts, was the cause of the attack" upon these three senators (*Cong.
Globe,* 34 Cong., 1 Sess., 1,403–4), for Sumner and his friends thought he had
come off triumphant in the earlier fray. Ben: Perley Poore, a not too trustworthy
friend, claimed that Sumner told him the attack on Douglas, Mason, and Butler
was a necessary "demonstration to satisfy those who had elected him" (Poore to
Pierce, Nov. 18, 1875, Pierce MSS.), but such candid cynicism was not all like
Sumner.

There is no reason to believe that Sumner intended to invite physical retalia-
tion for his hard words. He wanted to be as frank as possible "within the limits
of parliamentary propriety" (*Crime Against Kansas,* p. 6). Unaware of the power
of his own words, he could not anticipate how offensive they would seem to his
opponents. Long afterward he used to ask his secretary "with perfect simplicity
what it was in the speech . . . that Butler's friends objected to. . . ." (Dawes:
Sumner, p. 113).

Feeling that the occasion was "the greatest . . . that has ever occurred in our history," Sumner wanted the form as well as the content of his oration to measure up to the challenge. Painstakingly he wrote out his speech, which in a printed version runs to 112 pages, working in not merely the usual citations from British parliamentary debates, the *Congressional Globe*, and the *Statutes at Large*, but also quotations from Florus, Cicero, Livy, Vergil, Dante, and Milton. He tested the cadences of his elaborately balanced sentences:

A few short months only [he planned to say, early in the oration] have passed since this spacious mediterranean country [Kansas] was open only to the savage, who ran wild in its woods and prairies; and now it has already drawn to its bosom a population of freemen larger than Athens crowded within her historic gates, when her sons, under Miltiades, won liberty for mankind on the fields of Marathon; more than Sparta contained when she ruled Greece, and sent forth her devoted children, quickened by a mother's benediction, to return with their shields or on them; more than Rome gathered on her seven hills, when, under her kings, she commenced that sovereign sway, which afterwards embraced the whole earth; more than London held, when, on the fields of Crecy and Agincourt, the English banner was carried victoriously over the chivalrous hosts of France.

For his peroration he closely imitated a passage from Demosthenes's "On the Crown," which he had just borrowed from the Library of Congress.[7] Then he thoroughly memorized the entire oration so that he would not have to refer to his manuscript once during his delivery. After reading the whole address to Seward —ostensibly to get the New Yorker's advice; actually, one suspects, to practice before an audience—he had the congressional printer set it up in type. He was ready to denounce "The Crime Against Kansas."

• 1 •

"Mr. President," Sumner commenced sonorously when he gained the floor at one o'clock on the afternoon of May 19. "You are now called to redress a great transgression. Seldom in the history

---

[7] Cf. Sumner: *Crime Against Kansas*, p. 22, and Demosthenes: *De Corona and de Falsa Legatione* (The Loeb Classical Lib., London: William Heinemann; 1926), pp. 155, 157. Receipts for Books, Library of Congress Records, 1855-7, p. 49.

of nations has such a question been presented. . . . A crime
has been committed, which is without example in the records of
the past. . . . It is the rape of a virgin territory, compelling it to
the hateful embrace of slavery. . . ."

Long heralded, Sumner's speech had drawn an unusually
large audience. "Not only were the galleries thronged to their utmost capacity with ladies and gentlemen, but all the doorways
were completely blocked up with listeners," the New York *Post*
correspondent reported. "It seemed even as if the members of
the other House had adjourned to crowd the lobbies of the Senate. No such scene has been witnessed in that body since the
days of Webster." Virtually every member of the Senate was in
his seat as Sumner began. During the first few minutes, while
Sumner announced his intention to exhibit the proslavery conspiracy against Kansas in its brutal nakedness, "without a single
rag, or fig-leaf, to cover its vileness," Douglas, Isaac Toucey, of
Connecticut, and Robert Toombs, of Georgia, made an ostentatious pretense of being totally preoccupied with letter writing or
engaged in loud and distracting conversation, but as the orator
launched into his fierce indictment, they subsided and, along
with the rest of the crowded chamber, listened intently.[8]

During the three hours Sumner spoke on May 19 he exposed
"The Crime Against Kansas," which, he insisted, originated in
"the *One Idea*, that Kansas, at all hazards, must be made a slave
State." It was for this very purpose that the Missouri Compromise
had been repealed and that "swindle," the Kansas-Nebraska Act,
passed. The word "swindle," Sumner apologized, had "not the authority of classical usage," but it had "the indubitable authority of
fitness," as no other word could adequately express "the mingled meanness and wickedness of the cheat." Under its malign
operations, Atchison, that "connecting link between the President
and the border ruffian," had invaded Kansas with his Missouri
banditti, and there had "renewed the incredible atrocity of the
Assassins and of the Thugs." Douglas's "Popular Sovereignty" had
thus "ended in Popular Slavery."[9]

The apologies for this hateful atrocity, Sumner continued,

[8] Washington Correspondence of New York *Evening Post*, May 21, 1856, in
W. S. Thayer MSS.; New York *Tribune*, May 21, 1856.
[9] *Crime Against Kansas*, pp. 6–8, 11, 12, 15.

were "four in number, and four-fold in character." First was Douglas's "Apology *tyrannical*," that the proslavery legislature in Kansas had been properly authenticated by law and, "whatever may have been the actual force or fraud in its election, . . . the whole proceeding is placed under the formal sanction of law." Such an argument, Sumner contended, placed "the certificate above the thing certified" and gave "a perpetual lease to violence and fraud, merely because at an ephemeral moment they were unquestioned." The "Apology *imbecile*," that there was an "alleged want of power in the President to arrest the Crime," Sumner refuted by noting that Pierce had found no such constitutional obstacle to enforcing the fugitive slave acts in the Burns case. "Where there is a will, there is a way." The "Apology *absurd*" cast the blame for Kansas disorders upon an alleged free-soil Kansas Legion, a "poor mummery of a secret society." Finally, the "Apology *infamous*" blamed the New England Emigrant Aid Company for the civil war threatening the territory. The company, Sumner declared, not quite accurately, "supplied no arms of any kind to anybody." [1] Its planned emigration was entirely legal—just as legal as was Massachusetts' determination to support freedom in the territory. "I am proud to believe," Sumner concluded his first day's remarks, "that you may as well attempt, with puny arm, to topple down the earth-rooted, heaven-kissing granite which crowns the historic sod of Bunker Hill, as to change her fixed resolves for Freedom everywhere, and especially now for freedom in Kansas." [2]

When Sumner resumed on May 20, he examined "*the various remedies proposed*" for the Kansas difficulties, which, by careful rhetorical planning, were four-fold like the apologies he had just discussed. To "the *Remedy of Tyranny*," President Pierce's proposal to compel obedience to the "Law and Order" government, Sumner replied that he would "not consent to wad

---

[1] In response to Sumner's inquiry, the secretary of the company told him "the company had never sent, or paid for sending guns, cannon, pistols or other weapons to Kansas." If the company was technically innocent, its directors and officers individually contributed heavily to supplying the Kansas migrants with rifles. W. H. Iseley: "The Sharps Rifle Episode in Kansas History," *American Historical Review*, XII (1906–7), 546–66. The best modern account of the New England Emigrant Aid Company is Samuel A. Johnson: *The Battle Cry of Freedom* (Lawrence: University of Kansas Press; 1954).

[2] *Crime Against Kansas*, pp. 15–20, 22.

the National artillery with fresh appropriation bills, when its murderous hail is to be directed against the constitutional rights of my fellow-citizens." The *"Remedy of Folly,"* the suggestion that the free-state settlers should be deprived of their arms, would "trample on one of the plainest provisions of constitutional liberty." If Congress adopted "the *Remedy of Injustice and Civil War,"* the proposal that the "Law and Order" legislature be authorized to call a constitutional convention, it would, Sumner protested, "put the infant State . . . to suckle with the wolf, which you ought at once to kill." This solution would "be the beginning of civil war." There remained, then, only the *"Remedy of Justice and Peace,"* Seward's proposal to admit Kansas immediately as a free state. This remedy, Sumner argued, was justified "on every ground of precedent, whether as regards population or forms of proceedings; also on the vital principle of American institutions; and, lastly, on the absolute law of self-defense." [3]

Such was the argument of Sumner's "Crime Against Kansas" oration, and if the address had contained nothing more, it could hardly have been reckoned among the senator's more notable productions. But, in addition, Sumner felt it necessary to "say something of a general character"—"not," as he admitted, "belonging to the argument"—"in response to what has fallen from Senators who have raised themselves to eminence on this floor in championship of human wrongs," and he included his carefully rehearsed personal attacks upon Senators Douglas, Butler, and Mason.

On the first day Sumner spoke, he branded Senator Butler, who was absent in his native South Carolina, as the Don Quixote of slavery, who "has chosen a mistress to whom he has made his vows, and who, though ugly to others, is always lovely to him; though polluted in the sight of the world, is chaste in his sight . . . the harlot, Slavery," and labeled Douglas "the squire of Slavery, its very Sancho Panza, ready to do all its humiliating offices." [4]

Many senators were surprised at the venom of Sumner's remarks, but, largely because of the complexity and confusion of the Senate rules, no one called the speaker to order. Douglas,

[3] Ibid., 22–4, 28.
[4] Ibid., pp. 3, 5.

pacing irritatedly across the rear of the Senate Chamber, muttered: "That damn fool will get himself killed by some other damn fool." [5]

On the second day of his oration, Sumner continued and extended his personal references. Once again he attacked the absent Butler. Uncharitably referring to the effects of the slight labial paralysis from which the elderly South Carolina senator suffered, Sumner charged that he "with incoherent phrases, discharged the loose expectoration of his speech" upon the representatives of free Kansas. "There was no extravagance . . . which he did not repeat; nor was there any possible deviation from truth which he did not make. . . . But the Senator touches nothing which he does not disfigure—with error, sometimes of principle, sometimes of fact. He shows an incapacity of accuracy. . . . He cannot ope his mouth, but out there flies a blunder." Yet, this senator, Sumner complained, had dared rush "forward in the very ecstasy of madness" to compare his State of South Carolina, with "its shameful imbecility from Slavery," to the free territory of Kansas. "Were the whole history of South Carolina blotted out of existence, from its very beginning down to the day of the last election of the Senator to his present seat on this floor, civilization might lose—I do not say how little, but surely less than it has already gained by the example of Kansas, in its valiant struggle against oppression."

Sumner concluded with a rapid assault upon Senator James M. Mason, "who represents that other Virginia, from which Washington and Jefferson now avert their faces, where human beings are bred as cattle for the shambles." [6]

As Sumner resumed his seat, Cass, dean of the Senate, rose solemnly to pronounce Sumner's speech "the most un-American and unpatriotic that ever grated on the ears of the members of this high body." Douglas followed with a complaint that Sumner had merely rehashed old arguments, adding nothing new to the debate but "personal assaults and . . . malignity" and a series of "classic allusions, each one only distinguished for its lasciviousness and obscenity—each one drawn from those portions of the

[5] *Cong. Globe*, 34 Cong., 1 Sess., 1,477 ff., esp. 1,483. (All subsequent references to the *Congressional Globe* in this chapter are to the proceedings of this session.) Milton: *Eve of Conflict*, p. 233.
[6] *Crime Against Kansas*, p. 29.

classics which all decent professors in respectable colleges cause
to be suppressed, as unfit for decent young men to read." [7] These
"libels" and "gross insults" were the more objectionable as they
did not rise in the give-and-take of debate, but had been "conned
over, written with cool, deliberate malignity, repeated from night
to night in order to catch the appropriate grace." "Is it his object
to provoke some of us to kick him as we would a dog in the street,
that he may get sympathy upon the just chastisement?" Douglas
asked.

Mason rose loftily to explain: "I am constrained to hear here
depravity, vice in its most odious form uncoiled in this presence,
exhibiting its loathsome deformities in accusation and vilification
against the quarter of the country from which I come . . . because it is a necessity of my position, under a common Government, to recognize as an equal, politically, one whom to see
elsewhere is to shun and despise."

Regaining the floor for a rebuttal, Sumner made one of his
rare impromptu efforts, doubtless allowing the excitement of his
oratorical success to carry him further than he had originally intended. Cass, his oldest acquaintance in the Senate, he passed
over in silence. "To the Senator from Illinois I should willingly
leave the privilege of the common scold—the last word," Sumner continued, but Douglas should "remember hereafter that the
bowie-knife and bludgeon are not the proper emblems of senatorial debate. . . . I say, also, to that Senator . . . that no person
with the upright form of man can be allowed—" and he hesitated.

Douglas blustered: "Say it."

"I will say it," Sumner went on; "no person with the upright
form of man can be allowed, without violation of all decency, to
switch out from his tongue the perpetual stench of offensive
personality. . . . The noisome, squat, and nameless animal, to
which I now refer, is not the proper model for an American Senator. Will the Senator from Illinois take notice?"

"I will," Douglas retorted; "and therefore will not imitate you,
sir."

[7] This charge against Sumner, which historians have often repeated, had no
basis in fact. There was nothing obscene about any of his allusions, or anything
lascivious about his quotations. It is hard to believe that Douglas, a rough
Westerner, was so shocked by a word like "harlot."

"Mr. President," Sumner replied haughtily, "again the Senator has switched his tongue, and again he fills the Senate with its offensive odor."

Turning finally upon Mason, Sumner reminded him that "hard words are not argument; frowns not reasons; nor do scowls belong to the proper arsenal of parliamentary debate."

Reporters understood Mason to mutter: "The Senator is certainly *non compos mentis*," and the debate closed.[8]

· 2 ·

"Mr. Sumner has added a cubit to his stature," the New York *Tribune* declared, as the debate ended. Letters of praise began pouring in. About half of them lauded "the inspiring eloquence and lofty moral tone which characterized and ran through this triumphant senatorial achievement," and the rest rejoiced in the way Sumner *"Lashed Those Demagogues."* "Your speech," the loyal Longfellow wrote, "is the greatest voice on the greatest subject that has been uttered." [9]

Many politicians, however, were troubled by the harshness of Sumner's language. Seward had advised Sumner to eliminate all his personal attacks and disapproved also of his gratuitous assault against the honor of South Carolina. Even Republican stalwarts like Wilson and Ben Wade regretted the vindictiveness of Sumner's tone. "Language equally intemperate and bitter is sometimes heard from a notorious parliamentary blackguard," Edward Everett thought, "but from a man of character of any party I have never seen any thing so offensive." [1]

Most Democrats and nearly all Southerners were outspokenly hostile. The Washington *Star* declared that Sumner's "personal vilification and abuse of Senator Butler . . . caused a blush of shame to mantle the cheeks of all present who respect the character of the body before whom it was uttered; because it was wholly unjust and untrue, and, in style, far better suited to

---

[8] *Cong. Globe*, Appendix, 544–7; New York *Tribune*, May 21, 1856.

[9] New York *Tribune*, May 20–1, 1856; New York *Evening Post*, May 21, 1856; W. W. Leland to Sumner, May 21, 1856, Sumner MSS.; Longfellow to Sumner, May 28, 1856, copy, Longfellow MSS.

[1] *Cong. Globe*, Appendix, 664; Everett, Diary, May 25, 1856, and June 18, 1857; A. G. Riddle: *The Life of Benjamin F. Wade* (Cleveland: The Williams Publishing Co.; 1888), p. 242.

some low doggery." In street-corner conversations in Washington, always a hotbed of proslavery interests, Southerners could discuss only the insults Sumner had offered the South and the redress that should be taken. One Tennessee Congressman announced: "Mr. Sumner ought to be knocked down, and his face jumped into." [2]

The danger that these sentiments might erupt in personal violence against Sumner was not lost upon his friends. Troubled by Douglas's question: "Is it his object to provoke some of us to kick him . . . ?" Representative John A. Bingham, a Republican from Ohio, warned Wilson just after the speech to protect his colleague. Wilson gathered Anson Burlingame and Schuyler Colfax, both Republicans in the House, and told Sumner: "I am going home with you to-day—several of us are going home with you."

Unafraid, and rather vexed by what he considered unnecessary precautions, Sumner replied: "None of that, Wilson." He slipped out a side door of the Capitol unattended, accompanied Seward, who was on his way to catch the omnibus, a few blocks, and then walked to his lodgings alone. [3]

But the alarm of Sumner's friends was not excessive. Though no attacks were made upon him on May 20, Southerners were still angrily discussing his speech. A South Carolinian, it was said, "could not go into a parlor, or drawing-room, or to a dinner party, where he did not find an implied reproach that there was an unmanly submission to an insult to his State and his countrymen." [4]

Congressman Preston S. Brooks, of South Carolina, flinched sensitively under these reproaches. Now serving his second term in the House of Representatives, Brooks was not known as one of the Southern fire-eaters. He had pursued a moderate course during the Kansas-Nebraska debates of 1854 and was even taunted in his home state for being "a little too national." A man of very moderate ability, his one claim to fame was his half-humorous proposal that congressmen be required to check their firearms in the cloakroom before appearing on the House floor. Six feet tall and weighing about 170 pounds, with a proud military bearing that

[2] *Star*, quoted in Boston *Post*, May 24, 1856; *Cong. Globe*, Appendix, 631–2; *Alleged Assault upon Senator Sumner* (*House Report*, No. 182, 34 Cong., 1 Sess.), p. 66. Hereafter this document is cited as *Sumner Assault*.
[3] *Sumner Assault*, pp. 25, 42.
[4] *Cong. Globe*, Appendix, 632.

reminded observers of his Mexican War service, and a handsome, though rather juvenile, face, the thirty-six-year-old Brooks had won many friends in Congress "by his obliging disposition and his conciliatory temper, not less than by his cordial and agreeable manners." But, under his placid exterior, there burned a smoldering hatred of abolitionists, a proud devotion to the South and to South Carolina, an intense loyalty to his family, and a determination to live by the code of a gentleman.[5]

Along with many other representatives, Brooks had gone over to the Senate chamber on May 19, when Sumner began his oration, and he remained long enough, apparently, to hear Sumner call Butler, who was Brooks's cousin, the Don Quixote of slavery. Of Sumner's remarks on the second day Brooks knew only by report, but that apparently was enough to convince him that the Massachusetts senator had "insulted South Carolina and Judge Butler grossly." By the code of Southern chivalry Butler, when he returned from South Carolina, would be obliged to flog Sumner. Realizing that his cousin was old and that Sumner was "a very powerful man," Brooks concluded: "I felt it to be my duty to relieve Butler and avenge the insult to my State." But with curious deliberateness he waited until he could read the published version of Sumner's speech, on May 21, before definitely deciding to take action.[6]

Finding the speech as offensive as rumor had reported, Brooks determined to proceed according to the Southern code duello. Though he believed Sumner's remarks clearly slanderous, he did not even think of bringing legal action. No Southern gentleman considered a law suit the proper redress for a slur upon his own good name or upon that of a member of his family. Though Brooks had fought a duel in his youth, he did not consider challenging Sumner to a fight. In the first place, he knew that Sumner

[5] James E. Walmsley: "Preston S. Brooks," in Allen Johnson and Dumas Malone (eds.): *Dictionary of American Biography* (New York: Charles Scribner's Sons; 1929), III, 88; Harold S. Schultz: *Nationalism and Sectionalism in South Carolina, 1852–1860* . . . (Durham: Duke University Press; 1950), pp. 115–16; *Cong. Globe*, Appendix, 876.

[6] *Cong. Globe*, Appendix, 886; Brooks to his brother, J. H. Brooks, May 23, 1856, in Robert L. Meriwether (ed.): "Preston S. Brooks on the Caning of Charles Sumner," *South Carolina Historical and Genealogical Magazine*, XII (1951), 2 [hereafter cited as "The Caning of Sumner"]; *Sumner Assault*, pp. 61–2; "Statement by Preston S. Brooks," May 28, 1856, *MHSP*, LXI (1927–8), 221.

would not accept, as "the moral tone of mind that would lead a man to become a Black Republican would make him incapable of courage." Secondly, he thought that Sumner might report the challenge to the police, in which event Brooks would become liable "to legal penalties more severe than would be imposed for a simple assault and battery." But chiefly Brooks refrained from challenging Sumner because, according to the code of the Old South, a duel must be between social equals; to call Sumner out to the field of honor would be to give him, in Southern eyes, a social respectability he could not otherwise attain.[7]

"To punish an insulting inferior," the Southern code ruled, "one used not a pistol or sword but a cane or horsewhip." Brooks coolly explored these possibilities. "I . . . speculated somewhat as to whether I should employ a horsewhip or a cowhide," he declared later; "but knowing that the Senator was my superior in strength, it occurred to me that he might wrest it from my hand, and then . . . I might have been compelled to do that which I would have regretted the balance of my natural life." In other words, "it was expressly to avoid taking life that I used an ordinary cane." The instrument he selected was a gutta-percha walking stick, presented to him several months earlier by a friend. Weighing eleven and one-half ounces, the cane had a gold head; it tapered from a thickness of one inch at the large end to three quarters of an inch at the small, and had a hollow core of about three eighths of an inch.[8]

Having selected his weapon, Brooks had merely to pick the time and place for chastising Sumner. On Wednesday morning, May 21, he chose a seat in the Capitol grounds, waiting for Sumner to pass on his way to the Senate, and paced back and forth between it and the steps of the Capitol. Meeting him as he turned away from the steps, Representative Henry A. Edmundson, of Virginia, hailed him: "You are going the wrong way for the discharge of your duties." Brooks asked his friend to walk with him, and as they paced along, he declared that "Sumner had been very

[7] Brooks, in the Carolina *Times*, Aug. 30, 1856, clipping in Parker-Sumner Scrapbook; *Cong. Globe*, Appendix, 832. Cf. Charles S. Sydnor: "The Southerner and the Laws," *Journal of Southern History*, VI (1940), 3–23; and Jack Kenny Williams: "The Code of Honor in Ante-Bellum South Carolina," *South Carolina Historical Magazine*, LIV (1953), 113–28.
[8] *Cong. Globe*, Appendix, 832; *Sumner Assault*, pp. 73, 75.

insulting to his State, and that he had determined to punish him, unless he made an ample apology." "It was time," he continued, "for southern men to stop this coarse abuse used by the Abolitionists against the southern people and States, and . . . he should not feel that he was representing his State properly if he permitted such things to be said." Edmundson asked how he could be of assistance. "I wish you merely to be present, and if a difficulty should occur, to take no part in it," Brooks replied. "Sumner may have friends with him, and I want a friend of mine to be with me to do me justice." The two representatives remained at their observation post until twelve thirty, but when Sumner did not appear, they concluded that their prey had eluded them, and they walked into the Capitol.

Foiled, Brooks spent the rest of the day brooding about the "insult" to his state and his family, and he grew more than ever resolved that "it ought to be promptly resented." That night he told Representatives Lawrence M. Keitt and James L. Orr, both close political associates from South Carolina, of his purpose "to 'disgrace' the Senator with the South by a flagellation." What they advised is not known, but Brooks left them resolved "that he could not overlook the insult." So angry that he slept scarcely at all, he was up early the next morning to seek his revenge.

By eleven o'clock he was waiting in the porter's lodge at the entrance to the Capitol grounds, again ready to intercept Sumner as he entered the building. He planned to assault the senator there, if Sumner followed his customary practice and walked to the Capitol; if he came by carriage, Brooks intended to cut through the grounds, run up the flight of steps and through the Capitol so as to meet him in the space behind the building where the carriages stopped. Passing by the lodge on his way to the House, Edmundson spied Brooks and greeted him: "You are looking out." When Brooks explained his plan, the Virginia congressman cannily suggested a flaw: "The exertion and fatigue of passing up so many flights of steps would render him unable to contend with Mr. Sumner, should a personal conflict take place," especially as "no doubt Mr. Sumner was physically a stronger man than himself." [9]

[9] *Sumner Assault*, p. 59; *MHSP*, LXI, 221–3; Boston *Commonwealth*, Feb. 22, 1873.

Perhaps the reasoning convinced Brooks, or perhaps he concluded, as the noon hour for the convening of Congress approached, that he had again missed his quarry. In either case, he
walked along with Edmundson up to the Capitol rotunda, where
the Virginian went to his duties in the House, and Brooks "determined to keep [an] eye on Mr Sumner." He found the Senate in
session, but both houses were scheduled to adjourn at an early
hour because of the recent death of Representative John G. Miller,
of Missouri. While Senator Henry S. Geyer pronounced a eulogy
upon his deceased colleague, Brooks stood in the lobby on the opposite side of the main aisle from where Sumner was sitting.

As the House adjourned earlier than the Senate that day,
Edmundson came over to the Senate chamber, where he saw
Brooks and where, in the vestibule, he met Keitt and proposed
that they leave. "No," said Keitt, "I cannot leave till Brooks does,"
and he disappeared behind the screen back of the Vice-President's chair, where he began talking with one of his constituents.[1]

At 12:45 the Senate adjourned, and most of the members
left the chamber, though several stood talking in the vestibule and
in the cloakroom. Sumner stayed at his desk, pen in hand, franking copies of his "Crime Against Kansas" speech. Several visitors
tried to interrupt him, but he promptly and briefly dismissed
them, declaring that he was busy.[2]

Impatiently Brooks awaited his opportunity. Until the room
could be cleared, he took a desk in the back row of the chamber,
across the aisle and three seats removed from Sumner. Wilson,
when leaving, caught his eye, recognized him, and gave a polite
bow. When Edmundson came up and jokingly asked Brooks if he
were now a senator, the South Carolinian, fuming with anger, replied that he could not approach Sumner while there were ladies
present, and he pointed to a pretty but persistent female conver-
sationalist who had taken a seat in the lobby not far from where
Sumner was sitting. He had already tried, unsuccessfully, to get
the sergeant-at-arms to remove the lady. Finally, exclaiming that
"he would stand this thing no longer," he rose and went into the
vestibule, where he planned to send a message asking Sumner to

---

[1] *MHSP*, LXI, 221–3; *Sumner Assault*, pp. 60, 63; *Cong. Globe*, 1,292.
[2] *Sumner Assault*, p. 23.

come outside. Edmundson, following him, argued that such a move would do no good, as Sumner undoubtedly would only send for Brooks to come to his desk. When Edmundson stopped to speak to a friend, Brooks went back into the Senate, where Sumner was still busily writing.[3]

Finding the lobby at last clear of women, Brooks proceeded upon his errand. Operating, as he thought, "under the highest sense of duty," he approached the front of the desk where Sumner still sat behind a large pile of documents, "writing very rapidly, with his head very close to the desk," his armchair drawn up close and his legs entirely under the desk. With cool self-possession and formal politeness, Brooks addressed him: "Mr. Sumner." [4]

Sumner did not get up, but merely raised his head to identify his visitor. Nearsightedness, for which he was too vain to wear glasses, made the figure before him indistinct, but perfect vision would not have warned him, as he did not know Brooks by sight.[5]

"I have read your speech twice over carefully," Brooks began in a low voice. "It is a libel on South Carolina, and Mr. Butler, who is a relative of mine—" [6] As Sumner seemed about to rise, Brooks interrupted himself to give Sumner "a slight blow" with the smaller end of his cane. Stunned, Sumner instinctively threw out his arms to protect his head, and Brooks felt "compelled to strike him harder than he had intended." He began to rain down blows, and, he boasted: "Every lick went where I intended." In the excitement, Brooks forgot that he had set out only to flog Sumner, and began to strike him on the head "as hard as he could." [7]

Dazed by the first blow, Sumner of course could not remember that in order to rise from his desk, which was bolted to the

---

[3] Ibid., pp. 42, 60, 79.

[4] The Carolina *Times*, Aug. 30, 1856, in Parker-Sumner Scrapbook; Sumner: *Works*, IV, 269; *Sumner Assault*, p. 57.

[5] H. W. Beecher, in New York *Tribune*, May 31, 1856; *Sumner Assault*, p. 26.

[6] It is difficult to determine precisely what words Brooks used. The version here given is that remembered by Sumner himself, who asserted that Brooks began striking while uttering these words; he also recalled that Brooks had used the phrase "old man." *Sumner Assault*, pp. 23–4. Brooks claimed that he used more elaborate phraseology: "Mr. Sumner, I have read your Speech with care and as much impartiality as was possible and I feel it my duty to tell you that you have libeled my State and slandered a relative who is aged and absent and I am come to punish you for it." "Caning of Sumner," p. 2. For other variants see *MHSP*, XLI, 221–3; *Sumner Assault*, p. 81. I accept Sumner's version both because the senator's memory was remarkably precise and because the phrasing is shorter and less "literary." In any case, the difference is not great, for Brooks admitted that he struck before he ended his sentence.

[7] *MHSP*, LXI, 222; *Sumner Assault*, pp. 27, 35.

floor by an iron plate and heavy screws, he had to push back his chair, which was on rollers.[8] Perhaps half a dozen blows fell on his head and shoulders while he was still pinioned. Eyes blinded with blood, "almost unconsciously, acting under the instinct of self-defence," he then made a mighty effort to rise, and, with the pressure of his thighs, ripped the desk from the floor. Staggering forward, he now offered an even better target for Brooks, who, avoiding Sumner's outstretched arms, beat down "to the full extent of his power." So heavy were his blows that the gutta-percha cane, which he had carefully selected because he "fancied it would not break," snapped, but, with the portion remaining in his hand, he continued to pour on rapid blows. The strokes "made a good deal more noise after the stick was broken than before. They sounded as if the end of the stick was split."[9]

As soon as Sumner was free from the desk, he moved blindly "down the narrow passage-way, under the impetuous drive of his adversary, with his hands uplifted." As "Brooks continued his blows rapidly with the part of the stick he held in his hand," Sumner lost consciousness and "was reeling around against the seats, backwards and forwards." "His whole manner seemed . . . like a person in convulsions; his arms were thrown around as if unconsciously." Knocking over another desk, diagonally in front of his own, he seemed about to fall when Brooks reached out and with one hand held Sumner up by the lapel of his coat while he continued to strike him with the other. By this time the cane had shivered to pieces. Sumner, "entirely insensible" and "reeling and staggering about," was about to fall in the aisle. "I . . . gave him about 30 first rate stripes," Brooks summarized. "Towards the last he bellowed like a calf. I wore my cane out completely but saved the Head which is gold."[1]

The beating had taken place in less than one minute. The sound made by Brooks's cane had at once attracted the attention of everyone who remained in the Senate chamber, and most of them began rushing toward the fracas. Representatives Ambrose S. Murray and Edwin B. Morgan, who had been in con-

[8] I have been permitted to inspect Sumner's desk and chair, which are preserved in the Massachusetts Historical Society, through the courtesy of the Director, Mr. Stephen Riley.

[9] *Sumner Assault*, pp. 23–4, 32, 35, 56, 65, 79; *MHSP*, LXI, 222.

[1] *Sumner Assault*, pp. 27, 32, 37, 38, 40, 71, 80; "The Caning of Sumner," pp. 2–3.

versation behind the screen that separated the Senate seats from the vestibule, were the first to arrive. While Morgan caught Sumner, Murray seized Brooks by the arm while in the act of striking, and tried to draw him back from his foe.[2]

While Brooks struggled against this unexpected interference, the elderly Whig senator from Kentucky, John J. Crittenden, came up the aisle, expressed his "disapprobation of such violence in the Senate chamber," and warned Brooks: "Don't kill him." Brooks, apparently realizing that he had far exceeded his original purpose, muttered: "I did not intend to kill him, but I did intend to whip him." [3]

Just as Crittenden was warning Brooks, Keitt, who had been near the clerk's desk at the outset of the attack, bounded up the center aisle, with his "small cane . . . lifted above his head, as if he intended to strike." "Let them alone, God damn you," he shouted at Crittenden.[4]

By this time Toombs, of Georgia, had come up, and he warned the infuriated Keitt not to strike Crittenden. He did nothing, however, to restrain Brooks, still struggling to escape from Murray and renew the assault on Sumner; "I approved it," said Toombs later. Nor did Douglas, summoned from the anteroom by the scuffling, interfere. He at first thought of trying to "help put an end to the affray," he declared, but "it occurred to my mind, in an instant, that my relations to Mr. Sumner were such that if I came into the Hall, my motives would be misconstrued, perhaps, and I sat down again." [5]

In a few seconds, friends led Brooks off into a side room, where they washed a small cut he had received above his eye from the recoil of his stick. Minutes later he and Keitt were walking together down Pennsylvania Avenue.[6]

Meanwhile, Morgan, who had arrived at the same moment as Murray, had caught Sumner so that he was "saved . . . from falling as heavily upon the floor as he would otherwise have done." While Brooks was being led off, Sumner, partially supported by Morgan, lay "at the side of the center aisle, his feet in the aisle, and he leaning partially against a chair." He remained "as sense-

[2] *Sumner Assault*, pp. 38–40, 48.
[3] Ibid., pp. 30, 33, 49, 57; Boston *Commonwealth*, Feb. 22, 1873.
[4] *Sumner Assault*, pp. 29, 58.
[5] *Cong. Globe*, 1,305.
[6] *Sumner Assault*, pp. 50, 71.

less as a corpse for several minutes, his head bleeding copiously from the frightful wounds, and the blood saturating his clothes." [7]

Within a few minutes Sumner regained consciousness. One of the pages gave him a glass of water, and somebody suggested that he should be carried to a sofa in the anteroom. Sumner said that he thought he could walk, requested that his hat be found and that the documents on his desk be taken care of, and, leaning upon Morgan and another man, stumbled into the anteroom. His face was covered with blood as he passed Louisiana Senator John Slidell, who "did not think it necessary to . . . make any advances toward him" or to express any sympathy. A few minutes later Dr. Cornelius Boyle, who had been hastily summoned, dressed the wounds, which were still bleeding profusely, and put two stitches in each. [8]

Just as the doctor was finishing, Wilson, who had heard of the attack and had rushed back to the Capitol, arrived, and, helping Sumner into a carriage, took him to his lodgings and put him to bed. Sumner's "shirt around the neck and collar was soaked with blood. The waistcoat had many marks of blood upon it; also the trowsers. The broadcloth coat was covered with blood on the shoulders so thickly that the blood had soaked through the cloth even through the padding, and appeared on the inside; there was also a great deal of blood on the back of the coat and its sides." [9]

About an hour later Dr. Boyle came to Sumner's rooms to make a more thorough examination. He told the anxious friends waiting there "that such was the condition of Mr. Sumner it was absolutely necessary that he should be kept quiet, for he could not tell the extent of his injuries at that time." [1]

Before falling into a dazed sleep, Sumner remarked: "I could not believe that a thing like this was possible." [2]

· 3 ·

Arrested on a charge of assault, Brooks was immediately freed under a $500 bail, and he became the hero of the extreme pro-

[7] Ibid., 38–40; *Cong. Globe*, 1,305; Morgan, in New York *Tribune*, May 31, 1856.
[8] *Sumner Assault*, pp. 35–6, 41–2, 51; *Cong. Globe*, 1,305.
[9] *Sumner Assault*, p. 26.
[1] Ibid., p. 67.
[2] Johnson: "Recollections of Charles Sumner," *Scribner's Monthly*, VIII (1874), 482.

slavery clique. Armed and menacing, Southern fire-eaters talked of imitating Brooks's example, and made violent threats against other Northern leaders. "It would not take much to have the throats of every Abolitionist cut," Brooks thought. "If the northern men had stood up," Keitt wrote scornfully a few days later, "the city would now float with blood. . . . Everybody here feels as if we were upon a volcano." Southerners said that if Congress dared discuss Brooks's actions, the House of Representatives would "ring with vollies [sic] from revolvers." [3]

The Senate made no move to redress Sumner's injury. The Republican caucus, which met shortly after the assault, decided that it would be best not to make a party issue of the attack and that Massachusetts congressmen should not take the lead in any investigation. With these party injunctions restraining his natural indignation, Wilson took the floor on May 23 and made a brief, factual explanation of his colleague's absence. He submitted no motion, but left it "to older Senators" to devise "measures to redress the wrongs of a member of this body, and to vindicate the honor and dignity of the Senate." There was a pause, and nobody stepped forward. As the President pro tempore was about to go on to other business, Seward moved for the appointment of an investigating committee. Elected by the Senate, it contained not one Republican. Its report, made on May 28, declared that "this assault was a breach of the privileges of the Senate," but, as Brooks was a member of the other house, "it is not within the jurisdiction of the Senate, and can only be punished by the House of Representatives." [4]

Meanwhile, the House, less dignified but more active, had already appointed an investigating committee of its own, a majority of whose members were Republicans, and it began taking the testimony of twenty-seven witnesses, starting with Sumner himself, who was interviewed at his lodgings.

While Congress was investigating, the public had already made up its mind. For most Northerners, news of the attack upon Sumner came as an electrifying shock. The deep sense of Northern outrage can best be judged not from the reactions of party

[3] "The Caning of Sumner," p. 3; Schultz: *Nationalism and Sectionalism*, pp. 117–18; H. A. Wise to Everett, May 31, 1856, Everett MSS. Cf. Wilson in *The Collector*, XLII (1927), 525.
[4] *Cong. Globe*, 1,279, 1,317.

politicians, whose responses could be anticipated, but in the letters and diaries of unimportant citizens. "The instant Papa told
me," one Massachusetts maiden wrote, "it seemed exactly as if a
great, black cloud was spread over the sky. . . . I keep always
thinking about it, and no matter what I am doing I have a sort of
consciousness of something black and wicked." "Mr. Brooks is a
very naughty man," little Mary Rosamond Dana, daughter of
Sumner's friend, decided, "and if I had been there I would have
torn his eyes out and so I would now if I could." "We are in great
indignation here," a Connecticut schoolgirl told her parents. "I
don't think it is of very much use to stay any longer in the High
School, as the boys would better be learning to hold muskets, and
the girls to make bullets." [5]

Hundreds wrote Sumner of their sympathy. "My life is at
your service," declared one New Yorker. "The news of the most
foul, most damnable and dastardly attack . . . perfectly overwhelmed me with indignation and rage," a Chicago German wrote.
"Even if they succeed in killing you now, you have achieved renown with posterity," another correspondent comforted Sumner.
"You are glorious now," still another echoed. "The crown of martyrdom is *yours*. . . . Every noble crown is, and ever has been, a
crown of thorns' and *you* have been found meet to wear the one
the Savior wore—Oh thank God and murmur not." As is always
the case in times of deep emotional stress, dozens of writers resorted to tried phrases that in other circumstances would have
seemed clichés. The assault "made my blood boil." I should have
"fought like a tiger for you." "My blood is boiling." "This murderous outrage . . ." ". . . the mean and dastardly attack on your
person." "The blood boils in my veins." ". . . this detestably
cowardly assault." "For four days my blood overboils. . . ."
". . . my warmest sympathy." ". . . the cowardly assault upon
your person." As Horace Mann simply summarized: "We are not
only shocked at the outrage committed upon you, but we are
wounded in your wounds, and bleed in your bleeding." [6]

[5] Lilian R. Clarke to Sumner [May 1856], Sumner MSS.; Mary R. Dana to
Sumner [June 1856], ibid.; A. Augusta Dodge (ed.): *Gail Hamilton's Life in
Letters* (Boston: Lee and Shepard; 1901), I, 123.
[6] Mann to Sumner, May 27, 1856, Sumner MSS. The other quotations in the
above paragraph are phrases chosen at random from the hundreds of letters
Sumner received between May 21 and May 26, ibid.

Virtually every Northern city held a public meeting to protest the assault. There were rallies not merely in New York, Philadelphia, and Boston, not merely in Albany, Cleveland, Detroit, New Haven, Providence, and Rochester, but in Newmarket, New Hampshire, Lockport, New York, Rahway, New Jersey, Berea, Ohio, Burlington, Iowa, and in dozens of other towns.[7] The New York meeting, on May 30, was the most conspicuous of these gatherings. "It was the most remarkable and significant assembly I ever attended," one of Sumner's correspondents told him; "4000 of the most substantial citizens of N. York spoke as *one man* in terms and tones which would make Southern sneaks and bullies tremble in their shoes." "A vast crowd, earnest, unanimous, and made up of people who don't often attend political gatherings" thronged the Tabernacle. Though an effort had been made to keep the meeting out of radical antislavery men's hands by asking New York merchants, of Whig background, to preside, the audience was ready for strong talk. Whenever William M. Evarts, who read the resolutions, mentioned Sumner's name, "Peal after peal, cheer after cheer, succeeded each other like the discharge of heavy artillery," and there was "a spontaneous outburst of groaning and hissing at the sound of 'Preston S. Brooks.' " [8]

In Massachusetts, naturally, the feeling ran deepest. "When the intelligence of the assault on Mr. Sumner . . . reached Boston," declared Edward Everett, who was not given to exaggeration, "it produced an excitement in the public mind deeper and more dangerous than I have ever witnessed. . . . If a leader daring and reckless enough had presented himself, he might have raised any number of men to march on Washington." [9]

For a moment it seemed as if political lines and past differences had been obliterated in Massachusetts. "There is a great de-

[7] New York *Herald,* May 31, 1856; Boston *Advertiser,* May 26, 1856; New York *Tribune,* May 30, and June 2–3, 9, and 11, 1856; Rochester *Democrat,* May 31, 1856; *Zachariah Chandler: An Outline Sketch of His Life and Public Services* (Detroit: The Post and Tribune Company; 1880), pp. 119–20; Francis and H. L. Wayland: *A Memoir of the Life and Labors of Francis Wayland* . . . (New York: Sheldon and Company; 1867), II, 154; *Annals of Cleveland, 1818–1935,* XXXIX, items 2,847–8, 2,854; William Salter: *The Life of James W. Grimes* . . . (New York: D. Appleton and Company; 1876), pp. 80–1.

[8] G. P. Putnam to Sumner, May 30, 1856, Sumner MSS.; J. A. Briggs to George Sumner, May 31, 1856, ibid.; Allan Nevins and Milton Halsey Thomas (eds.): *The Diary of George Templeton Strong* (New York: The Macmillan Co.; 1952), II, 276; New York *Herald* and New York *Tribune,* May 31, 1856.

[9] Everett to Horace Maynard, Oct. 3, 1857, copy, Everett MSS.

sire for a public meeting to express the outraged feelings of all classes of our citizens," one Bostonian reported to Sumner. The organizers of the Faneuil Hall rally on May 24 were careful to invite men of all political views. A dense throng, estimated at 5,000 persons, crowded in and around the ancient building, to hear Governor Henry J. Gardner declare that he would "rise above party feeling and party bias" and stand by Sumner "as a representative of Massachusetts, under every circumstance, in this, his hour of trouble"; to listen to Hillard, long estranged from Sumner politically, pronounce the attack the "act of an assassin" and, "after a friendship of twenty years," praise Sumner as "a most amiable, gentle and kindly man"; and to roar approval of resolutions condemning Brooks's attack "not only as a cowardly assault upon a defenceless man, but as a crime against the right of free speech and the dignity of a free State." [1]

This appearance of unanimity was superficial; it was too much to expect that all the antagonisms Sumner had aroused could be forgotton in a moment. Fletcher Webster, the embittered son of Daniel Webster, said cynically that if Sumner "would indulge in such attacks . . . he ought at least to take the precaution of wearing an iron pot on his head." Some of the conservative Curtis family muttered, when they heard the news: "Served him right," and "I wish they had killed him." Sumner himself received a very few letters from Northerners who announced: "I am happy that one man was found who chastised you, but . . . you did not get one half what you merit." [2]

The political implications of the Brooks assault were immediately apparent. The chance fact that Brooks's attack had occurred almost simultaneously with a Southern raid on the free-state town of Lawrence, Kansas (May 21, 1856), gave the Republicans the perfectly matched themes of "Bleeding Sumner" and "Bleeding Kansas" for the coming presidential campaign. Astute observers like Secretary of State William L. Marcy predicted that the Sumner-Brooks affair, as ceaselessly exploited in the New

[1] George White to N. P. Banks, June 10, 1856, Banks MSS.; J. W. Stone to Sumner, May 22, 1856, Sumner MSS.; J. A. Dresser to Sumner, May 25, 1856, ibid.; Boston *Advertiser*, May 25, 1856.

[2] Charles T. Congdon: *Reminiscences of a Journalist* (Boston: James R. Osgood and Company; 1880), p. 85; R. E. Apthorp to Sumner, May 29, 1856, Sumner MSS.; "A Pennsylvanian who is opposed to Slavery" to Sumner, May 25, 1856, ibid.

York *Tribune* and other antislavery newspapers, would cost the Democratic party 200,000 votes in the fall election. On the very day after the beating, Sumner received a telegram from Michigan: "Every blow from the ruffian Brooks gives ten thousand [votes] to liberty." New Jersey Republicans reported that the assault on Sumner was the only force galvanizing antislavery opinion. Sourly Winthrop concluded: "Brooks and Douglas deserve statues from the Free-Soil party. The cane of the former and the Kansas Bill of the latter . . . have secured a success to the agitators." [3]

Republican strategists tried to take full advantage of the popular indignation. Perhaps a million copies of Sumner's "Crime Against Kansas" speech were distributed. The New York *Tribune* printed them at twenty cents a dozen, twenty dollars a thousand. Desiring the people to read Sumner's speech, Republican managers were, nevertheless, anxious not to have too much discussion of his arguments. By stressing the Brooks assault itself, they felt, Northern differences of opinion could be minimized and "the instincts, passions and sense of liberty of the free states" could be "roused against the enormous pretensions and villainous acts of the South." The main point to stress, the Springfield *Republican* urged, was: "The remedy for ruffianism resides in a united North. Old party names must be forgotten, old party ties surrendered." [4]

Massachusetts Republican leaders shrewdly capitalized upon the intense popular excitement. Keeping abolitionists and the recognized leaders of their party from taking too active a role in the protest rallies, they tried to give the impression that "prominent men of all parties" joined in condemning the assault. Then, as the movement was allegedly nonpartisan, they could exert immense pressure upon those who refused to participate in it. When Edward Everett, for example, declined to serve as vice-president of the Faneuil Hall rally on the ground that he had retired from politics, his refusal was widely publicized as a tacit endorsement

[3] Rochester *Democrat*, Sept. 3, 1857; J. G. Hudson to Sumner, May 23, 1856, Sumner MSS.; Everett to H. A. Wise, June 2, 1856, Everett MSS.; "Wales" to N. P. Banks, July 21, 1856, Banks MSS.; Ruhl Jacob Bartlett: *John C. Fremont and the Republican Party* ("Ohio State University Studies: Contributions in History and Political Science," No. 13, Columbus: Ohio State University Press; 1930), p. 61.
[4] Pierce, III, 458; E. P. Whipple to George Sumner, June 14, 1856, Sumner MSS.; George S. Merriam: *The Life and Times of Samuel Bowles* (New York: The Century Co.; 1885), I, 148.

of Brooks, his lecture invitations throughout New England were canceled, and he had to make a public statement of his "decided condemnation of the outrages." Conservative Whigs fumed impotently under the Republicans' pressure. "It is not enough that you agree with them," ex-governor Emory Washburne complained, "you must say your creed in their words with their intonation and just when they bid you or they hang or burn you as a heretic." [5]

Sumner's friends used Massachusetts indignation over the assault to bolster his shaky political prospects. The news of the attack reached Boston just in time to give Sumner's supporters a face-saving victory over Governor Gardner, who was trying to emasculate the personal liberty law Sumner had helped draft. By astute management Republicans forced through the legislature resolutions not merely condemning Brooks's actions, but endorsing "Mr. Sumner's manliness and courage in his earnest and fearless declaration of free principles, and his defence of human rights and free territory." John A. Andrew almost gave their game away when he blurted out at the Faneuil Hall rally that in order to secure "liberty of speech—nay, liberty itself," Sumner must be reelected, for Republicans were unobtrusively working toward precisely that end. "Providence itself seems to be on the side of the republican party," Hillard lamented. "Sumner is not merely their champion but their martyr, and his election for the next six years is now certain." A New Yorker, more prescient, declared that Sumner "is made by this act, senator for life." [6]

Sumner's political opponents tried to minimize the effects of the assault by balancing their denunciation of Brooks with criticism of Sumner. The Boston *Post*, a Democratic paper, forthrightly called Brooks's action "disgraceful," but it also complained of "the bitter tirade of personality, the wanton vituperation of high personal character, the absolute vulgarity of language" in Sumner's speech. The Boston *Courier*, an inveterate opponent of Sumner's, declared: "The member from South Carolina transgressed every rule of honor which should animate or restrain one gentleman in his connexions with another, in his ruffian assault

[5] Everett, Diary, May 24, 28, and 31, and June 2, 1856, Everett MSS.; Frothingham: *Everett*, p. 405; Washburne to Winthrop, June 7, 1856, Winthrop MSS.
[6] Bean: "Party Transformations," pp. 331–3; Boston *Advertiser*, May 26–7, 1856; *Cong. Globe*, Appendix, 630; Hillard to Lieber, May 28, 1856, Lieber MSS.; James E. Harvey to John McLean, May 30, 1856, McLean MSS.

upon Mr. Sumner," but added that "The Crime Against Kansas" speech was "excessively insulting and provoking, and not only highly indiscreet in sentiment and language, but unjustifiable, in any view in which it can be regarded." [7]

The significant thing, however, is the fact that virtually every Northern public man, however much he disapproved of Sumner or his speech, expressed sharp condemnation of Brooks. Even George Ticknor called the assault "brutal," and Winthrop exclaimed: "But how could any highminded and honorable man, as Mr. Brooks is represented to be considered in Carolina, have taken such a mode and place of redress, and have proceeded to such extreme violence!" The strength and unanimity of Northern opinion can best be gauged by the actions of that wily, unprincipled Democratic operator, Benjamin F. Butler. While the other members of the Massachusetts delegation to the Democratic national convention, passing through Washington in late May, carefully had nothing to do with Sumner, Butler, more sensitive to public opinion, paid a conspicuous visit of sympathy to the wounded senator, openly praised him as "a chivalric citizen of the Puritan commonwealth," and denounced Brooks as "a coward and an assassin." [8]

· 4 ·

Simultaneously the opposite pattern of public opinion was appearing in the South. Brooks, virtually unknown before the assault, suddenly found himself a sectional hero. "Every Southern man sustains me," he confidently wrote his brother. "The fragments of the stick are begged for as *sacred relicts* [sic]." His constituents in Newberry, at a public meeting on May 24, voted the congressman a "handsome gold headed cane" and endorsed his action:

Our Senators and Representatives in Congress have for a series of years patiently submitted to these tirades of calumny and vituperation, and they have in vain attempted to meet insults by argument and reason. . . . The aggravated insults given by the Senator from Massachusetts . . . furnish an ample justification of our Representative.

[7] Boston *Post*, May 24, 1856; Boston *Courier*, May 24, and 26, 1856. Cf. D. D. Barnard to Hamilton Fish, May 26, 1856, Fish MSS.

[8] Ticknor: *Life, Letters and Journals*, II, 296; Winthrop to John J. Crittenden, June 3, 1856, Crittenden MSS.; Conger: *Reminiscences*, pp. 89–90; Lowell *Evening Advertiser*, June 10, 1856; Butler to F. P. Rice, Feb. 15, 1886, Butler MSS.

Charleston, South Carolina, merchants contributed to buying Brooks a cane, inscribed: "Hit him again." "One of Carolina's truest and most honored matrons" wrote Brooks that "the ladies of the South would send him *hickory* sticks, with which to chastise Abolitionists and Red Republicans whenever he wanted them." In Columbia the governor of South Carolina headed the subscription list for "a splendid silver pitcher, goblet and stick" to be presented to Brooks, and even the slaves in the South Carolina capital collected money to buy him "an appropriate token of their regard." At the University of Virginia, students arranged to send Brooks a cane that should "have a heavy gold head, which will be suitably inscribed, and also bear upon it a device of the human head, badly cracked and broken." [9]

In their private correspondence, as well as in their public utterances, Southerners almost unanimously supported Brooks's actions. "Were I in the House I should certainly propose a vote of thanks to Mr. Brooks," Braxton Bragg, of Louisiana, wrote a friend. "You can reach the sensibilities of such dogs only through . . . their heads and a big stick." Paul Hamilton Hayne, the Southern poet, thought that Sumner, far from being "a martyr," should rather have been willing to "burn a hundred years in Hell than submit to a Public indignity—and *such* an indignity." "The Yankees seem greatly excited about Sumner's flogging," Toombs sneered. "They are afraid the practice may become general and many of [their] heads already feel sore. Sumner takes a beating badly." [1]

"In the main," announced the Richmond *Enquirer*, "the press of the South applaud the conduct of Mr. Brooks, without condition or limitation." A very few Southern papers boldly denounced the assault. The obscure Minden (Louisiana) *Herald* forthrightly condemned Brooks. The Memphis *Bulletin*, after complaining that

[9] "The Caning of Sumner," p. 3; Schultz: *Nationalism and Sectionalism*, p. 119; Columbia *South Carolinian*, May 28, 1856; Richmond *Enquirer*, May 30, 1856; Thomas Shelton Fox to W. H. Fox, June 1, 1856, John Fox MSS.
[1] Ulrich Bonnell Phillips (ed.): *The Correspondence of Robert Toombs, Alexander H. Stephens, and Howell Cobb* (*Annual Report of the American Historical Association*, 1911, Vol. II), p. 365; Bragg to "Dear General," May 31, 1856, George Hay Stuart MSS.; Hayne to Horatio Woodman, Sept. 8, 1856, Woodman MSS. Cf. Wilson: *Slave Power*, II, 490; J. F. H. Claiborne: *Life of John A. Quitman* . . . (New York: Harper & Brothers; 1860), II, 318–20. Of course, Southern opinion was not really unanimous, but the few Southerners who expressed regret over Brooks's actions did so privately. For example see Felton to Sumner, Nov. 8, 1860, Sumner MSS.; Everett, Diary, June 9, 1856, Everett MSS.; Phillips (ed.): *Toombs Correspondence*, p. 336.

Sumner was "a low, grovelling, wicked demagogue," called the attack "wholly inexcusable upon any grounds whatever." Especially in border cities like Baltimore, Louisville, and St. Louis some newspapers branded the "wanton and unjustifiable" assault as an "outrage and desecration" of the Senate chamber which called for "the prompt expulsion . . . of Mr. Brooks." [2]

A great many more Southern newspapers criticized not the principle upon which Brooks acted, but the time, place, and manner of its execution. Some Southern editors doubted the chivalry of attacking "a man whilst seated at his desk engaged in writing, and who has not had time to place himself face to face with his opponent." "The Senate Chamber is not the arena for exhibitions of this character," the Wilmington (North Carolina) *Herald* chided. "It is a shock to every man's sense of right and propriety to think of . . . a Senator in his seat subjected to such ignominious and hostile treatment," the Mobile *Advertiser* agreed. The Macon (Georgia) *Telegraph* argued that Brooks's action would give "a stronger impetus to Black Republicanism than anything else which could be imagined of a hundred times its importance." [3]

These Southern reservations came mostly from Whig editors, largely in the border states and in the larger port cities along the Mississippi River and the Gulf of Mexico. Perhaps they reflected Southern conservatives' positive dislike for Brooks's rash deed, their distrust of fire-eating, and their hope for peaceable adjustment of sectional conflicts, but it is notable that they were arguments against the policy, not the principle, of the Brooks assault. Southern dissenters, like the Northerners who had private reservations about Sumner's speech, were obliged to give at least lip service to the dominant sentiment of their section. [4]

[2] Richmond *Enquirer*, June 2, 1856; Minden (La.) *Herald*, clipped in Sumner Scrapbooks; Memphis *Bulletin*, Baltimore *Clipper*, Baltimore *Sun*, and Baltimore *Maryland*, all quoted in New York *Herald*, June 11, 1856.

[3] Charlottesville (Va.) *Advocate*, and Mobile *Advertiser*, quoted in New York *Herald*, June 11, 1856; Huntsville *Southern Advocate*, and Macon *Telegraph*, quoted in Avery O. Craven: *The Growth of Southern Nationalism*, *1848–1861* (Vol. VI of *A History of the South*, ed. by Wendell H. Stephenson and E. Merton Coulter, Baton Rouge: Louisiana State University Press; 1953), pp. 233–5; Wilmington *Herald*, clipped in Parker-Sumner Scrapbook.

[4] Avery O. Craven in *The Growth of Southern Nationalism* has made a careful analysis of Southern newspaper reactions to the Brooks assault, which I have found valuable. But Professor Craven's very laudable desire to show the diversity of Southern opinion has led him, as it seems to me, to give disproportionate space to the newspapers that did not approve the attack. In quoting from

That feeling was one of enthusiastic approval of Brooks. Aside from a momentary deviation by the Charleston *Mercury,* every South Carolina newspaper unqualifiedly praised the assault. "*A Good Deed,*" exclaimed the Richmond *Whig.* "The only regret we feel is, that Mr. Brooks did not employ a horsewhip or a cow-hide upon his slanderous back, instead of a cane." "We consider the act good in conception, better in execution, and best of all in consequences," the Richmond *Enquirer* said. "These vulgar aboli-tionists in the Senate . . . must be lashed into submission. Sum-ner, in particular, ought to have nine-and-thirty early every morn-ing. He is a great strapping fellow, and could stand the cowhide beautifully." "Far from blaming Mr. Brooks," added the Richmond *Examiner,* "we are disposed to regard him as a conservative gentleman, seeking to restore to the Senate that dignity and re-spectability of which the Abolition Senators are fast stripping it." The *South-Side Democrat,* of Petersburg, Virginia, expressed grat-itude for "the *classical* caning which this outrageous Abolitionist received . . . at the hands of the chivalrous Brooks," and an-other Petersburg editor concluded: "If thrashing is the only rem-edy by which the foul conduct of the Abolitionist can be controlled . . . it will be very well to give Seward a double dose at least ev-ery other day until it operates on his political bowels." [5]

With public opinion so aroused, congressional discussion of the Brooks assault inevitably became a field day for the excited, the oratorical, and the politically ambitious. When Wilson in the Senate denounced the "brutal, murderous, and cowardly assault," Butler, who had hurried to Washington in order to defend his young relative as "a man acting under sensibility and under the dictates of high honor," interrupted with: "You are a liar!" Two days later Brooks challenged Wilson to a duel, but the Massachu-setts senator scornfully declined, declaring that dueling was "the lingering relic of a barbarous civilization, which the law of the country has branded as a crime." [6]

them, he does not give sufficient recognition to the rhetoric demanded of Southern editors everywhere except in a few border cities. They were free to question the time, place, and expediency of Brook's actions, but not his correctness in fol-lowing the code duello.

[5] Schultz: *Nationalism and Sectionalism,* p. 119; Richmond *Whig* and Petersburg *Intelligencer,* clipped in Parker-Sumner Scrapbook; Richmond *En-quirer,* June 2, 1856; Richmond *Examiner,* May 30, 1856; Petersburg *South-Side Democrat,* May 24, 1856.

[6] *Cong. Globe,* 1,306, and Appendix, 631; Wilson: *Slave Power,* II, 486;

In the House the debates presented an even more threatening aspect. On June 2 the investigating committee, by a strict party vote, recommended the expulsion of Brooks and the censure of both Edmundson and Keitt; the minority, two Southerners, declared that the House had no jurisdiction and should express no opinion on the subject. The reports excited heated debate. Every member of the South Carolina delegation in Congress felt it his duty to defend Brooks. Republicans filled the pages of the *Congressional Globe* in reply. The angriest of the Northern speeches was that by Anson Burlingame, a friend of Sumner's, whose Boston constituency seemed likely to repudiate him in the fall election. Defiantly he charged that Brooks had stealthily approached Sumner and had struck him down "as Cain smote his brother." When Brooks promptly challenged him to a duel, Burlingame accepted—but picked as the location the Canadian side of the Niagara Falls, to which Brooks could not go unless he defied the mobs that would threaten him in New York and Philadelphia.[7]

After protracted, bitter argument, the motion to expel Brooks came to a vote on July 14. It passed the House by 121 to 95, but as the requisite two-thirds was lacking, Brooks was not expelled. The next day the House acquitted Edmundson and censured Keitt. After making defiant speeches, both South Carolina representatives promptly resigned, returned to their constituencies, and were triumphantly re-elected. Brooks was at length fined $300 in the district court at Baltimore for his assault.

· 5 ·

The vote on Brooks's expulsion revealed an ominous pattern: every Southern congressman but one voted against expulsion. The vote was a crystallization of what had become apparent in the debates. "In determining this question," one troubled representative found, "members from the South are rallying in a body to one legal conclusion, while members from the free States are concentrating with like unanimity in the other direction, as if there was any-

Elias Nason and Thomas Russell: *Life and Public Services of Henry Wilson, Late Vice-President of the United States* (Boston: B. B. Russell; 1876), p. 188.

[7] *Cong. Globe*, Appendix, 656; James E. Campbell: "Sumner—Brooks—Burlingame, or, The Last of the Great Challenges," *Ohio Archaeological and Historical Quarterly*, XXXIV (1925), 435–73, an article sharply hostile to Burlingame.

thing in climate, latitude, or longitude, which ought to control the judgment of a lawyer in determining a legal question." [8]

The same polarization had already appeared in newspaper opinion and in public and private reactions to the assault. To thoughtful observers it was apparent that something dangerous was happening to the American Union when the two sections no longer spoke the same language, but employed rival sets of clichés to describe the Brooks-Sumner affair.

In Southern parlance, Preston Brooks had inflicted a caning, or a whipping, upon that blackguard Sumner in order to chastise him for his unprovoked insults to the hoary-headed Senator Butler and for his foul-mouthed denunciation of South Carolina.[9] There was no conspiracy, and Brooks had no coadjutors. He acted not for political reasons, but solely to redress a personal wrong. In caning Sumner, he neither violated the privileges of the Senate nor broke the Constitutional guarantee of free speech to congressmen.[1] His weapon was nothing but a common walking stick, such as gentlemen frequently use. After sufficiently warning Sumner, Brooks lightly struck him across the face with a blow that was but a tap, intended to put him on his guard. As Sumner promptly rose to defend himself, Brooks naturally applied the stick with more force. After the first blow, Sumner bellowed like a bull calf and quickly fell cringing to the floor, an inanimate lump of cowardice. Though Sumner suffered only flesh wounds, he absented himself from the Senate because of mortification of feeling and wounded

[8] *Cong. Globe*, Appendix, 822.

[9] Virtually every word in these next paragraphs might well be put in quotation marks, or in multiple quotation marks, for all the key phrases constantly recurred in the public and congressional discussions of the attack.

[1] Though my purpose here is to show what men thought and felt, I am obliged to add that this contention was most dubious. Brooks's defenders argued that the Senate was not in session when he struck Sumner; that he chastised the senator not for words uttered in debate, but for libelous words printed in advance of delivery and read, not heard, by Brooks; and that in any event senatorial privilege, as guaranteed in the Constitution (Art. I, sec. 6) does not cover defamation of character. But American courts have consistently ruled (4 Mass. 27; 103 U.S. Reports 200; 341 U.S. Reports 367) that the immunity of congressional speech is absolute. See Leon R. Yankwich: "The Immunity of Congressional Speech—Its Origin, Meaning and Scope," *University of Pennsylvania Law Review*, XCIX (1950–1), 960–77. But, for dissenting views see *Stockdale* v. *Hansard* (112 Eng. Rep. 1,112); Story's *Commentaries on the Constitution*, sec. 863; Justice W. O. Douglas, in *Tenney* v. *Brandhove* (341 U.S. Reports 381), and Oliver P. Field: "The Constitutional Privileges of Legislators," *Minnesota Law Review*, IX (1924–5), 442–6.

pride. Brooks, with conspicuous gallantry, promptly reappeared in the House of Representatives, ready to face all accusers.

In Northern language, the affair bore an entirely different aspect. Bully Brooks had made a brutal assault upon Sumner with a bludgeon. The act had no provocation; on the contrary, Sumner for years had silently endured a harsh stream of unparliamentary personalities from Butler and other defenders of the slave power.[2] The alleged cause of the assault, Sumner's speech, was marked by the classic purity of its language and the nobility of its sentiments. The fearlessness of Sumner's ideas had, in fact, been what singled him out for assassination. Brooks was the mere tool of the slave-holding oligarchy. While fellow conspirators gathered around him to prevent interference, the South Carolinian stealthily approached Sumner and committed his brutal and barbarous outrage upon an unarmed man. Though Sumner courageously tried to defend himself,[3] the ruffian took advantage of his defenseless position and of the surprise, beat Sumner senseless, and continued to strike him after he collapsed on the floor. For most Northerners a versifier in the New York *Evening Post* summarized the matter:

> Who, like a caitiff, base and low,.
> Came treacherously upon his foe,
> And stunned him with a murderous blow?
>   *Preston Brooks!*

. . .

[2] Wilson and Representative W. S. Damrell, of Massachusetts, both made elaborate attempts to prove that in the matter of personalities Butler was the aggressor. (*Cong. Globe*, 1,400–3, and Appendix, 872–5). They showed that Butler in previous debates had referred to Sumner as a "plunging agitator," a "rhetorical advocate," guilty of "sickly sentimentality" and of "flagrant misrepresentation" of history and that he had once declared: "I know [Sumner] is not a tactician, and I shall not take advantage of the infirmity of a man who does not know half his time exactly what he is about." On the whole, however, their argument is not convincing. Butler had indeed said sharp things about Sumner, but they were intended to make him appear ridiculous, not to assail his moral character; in any case, they were made in the course of extemporaneous debate when Butler may have been carried away by his own rhetoric. Sumner's attack on Butler, on the other hand, was carefully and deliberately prepared in advance, and it made inexcusable personal references to Butler.

[3] After some Northern papers expressed "contempt for a man who has not spunk enough for either resistance or revenge," Sumner's friends heavily stressed this point. Sumner later declared that he would "most certainly" have defended himself "to the best of my ability, and the last extremity," had he been able. Letter of Jane G. Swisshelm to New York *Tribune*, Aug. 23, 1856, clipping in Sumner Scrapbooks. According to Wilson, as Sumner was led bleeding from

> *Who, when his victim senseless lay,*
> *Cold and inanimate as clay,*
> *His brutal hand refused to stay?*
>   *Preston Brooks!*

While Brooks's coadjutors triumphantly led their champion out of the Senate, Sumner lay prostrate and suffering, his head a mass of beaten flesh, a martyr to the cause of Liberty and Free Speech.

Northern spokesmen drew a significant contrast between the character of the assailant and the assailed. Brooks, they said, was a coward. When Burlingame called his bluff by accepting his challenge to a duel, the South Carolinian quickly showed his true metal:

> *To Canada Brooks was asked to go,*
> *To waste a pound of powder or so,*
> *But he quickly answered, No; No; No.*
> *For I'm afraid, afraid, afraid,*
>   *Bully Brooks's afraid.*

What else could one expect, Ralph Waldo Emerson asked, from a product of the slave system, where man was but "an animal, given to pleasure, frivolous, irritable, spending his days in hunting and practising with deadly weapons to defend himself against his slaves and against his companions brought up in the same idle and dangerous way?" Sumner, on the other hand, was the ripe product of Northern scholarship and culture. No enemy could accuse him of "drunkenness, nor debauchery, nor job, nor peculation, nor rapacity, nor personal aims of any kind." Sumner, declared Emerson, in the words Bishop Burnet had applied to Isaac Newton, was "the whitest soul I ever knew."

When the two sections no longer spoke the same language, shared the same moral code, or obeyed the same law, when their representatives clashed in bloody conflict in the halls of Congress, thinking men North and South began to wonder how the Union could longer endure. "I do not see how a barbarous community and a civilized community can constitute one state," Emerson gravely declared. "I think we must get rid of slavery, or we must get rid of freedom." [4]

---

the Senate chamber, he declared: *"When I recover I will meet them again, and put it to them again."* Boston *Courier*, June 10, 1856.

[4] Rusk: *Emerson*, p. 389; *The Liberator*, XXVI (June 6, 1856), 91.

CHAPTER XII

The Vacant Chair

W HILE CONGRESS and the public were angrily debating the
Brooks assault, Sumner was trying to regain his health. It was
more than three years before he was able regularly to resume his
Senate duties. During this unhappy period he wandered restlessly
from one health resort to another, fretting impatiently at the slowness of his recovery and experimenting with any cure, however
rigorous, that might promote it. These three years were filled with
exciting developments in national politics: James Buchanan was
inaugurated; the Supreme Court handed down the Dred Scott decision; Douglas broke with the administration over its Kansas policy; Abraham Lincoln challenged the "Little Giant" in his home
state; John Brown's raid sent panic through the South. On all
these subjects Sumner's voice was unheard in the Senate chamber. His only consolation for his enforced abstinence from politics
was his conviction that "to every sincere lover of civilization his
vacant chair was a perpetual speech." [1]

· 1 ·

When Sumner was led bleeding from the Senate chamber on May
22, 1856, nobody anticipated that his recovery would be thus protracted. To be sure, his injuries were painful. He had three
wounds on his head: one very slight and requiring no medical attention; another on the left side, "two and a quarter inches long,
cut to the bone—cut under, as it were, and very ragged"; and still
another on the right side, "rather in front," not quite two inches
long, cut also to the bone. In addition, he had bruises on both his

---

[1] Sumner: *Works*, IV, 409.

hands, on his arms, and on his shoulders, and there was a heavy black bruise across his thighs, made as he wrenched his desk from its bolts.[2]

During the first three days after the assault, Sumner seemed to be recovering rapidly. Though he remained in bed most of the time, under the care of his brother George, who hastily came down from Boston to act as nurse, Dr. Cornelius Boyle, his physician, thought that he was "doing very well." Sumner's injuries, the doctor told congressional investigators a few days later, were "simply . . . flesh wounds"—"nothing but flesh wounds." They did not, he declared, "necessarily confine him one moment. . . . Mr. Sumner might have taken a carriage and driven as far as Baltimore on the next day [after the beating] without any injury."[3]

Dr. Marshall S. Perry, who was sent down from Boston by wealthy Republican manufacturer George L. Stearns so as to be sure Sumner would receive the best medical treatment, also found the patient in very satisfactory shape on May 25. The wound on the left side of his head had nearly healed, but "in the one on the right side there was perhaps an inch, or three quarters of an inch, which had not adhered." Troubled by "a pulpy feeling" on the right side of Sumner's head and by the senator's "unnaturally excited state," Perry recommended that he keep very quiet and get complete rest.

On the following day Sumner still appeared to be progressing satisfactorily, though the wound on the right side of his head began suppurating. He felt able to make a statement to the House investigating committee, which called at his rooms. That evening Dr. Boyle "applied collodion, which prevented the escape of pus." He was still "pretty comfortable" on the morning of May 27, though he complained of more pain. Giddings, who visited him that afternoon, found him sitting up. "His countenance appeared natural, and his conversation was cheerful." With little or no fever, he "insisted that he would resume his seat in a few days."[4]

That evening he suffered a relapse. Dr. Perry found him

---

[2] *Sumner Assault*, pp. 51, 55.
[3] Ibid., pp. 51–3.
[4] *Sumner Assault*, pp. 68–9; undated statement of Dr. Perry, Sumner MSS.; Perry: *Case of Hon. Charles Sumner* (a communication to the Boston Society for Medical Improvement, Dec. 8, 1856; 7-page pamphlet in Parker-Sumner Scrapbook), pp. 1–2; *Cong. Globe*, 34 Cong., 1 Sess., Appendix, 1,119.

with "more fever than at any time before, skin hotter than natural —pulse between 80 and 90, fuller and harder than at any time before." During the evening his pain, "principally confined to the posterior part of the head," became quite intense, and, restless and uneasy, he passed a sleepless night. The next morning Dr. Boyle found Sumner "excited and feverish, his pulse about a hundred." The glands on the back of his head and neck had begun to swell. Almost certainly septicemia had set in. Dr. Boyle decided that the patient's discomfort resulted from the "cuticle" (a solution of gun cotton and chloroform) he had applied to the wound on the previous day, and, removing it, found "about a table-spoonful of pus, . . . which had gathered under the scalp." He then poulticed the wound, and Sumner, under an opiate, was able to get several hours of sleep.[5]

At this point George Sumner dismissed Dr. Boyle. He felt that the treatment of his brother had been unskillful, and perhaps he was displeased when the doctor told congressional investigators that his patient suffered only "flesh wounds."[6] Dr. Perry took complete charge of the case, and he promptly called in Dr. Harvey Lindsly, a Washington physician, as consultant. They permitted the wound to suppurate freely, and soon Sumner felt "very nearly free from pain in the head—more calm and composed than he had been." On May 29 George was able to write Longfellow: "The crisis has passed and our noble fellow is safe."[7]

During the next two weeks Sumner "was very weak, had some fever, especially when excited, and was confined mostly to his bed." He felt debilitated; he "lost flesh and strength, his appetite was irregular, and his nights wakeful—sometimes lying awake all night, or when sleeping, disturbed." Anemia had probably followed his septicemia.[8] Sumner no longer complained of much pain from the wounds on his head, which were healing over, but he began exhibiting other, more disturbing symptoms. A

[5] Perry's Statement, Sumner MSS.; *Sumner Assault,* pp. 69–70.
[6] George Sumner claimed that he dismissed Boyle before hearing of his testimony. *Cong. Globe,* 34 Cong., 1 Sess., 1,438. Southerners insisted that he did so because Boyle would not exaggerate the nature of Sumner's wounds. Ibid., Appendix, 806; New York *Herald,* June 22, 1856.
[7] Perry's Statement, Sumner MSS.; George Sumner to Longfellow, 4 a.m., Thursday [May 29, 1856], Longfellow MSS.
[8] For this diagnosis, as for much of the other medical opinion incorporated in this chapter, I am indebted to Dr. Julia L. Schneider, of the Neurological Institute of New York.

neuralgic pain in the back of his head came on in paroxysms. He had "a feeling of oppressive weight or pressure on the brain," which he repeatedly described as "a 56-pounds weight" upon his skull. "Increased sensibility of the spinal cord, and a sense of weakness in the small of the back" made his walking so irregular and uncertain that "after slight efforts he would lose almost entire control of the lower extremities." [9]

By the middle of June, Sumner was able to move to Francis P. Blair's tree-shaded home at Silver Spring, on the outskirts of Washington, where he could escape some of the capital's midsummer heat. For a while he "lay 22 hours out of the 24 on his back," but by June 23 he was "able to totter a mile around the garden . . . hoping daily for strength which comes slowly." But Silver Spring was too close to Washington. When Sumner went into the capital, on June 25, he overexerted himself and had a relapse. When he remained at the Blairs', numerous visitors came to see him, and he was "exhausted by his efforts to entertain them." On July 4 Seward found him much prostrated, his elasticity and vigor gone, moving "like a man whose sight is dimmed, and his limbs stiffened with age." [1]

It was clear that Sumner needed less exciting and more salubrious surroundings, and, after arranging his affairs in Washington, he left for the North. At Philadelphia he consulted the distinguished physician, Dr. Caspar Wister, who found that Sumner was in "a condition of extreme nervous exhaustion, his circulation feeble, and in fact every vital power alarmingly sunken." At Dr. Wister's advice, he went to Cape May, where for a week he seemed to do very well, though the water was too cool for bathing, but an unaccountable setback sent him seeking other remedies. In early August he found the secluded health resort of Dr. R. M. Jackson, high in the mountains at Cresson, Pennsylvania, where he was put on a regimen of "judicious diet, mild tonic agents, constant exercise in the open air on horse back or in a carriage." [2]

[9] Perry: *Case of Sumner*, p. 2.
[1] Smith: *Blair Family*, I, 348–9; Sumner to Howe, June 23 [1856], Sumner MSS.; A. B. Johnson to George Sumner, July 7, 1856, ibid.; Seward: *Seward at Washington, 1846–1861*, p. 282.
[2] Wister to M. S. Perry, Oct. 14, 1856, in Perry: *Case of Sumner*, p. 3; R. M. Jackson to Henry Wilson [Sept. 1856], Sumner MSS.

Sumner still gave some outward evidence of illness. Though his general health seemed "partially restored, his appetite reasonably good, and his mind ever glowing," he "had the appearance of a man who had been sick for a length [of] time, and was still extremely unwell." He had lost weight; his lips and face were pale; there was "a slight redness around the cicatrices of the recently healed cuts, also some morbid sensibility on pressure." Most conspicuous of all was his "tottering and uncertain gait"; he had difficulty in rising from a chair, and he walked like a man "creeping through a darkened chamber under the influence of a paroxysm of nervous headache." [3]

With the invigorating mountain air, the exercise, and Dr. Jackson's mild remedies, these outward symptoms gradually began to disappear, leaving Sumner to wrestle with more subtle and frightening warnings of illness. Walking (but not horseback riding) or the slightest mental exertion continued to produce the sense of pressure on the top of his head. His thigh muscles continued to be weak. When fatigued, he often involuntarily relived the trauma of the assault. His secretary described his symptoms: "At times he feels as tho' the blows were raining upon his head again; then will feel a numbness in the scalp; then again acute pains; then a sense of exhaustion that prevents any physical or mental effort." [4]

Restless and unable to sleep at night, Sumner feared that these symptoms might mean that he was losing his mind. He had always dreaded incapacitating disease more than death itself.[5] Now, he told Giddings: "I sometimes am led to apprehend that I may yet be doomed to that heaviest of all afflictions, to spend my time on earth in a living sepulcher." George Sumner's indiscreet reminiscences of mental cases he had seen in Paris hospitals undoubtedly contributed to Sumner's state of mind. So did Dr. Wister's disclosure that he was uncertain as to whether Sumner's brain "was deranged *organically* or only *functionally*." "Had it been the former," Sumner wrote Howe, "then, as you know, death would have been my best friend." [6]

[3] Rochester *Democrat*, Aug. 19, 1856; R. M. Jackson to Henry Wilson [Sept. 1856], Sumner MSS.; Jane G. Swisshelm to New York *Tribune*, Aug. 23, 1856, clipping in Sumner Scrapbooks.

[4] A. B. Johnson to George Sumner, July 7, 1856, Sumner MSS.

[5] See above, p. 97.

[6] *Cong. Globe*, 34 Cong., 1 Sess., Appendix, 1,119; Sumner to Howe, July 2, and Sept. 26, 1856, Sumner MSS.

In this state of anxiety, Sumner closely watched his symptoms, and every weakness, every ache, every bout of insomnia
reinforced his troubled conviction that his brain was affected.
After a month he found the isolation of Cresson unbearable and,
against Dr. Jackson's advice, he returned to Philadelphia. He explained that he wanted to be nearer his Senate duties; perhaps
he also wanted something to distract his mind.

The change brought only partial relief. Though he felt very
comfortable some days, his nerves were "still painfully sensitive,"
his nights were often sleepless, and his "legs and arms seemed all
jangled." "I left the Mountain prematurely," he confessed to
Dr. Jackson, "before my system had hardened into health, and
have had some weakness and nervous sensibility since, incapacitating me for work." Dr. Perry, who re-examined Sumner at the
end of September, concluded: "From the time of the assault to
the present, Mr. Sumner has not been in a situation to expose
himself to mental or bodily excitement without the risk of losing
his *life*." [7]

· 2 ·

These sufferings, of course, did not go unobserved. Newspaper
correspondents followed Sumner from one health resort to another and filled Northern newspapers with stories of interviews
with "the Martyr Senator." So great was popular enthusiasm
for Sumner that the New York *Tribune* and the Cleveland
Leader urged that he be named as the vice-presidential candidate on the Republican ticket, along with John C. Frémont, who
was slated to fill the first place. At the Republican national convention in June Sumner received thirty-five votes in the balloting
for vice-presidential nominees—a sizable tribute, though considerably less than the number cast for Illinois's Abraham Lincoln or for New Jersey's William L. Dayton, who was nominated. [8]

Sumner had no desire to be Vice-President, but he was
"much in hopes that some benefit to the anti-slavery cause might

[7] Sumner to Dana, Sept. 16, 1856, Dana MSS.; Sumner to Howe, Sept. 11,
1856, Sumner MSS.; Sumner to R. M. Jackson, Oct. 11, 1856, MS. owned by
Mrs. Edward C. Reeve, Clearfield, Pennsylvania; Statement of Dr. M. S. Perry,
Sept. 30, 1856, Sumner MSS.

[8] New York *Tribune*, June 17, 1856; Buffalo *Commercial Advertiser*,
June 18, 1856; Cleveland *Leader*, June 11, 1856; New York *Herald*, June 20,
1856.

accrue from the affair" with Brooks. With his faith in the power of oratory, he longed to take the stump for the Republican candidates, but his physicians absolutely forbade all public appearances. The advice of Republican politicians agreed with that of the doctors; they shrewdly realized that Sumner whole had less popular appeal than Sumner wounded. Reluctantly the senator abandoned his hope of campaigning. "Never before could I exert so much influence by speaking," he lamented in October; "and now nearly five months have been consumed—a large slice of human life—and I have been compelled to silence." He was obliged to content himself with writing spirited public letters endorsing "those candidates who are openly and unequivocally hostile" to the criminal plot "to subjugate Kansas and install the slave Oligarchy in the permanent control of the National Goverment." [9]

Massachusetts Republicans wanted to take the fullest advantage of public interest in Sumner. They did not support his vice-presidential candidacy because they were unwilling to lose so overwhelmingly popular a figure from state politics. Instead they talked for a time of capitalizing upon Sumner's martyrdom by running him for governor; thus simultaneously they could give "a tremendous rebuke of S. Carolina and the South" and could kill off the sinister Henry J. Gardner. Only the senator's firm refusal quashed the scheme. [1]

Within limits Sumner was willing to help his party. As it seemed probable that Anson Burlingame was going to be defeated in his fight for re-election, Sumner, who privately distrusted the young congressman and thought that by accepting Brooks's challenge he had "deliberately discarded the standards of Northern civilization to adopt the standards of Southern barbarism," staged an affectionate interview with him at Cresson, where newspaper correspondents thought that the senator and

[9] Seward: *Seward at Washington, 1846–1861*, p. 272; Sumner to Wendell Phillips, Oct. 7, 1856; MS. in private hands (photostat supplied through the courtesy of Prof. Irving Bartlett, of M. I. T.); Sumner to the chairman of the meeting at Faneuil Hall, Oct. 29, 1856, photostat in Alexander William Armour MSS. Cf. Sumner to W. M. Whitehead et al., Oct. 10, 1856, C. G. Leland MSS.

[1] Adams, Diary, June 16–17, 1856, Adams MSS.; John Bigelow to Sumner [Aug. 22, 1856], Sumner MSS.; E. D. Moore to Wilson, Aug. 9, 1856, ibid. See also James Lodge to Sumner, June 10, 1856, ibid.; Boston *Post*, Aug. 4, 1856; J. G. Fuller to N. P. Banks, Aug. 14, 1856, Banks MSS.; Anderson: "Slavery Issue," p. 210.

the representative acted "like father and son." [2] When not even a strong public letter endorsing Burlingame seemed sufficient, Sumner yielded to heavy pressure and, against the advice of his physicians, returned to Boston, ostensibly to receive a giant public reception, actually to promote the chances of Republican candidates.

On November 3 most of Boston joined enthusiastically in what the newspapers called "an earnest, heartfelt ovation to the ORATOR, STATESMAN, the SCHOLAR, and 'CHAMPION OF FREEDOM.'" The procession started from the Brookline house of Amos A. Lawrence, who for the time forgot his political hostility to Sumner, and moved to the Boston city line, where the aged Josiah Quincy, on the same spot where he had welcomed Lafayette as the honored guest of the city in 1824, greeted Sumner "as one to whom the deliverance, which we hope may yet be destined to our country will be greatly due." Then the parade proceeded toward Beacon Hill. Many homes and stores were decorated with greetings: "MASSACHUSETTS LOVES, HONORS, AND WILL SUSTAIN HER NOBLE SUMNER"; "Welcome, thrice Welcome"; "May 22, 1856" (in black); "WELCOME, FREEDOM'S DEFENDER." As Sumner's carriage passed, "spontaneous cheers would rise from the crowds, and ladies waved their handkerchiefs, making a very animated scene."

At the State house Governor Gardner welcomed the senator. This, he took pains to declare, was "no political ovation," but he pledged that Massachusetts "does stand by you today. She will stand by you tomorrow; (enthusiastic cheers) and she will stand by you, in her defense, forever (loud cheering)."

Sumner, who still looked "like an invalid—pale and suffering from weakness," replied "in a very low tone, and was evidently laboring under great physical disability." After only a few sentences he had to stop, and handed the remainder of his intended remarks to the reporters for newspaper publication. His ostensibly nonpartisan address of thanks for the welcome he had received actually made two principal points: that Sumner, though still an invalid, expected soon to "be permitted, with unimpaired vigor, to resume all the responsibilities of his position";

[2] Sumner to Giddings, July 22, 1856, Sumner MSS.; Jane G. Swisshelm to New York *Tribune*, Aug. 23, 1856, clipping in Sumner Scrapbooks.

and that the opponents of the Republican party in Massachusetts were "in sympathy, open or disguised, with the vulgar enemy, quickening everywhere the lash of the taskmaster, and helping forward the Satanic carnival" of slavery.[3]

Though Sumner suffered a relapse immediately after this public appearance and once again reported his "brain, shoulders and back all sensitive," his exertions were not in vain. Frémont received an overwhelming majority in Massachusetts. Burlingame was re-elected by the narrowest of margins. What was more important, an immense amount of enthusiasm had been generated for Sumner himself. As the Boston *Atlas* explained: "The personal appearance of Mr. Sumner, so haggard and careworn, the eye, once so beaming, now languid, the healthful cheek, now pale and thin, and the dark lines around the brow, chilled the hearts of all who beheld him. . . . Strong, athletic men, unaccustomed to emotion, drew stifled breaths, and were not ashamed to let it be known that they, too, suffered with Mr. Sumner." All this emotion had an immediate political point, as when the Boston *Herald*, hitherto opposed to Sumner, now changed its policy and urged: "If now we were a member of the legislature, we would be unwilling to enter upon any business after the organization, till Charles Sumner was re-elected to the seat where he was assaulted; we should not care what his political opinions were; if we disagreed with them ten thousand times more than we ever did, still would we give him our earnest and hearty support." [4]

Though Sumner professed total indifference to his re-election, he was in fact very keenly interested. He kept a close watch on the intrigues of Gardner, again re-elected governor in 1856 with Republican connivance, of Burlingame, and of others who aspired to succeed him. Though he sometimes talked in private of resigning his Senate seat, in order to go to Europe and regain his

[3] This account is based upon Sumner: *Works*, IV, 368–85, the Boston *Advertiser*, Nov. 4, 1856, Boston *Herald*, Nov. 2, 1890, and reports in the Boston *Bee, Journal, Transcript, Atlas, Courier*, and *Traveller*, clipped in Sumner Scrapbooks. I cannot verify the story that all but two of the houses on Beacon Street were tightly shuttered during the reception to show disapproval of Sumner. Dawes: *Sumner*, p. 120.

[4] Sumner to Howe, Wednesday [1856], MS., Huntington Lib.; Boston *Herald*, Nov. 5, 1856.

health, he always accompanied such suggestions with a reminder of "Gardner's intrigues, and the prospect of putting into
the vacancy a lower toned and unfaithful man." He spoke of his
willingness to give up his office if only Charles Francis Adams
could be his successor—a choice he well knew was politically
impossible—and then quickly permitted himself to be persuaded
that resignation would embarrass his party. Learning that Gardner was promoting a rumor that he was an incurable invalid, the
senator quietly dropped a passage from his remarks at the Boston
reception suggesting "the probability that he might not be able to
take his seat the next session," and, though actually very unwell,
he announced, just as the new legislature assembled in January
1857, that he would resume his duties by the end of the month.
"All of us must persevere," he wrote to correspondents who expressed sympathy for his continued feebleness, "and I assure you
that I have no intention of abandoning the field of duty in which
I have been placed." [5]

Sumner could remain publicly aloof from the re-election
contest because his friends were working assiduously for him.
The most effective of these was that "*straight* and *impracticable*
Republican," Frank Bird, a paper manufacturer of East Walpole,
who, as a friend said, could not "be coaxed, bought, told nor
bullied." Active in antislavery politics since 1848, Bird had
started having lunch every Saturday with John A. Andrew, the
young Free Soil lawyer, James W. Stone, one of the Free Soil
ward bosses in Boston, and William S. Robinson, the Boston correspondent of the Springfield *Republican*, in order to talk over
political prospects. Other antislavery stalwarts, such as Howe,
George L. Stearns, and Wilson, had joined them, and, moving to
Parker's Hotel, they held a kind of irregular weekly antislavery
caucus, attended by as many of its thirty or forty members as
might be in town and might want to share the simple Saturday
lunches, which cost each man a dollar, with wine extra. By 1856
the "Bird Club," as the group was called, exerted an immense, if
informal, influence in Massachusetts politics, and fortunately
for Sumner it enthusiastically supported his re-election by nomi-

[5] Adams, Diary, Oct. 11, Nov. 8, 13, and 20, and Dec. 25, 1856, Adams MSS.;
Sumner to E. C. Dawes, Dec. 11, 1856, MS., William L. Clements Lib.

nating pro-Sumner candidates for the legislature, by spying out Gardner's plots, and by careful canvassing of the legislators.[6]

When the new legislature met in January 1857, Bird's planning brought prompt results. Announcing that "there was one particular thing for which the members of the present Legislature were sent here, and that was to choose a United States Senator," the Republicans in the House of Representatives forced a vote on January 9, even before Governor Gardner could send in his inaugural message, which they feared might contain distracting proposals. Out of the 345 votes cast, Sumner received all but twelve. Four days later, against protests over their unseemly haste, Republicans in the Senate adopted a rule for viva-voce voting on the senatorial election, and, as public opinion could thus be brought to bear upon each member, Sumner received the unanimous vote of the upper house.[7]

Welcoming the vote as a "sign, that the people of Massachusetts, forgetting ancient party hates, have at last come together in support of a sacred cause, compared with which the fate of any public servant is of small account," Sumner began his second six-year term in the Senate in his favorite role of the statesman called by popular acclaim to his duties. "The election here has not cost me one moment's solicitude," he assured Seward. "I sought nobody, and said nothing, pursuing now the course which I adopted six years ago. . . . What has been done has been the utterance of the State, without a hint from me." [8]

· 3 ·

If Sumner's health was of great concern to his friends, both personal and political, it was of equal interest to his opponents, who from the beginning found something suspicious about his invalidism. As it was part of the standard Southern interpretation of the assault that Brooks had only "chastised" Sumner with a "light

[6] Howe to Palfrey, Aug. 10 [1859], Palfrey MSS.; John A. Andrew's endorsement, on P. W. Chandler to Andrew [Mar. 1862], Andrew MSS. On Bird and the "Bird Club" see: Stearns: *Cambridge Sketches*, pp. 162–79; Schurz: *Reminiscences*, II, 130; Pearson: *Andrew*, I, 58–60; Harrington: *Banks*, p. 41; Boston *Commonwealth*, July 29, and Aug. 5, 1865, Nov. 5, 1870.

[7] Clippings from Boston *Advertiser* and Boston *Atlas*, Sumner Scrapbooks.

[8] Sumner: *Works*, IV, 394; Seward: *Seward at Washington, 1846–1861*, p. 296.

walking cane," proslavery congressmen never accepted as a fact that Sumner had been seriously injured. Their suspicions were confirmed when Dr. Boyle testified to the House investigating committee on May 27 that Sumner's injuries were "nothing but flesh wounds." When Senator Butler spoke in defense of Brooks on June 12, he argued: "For anything that appears in that testimony, if [Sumner] had been an officer of the Army, and had not appeared on the next day [after the attack] on the battle-field, he would have deserved to be cashiered." [9]

After Republicans made "Bleeding Sumner" one of the principal issues in the 1856 presidential campaign, supporters of both Buchanan, the Democratic nominee, and Fillmore, the American candidate, openly charged that the senator was shamming. His wounds, they noted, offered a most convenient political martyrdom. As Sumner was not too ill in June to prepare a carefully revised edition of "The Crime Against Kansas," the Boston *Courier* decided that he was "playing the political possum." In July the Washington *Union*, the official organ of the Pierce administration, charged that Sumner's wounds were entirely healed, but that he stayed away from the Senate because of "his wounded pride and his irrepressible anger and indignation." The Boston *Post* suggested that Sumner's doctors were conspiring to picture the senator as an invalid until just prior to election, when he could reappear before the public and capitalize "very much upon the interest his protracted absence from public duty [would] excite to see and hear him, for party effect." By fall the Washington *Union* had uncovered an even worse plot: physicians were "nursing the disease, lest it should die a natural death," because Sumner was "resolved not to recover until after the next Senatorial election in Massachusetts." Noting that Sumner miraculously recuperated just in time to address the citizens of Boston on the day before the elections, the Philadelphia *News* concluded: "The Senatorial sophomore has no doubt done more by playing possum than if he had stumped the entire North with re-hashes and plagiarisms from Demosthenes." [1]

Sumner was furious over these accusations. "While thus

---

[9] *Cong. Globe*, 34 Cong., 1 Sess., Appendix, 625. Cf. ibid., 806.

[1] Boston *Courier*, June 21, 1856; Boston *Post*, Aug. 21, 1856; Washington *Union*, and Philadelphia *News*, quoted in *The Liberator*, XXVI (July 25, 1856), 118, and XXVI (Nov. 28, 1856), 189.

suffering for more than four months," he exclaimed in September, "I have been charged with the ignoble deed of *shamming illness!* It seems to me, if any thing could add to the character of the original act it is this supplementary assault on my character." Republican politicians were also seriously troubled over these slanders, which seemed to attract much credence in the Northwest, and they urged Sumner to collect affidavits from his other physicians to counteract the influence of Dr. Boyle's damaging testimony. Wilson helped Sumner gather statements from Dr. Lindsly, Dr. Wister, Dr. Perry, and Dr. Jackson, all declaring that Sumner's brain had "received a shock from which it might not recover for months" and all emphatically affirming that Sumner was unable to resume his Senate duties. This combined medical statement, Sumner himself declared in private, "was specially intended for Indiana, where the calumny had been employed; and . . . it was necessary that it should be circulated before the Election. . . ." [2]

The publication did not down the suspicion of fraud. Throughout the next three years, while Sumner was generally absent from the Senate, hostile newspapers carried occasional stories that he was "malingering" with a "sham sickness." Sumner, declared the New York *Atlas* in 1858, "is rapidly acquiring the reputation of a charlatan, who, preceded by his servant in motley, with a trumpet and drum, cries his injuries and sufferings in the cause of freedom as saleable wares, for the purpose of putting money in his purse." "This most ridiculous of humbugs," announced another editor, "fairly stinks in the nostrils of the American people." [3]

This accusation, which has found some defenders among later historians of pronounced antiabolitionist sympathies,[4] rests upon very flimsy evidence. The only medical testimony that sup-

---

[2] Sumner to Mrs. Hamilton Fish, Sept. 27, 1856, Fish MSS.; Lyman Trumbull to George Sumner, June 13, 1856, Sumner MSS.; W. H. Furness to R. M. Jackson, Oct. 10, 1856, MS. in the possession of Mrs. Edward C. Reeve; Sumner to R. M. Jackson, Oct. 11, 1856, ibid. The statements of Drs. Lindsly, Perry, Wister, and Jackson, all dated in September 1856, are in the Sumner MSS.

[3] New York *Atlas*, quoted in *The Liberator*, XXVIII (July 2, 1858), p. 105; Richmond *Whig*, Dec. 27, 1856; Charleston *Courier*, quoted in Boston *Advertiser*, Sept. 16, 1858.

[4] E.g., Milton: *Eve of Conflict*, pp. 236–7. Avery Craven: *The Coming of the Civil War* (New York: Charles Scribner's Sons; 1942), pp. 367–8, is slightly less hostile to Sumner.

ports it is the statement of Dr. Boyle, a Southern physician, strongly opposed in politics to Sumner and very friendly to both Senator Butler and Preston Brooks. Even if Dr. Boyle had been an unprejudiced observer, his testimony as to Sumner's superficial wounds, lack of fever, etc., would have only limited medical value, for it was given on May 27, before septicemia was apparent. In his frequently overlooked testimony on the following day, Dr. Boyle added that Sumner had begun to run a fever, that infection had set in, and that he had prescribed opiates.[5] If Dr. Boyle's testimony is accepted in its entirety, it proves only what no one ever denied: that Sumner seemed to be recovering quite satisfactorily during the first few days after the assault, but that infection set in on the evening of May 27.

Opposed to Dr. Boyle's slight evidence are elaborate, sworn statements by the four physicians who were in charge of Sumner's case from May 27 until the end of the year. Dr. Harvey Lindsly declared that when he came on the case, Sumner was unable to resume his public duties, and that he had urged him to go to the seashore or to the mountains to recuperate. Dr. Caspar Wister, of the eminent Philadelphia family of physicians, opposed in politics to Sumner, made an early diagnosis that Sumner's recovery depended upon his "entire abstraction from all excitement" and, on re-examining him in late September, held that he was "still an invalid," requiring constant medical care. Dr. R. M. Jackson, who was a Democrat, swore that Sumner was "still extremely unwell" when he came to the Pennsylvania mountains and that he left Cresson prematurely, "still an invalid." Dr. Marshall S. Perry, one of the most respected doctors in Boston, was positive that Sumner was so badly injured that mental or bodily exertion would cost him his life.[6]

[5] *Sumner Assault*, pp. 50–4, 71. When George Sumner peremptorily dismissed Dr. Boyle, the physician grew very angry at what he considered a slur upon his professional integrity, and tried to collect other evidence to prove that Sumner had not been dangerously injured. The best he could do was to get an offhand remark from Dr. Lindsly to the effect that there was "not much the matter" with Sumner—an opinion that Dr. Lindsly presently contradicted in a affidavit—and a letter from Dr. Thomas Miller, who helped drain Sumner's wounds on May 30, declaring that he did not think "Mr. Sumner in any danger." *Cong. Globe*, 34 Cong., 1 Sess., 1,414.

[6] The statements of these four doctors, dated Sept. 22–30, 1856, are in the Sumner MSS. Dr. Jackson, who was postmaster at Cresson, was removed by the Pierce administration for his statement that Sumner was an invalid. Sumner to R. M. Jackson, Dec. 20, 1856, in the possession of Mrs. Edward C. Reeve.

There is a notable lack of evidence to support the theory that Sumner was pretending to be ill. Certainly not one word he ever uttered or wrote, even to his closest friends and to his brother, could be interpreted as lending support to such a charge. If there was a plan to have Sumner feign sickness until after the 1856 elections, somebody must have been in on the plot. But there is not a known scrap of evidence, in the correspondence of any of his friends, in the papers of any Republican leader, or even in any belated reminiscence, which lends credence to the theory. If there was a plot, it was one of the best kept secrets in American history.

Those who charged Sumner with shamming relied upon logic as defective as their evidence. If he was pretending invalidism in order to aid the Frémont campaign or to promote his own re-election to the Senate—and there is no question but that his illness was skillfully exploited for both purposes—surely by January 1857 the game should have been over and Sumner should have resumed his seat. In fact, Southerners were puzzled at his failure to do so. Recognizing that after 1856 neither Sumner nor the Republican party had anything to gain by continuing a charade of this kind, proslavery men changed their attack and, during the next two years, attributed Sumner's absence from Washington to embarrassment at having been detected in his sham or to cowardice.[7]

· 4 ·

If the charge that Sumner was malingering must be dismissed as illogical theorizing upon insubstantial evidence, it must be admitted that the precise nature of Sumner's ailment was mysterious.[8] He looked well in the face, his voice was as firm and manly as usual, his intellect was bright and strong; but, when he tried to rise from his chair, he had to reach out for support, and he

[7] E.g., Lieber to Hillard, Dec. 13, 1856, Lieber MSS.
[8] In the following discussion of Sumner's medical problems, I have been fortunate to secure the advice of two leading specialists, Dr. Bronson S. Ray, of the Cornell Medical Center, and Dr. Julia L. Schneider, of the Neurological Institute of New York. Giving generously of their time, both Dr. Ray and Dr. Schneider read through a 30-page memorandum I had prepared, listing in objective fashion Sumner's symptoms and the treatments prescribed for them. The judgments of these two eminent specialists, made quite independently and without any consultation between themselves, coincided at every point.

"walked with a cane and quite feebly, instead of his peculiarly vigorous stride." His progress toward recovery was disturbingly unpredictable. "Sometimes I think at last it has come," he wrote in January 1857, "and then before the day is over I am admonished that I can do but little." [9]

Disturbed over these setbacks, he postponed returning to Washington until late February, when Massachusetts businessmen demanded that he vote on the new tariff bill. Republican colleagues greeted Sumner warmly as he resumed his seat, as did the two Democratic senators from Rhode Island; the rest, including Douglas, Toombs, Slidell, and Cass, "passed and repassed Mr. Sumner's seat and neither gave nor received a look of recognition." After casting the deciding vote against a proposed increase in import duties on raw wool, a proposal naturally opposed by Massachusetts woolen manufacturers who desired cheap raw materials, Sumner felt too unwell to continue in his place. "I have sat in my seat only one day," he reported to Theodore Parker on March 1. "After a short time the torment to my system became great, and a cloud began to gather over my brain. I tottered out and took to my bed." [1]

He decided to go to Europe for his health. Delaying in Washington only long enough to be sworn in on March 4, the beginning of his second Senate term, he sailed from New York three days later. Though he was seasick, his other symptoms began to disappear. By the end of the voyage he could rise from a seat without difficulty, and, aided only by a cane, he walked the decks for hours.

Landing at Le Havre on March 21, Sumner spent the next seven months in an exhausting round of visiting and sight-seeing.[2] The twenty years that had passed since his first trip to Eu-

[9] Lydia M. Child to Whittier, Jan. 2, 1857, Child MSS.; Mary Thatcher Higginson (ed.): *Letters and Journals of Thomas Wentworth Higginson, 1846–1906* (Boston: Houghton Mifflin Co.; 1921), p. 78; Sumner to William Schouler, Jan. 6, 1857, James Schouler MSS.

[1] W. B. Spooner to Sumner, Feb. 24, 1857, Sumner MSS.; John E. Lodge to Sumner, Mar. 4, 1857, ibid.; Washington correspondence of Boston *Traveller*, Feb. 27, 1857, clipping in Sumner Scrapbooks; Pierce, III, 519. For Sumner's votes on the tariff bill see *Cong. Globe*, 34 Cong., 3 Sess., Appendix, 354, 356, 358. Cf. Edward Stanwood: *American Tariff Controversies in the Nineteenth Century* (Boston: Houghton Mifflin Co.; 1903), II, 97–108.

[2] Sumner kept a rather bare, day-by-day account of his itinerary in his Travel Journal, MS., Wellesley College. The essential portions were printed in Pierce, III, 529–55.

rope had dimmed none of his enthusiasm for historic sights or his admiration for eminent persons. Though some of the friends he had made on his former visit were dead, there were still many who remembered him and who flooded him with calls and invitations. Guizot, Lamartine, Drouyn de Lhuys, Michel Chevalier, Tocqueville, and Turgenev welcomed him in Paris. In London he had barely registered at Maurigy's Hotel, in Regent Street, when Lord Brougham and Lord Chancellor Cranworth called. The Duchess of Sutherland entreated him to make Stafford House his home; her daughter, the Duchess of Argyll, took a fond interest in Sumner's health, and, with her husband, persuaded him to pay a visit to Inverary. Nassau Senior, George Grote, Henry Reeve, Charles Kingsley, William Makepeace Thackeray, and Thomas Babington Macaulay entertained him. He met Lord Palmerston, who "seemed to have the gift of perpetual youth," lunched with Lord John Russell, and dined with William E. Gladstone. He renewed his acquaintance with Richard Cobden and met John Bright for the first time.

During the entire trip Sumner kept up a rigorous schedule of sight-seeing which would have exhausted a man half his age. Despite a cold that persisted for the two months he remained in Paris, he saw everything and everybody in the French capital. On May 24 he went on a tour of the French provinces and visited Orleans, Blois, Chambord, Tours, Angers, Nantes, La Haye, Poitiers, Bordeaux, Bayonne, Toulouse, Lyons, and Dijon—as well as a number of intervening places—in something less than three weeks. Then followed two months of frenzied social life and sight-seeing in London. Returning to the Continent, Sumner then went to Rheims, Strasbourg, Basle, Berne, Lucerne, Turin, the Hospice of St. Bernard, Geneva, Heidelberg, Frankfurt, Cologne, Amsterdam, the Hague, and Brussels, all within a month and without missing one of the starred attractions in his Baedeker. Returning to London for a week in September, during which he had five dinner engagements, Sumner then traveled to Manchester, Leeds, Edinburgh, Glasgow, Aberdeen, and Llandudno before sailing from Liverpool on November 7.[2a]

The mere recital of this exhausting peregrination is enough

[2a] For detailed accounts of these English engagements, see six letters from Sumner to Baron Hatherton, Aug. 10–Nov. 7, 1857, Hatherton MSS.

to prove that Sumner, while in Europe, was not severely troubled by the effects of the Brooks assault. Though he occasionally complained that his health was "not yet firm" and that he had "a morbid sensibility of the spinal system," everybody reported that he looked remarkably well. Young Henry James never forgot his disappointment when Sumner turned up in Paris "with wounds by that time rather disappointingly healed," and not even the senator's "visible, measurable, unmistakeable greatness" could quite compensate for that defect.[3]

Toward the end of his European tour, however, Sumner's health received a setback, which was of psychological rather than physiological origin. Convinced that he had received "injuries to the brain" during Brooks's assault, he was uncertain about whether he should resume his place in the Senate when the new session of Congress began in December. Instead of asking the advice of any of several distinguished British physicians, he solicited the opinion of George Combe, whose writings on phrenology he had at a much earlier day admired. Combe, who was not a doctor and who was now nearly seventy years old, wrote out an account of what he took to be Sumner's symptoms and submitted them to Sir James Clarke, the Queen's physician. Clarke, without making any examination himself—indeed, without even seeing Sumner—gave as his considered judgment: "I have no hesitation in affirming, that, if he returns to mental labor in less than a year from this time he will soon become a permanent invalid, if he does not lose his life." Passing the diagnosis along to the senator, Combe added his personal opinion that Sumner's "brain, although apparently functionally sound, . . . would give way under the pressure of public life in America."[4]

Bearing these medical warnings always in mind, Sumner returned to America torn between conflicting desires. With all his conscious will he wanted to reappear in the Senate and further to expose the villainies of the slavocracy. From the very

[3] Sumner to Longfellow, Apr. 2, 1857, Longfellow MSS.; Sumner to Mrs. W. H. Seward, July 23, 1857, Seward MSS.; *The Liberator*, XXVII (Oct. 30, 1857), 175; Edward Waldo Emerson: *The Early Years of the Saturday Club, 1855–1870* (Boston: Houghton Mifflin Co.; 1918), p. 306.

[4] Sumner to Bird, Sept. 11, 1857, Bird MSS.; Combe to Clarke, Oct. 8, 1857, copy, Combe MSS.; Clarke to Combe, Oct. 9, 1857, ibid.; Combe to Henry D. Rogers, Oct. 19, 1857, Sumner MSS.

day after the Brooks assault he had expressed "the constant wish . . . that he might be speedily restored so as to take his seat again in the Senate, from which . . . he had never before been absent for a single day." Compelled to be silent during the 1856 presidential campaign, he vowed on the day of his re-election to the Senate that he would return to Washington and "paint in its true colors, that institution, whose barbarism had with its own peculiar instrument enforced silence upon him." He told Theodore Parker that he expected to deliver an oration "in the Senate which shall tear Slavery open from its chops to its head— from its bully chops down to its coward heel!" "If I ever get back to Washington," he promised Thomas Wentworth Higginson, "the speech that I shall make when I do get there . . . will be to my last speech in the Senate of the United States as first proof brandy to molasses and water." [5]

Perhaps the very frequency and intensity of such statements suggest the inner reluctances that Sumner also felt about returning to the Senate. The more Sumner committed himself to delivering another powerful attack on slavery, the less he could forget the likely consequences. All along he had been convinced that a new attempt would be made against his life. He believed such letters as that signed by "A South Carolina Plug Uglie," who wrote "to say if you value your life not to visit Washington the coming session. . . . You may take the whole of Boston as your body guard but it wont make a damn bit of difference I am willing to sacrifice my life for the honor of my native state." "I suppose I shall be shot," Sumner told Higginson as he talked of going back to his seat. "I don't see what else is left for them to do." [6] Now to these fears the English physicians added another and, in his eyes, even greater danger—one that had never been entirely absent from his thoughts—the likelihood that if he re-

[5] Harvey Lindsly to Wilson, Sept. 22, 1856, Sumner MSS.; J. W. Atwood to Sumner, June 21, 1860, ibid.; Weiss: *Parker*, II, 218; Worcester correspondence of New York *Tribune*, Jan. 17, 1857, clipping in Sumner Scrapbooks. Sumner was unhappy that Higginson revealed these intentions. Sunmer to "My dear friend," Jan. 25, 1857, MS., Yale Univ. Lib.

[6] "A South Carolina Plug Uglie" to Sumner, Nov. 23, 1857, Sumner MSS.; Worcester correspondence of New York *Tribune*, Jan. 17, 1857, clipping, Sumner Scrapbooks. Cf. Lydia Maria Child: *Letters* . . . (4th ed.; Boston: Houghton Mifflin Co.; 1884), p. 88; Wilson to Sumner, Jan. 29, 1857, Sumner MSS.; Ames: *Life* . . . *of Peter and Susan Lesley*, I, 319.

turned to the Senate, it would be "at the peril of his intellect." [7]

When the new session of Congress opened in December 1857, Sumner was able to force himself to attend, but he could not take much interest in politics. The feud between President Buchanan and Senator Douglas over the Kansas question, which threatened to split the Democratic party, attracted only his most cursory attention; like any other invalid, he was concerned chiefly with his own health. He found that listening to the Senate debates jangled his nervous system. After only a few days of attendance he felt "the weight spreading over his brain." He thought that it might help if he kept away from the Senate, though remaining within call if his vote was needed, but still he grew no better. [8]

Tense and worried by his absence from duty during the day, he now spent sleepless nights, for a bladder condition, probably prostatitis, obliged him to rise three or four times during each night. Sumner connected this new affliction—quite incorrectly, and contrary to Dr. Perry's very sound diagnosis—with the injuries produced by Brooks's assault. Here was just one more bit of evidence that the English doctors had been correct, and he began worrying even more about having "paralysis or softening of the brain." "I cannot work with the mind, except in very narrow limits," he wrote the Duchess of Argyll in despair. "To sit in the Senate is exhausting, even though I renounce all special interest in the debate and leave every thing to others. This is hard— very hard. It is hard to be so near complete recovery and still to be kept back." [9]

On December 20 Sumner left Washington, and he remained away during most of the next five months. As soon as he left the "vileness and vulgarity" of the capital, he noted a considerable improvement in his health. To occupy his time he started studying engravings, a large collection of which had just been presented to Harvard College, and his enthusiasm and energy in his new recreation exhausted his friends. "Verily, he goes thoroughly through the work," Longfellow complained. "For

[7] Adams, Diary, Nov. 20, 1857, Adams MSS.
[8] Pierce, III, 558–9.
[9] M. S. Perry to Sumner, Dec. 10, and 18, 1857, Sumner MSS.; Sumner to Duchess of Argyll, Dec. 22, 1857, Argyll MSS.

my part I cannot take in so much at once." But, guided by Dr. Louis Thies of Harvard, Sumner examined every engraving at the college. Then he studied private collections, first in Boston, then in New York and Philadelphia.[1]

Once Sumner was away from Washington, his interest in public affairs picked up. He longed to show that the continuing "injustice, cruelty and meanness" of Buchanan's Kansas policy was "the natural fruit of slavery—which makes men unjust, cruel and mean." He yearned also to denounce William Walker's filibustering expedition against Nicaragua as a new attempt to spread slavery. He worried fretfully over Southern schemes to seize Cuba. In letter after letter he urged the Duchess of Argyll and his other English friends to have the British government persuade Spain to emancipate the slaves in Cuba, for such an action would end the illegal American slave trade, stop filibustering in the Caribbean, and "humble forever the whole slave-interest in the United States."[2] When Lord Napier, the British minister in Washington, failed to agree with Sumner, but instead fraternized with the Southern Democrats, Sumner pungently reported his deficiencies to English friends. When Napier was recalled in 1858, the American press gave Sumner the credit.[3]

Every time Sumner had to go to Washington, all his old symptoms returned. In February 1858 Wilson summoned him to the capital for a few days to vote against Buchanan's Army Bill, "giving soldiers to a wicked Government" for use in Kansas, but, though Sumner tried to spend most of his time in the Smithsonian Institution and in the Library of Congress, the strain was too great and he had to return to New York. Brought down again in April, he arrived too late to give his vote for the free-state cause in Kansas, but, during the several days he remained, the

---

[1] Sumner to Longfellow, Feb. 22, 1858, Longfellow MSS.; Longfellow, Diary, Jan. 22, and 26, 1858, ibid.

[2] Sumner to Gerrit Smith, Jan. 17, 1858, Smith MSS.; Sumner to Duchess of Argyll, Jan. 12, 1858, Argyll MSS.; Sumner to Duchess of Sutherland, Apr. 30, 1858, ibid.; Sumner to Nassau Senior, June 22, 1858, MS., Huntington Lib.; Sumner to Lord Brougham, Apr. 21, and June 30, 1858, Brougham MSS.

[3] Sumner to Duchess of Argyll, Dec. 22, 1857, Jan. 12, and Feb. 15, 1858, Argyll MSS.; Duchess of Argyll to Sumner [Mar. 1858] and June 19 [1859], Sumner MSS.; New York Times, Dec. 16, 1858; A. B. Johnson to Sumner, Apr. 21, and 26, 1858, Sumner MSS. Sumner denied the rumor that he brought about Napier's recall. "I could never think of any such interference . . . even if its impotence were not too glaring." Sumner to Seward, Apr. 19, 1858, Seward MSS.

tense bitterness of the Senate debates once again affected him. Without warning his old enemy struck. While reading in the stacks of the Library of Congress, he was called to the Senate to cast a vote. Perhaps he rose too quickly or walked too rapidly to the Senate chamber, for the afternoon found him prostrate with exhaustion. For the next three or four days he suffered back ailments and could rise from his chair only with great difficulty. At Wilson's insistence, he again left Washington. "All my plans are clouded," Sumner gloomily wrote Howe. "I had hoped to do something—indeed to strike a blow before this session closed." "Two years gone already! How much more!" [4]

Dr. Wister, whom Sumner consulted again in Philadelphia, found his condition serious and warned that he "must resolutely renounce all idea of doing any thing till next winter." The advice confirmed Sumner's fears. "The English physicians understood my symptoms better than I did," he once more began to think. There must be a "deep-seated disease," the softening of the brain and the paralysis suggested by Sir James Clarke.[5]

"Never before was I so uncertain what to do or where to go," Sumner lamented. He had no faith in his American doctors. Dr. Perry's diagnosis that his symptoms were caused by his "generous diet and little exercise," by his urinary complaint, and by that "depressing passion," fear, which acted "sadly upon the nervous system," seemed shallow to him. Both Dr. Perry and Dr. Wister advised him to go abroad again, but, after all, he had tried that remedy. "Where shall I go? What do?" he desperately queried. "Europe? where in Europe? baths there? water-cure there? extensive travel there? Switzerland and baths there? . . . the Pyrenees, and baths there? . . . Spain? Russia? . . . Where shall I go and what do? I know not, nor can I divine." [6]

· 5 ·

When Sumner sailed again for Europe on May 22, 1858, all his friends and most of his enemies were convinced that his sena-

[4] Sumner to Longfellow, Feb. 22, 1858, Longfellow MSS.; Boston *Advertiser*, Apr. 3, 1858; Sumner to Howe, Apr. 16–17, 1858, Sumner MSS.
[5] Sumner to Duchess of Argyll, June 1, 1858, Argyll MSS.; Sumner to Pierce, Apr. 24, 1858, Sumner MSS.
[6] M. S. Perry to Sumner, Apr. 29, 1858, Sumner MSS.; Sumner to Longfellow, May 10, 1858, Longfellow MSS.

torial career was closed. People said that his case was hopeless; the fact that, on the train from Washington, he allowed his pocket to be picked of a $2,000 note of Longfellow's suggested that "his mind was somewhat weakened." Shedding hypocritical tears over "Mr. Sumner's physical infirmity," the Boston *Courier* joined the Boston *Herald* in demanding that a senator so incapacitated should resign.[7]

Sumner's appearance at this time justified the most ominous forebodings. He walked only with the greatest difficulty. "When he tried to move forward he was compelled to push one foot slowly and gently forward but a few inches, and then drag the other foot to a level with the first, holding his back at the same time to diminish the pain that he had there." Only after moving about for fifteen minutes or so in this slow and stiff fashion did the pain abate, so that he would walk more easily. More disturbing was the fact that "he could not make use of his brain at all. He could not read a newspaper, could not write a letter. He was in a frightful state as regards the activity of the mind, as every effort there was most painful to him. It seemed to him at times as if his head would burst; there seemed to be some great force within pushing the pieces away from one another." [8]

His physicians did not agree on the causes of these distressing complaints. After some hesitation, Dr. Wister finally concluded that there was "no evidence of organic disease." Sumner suffered, he thought, from "extreme nervous prostration"; "the injuries he originally received on the floor of the Senate had been aggravated by the peculiar condition of his nervous system at the time, a condition induced by severe mental and nervous tension from the loss of sleep for several consecutive nights, also by the peculiar susceptibility of his temperament, which is highly nervous." Dr. Jackson, on the other hand, was certain that Brooks's blows had caused "either congestion, or concussion followed by congestion, or positive inflammation of the brain or its investing membranes" and that Sumner's "brain and spinal cord had been the seat of a grave and formidable lesion." Though not so posi-

[7] Howe to M. F. Conway, June 27, 1858, Howe mss.; Hillard to Lieber, Apr. 27, and May 26, 1858, Lieber mss.; Boston *Courier*, May 24, 1858; Anderson: "Slavery Issue," p. 242.

[8] Dr. Charles Edward Brown-Séquard, in New York *Tribune*, Mar. 18, 1874.

tive, Dr. Perry also believed "that the base of the brain, as well as the spinal cord, has been the seat of some serious lesion." But, when Sumner was examined in Paris, his physician was emphatic in declaring that he "never had a brain affection" and that he "had no paralysis." [9]

It is difficult to appraise the medical validity of these conflicting statements. Unfortunately Sumner never had a complete neurological examination, for he never consulted Dr. S. Weir Mitchell, of Philadelphia, the one specialist in the United States competent to make such a study. As Sumner's friends refused to permit an autopsy of his brain and spinal cord after his death in 1874, the question of his injuries can never be settled with absolute certainty. Fortunately, however, Sumner kept such elaborate records of his health, his physicians' opinions, and even his medical prescriptions that modern neurologists and brain specialists can agree on the nature of his affliction.

These physicians declare that Sumner's reactions during the first few days after the Brooks assault were precisely what they would expect in a patient who had received a nasty blow on the head.[1] He did not have either a fractured skull or a concussion, for he did not suffer the severe headaches, changes in state of awareness, and somnolence which accompany brain traumas; instead, his condition was feverish and excited. Septicemia developed in his wounds and left him considerably debilitated, perhaps suffering from anemia. The symptoms of which he subsequently complained—pressure on the skull, weakness of the spine, difficulty in walking—could not, from a neurological point of view, possibly have been the results of blows he received on his head or even of a spinal lesion. The urinary condition that caused Sumner so much distress had no medical connection with the Brooks assault. At the same time no physician who has

---

[9] Wister to Wilson, Sept. 25, 1856, Sumner MSS.; Perry: *Case of Sumner*, pp. 5–7; C. E. Brown-Séquard to J. Collins Warren, Mar. 21, 1874, MS., Mass. Hist. Soc.; *Boston Medical and Surgical Journal*, Mar. 26, 1874.

[1] Sumner's remarkably complete medical record includes diagnoses by Drs. Boyle, Wister, Lindsly, Jackson, Perry, Brown-Séquard, and George Hayward; prescriptions and medical instructions given Sumner by Brown-Séquard, Hayward, Perry, and Jackson; and elaborate day-by-day accounts of Sumner's appearance and symptoms by Sumner himself, by interested friends, and by political and personal opponents.

studied the voluminous medical documents in Sumner's case has
the least suspicion that Sumner was malingering; his sufferings
were intense and genuine.

The diagnosis, then, is that Sumner was not shamming, but
that his ailments were not, neurologically, the result of Brooks's
beating. Cases of this sort are far from rare in medical history,
and modern specialists classify Sumner's illness as "post-traumatic syndrome," in which numerous symptoms without objective causes follow a traumatic experience, such as an accident
(physical trauma) in which the patient is not seriously injured.
The precise nature of such a post-traumatic syndrome is not
entirely clear; most neurologists believe it to be largely psycho-
genic. Patients suffering from such symptoms have great difficulty in reassuming their obligations to their families, their
friends, and their employers.

In Sumner's case it is clear that the Brooks assault produced
psychic wounds that lingered long after the physical injuries had
disappeared. The pressure he felt on his head was a mental reenactment of the beating. Bearing in mind that the attack occurred in 1856, one is not so puzzled that he felt the weight on
his skull to be precisely fifty-six pounds. The pain in his thighs
was reminiscent of his tearing up his desk as he sought to rise
under Brooks's lashing. It is at least suggestive that the senator
who had for years been demanding a political party with "Back-
bone" should suffer mysterious spinal complaints. All these
symptoms occurred chiefly, though not exclusively, when Sumner turned his mind to public affairs or tried to return to his Senate duties. The incredibly unprofessional and unscientific warnings of his English physicians that mental exertion might
permanently impair his brain added to his tension on these occasions, as did his strong belief that the Southerners would shoot
him. Hitherto Sumner had driven himself with his inflexible will
to maintain impossibly high standards, despite overwork and
mental strain; now he was faced with rebellion on the part of
his body and of an unconscious segment of his mind.

As the ordinary remedies of rest and exercise were ineffectual for a malady of this sort, Sumner did not know what further
steps to take for recovery; he was ready for desperate measures.
In June 1858 an American merchant residing in Paris suggested

that he visit Dr. Charles Edward Brown-Séquard, the French-American physician who was already famed for his pioneer work in the dissection of the spinal cord and for his discovery of the vasomotor nerves. Though Brown-Séquard was not then in general practice, he welcomed a case so interesting and important as Sumner's. "There is," he wrote the senator, "hardly a single human being,—my own family included,—whom I would so heartily rejoice to relieve from pain or disease, as Mr. Charles Sumner." [2]

On June 10 Brown-Séquard gave Sumner a three-hour examination. After noting his more obvious symptoms, the doctor tested the sensitivity of Sumner's spine, first with ice, then with boiling water, and finally with an esthesiometer, and he repeated his experiments again and again to ascertain the precise range of the disease in the spine and the neck. He found two "exquisitely tender" spots on the spine, one "situated at the junction of the cervical and dorsal regions, the other at that of the dorsal and lumbar." The brain itself he declared "free of any serious remaining injury," though there was still "an effusion of liquid about the brain and . . . a slight degree of congestion, chiefly if not only confined to the membrane around the brain." [3]

Sumner had instant and complete faith in this "most careful, skilful, learned and devoted physician," whose every word was reinforced by his worldwide reputation. He felt enormously relieved to be assured, by such an authority, that his brain was unaffected. He could easily accept Brown-Séquard's explanation, in simple, everyday language, of the symptoms from which he suffered. His back ailments, the doctor told him, were "the effect of what is called *contre-coup*. Mr. Sumner being seated and inclined over his desk at the time of the assault, the blows on his head took effect by *counter-stroke*, or communicated shock in the spine." "It is the nature of this disease," he added, "that, when the blow is struck upon the head, especially when the person struck is in a sitting posture, that the shock follows the spinal column until it reaches what is termed the point of resistance. Here the shock stops, and at this point there arises the germ of

[2] Brown-Séquard to Sumner, June 9, 1858, Sumner MSS.
[3] Sumner to Nassau Senior, June 22, 1858, MS., Huntington Lib.; Sumner to Longfellow, June 27, 1858, Longfellow MSS.; *Boston Medical and Surgical Journal*, May 21, 1874; New York *Tribune*, July 9, 1858.

future trouble." It was, Brown-Séquard explained, just like trying to drive a nail into very hard wood; the blow of the hammer
bent not the head of the nail, but the weakest spots in its shaft.
So, the thick bones of the skull had protected Sumner's brain,
but the shock had injured the spine at the two points that were
now so sensitive. The upper irritation was "the cause of the
whole mischief as regards the function of the brain"; the lower
"caused the pain which gave the appearance of paralysis" in the
legs.[4]

Having diagnosed the case, Brown-Séquard proposed a cure.
"Fire" was his remedy. If he applied counter-irritants to the two
sprains, these would "produce the absorption of the excess of
fluid effused about the brain, and diminish the congestion of the
membranes of this organ," and would thus lessen "the degree of
pain, if not altogether render the sensibility normal, so as to allow walking and other movements to take place without pain."
The most effective counter-irritant, Brown-Séquard told his patient, was the moxa, a treatment of Japanese origin, in which
the naked skin was burned with inflamed agaric (*amadou*), cotton wool, or some other very combustible substance. The medical
records do not show which form of moxa Brown-Séquard favored, but the standard one in use at the time was formed of
"cotton, rendered downy by carding, and made into a roll an inch
long, and from half an inch to two inches in diameter." The
treatment, Brown-Séquard warned, would be most painful, but
without it Sumner must remain "a permanent invalid, always
subject to a sudden and serious relapse."[5]

Brown-Séquard's "examination and report gave me such
confidence," Sumner wrote Howe, "that I put myself at once in
his hands." He asked the doctor when he could apply the first
moxa.

"To-morrow, if you please," said Brown-Séquard.

[4] Sumner to Mrs. W. H. Seward, June 27, 1858, Seward MSS.; New York
Tribune, July 9, 1858; Brown-Séquard, in New York *Tribune*, Mar. 18, 1874, and
in Meadville *Republican*, Mar. 20, 1874. At another time Brown-Séquard suggested a slightly different origin of these "two sprains of the spine." "The upper
one was caused by the blows on the head, the lower by the violent effort which
Mr. Sumner made to rise during the assault." *Boston Medical and Surgical
Journal*, May 21, 1874.

[5] Sumner: *Works*, IV, 330; Sumner to Longfellow, June 27, 1858, Longfellow MSS.; New York *Tribune*, June 23, 1858. On the moxa then used see *Cyclo-
pedia of Practical Medicine* (1833), I, 492.

"Why not this afternoon?" countered Sumner eagerly.

The doctor prepared to give his patient chloroform to ease the pain. Sumner objected: "If you say positively that I shall derive as much benefit if I take chloroform as if I do not, then of course I will take it; but if there is to be any degree whatever of amelioration in case I do not take it, then I shall not take it." Believing that the greater Sumner's pain, the better his chances of recovery, Brown-Séquard did not give him the anesthetic, but burned the moxa on his bare back.[6]

During the next thirteen days Brown-Séquard gave Sumner the moxa treatment five additional times, each time without anesthetic. "I have never seen a man bearing with such fortitude as Mr. Sumner has shown, the extremely violent pain of this kind of burning," he declared at the time, and many years later he still felt that he had submitted Sumner "to the martyrdom of the greatest suffering that can be inflicted on mortal man." Sumner bore the pain stoically. "The torment is considerable," he wrote Howe, in marked understatement, "but that is over in 5 or 10 minutes. But then come the annoyances and inflammations which . . . are incident to burns. Of course, I walk with pain; lie down with pain; rise with pain." [7]

After six moxae Brown-Séquard gave his patient a two-month respite from burning, but, in the ninety-degree heat of Paris, Sumner got little benefit from the rest. The six open suppurating wounds resulting from his burns kept him in torment. "For 5 weeks," he lamented, "I have not been able to lie on my back or to turn over in my bed." He began complaining that the fire had driven his pains into one of his legs, which was "sadly disabled." [8]

On July 20 the meaning of that last symptom appeared. In the middle of the night "neuralgic, constringing and oppressing" pain in his chest woke him up. He could neither lie down nor stand up. Finally he managed to prop himself up with cushions in a chair, so as to get a little relief. Alone in his hotel, unattended except by servants, he had to wait in this position from

6 Sumner to Howe, June 24, 1858, Sumner mss.; Sumner: *Works*, IV, 330–1; New York *Tribune*, Mar. 18, 1874.
7 New York *Tribune*, June 28, 1858, and Mar. 18, 1874; Sumner to Howe, June 24, 1858, Sumner mss.
8 Sumner to Longfellow, July 19, 1858, Longfellow mss.

four o'clock in the morning until six in the evening, when Brown-
Séquard arrived. Finding the pain "almost without precedent,"
the doctor attributed it to "the original concussion" of the Brooks
assault and rather proudly decided that Sumner's case was "one
of the most interesting in the history of science." Giving Sumner
opiates for immediate relief, he prescribed belladonna and decided to postpone indefinitely further moxa treatments.[9]

Sumner was apparently entirely satisfied with Brown-
Séquard. If he had any doubts about his treatment, they were
dispelled when George Hayward, a Boston physician then practicing in Paris, not only endorsed it, but reported that four of
"the most eminent medical authorities in England," Sir Benjamin
Brody, Sir James Clarke, Sir Henry Holland, and Dr. Lawrence,
also approved it. Many of Sumner's American friends, however,
were very dubious about Brown-Séquard and his remedies.
Dr. Perry was sure that "a life of perfect repose would be more
beneficial . . . than the application of hot irons." Howe, who
was a doctor himself, thought that his friend had fallen into the
hands of quacks who were "certainly tormenting and injuring
him in the pursuit of a baseless theory." [1]

From a medical point of view, Brown-Séquard's critics
were entirely correct. His neurological examination of Sumner
had been wholly inadequate, and his diagnosis of spinal sprains
brought about by *contre-coups* was medical nonsense. The moxa
treatment was, therapeutically, no treatment at all; it was merely
a terribly painful experience. Application of moxae could no
more give permanent benefit to a brain or spine injury than
could a strong liniment. Brown-Séquard's theory that the con-
strictive pressure in Sumner's chest was somehow an extension
of the spinal injury "through the avenue of the nearest network
of veins . . . from the spinal column to the heart" is anatomically ridiculous.[2] In fact, Sumner had his first attack of angina

[9] Sumner to Howe, July 22, 1858, Sumner MSS.; New York *Tribune*, Aug. 10,
1858.
[1] Sumner to Seward, July 19, 1858, Seward MSS.; Hayward to Sumner,
Nov. 20, 1862, Sumner MSS.; G. R. Russell to Sumner, Aug. 15, 1858, ibid.;
Howe to Palfrey, Sept. 2, 1858, Palfrey MSS.; Howe to Sumner, July 11, 1858,
Howe MSS.
[2] Meadville *Republican*, Mar. 20, 1874. Brown-Séquard had the grace to
admit that "this theory did not admit of demonstration." *Boston Medical and
Surgical Journal*, Mar. 26, 1874.

pectoris, perhaps brought on by—though not caused by—the shock and discomfort of the moxa treatment; Brown-Séquard quite properly prescribed belladonna for it.

If from a physiological point of view Brown-Séquard's treatment—which, it must be remembered, was in keeping with the most advanced medical thought of the time—was worse than worthless, it is possible that it benefited Sumner in other ways. His sufferings, which were widely publicized in American newspapers, gave the lie, once and for all, to charges that he was shamming; moreover, the same very real and demonstrable pain freed Sumner himself from his worried sense of guilt at being absent from his post of duty. He even gained some psychic income from his torture. While his back was being burned, he allowed his mind to wander, and he "thought sometimes of St. Lawrence on the gridiron—sometimes of Prometheus with the vulture at his liver, and also of many others in the list of fire-sufferers." Identifying himself with the martyrs of the past, he erased any unconscious doubts about the correctness of his course; never again in the future would he feel lost without the unstinted approbation of his peers. Having, as Prescott observed, enjoyed "quite contrary to usage—the crown of martyrdom during his own lifetime," Sumner came to be, even in his own eyes, less a fallible human being than a symbol of a righteous cause. He found it easy to suppress any expression of resentment against Preston Brooks, who, in this new mood, seemed only "the unconscious agent of a malign power." Not even the death of the South Carolina congressman of an agonizing disease in March 1857 evoked a bitter word from Sumner. "The Almighty has settled this," he told a friend, "better than you or I could have done." [3]

Secure in his faith that his and the Almighty's ways were identical, Sumner began to mend. Gradually the sores on his back healed, and he could ride comfortably in a carriage. His

[3] Sumner to Howe, July 1, 1858, Bird MSS.; Ticknor: *Prescott*, p. 423; Pierce, III, 524; J. L. Bennett to Sumner, June 7, 1860, Sumner MSS. Still Sumner did speak of the assault as attempted "murder" (Earl of Carlisle, Diary, Oct. 29, 1857, Carlisle MSS.), and his devoted secretary declared: "Mr. Sumner largely refrained from talking of Brooks, except to say he had no more personal feeling against him than against the stick he used—but I was sensible that he was not unwilling to have me talk of him." A. B. Johnson to Pierce, Feb. 12, 1886, Pierce MSS.

"neuralgia," as Brown-Séquard persisted in calling his angina pectoris, was an ever present danger; on a little excursion to St. Germain in August he suffered "those terrible pains" in his chest four times. Still he could now receive callers, make occasional visits, and listen to lectures. At the end of the summer he went to Aix-en-Savoie to try the famous mineral baths. After his experience with Brown-Séquard, he found the treatment of hot and cold douches a positive luxury. The regimen palled after about a month, and he "rushed through Switzerland," visited Milan, Verona, Padua, and Venice all too briefly, and then came north by way of Vienna, Prague, Dresden, and Berlin. "All my time," he explained, "has been devoted simply to regaining my lost health." [4]

· 6 ·

On his return to Paris in November 1858, Sumner received disquieting political intelligence from home. A number of Massachusetts citizens were becoming bored by what they considered the undue length of Sumner's martyrdom. Henry David Thoreau recorded that one Massachusetts woman, with feeble curiosity, asked: "How is that young man who had his head hurt? I haven't heard anything about him for a good while." Others felt that they had heard far too much about Sumner's wounds, treatments, and sufferings. "We hope," declared the stanchly Republican New York *Times*, "that Mr. Sumner's friends will not consider it necessary hereafter to send bulletins of his health to the Press upon the arrival of every steamer; these . . . are getting to be monotonous." [5]

By the summer of 1858 a strong sentiment had developed that Sumner ought to resign. Republicans as diverse as Howe, Charles Francis Adams, and William Pitt Fessenden shared it. [6] Active leadership in the movement, however, fell to Governor

---

[4] Sumner to Felton, Aug. 5, 1858, Sumner MSS.; Sumner to Longfellow, Sept. 15, 1858, Longfellow MSS.; Sumner to Duchess of Argyll, Dec. 2, 1858, Argyll MSS.; Sumner to Lyman Trumbull, Sept. 12, 1858, MS., Illinois State Hist. Lib.

[5] Bradford Torry (ed.): *The Writings of Henry David Thoreau* (Boston: Houghton Mifflin Co.; 1906), XII, 447; New York *Times*, Dec. 16, 1858.

[6] Howe to Sumner, May 18 [1858], Howe MSS.; Adams, Diary, Dec. 18, 1858, Adams MSS.; Fessenden to Hamilton Fish, Dec. 18, 1858, Fish MSS.

N. P. Banks, that "bobbin boy of Waltham," who had managed to
secure the combined nominations of the Republican and American parties in 1857 and to defeat the obnoxious Henry J. Gardner.[7] Ambitious and necessitous, Banks was hardly inaugurated
before he began to think longingly of the security of a six-year
Senate term. To others Sumner's vacant chair might be a "perpetual speech"; to Banks it was a perpetual reminder of a political opportunity.

As Sumner's popularity was still great, Banks moved
stealthily. First he carefully disseminated a rumor that Sumner
had already submitted his resignation. Then, at the Republican
state convention in September 1858, Banks's friends presented
an apparently innocuous resolution to the effect that "It is the
first duty of a Representative to attend the sessions of the body
of which he is a member." Actually Banks had written the resolution himself and wanted it to serve as a trial balloon. If it met
with popular approval, the governor would interpret it as applying to the absent senator; if there was popular resentment
against it, he could swear that it was intended to refer only to
the state legislature.[8]

Frank Bird, who hated Banks as much as he loved Sumner,
was instantly alert to the plot. He countered Banks's ambiguous
resolution with another, very positive one: "That . . . Charles
Sumner, though separated from us by the broad Atlantic—seeking in foreign lands for the restoration of health, impaired by
ruffian violence in the Senate House—has our undivided affection, our high regard, and our constant prayer for his speedy
restoration to health." Faced with such a challenge, Banks's
stratagem failed—but not his desire to become senator.[9]

Sumner, who had been completely out of touch with American news for months, was distressed to hear of Banks's intrigues.
Though Republican leaders in Boston assured him that the plot
to replace him was "confined to the meanest hunkers and the

[7] On Banks's rise to power see Harrington: *Banks,* pp. 42–4; Bean: "Party
Transformations," pp. 357–64; clippings from Massachusetts newspapers for
1857 campaign, W. S. Robinson Scrapbooks.
[8] Howe to Sumner, Nov. 6, 1858, Howe MSS.; Bird to Sumner, Sept. 14,
1858, Sumner MSS.; A. G. Browne to Sumner, Sept. 14, 1858, ibid.; Anderson:
"Slavery Issue," p. 242.
[9] The Worcester *Spy* (Dec. 29, 1858) and the Boston *Advertiser* (Sept. 18,
1858) denounced Bank's intrigue as "inconsiderate and premature."

smallest of trading politicians with the exception of a very few cold-blooded and selfish scamps like Banks," Sumner also bore in mind the advice of his personal supporters: " 'Political friends' are ungrateful scoundrels, and if they huzza you to day they will talk of your successor tomorrow." [1]

Sumner refused to allow Banks's "heartless" plot to force him into resigning. He needed his Senate salary for his medical and traveling expenses; [2] his best friends urged him not to resign; he could not surrender his seat without also giving up faith in his permanent recovery. Most important of all, he now completely identified his own personal prospects with the future of the antislavery cause. "If my position were merely political, I should resign at once," he assured Howe, "but I am unwilling to renounce the opportunity of again meeting the enemies of freedom in the Senate. My resignation would delight the slave-drivers, and . . . it would pain, the true Anti-Slavery men of the country. . . . That delight and that pain shall not come from me." [3]

Unwilling to resign, Sumner still felt unable to resume his duties. In November 1858 he issued a new public statement of his disabilities and prospects. Dr. Brown-Séquard and Dr. Hayward now brought in the eminent physician, Armand Trousseau, as a consultant; the three declared that Sumner "was still suffering from the injuries he received more than two years and a half ago," that they considered it "unadvisable for him to return to his public duties during the present winter," but that they had "great confidence, *that he would surely recover*." The timing of the statement suggests that it was designed to check Banks's

---

[1] Bird to Sumner, Sept. 14, 1858, Sumner MSS.; A. G. Browne to Sumner, Sept. 14, 1858, ibid., G. R. Russell to Sumner, Aug. 15, 1858, ibid.

[2] C. F. Adams to J. T. Furness, Jan. 17, 1858, copy, Adams MSS. Sumner continued regularly to draw his Senate pay while absent in Europe. The expenses of his European travels were large. During his 1858–9 trip alone he had a letter of credit on the House of Baring for £2000; apparently he spent all of this and owed the bankers at the end of his trip $206.40 more. His financial records, with numerous receipted bills for large purchases of hand-tailored clothing, *objets d'art*, etc., are in the Sumner MSS. Howe, as numerous letters to Sumner in the Howe MSS., 1858–9, indicate, managed his finances while he was abroad.

[3] Sumner to Howe, Nov. 24, 1858, Sumner MSS. Cf. Sumner to Carlos Pierce, July 19, 1858: "It is hard to endure pain long continued; but it is harder still to see life glide away and precious opportunities disappear . . . and there is a new pang added by the baseness of men." MS. in the possession of Mr. George H. Wettach, Fair Lawn, N. J.

plot; the carefully balanced wording indicates that the doctors had been asked to speak of the senator's injuries as serious, but not permanently incapacitating.[4]

Though Brown-Séquard wanted to resume the moxa treatments, the three doctors finally agreed that Sumner should spend the winter in retirement in southern France. He selected the placid university town of Montpellier, where he would be almost completely isolated from disturbing news from America. "Away from care, responsibility or excitement," he settled into a three-month round of *"ventouse seches* and *capsules* and *pilules."* Though not entirely free from angina pectoris, and obliged to spend much of his time in bed, he enjoyed this "most retired and tranquil life." He found the climate "exquisite,—a perpetual spring"; the promenades were "the finest in France"; the professors at the university were "charming." [5]

Best of all, his health was improving. Though overexertion occasionally produced some of his old symptoms, he suffered no real relapses during his quiet winter. By spring he was feeling almost well again. "Many gloomy hours I have passed, and much pain I have endured," he triumphantly wrote Howe in March 1859. "But I believe this is past." [6]

By April he felt able to visit Italy. In Naples he met George Bemis, a young and sympathetic Boston lawyer, and they joined forces in sight-seeing. Though Bemis wrote home that the senator was "not a well man yet," as he had to use a cane, became tired if he walked a considerable distance, and still had "to disturb himself three or four times" each night because of his bladder condition, the lawyer's diary shows that Sumner was capable of vigorous exertions. They visited museums, inspected the cathedral, went out to Vergil's grotto, climbed Vesuvius, drove to Herculaneum and Pompeii, took a horseback trip to St. Elmo, during which Sumner "indulged himself in a glass of goat's milk, much to the amusement of the by-standers," and went through the royal palace, including even the coach house.

All the while Sumner talked and talked. He discussed litera-

---

[4] New York *Tribune*, Dec. 16, 1858.
[5] Sumner to W. W. Story, Dec. 11, 1858, MS., Huntington Lib.; Sumner to Duchess of Argyll, Feb. 10, 1859, Argyll MSS.; Sumner to Longfellow, Mar. 4, 1859, Longfellow MSS.
[6] Sumner to Howe, Mar. 8 [1859], Sumner MSS.

ture with Bemis—"e.g., Hannibal's campaign, Italian writers, French and Italian morals, Manzoni's Promesi Sposi—love, including some of Sumner's experiences—Society, wherein Sumner told . . . a great deal of his English and foreign acquaintances—Law, including Sumner's relations with G. T. Curtis, B. F. Hallett, R. C. Winthrop, G. S. Hillard, etc.—Persons, including Prescott, Bancroft, Lord Brougham, Bunsen, de Tocqueville, Judge Fletcher etc., etc. . . . criminal law theories . . . curious chapters in Franklin's history . . . English peculiarities of pronunciation . . . Lord Palmerston's intrigues and marriage . . . Michelet on Amour (Love). . . ." Bemis, the good listener, reported that Sumner, as he left Naples, "spoke as if he had enjoyed our intercourse." [7]

Then Sumner spent three glorious weeks in Rome, where William Wetmore Story, the artist son of Justice Story, accompanied him to the galleries and the churches and the art studios. Sumner's enthusiasm exhausted the Storys, the Robert Brownings, and the Nathaniel Hawthornes, for what he lacked in appreciation of art he made up with zeal. Leaving reluctantly, he wrote Story: "Rome haunts me perpetually, and I wish to ask you a hundred questions which I forgot." [8]

He arrived in northern Italy just as Napoleon III's troops were driving out the Austrians. At Turin he rejoiced equally in the courage and hope he found among all classes in the Kingdom of Savoy and in the firm competence of Count Cavour, who granted him a private interview. "Three cheers for Italy," Sumner exclaimed as he left the capital of the Piedmont, "and may the Austrian empire cease to exist." [9]

Back in Paris in June, Sumner had another examination by Brown-Séquard and went on another round of sight-seeing. Theodore Parker, who had come to Europe in what proved to be a vain hope of combatting the tuberculosis that afflicted him, found him "the same dear old Sumner as he used to be before that scoundrel laid him low." "He walks on those great long legs of

[7] Bemis to Jonathan Bemis, Apr. 23, 1859, Bemis MSS.; Bemis, Diary, Apr. 19, and 24, 1859, ibid.
[8] Sumner to W. W. Story, May 14, 1859, MS., Huntington Lib.; James: *Story*, II, 40–1.
[9] James: *Story*, II, 36–41; Sumner to Duchess of Argyll, May 20, 1859, Argyll MSS.

his at the rate of four or five miles an hour; his countenance is good, good as ever; he walked upright and sits upright; all the trouble has vanished from his brain. . . ."[1]

As the time for his departure drew near, Sumner dreaded leaving the "Elysium" of Europe for an America "befouled by slavery." Even the Italians, oppressed by centuries of despotism, were proving themselves more worthy of liberty than the "Americans with four millions of slaves, and with a leaven of slaveholding tyrants, and foreign immigrants who cannot speak our language." Sumner joined his European friends in laughing at the notion that slaveholding America could claim "All men are created equal"; he was so bitter against his country that one irate fellow citizen thought him "Mrs. Trollope in disguise."[2]

Anticipating his return to Washington, where he would be "amidst tobacco-spitting, swearing slave-drivers, abused by the press, insulted so far as it is possible, pained and ransacked by the insensibility about him to human rights and the claims of human nature," Sumner tried to enjoy every moment of his last months abroad.[3] An exciting fling in London society, six weeks at the salt-water baths near Le Havre, a brief tour of Brittany, a final few days in Paris, where he spent about $1,500 in buying, generally at outrageous prices, bronzes, china, books, engravings, manuscripts, and other alleged antiques, and a short, happy trip through rural England completed his European travels. On November 5 he sailed from Liverpool.

"I return," he wrote to Bemis, "with mingled feelings— happy in the consciousness of health regained, and yet with a certain solicitude as to how I can stand the strain and tug of the work and responsibility before me." Of the nature of that work and the extent of his responsibility he had no doubt. While suffering from the moxa treatment, he had sworn: "If health ever returns I will repay to slavery and the whole crew of its supporters every wound, burn, . . . ache, pain, trouble, grief which I have suffered. That vow is registered."[4]

[1] Weiss, *Parker*, II, 294–5.

[2] Sumner to Longfellow, July 19, 1858, Longfellow MSS.; Weiss, *Parker*, II, 336; F. Schrœder to Hamilton Fish, July 7, 1859, Fish MSS.

[3] James: *Story*, II, 45.

[4] Sumner to Bemis, Nov. 5, 1859, Bemis MSS.; Sumner to Howe, July 22, 1858, Sumner MSS.

CHAPTER XIII

If Mr. Lincoln
Stands Firm

❧

W HAT A DIFFERENCE between this place and Rome!" Sumner lamented as he returned to Washington in December 1859. The American capital looked more than ever bare and grotesque. At one end of Pennsylvania Avenue rose the architecturally improbable Capitol with its unfinished dome; at the other, Clark Mills's "caricature" of General Jackson imperturbably saluting from the saddle of an anatomically impossible horse. Sumner blushed when courtesy required him to show the sights of Washington to visiting Englishmen. Constantly he wished for "A walk in the streets of Rome, a stroll on the Pincian, a visit to the Vatican, a sight of St. Peter's—oh, for an hour, one brief hour, of any of these!" [1]

Politically, too, Washington seemed worse than ever. Embittered by John Brown's raid on Harpers Ferry, the Southerners had become more extreme in their defense of slavery. Even a moderate like Jefferson Davis demanded federal protection for slavery in all the territories. Albert Gallatin Brown, the other senator from Mississippi, boldly announced that "slavery is a great moral, social, and political blessing—a blessing to the slave, and a blessing to the master." Senator Mason, of Virginia, agreed "that the condition of African bondage elevates both races," and

---

[1] James: *Story*, II, 48; Boston *Commonwealth*, Mar. 7, 1874; Gordon N. Ray (ed.) *The Letters and Private Papers of William Makepeace Thackeray* (Cambridge: Harvard University Press; 1946), III, 195.

R. M. T. Hunter, from the same state, argued: "There is not a respectable system of civilization known to history, . . . whose
foundations were not laid in the institution of domestic slavery." [2]

Southern hostility toward Sumner had not diminished during his years of absence. Some young Virginians talked of kid-
napping him for the purpose of offering him some physical
indignity. "We see plainly that you are spoiling fast for another
licking," a "Southern Mazzini or Plug Ugly" wrote him, "and it is
quite evident that you are flattering yourself with the idea that
no Southerner dare lay hands on *you* for fear of mighty vengeance of the northerners in defence of their sand-box dollybaby
Senator. . . . What in Hell do we care for the Vengeance of the
Yankees. Why a dissolution and a fight is what we are after. And
if giving you *another pummelling* will be the means of bringing it
about then here gos [*sic*] it." [3]

"This is a barbarous place," Sumner felt. "The slave-masters
seem to me more than ever *barbarians*—in manner, conversation, speeches, conduct, principles, life. All things indicate a
crisis." [4]

• 1 •

Sumner was slow to resume an active part in the sectional contest. His health, he felt, was still precarious. Unable to reconcile
himself to the fact that at forty-eight years of age he did not have
the vigor of an adolescent, he worried because he could no longer
race along the streets at a pace that approached a gallop and because he was obliged to walk, rather than run, up the steps of
the Capitol. [5]

His role in the Republican party was as uncertain as his
health. During his absence Republican leaders seemed to have
become more concerned with respectability than with human
rights. Feeling sure of the antislavery vote in the 1860 elections,

---

[2] *Cong. Globe*, 36 Cong., 1 Sess., 596, 1,004, and Appendix, 106.
[3] Sumner to J. A. Andrew, Dec. 9, and 12, 1859, Andrew MSS.; "Southern
Mazzini" to Sumner, Apr. 19, 1860, Sumner MSS.
[4] Sumner to "My dear Sir," Mar. 24, 1860, Segal Coll.; James: *Story*, II, 48.
[5] George Sumner to Chase, Nov. 20, 1859, Chase MSS., Hist. Soc. of Penn.;
Richards: *S. G. Howe*, II, 477.

they were cultivating a moderate stand in order to win over former Whigs and Know-nothings. They went out of their way to condemn John Brown's raid; Seward repressed his "irrepressible conflict" doctrine and talked blandly of differences between "capital states" and "labor states"; there was even doubt about whether the Republicans, in their national convention of 1860, would dare endorse the Declaration of Independence. Sumner cared nothing for the protective tariff, the land grants to agricultural colleges, the chartering of a Pacific railroad, and other economic legislation with which Republicans now concerned themselves.

Even when Congress discussed questions relating to slavery, Sumner's consuming interest as a senator, he found himself unfamiliar with issues. He knew only what the newspapers told him about John Brown's raid, which had occurred before he returned from Europe. Sumner's attention had been so centered upon his own suffering that he apparently forgot that he had once met Brown, in early 1857, when the Kansas free-state leader, already notorious for the bloody massacre of Southerners on Pottawatomie Creek, visited him in Boston and asked to see the coat he was wearing when Brooks assaulted him. Painfully Sumner had hobbled to his closet and handed the garment, still stiff with blood, to Brown, who closely examined it and "said nothing . . . but . . . his lips compressed and his eyes shown like polished steel." [6] Sumner had forgotten, too, his endorsement of Hugh Forbes, the Englishman who had served for a time as Brown's drillmaster, but had broken with him over his plan to seize the Harpers Ferry arsenal. [7]

Suniner found it hard to make up his mind about Brown's raid, which occupied so much of the time of the Thirty-Sixth Congress. Convinced that Brown was "almost mad" and that "of course his act must be deplored," he could not help admiring "the singular courage and character shewn by its author," in whom he found "much of the Convenanter, the Puritan and even the early Christian martyr." "For a practical statesman, believing

[6] James Redpath to Elias Nason, Apr. 10, 1874, MS. owned by Mr. Boyd B. Stutler; Springfield *Republican*, Feb. 6, 1857. Cf. Nason: *Sumner*, pp. 250–1; James Freeman Clarke: *Anti-Slavery Days* . . . (New York: R. Worthington; 1884), pp. 153–4; Clarke: *Memorial and Biographical Sketches* (Boston: Houghton Mifflin Co.; 1878), 101–2.
[7] Sumner to Rev. Dr. Francis, Oct. 24 [1858], Washburn MSS.

slavery a wrong, the subject is not without its difficulties," he confessed. "Not, indeed, that I hesitate to judge the *act;* but how can I refuse my admiration to many things in the *man?*" He refrained from entering the debates on Brown's raid, giving as his reason his doctor's advice against overexertion.[8]

Such silence was what Republican managers most wanted from Sumner as the presidential election of 1860 drew near. Hoping to widen the split in the Democratic party, they feared any word or act which might give Stephen A. Douglas an opportunity to step forward as the defender of the South. Almost as fervently they hoped that nothing would be said in the Senate to alienate any of the Northern Whigs and Know-nothings who seemed ready to join the Republicans. So obvious was the Republican desire to play down antislavery agitation that Sumner grew distressed over "the hollowness of our own professing friends." "Half of our republicans need conversion to first principles," he decided.[9]

Sumner was willing to go along with his party leaders, however, at least until after the Republican nominee was selected. He had no thought of being a candidate himself. "It is hard for a person, who has been in the Senate, exposed to bitter opposition and also to jealousies and rivalries, to rally for himself the whole party," he realized, "and perhaps the very brilliancy of his position is against him. He is too much known, and the neutral men, whose votes are wanted, cannot sustain him." [1] Like most Republicans, he expected the Chicago convention to nominate William H. Seward, and he was well pleased with the prospect. Though he regretted that Seward's recent speeches had become increasingly conservative on slavery questions, he recognized that the New Yorker was trying "to plead the good cause, and at the same time to avoid disturbing the prejudices of those who differed from him," and he remained confident of Seward's basic soundness.[2]

[8] Sumner to Duchess of Argyll, Dec. 20, 1859, Argyll MSS.
[9] Sumner to Palfrey, Apr. 26, 1860, Palfrey MSS.; Stearns: *Stearns,* p. 214.
[1] Sumner to Duchess of Argyll, May 22, 1860, Argyll MSS. Sumner was explaining the reasons why the Republican party failed to nominate Seward, but his words also applied to himself.
[2] Adams, Diary, May 7, 1860, Adams MSS.; Sumner to W. W. Story, May 8, 1860, MS., Huntington Lib.; Sumner to Duchess of Argyll, Mar. 2, 1860, Argyll MSS.

To Sumner's surprise, however, the Republican convention, which met at Chicago on May 16, passed over Seward and nominated Abraham Lincoln, of Illinois, who was personally unknown to Sumner—and, indeed, to most Eastern Republicans. To the Duchess of Argyll, who watched American politics closely, he tried to show the nomination in the best possible light. Lincoln, he assured her, was "a good honest Anti-Slavery man," who would bring strength to the party in the Northwest and in Pennsylvania, where Seward's chances would have been doubtful. "Those who know him speak of him as a person of positive ability and of real goodness," he added, though he was obliged to admit that the nominee had "very little acquaintance with Government" and was quite ignorant of foreign affairs. Still, he added cheerfully: "We think he will be the next President." [3]

Sumner thought that the nomination of Lincoln, whose views on slavery were believed to be moderate, required an explicit, radical restatement of Republican doctrines. Any hesitation he might have had on the ground of expediency was removed when he learned that the Democrats had irreparably split, with Douglas the nominee of the Northern wing of that party, John C. Breckinridge that of the Southern. The existence of a feeble fourth ticket, calling itself Constitutional Unionist, which sought to rally conservative Whigs behind John Bell and Edward Everett, made Republican success more certain. Winning the election was now less Sumner's concern than keeping his party faithful to its principles.

· 2 ·

Political considerations dictated the timing of Sumner's new assault upon the South, but the intention had been fixed in his mind ever since the Brooks assault. So evident was the vindictive-

---

[3] Sumner to Duchess of Argyll, May 22, 1860, Argyll MSS. I have found nothing to confirm the belated reminiscence of Blair Lee that Sumner, meeting his mother on the streets of Washington just after Lincoln's nomination, said: "Mrs. Lee, we are wholly ruined." (Smith: *Blair Family*, I, 485.) Sumner's letter consoling Seward upon the loss of the nomination (May 20, 1860, Seward MSS.) certainly reflects disappointment, but not despair. In the balloting at Chicago for presidential nominees, Sumner himself received a single vote, from a Kentucky delegate. *Proceedings of the First Three Republican National Conventions of 1856, 1860 and 1864* . . . (Minneapolis: Charles W. Johnson; 1893), p. 149.

ness he had stored up that even loyal friends like Howe and Longfellow thought he was "too full of fight," and they warned him
"against saying a word not qualified by benevolence and charity." [4] Others urged him not to make any reference to his sufferings when he spoke and to ignore his Southern assailants. "You
have floored those dirty fellows," T. P. Chandler advised, "and I
would not stop to piss on them while they are down." [5]

Sumner was not to be diverted by these appeals. "There is a
time for every thing," he informed Howe severely, "and when
crime and criminals are thrust before us they are to be met by
all the energies that God has given us by argument, sarcasm,
scorn and denunciation. The whole arsenal of God is ours, and I
will not renounce one of the weapons—not one!" [6]

With his mind fully made up, Sumner waited for an opportunity to claim the Senate floor. A bill for the admission of Kansas as a free state afforded a suitable occasion, and on June 4,
at precisely twelve o'clock, he appeared in the Senate in full evening dress, including white gloves, to launch into his four-hour
oration on "The Barbarism of Slavery."

The news that Sumner was to speak had attracted a respectable, but not crowded, audience to the Senate galleries, and at
the same time had driven most of the Democratic members to
absent themselves conspicuously from the chamber. Gathering
at the bars in the Senate lobby, they made a considerable amount
of noise as Sumner spoke. Senator Louis T. Wigfall, a Texas
fire-eater, strolled ominously up and down the aisle near the
speaker, his "dark, deeply-set eyes, glaring from beneath his
heavy, shaggy brows" at Sumner. Douglas squirmed restlessly in
his seat, and Mason exhibited his exasperation by chewing an
immense quantity of tobacco, so that by the end of the oration,
his quids lay around him in a semicircle. [7]

There was great curiosity to see whether Sumner's strength
would be equal to another long oration, and there was an even
more sensitive interest to learn whether he would refer to him-

[4] Richards: *S. G. Howe*, II, 445.
[5] Chandler to Sumner, Feb. 24, 1860, Sumner MSS.
[6] Sumner to Howe [Jan. 1860], Sumner MSS.
[7] Undated clipping from Cincinnati *Commercial*, Pierce Scrapbooks; Boston
Atlas & Bee, June 5, 1860; New York *Herald*, June 6, 1860; George Sumner to
Longfellow [June 1860], Longfellow MSS.

self and his own sufferings. Quietly he began: "I have no personal griefs to utter. . . . I have no personal wrongs to avenge; only a barbarous nature could attempt to wield that vengeance which belongs to the Lord. The years that have intervened and the tombs that have been opened since I spoke have their voices too," he declared, in his only public reference to the recent deaths of Preston Brooks and Andrew P. Butler. "Besides, what am I—what is any man . . . compared with the Question before us?" [8]

Without further preliminary he launched into his elaborate philippic, which marked an innovation in his oratorical technique. Hitherto he had carefully memorized each major speech and had addressed his remarks to his fellow senators in the hope of influencing their votes. Now he did not wish to overtax his strength by committing to memory an address that, when published, filled forty-two closely printed columns of the *Congressional Globe*. Moreover, experience had taught him that "no senator is reached by any argument" and that his orations could have an effect only if "addressed somewhat as harangues to the whole country." As he intended them "for circulation as tracts," he wanted them to be "full and almost scholastic in form" and to have "more of the completeness and elaborateness of an article, with, however, the form of a speech." Consequently he made no concessions whatever to his listeners, but read all the 35,000 words of his address, including elaborate statistics and lengthy quotations, from galley proofs he held in his hand. [9]

As if recognizing that his new technique lacked brilliance in delivery, Sumner compensated by resorting to increased violence of language. Over half his oration was a refutation of Southern senators' claims that slavery was a beneficent institution, productive of a high civilization. Sumner retorted bluntly that a slave society was no civilization at all. "Barbarous in origin; barbarous in its law; barbarous in all its pretensions; barbarous in the instruments it employs; barbarous in consequences; barbarous in spirit; barbarous wherever it shows itself, Slavery must breed Barbarians." The real character of Southern slavery appeared

[8] Sumner: *The Barbarism of Slavery* . . . (Washington: Thaddeus Hyatt; 1860), p. 1.

[9] Sumner to Theodore Tilton, June 22, 1860, Tilton MSS.; Sumner to Duchess of Argyll, July 31, 1860, Argyll MSS.

in the laws regulating the "peculiar institution." A Southern Negro might "be marked like a hog, branded like a mule, yoked like an ox, maimed like a cur, and constantly beaten like a brute; all according to law." Moreover, "by the license of Slavery, a whole race is delivered over to prostitution and concubinage, without the protection of any law."

The practical consequences of slavery were as barbarous as its laws. In relentless statistical detail Sumner compared the populations and the economies of the free and the slave states. He found that through the influence of slavery "population, values of all kinds, manufactures, commerce, railroads, canals, charities, the post office, colleges, professional schools, academies, public schools, newspapers, periodicals, books, authorship, inventions" in the South were "all stunted." Mercilessly he singled out South Carolina for scorn. Despite that state's lofty pretensions to culture, a smaller percentage of her white population than of the Massachusetts free Negroes attended school.

Even more shocking, Sumner found, was the influence of slavery upon the character of the slaveholders. "Every Slavemaster on his plantation is a Bashaw, with all the prerogatives of a Turk." "Six thousand skulls of infants are said to have been taken from a single fish-pond near a nunnery, to the dismay of Pope Gregory," Sumner asserted. "Under the law of Slavery, infants, the offspring of masters 'who dream of Freedom in a slave's embrace,' are not thrown into a fish-pond. . . . They are sold."

How could one expect civilized leaders to emerge from such a society? Naturally these "modern imitators of Cain" in the Southern United States adopted "the bludgeon, the revolver, and the bowie-knife" as their constant companions; naturally they turned to the cowardly duel; naturally they desired "the suppression of all freedom of speech or of the press." Naturally, too, these slaveholders, when they became members of Congress, heaped "reproach, contumely, violence even unto death" upon anyone who disagreed with them. Sumner reviewed the history of the violence committed by these congressional "bludgeon-bearers of Slavery"—conspicuously omitting any reference to 1856.

These Southern slaveholders were not merely barbarians; they seemed to rejoice in their degraded condition. "No New Zealander exults in his tattoo, no savage of the Northwest exults in his flat head, more than the Slave-master in these latter days . . . exults in his unfortunate condition."

In the second, much briefer section of his oration, Sumner contested the Southern argument that slaveholders had a right to take their "property" into the national territories. "There is no sanction for such pretension; no ordinance for it, or title," he asserted. The Southern claim of superiority for the white race, if true, was no justification for extending slavery. "If the African race be inferior, as is alleged, then is it the unquestionable duty of a Christian Civilization to lift it from its degradation, not by the bludgeon and the chain . . . but by a generous charity." The argument that the Bible justified slavery was both ridiculous and unhistorical. The Southern contention that the Constitution protected their peculiar property was equally unfounded; the Constitution contained "not one sentence, phrase, or word—not a single suggestion, hint, or equivocation, even" to justify such a proslavery interpretation. The true principle, Sumner concluded, in almost the same words used in his first antislavery speech in Congress in 1852, was to make "Freedom *national* and Slavery *sectional*" by establishing everywhere under federal jurisdiction "the law of impartial Freedom without distinction of color or race." [1]

As Sumner concluded, Senator James Chesnut, of South Carolina, rose to explain why the Southern senators had listened quietly to Sumner's diatribe. "After ranging over Europe, crawling through the back doors to whine at the feet of British aristocracy, craving pity, and reaping a rich harvest of contempt," Sumner, "the incarnation of malice, mendacity, and cowardice," had reappeared in the Senate, neither wiser nor better for his experience. Unwilling "to increase the devotees at the shrine of this new idol," the Southerners were "not inclined again to send [him] forth the recipient of punishment howling through the world, yelping fresh cries of slander and malice."

[1] All quotations in the above paragraphs are from Sumner: *The Barbarism of Slavery*. See pp. 3–6, 12, 14–18, 20, 24–5, 27–8, 31. On Sumner's use of the Civilization-Barbarism antithesis to characterize the sectional struggle see Charles A. and Mary R. Beard: *The American Spirit: A Study of the Idea of Civilization in the United States* (*The Rise of American Civilization*, Vol. IV New York: The Macmillan Co.; 1942), pp. 301–7.

Sumner, though very weary from his exertions, replied that he planned to print Chesnut's remarks in an appendix to his speech as another illustration of the barbarism he had just described.[2]

· 3 ·

Washington seethed with excitement as the news spread of Sumner's fresh, bitter attack upon the South. Wherever Southerners gathered, they asked each other whether "Sumner's got it yet." Four days after the oration a drunken clerk from the patent office forced his way into Sumner's chamber and threatened that his friends would cut the senator's "d——d throat before the next night."

Alarmed, the Massachusetts delegation to Congress rallied to protect their senator, and some Kansas admirers constituted themselves his bodyguard. Though in "a state of not unnatural excitement" over the danger, Sumner refused to arm himself and tried to dissuade protectors from carrying firearms. But, for more than three weeks they kept the senator closely guarded. "Two men sleep on the floor of my front room," he reported to Longfellow; "they have watched me at leaving the Senate, and, if not by my side, have kept within a short distance, so as to be near if any attack should come. All this has been done without any hint from me, and hardly with my approval. . . . Think of such precautions in a place which calls itself civilized!"[3]

Events proved that Sumner was more in need of protection from his Northern friends than from his Southern enemies. Of course the Southerners were irritated by his speech, and probably most agreed with the editor of the New Orleans *Crescent* that Sumner was "a pestilent knave and low demagogue, who, from the meanest of motives, is trying to create sectional hatred in the country." But the vituperativeness of Sumner's analysis

[2] *Cong. Globe*, 36 Cong., 1 Sess., 2,603–4.

[3] Clippings from New York *Evening Post* and other newspapers, Sumner Scrapbooks; *The Liberator*, XXX (June 18, 1860), 94; A. B. Johnson to George Sumner, June 6, 1860, Sumner MSS.; Adams, Diary, June 9, 1860, Adams MSS.; Sumner to Longfellow, June 29, 1860, Longfellow MSS. The story that Sumner himself asked the Massachusetts delegation to defend him (Dawes: *Sumner*, pp. 146–7) is untrue. A. B. Johnson to Pierce, Aug. 8, 1892, Pierce MSS.

of slavery made it possible for many Southerners to dismiss his speech as just another abolitionist harangue, no more worthy of consideration than the rantings of Garrison or Wendell Phillips.[4]

In the North, however, Sumner's oration could not be so easily dismissed. The senator was, after all, a principal figure in the Republican party. He could claim, with justice, to have been one of the founders of the party; his sufferings at the hands of Preston Brooks had been potent Republican ammunition in 1856; now, as one of the senior Republicans in the Senate, he was certain to be a powerful figure if Lincoln was elected. Surely he spoke not for himself alone, but for his party.

Such an interpretation was precisely what most Republican leaders feared. Few Republicans in Congress approved his speech. "As a bitter, denunciatory oration, it could hardly be exceeded in point of style and finish," Senator James W. Grimes, of Iowa, thought. "But . . . it sounded harsh, vindictive, and slightly brutal. . . . His speech has done the Republicans no good." Party leaders outside of Congress were equally disturbed by Sumner's incendiary tone. When the senator sent a copy to Abraham Lincoln, the presidential nominee cagily acknowledged it in a noncommittal note: "I have not yet found time to peruse the speech; but I anticipate much both of pleasure and instruction from it."[5]

Republican newspapers were outspoken in criticizing the speech. Horace Greeley could not find room for the oration in his New York *Tribune* (though he later printed it in his weekly edition, which circulated in the strongly antislavery rural areas of the North and the West). Faintly praising it as "doubtless a strong and forcible speech," the *Tribune* editor wished "he had made it on some other bill than that providing for the Admission of Kansas," which it would, in fact, help to defeat. The New York *Times* was even more unsympathetic. Judging that Sumner had devoted his "four leisure years . . . to collecting every instance of cruelty, violence, passion, coarseness, and vulgarity recorded as having happened within the Slave States," it asked: "Aside from

[4] Dwight Lowell Dumond (ed.): *Southern Editorials on Secession* (New York: The Century Co.; 1931), pp. 129, 131.

[5] Salter: *Grimes*, p. 127; Roy P. Basler (ed.): *The Collected Works of Abraham Lincoln* (New Brunswick: Rutgers University Press; 1954), IV, 76.

its utter irrelevancy to the Kansas Question, what general good
can be hoped from such envenomed attacks upon the Slave
States?" [6]

Even Massachusetts Republicans received "The Barbarism
of Slavery" coolly. The Boston *Advertiser,* a former Whig journal
that now represented the conservative wing of the Republican
party in eastern Massachusetts, thought well of the "careful and
patient labor" which had gone into the speech, but asked "whether
the occasion called for such a display of power, whether the object of attack needed such ponderous blows." The Springfield *Republican,* the most powerful party paper in western Massachusetts, was more blunt: "We do not think Charles Sumner a statesman and we doubt if he ever can become one, or has any bent in
that direction." [7]

Sumner's opponents gleefully attacked the speech. Boston
patricians, ousted from political power, but still cherishing their
hatred of Sumner, which they now could exhibit only in carping
at his use of classical quotations or in repeatedly blackballing him
for membership in the Massachusetts Historical Society,[8] welcomed the oration as evidence "no less [of] his total unfitness
for public station than [of] his utter inaptitude for political warfare." The Boston *Courier,* for which his former friend Hillard
now wrote, branded the speech as "an insidious and faithless
blow at the Constitution." Boston Democrats denounced the "ped-
antry, egotism, fortuitous hypothesis, malice, rhapsody, and ver-
bosity" which characterized the address, and Catholic papers,
alarmed by Sumner's gratuitous reference to alleged immoralities

[6] New York *Tribune,* June 5, 1860; New York *Times,* June 6, 1860. For
other, similar newspaper reactions see Sumner: *Works,* V, 132–7.

[7] Boston *Advertiser,* June 6, 1860; Springfield *Republican,* quoted in Laura
A. White: "Charles Sumner and the Crisis of 1860–61," in Avery Craven (ed.):
Essays in Honor of William E. Dodd (Chicago: University of Chicago Press;
1935), p. 139.

[8] When Sumner declared that Senator Mason's conduct as chairman of the
committee investigating John Brown's raid reminded him of what "an ancient
poet said of a judge in hell, that he punished first and heard afterwards,—
'castigatque auditque'" (Sumner: *Works,* IV, 450), the Boston *Courier* professed to be terribly shocked at his "offensive and insulting language . . . unfit
to be employed by any person worthy of such a place." *The Liberator,* XXX
(Apr. 27, 1860), 65. C. F. Adams repeatedly sponsored Sumner for membership
in the Historical Society, but Winthrop always blocked his election. Adams,
Diary, Dec. 10, 1857, Mar. 11, and Dec. 9, 1858, and Feb. 1, 1859, Adams MSS.

in monasteries, agreed that "a speech more destitute of states-manship, in every point of view, was never given to the public in any form." [9]

James Gordon Bennett, the pro-Southern editor of the New York *Herald,* was more cunning that these forthright opponents of Sumner's. He printed "The Barbarism of Slavery" in full on the front page of the *Herald* and day after day gave it a great play. Bennett argued that Sumner, who possessed "the philosophical acumen of Mr. Seward, without his cautious reserve as a politi-cian; the honesty of Lincoln, without the craft of a candidate in nomination [;] and literary culture, political zeal, and the gift of eloquence," was "in the very foremost rank as a leader and expo-nent of the black republican ideas." Hence Sumner's oration re-vealed the true plans of his party, whose success in November would mean "carnage and the flames of war," "swords dripping with fraternal gore, torches put to the homes of brothers, deso-lation spread over happy and prosperous States, for opinion's sake." [1]

Sumner angrily resented these criticisms. Neither the at-tacks of the Southerners, whom he now considered beyond the reach of reason, nor the jibes of Northern Democrats, those open compurgators of Preston Brooks, troubled him so much as the "cold shoulderism, heartlessness, dirty-water and paving stones" with which Republicans had received his ideas. Indig-nantly he denied the charge, which even *The Times* of London echoed, that he had spoken in a spirit of "personal irritability." "The Barbarism of Slavery" was "almost a necessity," he explained defensively; he had avoided "all personality and . . . absolutely all allusion to his own experience." Of course he had used strong language, but it was not his words but the facts that branded slavery as barbaric. Critics failed to see the symbolic purpose in his speech: he was no mere senator, but the Spokesman of a Righteous Cause, who had acted "to vindicate Freedom of debate

[9] *The Liberator,* XXX (June 22, 1860), 97; Sumner: *Works,* V, 136; Ander-son: "Slavery Issue," pp. 286–7.
[1] New York *Herald,* June 5–6, 1860. After building Sumner up, Bennett proceeded joyfully to demolish him, arguing, with some justice, that the crimes he attributed to slavery were unrepresentative and that he ignored "the record of divorces, elopements . . . the overcrowded prisons; the penal hospitals . . . the notorious insecurity of life in the great cities," and other evidences of "barbarism" in the North. *Ibid.,* June 7, 1860.

struck down in my person; and this I wished to do not by words and mere declamations, but by a speech, which, as a practical exercise of this right, should be a precedent and an example." [2]

Instead of praise for this service, Sumner felt that he was rewarded with obloquy and indifference. "Perhaps no person has ever received so many attacks—with so little of real assistance in his defence," he complained. "Others, who have become equally obnoxious, have had earnest [newspaper] presses to beat back the enemy. I have none; not one that does not give the enemy something to hurl at me." "Perhaps," he added, in his martyr tone, "I deserve it. At all events, I have labored for the truth, and I accept the consequences." [3]

With the new, inner security Sumner had developed during his long illness, he was undeterred by criticism. "*That* speech," he vowed, "will yet be adopted by the Republican party." Long after Congress adjourned, he remained in sweltering Washington franking thousands of copies for distribution all over the country. Determined to maintain the offensive, he accepted an invitation to speak before the Young Men's Republican Club of New York, the radical anti-Seward wing of the party, on July 11. Aside from adding juicy details on "the roasting of slaves alive at the stake" in the South, a tribute to Lincoln, "whose ability, so conspicuously shown in his own State, attracted at once the admiration of the whole country," and a prediction that with Republican success slavery would die "as a poisoned rat dies of rage in its hole," he mostly repeated the argument of "The Barbarism of Slavery." By reiteration he hoped to gain broader acceptance of his ideas, so as to maintain the Republican principles "in purity and power." [4]

Loyally Sumner's friends supported his efforts. Howe solicited subscriptions on the streets of Boston in order to finance a wide distribution of the speech. Frank Bird mailed a copy to each voter in his district. E. L. Pierce interviewed every editor in his congressional district and secured pledges that they would back

[2] Sumner to Elizur Wright [June 1860], copy, Wright MSS.; Robinson: *Pen Portraits*, p. 91; *The Times* (London), June 18, 1860; Sumner to Duchess of Argyll, July 31, 1860, Argyll MSS.

[3] Sumner to Theodore Tilton, July 21, 1860, Tilton MSS.

[4] Sumner to Howe, June 12, 1860, MS., Huntington Lib.; Sumner to Pierce, July 6, 1860, Sumner MSS.; Sumner to Theodore Tilton, July 21, 1860, Tilton MSS.; Sumner: *Works:* V, 210, 225, 229.

Sumner's stand. Then the Bird Club backed resolutions in the Massachusetts House of Representatives praising the senator "for his recent manly and earnest assertion of the right of free discussion on the floor of the United States Senate" and approving "the thorough, truthful and comprehensive examination of the institution of Slavery embraced in Mr. Sumner's recent speech." "There was," Howe reported with delight, "much *squeaming* among the party hacks at the State House about endorsing the speech; and they only lacked the pluck—(not will) to refuse to do it." But, under the remorseless pressure of Bird's machine, both houses of the legislature passed the resolutions by overwhelming majorities. Triumphantly Pierce wrote Sumner: "If the politicians disown you, they will have to disown Massachusetts—for Massachusetts will sustain both you and your speech —and you will without question be reelected at the expiration of your present term." [5]

After a few weeks, Sumner's exertions to circulate and publicize his speech began to pay off. Though the more sophisticated Republican Eastern cities had repudiated it, the rural areas of the North and West welcomed it. To these Republicans, whose antislavery principles were ingrained, Sumner's address was an assurance that their party stood for something more significant than enacting a protective tariff, building a Pacific railroad, or even electing a presidential candidate. Practically every small-town newspaper in Massachusetts, most of those throughout the rest of New England, and a great many others stretching out to the western frontier—in fact, wherever New Englanders had settled—enthusiastically praised both the speech and the senator. Equally significant were the hundreds of adoring letters which poured in upon Sumner. While Republican chieftains, with the notable exception of Salmon P. Chase, were silent, insignificant members of the party thanked Sumner for his oration "in the name of our common humanity, in the name of justice, in the name of righteousness and of the God of all excelence [sic]. "Behind you," pledged a Pittsburgh admirer, "stand a mil-

---

[5] Howe to Sumner, June 5, and 15, 1860, Howe MSS.; Bird to Sumner, June 30, 1860, Sumner MSS.; Pierce to Sumner, June 20–1, 1860, ibid.; "Resolves Relating to Freedom of Speech," passed by the Massachusetts legislature, and transmitted to Sumner, June 16, 1860, ibid.

lion of your fellow-citizens in whose hearts your speech finds an echo." [6]

So great was the reaction in Sumner's favor that the same party managers who treated him coolly in June warmly solicited his aid in August. The congressional Republican committee decided to circulate "The Barbarism of Slavery" as a campaign document at two dollars a hundred. Thurlow Weed, who, like Seward, had been aghast at the impolicy of the speech when it was delivered, now begged Sumner to campaign through upstate New York. From Illinois, Maine, and Ohio Sumner received urgent invitations to speak. So popular was the senator now that a mere letter from him, supporting the candidacy of Republican J. M. Ashley in Ohio, was credited with playing a major role in defeating the Democratic candidate.[7]

Sumner refused to campaign outside of Massachusetts, for he had urgent business at home. The murmur of criticism evoked by his "Barbarism of Slavery" speech reminded him that he must reassert leadership in his own state Republican party—a task the more urgent as his own re-election to the Senate was only two years away. As the Republicans were certain to carry Massachusetts by an overwhelming majority in 1860, Sumner and his friends thought the occasion most opportune to weed out party leaders whose antislavery zeal was dubious.

Governor N. P. Banks, handsome, dapper, and plausible, was marked for slaughter. Ever since Banks had intrigued for Sumner's seat, the senator's friends had been undercutting him. They had not been able to keep him from winning renomination in 1859, but they kept the choice from being unanimous. With Sumner's tacit connivance, they undermined the governor's hopes for the Republican presidential nomination in 1860 by splitting the Massachusetts delegation and making John A. Andrew, Sumner's warm partisan, chairman. Banks decided to retire temporarily from politics in order to become resident director of the Illinois Central Railroad, but he had his eye on 1864 and wanted to leave the Massachusetts Republican party in friendly

[6] Sumner preserved clippings from dozens of small-town newspapers in his scrapbooks. For extracts from the correspondence evoked by the speech see Sumner: *Works*, V, 146–73. Hundreds of other letters are in the Sumner MSS.

[7] Ashley to Sumner, Oct. 13, 1860, Sumner MSS.

hands. Consequently he kept his decision not to run again for governor a secret until his henchmen could organize support for the nomination of his friend, Congressman Henry L. Dawes. Then, only five days before the state convention was to meet at Worcester, he publicly announced his withdrawal in a statement carefully timed to reach the rural districts, where Sumner's friends were strongest, too late to influence the choice of delegates.

But, William Claflin, a member of the Bird Club and a state senator, got wind of Banks's intention one day before he made his public announcement and, though it was late at night, went at once to Sumner's house on Hancock Street. "Give me my boots," exclaimed Sumner when he heard the news. "John A. Andrew must be the next governor of Massachusetts." During the next five days Sumner and the members of the Bird Club were incessantly active, buttonholing delegates, arranging caucuses, planning tactics. Strongly as they desired Andrew's nomination, Sumner's faction had in mind something "more important than the mere nomination of governor"; they intended to purify the Republican party in Massachusetts, to endow it with "the spirit of liberty"—and to align it squarely behind Sumner himself.[8]

When the Republican convention met at Mechanic's Hall in Worcester on August 29, every detail had been prearranged, including Sumner's carefully delayed appearance, at which the delegates rose and cheered. Before the nominations began, the senator was invited to address the meeting. After the enthusiastic shouts of welcome died out, Sumner launched into a vindication of the Republican party against "the Proslavery non-committalism of Bell, the Proslavery dogma of Breckinridge, and the Proslavery dodge of Douglas." Ostensibly standing aloof from the gubernatorial nomination the convention was about to make, Sumner, in fact, warmly endorsed Andrew. "Let not fidelity to those principles which give dignity and glory to Massachusetts, and to our common country, be an argument against him," he urged, referring to the unnamed candidate; in obvious reference

[8] For an excellent account of these maneuvers see Harrington: *Banks*, pp. 47–51. See also Pearson: *Andrew*, I, 120–1; C. M. Ellis to Sumner, Aug. 25 [1860], Sumner MSS.

to Andrew, who had approved of John Brown and had subscribed money to defend the raiders, Sumner cited the verses of Jonathan Swift:

> *That stupid cant, "He went too far," despise,*
> *And know that to be brave is to be wise.*

Partly by preconvention maneuvering, partly by Sumner's oratory, the Bird Club frustrated Banks's efforts to name his successor, and the convention chose Andrew by a vote of 723 to 327.[9]

Enthusiastically Sumner threw himself into the campaign to elect Andrew, whose "unquestioned abilities, extensive attainments, and rare aptitude for affairs" would make him an ideal governor. Almost every day he addressed Republican rallies in speeches that had a force and directness markedly in contrast with his Senate oratory. The choice before the voters, he said, was simply that between Northern civilization and Southern barbarism, between the doctrines of John Quincy Adams and those of John C. Calhoun, between the Mayflower and the first "Slave-Ship, with its fetters, its chains, its bludgeons, and its whips." "Choose ye, fellow-citizens, between the two." [1]

In November the voters of Massachusetts chose. By almost unprecedented majorities they elected John A. Andrew governor and gave their electoral votes to Abraham Lincoln for President.

· 4 ·

In the secession crisis that followed Lincoln's election in 1860 Sumner's course was an erratic one.[2] Though he later recalled

---

[9] Contemporary newspaper accounts of the convention are clipped in the W. S. Robinson Scrapbooks. Cf. Sumner: *Works*, V, 240–68.

[1] Sumner: *Works*, V, 277, 286; Boston *Advertiser*, Nov. 6, 1860.

[2] The following pages cover the period treated in Laura A. White's "Charles Sumner and the Crisis of 1860–61," the only portion of a projected biography Professor White published before her death. In her critical and stimulating essay Miss White argued that "Sumner's central idea at this time seems to have been . . . the *permanent* separation of all slave states and the organization of two confederacies—one slave, one free." I cannot agree with this interpretation for the following reasons: (1) I am unwilling to trust the anonymous Washington newspaper correspondents, particularly those of the venemously anti-Sumner New York *Herald*, upon whom Miss White heavily relied; (2) I agree with Professor Frank Maloy Anderson (*The Mystery of 'A Public Man': A Historical Detective Story* [Minneapolis: University of Minnesota Press; 1948]) that "The Diary of a Public Man" (*North American Review*, CXXIX (1879), 125–40, 259–73, 375–88, 484–96), upon which Miss White depended, is "a semi-fictional

that he had, from the very beginning, insisted that the Federal Union must be preserved, even at the cost of coercing the seceding states, contemporary evidence shows that his ideas were confused and contradictory. Like most Republicans, he failed at the outset to understand the seriousness of the crisis. He had heard threats of disunion so often that he had ceased to credit them. Like Greeley, Seward, and Thurlow Weed, Sumner, during the 1860 campaign, had sneered at Southern talk of disunion as mere "weapons of political warfare," "threats, and nothing more," "one supreme absurdity." [3]

Even after Sumner arrived in Washington in December 1860, and learned that South Carolina, Georgia, Florida, Alabama, Mississippi, Louisiana, and Texas would almost certainly be out of the Union before Lincoln could be inaugurated, he found it difficult to decide what policy to pursue. A sincere advocate of peace, he could not share Ben Wade's enthusiasm for forcing the Southern states back into the Union, or join Zachariah Chandler in asserting: "Without a little blood-letting this Union will not . . . be worth a rush." The other alternative, further concessions to the South, was even less palatable. If the history of the United States taught anything, Sumner felt, it was that appeasement of slaveholders was impossible. The Missouri Compromise, the Compromise of 1850, the Kansas-Nebraska Act had all been abdications of Northern principle in order to placate the South, but the slaveholders remained insatiable. Concessions, furthermore, would demoralize the forces of freedom in the North. "The enmity of Slavery may be dangerous," Sumner warned, "but its friendship is fatal." [4]

---

production," which "ought not to be regarded as a reliable source"; (3) I have found new materials in the Adams MSS. and the Argyll MSS., which, of course, were not available to Miss White, contradicting her thesis; (4) I believe that Miss White, by confining her researches to Sumner alone, failed to realize that his position on peaceful secession was very similar to Greeley's, which David M. Potter has so incisively analyzed: "When confronted by a choice between compromise and peaceable secession, Greeley chose peaceable secession; but when confronted by a choice between war and peaceful secession, Greeley chose war" ("Horace Greeley and Peaceable Secession," *Journal of Southern History*, VII [1941], 145–9). (5) It seems to me that Miss White confused Sumner's prophecies about the spread of secession with a desire to see it spread.

[3] Boston *Advertiser*, Oct. 9, 1860; Sumner: *Works*, V, 296, 305. In the following pages I am heavily indebted to Professor David M. Potter's admirable monograph, *Lincoln and His Party in the Secession Crisis* (New Haven: Yale University Press; 1942).

[4] Sumner: *Works*, V, 342.

Tentatively Sumner brought himself to think that the temporary secession of the Gulf states might not be a bad thing. He never went as far as President-Elect Lincoln, who said that he was "rather glad of this military preparation in the South" because it would "enable the people the more easily to suppress any uprisings there which [the secessionists'] misrepresentations . . . may have encouraged," [5] but he did recognize that secession—"the mild phrase for treason"—might have compensations. Withdrawal of the congressional delegations from the Deep South would make it easier for the Republicans to gain complete control of the national government. Perhaps during the absence of the slaveholders the United States could take advantage of the unrest in British North America, and Sumner again toyed with one of his oldest and most persistent ideas, the "magnificent project of the . . . acquisition of Canada." [6]

What was more important, the seceding Southerners, sailing off into independence "with the black flag at the mast-head," would promptly find that "Slavery could not gain" from their venture. They would learn that "the civilization of the Christian world, speaking with the innumerable voices of the press, and constituting a Public Opinion of irresistible energy," was hostile to the creation of a new slave power. Europe would "refuse to recognize it in the Family of Nations." Out of the Union, and unprotected by federal armies, these states of the Deep South would inevitably face "servile insurrection, ending in Emancipation—perhaps, as in Santo Domingo." As a lover of peace Sumner shuddered at this prospect. "Much as I desire the extinction

---

[5] Quoted in Potter, *Lincoln and His Party*, p. 141.

[6] Everett, Diary, Jan. 29, 1861, Everett MSS. The New York *Herald* charged that Republicans actually desired "to prevent the seceding States from returning to the Union, and to force the rest of the slave States out of it, . . . with a view of annexing the British colonies, which would have nothing to do with the confederacy so long as slavery was tolerated within its borders, but which, with that insuperable objection removed, will be glad to unite . . . with their Anglo-Saxon brothers" (Feb. 4, 7, and 17, 1861). Cf. Gardner Brewer to Sumner, Jan. 30, 1861, Sumner MSS. For Canadian opinion on annexation see Helen G. MacDonald: *Canadian Public Opinion on the American Civil War* ("Columbia University Studies in History, Economics, and Public Law," Vol. CXXIV, New York: Columbia University Press; 1926), p. 85 ff. As early as 1849 Sumner wrote Richard Cobden of the "inevitable . . . annexation to the United States" of Canada. Pierce, III, 42. He told the Earl of Carlisle that the acquisition of Canada by the United States "would 'redress the balance,' which has been turned in favor of Slavery by the annexation of Texas." Sumner to Earl of Carlisle, Jan. 8, 1850, Carlisle MSS.

of slavery," he protested, "I do not wish to see it go down in blood." Yet he could not resist a certain grim satisfaction in watching the slaveholders "rush upon their destiny." All in all, then, he began to think that a temporary secession of the Gulf states could be endured quite cheerfully. "The difficulties in the way of the *seceders* are so great," he wrote Howe in December 1860, "that I fear we shall not get rid of them *long enough*. My desire is that 4 or 5 should go out *long enough* to be completely humbled and chastened and to leave us in the control of the Government." [7]

"If the secession can be restrained to the 'Cotton States,'" Sumner wrote the Duchess of Argyll shortly after Congress convened, "I shall be willing to let them go. But can it be stopped there?" That "if" and that question were weighing on all minds. Sumner was convinced that a proper Northern policy could keep the slave states of the Upper South peaceably in the Union until the Gulf states, after an unsuccessful attempt at independence, asked readmission. Considering "the whole slave-holding class as a combination of ruffianism and bluster, whiskey-drinking and tobacco-chewing," Sumner, as Charles Francis Adams, Jr., shrewdly observed, thought that the secessionists of the Upper South would, "like petulant, passionate children, prone to violence," yield in face of Northern firmness. Convinced that "the large mass of people even in the Slave States do not desire disunion," Sumner felt that the Republicans must strengthen the hands of such Southern antislavery men as the Blairs in Maryland and Missouri, and Cassius M. Clay in Kentucky. The potential unionist majority in the Upper South must not be "debauched" by concessions or compromises. To the suggestion that his policy might make the Southerners resort to arms, Sumner exclaimed: "Never! They are too crafty! Bullies! Braggarts! They would be assassins some of them if they dared—but fair fight, never!" [8]

Positive that he had worked out a proper policy for coping with secession, Sumner was appalled to discover that Congress

[7] Sumner: *Works*, V, 304, 482–3; Sumner to Duchess of Argyll, Dec. 14, 1860, Argyll MSS.; Sumner to Howe, Dec. 16, 1860, Sumner MSS. Cf. Ellis Yarnall: *Wordsworth and the Coleridges* . . . (New York: The Macmillan Co.; 1899), p. 8.

[8] Sumner to Duchess of Argyll, Dec. 14, 1860, Argyll MSS.; C. F. Adams, Jr.: *Autobiography*, pp. 85–6; Sumner: *Works*, V, 302; W. H. Russell: "Recollections of the Civil War," *North American Review*, CLXVI (1898), 241–2.

was seriously considering compromise as a means of relieving the crisis. Senator Crittenden, Henry Clay's successor, proposed irrevocable constitutional amendments that, among other things, would guarantee slavery in "all the territory of the United States now held, or hereafter acquired, below the latitude of 36° 30′." Stephen A. Douglas was working indefatigably to support compromise. So strong was the desire for adjustment that the House of Representatives appointed a Committee of Thirty-three and the Senate a Committee of Thirteen to work out remedies for the sectional crisis.

Believing that his own program would ensure peace, liberty, and union, Sumner gave no countenance to such talk of appeasement. He was unmoved by appeals from the Boston mercantile community, hard hit by the cutting off of Southern cotton. If businessmen failed to support his plan, Sumner announced that he would appeal to the soundly antislavery elements in Massachusetts, "the farmer, the mechanic, the laborer." He refused to believe impressive evidence that popular sentiment even in his own state favored compromise. In Boston itself a rowdy mob showed its sympathies with the South by breaking up a meeting commemorating the execution of John Brown, manhandled some Negroes who were in attendance, threatened Wendell Phillips's life, and hooted at Sumner's house in Hancock Street. At local elections held in December the Republican vote fell off sharply; the party lost Worcester and Newburyport and had far smaller strength in Boston, Charlestown, and Lowell. Boston workingmen favored compromise and bitterly condemned Sumner for opposing it. Mammoth petitions supported Crittenden's proposals; in Boston, with only 19,000 voters, 14,000 persons endorsed the compromise amendments.[9]

To all such agitation Sumner professed himself totally indifferent. To the intense irritation of the sponsors of the Crittenden petition, he declared that most of the Massachusetts signers must have been "seduced" by the Kentucky senator's rep-

9 Sumner: *Works*, V, 473; Maria Weston Chapman to Sumner [Dec. 1860], Sumner MSS.; Mary Scrugham: *The Peaceable Americans of 1861* ("Columbia University Studies in History, Economics, and Public Law," Vol. XCVI, New York: Columbia University Press; 1921), pp. 70–1; Mrs. Chapman Coleman: *The Life of John J. Crittenden* (Philadelphia: J. B. Lippincott & Co.; 1873), II, 238–40, 262.

utation and have "put their names to a petition which . . . they did not, in all respects and in all its bearings, fully understand." Anyway, as most of the signers lived in the cities, especially in Boston, they did not represent the true spirit of the Commonwealth, "for it is only when you get off those pavements, away from the paving stones, that you find the true sentiment of Massachusetts." [1]

Naturally Sumner showed no sympathy for the committee of distinguished Bostonians who arrived in Washington to present their huge petition, patriotically wrapped in a United States flag, in favor of the Crittenden compromise, and the choice of Edward Everett, A. A. Lawrence, and Robert C. Winthrop to head the group was scarcely designed to win his confidence. When Sumner met members of the committee accidentally on the evening of their arrival, he scornfully refused to speak to Winthrop, but told the others that their petition was "mere *wind*, —nothing better than a penny-whistle in a tempest." During the next few days, while the committee tried to drum up support for the compromise, Sumner ignored their existence. Not until Edward Everett cunningly played upon the senator's vanity by telling him that he alone could introduce a successful compromise bill did Sumner unbend to the extent of explaining, in an incoherent, excited fashion that Everett thought "approaching to insanity," his own program for solving the crisis. Not even Everett's flattery could induce him to support Crittenden's proposals. Sententiously he explained: "You are mistaken in supposing that I might have success with compromise, if I could bring it forward. If I am strong with the North, it is because of the conviction that I cannot compromise; but the moment I compromised, I, too, should be lost."

Toward Winthrop, Sumner remained implacable. When Winthrop and Everett, as former members, were admitted to the Senate chamber, where most of the members they had known in previous years cordially welcomed them, Sumner came up, thrust himself between the two men on the sofa where they were seated, and, rudely turning his back upon Winthrop, proceeded to talk

---

[1] George T. Brown and others to Sumner, Feb. 13, 1861, copy, Crittenden MSS.; C. B. Allen to J. J. Crittenden, Feb. 13, 1861, ibid.; Sumner: *Works*, V, 472, 474; White: "Sumner and the Crisis," p. 167.

with Everett. Eager to do anything he could to help promote compromise, Winthrop had other members of the committee tell
Sumner that he was willing to forget the past. Loftily Sumner
refused to speak to him until he made an apology. "I did not understand *for what* the apology was to be," Winthrop noted in his
journal, "but as I had always considered him as the offending
party I had nothing further to do but to forgive him (as I did)
and let him go." [2]

If the Massachusetts Union-savers found Sumner intracta-
ble, President Buchanan learned that he was immovable. Convinced that "The President is a traitor, who lets the vessel drift
to destruction," Sumner did not willingly speak to Buchanan, but,
when Governor Andrew requested him to have a formal interview with the President, he reluctantly went to the White House
on February 2. The feeble Buchanan was distraught by the crisis;
believing that no state had the right to secede and that the federal government could not coerce a seceded state, he longed for
compromise and, though he probably knew it was in vain, tried
to influence Sumner. When the senator had completed his official business, he remained to ask: "Mr. President, what else can
we do in Massachusetts for the good of the country?"

There was a pause. Then Buchanan heavily sighed: "Much,
Mr. Sumner—no state more."

"What?"

"Adopt the Crittenden propositions," said Buchanan.

"Is that necessary?"

"Yes."

Firmly Sumner replied: "Massachusetts has not yet spoken
directly on these propositions; but . . . such are the unaltera-
ble convictions of her people, they would see their state sink below the sea and become a sandbank before they would adopt
those propositions acknowledging property in man." [3]

[2] For a day-by-day account of the committee's reception in Washington see
Winthrop's "Memorandum, January 1861," Winthrop MSS. See also Everett,
Diary, Jan. 29, 1861, Everett MSS.; Sumner: *Works*, V, 444; George W. Curtis,
in *A Memorial of Charles Sumner* (Boston; 1874), pp. 141–2.

[3] Sumner to Thomas Gaffield, Dec. 29, 1860, MS., Huntington Lib.; Sumner
to Andrew, Feb. 3, 1861, Andrew MSS.; Springfield *Republican*, Feb. 6, 1861.

· 5 ·

Sumner gained a certain fierce satisfaction from such encounters with political opponents, to whom he owed nothing and from whom he could expect less, but he grieved to find that members of his own party were also endorsing concessions to the South. It was bad enough for moderate Republicans like John Sherman to advocate compromise, or for Thurlow Weed, whom Sumner dismissed as "a *politician*—not a *statesman*," [4] to talk of extending the Missouri Compromise line. But, when leading spokesmen of the party, hitherto distinguished for their antislavery principles, also favored yielding to the South, Sumner became almost frantic over their backsliding.

He found Seward's position both incomprehensible and unpardonable. The foxy New Yorker, who was expected to become the "premier" of the incoming Lincoln administration, was too clever to expose his hand, but everybody believed that he was co-operating with Douglas and Crittenden to work out a new compromise scheme. Hoping to win Sumner over, Seward asked his opinion of the major policy statement he planned to make in the Senate on January 12, favoring a modification of the Northern personal liberty laws, guaranteeing by constitutional amendment that Congress would never interfere with slavery in any state, and endorsing a somewhat obscure plan that appeared to mean that the New Mexico–Arizona territory would be admitted as another slave state. Sumner was appalled. He thought that Seward's speech would encourage the fire-eaters of the Deep South and undermine the strong unionism of the border states. These concessions would cost the country everything. He pleaded with Seward, "he . . . prayed him, besought him, implored him by his past record, his good name, his memory hereafter," to delete "every word of compromise, concession, or offer to the traitors." All Seward needed to do was "simply to declare that Mr. Lincoln would be inaugurated on the 4th March, President of the United States, and to rally the country to his support." [5]

[4] Sumner to Andrew, Jan. 8, 1861, Andrew MSS.
[5] C. F. Adams, Jr.: *Autobiography*, p. 81; Sarah Forbes Hughes (ed.): *Letters and Recollections of John Murray Forbes* (Boston: Houghton Mifflin Co.; 1899), I, 186; Sumner to Andrew, Jan. 17, 1861, Andrew MSS. For a discussion of Republican intraparty strife, by an admirer of Seward, see Henry Adams: "The Great Secession Winter of 1860–61," *MHSP*, XLII (1909–10), 660–87.

When Seward ignored the advice and made his speech, Sumner became frantic with anxiety. He could not sleep nights; his health was impaired; his concern over compromise became obsessive. He "talked like a crazy man," the hostile Charles Francis Adams, Jr., remembered, "orating, gesticulating, rolling out deep periods in theatrical, whispered tones,—repeating himself, and doing everything but reason." He could not be diverted from his concern over Seward's defection; at an interruption of his monologue he did not go off the track, but "merely gave a bump and a jerk, and went on fiercer in his utter disregard of logic and policy." Seward, he declaimed, had "never been aware of the real peril"; Seward "had throughout the session been demented, . . . wholly ignorant of the true nature of the question and of the feeling of the South." Seward "was demoralizing the North. If he had but held firmly to his position, and refused all parley with secessionists, all would have been well. An appeal should have been made to the loyal, Union-loving feeling of the border Slave States, and all would have been well." Firmness would have kept the North united; it would have held the border states in the Union; it would have brought the Gulf states back with their pride humbled and their slaves freed. "I am sure," Sumner whispered excitedly, "I am certain—I see my way so clearly; such a glorious victory was before us; right was with us, God was with us—our success was sure did we only hold firmly to our principles." [6]

Disturbed by Seward's course, Sumner became positively frenetic when he discovered that the compromise spirit was spreading to the Massachusetts congressional delegation and that his old friend Charles Francis Adams was infected. Adams, of all men, in Sumner's opinion should have rejected concessions to the slavocracy. He was a Massachusetts man. He was a man of principle. The son of John Quincy Adams, the grandson of John Adams, Charles Francis was, in Sumner's opinion, "as great a man as his father or his grandfather," [7] and he should have exhibited their moral stamina. He owed much to Sumner, who had overridden the opposition of Wilson and other party hacks to

---

[6] C. F. Adams, Jr.: *Autobiography*, pp. 79–82; Sumner to Andrew, Jan. 17, 1861, Andrew MSS.

[7] Charlton Yarnall (ed.): *Forty Years of Friendship . . .* (London: The Macmillan Co., Ltd.; 1911), p. 66.

force his nomination to Congress in 1858. He should have reflected Sumner's ideas, for the senator took great pains to indoctrinate him every Sunday when he had dinner with the Adams family.

Instead, Adams, starting from premises identical to Sumner's, arrived at precisely opposite conclusions as to how the secession crisis could be handled. Whereas Sumner thought firmness would develop the unionist sympathies of the border states, Adams, who was a member of the Committee of Thirty-three from the House, concluded that the moderate old Whigs like Crittenden were the only border-state unionists who had any political power and that they would be repudiated by their states unless they could show that the North was willing to make concessions. Adams concluded that Sumner's policy of "rigid dignity and listless inactivity," of "railing at the rebellion and repulsing all sympathy with the hesitating and timid but honest citizens of the slave states," could only lead to the secession of the border states and the Confederate capture of Washington before Lincoln's inauguration. First in the House committee, then in a major speech on January 31, Adams indicated the concessions that he, along with others in the Seward wing of the Republican party, was willing to make to the border states: modification of the personal liberty laws; a constitutional amendment prohibiting federal interference with slavery in the states; admission of New Mexico as a slave state.[8]

To Sumner all these concessions seemed derelictions of principle. The Massachusetts personal liberty law, which he and Dana had originally drawn up, which had been saved from repeal by the Brooks assault, was "one of the glories of our Commonwealth"; moreover, its repeal would *not have the slightest influence in satisfying the slave states.* To admit New Mexico as a slave state would be *"a fatal dismal mistake,"* "an abandonment of principle." It did not matter if, as Adams argued, the number of slaves in New Mexico would always be small. *"To sanction the enslaving of a single human being,"* Sumner passionately believed, "is an act which cannot be called small, unless the whole

[8] This analysis of Adam's course in the secession crisis is based on his unpublished diary and on his letterbooks of the period. See, especially, his Diary, Dec. 20, 1860, and his letter to Dana, Feb. 9, 1861, Adams MSS.

moral law which it overturns or ignores is small." To add an amendment guaranteeing slavery would undermine the basis of Sumner's entire antislavery argument, that the Constitution no-where recognized property in man. "Ignoble will it be in us," he argued, "to concede beyond the Constitution, which . . . em-bodies all that our fathers would concede." [9] Worst of all, even if the North humiliated itself by making the concessions Adams proposed, the slaveholders, "Punic in faith, Punic in character," would not be satisfied. *"They are all essentially false, with trea-son in their hearts, if not on their tongues."* [1]

Vainly Sumner tried to convince Adams of the error that he and Seward were making. But, Adams, busy with the practical work of the Committee of Thirty-three, never really tried to un-derstand the senator's plan for coping with the secession crisis and tended to dismiss him as an impractical theorist. Since Sum-ner, as Henry Adams said, could "no more argue than a cat" and was unable to reason with his friend, he orated at him. His for-merly peaceful Sunday dinners with the Adams family now be-came occasions of violent political wrangling. One Sunday after Seward's speech, for example, Sumner and Senator Preston King, of New York, dined with the Adamses, and, after the ladies retired, fat, amiable King in his genial way deplored the plan to admit New Mexico as a slave state. Sumner sustained him in round, rhetorical periods. As the discussion grew warmer, with King and Adams each attacking the other's logic, Sumner inter-posed "with a re-assertion of our being right, and that the South must be made to bend." Sharply Adams rebuked him: "Sumner, you don't know what you're talking about. Yours is the very kind of stiff-necked obstinacy that will break you down if your per-severe." [2]

Offended, Sumner did not answer Adams; he thought that events were already doing so. Prior to December 21, when Adams had first endorsed the admission of New Mexico as a slave state, only South Carolina had seceded; during the six weeks following that concession Mississippi, Florida, Alabama, Georgia, Louisi-

---

[9] Sumner to Dana, Jan. 20, 1861, Dana MSS.; Sumner to H. L. Pierce, Jan. 29, 1861, MS., Houghton Lib.; Worthington C. Ford (ed.): "Sumner's Letters to Governor Andrew, 1861," *MHSP*, LX (1926–7), 227–8; Hughes: *Forbes*, I, 186.

[1] Sumner to Andrew [Jan. 1861], Andrew MSS.

[2] Ford (ed.): *Letters of Henry Adams*, pp. 79–80.

ana, and Texas had moved toward secession, and Virginia and Tennessee were about to summon conventions. With a feeling approaching satisfaction, Sumner observed the progress of disunion during the month of January; these developments were precisely what he had predicted would result from compromise of any sort. The cotton states were lost already, he told Governor Andrew. "Virginia will go, and will carry with her Maryland and Kentucky." *"They will all go."* [3]

Pleased to have his prophecies fulfilled, willing to believe the worst of the "barbarous" slaveholders, Sumner seemed at times to look "forward to the violence and slaughter of civil war, with the consequences of insurrection in the South almost with a grim satisfaction." He was entirely willing to credit Edwin M. Stanton, Buchanan's new attorney general, who told him in excited, conspiratorial tones: "that every thing was bad as could be—that Virginia would certain secede—that the conspiracy was the most wide-spread and perfect—that all efforts to arrest the movement there by offers of compromise . . . were no more than that" (snapping his fingers). Stanton, who more than anybody else in Washington seemed to have a "strong . . . grasp of the whole terrible case," further convinced Sumner that the Peace Conference, which Virginia had summoned to meet in the capital on February 4, was intended not to preserve the Union, but "to constitute a Provisional Government which was to take possession of the capital and declare itself the nation." [4]

Adams's and Seward's concessions, Sumner reflected bitterly, had already undermined Southern unionism and had frustrated his own plan for coping with the crisis. All the North could do now was to maintain its principles and await events. There must be no further Republican gestures toward compromise; they would be futile in restraining the slave states, but would be potent in demoralizing the North. But, while the North remained inflexible, it must take no move that could be considered aggressive; it must not even send troops to defend the national capital, for that would provoke bloodshed. "If possible," Sumner coached

[3] Sumner to Andrew, Jan. 8, 1861, Andrew MSS.
[4] Adams, Diary, Jan. 6, 1861, Adams MSS.; Sumner to Andrew, Jan. 26, 1861, Andrew MSS.; Henry Wilson: "Jeremiah S. Black and Edwin M. Stanton," *Atlantic Monthly*, XXVI (Oct. 1870), 466.

Andrew, "we must avoid civil war; indeed, to avert this dread calamity, I will give up, if necessary, territory and state; but I will not give up our principles." [5]

With Seward and Adams among the compromisers, Sumner felt that he must exert his every power to keep Massachusetts Republicans firm against all concession to the South. His letters home became constantly shriller in his effect to counteract Adams's influence. Almost daily he wrote Governor Andrew not to concede so much as a "pepper-corn" to the slaveholders. "My earnest prayer," he informed his Boston friends, "is that the state where I was born, and which I now honorably represent may not join in the surrender of those principles which constitute her glory." The italics and the exclamation marks with which Sumner peppered his numerous letters during the secession crisis attest the passion he felt on this subject. "Pray," he besought Andrew, "keep Massachusetts sound and *firm*—FIRM—FIRM—against every word or step of concession." [6]

· 6 ·

Had Sumner's conflict with Adams been a purely intellectual difference, it could have been smoothed over, but behind their arguments lurked wounded personal feelings and latent political rivalries. Adams inevitably was irked by his role as Sumner's protégé in Washington. The senator's ponderous homilies, his ostentatious culture, his rhetorical flourishes, his unvarnished egotism all became increasingly insufferable. Adams, who could never forget his distinguished ancestry, found intolerable Sum-

[5] Sumner to Andrew, Jan. 8, 1861, Andrew MSS. I do not agree with Miss Laura A. White's conclusion ("Sumner and the Crisis," p. 156) that this statement proves that Sumner desired a permanent disruption of the United States. As a peace advocate he wanted to avert war; as an antislavery man he feared compromise more than secession. I know of no authenticated statement by Sumner indicating that he ever considered the *permanent* division of the nation possible or desirable. There is no reason to accept statements in the New York *Herald* to the contrary, and the opinion of William B. Read, of Philadelphia, that "Sumner and his peculiar school [were] preaching peace and recognition" of the Confederacy (Read to Joshua Baring, Apr. 25, 1861, House of Baring MSS.) is based on nothing but hearsay.

[6] Sumner to Dana, Jan. 20, 1861, Dana MSS.; Sumner to Charles G. Loring, Jan. 26, 1861, Loring MSS.; Sumner to Andrew, Jan. 17, 1861, Andrew MSS. Cf. Ford (ed.): "Sumner's Letters to Andrew."

ner's conviction that "his great services, his superiority in education, his oratorical power, his political experience, his representative character at the head of the whole New England contingent,
and, above all, his knowledge of the world, made him the most
important member of the Senate."[7]

Sumner, for his part, bore his differences with Adams with
unusual docility until he thought his own political position was
imperiled. He had been disturbed to find that Adams was the
only member of the Massachusetts delegation in either house
given a place on the committees formulating compromise proposals. The fact that the Massachusetts newspapers that had
always been most suspicious of Sumner voiced such hearty approval of Adams's course during the secession crisis was alone
enough to arouse the senator's apprehensions, and Boston talk
about Adams as an ideal candidate to oppose Sumner in 1862 did
nothing to allay them.[8]

Always secretive when his own personal prospects were at
stake, Sumner moved cautiously against Adams, giving no overt
cause for hostility. In January, when a strong Massachusetts
movement developed for putting Adams into the cabinet, the letter making the recommendation to President-Elect Lincoln was
circulated to every other member of the delegation before it
reached Sumner. Rather than cause an open break, Sumner
"most sincerely and cordially" endorsed Adams's candidacy—
but a close friend of Lincoln's reported: "Not quite *all* the Massachusetts delegation are for Mr. Adams," and Wilson, who was
working very closely with Sumner, wrote Lincoln that he would
"cheerfully bow" to a decision "passing over Massachusetts" for a
cabinet post.[9]

[7] Henry Adams: *Education*, p. 102.
[8] White: "Sumner and the Crisis," pp. 140, 165–6; John E. Lodge to Sumner, Mar. 4, 1861, Sumner MSS.
[9] Letter signed by all members of the Massachusetts delegation to Abraham
Lincoln, Jan. 4, 1861, R. T. Lincoln MSS.; Leonard Swett to Lincoln, Jan. 5,
1861, ibid.; Wilson to Lincoln, Jan. 5, 1861, ibid. There is nothing to suggest that
Sumner himself wished to go into the cabinet at this time, though there was
some newspaper speculation that he might become Secretary of State. William
E. Baringer: *A House Dividing: Lincoln as President Elect* (Springfield: The
Abraham Lincoln Association; 1945), pp. 45, 86–7. New England conservative
Republicans for months had been organizing to defeat any such possibility. L. E.
Chittenden to Thomas H. Dudley, Nov. 1, 1860, Dudley MSS.

Conscious of his own rectitude, Adams did nothing to placate Sumner. On January 28 he drew up a letter urging Governor Andrew to send delegates to the Peace Conference recently summoned by Virginia, and persuaded most of the other Massachusetts congressmen to sign it. Perhaps it was not entirely by accident that he approached Sumner last. Angered at again being confronted with a *fait accompli,* worried by Stanton's information that the proposed conference was really "a treacherous and violent assemblage, which . . . was to be the nucleus of the assault upon the city," and prickly with pride because he had just written Andrew not to send delegates, Sumner hotly refused to sign. After exchanging sharp words with his friend, Adams mailed the letter anyway and went back to his seat in the House. Sumner promptly followed and called aside one Massachusetts representative after another to convince them of the error they had committed. Adams inevitably was drawn into one of these conversations, and, flying into a passion, he denounced Sumner's course as "insulating Massachusetts." The next day Sumner tried to renew the discussion, declaring that he was "much pained" by Adams's expressions, which seemed to cast doubt upon the purity of his motives, but Adams, though expressing regret that he had offended the senator, refused to budge from his position.[1]

Two days later, when Adams made his important speech in the House endorsing compromise, Sumner was conspicuous by his absence. The following Sunday, for the first time since the session opened, he did not dine with the Adamses. Though the Adams family tried to conciliate him, he coolly rebuffed them. "To bring him round is impossible," Henry Adams exclaimed. "God Almighty couldn't do it. . . . He will stand on his damned dignity." Twice more, at Mrs. Adams's urgent insistence that it was necessary to quash public reports of a quarrel, Sumner had dinner with his former friends, and late in March he called on them at Quincy, where, finding Charles Francis Adams away on business, he condescended to inform Mrs. Adams that he believed "Mr. Adams meant to be honest" in his mistaken course. But their friendship was already dead. Sumner, as usual, con-

[1] Sumner to Andrew, Jan. 26, 1861, Andrew mss.; Adams, Diary, Jan. 28–9, 1861, Adams mss.; Ford (ed.): *Letters of Henry Adams,* pp. 85–6.

cealed his feelings about the break, but Adams recorded in his diary that he had "a sense of relief," as Sumner had "ceased to be an agreeable companion." [2]

Adams tried to keep the public pretense that his differences with the senator were not over important principles, but were "mainly as to policy," but Sumner thought otherwise and promptly began to undermine Adams's position in the Massachusetts Republican party. After their quarrel, he entered into the debates on the Crittenden resolutions for the first time and, hoping to rally public opinion against Adams, demanded "plainly and unequivocally . . . two things, all-sufficient for the present crisis . . . : first, that the Constitution of the United States, as administered by George Washington shall be preserved intact and blameless in its text, with no tinkering for the sake of Slavery; and, secondly, that the verdict of the people last November, by which Abraham Lincoln was elected President of the United States, shall be enforced without price or condition." [3] On March 4 his vote helped finally defeat the Crittenden Compromise.

For once Sumner did not rest in his belief that a good speech was an action; he sent out dozens of letters to his friends in Massachusetts, carefully not mentioning Adams by name, but ardently opposing every one of the compromise proposals Adams supported. Those who favored amending the personal liberty law—like Adams, his correspondents were supposed to add—he termed men who placed *property* above *Human Freedom*." Congressmen who talked of compromise—again like Adams, Sumner's readers were expected to supply—failed to understand that "all propositions of adjustment, unless they assume the form of absolute 'surrender' are absolutely in vain." After stirring up antiAdams opinion at home, Sumner then turned his attention to the other members of the Massachusetts delegation in Congress. Confidentially he assured them that Adams and Seward were "Ishmaelites," that the former was now condemned everywhere

[2] Adams, Diary, Jan. 31, Feb. 3, and 7, and Apr. 27, 1861, Adams MSS.; Ford (ed.): *Letters of Henry Adams*, p. 87; Pierce, IV, 3; C. F. Adams, Jr.: *Autobiography*, pp. 102–3; Frederic Bancroft (ed.): *Speeches, Correspondence, and Public Papers of Carl Schurz* (New York: G. P. Putnam's Sons; 1913), VI, 286.

[3] Adams to Bird, Feb. 11, 1861, copy, Adams MSS.; Boston *Advertiser*, Feb. 6, 1861; Sumner: *Works*, V, 471; *Cong. Globe*, 36 Cong. 2 Sess., 863.

in the Bay State as "weak-kneed," and that were he now running
for re-election, he could not "get a corporal's guard to vote for
him." [4]

On the specific question of sending Massachusetts commissioners to the Peace Conference, Sumner acted adroitly. In
newspaper interviews, which he could always repudiate, he
branded the proposed convention as "part of the treasonable conspiracy against the general government." In private letters to his
personal followers he warned that the conference would be "a
first step toward 'surrender.' " At his suggestion E. L. Pierce and
other members of the Bird Club published editorials attacking
Adams's proposal to send delegates. But, uncertain about just
how great the appeal of a peace conference would be in Massachusetts, and recognizing that Governor Andrew was under
heavy pressure, Sumner carefully did not test his strength by demanding that the governor refrain from appointing Massachusetts commissioners. Instead, he advised Andrew "to keep the
delegation a *Unit*" by appointing only delegates hostile to compromise. The result was that though Adams won a small victory
when the governor appointed commissioners, the delegates were
completely under Sumner's influence when they got to Washington. He saw to it that they were protected from contact with
compromise, including contact with Adams himself, and could
later report with joy that they were satisfactorily intransigent
in the Peace Conference.[5]

As Sumner's campaign against Adams got under way, his
friends, perhaps without direct inspiration from the senator himself, planned to push it further. By February it was too late to
urge Sumner for a seat in the cabinet; anyway, everybody already
knew that not Adams, but Gideon Welles, of Connecticut, would
be the one New Englander called to Lincoln's council. But, as
Adams was now frequently suggested as United States minister
to England, Sumner's intimates began to wonder whether this
important assignment could not go to a person more worthy. His

[4] Sumner to H. L. Pierce, Jan. 29, 1861, MS., Houghton Lib.; Sumner to
Dana, Feb. 1, 1861, Dana MSS.; Samuel Hooper to N. P. Banks, Feb. 1, 1861,
Banks MSS.

[5] New York *Evening Post*, Jan. 30, 1861; Boston *Transcript*, clipped in
Stephen Higginson to Sumner, Jan. 31, 1861, Sumner MSS.; Sumner to William
Claflin, Feb. 4, 1861, Claflin MSS.; Sumner to Andrew, Jan. 28, and Feb. 20,
1861, Andrew MSS.; Adams, Diary, Feb. 8, 1861, Adams MSS.

brother George took the most active role in soliciting letters of recommendation, but John E. Lodge and Longfellow also did their part. They put pressure on Senators Wilson and Fessenden to support Sumner's appointment, and they persuaded Governor Andrew and former Governor Boutwell that Sumner, with his advantages and experience, would "*begin* a diplomatic career in England, as far forward, as most men would leave off, at the end of four years." [6]

Sumner himself stood carefully aloof from the movement. "I shall neither say or do anything on the matter," he coyly told Andrew, "but I shall continue in position to act hereafter, as I have always tried to do, according to the requirements of duty." But George Sumner more forthrightly declared: "There is no doubt now the thing would be *agreeable* to Charles—but ACTION is wanted." [7]

· 7 ·

The fate of Sumner's efforts to block Adams both on compromise and on the English mission lay in the hands of Abraham Lincoln. Anxiously he looked toward Springfield. The little news that reached him about the President-Elect seemed encouraging. His brother George, who was lecturing in the West, wrote him that Lincoln had pledged not to let the Republican party become "a mere sucked egg, all shell and no meat,—the principle all sucked out." Though Sumner himself was not in correspondence with the incoming President, he doubtless had heard that Lincoln was privately advising other congressmen to "entertain no proposition for a compromise in regard to the *extension* of slavery," as "the tug has to come, and better now, than any time hereafter." Hopefully Sumner read the speeches Lincoln made during his circuitous February journey to Washington. Along with Fessenden and other Republicans opposed to compromise, he pre-

[6] George Sumner to Longfellow [Mar. 12, 1861] and Mar. 18, 1861, Longfellow MSS.; Lodge to Sumner, Mar. 4, and 8, 1861, Sumner MSS.; *MHSP*, LXII, 209–10; Longfellow to Fessenden, Feb. 26, 1861, photostat, Longfellow MSS.; Andrew to Abraham Lincoln, Mar. 12, 1861, Appointment Papers, Department of State Records; Boutwell to Lincoln, Mar. 18, 1861, ibid.; Andrew to Wilson, Mar. 11, 1861, copy, Andrew MSS.

[7] Sumner to Andrew, Mar. 10, 1861, Andrew MSS.; George Sumner to Longfellow [Mar. 12, 1861], Longfellow MSS.; New York *Herald*, Mar. 13, 1861.

pared to exercise his utmost charm upon the President-Elect when he arrived. "If Mr. Lincoln *stands firm*," Sumner told Andrew, "I do not doubt that our cause will be saved. All that we hear testifies to his character." "But," he reflected, *"he is a man!"* [8]

 On the day after Lincoln reached the capital, Sumner called on him at Willard's hotel. In the antechamber he frostly met Charles Francis Adams, also bent on influencing the President-Elect. Both men had their interviews, and both left puzzled. Adams went away feeling that this "tall, illfavored man, with little grace of manner or polish of appearance" had nevertheless "a plain, goodnatured, frank expression which rather attracts one to him." Sumner was "greatly amazed" to find Lincoln so wanting in the dignity, the social poise, the breadth of culture requisite for a President. Now and then he noticed in Lincoln's conversation "flashes of thought and bursts of illuminating expression which struck him as extraordinary," but he was baffled by his droll Western sense of humor. When the President-Elect, admiring the senator's height, offered to "measure backs" to determine who was the taller, Sumner, unamused, stiffly replied that this was "the time for uniting our fronts against the enemy and not our backs." After they parted, Lincoln is supposed to have said: "I have never had much to do with bishops where I live, but, do you know, Sumner is my idea of a bishop." Sumner, on his part, "could not get rid of his misgivings as to how this seemingly untutored child of nature would master the tremendous task before him." [9]

Eagerly Sumner waited for Lincoln's inaugural address to reveal the policy of the new administration. Though March 4, 1861, was a raw day, Sumner stood in the dust-laden, rasping wind to witness the swearing in of the first Republican president. Rejoicing that the inauguration had come off without disturbance from Southern sympathizers and even more that Lincoln's address, though ambiguous in parts, offered the South no new compromise proposals, Sumner strode home from the Capitol in

[8] Pierce, IV, 16; New York *Herald*, Feb. 23, 1861; Sumner to Andrew, Feb. 20, 1861, Andrew MSS.

[9] Adams, Diary, Feb. 24, 1861, Adams MSS.; Schurz: *Reminiscences*, II, 240–1; Ben: Perley Poore, in Allen Thorndike Rice (ed): *Reminiscences of Abraham Lincoln by Distinguished Men of His Time* (New York: *North American Review*; 1888), 223. Cf. the "Diary of a Public Man," quoted in Anderson: *The Mystery of "A Public Man,"* pp. 215–18.

high spirits. To Charles Francis Adams, Jr., who met him, he remarked: "I do not suppose Lincoln had it in his mind, if indeed
he ever heard of it; but the inaugural seems to me best described
by Napoleon's simile of 'a hand of iron and a velvet glove.' " [1]

Happy in his belief that Lincoln's first inaugural had killed
off Adams's "demented" scheme of appeasing the South, Sumner
was willing to accept, without too much grumbling, the new
President's attempts to placate the pro-compromise wing of the
Republican party through patronage. He offered no resistance
when Lincoln thwarted a last-minute move he and other antislavery Republicans made to block Seward's nomination as Secretary of State. Nor did he protest when Adams was named minister to Great Britain. He recognized that the nomination was not
intended as a slap at himself; Lincoln had apparently made up
his mind before the recommendations for Sumner reached him,
and he appointed Adams simply because Seward insisted on it. [2]

If either of these rebuffs wounded Sumner's vanity, he was
pacified by his selection as chairman of the Senate Committee on
Foreign Relations, a post which he was to make more important
than that of any ambassador and more influential than that of
most Secretaries of State. Even the usually hostile New York *Herald* had to admit that Sumner dserved the chairmanship: "He
is probably one of the most accomplished linguists in the United
States, and his present relations with the foreign ministers are of
the highest social order." [3]

Partly because Sumner was suspected of being "grouty" over
the English mission, Lincoln gave him as free a hand as possible
in other patronage. "Sumner's influence is very potential—more
than any body's else put together," Congressman John B. Alley
warned a Massachusetts office-seeker. Though the senator constantly lamented that he was powerless to aid his true antislavery
friends, he actually controlled an extraordinary number of the

[1] Charles Francis Adams, Jr.: "Lincoln's First Inauguration," *MHSP*, XLII
(1908–9), 148–50; Adams: *Autobiography*, pp. 97–8.
[2] Aaron Goodrich to Frederick W. Seward, Feb. 20, 1861, Seward MSS.; Wilson to Andrew, Mar. 14, 1861, Andrew MSS.; Seward to Lincoln, Mar. 11 [1861],
R. T. Lincoln MSS. Sumner telegraphed Adams the news when the Senate confirmed his appointment. Adams, Diary, Mar. 20, 1861, Adams MSS.
[3] New York *Herald*, Mar. 7, 1861. "That you should displace Mason as the
head of Foreign Relations!" Dana exulted. "Who would have dreamed it in
1856 . . . ?" Dana to Sumner, Mar. 9, 1861, Sumner MSS.

federal offices in Massachusetts, and he filled them not with Bostonians, but with Republicans from the central and western counties, which had always been the source of his political strength. The new collector of customs at Boston, who hired more employees than any other federal office-holder in the state, was John Z. Goodrich, of Stockbridge, in far western Massachusetts. His previous services to the party would probably have gained him his appointment in any event, but Sumner's intervention was given credit for his final selection.[4]

Of almost equal political importance to Sumner was the postmaster at Boston, whose office employed 127 clerks. When Lincoln asked Sumner to fill the office, the senator, unaccustomed to handling patronage, laughed that it was "an elephant on his hands," but he took the greatest care to select a postmaster who would be politically useful. Avoiding all the outstanding Republican candidates, as their loyalty to him personally was doubtful, Sumner chose John G. Palfrey, his political ally since Free Soil days. Palfrey's plaintive appeals for an appointment, his literary eminence, and his complete trustworthiness no doubt were the influences determining Sumner's selection, but he also took into account Howe's observation: "It is not in *you* to ask or wish any thing of a post master that the Doctor [Palfrey] would not accede to." [5]

In making foreign appointments, Sumner's influence was equally powerful. Believing that "it is of incalculable importance, that our cause should be represented at every European Government with all of character, skill and persuasion which we can command," Sumner repeatedly urged Lincoln to appoint American men of letters to diplomatic posts. Though he did not succeed in securing a consulate for Herman Melville, he did promote the appointments of George Perkins Marsh as minister to Italy and of John Lothrop Motley as minister to Austria. Restive under the frequent claims Sumner made for Massachusetts citizens, Lincoln protested: "I suppose you . . . think your State

[4] Bigelow: *Retrospections*, IV, 275; Alley to William Schouler, Apr. 14, 1861, William Schouler MSS.; Sumner to Elizur Wright, Mar. 7, 1861, Wright MSS.; New York *Herald*, Mar. 27, and Apr. 6, 1861; Stearns: *Stearns*, p. 244.

[5] New York *Herald*, Mar. 14, 1861; C. F. Adams, Jr.: *Autobiography*, pp. 101–3; Sumner to Bird, Mar. 10, 1861, Bird MSS. See also letters from the following in the Sumner MSS.: Andrew, Mar. 11, and 21, 1861; Dana, Mar. 13, 1861; John B. Alley, Mar. 15, 1861; Pierce, Apr. 2, 1861; Howe, Mar. 13 [1861].

could furnish suitable men for every diplomatic and consulate station the Government has to fill," but he gave to Massachusetts, and to Sumner, a very large share.[6]

Sumner professed to be "weary, disheartened and unhappy" at having to participate in these struggles for power. "From early morning till late at night I see nothing but the contest of politicians, and the incapacity of men in power," he lamented, "and I long for my old place in Opposition, free, open, unembarrassed." As a matter of fact, there is a good deal of evidence to show that he found it wonderfully exciting to be in power and at the center of events. Even if the office-seekers were as thick as "the buffaloes on the plains at the foot of the Rocky Mountains," he liked to help give out jobs, for he could now end the ostracism that Southerners had too long imposed upon the enemies of slavery. He also enjoyed having a friendly administration in the White House, and he grandly showed his constituents over the executive mansion and introduced them to the President. Best of all, he liked to know the latest gossip, and he regaled his dinner companions with tales of how Lincoln "was meddling with every office in the gift of the Executive" and how Mrs. Lincoln had interfered with the selection of a naval officer at the Boston customs house.[7]

Absorbed by the distribution of the spoils, Sumner virtually abandoned his earlier, excited attention to the problems of secession. As he knew nothing of Seward's elaborate, abortive efforts to arrange for the surrender of Fort Sumter, in Charleston harbor, to the Confederates, Sumner thought that the Lincoln administration had given up all thought of compromise. Consequently he was willing to trust the President. When Senator Wade at a secret Senate caucus on March 11 proposed to demand that Lincoln hold Fort Sumter even if it cost 100,000 lives, Sumner helped quash the resolution, declaring that evacuation

[6] Sumner to Bird, Mar. 10, 1861, Bird MSS.; Jay Leyda: *The Melville Log* (New York: Harcourt, Brace & Co.; 1951), II, 634–9; George William Curtis (ed.): *The Correspondence of John Lothrop Motley* (New York: Harper & Brothers; 1889), II, 30–1; Sumner to Duchess of Argyll, Nov. 11, 1861, Argyll MSS.; J. B. Alley, in Rice (ed.): *Reminiscences of Abraham Lincoln*, pp. 577–9.
[7] Sumner to Howe, Apr. 7, 1861, Sumner MSS.; Sumner to Elizabeth Peabody, Apr. 7, 1861, Mann MSS.; Sumner to Longfellow, Jan. 23, 1861, Longfellow MSS.; New York *Herald*, Apr. 11, 1861; C. F. Adams, Jr.: *Autobiography*, pp. 102–3; Adams, Diary, Mar. 16, 1861, Adams MSS.

of the forts was a purely military question, in which the Senate had no right to meddle.[8]

In the complex sequence of events which led up to the Confederate attack on Fort Sumter, on April 11, Sumner played no role.[9] Early recognizing that "Everything tends . . . to a break-up of the Union," [1] he was not surprised when the Southerners rashly precipitated war. His regret at hearing the news was tinctured with irony that he, "loving Peace, vowed to Peace, should be called to take such great responsibility in an awful ghastly civil war." "My system," he told Longfellow, "would have made it unnecessary." [2]

If Sumner had been given to self-criticism, the firing on Fort Sumter might have caused him to ponder what part he himself had played in bringing on the sectional conflict. In the minds of many Southerners, extremists like Sumner were responsible for the break-up of the Union. As a Conscience Whig, he had helped kill the national Whig party, which had once bound together conservatives of both North and South. As Free Soil senator, he had seized every opportunity to attack the South and to embitter sectional feelings. As Republican martyr, he had been instrumental in keeping his party committed to an antislavery course and in scotching efforts at compromise. "By degrees," as Carl Sandburg has remarked, "Sumner had come to stand for something the South wanted exterminated from the Union; he was perhaps the most perfect impersonation of what the South wanted to secede from." [3]

He might also have reflected upon the role that chance had played in elevating him to his prominent position. He had stumbled into politics largely by accident. He rose to leadership in the Massachusetts Free Soil movement as much through the unavailability of his rivals as through his own talents and exertions. Can-

[8] Rudolph Schleiden, Despatch No. 34, to the Hanseatic government at Bremen, Mar. 12, 1861, Lib. of Cong.
[9] See the thorough analyses of the Sumter crisis in Randall: *Lincoln the President* (New York: Dodd, Mead & Co.; 1945), I, Chap. xii; Kenneth M. Stampp: *And the War Came* (Baton Rouge: Louisiana State University Press; 1950), Chap. xiii; Allan Nevins: *The War for the Union* (New York: Charles Scribner's Sons; 1959), I, Chap. iii.
[1] Pierce, IV, 17.
[2] Sumner to Longfellow, Apr. 17, 1861, Longfellow mss.
[3] Carl Sandburg: *Abraham Lincoln: The War Years* (New York: Harcourt, Brace & Co.; 1939), I, 104.

didate of a minority party, he was first chosen to the Senate
through the devious workings of a political coalition. At nearly
any point during his first five years in office, had he been up for
re-election, he would almost certainly have been defeated. Then
Preston Brooks's attack gave him his second term in the Senate
and thereby assured him seniority and prestige within the
Republican party. Never chosen by direct popular vote for any
office, Sumner, by 1861, nevertheless had become one of the
most powerful men in the United States.

But Sumner was not introspective, and he would brusquely
have dismissed both these lines of thought. In his own mind he
bore no responsibility whatever for the coming of the Civil War.
The voice of puritanism in politics, he had merely spoken out for
Truth and Justice. Not he, but the treasonable leaders of the
South, madly intent upon defending their barbarous institution,
had caused the war. Nor would Sumner have agreed that he
owed his own commanding political position to chance. True, he
would admit that high office had been thrust upon him, without
his solicitation and even against his will. But the fact that despite
the intrigues of the Boston magnates, the propaganda of the newspaper editors, and the maneuvers of the politicians, Massachusetts
had twice chosen him senator proved that the plain people of the
Commonwealth were sound on the slavery question.

Far from brooding over the past, Sumner looked toward the
future. At once he recognized that the coming of the Civil War,
despite all its attendant horrors, would solve many problems. No
longer would he have to endure the arrogance of Southern slaveholders in the United States Senate. No longer would he have to
fight to keep members of his own party firm against compromise.
No longer need he fear a movement to write slavery into the
Constitution. Indeed, the war offered new opportunities for the
antislavery crusade. As soon as Sumner heard of the firing on
Fort Sumter, he instantly thought back to John Quincy Adams's
teaching that emancipation was one of the President's war powers. At once he went to the White House, pledged Lincoln his
support, "heart and soul," and indicated his own program for
winning the Civil War: "I . . . told him . . . that under the
war power the right had come to him to emancipate the slaves." [4]

---

[4] Yarnall: *Wordsworth and the Coleridges*, pp. 7–8. Cf. Julian: *Giddings*,
p. 385.

List of Manuscript Collections
and Scrapbooks Cited

THE PURPOSE of this list is to indicate the location of manuscript collections cited in the previous pages. It does not include numerous collections which I have searched but from which I have not quoted, nor does it enumerate detached or scattered manuscript items, the locations of which are given in the footnotes.

Adams Family MSS., Massachusetts Historical Society, Boston. Diaries and papers of John Quincy Adams and of Charles Francis Adams.

Aldrich, Charles, MSS., Iowa State Department of Archives and History, Iowa City.

Andrew, John Albion, MSS., Massachusetts Historical Society.

Appleton, Nathan, MSS., ibid.

Argyll MSS., Henry E. Huntington Library, San Marino, California. Papers of George Douglas Campbell, 8th Duke of Argyll, and of his wife, Elizabeth.

Armour, Alexander William, MSS., Library of Congress, Washington, D.C.

Bancroft, George, MSS., Massachusetts Historical Society.

Banks, Nathaniel P., MSS., Essex Institute, Salem, Massachusetts.

Bemis, George, MSS., Massachusetts Historical Society.

Bird, Francis W., MSS., Houghton Library, Harvard University, Cambridge, Massachusetts.

Brougham MSS., University College of London. Papers of Henry Peter Brougham, Baron Brougham and Vaux.

Butler, Benjamin F., MSS., Library of Congress.

Carlisle MSS., Castle Howard, Yorkshire. Papers of George William Frederick Howard, Lord Morpeth and later 7th Earl of Carlisle.

Chamberlain, Mellen, Jr., Diary, Boston Public Library.

Chase, Salmon P., MSS., Historical Society of Pennsylvania, Philadelphia.

Chase, Salmon P., MSS., Library of Congress.

Child, Lydia Maria, MSS., ibid.

Claflin, William, MSS., Rutherford B. Hayes Library, Fremont, Ohio.
Clarendon MSS., Bodleian Library, Oxford University. Papers of
George Frederick Villiers, 4th Earl of Clarendon.
Clarke, James Freeman, MSS., Houghton Library.
Cleveland, Henry R., MSS., Berg Collection, New York Public Library.
Combe, George, MSS., National Library of Scotland, Edinburgh.
Crittenden, John Jordan, MSS., Library of Congress.
Curtis, Benjamin R., MSS., ibid.
Cushing, Caleb, MSS., ibid.
Dana, Richard Henry, Jr., MSS., Massachusetts Historical Society.
Daveis, Charles S., MSS., Columbia University, New York, N.Y.
Davis, John, MSS., American Antiquarian Society, Worcester, Mass.
Dawes, Henry L., MSS., Library of Congress.
Department of State, Appointment Papers, The National Archives,
Washington, D.C.
Dix, Dorothea L., MSS., Houghton Library.
Dudley, Thomas H., MSS., Huntington Library.
Dunlap, Andrew, MSS., Essex Institute.
Ellis, G. E., MSS., Massachusetts Historical Society.
Everett, Edward, MSS., ibid.
Fields, James T., MSS., ibid.
Fillmore, Millard, MSS., Buffalo Historical Society, Buffalo, N.Y.
Fish, Hamilton, MSS., Library of Congress.
Folsom, Charles, MSS., Boston Public Library.
Fox, John, MSS., Duke University, Durham, N.C.
Fuller Family MSS., Houghton Library.
Papers of Margaret Fuller.
Garrison, William Lloyd, MSS., Boston Public Library.
Garrison, William Lloyd, MSS., Smith College, Northampton, Mass.
Giddings, Joshua R., MSS., Ohio Archaeological and Historical So-
ciety, Columbus, Ohio.
Giddings-Julian MSS., Library of Congress.
Greene, George W., MSS., Houghton Library.
Harvard College Faculty Records, Harvard University Archives, Cam-
bridge, Mass.
Harvard College Library Charge Books, ibid.
Harvard College Papers, ibid.
Harvard College Records, ibid.
Hasty Pudding Club, Secretary's Records, ibid.
Hatherton MSS., Staffordshire County Record Office, Stafford. Papers
of Edward John Littleton, First Baron Hatherton.
House of Baring MSS., Public Archives of Canada, Ottawa.
Howe Family MSS., Houghton Library.
Papers of Samuel Gridley Howe and Julia Ward Howe.

Kent, James, MSS., Library of Congress.

Lawrence, Amos A., MSS., Massachusetts Historical Society.

Library of Congress Records, Receipts for Books, Library of Congress.

Lieber, Francis, MSS., Huntington Library.

Lincoln, Robert Todd, MSS., Library of Congress.

Longfellow, Henry Wadsworth, MSS., Craigie House, Cambridge, Mass.

Loring, Charles G., MSS., Houghton Library.

Lowell, James Russell, MSS., ibid.

McLean, John, MSS., Library of Congress.

Mann, Horace, MSS., Massachusetts Historical Society.

Morton, Marcus, MSS., ibid.

Norton, Charles Eliot, MSS., Houghton Library.

Paine, Byron, MSS., Wisconsin State Historical Society, Madison.

Palfrey, John Gorham, MSS., Houghton Library.

Parker-Sumner Scrapbook, Boston Public Library.

Pierce, Edward L., MSS., Houghton Library.

Pierce Scrapbooks, ibid.

Prescott, William H., MSS., Massachusetts Historical Society.

Raymond, Henry J., MSS., New York Public Library.

Robie-Sewall MSS., Massachusetts Historical Society.

Robinson, William S., Scrapbooks, Boston Public Library.

Rockwell, A. F., MSS., Library of Congress.

Rockwell, Julius, MSS., New York Historical Society, New York, N.Y.

Sargent, Epes, MSS., Boston Public Library.

Sargent, John O., MSS., Massachusetts Historical Society.

Schouler, James, MSS., ibid.

Schouler, William, MSS., ibid.

Segal, Charles, Collection.

> Over 100 letters from Sumner in the private possession of Mr. Charles M. Segal, Brooklyn. N.Y.

Seward, William H., MSS., University of Rochester, Rochester, N.Y.

Shattuck, George C., MSS., Massachusetts Historical Society.

Smith, Gerrit, MSS., University of Syracuse, Syracuse, N.Y.

Sparks, Jared, MSS., Houghton Library.

Stevenson, Andrew, MSS., Library of Congress.

Story, Joseph, MSS., ibid.

Stuart, George Hay, MSS., ibid.

Sumner Autograph Collection, Houghton Library.

Sumner, Charles, MSS., ibid.

Sumner, Charles Pinckney, MSS., Massachusetts Historical Society.

Sumner-Appleton MSS., Boston Public Library.

Thayer, William Sydney, MSS., Library of Congress.

Ticknor, George, MSS., Dartmouth College, Hanover, N.H.

Tilton, Theodore, mss., Buffalo Public Library, Buffalo, N.Y.

Tower, Charlemagne, mss., Columbia University.

Van Buren, Martin, mss., Library of Congress.

Vaughan, Sir Charles, mss., Codrington Library, All Souls College, Oxford.

Walker, Amasa, mss., Massachusetts Historical Society.

Warden, David B., mss., Maryland Historical Society, Baltimore.

Washburn Autograph Collection, Massachusetts Historical Society.

Waterston, Robert C., mss., ibid.

Wayland, Francis, mss., Brown University, Providence, R.I.

Webster, Daniel, mss., Dartmouth College.

Webster, Daniel, mss., Houghton Library.

Webster, Daniel, mss., Library of Congress.

Weed, Thurlow, mss., University of Rochester.

Weston, Maria (Chapman), mss., Boston Public Library.

Whittier, John Greenleaf, mss., Houghton Library.

Wilson, Henry, mss., Library of Congress.

Winthrop, Robert C., mss., Massachusetts Historical Society.

Woodman, Horatio, mss., ibid.

Wright, Elizur, mss., Library of Congress.

INDEX

Blair, Francis Preston, Sr.: entertains Sumner, 210; helps organize Republican party, 276; offers Sumner hospitality, 315; as Southern Unionist, 368

Blessington, Countess of, 55

Booth, Sherman M., 272

Boston *Advertiser,* 238; publishes Sumner's letters, 81, 100; opposes Conscience Whigs, 142; defends Winthrop, 144; attacks Palfrey, 161; criticizes "Justice to the Land States," 213; opposes plan to unseat Sumner, 276; deprecates "Barbarism of Slavery," 359

Boston *Atlas,* 238; opposes Conscience Whigs, 142; attacks Palfrey, 161; attacks Coalition, 183; criticizes Webster, 184–5; reports Sumner's first Senate speech, 211; dislikes "Justice to the Land States," 213; opposes plan to unseat Sumner, 276; describes Sumner, 320

Boston *Commonwealth:* founded, 193–4; praises Sumner, 196; publishes "Justice to the Land States," 213; defends Sumner in Drayton and Sayres case, 221; supports Sumner, 225–6; prints "Landmark of Freedom," 256

Boston *Courier:* is cool to Conscience Whigs, 142; publishes Sumner's letters, 144–6, 161; taunts Sumner for silence, 276; on Brooks assault, 303–4; accuses Sumner of shamming, 323; urges Sumner to resign, 334; condemns "Barbarism of Slavery," 359

Boston *Herald,* 320, 334

Boston *Post,* 238; attacks "True Grandeur of Nations," 112; attacks Sumner, 226; welcomes plan to unseat Sumner, 276;

Boston *Post* (*continued*) on Brooks assault, 303; accuses Sumner of shamming, 323

Boston Prison Discipline Society: work of described, 121; controversy over policy of, 122–8

Boston Public Latin School, 9

Boston *Transcript,* 256

Boston *Whig:* becomes Conscience Whig organ, 141–2; attacks Winthrop, 144; defends Palfrey, 161

Boutwell, George S.: Coalition candidate for governor, 189; endorses Compromise of 1850, 191; elected, 192; attitude toward Coalition, 193; attacked by Free Soilers, 196; in constitutional convention, 245, 247; urges Sumner's appointment as minister to Great Britain, 382

Boyle, Cornelius, 324; dresses Sumner's wounds, 297; describes Sumner's injuries, 313; dismissed, 314; belittles Sumner's sufferings, 323, 325

Bragg, Braxton, 305

Breckinridge, John C., 352, 364

Bridgman, Laura, 87

Bright, John, 328

Brody, Benjamin, 340

Brooks, Charles, 102–3

Brooks, Preston S.: characterized, 289–90; plans attack on Sumner, 290–4; assaults Sumner, 294–6; arrested, 297; congressional investigation of assault by, 298; Northern reaction to assault by, 298–301; political implications of assault by, 301–4; Southern attitudes toward assault by, 304–7; challenges Wilson to duel, 307; investigated by Congress, 307–8; resigns and is re-elected, 308; Southern interpretation of assault by, 309–10; Northern in-

ABOUT THE AUTHOR

David Herbert Donald, who has twice been awarded the Pulitzer Prize for Biography, is Charles Warren Professor of American History and Professor of American Civilization at Harvard University. His many books include *Lincoln's Herndon, Lincoln Reconsidered, The Politics of Reconstruction, Charles Sumner and the Rights of Man,* and *Look Homeward: A Life of Thomas Wolfe.*